The SGML Handbook

Charles F. Goldfarb
IBM Almaden Research Center

Edited and with a foreword by
Yuri Rubinsky,
SoftQuad Inc.

CLARENDON PRESS · OXFORD
1990

Oxford University Press, Walton Street, Oxford OX2 6DP

Oxford New York Toronto
Delhi Bombay Calcutta Madras Karachi
Petaling Jaya Singapore Hong Kong Tokyo
Nairobi Dar es Salaam Cape Town
Melbourne Auckland

and associated companies in
Berlin Ibadan

Oxford is a trade mark of Oxford University Press

Published in the United States
by Oxford University Press, New York

British Library Cataloguing in Publication Data
Goldfarb, Charles F.
The SGML handbook
1. Publishing. Applications of computer systems
I. Title
070-50285
ISBN 0–19–853737–9

Library of Congress Cataloging in Publication Data
Goldfarb, Charles F.
The SGML handbook.
Includes bibliographical references and index.
1. Electronic publishing. 2. SGML (Computer program
language) I. Rubinsky, Yuri. II. Title.
Z286.E43G64 1990 686.2'2544536 90–7783
ISBN 0–19–853737–9

Produced from CRC supplied by the author
Printed and bound in Great Britain
by Bookcraft Ltd., Midsomer Norton, Avon

To Linda

but for whom life would be like SGML without an application –
all form and no meaning.

Contents

Figures

Foreword

Over the next five years, computer users will be invited to abandon their worst habits: They will no longer have to work at every computer task as if it had no need to share data with all their other computer tasks; they will not have to act as if the computer is simply a complicated, slightly-more-lively replacement for paper; not have to spend days trying to make dissimilar computers communicate, dissimilar operating systems cooperate; not have to appease software programs that seem to be at war with one another.

To a very great extent, the Standard Generalized Markup Language is the revolution that is enabling this progress. SGML's early adopters are building information environments today that will serve them well into the foreseeable future, and probably into the unforeseeable too.

Real standards do not suddenly appear. They *emerge* from one of two processes, informal or formal, during which a proposed standard is recognized as reflecting real needs.

In the informal case, a single corporation may announce a "standard" — and many have — but it is only when a sufficiently large (or sufficiently impressive) group of corporations and users agree to go along that the purported standard really becomes one. In the background, perhaps, are questions of quality or applicability. In the foreground are business and market advantage. How universally effective such a standard is may have no influence on its acceptance.

In a formalized procedure, on the other hand, through the consensus of national standards bodies, industry experts and potential users establish a set of requirements, agree (eventually) on standards that satisfy those requirements, and make them available to the world. If the world is interested, takes notice, suggests improvements, begins implementation, and begins to adopt the standard, then the process has been successful, *then* the user requirements have been met.

These are the quiet steady steps that SGML has taken; the results are beginning to have an impact on paper and electronic publishing throughout the world.

During the decade in which the Standard Generalized Markup Language developed, countless hours of discussion and analysis created a group of SGML experts within the international standards-setting community. Software developers interested in building SGML tools were able, in those days, to contribute to the creation of the standard, and to learn directly from the individuals responsible how to interpret various clauses and constructs and the relationships between them. At the center of this activity, co-ordinating the technical work at the international level, drafting and re-drafting, assimilating and synthesizing the contributions and requirements of experts in computer science, text processing and information management, was Dr. Charles Goldfarb, astonishingly accessible at standards meetings, conferences, over the telephone and via electronic mail.

THE SGML HANDBOOK hopes, among other goals, to give those people who weren't part of SGML's development access to Dr. Goldfarb's thoughts on every clause in the standard, by guiding the reader through the Standard Generalized Markup Language as no one but he could.

The book is, first and foremost, a practical aid for people who want to understand, use and implement ISO 8879 — the SGML standard. The standard is a technical document, detailing precisely what SGML is and therefore how an SGML parser must behave. The Handbook's job is to "flesh out" the legalistic terminology of the standard, to provide depth and connections between the parts.

For there is considerably more to the standard than its legalities and its technicalities. Much of what is most exciting about SGML is to be found between the lines of ISO 8879 and in the applications that people are now developing. For example:

— The standard explains the consistent manner in which an SGML system must declare the character set being used for the storage of data. The implications of this simple statement are far-reaching: SGML is thereby independent of all the "proprietariness" that has traditionally been associated with hardware and software.

— The standard describes how delimiting characters allow software to distinguish the contents of information from characters which may indicate the structure of that information. This adds a new dimension to the files we have — a dimension of information about the information that lets text's elemental structure be used simultaneously for traditional word processing and formatting operations as well as with the powerful retrieval technologies that we associate with database management systems. This, in turn, implies that documents can be "pulled together" on the fly, gathered up from a variety of components for use in new contexts.

— The standard mandates how one declares a set of elements, attributes and entities for a specific purpose and then uses these declared constructs to mark up content. *Together*, the declarations and marked-up content are the document. This powerful idea, for me, is the reason that SGML has been and will continue to be so successful. ISO 8879 never describes SGML as a meta-language, but everything about its system of declarations and notations implies that a developer has the tools to build exactly what is required to indicate the internal structure of any type of information in a common tool-independent manner.

I give this small set of examples to serve as a guidepost for the reader. The most rewarding approach to this book is to read it with a vested interest, with a specific task to accomplish, and with an imagination that takes advantage of the constructs in the standard and the insights in the annotations to see the implications for one's own applications and systems.

Already, at this early stage in SGML's history, an extraordinary range of people are working with it: novelists, technical writers, computational linguists, biblical scholars, dictionary-makers, parliamentarians, paper publishers, electronic publishers, Braillists, musicians, builders of hypertexts, of expert systems, of airplanes and helicopters, of automatic translation software.

SGML is a success because it is a language for building the architectures required to accommodate such variety. It will continue to attract governments, corporations and industry groups because it is an approved, published international standard whose timing is right: Communicating, open systems are now offered by every computer vendor and such links are useless without the exchange of *content* that SGML enables.

As Dr. Goldfarb makes clear in the Acknowledgements section of this book, SGML was (and continues to be) the work of a large and dedicated group of individuals, but all of them would agree that Charles Goldfarb is the real inventor of the language and that the strength of his vision, throughout the decade-long creation process, is what gives SGML its focus and its clarity of purpose. Accordingly, the publication of THE SGML HANDBOOK is of critical importance. SGML is a rich, multi-purpose standard, and is appropriately sophisticated: It is providing an essential service by making possible the exchange of information at any level of complexity between software, hardware, storage and presentation systems. Like SGML itself, THE SGML HANDBOOK is an enabling mechanism. SGML will improve the productivity and competitiveness of everyone who uses computers if its sophistication is now harnessed by a generation of developers of SGML systems and applications. Those are the people who will find this book an invaluable companion, and, most important, the authoritative voice.

Yuri Rubinsky
Toronto, Ontario
August, 1990

Preface

There is a wonderful poem by John G. Saxe called "The Blind Men And The Elephant" that begins:

> It was six men of Indostan
> To learning much inclined
> Who went to see the elephant
> (Though all of them were blind),
> That each by observation
> Might satisfy his mind.

I don't remember the words, but I recall that each of the blind men approached a different part of the beast. One stroked the tail and decided the elephant was like a rope. Another touched its side and concluded that elephants were like walls.

One blind man grabbed the trunk and determined it was another form of snake. The fourth put his arms around one of the elephant's legs and declared elephants to be like trees.

The fifth man, I think, felt the elephant's ear and decided it was a poorly tailored leather jacket or some such, and I don't remember what the sixth did at all. In any event, they all wound up arguing about the true nature of the elephant, with each being partly right and all of them being wrong.

Saxe's poem was intended as a dig at theologians, who necessarily argue about something that none of them can see. However, it can apply just as well to some of today's high tech community. Faced with something new and unusual, these experts and specialists, though sighted, sometimes fail to see any more than what they have been trained to expect.

Which brings us to the subject of this book. The Standard Generalized Markup Language has in many respects been a victim of this modern form of blindness. There has been a dismaying tendency to characterize SGML solely in terms of the aspect with which one happens to make contact:

— It is a tagging language.

— It handles logical structures.

— It is a file linking and addressing scheme.

— It is a data base language for text.

— It is a foundation for multimedia and hypertext.

— It is a syntax for text processing style sheets.

— It allows coded text to be reused in ways not anticipated by the coder.

— It is a document representation language for any architecture.

— It is a notation for any kind of structure.

— It is a metalanguage for defining document types.

— It represents hierarchies.

— It is an extensible document description language.

— It is a standard for communication among different hardware platforms and software applications.

SGML is and does all of these things, but the whole is much more than the sum of the parts. Moreover, it is only by understanding the whole that one can make the best use of SGML.

I think that a high tech version of Saxe's poem would have a dramatic ending: The elephant eventually gets irritated by all the poking and fumbling and runs off, trampling the six blind men in the process.

The moral, of course, is that if you are going to mess around with something powerful that you do not fully understand — even something benign — you had better do it with your eyes open.

I hope THE SGML HANDBOOK will be the eye-opener that lets you see the elephant.

Acknowledgments

This book is the culmination of some twenty years of work on SGML, and on its precursor, IBM's GML, so I have a lot of people to thank.

For joining me at the start of the whole thing I continue to be grateful to: Ed Mosher and Ray Lorie, who put the "M" and "L" (respectively) into GML; Truly Donovan, the first professional document type designer, who taught me never to forget the user's perspective; and Neal Eisenberg and Jack Steitz, whose programming expertise proved, in a variety of pioneering projects, that generalized markup really worked.

It is a long way from an initial language design — even one with a proven precursor — to an International Standard of the calibre of ISO 8879. There were many travelers on that journey, some hundreds of experts around the world who contributed to the standard during the last twelve years. In 1983 I found a way to acknowledge the effort of the major contributors in a more enduring and "standardized" way than I could possibly do here. The results can be found in annex C.1.4 ⟨ 82 ⟩, which was revised over the years to reflect notable contributions by people who came later to the project.

Even so I must pay particular thanks to some of that number. Joe Gangemi was, during the most crucial years of the standard's development, an ever-available critical sounding-board and design partner — the first to hear about any new idea, and the last with whom I discussed the ones that were to go no further. Bill Davis, Jim Mason, and Sharon Adler were three of the earliest and most active SGML developers; each has gone on to become a chairman of one of the principal committees contributing to SGML — ANSI X3V1.8, ISO/IEC JTC1/SC18/WG8, and GCA GenCode, respectively.

I must also acknowledge the people who helped me, as a novice standards editor, to run the tortuous political path from technical completion to formal approval: Bill Tunnicliffe, the first chairman of ISO/TC97/SC18/WG8 (and, not incidentally, the father of generic coding); Fran Schrotter and Bernadette St. John of ANSI, who made sure that ISO 8879 progressed in accordance with ISO procedures, but could always find a non-standard solution when a problem called for one; and Millard Collins, the chairman of ANSI X3V1, for his invaluable assistance. I am especially grateful to Mary Anne Gray, who provided guidance and support in two capacities: as chairman of SC18 and as IBM's Director of Standards Relations.

A standard can succeed only if there is broad participation in its development and widespread understanding of its usefulness after it has been developed. I must thank two people in particular for their extraordinary efforts in developing a broadly-based knowledgeable constituency for SGML: Norm Scharpf, Director of the Graphic Communications Association, has for more than twenty years led the North American publishing community's efforts to achieve standardized generic coding (see Appendix A (567)). Joan Smith, founding President of the SGML Users' Group, has more than anyone been responsible for achieving the high level of European interest in SGML.

I also have Joan to thank for encouraging me to meet the staff at ISO Central Secretariat. One could be forgiven for thinking that the very center of international standardization would be a hide-bound bureaucracy, but nothing could be further from the truth. I am indebted to Peter Jones, Keith Brannon, and Mike Smith, who served at various times as Technical Officers and Central Secretariat Editors for ISO 8879, for their great help in the polishing of the standard and its progression to final aproval; to Michael Leaman, Director of Standards Publishing and Methodology, for his flexibility in accommodating the first ISO standard written in the American language; and to Jacques Olivier Chabot, Director of Administration and Finance, for smoothing the way in general, and in particular for exercising his considerable diplomatic skills to remove the last obstacle to publication. I am especially indebted to Jacques for making this book possible.

It was during a meeting at ISO Central Secretariat that I first met Anders Berglund, then of the European Particle Physics Laboratory (CERN), who figures in a wildly improbable story about the publication of ISO 8879. The story claims that I shipped the unformatted SGML source files to Anders over a computer network, got on a plane to Geneva, and found the standard — formatted to full ISO publishing specifications — waiting when I arrived at my hotel. I would now like to confirm that the story is indeed true, and to thank Anders for his extraordinary text programming effort. (I am happy to add that the ISO was also impressed, and that both SGML and Anders — the latter in the capacity of Director of Information Processing — are now vital constituents of the ISO publishing operation.)

Editing standards and writing books are time-consuming tasks. That time has to come from somewhere. In my case, most of it came from my employer for those twenty years — IBM. In particular, it came from Bobby Lie, Manager of the Computing Facility at the IBM Almaden Research Center, a man of unusual patience and long-term vision.

I would also like to thank my manager, Norm Pass, for his encouragement and support at every phase of the standardization and book writing. I can say that because, through the kind of strange (and in my case, fortunate) quirks that happen in IBM, Norm has been my manager at three different times during these projects, including the inception of the standards work and now — twelve years later — the publication of this book. In between, the role has been filled by Wes Christiansen, Mike Kay, Don Raimondi, and Steve Zilles; I thank all of them for their help. My special thanks, also, to Debbie Perez, for her unfailingly cheerful logistical and moral support.

Two people made special contributions to this book: Harvey Bingham contributed the idea for the format of the syntax productions, with their built-in cross-references. Robert Tischer wrote an insightful explanation of the fine line that SGML walks between humanism and science (see annex H [*556*]).

For my last acknowledgments I will borrow the words of the anonymous twelfth-century calligrapher who, describing the task of copying an entire book by hand, wrote:

> A man who knows not how to write may think this no great feat. But only try to do it yourself and you shall learn how arduous is the writer's task. It dims your eyes, makes your back ache, knits your chest and belly together. It is a terrible ordeal for the whole body.

In the electronic publishing age, that ordeal falls on the bodies of the pre-press production team. I gratefully acknowledge the intelligent and meticulous transcription of my taped dictation by Daniel Neff, the conscientious and skillful production of the index by Murray Maloney, and the wizard-level text programming of Ben Thomas that transformed my dream of a paper hypertext into reality.

But I owe a special debt of thanks to Yuri Rubinsky, the organizer and leader of that team. He stepped in as editor, indexer, cross-referencer, designer, and production manager at a time when it appeared that a surgeon's knife had permanently cut out any likelihood of completing the book. Without Yuri the elephant would still be trapped inside my head.

And a final word of thanks to my family: to Linda, Edward, and Andrew, for their unflagging and moderately successful attempts to keep me sane and healthy throughout it all; and to the world's most beautiful cat, for companionship during those long hours of the night when even Linda had given up on me.

Charles F. Goldfarb
Saratoga, California
August, 1990

How to Use This Book

Please take the time to read this section — it is like the READ.ME file that comes with your PC software, without which the 500 pages of documentation and seven megabytes of program code are useless.

THE SGML HANDBOOK is a complex book and this section is your guide to it. It will show you how to distinguish the text of ISO 8879 from my annotations, and how to identify the material that will best help you to evaluate, use, and/or implement SGML. It includes an explanation of the editorial conventions of ISO standards that you must read if they are not familiar to you. This section also explains the unique "push-button access" system that allows THE SGML HANDBOOK to function as a paper hypertext.

The Basics

THE SGML HANDBOOK contains all of the text of ISO 8879 — the SGML standard — extensively annotated, together with a structured overview and additional tutorial and reference material. A system of cross-references has been introduced within and between the ISO and non-ISO text. There is also a comprehensive index.

The ISO text in this book is the complete official text of ISO 8879, with the amendment of 1988 integrated into it. The clarifications recommended by SGML committee document N1035 have also been adopted, which chiefly affects the definitions. These are indicated with change bars in the right margin.[1]

Unqualified references to "the standard", refer to ISO 8879. There are also two supporting standards that are described in Part Two of this book. They are ISO 9069, which standardizes "SDIF", the SGML Document Interchange Format, and ISO 9070, which standardizes registration

---

[1] In Appendix C (594) there is a complete description of the ISO text sources, together with any superseded text. The corrected text was used in the body of the book to maximize clarity for the reader.

procedures for SGML public text owner identifiers.

References to the "SGML committee" or "SGML developers", are references to ISO/IEC JTC1/SC18/WG8. This is the "Working Group" of international experts, sent by their national standards bodies, that is responsible for the development of SGML. WG8 actually has a much broader mandate — text description and processing languages — and therefore only some of its members are involved with the nitty-gritty of SGML. However, nothing done by the SGML "Special Working Group", as it is called, has any official status until it is approved by WG8.[2]

Structure and Organization

The book is organized into four parts.

— Part One: Tutorials

This part includes the three tutorial annexes from ISO 8879 (unannotated) plus an extensive new tutorial on the LINK feature.

— Part Two: A Structured Overview of SGML

The overview consists of nine chapters that discuss every aspect of SGML from the standpoint of its purpose and capabilities, rather than syntax details — the forest, in other words, not the trees. A top-down approach is followed, and every term in the SGML glossary[3] is introduced in context. You should read the overview to find out what SGML is all about, and whether it has the functions needed for your intended applications.

The overview is also useful prerequisite reading for some of the more complex areas of the standard. Anyone involved with concrete syntax design, for example, should find the chapter on character sets (Chapter 7 $\boxed{192}$) to be helpful (as should anyone working with fonts or coding in general, for that matter).

---

[2] The standards developed by WG8 are submitted to its parent body, Subcommittee 18 ("Text and Office Systems") of Joint Technical Committee 1 ("Information Processing") of the International Organization for Standardization (ISO) and the International Electrotechnical Commission (IEC). SC18 secures approval of standards by conducting mail ballots among its national member bodies. The national organizations usually have committees that correspond to those in SC18, and it is their members who prepare the ballot responses. Normally, some of those members are also members of the Working Group that did the technical work in the first place, so continuity is maintained.

[3] That is, the definitions clauses of ISO 8879, ISO 9069, and ISO 9070.

— Part Three: ISO 8879 Annotated

If Part Two is a map of the SGML forest, Part Three is the field guide to the trees. It contains the full text of the body of ISO 8879 — clauses 0 through 15 — with extensive annotations and cross-references added.

— Part Four: ISO 8879 Annexes

This part contains the full text (unannotated) of the non-tutorial annexes to ISO 8879: annexes D through I.

Each part begins with a detailed outline table of contents that in itself may be a useful reference or study aid. The outline for Part Two, for example, shows the semantic structure of SGML and where each glossary term fits into it. The outline for Part Three shows the syntactic structure and where each syntax production fits into that. The Part Three outline also includes a (relatively) concise alphabetical list of the definition terms.

In addition to the four parts, there are four appendices (not to be confused with ISO 8879 annexes!).

— Appendix A is a short history of the development of SGML.

— Appendix B is an SGML committee document, "N1035", which recommends editorial changes and clarifications to the standard.

— Appendix C describes how N1035 was used in preparing this book.

— Appendix D identifies sources of additional information on SGML.

To find your way around the book, you will want to keep in mind that Part One has tutorial annexes, Part Two has chapters, Part Three has clauses, Part Four has other annexes, and that there are also appendices and an index. The running headings are designed to serve as a reminder and navigational aid.

Typographic Conventions

ISO text, wherever it appears, is set in Helvetica, a sans-serif typeface favored by the ISO for its publications; non-ISO text, such as this section, is set in Palatino. If this distinction appears somewhat subtle, be reassured by the fact that ISO text lines are also numbered. If numbering, on the other hand, sounds like overkill, be reassured that the line numbers are also used by the push-button access system to pinpoint cross-references.

There are three exceptions to the above rule, but they are intuitive and I mention them only for the record:

— Headings are set in Helvetica throughout, but it is always clear from the context and the clause and annex numbers when they are ISO text.

— The public entity sets in annex D ⌞ 498 ⌟ and the public DTD in E.1 ⌞ 530 ⌟, which are ISO text, are set without line numbers. As everything in those annexes but the brief introduction is ISO text, there should be no confusion.

— SGML examples and public text are set in Courier, but in other respects are treated as ISO or non-ISO text, as described above. If a record in an example is too long to be set as a single line, it is broken at a syntactically correct point and continued on the next line (after a substantial indention). The break is indicated by a triangle symbol in the right margin.

The standard defines additional typographic conventions that are used within the ISO text (and occasionally within non-ISO text as well). They are described in clause 5 ⌞ 290 ⌟.

As that clause also indicates, the standard specifies SGML formally by using syntax productions, each of which defines a "syntactic variable". The definition of a syntactic variable is an expression that can include delimiter role names, constant strings, and other syntactic variables. In *THE SGML HANDBOOK*, the expressions are formatted so that each component appears on a separate line. If the component is a syntactic variable, the location of its definition appears in a "button" (explained below) set flush right at the end of the line. If the component is a delimiter role name, its assigned string in the reference concrete syntax appears in the button instead.

The Push-button Access System

A major difficulty in reading ISO 8879 is the inconvenience of tracking the many explicit and implicit cross-references. For example, to understand a syntax production, it can be helpful to read the definitions of the syntactic variables used in it. Unfortunately, ISO 8879 gives not a clue as to where they can be found — not the page number, nor even the sequential number of the syntax production.

The problem also arises when a syntactic variable occurs in normal ISO text. It is easily recognized as a syntactic variable because it is italicized, but no production number or page number is given for it. Even explicit cross-references, such as clause and figure numbers, suffer from the lack of location data, as the ISO style prohibits the use of page numbers because of possible interference with readability.

For *THE SGML HANDBOOK* I resolved to solve this problem. When using SGML with a modern electronic publishing system, it is relatively easy to capture the locations and other information about elements of interest. The difficulty lies in introducing this information into the text without sacrificing readability. In the case of ISO text, there is the additional problem of making it clear that the added cross-reference information is not part of the standard.

The solution — borrowed from interactive hypertext systems — is a stylized cartouche, or "button", that contains the added cross-reference information. The buttons are clearly not part of the text, but are fairly easy to ignore during normal reading. They contain location information that supplements the textual portion of the implicit or explicit cross-reference. For example, a syntactic variable or clause number will appear in the text in its normal form, but will be followed by a button containing the page and line number at which it can be found. Some examples have already appeared in the book.[4]

The reference button idea proved so helpful in the ISO text that it was extended to the annotations as well. In addition, special buttons — not connected with a visible reference — appear at the end of many paragraphs. These buttons associate the paragraphs with material in the tutorials, overview, or other annotations. Samples of the various button types, and the meaning of their contents, are shown in the following list:

Button	*Meaning of Contents*
[22] 15:10	production 22 on page 15, line 10
76:12	ISO text on page 76, line 12
92	ISO figure or non-ISO text on page 92

---

[4] And their meaning was so obvious you are wondering why I am taking your time to explain, right? Read on.

A-11.1 *45:6*	annotation of clause 11.1 on page 45[5]
O-4.236 *20:3*	overview discussion of definition 4.236 on p.20, line 3
T-B.12 *10*	tutorial B.12 on page 10

How to Read the Non-ISO Text

Appreciatively.[6]

There are just a few conventions to be aware of when reading the non-ISO text:

— The SGML vocabulary is used with the same strictness in the annotations as in the standard itself.

— The annotations are selective, and do not necessarily address everything in the clauses to which they apply. The objective was to supplement the standard when necessary, not to restate it. As a result, long but straightforward clauses will have few annotations while some very short clauses have pages of them.

— All delimiters in examples and in the text are from the reference concrete syntax, except when the contrary is stated. I may sometimes mention, for emphasis, that a delimiter string is from the reference concrete syntax, but my failure to do so does not imply that it is not.

How to Read the ISO Text

Carefully.[7]

Formal standards are complex documents in which every word can have both legal and technical significance. Moreover, standards are frequently translated into other languages. For these reasons, editorial conventions have been established to assure precision, accuracy, and clarity — often at the expense of readability by the uninitiated.

---

[5] Yes, I realize there is a line number in the button, but it is not necessary as the clause and page numbers are more than sufficient to locate a heading. The line number, if you must know, is that which would have been assigned to the clause heading had it been numbered as ISO text. True to Murphy's Law, I only saw that it was overkill too late to change anything but this footnote.

[6] Sorry. In the future I will attempt to confine untoward outbursts of jocularity to footnotes. However, I will continue to use footnotes for serious matters as well. Distinguishing between the two is left as an exercise for the reader.

[7] That was not jocularity — that was fair warning!

Key Principles

The key principles are:

— Precise and consistent definitions of terms.

— Distinguishing real requirements from mere commentary, explanations, or examples — and from definitions.[8]

The requirements and definitions are considered to be the "normative" text of the standard, while the remainder is considered merely "informative". Informative text in the body of a standard is identified as a "NOTE" or "NOTES". It is there to aid in understanding the standard, but does not change the requirements.

— Avoidance of redundancy.

If a requirement needs to be restated in order to clarify another part of the standard, the restatement is normally done in a note, to avoid the question of which text governs if the restatement is imperfect.

Structure of a Standard

A standard follows a prescribed structure:

— Clause 0 is an informative introduction (that is, it does not contain requirements).

— Clause 1 states what the standard includes.

— Clause 2 describes the expected uses of the standard.

— Clause 3 contains references to related standards.

— Clause 4 contains the definitions.

— Clause 5 and those following contain the actual requirements.

---

[8] Note that "requirements" here means the requirements imposed by the standard, not the user requirements that the standard was developed to satisfy.

There are also annexes containing information that was segregated from the body of the standard for convenience. Annexes are designated either "normative" or "informative". The former contain requirements and have the same force and effect as if they were in the body of the standard. The latter are just extended notes. All of the annexes of ISO 8879 are informative.

Formal Implications of Words

Some words have formal implications.

"Shall" and "must" mean that something is required. "Must" is used when referring to an unavoidable property of the subject matter — in this case, the SGML language; "shall" when there is a choice that can be made.

"Should" means that something is recommended, but not mandatory. Within normative text (as opposed to informative), it means the standard would like to have said "shall" but there was some rare situation in which the requirement could legitimately be ignored, or it was too burdensome to check for conformance.

"Deprecated" is the opposite of should. It means that something is technically allowed, but only rarely would it be a sensible thing to do.

Part One:

Tutorials

Part One: Tutorials

Annex A
Introduction to Generalized Markup

This tutorial consists of the full text of Annex A of ISO 8879 — the classic introduction to generalized markup concepts and to SGML in particular. The Annex started life as a paper on IBM's Generalized Markup Language (GML), upon which SGML is based, that was presented to an Association for Computing Machinery (ACM) conference on office automation in 1981. [1] In addition to discussing concepts, the paper describes the first commercial publication using GML.

(Dedicated trivia buffs can find more about the early history of GML and SGML in Appendix A ⌊ 567 ⌋.)

(This annex does not form an integral part of this International Standard.)

A.1 The Markup Process

2   Text processing and word processing systems typically require additional information to be interspersed among the natural text of
4   the document being processed. This added information, called "markup", serves two purposes:
6   a) Separating the logical elements of the document; and
    b) Specifying the processing functions to be performed on those
8   elements.

---

[1] Adapted from Goldfarb, Charles F., "A Generalized Approach to Document Markup", *SIGPLAN Notices*, June 1981, by permission of the author and the Association for Computing Machinery.

In publishing systems, where formatting can be quite complex, the markup is usually done directly by the user, who has been specially trained for the task. In word processors, the formatters typically have less function, so the (more limited) markup can be generated without conscious effort by the user. As higher function printers become available at lower cost, however, the office workstation will have to provide more of the functionality of a publishing system, and "unconscious" markup will be possible for only a portion of office word processing.

It is therefore important to consider how the user of a high function system marks up a document. There are three distinct steps, although he may not perceive them as such.

a) He first analyzes the information structure and other attributes of the document; that is, he identifies each meaningful separate element, and characterizes it as a paragraph, heading, ordered list, footnote, or some other element type.

b) He then determines, from memory or a style book, the processing instructions ("controls") that will produce the format desired for that type of element.

c) Finally, he inserts the chosen controls into the text.

Here is how the start of this paper looks when marked up with controls in a typical text processing formatting language:

```
.SK 1
Text processing and word processing systems
typically require additional information to
be interspersed among the natural text of
the document being processed. This added
information, called "markup," serves two
purposes:
.TB 4
.OF 4
.SK 1
1.#Separating the logical elements of the
document; and
.OF 4
.SK 1
2.#Specifying the processing functions to be
performed on those elements.
.OF 0
.SK 1
```

The .SK, .TB, and .OF controls, respectively, cause the skipping of
vertical space, the setting of a tab stop, and the offset, or "hanging
indent", style of formatting. (The number sign (#) in each list item
represents a tab code, which would otherwise not be visible.)

Procedural markup like this, however, has a number of
disadvantages. For one thing, information about the document's
attributes is usually lost. If the user decides, for example, to center
both headings and figure captions when formatting, the "center"
control will not indicate whether the text on which it operates is a
heading or a caption. Therefore, if he wishes to use the document
in an information retrieval application, search programs will be
unable to distinguish headings — which might be very significant in
information content — from the text of anything else that was
centered.

Procedural markup is also inflexible. If the user decides to change
the style of his document (perhaps because he is using a different
output device), he will need to repeat the markup process to reflect
the changes. This will prevent him, for example, from producing
double-spaced draft copies on an inexpensive computer line printer
while still obtaining a high quality finished copy on an expensive
photocomposer. And if he wishes to seek competitive bids for the
typesetting of his document, he will be restricted to those vendors
that use the identical text processing system, unless he is willing to
pay the cost of repeating the markup process.

Moreover, markup with control words can be time-consuming,
error-prone, and require a high degree of operator training,
particularly when complex typographic results are desired. This is
true (albeit less so) even when a system allows defined procedures
("macros"), since these must be added to the user's vocabulary of
primitive controls. The elegant and powerful TeX system (2), for
example, which is widely used for mathematical typesetting,
includes some 300 primitive controls and macros in its basic
implementation.

These disadvantages of procedural markup are avoided by a
markup scheme due to C. F. Goldfarb, E. J. Mosher, and R. A.
Lorie (3, 4). It is called "generalized markup" because it does not
restrict documents to a single application, formatting style, or
processing system. Generalized markup is based on two novel
postulates:

a) Markup should describe a document's structure and other
attributes rather than specify processing to be performed on

2   it, as descriptive markup need be done only once and will suffice for all future processing.

    b) Markup should be rigorous so that the techniques available for
4   processing rigorously-defined objects like programs and data bases can be used for processing documents as well.

6 These postulates will be developed intuitively by examining the properties of this type of markup.

A.2 Descriptive Markup

8 With generalized markup, the markup process stops at the first step: the user locates each significant element of the document and
10 marks it with the mnemonic name ("generic identifier") that he feels best characterizes it. The processing system associates the
12 markup with processing instructions in a manner that will be described shortly.

14 A notation for generalized markup, known as the Standard Generalized Markup Language (SGML), has been developed by a
16 Working Group of the International Organization for Standardization (ISO). Marked up in SGML, the start of this paper might look like
18 this:

```
    <p>
20  Text processing and word processing systems
    typically require additional information to
22  be interspersed among the natural text of
    the document being processed. This added
24  information, called <q>markup</q>, serves
    two purposes:
26  <ol>
    <li>Separating the logical elements of
28  the document; and
    <li>Specifying the processing functions
30  to be performed on those elements.
    </ol>
```

32   Each generic identifier (GI) is delimited by a less-than symbol (<) if it is at the start of an element, or by less-than followed by solidus
34 (</) if it is at the end. A greater-than symbol (>) separates a GI

from any text that follows it.[2] The mnemonics P, Q, OL, and LI stand, respectively, for the element types paragraph, quotation, ordered list, and list item. The combination of the GI and its delimiters is called a "start-tag" or an "end-tag", depending upon whether it identifies the start or the end of an element.

This example has some interesting properties:

a) There are no quotation marks in the text; the processing for the quotation element generates them and will distinguish between opening and closing quotation marks if the output device permits.

b) The comma that follows the quotation element is not actually part of it. Here, it was left outside the quotation marks during formatting, but it could just as easily have been brought inside were that style preferred.

c) There are no sequence numbers for the ordered list items; they are generated during formatting.

The source text, in other words, contains only information; characters whose only role is to enhance the presentation are generated during processing.

If, as postulated, descriptive markup like this suffices for all processing, it must follow that the processing of a document is a function of its attributes. The way text is composed offers intuitive support for this premise. Such techniques as beginning chapters on a new page, italicizing emphasized phrases, and indenting lists, are employed to assist the reader's comprehension by emphasizing the structural attributes of the document and its elements.

From this analysis, a 3-step model of document processing can be constructed:

a) Recognition: An attribute of the document is recognized, e.g., an element with a generic identifier of "footnote".

b) Mapping: The attribute is associated with a processing function. The footnote GI, for example, could be associated with a procedure that prints footnotes at the bottom of the page or one that collects them at the end of the chapter.

c) Processing: The chosen processing function is executed.

Text formatting programs conform to this model. They recognize such elements as words and sentences, primarily by interpreting

---

[2] Actually, these characters are just defaults. SGML permits a choice of delimiter characters.

spaces and punctuation as implicit markup. Mapping is usually via
2   a branch table. Processing for words typically involves determining
the word's width and testing for an overdrawn line; processing for
4   sentences might cause space to be inserted between them.[3]

In the case of low-level elements such as words and sentences the
6   user is normally given little control over the processing, and almost
none over the recognition. Some formatters offer more flexibility
8   with respect to higher-level elements like paragraphs, while those
with powerful macro languages can go so far as to support
10 descriptive markup. In terms of the document processing model,
the advantage of descriptive markup is that it permits the user to
12 define attributes — and therefore element types — not known to
the formatter and to specify the processing for them.

14 For example, the SGML sample just described includes the
element types "ordered list" and "list item", in addition to the more
16 common "paragraph". Built-in recognition and processing of such
elements is unlikely. Instead, each will be recognized by its explicit
18 markup and mapped to a procedure associated with it for the
particular processing run. Both the procedure itself and the
20 association with a GI would be expressed in the system's macro
language. On other processing runs, or at different times in the
22 same run, the association could be changed. The list items, for
example, might be numbered in the body of a book but lettered in
24 an appendix.

So far the discussion has addressed only a single attribute, the
26 generic identifier, whose value characterizes an element's semantic
role or purpose. Some descriptive markup schemes refer to markup
28 as "generic coding", because the GI is the only attribute they
recognize (5). In generic coding schemes, recognition, mapping,
30 and processing can be accomplished all at once by the simple
device of using GIs as control procedure names. Different formats
32 can then be obtained from the same markup by invoking a different
set of homonymous procedures. This approach is effective enough
34 that one notable implementation, the SCRIBE system, is able to
prohibit procedural markup completely (1).

36 Generic coding is a considerable improvement over procedural
markup in practical use, but it is conceptually insufficient.

---

[3] The model need not be reflected in the program architecture; processing of words, for example, could be built into the main recognition loop to improve performance.

Documents are complex objects, and they have other attributes
2 that a markup language must be capable of describing. For
example, suppose the user decides that his document is to include
4 elements of a type called "figure" and that it must be possible to
refer to individual figures by name. The markup for a particular
6 figure element known as "angelfig" could begin with this start-tag:

```
<fig id=angelfig>
```

8 "Fig", of course, stands for "figure", the value of the generic
identifier attribute. The GI identifies the element as a member of a
10 set of elements having the same role. In contrast, the "unique
identifier" (ID) attribute distinguishes the element from all others,
12 even those with the same GI. (It was unnecessary to say "GI=fig",
as was done for ID, because in SGML it is understood that the first
14 piece of markup for an element is the value of its GI).

The GI and ID attributes are termed "primary" because every
16 element can have them. There are also "secondary" attributes that
are possessed only by certain element types. For example, if the
18 user wanted some of the figures in his document to contain
illustrations to be produced by an artist and added to the processed
20 output, he could define an element type of "artwork". Because the
size of the externally-generated artwork would be important, he
22 might define artwork elements to have a secondary attribute,
"depth".[4] This would result in the following start-tag for a piece of
24 artwork 24 picas deep:

```
<artwork depth=24p>
```

26 The markup for a figure would also have to describe its content.
"Content" is, of course, a primary attribute, the one that the
28 secondary attributes of an element describe. The content consists
of an arrangement of other elements, each of which in turn may
30 have other elements in its content, and so on until further division is
impossible.[5] One way in which SGML differs from generic coding

---

[4] "Depth=" is not simply the equivalent of a vertical space control word. Although a
full-page composition program could produce the actual space, a galley formatter might
print a message instructing the layout artist to leave it. A retrieval program might simply
index the figure and ignore the depth entirely.
[5] One can therefore speak of documents and elements almost interchangeably: the
document is simply the element that is at the top of the hierarchy for a given processing
run. A technical report, for example, could be formatted both as a document in its own
right and as an element of a journal.

schemes is in the conceptual and notational tools it provides for
2 dealing with this hierarchical structure. These are based on the
second generalized markup hypothesis, that markup can be
4 rigorous.

A.3 Rigorous Markup

Assume that the content of the figure "angelfig" consists of two
6 elements, a figure body and a figure caption. The figure body in
turn contains an artwork element, while the content of the caption is
8 text characters with no explicit markup. The markup for this figure
could look like this: 6

```
10  <fig id=angelfig>
    <figbody>
12  <artwork depth=24p>
    </artwork>
14  </figbody>
    <figcap>Three Angels Dancing
16  </figcap>
    </fig>
```

18 The markup rigorously expresses the hierarchy by identifying the
— beginning and end of each element in classical left list order. No
20 additional information is needed to interpret the structure, and it
would be possible to implement support by the simple scheme of
22 macro invocation discussed earlier. The price of this simplicity,
though, is that an end-tag must be present for every element.

24 This price would be totally unacceptable had the user to enter all
the tags himself. He knows that the start of a paragraph, for
26 example, terminates the previous one, so he would be reluctant to
go to the trouble and expense of entering an explicit end-tag for
28 every single paragraph just to share his knowledge with the
system. He would have equally strong feelings about other element
30 types he might define for himself, if they occurred with any great
frequency.

---

6 Like "GI=", "content=" can safely be omitted. It is unnecessary when the content is
externally generated, it is understood when the content consists solely of tagged elements, and for data characters it is implied by the delimiter (>) that ends the start-tag.

With SGML, however, it is possible to omit much markup by
advising the system about the structure and attributes of any type
of element the user defines. This is done by creating a "document
type definition", using a construct of the language called an
"element declaration". While the markup in a document consists of
descriptions of individual elements, a document type definition
defines the set of all possible valid markup of a type of element.

An element declaration includes a description of the allowable
content, normally expressed in a variant of regular expression
notation. Suppose, for example, the user extends his definition of
"figure" to permit the figure body to contain either artwork or certain
kinds of textual elements. The element declaration might look like
this: [7]

```
<!--        ELEMENTS    MIN  CONTENT (EXCEPTIONS)  -->
<!ELEMENT fig            - -  (figbody, figcap?)>
<!ELEMENT figbody        - O  (artwork | (p | ol | ul)+)>
<!ELEMENT artwork        - O  EMPTY>
<!ELEMENT figcap         - O  (#PCDATA)>
```

The first declaration means that a figure contains a figure body and,
optionally, can contain a figure caption following the figure body.
(The hyphens will be explained shortly.)

The second says the body can contain either artwork or an
intermixed collection of paragraphs, ordered lists, and unordered
lists. The "O" in the markup minimization field ("MIN") indicates that
the body's end-tag can be omitted when it is unambiguously implied
by the start of the following element. The preceding hyphen means
that the start-tag *cannot* be omitted.

The declaration for artwork defines it as having an empty content,
as the art will be generated externally and pasted in. As there is no
content in the document, there is no need for ending markup.

The final declaration defines a figure caption's content as 0 or more
characters. A character is a terminal, incapable of further division.
The "O" in the "MIN" field indicates the caption's end-tag can be
omitted. In addition to the reasons already given, omission is

---

[7] The question mark (?) means an element is optional, the comma (,) that it follows the
preceding element in sequence, the asterisk (*) that the element can occur 0 or more
times, and the plus (+) that it must occur 1 or more times. The vertical bar (|) is used to
separate alternatives. Parentheses are used for grouping as in mathematics.

possible when the end-tag is unambiguously implied by the end-tag
of an element that contains the caption.

It is assumed that p, ol, and ul have been defined in other element
declarations.

With this formal definition of figure elements available, the following
markup for "angelfig" is now acceptable:

```
<fig id=angelfig>
<figbody>
<artwork depth=24p>
<figcap>Three Angels Dancing
</fig>
```

There has been a 40% reduction in markup, since the end-tags for
three of the elements are no longer needed.

— As the element declaration defined the figure caption as part
   of the content of a figure, terminating the figure automatically
   terminated the caption.
— Since the figure caption itself is on the same level as the
   figure body, the <figcap> start-tag implicitly terminated the
   figure body.
— The artwork element was self-terminating, as the element
   declaration defined its content to be empty.[8]

A document type definition also contains an "attribute definition list
declaration" for each element that has attributes. The definitions
include the possible values the attribute can have, and the default
value if the attribute is optional and is not specified in the
document.

Here are the attribute list declarations for "figure" and "artwork":

```
<!--        ELEMENTS     NAME     VALUE     DEFAULT -->
<!ATTLIST fig          id       ID        #IMPLIED>
<!ATTLIST artwork      depth    CDATA     #REQUIRED>
```

The declaration for figure indicates that it can have an ID attribute
whose value must be a unique identifier name. The attribute is
optional and does not have a default value if not specified.

---

[8] SGML actually allows the markup to be reduced even further than this.

In contrast, the depth attribute of the artwork element is required.
2   Its value can be any character string.

Document type definitions have uses in addition to markup
4   minimization.[9] They can be used to validate the markup in a
document before going to the expense of processing it, or to drive
6   prompting dialogues for users unfamiliar with a document type. For
example, a document entry application could read the description of
8   a figure element and invoke procedures for each element type. The
procedures would issue messages to the terminal prompting the
10   user to enter the figure ID, the depth of the artwork, and the text of
the caption. The procedures would also enter the markup itself into
12   the document being created.

The document type definition enables SGML to minimize the user's
14   text entry effort without reliance on a "smart" editing program or
word processor. This maximizes the portability of the document
16   because it can be understood and revised by humans using any of
the millions of existing "dumb" keyboards. Nonetheless, the type
18   definition and the marked up document together still constitute the
rigorously described document that machine processing requires.

A.4 Conclusion

20   Regardless of the degree of accuracy and flexibility in document
description that generalized markup makes possible, the concern of
22   the user who prepares documents for publication is still this: can
the Standard Generalized Markup Language, or any descriptive
24   markup scheme, achieve typographic results comparable to
procedural markup? A recent publication by Prentice-Hall
26   International (6) represents empirical corroboration of the
generalized markup hypotheses in the context of this demanding
28   practical question.

It is a textbook on software development containing hundreds of
30   formulas in a symbolic notation devised by the author. Despite the
typographic complexity of the material (many lines, for example,
32   had a dozen or more font changes), no procedural markup was
needed anywhere in the text of the book. It was marked up using a

---

[9] Some complete, practical document type definitions may be found in (4), although they are not coded in SGML.

language that adhered to the principles of generalized markup but
2 was less flexible and complete than the SGML (4).

The available procedures supported only computer output devices,
4 which were adequate for the book's preliminary versions that were
used as class notes. No consideration was given to typesetting until
6 the book was accepted for publication, at which point its author
balked at the time and effort required to re-keyboard and proofread
8 some 350 complex pages. He began searching for an alternative at
the same time the author of this paper sought an experimental
10 subject to validate the applicability of generalized markup to
commercial publishing.

12 In due course both searches were successful, and an unusual
project was begun. As the author's processor did not support
14 photocomposers directly, procedures were written that created a
source file with procedural markup for a separate typographic
16 composition program. Formatting specifications were provided by
the publisher, and no concessions were needed to accommodate
18 the use of generalized markup, despite the marked up document
having existed before the specifications.[10]

20 The experiment was completed on time, and the publisher
considers it a complete success (7).[11] The procedures, with some
22 modification to the formatting style, have found additional use in the
production of a variety of in-house publications.

24 Generalized markup, then, has both practical and academic
benefits. In the publishing environment, it reduces the cost of
26 markup, cuts lead times in book production, and offers maximum
flexibility from the text data base. In the office, it permits
28 interchange between different kinds of word processors, with
varying functional abilities, and allows auxiliary "documents", such
30 as mail log entries, to be derived automatically from the relevant
elements of the principal document, such as a memo.

32 At the same time, SGML's rigorous descriptive markup makes text
more accessible for computer analysis. While procedural markup

---

[10]On the contrary, the publisher took advantage of generalized markup by changing some of the specifications after he saw the page proofs.

[11]This despite some geographical complications: the publisher was in London, the book's author in Brussels, and this paper's author in California. Almost all communication was done via an international computer network, and the project was nearly completed before all the participants met for the first time.

(or no markup at all) leaves a document as a character string that has no form other than that which can be deduced from analysis of the document's meaning, generalized markup reduces a document to a regular expression in a known grammar. This permits established techniques of computational linguistics and compiler design to be applied to natural language processing and other document processing applications.

A.5 Acknowledgments

The author is indebted to E. J. Mosher, R. A. Lorie, T. I. Peterson, and A. J. Symonds — his colleagues during the early development of generalized markup — for their many contributions to the ideas presented in this paper, to N. R. Eisenberg for his collaboration in the design and development of the procedures used to validate the applicability of generalized markup to commercial publishing, and to C. B. Jones and Ron Decent for risking their favorite book on some new ideas.

A.6 Bibliography

1   B. K. Reid, "The Scribe Document Specification Language and its Compiler", *Proceedings of the International Conference on Research and Trends in Document Preparation Systems*, 59-62 (1981).

2   Donald E. Knuth, *TAU EPSILON CHI, a system for technical text*, American Mathematical Society, Providence, 1979.

3   C. F. Goldfarb, E. J. Mosher, and T. I. Peterson, "An Online System for Integrated Text Processing", *Proceedings of the American Society for Information Science*, 7, 147-150 (1970).

4   Charles F. Goldfarb, *Document Composition Facility Generalized Markup Language: Concepts and Design Guide*, Form No. SH20-9188-1, IBM Corporation, White Plains, 1984.

5   Charles Lightfoot, *Generic Textual Element Identification — A Primer*, Graphic Communications Computer Association, Arlington, 1979.

6   C. B. Jones, *Software Development: A Rigorous Approach*, Prentice-Hall International, London, 1980.

7   Ron Decent, *personal communication to the author* (September 7, 1979).

Annex B
Basic Concepts

This tutorial contains the full text of Annex B of ISO 8879. It covers such basics of SGML as document structure, markup recognition, attributes, entities, characters, data content notations, and marked sections.

(This annex does not form an integral part of this International Standard.)

2 This annex describes some of the basic concepts of the Standard Generalized Markup Language (SGML). Before beginning it, the
4 reader should consult annex A ⌈ 5 ⌉ to gain an initial familiarity with generic coding and generalized markup.

6 NOTE — The reader should be aware that this annex does not cover all basic SGML constructs, nor all details of those covered, and subtle distinc-
8 tions are frequently ignored in the interest of presenting a clear overview.

B.1 Documents, Document Type Definitions, and Procedures

The fundamental concept of generalized markup is the relationship
10 between documents, document type definitions, and procedures.

B.1.1 Documents

In generalized markup, the term "document" does not refer to a
12 physical construct such as a file or a set of printed pages. Instead, a document is a logical construct that contains a *document element*
14 ⌈ [12] *306:15* ⌉, the top node of a tree of elements that make up the document's *content* ⌈ [24] *320:1* ⌉. A book, for example, could contain

18

"chapter" elements that in turn contain "paragraph" elements and
2   "picture" elements.

Eventually, the terminal nodes of this document tree are reached
4   and the actual characters or other data are encountered. If paragraphs, for example, were terminal, their content would be charac-
6   ters, rather than other elements. If photographs were terminal they
would contain neither elements nor characters, but some nonchar-
8   acter data that represents an image.

The elements are distinguished from one another by additional
10 information, called *markup*, that is added to the data content. A
document thus consists of two kinds of information: data and
12 markup.

B.1.2 Document Type Definitions

An element's markup consists of a *start-tag* [14] *314:1* at its begin-
14 ning and an *end-tag* [19] *317:4* at its end. The tags describe the
characteristic qualities of the element.

16 One of these characteristics is the *generic identifier* [30] *325:17*,
which identifies the "type" of the element (manual, paragraph, fig-
18 ure, list, etc.). In addition, there can be other characteristics, called
"attributes", that further qualify the generic identifier.

20 An individual document's markup tags describe its structure of elements. That is, they indicate which elements occur in the docu-
22 ment's content, and in what order. That structure must conform to
rules that define the permitted structures for all documents of a
24 given type; that is, those documents having the same generic identifier.

26 The rules that define the possible structures are part of a *document
type definition* of that type of document. A document type definition
28 specifies:
    a) The generic identifiers (GIs) of elements that are permissible
30   in a document of this type.
    b) For each GI, the possible attributes, their range of values, and
32   defaults.
    c) For each GI, the structure of its content, including
34   i)   which subelement GIs can occur and in what order;
        ii) whether text characters can occur;
36   iii) whether noncharacter data can occur.

A document type definition does *not* specify:

2   a)   The delimiters that are used to indicate markup.

     b)   Anything about the ways in which the document can be

4   formatted or otherwise processed.

B.1.3 Procedures

Markup tags describe a document's structure of elements; they do

6 not say how to process that structure. Many kinds of processing are possible, one of which is to *format* the text.

8 Formatting can be thought of as mapping the element structure onto paper or a display screen with graphic arts conventions. For

10 example, the element "paragraph" could be displayed by setting the text of the element off from surrounding text with blank lines.

12 Alternatively, it could be displayed by indenting its first line.

Processing is handled by *procedures*, which are written in the

14 language of a formatter or other processing system. When a document is processed, a procedure is associated with each

16 generic identifier (that is, with each type of element). The procedure then processes the content of the element. In the case of

18 formatting, for example, the procedure performs the actions that render an element into printed text or another display form.

20 Thus, production of a document begins when a user creates the text, marking it up as a particular document type. One of the

22 facilities that can process that document is a formatter, which could have more than one set of procedures available.

24 For example, a document called "mybook", marked up as a "TechManual" document type, could be formatted in a number of

26 ways by using a different *procedure set* each time. One set could produce output in single column CRT display style, another set in

28 two column printed report style, and a third set in still another style.

When developing a completely new text application, then, a

30 designer would create document type definitions, using the Standard Generalized Markup Language. Probably, he would also

32 implement one or more procedure sets, using the languages of the systems that are to process the documents.

B.2 Markup

Markup is text that is added to the data of a document in order to convey information about it. In SGML, the markup in a document falls into four categories:

a) Descriptive Markup ("Tags")

Tags are the most frequent and the most important kind of markup. They define the structure of the document, as described above.

b) Entity Reference

Within a system, a single document can be stored in several parts, each in a separate unit of system storage, called an *entity*. (Depending on the system, an entity could be a file, a data set, a variable, a data stream object, a library member, etc.)

Separate entities are connected by *entity references* that can occur in a document's markup. An entity reference is a request for text — the entity — to be imbedded in the document at the point of the reference. The entity could have been defined either earlier within the document or externally.

The entity reference capability includes the functions commonly called *symbol substitution* and *file imbedding*.

c) Markup Declaration

Declarations are statements that control how the markup is interpreted. They can be used to define entities and to create document type definitions.

d) Processing Instructions

These are instructions to the processing system, in its own language, to take some specific action. Unlike the other kinds of markup, processing instructions are system-dependent, and are usually application-dependent as well. They normally need to be changed if the document is processed differently (for example, formatted in a different style), or on a different system.

An SGML system must recognize these four kinds of markup and
2   handle them properly: that is, it must have an "SGML parser". The
parser need not be a single dedicated program; as long as a
4   system can perform the parsing process, it can be said to have an
SGML parser.

6   Markup occurs in a document according to a rigid set of rules.
Some of the rules are dictated by SGML; they apply to all types of
8   document. Other rules are defined by the document type definition
for the type of document being processed.

10 Employing the rules of SGML, the markup parser must:
   a)   Scan the text of each element's content to distinguish the four
12   kinds of markup from one another and from the data.
         (Noncharacter content data is not scanned by the parser.)
14 b)   Replace entity references by their entities.
   c)   Interpret the markup declarations.
16 d)   Give control to the processing system to execute processing
         instructions.
18 e)   Interpret the descriptive markup tags to recognize the generic
         identifiers ("GIs") and attributes, and, following the rules of the
20   document type:
         i)   Determine whether each GI and its attributes are valid.
22   ii)   Track the location in the document structure.
   f)   Give control to the processing system to execute the
24   procedure associated with the GI. (Once again, there is no
         actual requirement for separate programs. "Giving control"
26   means only that the ensuing processing is not defined by this
         International Standard.)

B.3 Distinguishing Markup from Text

28 The markup discussed in this section applies to all document types.
The delimiter characters used are the delimiter set of the *reference*
30 *concrete syntax*. (They will be discussed as if there were only one
concrete syntax, although SGML allows variant concrete syntaxes
32 to be defined.)

B.3.1 Descriptive Markup Tags

Descriptive markup tags identify the start and end of elements.
34 There are three special character strings that are important (see
figure 9 [24]):

	STAGO	Start-TAG Open
2		This is a delimiter that indicates the beginning of a start-tag. In the figure, "<" is the **stago**.
4	**TAGC**	TAG Close
		The string from the **stago** to the **tagc** is called the
6		*start-tag* [14] *314:1*. In it the generic identifier ("GI") and all the attributes are given. In the figure, "quote"
8		was the GI and ">" is used for the **tagc**.
	ETAGO	End-TAG Open
10		This is a two-character delimiter that indicates the beginning of an end-tag. In the figure, "</" is the **etago**.
12		Between the **tagc** of the start-tag and the **etago** of the end-tag is the *content* [24] *320:1* of the element,
14		which can include data characters and subordinate elements. (Noncharacter data is kept separately; it will be
16		discussed later.) The end-tag contains a repetition of the GI to make the markup easier to read.

18 The scheme just described is the most general way of delimiting an element. SGML, though, allows a number of techniques of *markup*
20 *minimization* that allow the shortening of tags, and even their omission. These techniques, which are available as optional features,
22 will be described later.

B.3.2 Other Markup

An entity reference begins with an "entity reference open" (**ero**)
24 delimiter and ends with a "reference close" (**refc**). These are the ampersand and semicolon, respectively, in the following example:

26 `The &SGML; supports publishing and office systems.`

A markup declaration is delimited by "markup declaration open"
28 (**mdo**) and "markup declaration close" (**mdc**) delimiters, and a processing instruction by a "processing instruction open" (**pio**) and
30 a "processing instruction close" (**pic**).

    `here is an imbedded <!markup declaration> example`
32 `and an imbedded <?processing instruction> example`

To summarize:

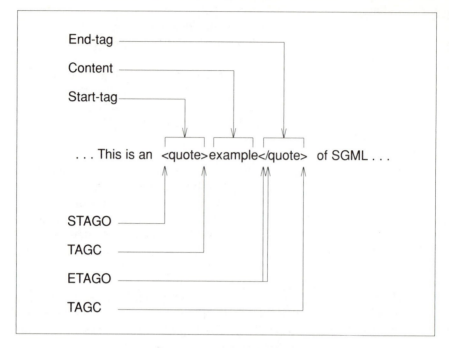

Figure 9 — Element Markup

	String	Name	Meaning
2	&	**ERO**	Opens a named entity reference.
	;	**REFC**	Closes a reference.
4	<!	**MDO**	Opens a markup declaration.
	>	**MDC**	Closes a markup declaration.
6	<?	**PIO**	Opens a processing instruction.
	>	**PIC**	Closes a processing instruction.

B.3.3 Record Boundaries

8   Not every text processing system breaks its storage entities into records. In those that do, the record boundaries are represented by
10 function characters known as the "record start" (**RS**) and "record end" (**RE**). The record boundaries could be used as general
12 delimiter characters in a variant concrete syntax, or as a special form of delimiter that serves as a "short entity reference". If a
14 record boundary is not a delimiter, its treatment depends on where it occurs.

B.3.3.1 Record Boundaries in Data

In attribute values (discussed later) and in the data content of an
element, record starts are ignored. The record ends, though, are
treated as part of the data because they might be significant to a
processor of the document. A formatter, for example, normally
interprets a record end as a space.

However, record ends are ignored when they are caused by
markup. That is:

— Record ends are ignored at the start or end of the content.
For example,

```
<p>
Short paragraph data.
</p>
```

is the same as

```
<p>Short paragraph data.</p>
```

— Record ends are ignored after a record that contains only
processing instructions or markup declarations. As a result,

```
<p>
Starting data
<?instruction 1>
<?instruction 2>
ending data.
</p>
```

and

```
<p>Starting data
<?instruction 1><?instruction 2>ending data.</p>
```

are equivalent. In other words, as far as the flow of data
characters is concerned, declarations and processing
instructions are simply ignored.

B.3.3.2 Record Boundaries in Markup

In tags or declarations, both record starts and record ends are

treated as spaces. They serve as internal separators within the
2   markup (as do horizontal tabs, incidentally).

The meaning of record boundaries within processing instructions
4   depends on the processing system.

B.4 Document Structure

SGML tags serve two purposes:
6   a)   They show the structural relationships among the elements of
         the document.
8   b)   They identify each element's generic identifier (GI) and
         attributes.
10   The rules for specifying structure and attributes are defined by
     SGML for all documents. (Some rules have already been
12   introduced; the others will be discussed later.) The *particular*
     elements and attributes allowed in a document, though, are defined
14   by that document's type definition.

B.4.1 Document Type Definitions

A generic identifier (GI) identifies an element as a member of a
16   class, or "type". A *document type definition* is a set of markup
     declarations that apply to all documents of a particular type.

18   The three most important kinds of declaration that can occur in a
     document type definition are:
20   a)   An *element declaration* [116] 405:6 , which defines the GIs
         that can occur in each element, and in what order.
22   b)   An *attribute definition list declaration* [141] 420:15 , which
         defines the attributes that can be specified for an element,
24   and their possible values.
     c)   An *entity declaration* [101] 394:18 , which defines the entities
26   that can be referred to in documents of this type. For
         example, entity references can simplify the keying of fre-
28   quently used lengthy phrases:

```
<!ENTITY SGML "Standard Generalized Markup Language">
```

30   To avoid repetitive keying, the document type definition is usually
     stored as a separate entity. It is then incorporated in each

2   document by means of a *document type declaration* [110] *403:1*
that identifies the document type and serves as a reference to the
external entity.

B.4.2 Element Declarations

4   Elements can occur in a document only according to the rules of
the document type definition. For example, unless the definition
6   allows a paragraph inside a figure, it would be an error to put one
there. The element declaration is used to define these rules.

B.4.2.1 Content Models

8   For each element in the document, the application designer
specifies two element declaration parameters: the element's GI and
10 a *content model* [126] *410:1* of its content. The model parameter
defines which subelements and character strings can occur in the
12 content.

For example, the declaration for a textbook might look like this:

14 `<!ELEMENT  textbook  (front, body, rear) >`

Here, "textbook" is the GI whose content is being defined, and
16 "(front, body, rear)" is the model that defines it. The example says
that a textbook contains the GIs "front", "body", and "rear". (The GIs
18 probably stand for "front matter", "body matter", and "rear matter",
but this is of interest only to humans, not to the SGML parser.)

20 A model is a kind of *group*, which is a collection of connected
members, called *tokens*. A group is bounded by parentheses, the
22 "group open" (**grpo**) and "group close" (**grpc**) delimiters. The
parentheses are required even when the model group contains but
24 a single token.

The tokens in a model group are GIs. There are also delimiters
26 called *connectors* that put the GIs in order, and other delimiters,
called *occurrence indicators*, that show how many times each GI
28 can occur.

B.4.2.2 Connectors and Occurrence Indicators

A connector is used *between* GIs, to show how they are
connected. The textbook model uses the "sequence" connector
(*seq*), the comma. It means that the elements must follow one
another in the document in the same sequence as their GIs occur
in the model.

An occurrence indicator is used *after* the GI to which it applies.
There are none in the textbook example: each element must
therefore occur once and only once. To make the front matter and
rear matter optional, the question mark, which is the optional
occurrence indicator (*opt*), would be used.

```
<!ELEMENT  textbook  (front?, body, rear?) >
```

So far only the top level of a textbook has been defined. The type
definition must also have structure declarations for "front", "body",
and "rear", then for the elements contained in "front", "body", and
"rear", and so on down to the data characters.

For the purposes of a simple example, the body can be assumed to
be just a sequence of many paragraphs. That is, the only GI
allowed in the body is "p" (for paragraph), but it can occur many
times. To indicate multiple paragraphs, the GI is followed by a plus
sign, which is the "required and repeatable" occurrence
indicator(*plus*).

```
<!ELEMENT body (p+) >
```

The plus sign indicates that there must be at least one paragraph in
the body. If, for some reason, it were desirable to allow a body to
have no paragraphs at all, the added symbol would be an asterisk,
which is the "optional and repeatable" occurrence indicator (*rep*).

```
<!ELEMENT body (p*) >
```

Suppose a textbook could have examples in the body, as well as
paragraphs. If the GI for an example were "xmp", "many
paragraphs or examples" would be indicated like this:

```
<!ELEMENT body (p | xmp) + >
```

The vertical bar is the "or" connector (*or*). The expression "p | xmp"
means "either a paragraph or an example".

Although a model group contains tokens, it is itself a single token to
2 which an occurrence indicator can apply. The grouping is needed in
the example because the occurrence indicators ("?", "+", and "*")
4 have higher precedence than the connectors ("," and "|").

Therefore, it would not be effective to say

6 `<!ELEMENT body (p+ | xmp+) >`

because it would mean "either many paragraphs or many
8 examples" rather than the desired "many intermixed paragraphs or
examples".

10 There is one more kind of connector to consider. Suppose the front
matter of the textbook had a title page that contained a title, an
12 author's name, and a publisher, but in *any* order. The **seq**
connector cannot be used because that requires a specific order.
14 Nor can the **or** connector, because that chooses only one of the
three elements.

16 Instead, the ampersand ("&"), which is the "and" connector(**and**)
should be used. It indicates that all of the GIs in the model group
18 must occur, but in any order.

```
<!ELEMENT titlepage (title & author & publisher) >
```

B.4.2.3 Entity References in Models

20 Suppose two elements have almost the same content model, but
not quite.

```
22  <!ELEMENT body (p | xmp | h1 | h2 | h3 | h4)+ >
    <!ELEMENT rear (p |      h1 | h2 | h3 | h4)+ >
```

24 Here, the body and rear matter both have paragraphs and
headings, but only the body can have examples.

26 Repetitive parts of markup declaration parameters can be handled
with entity references, just like repetitive text in a document. The
28 only difference is that entity references used in declaration
parameters ("parameter entity references") begin with a special
30 character, the percent sign ("%"), called the "parameter entity
reference open" delimiter (**pero**). The **pero** must also be used in

the entity declaration to show that the entity being defined is a
2 parameter entity (but as a separate parameter so it won't be
misinterpreted as a reference).

```
4  <!ENTITY % h1to4   "h1 | h2 | h3 | h4"  >
   <!ELEMENT  body    (p | xmp | %h1to4;)+ >
6  <!ELEMENT  rear    (p |        %h1to4;)+ >
```

B.4.2.4 Name Groups

There is another use for groups. The body matter and rear matter
8 might have the same structure declaration.

```
   <!ELEMENT body (p | xmp)+ >
10 <!ELEMENT rear (p | xmp)+ >
```

Keying effort could be saved and the similarity emphasized by
12 letting the declaration apply to a group of elements.

```
   <!ELEMENT (body | rear) (p | xmp)+ >
```

B.4.2.5 Data Characters

14 Up to now, all of the elements discussed contained only other
elements. Eventually, though, an application must deal with the
16 actual data, that is, the point where there are no more tags.

Data can be referred to in a model with the reserved name
18 "#PCDATA", which means "zero or more parsed data characters".
As it has, in effect, a built-in *rep* occurrence indicator, none can be
20 added to it explicitly. The declaration

```
   <!ELEMENT p (#PCDATA) >
```

22 says that a paragraph is a string of zero or more characters
(including record ends and spaces).

24 Incidentally, the reason "#PCDATA" is in upper-case is simply as a
reminder that it is defined by the markup parser. In the reference
26 concrete syntax, the markup parser ignores the case of all names,
except those of entities.

In most documents, elements that contain data characters can also
2   contain other tagged elements. Such elements normally include
short quotations, footnote and figure references, various types of
4   highlighted phrases, and specialized references or citations defined
for a particular document type.

6   For example, the structure of a paragraph might be defined as:

```
<!ENTITY % phrase    "quote | citation | reference" >
<!ELEMENT  p          (#PCDATA | %phrase;)*              >
```

These declarations indicate that a paragraph contains characters
10   mixed with "phrase" elements. There can be none or many of them.

The "#", incidentally, is a delimiter called the "reserved name
12   indicator" (***rni***) that is used whenever a reserved name is specified
in a context where a user-created name could also occur. The ***rni***
14   makes it clear that "#PCDATA" is not a GI.

B.4.2.6 Empty Content

An element can be defined for which the user never enters the
16   content: for example, a figure reference for which a procedure will
always generate the content during processing. To show an empty
18   element, a keyword is used to declare the content instead of the
usual parenthesized model group:

```
20   <!ELEMENT figref EMPTY >
```

An element that is declared to be empty cannot have an end-tag.
22   (None is needed, because there is no content to be ended by it.)

B.4.2.7 Non-SGML Data

If the body of the textbook contained photographs, the element
24   declaration could be

```
<!ELEMENT  body  (p | photo)+ >
```

26   A photo is typically represented by a string of bits that stand for the
colors of the various points in the picture. These bit combinations
28   do not have the same meaning as the characters in text and in
markup; they have to be interpreted as a unique notation that is not
30   defined by SGML.

As the markup parser does not scan non-SGML data, it must be
2   stored in a separate entity whose name is given by a special
attribute (discussed later). The element content will be empty.

4   `<!ELEMENT photo EMPTY >`

B.4.2.8 Summary of Model Delimiters

The following list summarizes the delimiters used in models and
6   their character strings in the reference delimiter set:

— Grouping:

String	Name	Meaning
8		
(	GRPO	Opens a group. The expression within
10		the group is treated as a unit for other operations.
12)	GRPC	Closes a group.

— Occurrence Indicators:

String	Name	Meaning
14		
?	OPT	Optional: can occur 0 or 1 time.
16 +	PLUS	Required and repeatable: must occur 1 or more times.
18 *	REP	Optional and repeatable: can occur 0 or more times.

20   — Connectors:

String	Name	Meaning
22 ,	SEQ	All of the connected elements must occur in the document in the same sequence
24		as in the model group.
|	OR	One and only one of the connected
26		elements must occur.
**& **	AND	All of the connected elements must occur
28		in the document, but in any order.

— Other:

String	Name	Meaning
30		
#	RNI	Identifies a reserved name to distinguish
32		it from a user-specified name.

B.5 Attributes

A descriptive tag normally includes the element's generic identifier
2 (GI) and may include attributes as well. The GI is normally a noun;
the attributes are nouns or adjectives that describe significant
4 characteristics of the GI. (The use of verbs or formatting
parameters, which are procedural rather than descriptive, is
6 strongly discouraged because it defeats the purpose of generalized
markup.)

8 The *particular* attributes allowed for a given element are defined by
the type definition, which also determines the range of values that
10 an attribute can have and what the default values are.

B.5.1 Specifying Attributes

A sample tag with two attributes is shown in figure 10 $\boxed{34}$.

12 The attributes follow the GI in the start-tag. Each attribute is
specified by giving its *name* $\boxed{\text{[55] } 346:17}$, the value indicator delim-
14 iter (*vi*), and the attribute *value*. In the example, the attribute
named "security" was given the value "Internal Use", and the attri-
16 bute "sender" was given the value "LTG".

B.5.1.1 Names

Attribute names, such as "security" and "sender" in the example,
18 share certain properties with other kinds of markup language
names already encountered, such as entity names and GIs. A
20 name must consist only of characters that have been designated as
"name characters", and it must start with one of a subset of the
22 name characters called the "name start" characters.

Normally (that is, in the reference concrete syntax), the name
24 characters are the letters, digits, period, and hyphen, and the name
start characters are the letters only. Lower-case letters in a name
26 are normally treated as though they were upper-case, so it makes
no difference in which case a name is keyed. In entity names,
28 though, the case is significant.

A name normally has a maximum length of eight characters, but a
30 system could define a variant *quantity set* $\boxed{\text{[194] } 470:1}$ in which

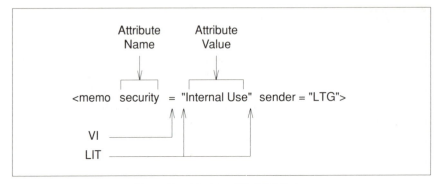

Figure 10 — Start-tag with 2 Attributes

name length and other quantitative characteristics of the language
2 could differ from the reference concrete syntax.

B.5.1.2 Attribute Values

The value of an attribute consists of data characters and entity
4 references, bounded by delimiters called "literal delimiters" (*lit*),
which are normally quotation marks ("). Alternative literal delimiters
6 (*lita*), normally apostrophes ('), can also be used, but the two types
cannot be paired with one another.

8 An empty attribute value is indicated by two *lit* delimiters in
succession:

10 `<listing name=Jones phone="555-1234" altphone="">`

Record ends and tabs in an attribute value are replaced by spaces.
12 Record start characters are ignored (that is, removed).

The following list summarizes the delimiter roles and their string
14 assignments in the reference delimiter set:

String	Name	*Meaning*
16 =	**VI**	Value Indicator
"	**LIT**	Literal Delimiter
18 '	**LITA**	Literal Delimiter (Alternative)

B.5.2 Declaring Attributes

For every element, the document type definition must contain
2 information that establishes the element's attributes. This is done
with an attribute definition list declaration. If there is no attribute
4 definition list for an element, then the element simply has no
attributes.

B.5.2.1 Attribute Definition Syntax

6 The attribute definition list declaration begins with the *associated
element type* [72] 377:1 to which the attribute definition list applies.
8 The declaration can specify a single GI or a group of them, in which
case the same attributes apply to all members of the group.

10 The declaration also includes, for each attribute, an attribute definition consisting of
12 a) the attribute name,
b) its allowable values (*declared value* [145] 422:6), and
14 c) a default value that will be used if the attribute is not specified
in the document and omitted tag markup minimization is in
16 effect (described later).

The attribute list has more parameters than the declarations that
18 have been shown up to now. When dealing with lengthy
declarations, it is helpful to add explanatory comments to them. In
20 a markup declaration, comments can occur between any
parameters, or a declaration could consist solely of comments.

22 Comments begin and end with two hyphens, the "comment
delimiter" (*com*). One use for comments is to put a heading over
24 the parameters:

```
<!--      ELEMENTS NAME     VALUE        DEFAULT -->
```

26 The attribute definition list requires that some of the parameters be
repeated for each attribute of the element. As declarations can
28 span record boundaries, a tabular form of entry can be used if
desired. The following declarations for the memo element in figure
30 10 [34] are in tabular form:

```
<!--      ELEMENTS     CONTENT                  -->
32 <!ELEMENT memo         (from, to, subject, body, sig,
                                    cc?)>
```

▼

```
      <!--       ELEMENTS NAME     VALUE          DEFAULT -->
  2   <!ATTLIST memo      status   (final|draft) "final"
                          security CDATA          #REQUIRED
  4                       version  NUMBER         "01"
                          sender   NAME           #IMPLIED
  6   >
```

The meaning of the attribute definition list is as follows:

8	**status**	The "status" attribute must have a value of "final" or "draft". As the attribute was not specified in
10		figure 10 ⟨ 34 ⟩, the parser will act as though the default value of "final" was entered.
12	**security**	The "security" attribute has a string of zero or more characters as its value. The keyword
14		"REQUIRED" in the default parameter indicates that the attribute must always be specified in the
16		document.
	version	The value of the "version" attribute must be a
18		string of 1 or more digits. The default value is the string "01".
20	**sender**	The "sender" attribute must have a syntactically valid SGML name as a value. The keyword
22		"IMPLIED" indicates that the attribute is optional, and that the value will be supplied by the applica-
24		tion if the attribute is not specified in the docu- ment. (In figure 10 ⟨ 34 ⟩ it was specified as
26		"LTG".)

Note that delimiters can be omitted from the default value when it is
28 composed entirely of name characters. (The default value parameter keywords begin with the *rni*, so they cannot be confused with
30 application-defined names.) In the above example, the default values "final" and "01" could have been entered without delimiters.

32 Since the topic of comments was introduced, it should also be
noted that an empty markup declaration ("<!>") is also a comment.
34 It can be used to separate parts of the source document with no
danger of being misinterpreted as a use of the "short reference"
36 feature (discussed later), as a blank record might be.

B.5.2.2 Complex Attribute Values

An attribute value might logically consist of a number of elements.

For example, an illustration of output displayed by a computer could
have two colors associated with it: green and black. As an attribute
can be specified only once in a tag,

```
<display color=black color=green>
```

could not be entered, as it would be an error.

However, by declaring the value "NAMES" for the "color" attribute,
both colors can be specified in a single attribute value:

```
<!ELEMENT display (p+)>
<!ATTLIST display color NAMES "white black">
<!>
<display color="black green">
```

The "NAMES" keyword means "a list of one or more SGML names,
separated by spaces, record ends, record starts, or horizontal tab
characters". Some other declared value keywords that allow lists
are:

NUMBERS   a list of one or more numbers.

NMTOKENS   a list of one or more name tokens (like
                     names, but they need not start with a name
                     start character: for example, "-abc 123 12.3
                     123a .123").

NUTOKENS   a list of one or more number tokens (like
                     name tokens, but the first character must be
                     a digit: for example, "123 12.3 123a 0.123",
                     but not ".123 456").

The singular forms "NMTOKEN" and "NUTOKEN" can be used
when only a single token is permitted. (Note that an *rni* is not
needed for the declared value parameter keywords, as a user-
defined name cannot be specified for that parameter.)

A complex attribute could be avoided altogether in this case by
defining two separate attributes:

```
<!ELEMENT display (p+)>
<!ATTLIST display bgcolor NAME "white" fgcolor NAME
                                       "black">
<!>
<display bgcolor=black fgcolor=green>
```

B.5.2.3 Name Token Groups

An attribute value can be restricted to a member of a group of
unique names or name tokens, called a *name token group*
[68] *374:1* :

```
<!--       ELEMENTS    CONTENT              -->
<!ELEMENT memo         (from, to, subject, body, sig,
                                        cc?)>
<!--       ELEMENTS NAME    VALUE          DEFAULT -->
<!ATTLIST memo     status  (final|draft)"final">
```

Given the above declaration, either

```
<memo status="draft">
```

or

```
<memo status="final">
```

can be specified. Any other value for the "status" attribute would be
incorrect.

A name token can appear only once in the attribute definition list
that applies to a single element type. It is translated to upper-case
in the same way as a name.

B.5.2.4 Changing Default Values

If the default value is specified as "CURRENT", the default will
automatically become the most recently specified value. This allows
an attribute value to be "inherited" by default from the previous
element of the same type. (This effect should be kept in mind when
adding or deleting tags that specify a current attribute.)

B.6 Entities

Entity references and parameter entity references have figured
prominently in some of the examples that have already appeared.
Although an entity has a superficial resemblance to a programming
language variable, it is actually a portion of the document, and as
such, it is a constant. References permit a number of useful
techniques:

a) A short name can be used to refer to a lengthy or text string, or to one that cannot be entered conveniently with the available keyboard.

b) Parts of the document that are stored in separate system files can be imbedded.

c) Documents can be exchanged among different systems more easily because references to system-specific objects (such as characters that cannot be keyed directly) can be in the form of entity references that are resolved by the receiving system.

d) The result of a dynamically executed processing instruction (such as an instruction to retrieve the current date) can be imbedded as part of the document.

B.6.1 Entity Reference Syntax

There are two kinds of named entity reference. A general entity reference can be used anywhere in the content of elements and delimited attribute values. Parameter entity references can be used within markup declaration parameters that are delimited with *lit* or *lita* delimiters. They can also be used to refer to consecutive complete parameters or group tokens, with their intervening separators.

A general entity reference is a name delimited by an "entity reference open" (*ero*), normally an ampersand, and a "reference close" (*refc*), normally a semicolon:

```
printed at &site; on
```

If an entity reference is followed by a space or record end, the *refc* can be omitted:

```
printed at &site on
```

A parameter entity reference is the same, except that it begins with a "parameter entity reference open" (*pero*), normally a percent sign. (Incidentally, "normally", in the context of delimiter strings, means "in the reference delimiter set".)

The distinction between general and parameter entities is made so that the document preparer can make up entity names without having to know whether the same names were used by the support personnel who created the markup declarations for the document type.

The following list summarizes the delimiters used in entity references and their character strings in the reference concrete syntax:

String	Name	Meaning
&	**ERO**	Entity Reference Open
%	**PERO**	Parameter Entity Reference Open
;	**REFC**	Reference Close

B.6.2 Declaring Entities

Before an entity can be referred to it must be declared with an entity declaration. There are two main parameters: the *entity name* [102] 395:1 and the *entity text* [105] 396:18 . The declaration

```
<!ENTITY uta "United Typothetae of America">
```

means that a reference to the name "uta" (that is, "&uta;") in the document will be the equivalent of entering the text "United Typothetae of America". The entity text is delimited by *lit* (or *lita*) delimiters (like an attribute value), and is known as a "parameter literal".

An entity does not inherently begin with a record start or end with a record end. If record boundaries are wanted around an entity, they should be put around the entity reference. The source

```
<p>The &uta; is a printing organization.</p>
```

resolves to

```
<p>The United Typothetae of America is a printing
                                    organization.</p>
```

while the source

```
<p>Printing organizations:
&uta;
Society of Scientific, Technical, and Medical Publishers
</p>
```

resolves to

```
  <p>Printing organizations:
2 United Typothetae of America
  Society of Scientific, Technical, and Medical Publishers
4 </p>
```

However, if a record end, rather than a **refc**, is used to terminate
an entity reference, the following record is concatenated to the
entity.

```
8 &uta
  , Inc.
```

resolves to

```
United Typothetae of America, Inc.
```

B.6.2.1 Processing Instructions

A processing instruction can be stored as an entity. It will be
ignored when the entity is created but executed when a reference
to the entity occurs.

```
<!ENTITY page PI "newpage; space 3" >
```

The keyword "PI" indicates that the entity will be interpreted as a
processing instruction when referenced.

B.6.2.2 Entities with Entity References

A parameter entity is declared by specifying a **pero** as the first
parameter, ahead of the entity name:

```
20 <!ENTITY % bullet "o" >
```

Parameter entities can be referenced within a parameter literal:

```
22 <!ENTITY prefix "%bullet;   " >
```

The reference to "%bullet;" is resolved when the "prefix" entity is
declared. It is not resolved on each reference to the "prefix" entity.

B.6.2.3 External Entities

In many text processing systems, there are multiple classes of
2   storage, such as files, library members, macro definitions, and
symbols for text strings. Such system dependencies can be kept
4   out of the body of the document by referencing external storage
objects as entities:

```
6   <!ENTITY part2 SYSTEM>
```

If the entity name is not sufficient to enable the system to identify
8   the storage object, additional information (called the "system
identifier") can be specified:

```
10   <!ENTITY part2 SYSTEM "user.sectionX3.textfile" >
```

The system identifier is delimited in the same manner as a
12   parameter literal. The nature and syntax of the system identifier
depends on a component of an SGML system called the "entity
14   manager", whose job it is to convert entity references into real
system addresses.

B.6.2.4 Public Entities

16   An external entity that is known beyond the context of an individual
document or system environment is called a "public entity". It is
18   given a "public identifier" by an international, national, or industry
standard, or simply by a community of users who wish to share it.

20   One application of public entities would be shared document type
definitions. Another would be shared "entity sets" of entity
22   declarations that support the graphic symbols and terminology of
specialized subject areas, such as mathematics or chemistry.

24   Public entities are declared in a manner similar to other external
entities, except that a "public identifier specification" replaces the
26   keyword "SYSTEM":

```
    <!ENTITY % ISOgrk1
28          PUBLIC "ISO 8879-1986//ENTITIES Greek
                                       Letters//EN">
```

30   The specification consists of the keyword "PUBLIC", the public

2   identifier, which is delimited like a literal, and an optional system identifier (omitted in the example). The public identifier can contain only letters, digits, space, record ends and starts, and a few special
4   characters; they are collectively known as the "minimum data" characters.

B.7 Characters

6   Each character in a document occupies a position in the document's *character set*. The total number of positions depends
8   on the size of the *code set*; that is, on the number of binary digits ("bits") used to represent each character.

10   For example, the character set known as ISO 646 International Reference Version (ISO 646 IRV) is a 7-bit set. There are 128 *bit*
12   *combinations* possible with 7 bits, ranging from the values 0 through 127 in the decimal number base. In 8-bit sets, 256 bit
14   combinations are possible. The position number, or *character number* [64] 357:1 , is the base-10 integer equivalent of the bit
16   combination that represents the character.

   It is also possible to employ "code extension techniques", in which
18   a bit combination can represent more than one character. Use of such techniques with SGML is discussed in E.3 537 .

B.7.1 Character Classification

20   Many character sets have been defined, to accommodate a variety of national alphabets, scientific notations, keyboards, display
22   devices, and processing systems. In each, the sequence of bit combinations is mapped to a different repertoire of digits, letters,
24   and other characters. Any character set large enough to represent the markup characters (name characters, delimiters, and function
26   characters) and the minimum data characters, can be used in an SGML document.

28   SGML classifies the characters as follows:

function characters	The record end and record start,
30	which have already been explained, are function characters, as is the
32	space. The reference concrete

syntax adds the horizontal tab (*TAB*), which is used to separate tokens in markup declarations and tags (along with the space, *RS*, and *RE* characters). Function characters can also serve as data characters, and can occur in short reference delimiters (explained later).

name characters   These are characters that can be used in a name. They always include the upper-case and lower-case letters A through Z and the digits 0 through 9; the reference concrete syntax adds the period and hyphen. Each name character (other than the digits and upper-case letters) has an associated upper-case form that is used for case substitution in names (except for entity names, in the reference concrete syntax). A subset of the name characters, called the *name start characters*, consists of the lower-case and upper-case letters, plus any other characters that a concrete syntax allows to start a name.

delimiter set   These are characters that, in varying contexts, will cause the text to be construed as markup, rather than as data.

non-SGML characters   These are characters that a document character set identifies as not occurring in SGML entities, chosen in part from candidates specified by the concrete syntax. The reference concrete syntax, for example, classifies the control characters in this way (except for the few that are used as function characters). Non-SGML characters occur in non-SGML data (such as images) that are in external entities, and in the "envelope" of the file

2 systems, data streams, etc., that contain or transmit the document. A system can also use them for its
4 own purposes, such as padding or delimiting during processing, as
6 there is no possibility of confusing them with markup or data
8 characters.

data characters All other characters, such as
10 punctuation and mathematical symbols that are not used as
12 delimiters, are data characters. (Markup characters can also be
14 data, when they occur in a context in which they are not recognized as
16 markup. Such data is called "parsed character data".)

B.7.2 Character References

18 It is rarely convenient, or even possible, to enter every character directly:

20 a) There may be no key for it on the entry device.
   b) It may not be displayable.
22 c) It may be a non-SGML character that cannot occur directly as a markup or data character.
24 d) It may be a function character that you want treated as data, rather than given its SGML function.

26 For such situations, a technique called a "character reference" is available to enter the character indirectly. (For visibility, the
28 following illustrations will use a character that could have been keyed, the hyphen.) The two declarations in the following example
30 are equivalent in any character set in which the hyphen is character number 45:

```
32   <!ENTITY hyphen "-" >
     <!ENTITY hyphen "&#45;" >
```

34 In the entity declarations illustrated so far, the literals contained only *character data* [47] *344:1* as the entity text. In the above
36 example, the second declaration contains a character reference. The character reference begins with a "character reference open"
38 delimiter (*&#*) and ends with a *refc* delimiter, but instead of a name

it contains a character number.

2   A literal can have a mix of character data and character references.
The following declarations are also equivalent:

4   ```
<!ENTITY finis "-|-" >
<!ENTITY finis "-|-" >
```

6   Character references can also be entered directly in attribute
values and data content, just as entity references can.

8   The function characters can also be referenced by named
character references: &#RS;, &#RE;, &#SPACE;, and &#TAB;.
10  This form of reference is used when the character's function is
wanted; the character number form is used to avoid the function
12  and enter the character as data.

The following list summarizes the delimiters used in character
14  references and their character strings in the reference concrete
syntax:

16  **String**      **Name**       *Meaning*

    **&#**          **CRO**        Character Reference Open
18  **;**           **REFC**       Reference Close

## B.7.3 Using Delimiter Characters as Data

The Standard Generalized Markup Language does not compel the
20  use of particular characters as delimiters. Instead, it defines
delimiter *roles* as part of an "abstract syntax" and allows character
22  strings to be assigned to them as part of a concrete syntax
definition. Although there are many such roles, the user's ability to
24  enter data characters freely is essentially unimpeded because:

    — Most of the delimiters occur only within markup declarations
26      or tags; only a few occur in the content of elements.
    — The same characters are used for more than one role.
28  — The delimiter roles that are meaningful in content are
        contextual; they will only be recognized when followed by an
30      appropriate contextual sequence (or are otherwise enabled).
        For example, the *ero* is only recognized when it is followed by
32      a name start character.
    — Most delimiters are multicharacter strings, which reduces the
34      chance of their occurring as data.
```

2 — A multicharacter delimiter or a "delimiter-in-context" will not be recognized if an entity starts or ends within it.

Because of the last point, ambiguity can always be avoided by
4 using a reference to enter the data character. Only two entities are needed for most situations in the reference delimiter set, and three
6 more will handle the special cases:

```
<!ENTITY amp    "&" >
8 <!ENTITY lt    "<" >
```

The entity references "&" and "<" can be used freely in text
10 whenever the ampersand or less-than sign are wanted, as the use of the reference terminates a delimiter-in-context.

12 `<!ENTITY rsqb  "]" >`

The right square bracket entity can be used similarly to avoid
14 recognition of a marked section end (discussed later).

`<!ENTITY sol CDATA "/" >`

16 The solidus is a valid delimiter only when the SHORTTAG feature is used (explained later), and even then it must specifically be
18 enabled for an element. As the delimiter is a single character and requires no contextual sequence, the entity reference alone is not
20 enough to assure that it will be treated as data. The "CDATA" keyword is therefore specified; it causes an entity's text to be
22 treated as character data, even though it may look like a delimiter.

`<!ENTITY quot  '"' >`

24 The """ (quotation mark) entity is needed only for the rare instance in which both the *lit* and *lita* delimiter characters occur as
26 data in the same literal. Normally, if a literal contained the *lit* character, it would be delimited with *lita* delimiters, and vice versa.

B.8 Marked Sections

28 A *marked section* [96] *392:9* is a section of a document that is entered as a parameter of a *marked section declaration*
30 [93] *391:13* in order to label it for a special purpose, such as disabling delimiters within it, or ignoring the section during certain pro-
32 cessing runs.

B.8.1 Ignoring a Marked Section

If a document is processed on two different systems, a processing
2   instruction that applies to one will not be understood by the other.
The markup parser can be made to ignore one of the instructions if
4   the section of the document that contains it is marked as a section
to be ignored:

```
6   <![ IGNORE [<?instruction for System A>]]>
```

The marked section declaration in the example consists of five
8   parts:
a) the *marked section start* ⌈**[94]** *392:3*⌋, which consists of the
10   **mdo** delimiter followed by the "declaration subset open" delimiter (**dso**), normally a left square bracket;

```
12  <![
```

b) the *status keywords*, in this case, the single keyword
14   "IGNORE";

```
IGNORE
```

16 c) another "declaration subset open" delimiter (**dso**) to indicate
the start of the marked section content;
18 d) the content;

```
<?instruction for System A>
```

20 e) and the *marked section end* ⌈**[95]** *392:6*⌋, consisting of the
"marked section close" delimiter (**msc**), normally two right
22   square brackets (to balance the two **dso** delimiters) followed
by the **mdc**.

```
24  ]]>
```

The processing instruction for the other system would be marked
26 as one to be included:

```
<![ INCLUDE [
28  <?instruction for System B>
]]>
```

30 Sending the document to system A requires exchanging the status
keywords for the two sections. This can be done most easily by

using two parameter entities, one for each processing system. One
entity would contain the character string "IGNORE" and the other
would contain "INCLUDE":

```
<!ENTITY % systema "IGNORE"  >
<!ENTITY % systemb "INCLUDE" >
```

The "IGNORE" keyword would not be used directly in any marked
section declaration. Instead, there would be a reference to one of
the two system-dependent entities. Given the previous
declarations, the instruction for "System A" in the following example
will be ignored, while the one for "System B" will be executed:

```
<![%systema;[<?instruction for System A>]]>
<![%systemb;[<?instruction for System B>]]>
```

Every other marked section in the document that refers to
"%systema;" or "%systemb;" will be affected similarly.

Now, if the two entity declarations are reversed, as follows,

```
<!ENTITY % systema "INCLUDE" >
<!ENTITY % systemb "IGNORE"  >
```

every marked section in the document that refers to "%systemb;"
will be ignored.

Note that even though the section content is ignored, enough
parsing is done to recognize nested marked section starts and
ends, so the correct end will be used for the section.

B.8.2 Versions of a Single Document

A document could be published in multiple versions whose text
differs slightly. SGML allows all versions of such a document to be
processed without duplicating the text of the common portions. The
version-dependent text is entered in marked sections, using the
technique just described, while the common text is not:

```
<![ %v1; [text for version 1]]>
<![ %v2; [text for 2nd version]]>
common text for both versions
<![ %v1; [more text for version 1]]>
<![ %v2; [more text for 2nd version]]>
```

Now, if the following entity declarations are defined:

```
2  <!ENTITY % v1 "INCLUDE" >
   <!ENTITY % v2 "IGNORE"  >
```

4 version 1 will be processed, as follows:

```
   text for version 1
6  common text for both versions
   more text for version 1
```

8 If the entity declarations are reversed:

```
   <!ENTITY % v1 "IGNORE"  >
10 <!ENTITY % v2 "INCLUDE" >
```

version 2 will be processed, as follows:

```
12 text for 2nd version
   common text for both versions
14 more text for 2nd version
```

B.8.3 Unparsable Sections

A marked section can be labeled as one that is not to be parsed:

```
16 <![ CDATA [
   <?instruction>
18 <p>A paragraph with an &entityx;
   reference that is not recognized.</p>
20 <?instruction>
   ]]>
```

22 The content of the section is treated as character data, so the two processing instructions and the entity reference will not be
24 recognized or processed as such.

If it is necessary to resolve entity references and character
26 references while ignoring other delimiters, the content can be treated as *replaceable character data* [46] *343:1* like this:

```
28 <![ RCDATA [
   <?instruction>
30 <p>A paragraph with an &entityx;
   reference that is recognized.</p>
```

```
   <?instruction>
2  ]]>
```

CDATA and RCDATA marked sections are not nestable, as are
4 IGNORE marked sections. The first marked section end will
terminate them.

B.8.4 Temporary Sections

6 A marked section can be flagged as temporary for easy
identification and removal:

8 `<![TEMP[<?newpage>]]>`

Such sections are useful for temporary "fixes" when a processor
10 does not get things quite right.

B.8.5 Keyword Specification

To facilitate keyword entry with entity references, the four status
12 keywords and "TEMP" can be used concurrently, and duplicates
are permitted. This allows multiple entity references to be used in a
14 single marked section declaration with no possibility of an error
being caused by their resolving to conflicting or duplicate keywords.

16 The status keywords are prioritized as follows:

```
       IGNORE
18     CDATA
       RCDATA
20     INCLUDE
```

If no status keyword is specified, "INCLUDE" is assumed.

B.8.6 Defining a Marked Section as an Entity

22 A marked section can be defined as an entity so it can be
incorporated at many points in the document:

```
24  <!ENTITY phrase1 MS
    "RCDATA[
26  a repeated phrase with
```

```
    a <tag> example
2   " >
```

Given this declaration, the input

```
4   This is &phrase1; in it.
```

will resolve to

```
6   This is <![RCDATA[
    a repeated phrase with
8   a <tag> example
    ]]> in it.
```

10 The "<tag>" was not recognized as markup because of the "RCDATA" keyword on the marked section declaration.

12 Note that there was no record start before the marked section nor a record end after it. The following example would have produced
14 them:

```
    This is
16  &phrase1;
    in it.
```

18 A marked section is not parsed or processed as such when the entity is defined. The marked section start and marked section end
20 are added automatically.

B.9 Unique Identifier Attributes

A *unique identifier* ("ID") is an attribute that names an element to
22 distinguish it from all other elements. An SGML markup parser can perform common processing for ID attributes, thereby minimizing
24 the implementation effort for procedures.

The purpose of IDs is to allow one element to refer to another: for
26 example, to allow a figure reference to refer to a figure. Normally, the procedure for the figure would associate some data with the ID
28 (such as the figure number). The figure reference procedure would retrieve the data and print it.

Although the markup parser is normally unaware of the meaning of
2 particular attributes, it can be told when an attribute is a unique
identifier:

```
4  <!--        ELEMENT          CONTENT              -->
   <!ELEMENT figure            (figbody, figcap)>
6  <!--        ELEMENT  NAME    VALUE        DEFAULT -->
   <!ATTLIST figure   id       ID           #IMPLIED>
```

8 Only one ID attribute is allowed for an element.

The value of a unique identifier attribute must be a name that is
10 different from the value of any other ID attribute in the document.
As with most names, the upper-case form is used, regardless of
12 how it was entered.

The element that does the referencing must have a "unique
14 identifier reference" attribute, indicated in the declared value by the
"IDREF" keyword:

```
16  <!--        ELEMENT          CONTENT              -->
   <!ELEMENT figref            EMPTY>
18  <!--        ELEMENT  NAME    VALUE        DEFAULT -->
   <!ATTLIST figref   refid    IDREF        #IMPLIED>
```

20 The value of an ID reference attribute must be a name that is the
same as that of some element's ID attribute. As usual, the upper-
22 case form of the name is employed.

B.10 Content Reference Attributes

Some documents are formatted and printed as separate chapters.
24 Separate formatting prevents automatic figure references across
chapter boundaries, although they would still be possible within a
26 chapter. An element definition could support the two types of figure
reference by specifying that the content could sometimes be empty
28 (the intra-chapter case), and that at other times it will be entered
explicitly (the cross-chapter case).

30 The condition for emptiness is the specification of an attribute that
is designated in the attribute definition as a "content reference"
32 attribute. (Everything else about the attribute behaves in its usual
manner.) The designation is made by entering the keyword
34 "#CONREF" as the default value:

```
     <!--         ELEMENTS         CONTENT                  -->
2    <!ELEMENT figref                (fignum, #PCDATA)>
     <!--         ELEMENTS  NAME    VALUE             DEFAULT -->
4    <!ATTLIST figref     refid    IDREF             #CONREF>
```

The keyword means that the attribute is a content reference
6 attribute, and also that it is an impliable attribute (the same as if the
default value were "#IMPLIED").

8 In the following example, the first "figref" has empty content, while
the second has both a "fignum" and a character string:

10 Here is text with a generated figure reference to
   <figref refid=figdavis>and a user-entered
12 reference to <figref><fignum>A-1</fignum>in the
   Appendix</figref> as well.

14 The first "figref" did not (and could not) have an end-tag because
the element was identified as empty by the explicit content
16 reference.

An element that just happens to be empty because its content
18 model is optional and no content is entered is not treated in this
way. Such an incidentally empty element must have an end-tag
20 (unless markup minimization is used, as explained later), because it
is impossible to tell from the start-tag whether an instance of the
22 element is actually empty.

It would be pointless (and is therefore prohibited) to designate a
24 content reference attribute for an element that is declared to be
empty.

26 To summarize (and expand slightly): content reference attributes
can be designated for any element type that is not declared empty.
28 When one or more such attributes has an explicit value specified on
the start-tag, that instance of the element is considered empty, and
30 no end-tag is permitted for it.

B.11 Content Model Exceptions

The content model specifies the elements that occur at the top level
32 of the content (the subelements). However, there are instances
when it may be necessary to refer to elements that are further

down. An optional parameter of the element declaration, called the
2 "exceptions" parameter, is used for this purpose.

B.11.1 Included Elements

In an indexed book, entry elements for the index could be
4 interspersed anywhere in the source. During formatting, the
procedures would collect, sort, and merge them, along with their
6 page numbers, and print the index.

It is cumbersome to express the relationship of the book to its index
8 entries in the usual way, as the entries would have to be included in
almost every model group. Instead, the exceptions parameter can
10 be employed:

```
   <!--        ELEMENTS  CONTENT (EXCEPTIONS)? -->
12 <!ELEMENT textbook  (front?, body, rear?) +(entry)>
```

The plus sign is the ***plus*** delimiter. Here it means that index entries
14 can occur anywhere in a textbook, even among the data
characters. This portion of an exceptions parameter is called an
16 "inclusion" group.

(Incidentally, the question mark on the heading comment is just a
18 reminder that the exceptions parameter is optional.)

B.11.2 Excluded Elements

It might be desirable to keep some element from showing up at *any*
20 level of an element being defined. For example, figures could be
kept from nesting with the following declaration:

```
22 <!--        ELEMENTS  CONTENT (EXCEPTIONS)? -->
   <!ELEMENT fig        (figbody, figcap?) -(fig)>
24 <!ELEMENT figbody    (artwork | p+)            >
   <!ELEMENT p          (#PCDATA | fig)           >
26 >
```

The content model clearly does not allow a figure to occur at the
28 top level of another figure, but the figure body could contain a
paragraph that could contain a figure. The exceptions parameter
30 with the ***minus*** prefix (hyphen) prevents such occurrences; it is
called an "exclusion" group.

A GI can be in an exclusion group only if its token in all affected
2   model groups has an *opt* or *rep* occurrence indicator, or is in an *or*
group or an applicable inclusion group. In other words, you cannot
4   exclude anything with an exclusion group that the model group
requires to be in the document. It follows from this that you cannot
6   use an exclusion group to change the required or optional status of
a token; for example, you cannot exclude all the members of a
8   required *or* group, thereby rendering it no longer required.

It is possible to specify both exclusion and inclusion exception
10   groups, in that order.

```
     <!--     ELEMENTS  CONTENT (EXCEPTIONS)? -->
12   <!ELEMENT fig      (figbody, figcap?) -(fig|xmp)
                                            +(gloss)>
```

14   If the same GI is in both an exclusion and an inclusion group,
whether in the same content model or in the content models of
16   different open elements, its presence in the exclusion group
governs.

B.12 Document Type Declaration

18   The document type of an SGML document is identified by a
"document type declaration", which occurs in the "prolog" of the
20   document, before any data. The element, attribute list, and other
declarations that have been discussed, which constitute the
22   document type definition, are grouped in a parameter called the
"declaration subset":

```
24   <!DOCTYPE manual [
       <!ELEMENT manual (front?, body, rear?) +(entry)>
26     <!-- Remainder of declarations constituting the
            document type definition go here. -->
28   ]>
```

The left and right square brackets are the "declaration subset open"
30   (*dso*) and "declaration subset close" (*dsc*) delimiters, respectively.

The part of an SGML document that occurs after the prolog, and
32   which contains the data and descriptive markup, is called an
"instance" of the document type (or just "document instance").

If, as is usual, a number of documents conform to the same
2   document type definition, a single copy of the definition can be kept
in an external entity and referenced from the documents. The entity
4   can simultaneously be declared and referenced by specifying an
external identifier on the document type declaration:

6   `<!DOCTYPE manual PUBLIC "-//Cave Press//DTD Manual//EN">`

Where the entire definition is external, as in the above example, no
8   declaration subset is needed. Normally, an external definition and a
subset are used together, with the subset containing things like
10 entity declarations that apply only to the one document.

```
    <!DOCTYPE manual PUBLIC "-//Stutely Press//DTD
12                                  Manual//EN" [
      <!ENTITY title "AIBOHPHOBIA: Fear of Palindromes">
14    <!-- Remainder of local declarations supplementing
            the document type definition go here. -->
16    ]>
```

The external entity is technically considered part of the subset, as if
18 a reference to it occurred just before the ***dsc***. This allows the
declarations in the document to be executed first, which gives them
20 priority over those in the external entity.

B.13 Data Content

The data content of a document is the portion that is not markup. It
22 has two major characteristics:
   a)   Its *representation* determines whether the markup parser can
24   scan it.

There are two main classes: character data, in which the bit
26   combinations represent characters, and bit data, in which the
bit combinations (singly or collectively) usually represent
28   binary values.
   b)   Its *notation* [146] 423:13 determines how the character or bit
30   strings will be interpreted by the procedures.

In a natural language notation, for example, the character
32   string "delta" might be interpreted as an English word, while in
a scientific notation it could be interpreted as a single graphic,
34   a Greek letter.

B.13.1 Data Content Representations

The Standard recognizes two data representations: character data
2 that conforms to the Standard, and non-SGML character or bit data
that does not.

B.13.1.1 Character Data (PCDATA, CDATA, and RCDATA)

4 In character data, each bit combination represents a character in
the document character set.

6 Before a character can be considered character data, it normally
must be parsed to determine whether it is markup. Such characters
8 are represented in a model group by the keyword "PCDATA".

In a paragraph with the following structure, a character could either
10 be data or part of a "phrase" or "quote" element tag:

```
<!ELEMENT p (#PCDATA | phrase | quote)* >
```

12 A character could also be part of a markup declaration, processing
instruction, entity reference, or other markup that is allowed in the
14 content of an element. Only if it is not a tag or other markup would
it be treated as data and passed to a procedure for processing.

16 A character used for markup is not normally passed to a procedure,
but when the optional "DATATAG" feature (discussed later) is used,
18 a character could be both markup *and* data. A space, for example,
could serve as the end-tag for a word and still be part of the data of
20 the sentence in which the word occurs.

It is also possible to enter character data directly, without it being
22 parsed for markup in the usual way. An element declaration can
declare its content to contain character data by specifying a
24 keyword, rather than a content model:

```
<!ELEMENT formula CDATA >
```

26 Note that no *rni* was required, because a user-defined name
cannot be specified for this parameter (except within model group
28 delimiters).

If an element contains declared character data, it cannot contain
30 anything else. The markup parser scans it only to locate an *etago*

or ***net***; other markup is ignored. Only the correct end-tag (or that of
an element in which this element is nested) will be recognized.

A variation of CDATA, called *replaceable character data*
[46] *343:1* , is specified with the keyword "RCDATA". It is like
CDATA except that entity references and character references are
recognized.

B.13.1.2 Non-SGML Data (NDATA)

Non-SGML data is data that is not parsable in accordance with this
Standard. It is either data in an undefined character set, bit data, or
some mix of the two. In undefined character set data, the bit
combinations represent characters, but not in the document
character set. In bit data, the bit combinations, although they can
be managed as characters, do not represent a character repertoire
in the usual way.

As non-SGML data cannot be scanned by the markup parser, and
may contain bit combinations that could, for example, erroneously
cause the operating system to terminate the file, it must be stored
in an external entity. Its location is made known to the parser by an
entity declaration, in the usual manner, except for additional
parameters identifying it as non-SGML data:

```
<!ENTITY japan86 SYSTEM NDATA kanji>
```

Non-SGML data can be entered only in general entities whose
declaration specifies the NDATA keyword and the name of a data
content notation (explained later). Such an entity can be referenced
with a general entity reference anywhere in the content that a
reference is recognized and a data character could occur.

If it is desired to associate attributes with the non-SGML data, a
dedicated element type can be defined for it. An NDATA element
must have empty content and an attribute definition for an
"ENTITY" ("general entity name") attribute whose value is the name
of the external entity.

```
<!ELEMENT japanese EMPTY>
<!ATTLIST japanese file    ENTITY            #REQUIRED
                   subject (poetry|prose) prose
>
```

The markup for a "japanese" element includes the entity name as
2 the value of the "file" attribute:

```
<japanese file="japan86">
```

4 An external entity attribute can be defined for any element, even
one with a content model. The application determines, as with all
6 attributes, how its value relates to the element content for the
processing being performed.

B.13.2 Data Content Notations

8 The difference between one type of non-SGML data and another
(or one kind of character data and another, for that matter) lies in
10 the data content notation. The notation is not significant to the
markup parser, but it is quite significant to humans and procedures.

12 An enormous number of data content notations are possible.
However, they tend to fall into a few distinct classes.

B.13.2.1 Notations for Character Data

14 Some common classes of notation for character data are natural
languages, scientific notations, and formatted text.

Natural Languages :

16 When a natural language notation is used, the procedures interpret
the characters as implicitly marked text elements. For example, a
18 sequence of characters bounded by interword spaces could be
recognized as a "word" element, a sequence of words terminated
20 by suitable punctuation as a "phrase" or "sentence" element, and
so on. In such notations, an ***RE*** is usually interpreted as an
22 interword space.

For additional flexibility, a natural language text notation can be
24 supplemented by explicit markup for specialized variants of
elements that are normally implicit (for example, quoted phrases,
26 programming keywords, emphasized phrases).

In conventional text processing systems, implicit markup
28 conventions and the trade-offs between explicit and implicit markup
are built in. In SGML, the data tag markup minimization feature

(discussed later) allows a user to specify the extent to which such
2   elements will be recognized by the markup parser and the extent to
which they will be interpreted by the procedures as part of the data
4   content notation.

Natural language notations occur in elements such as paragraphs,
6   list items, and headings. The content is usually *mixed content*
[25] *320:6* , in which data characters are intermixed with subele-
8   ments.

Scientific Notations :

These notations look like natural language notations, but the words
10 and phrases are meaningful to the application. In a mathematical
notation, for example, the phrase "3 over 4" could be interpreted as
12 the fraction "3/4".

Scientific notations occur in elements such as formulas, equations,
14 chemical structures, formal grammars, music, and so on. The
element content is usually CDATA or RCDATA, which allows
16 systems that cannot interpret the scientific notation to process the
element as if a natural language notation had been used.

Formatted Text :

18 Formatted text notations are similar to natural language notations,
and features of both might be incorporated in a single notation.
20 Their purpose is to identify elements of the "layout structure"
produced by a previous formatting application. Formatted text
22 notations include character sequences that identify formatted line
endings, spaces and hyphens introduced for alignment purposes,
24 font change codes, superscripts and subscripts, etc.

These notations are found in the same element types as natural
26 language notations (paragraphs, headings, etc.) and, when the
optional concurrent document type feature is used (discussed
28 later), in elements of the layout structure of the formatted
document. The content is normally mixed content.

B.13.2.2 Notations for Non-SGML Data

30 In NDATA entities, the bit combinations (singly or collectively) can
represent undefined characters, binary values, or a mixture of
32 binary values and characters.

Undefined Characters :

2 Natural language, scientific, and formatted text notations are found in NDATA just as in CDATA, but in other than the document character set. The data could, for example, employ code extension
4 techniques that assign multiple bit combinations to a single character, while the document character set does not. Such a
6 scheme is used for languages that require more characters than there are bit combinations in the document character set.

Binary Values :

8 Binary values can be interpreted as grey scale or color values for pixels in an image, digitized audio, musical wave forms, or as other
10 sets of numeric or logical values. The principal application of binary value notations in text processing is in the representation of
12 illustration elements: half-tones, photographs, etc.

Record boundaries are frequently ignored in binary notations, but
14 need not be.

Mixed Binary and Character :

A scientific or formatted text data notation could use a mixture of
16 characters and binary fields. Such notations are treated as unparsable NDATA notations because bit combinations in the
18 binary fields could erroneously be interpreted as markup delimiters.

B.13.2.3 Specifying Data Content Notations

The set of data content notations used in the document must be
20 declared with *notation declarations*. Each declaration specifies the name of a data content notation used in the document, together
22 with descriptive information about it:

```
    <!NOTATION eqn    PUBLIC "-//local//NOTATION EQN
24                                        Formula//EN">
    <!NOTATION tex    PUBLIC "-//local//NOTATION TeX
26                                        Formula//EN">
    <!NOTATION lowres SYSTEM "SCAN.MODULE" -- Low resolution
28                                        scan -->
```

2 An element's data content notation is specified with a notation attribute. The attribute's declared value is the keyword "NOTATION" followed by an additional parameter, a name group:

```
4   <!--        ELEMENTS        CONTENT                    -->
    <!ELEMENT formula          RCDATA>
6   <!--        ELEMENTS NAME VALUE              DEFAULT -->
    <!ATTLIST formula   data NOTATION(eqn|tex)  #REQUIRED>
8   <!>
    <formula data="eqn">3 over 4</formula>
```

10 The name group contains the valid values of the attribute.

B.14 Customizing

12 Many of the characteristics of the Standard Generalized Markup Language can be tailored to meet special needs.

B.14.1 The SGML Declaration

14 The tailoring of a document is described in its *SGML declaration* [171] 450:1 , a markup declaration that appears as the first thing in a document. The SGML declaration is normally provided automati-
16 cally by the markup parser, but if a document's tailoring differs from what a processing system expects, the SGML declaration must be
18 entered explicitly.

20 There are two main categories of tailoring: using optional features of SGML and defining an variant concrete syntax.

B.14.1.1 Optional Features

There are eleven optional features that can be used:

22 **SHORTREF**   Short entity reference delimiters
    CONCUR   Concurrent document type instances
24 **DATATAG**   Data tag minimization
    OMITTAG   Omitted tag minimization
26 **RANK**   Omitted rank suffix minimization
    SHORTTAG   Short tag minimization
28 **SUBDOC**   Nested subdocuments

	FORMAL	Formal public identifiers
2	**SIMPLE**	Simple link process
	IMPLICIT	Implicit link process
4	**EXPLICIT**	Explicit link process

They are described in annex C 66 .

B.14.1.2 Variant Concrete Syntax

6　The heart of SGML is the "abstract syntax" that defines the manner in which such markup constructs as generic identifiers, attributes,
8　and entity references are used. The delimiter characters, declaration names and keywords, length restrictions, etc., that have
10　been discussed in this Annex constitute a particular mapping of the abstract syntax to a real set of characters and quantities, known as
12　the "reference concrete syntax".

　　SGML allows a document to employ a variant concrete syntax to
14　meet the needs of system environments, national languages, keyboards, and so on. The characteristics of the concrete syntax
16　are declared on the SGML declaration in the following categories:
　　a) Delimiter assignments, including short entity reference
18　　　delimiters.
　　b) Character use, including identification of function characters
20　　　and candidates for non-SGML characters.
　　c) Naming rules, including name character alphabet and case
22　　　translation.
　　d) Definition of substitute declaration names, keywords, and
24　　　other reserved names.
　　e) Quantitative characteristics, such as the maximum length of
26　　　names and attribute values.

B.14.2 Impact of Customization

　　An SGML document that uses the reference concrete syntax and
28　no features (known as a "minimal SGML document") will be interchangeable among all SGML systems. Over time, though, it is
30　expected that other combinations of features and variant concrete syntaxes will come into wide use. Some possibilities are:
32　　a) Documents that are keyed directly by humans for publishing
　　　applications will probably use the SHORTREF, SHORTTAG,
34　　　and OMITTAG features. (Those that use only these features
　　　and the reference concrete syntax are known as "basic SGML
36　　　documents".)

b) Documents that will be used for linguistic analysis or in
2   connection with structured data bases will probably use the
DATATAG feature.
4 c) Documents produced by intelligent word processors will
probably use little minimization. Such systems will also
6   employ the concurrent document type feature so that
unformatted "logical structures" and formatted "layout
8   structures" can be represented simultaneously.
d) User organizations will define feature menus to meet their
10   special requirements.

B.15 Conformance

A document that complies with this International Standard in every
12 respect is known as a "conforming SGML document". A system
that can process such a document is known as a "conforming
14 SGML system". This International Standard sets no requirements
on the architecture, the method of implementation, or the handling
16 of markup errors, employed by conforming systems.

Annex C
Additional Concepts

This tutorial contains the full text of Annex C of ISO 8879. It covers the optional features of SGML, such as markup minimization. As the very powerful LINK feature receives only cursory treatment here, I have written a much fuller explanation of its capabilities and potential applications in Tutorial D 92.

(This annex does not form an integral part of this International Standard.)

2   This annex introduces the optional features that can be used in an SGML document. There are three categories: markup minimization,
4   link type, and other features.

    — Markup minimization features

6   These features allow markup to be minimized by shortening or omitting tags, or shortening entity references. Markup
8   minimization features do not affect the document type definition, so a minimized document can be sent to a system
10   that does not support these features by first restoring the omitted markup.

12   The features are SHORTTAG, OMITTAG, SHORTREF, DATATAG, and RANK.

14   — Link type features

      These features allow the use of "link process definitions",
16   which specify how a source document should be processed to produce a result document of another type (such as a
18   formatted document).

      Link processes are specified in *link type declarations*, which
20   are independent of document type declarations or any other

markup. However, they must be removed before sending a document to a system that does not support these features.

The link type features are SIMPLE, IMPLICIT, and EXPLICIT, which refer to the degree of control that can be exercised in specifying the result document.

— Other features

These features allow elements and entities to be redefined for different parts of the document, and public identifiers to be interpreted for automatic processing. They do affect the document type definition, so a document using these features may require modification before sending it to a system that does not support them.

The features are CONCUR, SUBDOC, and FORMAL.

Use of the optional features is indicated on the feature use parameter of the SGML declaration (except for SHORTREF, whose use is indicated by the concrete syntax, and by its own "short reference mapping" declarations).

C.1 Markup Minimization Features

The markup minimization features are:

SHORTTAG   means short tags with omitted delimiters, attribute specifications, or generic identifiers may be used.
OMITTAG   means some tags may be omitted altogether.
SHORTREF   means short reference delimiters may be used instead of complete entity references.
DATATAG   means data characters may serve simultaneously as tags.
RANK   means element ranks may be omitted from tags.

C.1.1 SHORTTAG: Tags With Omitted Markup

A short tag is one from which part or all of the usual markup has been omitted.

C.1.1.1 Unclosed Short Tags

The ***tagc*** can be omitted from a tag that is immediately followed by
2 another one.

For example, this markup:

4 `<chapter><p>A short chapter.</p></chapter>`

can be abbreviated to this:

6 `<chapter<p>A short chapter.</p</chapter>`

by omitting the ***tagc*** from the "chapter" start-tag and the "p" end-
8 tag.

C.1.1.2 Empty Tags

An empty short tag is one in which no GI or attributes are specified;
10 the tag consists solely of its delimiters. The parser assumes, for an
empty end-tag, that the GI is the same as that of the most recent
12 open element. For example, the following would be equivalent with
short tag minimization:

```
14  This is a <q>quoted</q> word.
    This is a <q>quoted</> word.
```

16 For empty start-tags, when the omitted tag feature is not also
enabled, the parser uses the GI of the most recently ended element
18 and the default values of the attributes. Using both empty start- and
end-tags, a list could be marked up as follows:

```
20  <!--       ELEMENTS  CONTENT                -->
    <!ELEMENT list      (item+) >
22  <!ELEMENT item      (p | list)*
    >
24  <list>
    <item>This is the first item (what else ?)</>
26  <>This is the second item.</>
    <>This is the third and last item.</>
28  </list>
```

(See C.1.2.6 `75` for use of the short tag feature when the omitted
30 tag feature is enabled.)

Markup can be reduced further by using the single character "null
2   end tag" (*net*) delimiter (normally "/") that is enabled by the short
tag feature. A *net* is interpreted as an empty end-tag only for an
4   element in which it was also used as (that is, in place of) the *tagc*
delimiter.

```
6   <p>This paragraph has
    a <q/quotation/ in it and
8   a solidus (/) that is data.</p>
```

The following list summarizes the delimiters used with the short tag
10   feature and their character strings in the reference delimiter set:

String	Name	*Meaning*
12 /	**NET**	Null end-tag.

C.1.1.3 Attribute Minimization

All or part of an attribute specification list can be omitted under the
14   following circumstances:

Value Delimiters :

The delimiters can be omitted from the specification of an attribute
16   value if the value is limited to name characters.

```
<standard security=public>
```

18   Note that entity references are not permitted in such attribute
values.

Defaulting :

20   If an attribute was declared with an actual default value, or the
keywords "#IMPLIED" or "#CONREF", the complete specification
22   for it can be omitted. The attribute will be treated as though the
default value had been specified for it. (This rule also applies to
24   current attributes after they have once been specified.)

Names :

2 An attribute's name and **vi** delimiter can be omitted if its declared value included a *name group* [69] *374:11* or *name token group* [68] *374:1* .

4 This form of minimization is useful when the attribute values imply the attribute name. A memo, for example, might have a "status" 6 attribute whose value was either "draft" or "final".

```
   <!--       ELEMENTS         CONTENT            -->
 8 <!ELEMENT memo              (from, to, subject, body,
                                    sig, cc?)>
10 <!--     ELEMENTS NAME     VALUE          DEFAULT -->
   <!ATTLIST memo      status    (final|draft) final  >
```

12 The usual markup for the attribute:

```
<memo status="draft">
```

14 would be cumbersome in this instance, since "draft" implies "status". With SHORTTAG minimization, however, either

```
16 <memo status="draft">
```

 or

```
18 <memo status=draft>
```

 or

```
20 <memo draft>
```

 could be entered in the document.

22 Omitting attribute names tends to make the document markup more ambiguous. This effect can be ameliorated if the groups are 24 kept small and the name tokens chosen are descriptive adjectives that imply the attribute name (for example, "NEW | REVISED", 26 "SECRET | INTERNAL | PUBLIC"). In the following example, the "compact" attribute is better from this standpoint than is 28 "emphasis":

```
   <!--       ELEMENTS         CONTENT              -->
30 <!ELEMENT list             (item*)>
```

```
<!--        ELEMENTS NAME      VALUE       DEFAULT -->
2 <!ATTLIST list     compact   (compact)   #IMPLIED
                     emphasis  (0|1|2|3)   0
4 >
```

C.1.2 OMITTAG: Tags May be Omitted

A type definition establishes the possible variations in structure
6 among documents of its type. An individual document, therefore,
need not contain as much markup.

C.1.2.1 Tag Omission Concepts

8 Assume that a class of magazine article documents, with a GI of
"article", has the following type definition:

```
10 <!--        ELEMENTS CONTENT                  >
   <!ELEMENT article  (title, body)            >
12 <!ELEMENT title    (#PCDATA)                 >
   <!ELEMENT body     (p*)                      >
14 <!ELEMENT p        (#PCDATA | list)*         >
   <!ELEMENT list     (item+)                   >
16 <!ELEMENT item     (#PCDATA, (p | list)*)  >
```

The full markup for an instance of an article might look something
18 like this:

```
   <article>
20 <title>The Cat</title>
   <body>
22 <p>A cat can:
   <list>
24 <item>jump</item>
   <item>meow</item>
26 </list>
   </p>
28 <p>It has 9 lives.
   </p>
30 </body>
   </article>
```

32 Note that the type definition says that a paragraph cannot

2   immediately contain another paragraph; it can contain only text characters and lists. Similarly, a list item cannot immediately contain another list item (even though it could contain another list).
4   As a result, the markup can be minimized by omitting many of the end-tags:

```
6   <article>
    <title>The Cat</title>
8   <body>
    <p>A cat can:
10  <list>
    <item>jump
12  <item>meow
    </list>
14  <p>It has 9 lives.
    </article>
```

16   It is possible to omit the item end-tag: the occurrence of another item indicates the end of the previous one (because an item cannot
18   contain an item). The paragraph end-tag is omissible by the same reasoning (a paragraph cannot contain another paragraph).

20   Finally, it is logical that the end of an element should also be the end of everything it contains. In this way, the article end-tag ends
22   the body and the last paragraph as well as the article.

      (The markup could be minimized still further, as the reader will no
24   doubt realize.)

C.1.2.2 Specifying Minimization

      Markup minimization is a good thing, but not if it makes it harder to
26   detect markup errors. In the last example, had the list end-tag been omitted, it would have been implied by the article end-tag, just as
28   the body end-tag was.

```
    <article>
30  <title>The Cat</title>
    <body>
32  <p>A cat can:
    <list>
34  <item>jump
    <item>meow
36  <p>It has 9 lives.
```

```
</article>
```

2 This would not have been the author's intention, though, as the last paragraph would erroneously have been made part of the last item
4 in the list.

To prevent such misinterpretations, there are two parameters on
6 the element declaration that specify the omitted tag minimization that is allowed for an element. When "OMITTAG YES" is specified
8 on the SGML declaration, the omitted tag feature is enabled, and the two minimization parameters are then required in all element
10 declarations.

C.1.2.3 End-tag Omission: Intruding Start-tag

An end-tag is omissible when its element's content is followed by
12 the start-tag of an element that cannot occur within it. This was the case for the paragraph and item end-tags in the article example.
14 The element declarations would look like this:

```
<!--          ELEMENTS  MIN  CONTENT                    >
16  <!ELEMENT p            - O  (#PCDATA | list)*          >
    <!ELEMENT list         - -  (item+)                    >
18  <!ELEMENT item         - O  (#PCDATA, (p | list)*) >
```

and have the following meaning:
20 a) The "MIN" heading identifies a pair of parameters for start-tag and end-tag minimization. Both parameters must be specified.
22 b) The "O" indicates that omitted tag minimization is allowed for the end-tag of the "p" and "item" elements.
24 c) The hyphen is the *minus* delimiter; it indicates that no minimization is allowed for the start-tags.

26 Recall that an end-tag must always be omitted if an element has empty content, because anything that follows the start-tag must
28 then be part of the containing element. Although this rule has nothing to do with markup minimization, it is helpful to mark the "O"
30 as a reminder that no end-tags will be found in the document.

```
<!ELEMENT figref - O EMPTY>
```

C.1.2.4 End-tag Omission: End-tag of Containing Element

A contained element's end-tag is omissible when it is followed by
the end-tag of an element that contains it.

```
<!--        ELEMENTS  MIN  CONTENT                  >
<!ELEMENT list        - -  (item+)                  >
<!ELEMENT item        - O  (#PCDATA)                >
```

The above declaration allows the end-tag of the third item to be
omitted from the following list, because it is implied by the list end-
tag:

```
<list>
<item>This is the first item (what else ?)</item>
<item>This is the second item.</item>
<item>This is the third and last item.
</list>
```

C.1.2.5 Start-tag Omission: Contextually Required Element

A start-tag is omissible when the element type is contextually
required and any other element types that could occur are
contextually optional.

Combined with the other minimization discussed previously, the
element declaration would be:

```
<!--        ELEMENTS  MIN  CONTENT                  >
<!ELEMENT list        - -  (item+)                  >
<!ELEMENT item        O O  (#PCDATA)                >
```

and the list could be marked up like this:

```
<list>
This is the first item (what else ?)
<item>This is the second item.
<item>This is the third and last item.
</list>
```

The start-tag was omissible for the first item because it was
required; it could not be omitted for the subsequent items because
they were optional.

2 Even when an element is contextually required, its start-tag cannot be omitted if the element type has required attributes or a declared content, or if the instance of the element is empty.

C.1.2.6 Combination with Short Tag Minimization

4 When short tag and omitted tag minimization are both enabled, empty start- and end-tags are treated uniformly: they are given the
6 GI of the most recent open element. The two forms of minimization can be used together, as in the following example:

```
8    <!--       ELEMENTS  MIN   CONTENT                  >
     <!ELEMENT p          - O   (#PCDATA | list)*        >
10   <!ELEMENT list       - -   (item+)                  >
     <!ELEMENT item       O O   (#PCDATA, (p | list)*) >
12   <list>
     <item>This is the first item (what else ?)
14   <>This is the second item.
     <>This is the third and last item.
16   </list>
```

Note that it was necessary to say "</list>" instead of "</>" at the
18 end, because the latter would have meant "item end-tag", rather than "list end-tag". Alternatively, "</></>" could have been entered
20 to mean "end the item, then end the list".

Now consider what happens when the markup is minimized further
22 by removing the first item start-tag:

```
     <list>
24   This is the first item (what else ?)
     <>This is the second item.
26   <>This is the third and last item.
     </list>
```

28 The identical results are achieved because when the first empty tag was encountered, "item" and not "list" was the open element, even
30 though "item" was implied by "O" minimization rather than entered explicitly.

C.1.2.7 Markup Minimization Considerations

32 Short tag minimization requires the user (and the markup parser) to know the current location in the document's structure, and to

understand attribute list declarations. Omitted tag minimization,
2   though, also requires knowledge of the element declarations.

This difference should be considered in deciding what kind of
4   minimization the user can be expected to handle properly, as
omitting a tag could result in a document that, while free of SGML
6   errors, is not what the user intended.

C.1.3 SHORTREF: Short Reference Delimiters May Replace Complete Entity References

Short references are single characters or short strings that can
8   replace complete delimited entity references. They can be used to
emulate common typewriter keyboarding and to simplify the entry
10 of elements with repetitive structures.

C.1.3.1 Typewriter Keyboarding: Generalized WYSIWYG

Some word processors offer text entry operators an interface
12 similar to that of the typewriters on which many operators were
trained. On typewriters, each function key produces an immediate
14 formatting result as it is struck: a carriage return starts a new line, a
tab key generates horizontal space, and so on. Word processors
16 that emulate this characteristic of typewriters are sometimes known
as "WYSIWYG" systems — for "what you see is what you get".

18 The characters produced by function keys are specific processing
instructions. Like all processing instructions, they limit a document
20 to a single formatting style, executable only on machines that
understand the instructions.

22 SGML, though, can offer the benefit of familiar typewriter
keyboarding while still maintaining the generality of the document.
24 With short references, typewriter function key characters can be
interpreted as descriptive markup. For example, the declarations

```
26  <!ENTITY   ptag     STARTTAG      "p"  >
    <!SHORTREF wysiwyg "&#TAB"       ptag
28                     "&#RS;&#RE;" ptag >
```

map both the tab and the line feed, carriage return sequence
30 (empty record) to the start-tag for a paragraph element. The actual
formatting for a paragraph depends, as always, on the application
32 procedure, just as if the start-tag had been entered explicitly. But

the entry device still produces the tabbing or extra line called for by
2 the function characters, thereby giving the user the immediate
visual feedback that is such an important aspect of WYSIWYG
4 systems.

The markup declarations have effectively created "generalized
6 WYSIWYG", in which typewriter function characters are interpreted
as generalized markup while retaining their visual effect. Moreover,
8 the user can freely intermix generalized WYSIWYG with explicit
tags, using whichever is most convenient for a particular part of the
10 document. This ability can be particularly helpful for complex
elements, such as multipage tables with running headings, where
12 typewriter functions do not offer a convenient and generally
accepted entry convention.

C.1.3.2 Typewriter Keyboarding Example: Defining a Short Reference Map

14 With short references, a user can create SGML documents with
common word processing entry conventions, rather than conscious
16 entry of markup. A large number of character strings are defined as
short reference delimiters in the reference concrete syntax. Those
18 containing "invisible" function characters and the quotation mark
are particularly useful for supporting common keyboarding; they
20 are:

String	Description
&#TAB;	Horizontal tab
&#RE;	Record end
&#RS;	Record start
&#RS;B	Leading blanks (record start, one or more spaces and/or tabs)
&#RS;&#RE;	Empty record (record start, record end)
&#RS;B&#RE;	Blank record (record start, one or more spaces and/or tabs, record end)
B&#RE;	Trailing blanks (one or more spaces and/or tabs, record end)
&#SPACE;	Space
BB	Two or more blanks (two or more spaces and/or tabs)
"	Quotation mark

Each short reference delimiter can be associated with an entity
name in a table called a "short reference map". A delimiter that is
not "mapped" to an entity is treated as data. Entity definition is
done in the usual manner, with an entity declaration. The mapping
is done with a "short reference mapping declaration". The following
example defines an empty record as a reference to the paragraph
start-tag:

```
<!ENTITY    ptag "<p>">
<!SHORTREF map1 "&#RS;&#RE;" ptag>
```

The "SHORTREF" declaration defines a map named "map1". The
map contains only one explicit mapping: the empty record short
reference is mapped to the entity "ptag". Whenever this map is
current (explained later), an empty record will be replaced by the
entity reference. For example,

```
Last paragraph text.
"
Next paragraph text.
```

will be interpreted as

```
Last paragraph text.
&ptag;
Next paragraph text.
```

which will instantaneously, upon resolution of the entity reference,
be reinterpreted as

```
Last paragraph text.
<p>
Next paragraph text.
```

As no other short reference strings were mapped, they will be
treated as data while this map is current.

C.1.3.3 Typewriter Keyboarding Example: Activating a Short Reference Map

Normally, a map is made current by associating its name with an
element type in a "short reference use" declaration. The following
example causes "map1" to become the current map whenever a
"chapter" begins:

```
<!USEMAP map1 chapter>
```

2 Whenever a chapter begins, map1 will become current and will remain current except within any nested subelements that are themselves associated with maps.

4 A short reference map need not be associated with every element type. An element that has none will simply use whichever map is
6 current at its start. In the following example, the quote and chapter elements have maps, but the paragraph element does not:

```
 8  <!ENTITY    ptag    "<p>"       -- paragraph start-tag -->
    <!ENTITY    qtag    "<quote>" >
10  <!ENTITY    qendtag "</quote>" >
    <!SHORTREF chapmap "&#RS;&#RE;" ptag
12                     '"'            qtag >
    <!SHORTREF qmap    '"'            qendtag>
14  <!USEMAP   chapmap chapter>
    <!USEMAP   qmap    q>
16  <!ELEMENT  chapter (p*)          >
    <!ELEMENT  p       (q|#PCDATA)* >
18  <!ELEMENT  q       (#PCDATA)    >
```

20 When a paragraph element begins, "chapmap" will remain current; it maps the quotation mark to the "qtag" entity, which contains the quote start-tag. Once the quote element begins, "qmap" becomes
22 the current map, and the quotation mark will be replaced by a reference to the "qendtag" entity, which contains the quote end-tag.
24 At the end of the quote, the paragraph element resumes, and with it the "chapmap" short reference map.

26 The markup

```
<chapter<p>Here is "a quotation" in the text.</p>
```

28 is now the equivalent of

```
<chapter<p>Here is <quote>a quotation</quote> in the
30                                              text.</p>
```

▼

32 The declarations allow the quotation mark to serve as the start-tag and end-tag of quotation elements, rather than being treated as data. Formatting procedures could therefore use opening and
34 closing curved quotation marks to distinguish the start and end of the quotation, which would not otherwise be possible with normal
36 typing conventions.

Incidentally, when declaring an entity whose replacement text is a tag, the following forms of entity declaration can be used:

```
2   <!ENTITY qtag     STARTTAG "quote" >
    <!ENTITY qendtag ENDTAG   "quote" >
```

4   The "STARTTAG" and "ENDTAG" keywords allow the tag delimiters
    to be omitted. They also allow a system to optimize the handling of
6   the entity because it knows it will most likely be used as a tag
    rather than as data.

8   Short entity references can be used only in elements whose
    content was defined by a model (that is, not in CDATA or
10 RCDATA). They cannot be used in attribute values or declaration
    parameters.

C.1.3.4 Tabular Matter Example

12 Many printable characters are defined as short reference delimiters
    in the reference concrete syntax (see figure 4 [364]). These char-
14 acters can be used as substitutes for the more lengthy general
    entity references, which allows a more concise and visual style of
16 markup when appropriate, as in tables:

```
    <!ENTITY    row       "<row><col>" >
18  <!ENTITY    col       "</col><col>" >
    <!ENTITY    endrow    "</col></row>" >
20  <!SHORTREF tablemap "(" row
                          "|" col
22                        ")" endrow >
    <!USEMAP    tablemap table>
24  <!ELEMENT   table     (row*)>
    <!ATTLIST   table     columns NUMBER #REQUIRED>
26  <!ELEMENT   row       (col+)>
    <!ELEMENT   col       (#PCDATA)>
28  <!>
    <table columns=3>
30  (row1,col1|row1,col2|row1,col3)
    (row2,col1|row2,col2|row2,col3)
32  (row3,col1|row3,col2|row3,col3)
    (row4,col1|row4,col2|row4,col3)
34  </table>
    <!>
```

36 The example allows the parentheses and the vertical bar (|) to be

used as entity references. (As short references are only recognized
in content, there is no danger of the vertical bar being construed as
an *or* connector.) The text will resolve to the following:

```
<table columns=3>
<row><col>row1,col1</col><col>row1,col2</col>
                         <col>row1,col3</col></row>
<row><col>row2,col1</col><col>row2,col2</col>
                         <col>row2,col3</col></row>
<row><col>row3,col1</col><col>row3,col2</col>
                         <col>row3,col3</col></row>
<row><col>row4,col1</col><col>row4,col2</col>
                         <col>row4,col3</col></row>
</table>
```

The "tablemap" is current only during the table so that the short
reference delimiters can be used as data in the rest of the
document.

C.1.3.5 Special Requirements

Although short reference maps are normally associated with
specific element types, it is possible to use a short reference use
declaration to select one arbitrarily:

```
<figure>
Opening text of figure (uses normal figure map).
<!USEMAP graphics -- Enable character graphics short
                                    refs -->
Remaining text of figure (uses "graphics" map).
</figure>
```

The map named in the declaration (here "graphics") replaces the
current map for the most recently started element (here "figure"),
just as if it had been named on a "USEMAP" declaration associated
with "figure" in the document type definition. However, it applies
only to this instance of a figure, not to any other. If the normal
figure map is required later in this figure, it must be activated with a
short reference use declaration, but for later figures it will become
current automatically.

It is possible to cancel all mappings by using the reserved map
name "#EMPTY" instead of a normal map name. The "empty" map,
which causes all short reference delimiters to be treated as data (or

separators), will be current under the same circumstances as a
2 normal map would have been.

Short references, though powerful, are not adequate for interpreting
4 arbitrary existing documents as if they had been marked up with
SGML. They are intended to let a user supplement normal SGML
6 markup with familiar word processing entry conventions. In
conjunction with the other markup minimization techniques, short
8 references make it possible to eliminate most conscious markup,
even without an "intelligent" word processor.

C.1.4 DATATAG: Data May Also be a Tag

10 The data tag minimization feature allows a content model to define
data characters that will be interpreted as tags while remaining part
12 of the data content.

The techniques of markup minimization discussed so far go a long
14 way toward creating text that appears almost free of markup. The
following list, for example, has no visible explicit markup within it:

```
16 <!ENTITY    itemtag    STARTTAG "jobitem"
                                   --JOBITEM start-tag-->
18 <!SHORTREF listmap    "&#RS;"  itemtag >
   <!USEMAP   listmap    joblist>
20 <!--        ELEMENTS  MIN      CONTENT  -->
   <!ELEMENT  joblist    - -      (jobitem+)>
22 <!ELEMENT  jobitem    - O      (#PCDATA)>
   <joblist>
24 Sharon Adler,          Vice Chairman
   Larry Beck,            Secretary
26 Anders Berglund,       Publisher
   Aaron Bigman,          Past Member
28 Jim Cox,               Past Member
   Bill Davis,            Chairman
30 Joe Gangemi,           Member
   Charles Goldfarb,      Editor
32 Mike Goodfellow,       Consultant
   Randy Groves,          Member
34 Charles Lightfoot,     Past Member
   Sperling Martin,       Past Member
36 Bettie McDavid Mason,  Consultant
   Jim Mason,             Member
38 Lynne Price,           Theoretician
```

```
    Stanley Rice,          Pioneer
2   Norm Scharpf,          Observer
    Craig Smith,           Theoretician
4   Joan Smith,            Publicist
    Ed Smura,              Member
6   Bill Tunnicliffe,      Member
    Kit von Suck,          Member</joblist>
```

8　The end-tag for each "jobitem" but the last is omissible because it is
followed by a jobitem start-tag. The last is implied by the end of the
10　list. The start-tags are present explicitly, but not visible, because
they are in entities referenced by a non-printing short reference
12　delimiter (the record start). The list thus appears completely
marked up with only two tags consciously entered by the user, but
14　there is more that could be done.

The element declaration states that a "jobitem" is merely a
16　sequence of characters. A reader, however, sees it as containing
separate "name" and "job" elements because the comma and
18　spaces identify the job title as clearly as a start-tag would have.
Such a situation, in which the conventions used in the data can
20　unambiguously identify elements within it, is known as *data tag
minimization*.

22　The SGML data tag feature allows these conventions to be
expressed in an element declaration through the use of a *data tag
24　pattern* [134] *416:9* :

```
    <!--          ELEMENTS   MIN    CONTENT  -->
26  <!ELEMENT    jobitem    - O    ([name, ", ", " "], job)>
    <!ELEMENT    name       O O    (#PCDATA)>
28  <!ELEMENT    job        O O    (#PCDATA)>
```

The declaration states (among other things) that:
30　a)　The start-tag for a "name" is omissible because it must be the
　　　first thing in a "jobitem".
32　b)　The "name" end-tag is omissible when it occurs in a "jobitem",
　　　because it is implied by the comma and spaces of the data
34　　　tag pattern.
　　c)　The "job" start-tag is omissible because a "job" element is not
36　　　allowed in a "name".
　　d)　The "job" end-tag is omissible because it is implied by the end
38　　　of the "jobitem".

The complete declaration for the "joblist" would appear as follows:

```
      <!ENTITY    itemtag    STARTTAG jobitem   --JOBITEM start-
2                                                       tag-->
      <!SHORTREF listmap    "&#RS;"   itemtag >
4     <!USEMAP   listmap    joblist>
      <!--        ELEMENTS  MIN       CONTENT   -->
6     <!ELEMENT  jobitem    - O       ([name, ", ", " "], job)>
      <!ELEMENT  name       O O       (#PCDATA)>
8     <!ELEMENT  job        O O       (#PCDATA)>
```

Characters are normally either data or markup, but not both. The
10 essence of data tag minimization is that characters are both data
and a tag at the same time. A data tag is an end-tag that conforms
12 to a *data tag pattern* [134] *416:9* that follows the data tag's element
in a *data tag group* [133] *415:16* in its containing element's model.
14 In the above example, the data tag group is

```
[name, ", ", " "]
```

16 The group is a **seq** group, bracketed by the "data tag group open"
(**dtgo**) and "data tag group close" (**dtgc**) delimiters (normally "["
18 and "]"), instead of the usual group delimiters, to indicate its special
nature. There are three tokens in the group:
20   a) The GI of the minimizable element:

```
      name
```

22   b) The *data tag template* [136] *416:26* , which in this case is a
single literal, but could also be an **or** group made up of liter-
24   als:

```
      ", "
```

26   The literal means "a comma followed by a space".
      c) A *data tag padding template* [137] *416:28* (which is optional):

28   " "

It means that zero or more spaces could follow the required
30   comma and space to constitute the data tag.
Thus, any string consisting of a comma and one or more spaces
32 that occurs after a "name" element begins in a "jobitem" will be
construed as the "name" end-tag. It will also, however, be
34 considered part of the data of the "jobitem".

Note the differences between a data tag and a short reference whose entity is an end-tag:

2 a) The short reference string is markup, not data.

   b) The short reference is recognized in any element whose map
4   has it mapped to an entity. The data tag is recognized only
       when its element is open and the containing element is that in
6   whose model the data tag group occurred.

   c) The short reference is a constant string; the data tag can be
8   any of a number of strings that conform to the data tag
       pattern.

10 The following list summarizes the delimiters enabled by the data
   tag feature and their character strings in the reference delimiter set:

12 **Char**	**Name**	*Meaning*
[	**DTGO**	Data tag group open.
14]	**DTGC**	Data tag group close.

C.1.5 RANK: Ranks May be Omitted from Tags

The rank of an element is its level of nesting. In many document
16 types, rank is only implied by the beginning and ending of nested
   elements, such as lists, and is never specified explicitly in the
18 document markup.

Some markup designers, though, prefer to use explicit rank
20 designations for some elements, such as headings and paragraphs
   (for example, p1, p2). Such elements tend to have declarations like:

```
22  <!--     ELEMENTS MIN CONTENT   -->
    <!ELEMENT p1      - O (#PCDATA, p2*)>
24  <!ELEMENT p2      - O (#PCDATA, p3*)>
    <!ELEMENT p3      - O (#PCDATA, p4*)>
26  <!ELEMENT p4      - O (#PCDATA)>
```

and document markup like:

```
28  <p1>Text of 1st level paragraph.
    <p1>Another 1st level paragraph.
30  <p2>Nested 2nd level paragraph.
    <p2>Another 2nd level paragraph.
32  <p1>Back to 1st level.
```

The SGML RANK feature offers a more convenient way of

specifying rank explicitly. An element can be designated a *ranked element* [118] *407:1* by dividing its GI into a *rank stem* [120] *407:17* and a *rank suffix* [121] *407:19*, which must be a *number* [56] *347:1*.

```
<!--          ELEMENTS MIN CONTENT   -->
<!ELEMENT p 1         - O (#PCDATA, p2*)>
<!ELEMENT p 2         - O (#PCDATA, p3*)>
<!ELEMENT p 3         - O (#PCDATA, p4*)>
<!ELEMENT p 4         - O (#PCDATA)>
```

When the rank feature is used, a rank stem can be entered in a tag instead of the complete GI. The complete GI will be derived from the stem and the last rank suffix specified for an element with that stem.

```
<p1>Text of 1st level paragraph.
<p>Another 1st level paragraph.
<p2>Nested 2nd level paragraph.
<p>Another 2nd level paragraph.
<p1>Back to 1st level.
```

A group of element types can share the same rank if they have identical content models. Such a group is called a *ranked group* [119] *407:5*. For example, if a document had normal paragraphs, numbered paragraphs, and bulleted paragraphs, each might contain any of the three at the next level down. The declaration

```
<!--          ELEMENTS  MIN CONTENT   -->
<!ELEMENT (p|n|b) 1 - O (#PCDATA, (p2|n2|b2)*)>
<!ELEMENT (p|n|b) 2 - O (#PCDATA, (p3|n3|b3)*)>
<!ELEMENT (p|n|b) 3 - O (#PCDATA, (p4|n4|b4)*)>
<!ELEMENT (p|n|b) 4 - O (#PCDATA)>
```

lets a document contain:

```
<p1>Text of 1st level paragraph.
<n>Numbered 1st level paragraph.
<p2>Nested 2nd level paragraph.
<b>Bulleted 2nd level paragraph.
<p1>Back to 1st level.
```

C.2 LINK Features: SIMPLE, IMPLICIT, and EXPLICIT

The discussion thus far has been confined to markup for a single
2 document type: the logical, or abstract, structure of a source
document that is to be processed. However, the result of
4 processing a document is also a document, albeit one that might
have a radically different document type definition.

6 For example, a document that conforms to a one-dimensional
source document type with a logical structure composed of
8 chapters, sections, and paragraphs, will, after formatting, also
conform to a two-dimensional result document type with a "layout"
10 structure whose elements are pages, columns, text blocks, and
lines.

12 The two document types will coincide at certain points, certainly at
the highest (document) level and possibly at others. A chapter in
14 the logical structure, for instance, might correspond to a "page set"
in the layout structure.

16 SGML supports multiple document types in two different ways:
  a) Link process definitions: document type definitions can be
18   linked to specify how a document can be transformed from
       one type (the "source") to another (the "result"); for example,
20   how the markup that would describe the data in terms of the
       result layout structure should be generated from the source
22   logical markup.
  b) Concurrent document instances: the markup for instances of
24   multiple document types can exist concurrently in a single
       document.

C.2.1 Link Process Definitions

26 Link set declarations can be used in applications such as formatting
to specify how logical elements in the source (for example,
28 paragraphs or list items) should be transformed into layout
elements in the result (for example, text blocks).

30 For example, if "para" and "item" elements were defined in the
source, and a "block" element were defined in the result with an
32 "indent" attribute, then

```
   <!LINK docset para block [ indent=3 ]
2                 item block [ indent=5 ]
   >
```

4 would cause a paragraph to be formatted as a text block with an
   indent of 3. List items would also be formatted as text blocks, but
6 with an indention of 5. The source text:

```
<item>Text of list item.</item>
```

8 would become the result text:

```
<block indent=5>Text of list item.</block>
```

10 For all other cases (assuming SHORTTAG minimization), all other
    attributes of the block would have their default values, as defined in
12 the block's element declaration.

    The LINK features are described in detail in clause 12 [433] .

C.3 Other Features

14 The remaining features are:

CONCUR   means that instances of the specified number
16   of document types (1 or more) may occur
                               concurrently with the base document type.
18 **SUBDOC**   means the specified number of open
                               subdocument entities (1 or more) may be
20   nested in the SGML document.
    FORMAL   means that public identifiers are to be
22   interpreted formally.

C.3.1 CONCUR: Document Instances May Occur Concurrently

    It is sometimes useful to maintain information about a source and a
24 result document type simultaneously in the same document, as in
    "what you see is what you get" (WYSIWYG) word processors.
26 There, the user appears to interact with the formatted output, but
    the editorial changes are actually made in the source, which is then
28 reformatted for display.

There are also cases in which even more than two such "views" of
2 the document can be useful, such as maintaining multiple formatted
results for instant display on both a CRT and a printer while still
4 having the logical document type available for other applications.

The concurrent document instance feature supports multiple
6 concurrent structural views in addition to the abstract view. It allows
the user to associate element, entity, and notation declarations with
8 particular document type names, via multiple document type
declarations.

10 The document type names are then prefixed to tags and entity
references, thus permitting multiple alternative sets of start-tags,
12 end-tags, and entities to be used in a document in addition to the
base set. Other markup and data can be associated with an
14 instance of a particular document type by means of marked
sections whose "INCLUDE" or "IGNORE" status is set by a
16 qualified keyword associated with that type.

In the previous example, if the layout document type were called
18 "layout", the concurrent markup for the formatted list item would be
(without markup minimization):

```
20  <(source)item>
    <(layout)block indent=5>Text of list item.
22  </(source)item>
    </(layout)block>
```

C.3.2 SUBDOC: Nested Subdocument Entities May Occur

24 A document in SGML is made up of one or more entities. The one
in which the document begins is called an "SGML document entity";
26 it is the one that contains the SGML declaration that identifies the
features and concrete syntax used throughout the document. The
28 SGML document entity also contains one or more document type
definitions, and is marked up to conform to one or more of those
30 definitions.

An entity that conforms to SGML markup is called an "SGML
32 entity". An SGML entity can contain references to "non-SGML data
entities" that contain only data that cannot be parsed, or to other
34 SGML entities that don't contain their own document type
definitions, called "SGML text entities".

When the subdocument feature is used, an SGML entity can also
contain references to "SGML subdocument entities", which do
contain their own document type definitions. An SGML
subdocument entity must conform to the SGML declaration of the
SGML document entity, but in other respects it establishes its own
environment. The document types and entity declarations of the
entity referencing a subdocument are suspended while the
subdocument entity is open, and restored when it ends. Current
rank begins anew in the subdocument, as do unique identifiers, so
there can be no ID references between the SGML document and
its subdocuments.

Subdocuments are referenced in the same manner as non-SGML
data entities. A general entity reference can be used anywhere in
content that it can be recognized, and where a data character could
occur (that is, in mixed content or in replaceable character data).
Alternatively, an element can be declared to have a general entity
name attribute that locates the subdocument entity:

```
<!ENTITY  art1          SYSTEM SUBDOC>
<!ELEMENT article - - EMPTY>
<!ATTLIST article       file ENTITY #REQUIRED>
<!>
<p>This topic is treated in the next article.</p>
<article file=art1>
```

Note that the element type need not be the same as the document
type of the subdocument entity. The latter is specified by the
document type declaration within it.

This feature allows separately created documents of various types
to be incorporated into a single document, such as an anthology.

C.3.3 FORMAL: Public Identifiers are Formal

When this feature is used, public identifiers have a formal structure
with a number of components:
  a) An owner identifier, which can be an ISO publication number,
     an identifier that conforms to a registration standard to
     guarantee uniqueness, or a private ("unregistered") identifier.
  b) A public text class, which identifies the kind of text being
     registered: SGML document, entity set, document type
     definition, and so on.

c) A public text identifier which names the registered text.

d) A designation of the natural language used, in the form of a standard two-character name.

e) An optional version, which identifies the output devices supported for device-dependent public text that is available in versions for more than one device. A system can automatically substitute the best version for the device in use during a given process.

Tutorial D
Link in a Nutshell

There exists an arcane area of Anglo-American law, called the "Rule Against Perpetuities", so complex that a California court once found an attorney to be innocent of malpractice on the grounds that no lawyer could be expected to understand it. My professor in Real Property at Harvard Law School, W. Barton Leach, was a well-known authority on the subject.[1] Prof. Leach wrote a famous article on the Rule whose title, "Perpetuities in a Nutshell", held out the promise that — California law to the contrary notwithstanding — the subject could be mastered. Since the LINK feature seems to have acquired some of that same aura of impenetrability, I thought it appropriate to borrow Prof. Leach's title. Unfortunately, to paraphrase what Leach said about perpetuities, the problem is not so much putting LINK in a nutshell as keeping it there.

The classical problem with a document that is marked up to describe logical structure is that the user cannot easily alter the formatting without compromising the generality of the document. Suppose he would like to specify an alternative set of formatting instructions in order to change the dingbats (bullets or whatever) that introduce the unordered list items.[2] He typically can do so either by inserting processing instructions, or by defining processing-oriented attributes. That is, either something like:

```
<ul>
<li>Item 1, with <q>normal</q> dingbat</li>
<?SET dingbat = "funny">
<?INDENT 7>
<li>Item 2, with <q>funny</q> dingbat</li>
```

---

[1] He was also well-known for a rumor that he drafted an unbreakable will for a Boston millionaire — and then broke it on behalf of a disgruntled heir.

[2] My 1959 *Webster's New World Dictionary of the American Language, College Edition* helpfully defines "dingbat" as "a doohickey".

```
<?SET dingbat = "normal">
<?INDENT 5>
<li>Item 3, with <q>normal</q> dingbat</li>
</ul>
```

or:

```
<ul>
<li>Item 1, with <q>normal</q> dingbat</li>
<li dingbat=funny indent="7">
Item 2, with <q>funny</q> dingbat</li>
<li>Item 3, with <q>normal</q> dingbat</li>
</ul>
```

Both of these techniques introduce process-specific information into the source document. The processing instructions are syntactically distinguishable from the descriptive markup, and can therefore be ignored easily. However, they can be rendered meaningless, or even disruptive, if the normal processing with which they interact should change.

The processing-oriented attributes are not distinguishable as such syntactically. Their interpretation is under the control of the application, which offers some additional flexibility. The main drawback of the technique is that multiple versions of the attributes (e.g., for different styles) cannot be supported. Moreover, if a new formatting process should require an additional attribute, the DTD would have to be modified. The modification could be inconvenient, or even impossible if the DTD were public.

SGML solves these problems with the LINK feature, which lets you specify formatting (or any other process) without distorting the logical structure markup. In a nutshell, LINK lets you associate processing-oriented attributes with a start-tag without actually putting them there.

Or, to put it another way, LINK allows you to associate style sheets and procedures with elements.

D.1 Link Sets

The processing-oriented attributes are called "link attributes" in SGML. They occur in a "link rule" that is expressed by a construct called a "link set" declaration in the document prolog. (You will see why it is a "set" a little later.)

The link sets, in turn, are grouped together in "link process definitions" (LPD), which can correspond to a particular formatting style, output device, or to a process other than formatting.

Here is a link set, named "lifunny", that gives list items additional indentions and funny dingbats:

```
<!LINK lifunny
      li [ dingbat=funny indent="7" ]
>
```

Even though link attributes do not actually occur on a start-tag, they are specified just as if they did. In the above example, the square brackets delimit text that is parsed as though it occurred in a start-tag, rather than in a declaration.

It should be noted, incidentally, that the dingbat and indent attributes are just examples. Link attributes are defined by an application with ATTLIST declarations, just like start-tag attributes. The only difference is that the declarations occur in an LPD, rather than in a DTD.

A single link set can include the link rules for a number of element types, hence the designation "set". For example:

```
<!LINK lifunny
      li    [ dingbat=funny indent="7" ]
      q     [ font=italic qmark=no ]
>
```

Here is another link set, named "linormal", that uses the normal indention and a normal dingbat for LIs:

```
<!LINK linormal
      li    [ dingbat=normal indent=normal ]
      q     [ font=roman qmark=yes ]
>
```

With these two link sets available, we can modify the format of an individual list item without resorting to processing instructions or processing attributes, simply by invoking the link sets with "link set use" declarations:

```
<ul>
<li>Item 1, with "normal" dingbat</li>
<!USELINK lifunny style1>
<li>Item 2, with "funny" dingbat</li>
<!USELINK linormal style1>
<li>Item 3, with "normal" dingbat</li>
</ul>
```

But USELINK declarations are rarely needed — the normal method of using link sets is much simpler and more powerful, as we will see shortly.

D.2 Link Types

In the preceding example, "style1" is a "link type"; that is, "style 1" is the name of the LPD in which the link sets are defined. A document could have many LPDs; at run-time, the user states which (if any) are active for that run. USELINK declarations for inactive link types are ignored.

Obviously, some link set had to be in effect at the start of the list, and at the start of the document, for that matter. This link set has the reserved name "#INITIAL", and there must be exactly one of them in an LPD.

Just as a DTD is expressed by markup declarations that occur within the declaration subset of a document type declaration, an LPD is expressed by declarations within a link type declaration. The declarations for the link process referred to as "style1" in the previous examples might look like the following:

```
<!LINKTYPE style1 general #IMPLIED [
  <!ATTLIST li   dingbat NAME normal indent CDATA normal>
  <!ATTLIST q    font    NAME roman  qmark  NAME  yes    >
  <!LINK #INITIAL
         li   [ dingbat=bullet indent=5 ]
         q    [ font=roman qmark=yes ]
  >
  <!LINK lifunny
         li   [ dingbat=funny indent="7" ]
         q    [ font=italic qmark=no ]
  >
  <!LINK linormal
         li   [ dingbat=normal indent=normal ]
         q    [ font=roman qmark=yes ]
  >
]>
```

This kind of LPD is called an "implicit link", because of the parameters of the LINKTYPE declaration. The first parameter, of course, is the link type name, "style1". The second is the document type on which the link process operates (the "source document type"); in the example, it is the general document type defined in E.1 [530]. The third parameter,

"#IMPLIED", means that the result of the process is implied by the application (hence "implicit link").

There is another form of link, called "explicit link", in which the document type resulting from the process is not implied, but is specified. There is also a form, called "simple link", in which neither document type is specified. Both of these will be discussed later, not because they are less important than implicit link, but because it is easier to deal with them once implicit link is understood.

Returning to our example, the attributes of the ordered list define the normal dingbat and indention for the list items (again, remember that these semantics are illustrative only — the application, not SGML, defines the relationship between attributes of different elements). List items are treated uniformly throughout the document, except when a particular item is modified in the document instance by a USELINK declaration.

D.3 Context-sensitive Processing

It is a first principle of SGML that variations in the style of a formatted document stem from variations in the logical structure. In other words, if a user decides that certain phrases should be in a different type font from others, it is because they contain a different kind of information — perhaps citations, foreign words, or the like. (Users also modify the format to accomplish copyfitting or to compensate for inadequacies in the formatter, but that is the exception that proves the rule.)[3]

Although one could obtain the desired format for special phrases by defining a link set and using USELINK declarations, that approach is not recommended. Instead, the special phrases should be tagged as the kind of elements they are, and the type font change should be part of the style for that special phrase.

However, there lies between the two extremes of (1) modifying each instance of an element individually, and (2) processing all elements of the same type uniformly, a third possibility — the context-sensitive style.

---

[3] This principle does not imply that all formatted instances of an element type will look identical — only that any differences will result from the uniform application of the same rule of style. For example, the layout of a page might require that paragraphs be cast off, in order, into a succession of areas of varying width. The paragraphs are all considered to be formatted in the same style, even though the result of applying that style causes them to look different from one another.

D.3.1 The USELINK Parameter

Suppose, in our example, we wanted all list items to be formatted normally in the body of the document, but we wanted funny dingbats and extra indention for all list items within the front matter. Such a style is equivalent to wanting the link set "linormal" to apply to list items occurring in the body, and the link set "lifunny" to apply in the front matter. SGML has a provision for such an automatic link set invocation, as follows:

```
<!LINKTYPE style2 general #IMPLIED [
   <!ATTLIST li  dingbat NAME normal indent CDATA normal>
   <!ATTLIST q   font    NAME roman  qmark  NAME yes    >
   <!LINK #INITIAL
          frontm #USELINK lifunny
          body   #USELINK linormal
   >
   <!LINK lifunny
          li    [ dingbat=funny indent=7 ]
          q     [ font=italic qmark=no ]
   >
   <!LINK linormal
          li    [ dingbat=bullet indent=5 ]
          q     [ font=roman qmark=yes ]
   >
]>
```

A USELINK parameter and link attributes could occur in the same link rule, although that situation does not arise in the example. Moreover, USELINK can be specified in any link set, not just the initial one, thereby allowing a hierarchy of context-sensitive processing specifications.

D.3.2 The POSTLINK Parameter

Suppose, in our example, we wanted all list items to be formatted normally except for the first in a list, for which we wanted funny dingbats and extra indention. Such a style is equivalent to wanting the link set "linormal" to apply to list items other than the first in a list, and the link set "lifunny" to the first. This form of automatic link set invocation is specified as follows:

```
<!LINKTYPE style6 general #IMPLIED [
```

```
<!ATTLIST li   dingbat NAME normal indent CDATA normal>
<!ATTLIST q    font    NAME roman  qmark NAME  yes   >
<!LINK #INITIAL
       ul   #USELINK lifunny
>
<!LINK lifunny
       li   #POSTLINK linormal [ dingbat=funny indent=7 ]
       q    [ font=italic qmark=no ]
>
<!LINK linormal
       li   [ dingbat=bullet indent=5 ]
       q    [ font=roman qmark=yes ]
>
]>
```

A USELINK parameter, a POSTLINK parameter, and link attributes could all be specified in the same link rule, although that situation does not occur in the example.

D.3.3 The Processing State

The source element structure is not the only context that could affect link rules — there is frequently a dependency on the state of processing as well. For example, the alignment of a heading might depend on whether the current output page is recto or verso, in addition to whether the heading occurs in the body or in the back matter.

SGML supports processing state dependencies by allowing a link set to contain more than one link rule for the same source element type. The only requirement is that link attributes must be specified in each of the rules, and that the application, by evaluating the attributes, must be able to determine which rule applies in any given instance.

An application, for example, could define a "usage" link attribute that would be specified for all conflicting link rules (but not if there were only one link rule for the element type): the first link rule for which it was "true" would apply. In an implementation, the application would have to communicate the selection back to the SGML parser, in case there was a USELINK or POSTLINK parameter.

In the following example, "curfont" is an application state variable that identifies the current font, and "EQ" and "NE" are relations in the application's expression language that test equality and inequality, respectively. The link set therefore specifies that list items will be set in bold italic if they occur when italic is the current font; if not, they will be set in italic.

```
<!LINK #INITIAL
        q       [ usage="curfont EQ italic"
                font=boldital qmark=no ]
        q       [ usage="curfont NE italic"
                font=italic qmark=no ]
>
```

D.3.4 Source Attribute Dependencies

An application could also permit the values of the source attributes to be tested in the same way as state variables. In the following example, "origin" is a source attribute of quotation elements that indicates whether they are direct quotes or attributions, and "val" is a function defined by the application's expression language that returns the value of a source attribute:

```
<!LINK #INITIAL
        q       [ usage="val(origin) EQ direct"
                font=boldital qmark=no ]
        q       [ usage="val(origin) NE direct"
                font=italic qmark=no ]
>
```

The example specifies that direct quotes will be set in bold italic and ordinary quotes in italic.

Obviously, an application could support a rich expression language that would allow combinations of tests of both source attributes and state variables.

D.4 Style Sheets and Procedures

In the examples up to now, all of the processing was specified directly in the link rules. This approach has the advantage of keeping all of the processing specifications in one place, with a uniform syntax. It effectively uses the link process definition as a formalized style sheet.[4]

For some applications, though, the richness of the specification possibilities calls for more flexibility than the link rule syntax offers. In these situations, the link set mechanism can be used to express the contexts in which the processing specifications change, while the specifications themselves would occur in external entities.

```
<!LINKTYPE style8 general #IMPLIED [
  <!ENTITY lifunny  SYSTEM -- Funny LI style sheet entity -->
  <!ENTITY linormal SYSTEM -- Normal LI style sheet entity    ▼
                              -->
  <!ATTLIST frontm style ENTITY #REQUIRED >
  <!ATTLIST body   style ENTITY #REQUIRED >
  <!LINK #INITIAL
          frontm [ style=lifunny  ]
          body   [ style=linormal ]
  >
]>
```

The style sheet entities could take a variety of forms. In a formatting process, for example, a style sheet entity could be:

— A traditional "typesetting order" in a natural language, intended to be read by a human compositor.

— A typesetting order in a system-independent formal language that will be translated algorithmically into processing instructions for a particular formatting program.

— Processing instructions for a particular formatting program.

— An executable macro or program.

In the second case, SGML could be used as the syntax of the formal language. In other words, the style sheet could itself be an SGML document.

```
<stylesht name=lifunny>
<descript>Provides funny formatting for LI elements.
<designer>U.N.Imaginative
```

---

4 The term "specification sheet" would perhaps better reflect the fact that the processing of SGML documents is not limited to conventional formatting — but "style sheet" is what everyone seems to call it.

```
<rule>
  <source>li
  <spec>dingbat<value>funny
  <spec>indent<value>7
<rule>
  <source>q
  <spec>font<value>italic
  <spec>qmark<value>no
</stylesht>
```

The above example is very simple. A real-world style sheet would likely have more complex means of referring to source elements and data, and of indicating values for specifications. It might also make extensive use of entities, such as for references to external resources and shared style sheet components. A real style sheet might also include additional descriptive elements to describe the intended effect of the specifications. Such elements would be useful to the designer in the same way that comments are useful to programmers. They would also be helpful to the end user if, for example, help screens or user manuals were formatted directly from the style sheets.

D.5 Mixing Manual and Automatic Link Set Activation

Note that the same definition mechanism is used for all link sets, regardless of whether they are invoked manually by USELINK declarations or automatically associated with element types by USELINK or POSTLINK parameters. In fact, the same link set can be activated by either technique at various points in the document.

When an element begins, the link set associated with it by the USELINK or POSTLINK parameter of the applicable link rule becomes the "current link set". If the link rule that applied to the element had no such parameter, then the current link set does not change.

When a USELINK declaration is used, it has the effect of changing the "current link set" for the open element. When the element ends, everything returns to normal, and the link sets for subsequent elements of that type will not be affected.

If it is desired to restore the normal current link set prior to the end of the element, a USELINK declaration with a reserved link set name of "#RESTORE" can be used:

```
<ul>
<li>Item 1, with "normal" dingbat</li>
<!USELINK lifunny style2>
<li>Item 2, with "funny" dingbat</li>
<!USELINK #RESTORE style2>
<li>Item 3, with "normal" dingbat</li>
</ul>
```

The same effect could be achieved without USELINK #RESTORE by explicitly naming the original current link set, but that technique is inferior for two reasons:

— The name of the original link set may not be easy to determine if there is a complex hierarchy of context-sensitive link sets.

— If, during revision of the document, the list were moved elsewhere, the original link set could change.

D.6 Avoiding USELINK Declarations (IDLINK)

A USELINK declaration has the drawback of introducing references to processing into the source document instance. Granted, it does not affect the descriptive markup as processing-oriented attributes do. Granted also, it is easily ignored if its process is not active, but there is still something intuitively uncomfortable about it.

The reason a USELINK declaration has this effect is not merely the syntactic device, but the effect that it is used to achieve. A USELINK declaration is only needed when the processing at some point in the document does not follow the normal rules. In some cases (probably including the preceding list item examples), the apparently anomalous instance really is rule-based, and could be handled by the LPD if the proper state variables and link sets were defined.

In other cases, though, separate processing might really be needed for individual elements because implementing a rule-based specification would be too complex. An example is specifying the size and position of figures, where the attribute values depend on a complex set of parameters including proximity of references to the figure, design of the page, position of other figures, etc.

SGML supports processing specifications for individual elements by means of an "ID link set declaration", in which each link rule is associated with the unique identifier attribute of an element, not just its type. In

the following example, there are two link rules for figure elements, one
for the figure whose ID is "fig1", and one for "fig2":

```
<!IDLINK fig1 figure [ pos="0 0"   size="10 10"]
         fig2 figure [ pos="15 30" size="20 40"]
>
```

An IDLINK declaration, because it refers to element IDs, is of little or
no use within an LPD that, presumably, could be used with more than
one document instance. The problem can be overcome by entering the ID
link set declaration in the link type declaration subset in the source document:

```
<!LINKTYPE style5a general #IMPLIED [
 <!ENTITY % style5 SYSTEM -- external LPD --> %style5;
 <!IDLINK fig1 figure [ pos="0 0"   size="10 10"]
          fig2 figure [ pos="15 30" size="20 40"]
 >
]>
```

Note that the previous example included an explicit entity declaration
and an entity reference to an external LPD. Normally, the declaration and
reference would be implied by an external identifier parameter in the link
type declaration, as in:

```
<!LINKTYPE style5b general #IMPLIED SYSTEM [
 <!IDLINK fig1 figure [ pos="0 0"   size="10 10"]
          fig2 figure [ pos="15 30" size="20 40"]
 >
]>
```

However, an implied external reference is resolved *after* the declaration subset, which in our case would mean that the ID link set would
occur (erroneously) prior to the definition of the link attributes that it
specifies.

The ID link set is the same as a normal link set in every respect but
one: it never becomes the current link set. Instead, its rules apply in preference to those of the current link set when an element is recognized
whose ID is associated with a link rule in the ID link set.

As with normal link sets, an ID link set can have conflicting link rules;
they would share the same unique identifier as well as the same element
type.

D.7 Explicit Link

When a document is processed, the result is another document, usually of a different type. For example, the process of hyphenation and justification of a magazine article could produce a "galley" document, and a subsequent casting-off process, performed on the galley, could produce a laid-out magazine page.

In the cases we have been considering, only the source document and the LPD were specified in SGML; the result document was left undefined. Or, to put it another way, the result document was implied by the semantics of the link process. However, it is also possible to specify the result document type explicitly in SGML. When that is done, the LPD is called an "explicit link".

Explicit links share all of the properties of implicit links, including USELINK and POSTLINK parameters. However, additional information can be specified in the link rules, as follows:

— If the processing of the source element causes the start of a result element, the result element type can be specified. If no result element is started, or if the result element type could vary, the keyword "#IMPLIED" is used.

— If a result element type is specified, attributes for it can also be specified. These attributes are not link attributes; they are properties of the result element and are defined in the result DTD. Specifying them in a link rule is equivalent to entering them in a start-tag if the result document were being created directly.

In the following example, a general document is linked to a formatted "volume" by the link process "style3". First-level headings in the source are linked to "block" elements in the result document type. On recto pages, the blocks are aligned right, and on verso pages they are aligned left.

```
<!LINKTYPE style3 general volume [
  <!ATTLIST h1   usage CDATA #IMPLIED >
  <!LINK #INITIAL
        h1 [ usage="page EQ recto" ] block  [ align=right ]
        h1 [ usage="page EQ verso" ] block  [ align=left ]
  >
]>
```

An explicit link process need not actually create an instance of the result element type. As always, the semantics of the markup are strictly left to the application. When explicit link is used, it simply reflects a judgment by the application designer that it is easier to specify processing in terms of both the source document and a conceptual result document, rather than in terms of the source alone.

D.8 Simple Link

An application designer may wish to offer only "global" style sheets, affecting the document as a whole with no context sensitivity. A link process for such a style sheet is termed a "simple link". It differs from implicit and explicit links in that it has no link sets, only link attribute definitions with fixed values, applicable to the document element.

```
<!LINKTYPE style4 #SIMPLE #IMPLIED [
  <!ATTLIST general dingbat NAME   #FIXED normal
                    indent  CDATA #FIXED normal
                    font    NAME  #FIXED roman
                    qmark   NAME  #FIXED yes>
]>
```

Simple links can also be used as supplements to implicit and explicit links. For example, a formatting style sheet might vary depending on the class of imaging device. Rather than develop multiple versions of the entire formatting LPD, it might be possible to isolate the device dependencies to a few global properties. Those properties could be expressed in simple LPDs, while the device-independent aspects of the style sheet would be expressed in a single implicit or explicit LPD. For a given processing run, one of the simple links would be active in addition to the formatting LPD.

In the following example, one simple LPD is defined for typesetters and another for video display devices. The links specify the layout, page size, and main and auxiliary font families. For the typesetters, the families are conventional type families; for the video displays, colors are used instead.

```
<!LINKTYPE typeset #SIMPLE #IMPLIED [
  <!ATTLIST general layout   NAME     #FIXED duplex
                    pagesize NUTOKENS #FIXED "8.5 11"
                    mainfont NAME     #FIXED Bodoni
                    auxfont  NAME     #FIXED Barnum>
```

```
]>
<!LINKTYPE display #SIMPLE #IMPLIED [
  <!ATTLIST general layout    NAME      #FIXED simplex
                    pagesize NUTOKENS #FIXED "9.75 6.5"
                    mainfont NAME      #FIXED blue
                    auxfont  NAME      #FIXED red>
]>
```

The simple links in the example could be used in conjunction with an LPD that did not specify the layout, pagesize, and font families, but instead referred to them as state variables maintained by the formatter. The formatter, of course, would set the variables in accordance with whichever of the two simple links was active for a given processing run.

D.9 Parsing with Respect to Active Links

If an SGML document contains link process definitions, one or more of them can be specified as "active" when the document is processed. Parsing is then performed with respect to the active LPDs and the base DTD.

An LPD can be active if:

a) it is a simple link; or

b) it is the only active implicit or explicit link; or

c) it is an explicit link that is part of a chain of processes in which the source document type of the first is the base document type, the source document type of the second is the result document type of the first, etc. The last link type in the chain can be either an explicit or implicit link.

In the case of a chain of processes, only one link is considered active at any point in the processing, and the document is at that point parsed with respect to that link and to its source DTD.[5]

---

[5] As with any explicit link process, there is no need actually to create instances of intermediate document types in a chain of links, nor must each link in the chain be processed completely before going on to the next. In practice, for example, a formatter might process part of a document to generate galleys, then process part of the generated galleys to produce pages, then go back to producing galleys again. An application could even use information gained during the page production process to re-do some of the earlier galley processing, perhaps at a different column width.

During the processing of a document, then, no more than one simultaneously active process can be an implicit or explicit link. The others (or all of them) must be simple links.

D.9.1 Entity References

Entities can be declared within a link type declaration subset. Such declarations (like everything else in an LPD) are effective only when the link type is active, in which case they are treated as though they had occurred at the start of the source DTD. As a result, entity declarations in an active LPD can change the meaning of entity references in both the source DTD and the document. Moreover, when links are active simultaneously (as opposed to chained), entity declarations in the LPDs appearing earlier in the prolog will preempt those in later LPDs.

SGML's treatment of entity declarations in LPDs offers substantial flexibility to the application designer. In the following example, entities defined in simple LPDs are used to specify default attribute values in an implicit LPD. (Only the relevant parts of the LPDs are shown.)

```
<!LINKTYPE typeset #SIMPLE #IMPLIED [
  <!ENTITY % layout  "duplex">
  <!ENTITY % pagesz  "8.5 11">
  <!ENTITY % mainfnt "Bodoni">
  <!ENTITY % auxfnt  "Barnum">
]>
<!LINKTYPE display #SIMPLE #IMPLIED [
  <!ENTITY % layout  "simplex">
  <!ENTITY % pagesz  "9.75 6.5">
  <!ENTITY % mainfnt "blue">
  <!ENTITY % auxfnt  "red">
]>
<!LINKTYPE style7 general #IMPLIED [
  <!ATTLIST (frontm|body|appendix|backm)
                  layout   NAME     %layout;
                  pagesize NUTOKENS %pagesz;
                  mainfont NAME     %mainfnt;
                  auxfont  NAME     %auxfnt;>
]>
```

D.9.2 Boilerplate Text

Boilerplate text can be made to vary from one process to another by declaring general entities within LPDs. In the following example, a single document is processed by two different LPDs to produce different versions of the product manual for two models of the product — the home version, in which the power switch is colored red, and the export version, in which it is green:

```
<!LINKTYPE home    #SIMPLE #IMPLIED [
  <!ENTITY color  "red">
]>
<!LINKTYPE export #SIMPLE #IMPLIED [
  <!ENTITY color  "green">
]>
<!DOCTYPE manual SYSTEM>
<manual><para>To begin, press the &color; power switch.
After 3 seconds, the rotor will turn.
```

The above technique works well when the number of variable text strings is limited and a distinct entity can conveniently be defined for each. In other cases, marked section declarations can be used, as in the following example:

```
<!LINKTYPE home    #SIMPLE #IMPLIED [
  <!ENTITY color      "red">
  <!ENTITY % status "INCLUDE">
]>
<!LINKTYPE export #SIMPLE #IMPLIED [
  <!ENTITY color      "green">
  <!ENTITY % status "IGNORE">
]>
<!DOCTYPE manual SYSTEM>
<manual><para>To begin, press the &color; power switch.
<![%status;[It is to the left of the display.]]>
After 3 seconds the rotor will turn.
```

Part Two:
A Structured Overview of SGML

Part Two: A Structured Overview of SGML

Chapter 1
Introduction

The tutorial introductions to SGML in Part One of this book were intended to impart a basic understanding of the language from the standpoint of a person marking up documents. This overview, in contrast, takes a more analytical approach, discussing every aspect of SGML in such contexts as:

— How SGML coordinates a document's abstract structure with its representation as a character string that is stored and interchanged in real systems.

— The relationship of SGML to a complete text processing application.

— How SGML can represent the full specification of processing for multiple applications without changing the source document.

The method used is to let the words of ISO 8879 speak for themselves; or more precisely, to let their definitions do the speaking. The standard contains more than 300 definitions. They are internally consistent and build upon one another, so that collectively they present most of the important concepts of SGML. Unfortunately, they appear in alphabetical order in ISO 8879, which may be useful for reference purposes, but which is hardly a logical structure for the rational exposition of SGML concepts.

This overview provides that logical structure, together with appropriate text to introduce and connect the definitions so that the key ideas are brought out.[1] Each definition is identified by its sequential number within the definitions clause of ISO 8879 or its companion standard, ISO 9069, the SGML Document Interchange Format (SDIF). The SDIF numbers are distinguished by the added suffix "S". The parts of the definitions that are merely illustrative or explanatory are, in accordance with ISO practice, identified as "notes", and the words in a defined term that can be omitted in order to form an abbreviation are parenthesized. In most cases, the abbreviated form of a term is also defined independently.

---

[1] The definitions are the property of the ISO and are used subject to the ISO copyright and grant of permission, as stated in the front matter of this book. However, the order of the definitions in this overview, the manner of organizing and presenting them, and the additional text that introduces and connects them, are not ISO property; they are part of the original material of this book and are protected by its copyright.

Chapter 2
Text Processing Application

SGML is a language for representing documents that are acted on by text processing applications.

The word "text" in "text processing application" does not have the usual dictionary connotations of "actual words of an author" as opposed to paraphrase, or "main portion of a book" as opposed to pictures, tables, and so on. The meaning here is derived from computer industry jargon — "text processing" as opposed to "data processing" — where data means "pure" information whose representation is optimized for processing and "text" refers to information in a form intended for human communication. It is not restricted to character text, but includes everything that can be perceived, including still and animated pictures, tables, photographs, music, and voice.

Characters are still of primary importance in text processing, not only because character text forms much of the subject matter, but because coded representations of characters are used to represent non-character text by associating different interpretations with them.

4.316 text: Characters.

2   NOTE — The characters could have their normal character set meaning, or they could be interpreted in accordance with a data content notation as the
4   representation of graphics, images, etc.

4.318 text processing application: A related set of processes
6   performed on documents of related types.

NOTE — Some examples are:

2   a)   Publication of technical manuals for a software developer: document
         types include installation, operation, and maintenance manuals;
4   processes include creation, revision, formatting, and page layout for a
         variety of output devices.

6   b)   Preparation of manuscripts by independent authors for members of
         an association of publishers: document types include book, journal,
8   and article; creation is the only defined process, as each publisher
         has its own methods of formatting and printing.

10 c)   Office correspondence: document types include memos, mail logs,
         and reports; processes include creation, revision, simple formatting,
12   storage and retrieval, memo log update, and report generation.

4.5 application: Text processing application.

14 **4.96 document:** A collection of information that is processed as a
    unit. A document is classified as being of a particular document
16 type.

NOTE — In this International Standard, the term almost invariably means
18 (without loss of accuracy) an SGML document.

4.102 document type: A class of documents having similar
20 characteristics; for example, journal, article, technical manual, or
    memo.

The processes referred to in the definition of text processing application can be quite complex, involving several distinct human and computerized subordinate processes. In SGML, the term "process" normally
refers to a subordinate process whose level of complexity is such that it
can be defined as a single task for a computer program. Such processes
are called "link processes" because they define the link between two different documents — the input to the process (the source document) and
the output (the result document).

22 **4.166 link process:** A process that creates a new instance of
    some document type (the result) from an existing instance of the
24 same or another document type (the source). Processes can be
    chained, so that the result of one is the source for the next.

26 NOTE — Examples of link processes include editing, in which the source
    and result document types are usually the same, and formatting, in which
28 they are usually different.

Chapter 3
SGML Application

3.1 Why SGML?

Historically, text processing applications were implemented by "marking up" manuscripts with instructions to an author, typist, or compositor. When computers took over part of the processing, the same model was followed, the markup now being added to the machine-readable representation of the document. Of necessity, the markup was specific to the processing being performed, and to the system that was performing it. The objective of SGML is to free markup from these dependencies and to regularize its use for modern text processing applications.

4.183 markup: Text that is added to the data of a document in order to convey information about it.

NOTE — There are four kinds of markup: descriptive markup (tags), references, markup declarations, and processing instructions.

4.178 mark up: To add markup to a document.

4.305 Standard Generalized Markup Language: A language for document representation that formalizes markup and frees it of system and processing dependencies.

4.278 SGML: Standard Generalized Markup Language

125

3.2 Specifying an SGML Application

SGML is a tool for defining and implementing some aspects of text processing applications; other tools are needed for the remainder. An SGML application is a particular use of SGML, but it normally includes processing specifications and other items that are not represented in SGML.

4.279 SGML application: Rules that apply SGML to a text
2 processing application. An SGML application includes a formal specification of the markup constructs used in the application,
4 expressed in SGML. It can also include a non-SGML definition of semantics, application conventions, and/or processing.

6 NOTES

1 The formal specification of an SGML application normally includes
8 document type definitions, data content notations, and entity sets, and possibly a concrete syntax or capacity set. If processing is defined by the
10 application, the formal specification could also include link process definitions.

12 2 The formal specification of an SGML application constitutes the common portions of the documents processed by the application. These
14 common portions are frequently made available as public text.

3 The formal specification is usually accompanied by comments and/or
16 documentation that explains the semantics, application conventions, and processing specifications of the application.

18 4 An SGML application exists independently of any implementation. However, if processing is defined by the application, the non-SGML
20 definition could include application procedures, implemented in a programming or text processing language.

22 **4.105 document (type) definition:** Rules, determined by an application, that apply SGML to the markup of documents of a
24 particular type.

NOTE — Part of a document type definition can be specified by an SGML
26 document type declaration. Other parts, such as the semantics of elements and attributes, or any application conventions, cannot be expressed
28 formally in SGML. Comments can be used, however, to express them informally.

30 **4.322 type definition:** Document type definition.

4.108 DTD: Document type definition.

2   **4.6 application convention:** Application-specific rule governing the text of a document in areas that SGML leaves to user choice.

4   NOTE — There are two kinds: content conventions and markup conventions.

6   **4.54 content convention:** An application convention governing data content, such as a restriction on length, allowable characters, 8   or use of upper-case and lower-case letters.

NOTE — A content convention is essentially an informal data content 10   notation, usually restricted to a single element type.

4.185 markup convention: Application convention governing 12   markup, such as a rule for the formulation of an entity name, or a preferred subset of allowed short reference delimiters.

3.2.1 Document Structure

SGML can represent documents of arbitrary structure. It does so by modeling them as tree structures with additional connections between the nodes. This technique works well in practice because most conventional documents are in fact tree structures, and because tree structures can easily be flattened out for representation as character sequences.

Except for the terminal nodes, which are "data", each node in an SGML document tree is the root of a subtree, called an "element". The descendants of a node are the "content" of that element. The document as a whole is termed the "document element".

14   **4.110 element:** A component of the hierarchical structure defined by a document type definition; it is identified in a document instance 16   by descriptive markup, usually a start-tag and end-tag.

NOTE — An element is classified as being of a particular element type.

18   **4.114 element type:** A class of elements having similar characteristics; for example, paragraph, chapter, abstract, footnote, 20   or bibliography.

4.9 attribute (of an element): A characteristic quality, other than 22   type or content.

3.2.2 Application Processing

An SGML application can include link process definitions that specify how elements are to be processed.

4.167 link process definition: Application-specific rules that apply
2 SGML to describe a link process. A link process definition includes
a formal specification, expressed in a *link type declaration*
4 [154] *434:1* , of the link between elements of the source and result,
including the definitions of source attributes applicable to the link
6 process ("link attributes").

NOTES

8 1   A link process definition can also include comments that describe the
semantics of the process, including the meaning of the link attributes and
10 their effect on the process.

2   There are three kinds of link process definitions: simple, implicit, and
12 explicit.

4.176 LPD: Link process definition.

14 **4.271 result document type (of a link):** A document type, a new
instance of which is created as the result of a link process.

16 **4.301 source document type (of a link):** A document type, an
existing instance of which is the source of a link process.

3.3 Implementation: The SGML System

An SGML application, like SGML itself, is an abstraction that could be realized in a variety of forms. For all practical purposes, however, the implementation of an SGML application occurs in a computer system that has the requisite software to qualify it as an "SGML system". That software includes an "SGML parser", which interprets the SGML markup, and an "entity manager", which allows the user to segment his documents, at his convenience, into arbitrary pieces, called "entities".

18 **4.287 SGML system:** A system that includes an SGML parser, an
entity manager, and both or either of:
20 a)   an implementation of one or more SGML applications; and/or

b) facilities for a user to implement SGML applications, with access to the SGML parser and entity manager.

4.285 SGML parser: A program (or portion of a program or a combination of programs) that recognizes markup in SGML documents.

NOTE — If an analogy were to be drawn to programming language processors, an SGML parser would be said to perform the functions of both a lexical analyzer and a parser with respect to SGML documents.

4.123 entity manager: A program (or portion of a program or a combination of programs), such as a file system or symbol table, that can maintain and provide access to multiple entities.

4.120 entity: A collection of characters that can be referenced as a unit.

NOTES

1   Objects such as book chapters written by different authors, pi characters, or photographs, are often best managed by maintaining them as individual entities.

2   The actual storage of entities is system-specific, and could take the form of files, members of a partitioned data set, components of a data structure, or entries in a symbol table.

3.4 Document Architecture

SGML establishes the representation of documents and the representation of processing specifications. It does not, however, codify the semantics of processing.[1]

As a result, an SGML application program might call on an SGML parser service that recognized processing specifications, but the application program itself would have to interpret and act on whatever was recognized. The processing semantics in such a case would be application-specific (even though the means of recognizing them are not), but as

---

[1] In other words, an SGML parser can recognize a processing specification when it sees one, but does not have the faintest idea of what it means!

long as all the users of a document have access to implementations of the application, no problems are presented.

Indeed, there are publishing situations where an SGML application can be useful with no processing specifications at all (not even application-specific ons), because each user will specify unique processing in a unique system environment.[2] The historical explanation for this phenomenon is that in publishing (unlike, say, word processing before the laser printer), the variety of potential processing is unlimited and should not be constrained.

On the other hand, there is sufficient commonality in text processing that the idea of common semantics has some appeal. Applications that followed the rules for such common semantics could be run on any system that implemented the semantics, thereby reducing the cost of application development and facilitating document interchange. A set of such rules for text processing applications is called a "document architecture".

4.97 document architecture: Rules for the formulation of text
2   processing applications.

NOTE — For example, a document architecture can define:
4   a)   attribute semantics for use in a variety of element definitions;
     b)   element classes, based on which attributes the elements have;
6   c)   structural rules for defining document types in terms of element
          classes;
8   d)   link processes, and how they are affected by the values of attributes;
          and/or
10   e)   information to accompany a document during interchange (a
          "document profile").

---

2 The Association of American Publishers (AAP) application is an example; it was the inspiration for the second note in the definition of "text processing application".

A document architecture could control every aspect of an application, or only a limited portion. In the latter case, a given application could conform to a number of document architectures at once.[3]

The relationship between SGML and document architectures represents a significant departure from the conventional approach to designing interchange representations, which is to define the desired semantics and then concoct an ad hoc encoding for documents conforming to the architecture. When SGML is used for the document representation, a number of benefits accrue that are independent of the architecture's processing semantics:

— Common utility programs that are unaware of a given architecture's semantics can operate on the structure of documents.

— Users can divide documents into arbitrary convenient pieces, transparently to the architecture.

— The SGML language can be used to extend a document's structure and data content to the extent permitted by the architecture or an application conforming to it.

— Hypertext links can be established within and among documents, either transparently to the architecture or under its control.

---

[3] At present, the ISO is standardizing a number of document architectures. One, called the "Office Document Architecture", or "ODA" (ISO 8613), is of the all-encompassing variety. The ODA standard governs the formatting, imaging, and interchange of office documents represented either in SGML, or in a binary encoding used by some telecommunication services. Another architecture, which specifically addresses the semantics of high-quality composition, is known as the "Document Style Semantics and Specification Language (DSSSL)"(ISO 10179). A third, the "Standard Page Description Language (SPDL)"(ISO 10180), defines only formatted documents, such as might be obtained by applying DSSSL to an SGML document.

Chapter 4
SGML Document

SGML represents three interrelated concurrent views of a document:

a) An element structure containing instances of one or more docu-
    ment types, reflecting, for example, the unformatted document, the
    document formatted for electronic display, the document formatted
    as camera-ready copy, etc..

b) An entity structure, reflecting the physical organization of the docu-
    ment into separately accessible pieces. Depending on the actual
    storage system, these pieces could be individual files, locations in
    memory, parts of a single file, etc.

c) A sequence of characters, formulated according to the rules of
    .SGML to represent both the element structure and entity structure.
    A character string is the simplest and most universal data structure,
    hence the most easily interchanged.

4.40 (character) string: A sequence of characters.

2 **4.308 string:** Character string.

4.1 Basic Concepts

4.282 SGML document: A document that is represented as a
4 sequence of characters, organized physically into an entity
structure and logically into an element structure, essentially as
6 described in this International Standard. An SGML document
consists of data characters, which represent its information content,

and markup characters, which represent the structure of the data
2 and other information useful for processing it. In particular, the
markup describes at least one document type definition, and an
4 instance of a structure conforming to the definition.

In practice, only a small portion of the markup need physically be present. Much of it can be omitted by using optional markup minimization features (discussed later).

4.1.1 Logical Organization

The element structure of a document consists of one or more hierarchies (tree structures), each conforming to a separate document type definition. Each non-terminal node is the root of a subtree that is an element, and each terminal node is data.

The children of any node are the "content" of an element. The content is "element content" if all the children are non-terminal, or "mixed content" if there is at least one terminal node. An individual terminal node is part (or all) of the "data content" of its parent. An individual non-terminal node is the root of a subelement of its parent.

Arbitrarily complex structures, such as hypertexts, are supported by attributes that represent various types of relationships among nodes and among documents.

4.113 element structure: The organization of a document into
6 hierarchies of elements, with each hierarchy conforming to a different document type definition.

8 **4.74 data content:** The portion of an element's *content* [24] *320:1* that is data rather than markup or a subelement.

4.1.2 Physical Organization

The entities that comprise an SGML document are simply collections of characters. There are two classes of entity: "SGML entities", whose characters are parsed according to ISO 8879, and "data entities", whose characters are interpreted according to notations specified by the application.

The first entity of a document that is parsed[1] must be a type of SGML entity called an "SGML document entity", as it contains the document type definition and other information that governs the parse.

4.126 entity structure: The organization of a document into one
2   or more separate entities.

NOTE — The first entity is an *SGML document entity* [[2] *295:13*] ; it con-
4   tains entity references that indicate where the other entities belong with respect to it.

6   **4.284 SGML entity:** An entity whose characters are interpreted as markup or data in accordance with this International Standard.

8   NOTE — There are three types of SGML entity: *SGML document entity*
[[2] *295:13*] , *SGML subdocument entity* [[3] *296:1*] , and *SGML text entity*
10   [[4] *296:5*] .

4.75.1 data entity: An entity that was declared to be data and
12   therefore is not parsed when referenced.

NOTES

14   1   There are three kinds: character data entity, specific character data entity, and non-SGML data entity.

16   2   The interpretation of a data entity may be governed by a data content notation, which may be defined by another International Standard.

4.1.3 Representation as a Sequence of Characters

An entity is simply a collection of characters. The characters that are permitted in both SGML entities and data entities are called "SGML characters". Each SGML character is either a markup character, which is interpreted by the SGML parser, or data, which is processed by the application.[2]

18   **4.280 SGML character:** A character that is permitted in an SGML entity.

---

[1] But this does not imply its position in actual storage.
[2] As the wording of the definitions suggests, this summary is an over-simplification. The details are covered later.

4.184 markup character: An SGML character that, depending on
2   the context, could be interpreted either as markup or data.

4.73 data character: An *SGML character* ⌈ **[50]** *345:1* ⌋ that is inter-
4   preted as data in the context in which it occurs, either because it
was declared to be data, or because it was not recognizable as
6   markup.

4.2 Text

4.2.1 Markup Declarations

The text of an SGML document is interpreted by an SGML parser, in
accordance with instructions given it by "markup declarations", which it
recognizes in the course of parsing.

4.186 (markup) declaration: Markup that controls how other
8   markup of a document is to be interpreted.

NOTE — There are 13 kinds: SGML, entity, element, attribute definition list,
10   notation, document type, link type, link set, link set use, marked section,
short reference mapping, short reference use, and comment.

12   **4.79 declaration:** Markup declaration.

4.2.1.1 Application-independent Instructions

Application-independent instructions to the parser occur in the
"SGML declaration", which is the first text parsed in an SGML document. Among these instructions are those that bind the "abstract syntax"
of SGML to the particular "concrete syntax" used in the document.

4.1 abstract syntax (of SGML): Rules that define how markup is
14   added to the data of a document, without regard to the specific
characters used to represent the markup.

16   **4.281 SGML declaration:** A markup declaration that specifies the
character set, concrete syntax, optional features, and capacity
18   requirements of a document's markup. It applies to all of the SGML
entities of a document.

4.48 concrete syntax (of SGML): A binding of the abstract syntax
2 to particular delimiter characters, quantities, markup declaration
names, etc.

One function of the concrete syntax is to assign delimiter strings to
delimiter roles. To minimize the chance that data will erroneously be
parsed as markup, many delimiter roles are not recognized unless their
delimiter strings occur in a specified context.

4 **4.88 delimiter role:** A role defined by the abstract syntax, and
filled by a character string assigned by the concrete syntax, that
6 involves identifying parts of the markup and/or distinguishing
markup from data.

8 **4.91 delimiter (string):** A character string assigned to a delimiter
role by the concrete syntax.

10 **4.87 delimiter-in-context:** A character string that consists of a
delimiter string followed immediately in the same entity by a
12 contextual sequence.

4.58 contextual sequence: A sequence of one or more markup
14 characters that must follow a delimiter string within the same entity
in order for the string to be recognized as a delimiter.

The concrete syntax also includes a quantity set that assigns values to
"quantities" that affect parsing. In many languages, such values are left
to the implementations, an approach that can impede portability signifi-
cantly. ISO 8879 defines a reference quantity set that is supported, *inter
alia*, by all conforming SGML systems (see figure 6 [470]).

16 **4.247 quantity set:** A set of assignments of numeric values to
quantity names.

18 **4.246 quantity:** A numeric restriction on some aspect of markup,
such as the maximum length of a name or the maximum nesting
20 level of open elements.

NOTE — Quantities are defined by the abstract syntax, but specific values
22 are assigned to them by the concrete syntax.

4.260 reference quantity set: The quantity set defined by this
24 International Standard.

4.2.1.2 Application-specific Instructions

Application-specific instructions to the SGML parser occur in the "prolog", which consists of declarations that express the document type and link process definitions. Not all document type and link process definitions will apply every time a document is processed. ISO 8879 says that the applicable ones are identified to the SGML parser by the system (which presumably was told about them by the user when he invoked the processing).

2   **4.2 active document type (declaration):** A document type that the system has identified as being active.

4   NOTE — An SGML entity is parsed with respect to its active document types, if any, or if not, with respect to its base document type and any active link types.

6   **4.21 base document type:** The document type specified by the first document type declaration in a prolog.

8   **4.3 active link type (declaration):** A link process that the system has identified as being active.

4.2.2 Descriptive Markup

When an SGML document is parsed, the parser recognizes an instance of the base document type and of each active document type, in which the element structure is delineated by descriptive markup tags.

10   **4.160 instance (of a document type):** The data and markup for a hierarchy of elements that conforms to a document type definition.

12   **4.100 document instance:** Instance of a document type.

14   **4.92 descriptive markup:** Markup that describes the structure and other attributes of a document in a non-system-specific manner, independently of any processing that may be performed on it. In

16   particular, SGML descriptive markup uses tags to express the element structure.

18   **4.314 tag:** Descriptive markup.

NOTE — There are two kinds: start-tag and end-tag.

2   **4.306 start-tag:** Descriptive markup that identifies the start of an element and specifies its generic identifier and attributes.

4   **4.119 end-tag:** Descriptive markup that identifies the end of an element.

6   **4.106 document type specification:** A portion of a tag that identifies the document instances within which the tag will be
8   processed.

NOTE — A *name group* [69] *374:11* performs the same function in an
10   entity reference.

In the usual case, in which there is only one document instance in the document, the document type specification is empty.

4.2.3 Other Markup

4.2.3.1 Reference

SGML incorporates a construct called a "reference" that performs typical substitution functions (copy, include, et. al.). At first blush, references appear to be purely lexical. However, there is a subtle context sensitivity in the design that helps to enforce clarity of markup.

4.256 reference: Markup that is replaced by other text, either an
12   entity or a single character.

4.124 entity reference: A reference that is replaced by an entity.

14   NOTE — There are two kinds: named entity reference and short reference.

4.37 character reference: A reference that is replaced by a single
16   character.

NOTE — There are two kinds: named character reference and numeric
18   character reference.

4.2.3.2 Separator

Markup constructs can be separated from one another by "white space" for readability. (There are also specialized separator strings that occur in markup declarations. They are discussed later.)

4.276 separator: A character string that separates markup
2   components from one another.

NOTES

4   1   There are four kinds: *s* [5] 297:23 , *ds* [71] 376:1 , *ps* [65] 372:1 , and *ts* [70] 375:3 .

6   2   A separator cannot occur in data.

4.273 s (separator): A separator, consisting of separator
8   characters and other non-printing function characters, that occurs in markup and in *element content* [26] 320:10 .

An s separator is commonly known as "white space".

4.2.3.3 Processing Instruction

Finally, as war is to diplomacy, there is the last resort of descriptive markup:

10   **4.234 processing instruction:** Markup consisting of system-specific data that controls how a document is to be processed.

4.2.4 Data

12   **4.72 data:** The characters of a document that represent the inherent information content; characters that are not recognized as
14   markup.

4.75 data content notation: An application-specific interpretation
16   of an element's data content, or of a data entity, that usually extends or differs from the normal meaning of the document
18   character set.

NOTE — It is specified for an element's *content* [**[24]** *320:1*] by a notation
2 attribute, and for a data entity by the *notation name* [**[41]** *333:33*] parameter
of the entity declaration.

It is now time to expand the earlier simplification regarding markup
characters and data characters, viz:

> Each SGML character is either a markup character, which is
> interpreted by the SGML parser, or data, which is processed
> by the application.

The correct statement is:

> Each SGML character is either:
>
> a) a markup character, which is parsed to determine
>   whether it is actually markup or is a data character
>   occurring in "parsed character data"; or
>
> b) a data character occurring in declared "character data".

4 **4.228 parsed character data:** Zero or more characters that occur
in a context in which text is parsed and markup is recognized. They
6 are classified as data characters because they were not recognized
as markup during parsing.

8 **4.229 PCDATA:** Parsed character data.

4.33 character data: Zero or more characters that occur in a
10 context in which no markup is recognized, other than the delimiters
that end the *character data* [**[47]** *344:1*]. Such characters are classi-
12 fied as data characters because they were declared to be so.

4.28 CDATA: Character data.

There are also forms of declared character data in which references are
recognized: "replaceable character data" and "replaceable parameter
data". The latter occurs only in markup declaration parameters.

14 **4.263 replaceable character data:** Character data in which a
general entity reference [**[59]** *350:17*] or *character reference*
16 [**[62]** *356:1*] is recognized and replaced.

2 NOTE — Markup that would terminate *replaceable character data* [46] *343:1* is not recognized in the replacement text of entities referenced within it.

4 **4.264 replaceable parameter data:** Character data in which a *parameter entity reference* [60] *350:22* or *character reference*
6 [62] *356:1* is recognized and replaced.

8 NOTE — Markup that would terminate *replaceable parameter data* [67] *373:8* is not recognized in the replacement text of entities referenced within it.

4.3 Entity Structure

4.3.1 Entity Declaration
10

Before an entity can be referenced, it must be declared by a markup declaration in the prolog.[3] An entity declaration associates an entity name (for use in references) with the text that will replace the reference.

12 **4.121 entity declaration:** A markup declaration that assigns an SGML name to an entity so that it can be referenced.

14 **4.127 entity text:** The entity declaration parameter that specifies the replacement text, either by including it in a parameter literal, or by pointing to it with an external identifier.

Sets of commonly-used entity declarations can be shared across systems and applications as "public text".

16 **4.125 entity set:** A set of entity declarations that are used together.

18 NOTE — An entity set can be public text.

---

[3] A defaulting mechanism for some kinds of undeclared entities is discussed later.

A useful technique for managing an entity set is to maintain it as an external entity. The set members can then be declared simply by declaring and referencing the entity that contains the set.

4.3.2 SGML Entities

There are three kinds of SGML entity:

a) The first entity to be parsed in a document is the "SGML document entity", of which there can be only one. It consists of a "prolog", which contains document type and link type declarations, and a "document instance set" with instances of one or more of the document types declared in the prolog. The SGML document entity can contain references to other SGML entities and to data entities.

b) An "SGML subdocument entity" has the same properties as an SGML document entity, except that it is not the first entity to be parsed and it does not have its own SGML declaration (or in any case, it is treated as though it had none).

c) An "SGML text entity" contains SGML markup but does not have its own prolog. It is parsed as though it were part of the entity from which it was referenced.

4.283 SGML document entity: The SGML entity that begins an
2 SGML document. It contains, at a minimum, an SGML declaration, a base document type declaration, and the start and end (if not all)
4 of a base document element.

4.286 SGML subdocument entity: An SGML entity that conforms
6 to the SGML declaration of the SGML document entity, while conforming to its own document type and link type declarations. It
8 contains, at a minimum, a base document type declaration and the start and end of a base document element.

10 **4.288 SGML text entity:** An SGML entity that conforms to the SGML declaration of the SGML document entity, and to the
12 document type and link type declarations to which the entity from which it is referenced conforms.

4.3.2.1 Prolog

The prolog contains at least one document type declaration, and (depending on the optional SGML features used in the document) may contain other document type declarations and link type declarations.

A document type declaration serves three functions:

— It identifies the element type of its document element.

— It contains, in its "declaration subset", the formal specification of a document type definition. The DTD can be in the same entity as the declaration (the "internal subset"), in an external entity that is implicitly referenced from the declaration (the "external subset"), or partly in both. An application designer can therefore establish a common DTD and permit (and control) local modifications to it.

— It can also contain, in its declaration subset, markup that is specific to the individual document; for example, declarations for entities that contain part of the document instance.

A link type declaration serves analogous purposes and has a similar structure. It identifies the source and result document types of the link, and its declaration subset contains the specification of the link process definition. A link type declaration can also modify its source DTD by including alternative declarations for entities. An application designer could use this mechanism, for example, to establish different default attribute values for different processes.

4.236 prolog: The portion of an SGML document or SGML
2   subdocument entity that contains document type and link type declarations.

4   **4.103 (document) type declaration:** A markup declaration that formally specifies a portion of a document type definition.

6   NOTE — A document type declaration does not specify all of a document type definition because part of the definition, such as the semantics of
8   elements and attributes, cannot be expressed in SGML. In addition, the application designer might choose not to use SGML in every possible
10   instance — for example, by using a data content notation to delineate the structure of an element in preference to defining subelements.

12   **4.170 link type declaration:** A markup declaration that contains the formal specification of a link process definition.

4.80 declaration subset: A delimited portion of a markup
2   declaration in which other declarations can occur

NOTE — Declaration subsets occur only in document type, link type, and
4   marked section declarations.

4.3.2.2 Document Instance Set

The "document instance set" is what you might comfortably think of
as the "real" document.

4.101 document instance set: The portion of an *SGML document*
6   *entity* [2] 295:13 or *SGML subdocument entity* [3] 296:1 in the
entity structure that contains one or more instances of document
8   types. It is co-extensive with the base document element in the element structure.

10   NOTE — When the concurrent instance feature is used, multiple instances
can exist in a document, and data and markup can be shared among them.

12   **4.99 document element:** The element that is the outermost
element of an instance of a document type; that is, the element
14   whose *generic identifier* [30] 325:17 is the *document type name*
[111] 404:4 .

16   **4.20 base document element:** A document element whose
document type is the base document type.

4.3.2.3 Records

An SGML entity is potentially divisible into "records", which allows
record boundaries to be given significance as markup characters. SGML
has precise rules for the parsing of record boundaries that are not delimiters:

— Record starts are ignored.

— Record ends are ignored for records that had no data.

— Other record ends are treated as data and passed to the application.

An application typically treats the data record ends as interword spaces. The SGML record boundary handling eliminates the problems of erroneous omission or insertion of such spaces that plague some text for-matters.

4.252 record: A division of an SGML entity, bounded by a record start and a record end character, normally corresponding to an input line on a text entry device.

NOTES

1   It is called a "record" rather than a "line" to distinguish it from the output lines created by a text formatter.

2   An SGML entity could consist of many records, a single record, or text with no record boundary characters at all (which can be thought of as being part of a record or without records, depending on whether record boundary characters occur elsewhere in the document).

4.253 record boundary (character): The record start (*RS*) or record end (*RE*) character.

4.255 record start: A *function character* [54] *346:8* , assigned by the concrete syntax, that represents the start of a record.

4.254 record end: A *function character* [54] *346:8* , assigned by the concrete syntax, that represents the end of a record.

4.3.3 Data Entities

Data entities are never parsed for SGML markup because their entity declarations declare them to contain only data characters.

4.3.3.1 Data Entity Classes

Data entities are classified by whether they are restricted to SGML characters, and therefore processable by SGML-based utilities (CDATA and SDATA entities), or whether they could potentially contain arbitrary bit combinations (non-SGML data entity).

4.34 character data entity: An entity whose text is treated as *character data* [47] *344:1* when referenced and is not dependent on a specific system, device, or application process.

4.29 CDATA entity: Character data entity.

2 **4.304 specific character data entity:** An entity whose text is treated as *system data* [45] *339:5* when referenced. The text is
4 dependent on a specific system, device, or application process.

NOTE — A specific character data entity would normally be redefined for
6 different applications, systems, or output devices.

4.275 SDATA entity: Specific character data entity.

8 **4.208 non-SGML data entity:** A data entity in which a non-SGML character could occur.

4.3.3.2 Data Content Notations

CDATA and SDATA entities are character data. Like all data characters in SGML documents, they could have their normal character set meanings, or they could have special meanings defined by a data content notation. In the latter case, they would be parsed by programs that recognize the notation. For SDATA entities, the "notation" is normally the system's processing language.

Data content notations are declared by "notation declarations", which associate a "notation name" for use in SGML markup with the "notation identifier" of the program that will interpret the data.

10 **4.212 notation declaration:** A markup declaration that associates a name with a notation identifier.

12 **4.214 notation name:** The name assigned to a data content notation by a notation declaration.

14 **4.213 notation identifier:** An *external identifier* [73] *379:1* that identifies a data content notation in a *notation declaration*
16 [148] *426:15* . It can be a *public identifier* [74] *379:8* if the notation is public, and, if not, a description or other information sufficient to
18 invoke a program to interpret the notation.

A data content notation could have "data attributes" defined for it. Their values serve as parameters to the notation parser. The notation name and the attribute values are specified in the entity declaration.

4.72.1 data attribute: An attribute of the data conforming to a
2   particular data content notation.

NOTE — In most cases, the value of the data attributes must be known
4   before the data can be interpreted in accordance with the notation.

4.3.3.3 Processing Instruction Entity

A processing instruction entity is like a data entity in that it is not parsed by an SGML parser. However, it differs from a data entity in that it is not considered to contain data.

4.235 processing instruction entity: An entity whose text is
6   treated as the *system data* 〔 **[45]** *339:5* 〕 of a *processing instruction*
〔 **[44]** *339:1* 〕 when referenced.

8   **4.230 PI entity:** Processing instruction entity.

The standard deprecates the use of processing instructions because they run counter to the SGML philosophy of rule-based processing, and because they introduce system-specific text into the document instance. For those occasions when the use of a processing instruction cannot be avoided, the standard recommends using an SDATA entity when the instruction returns data that is passed to the application, and a PI entity when it does not.

The distinction between a PI entity and an SDATA entity is important in the context of record end handling: a reference to a PI entity (like a processing instruction itself) is never considered to be data, while a reference to an SDATA entity is always considered to be data (even if the entity is empty).

4.4 Element Structure

When SGML entities are parsed in the entity structure, elements are opened and closed in the element structure.

4.220 open element: An *element* 〔 **[13]** *308:1* 〕 whose *start-tag*
10   〔 **[14]** *314:1* 〕 has occurred (or been omitted through markup minimization), but whose *end-tag* 〔 **[19]** *317:4* 〕 has not yet occurred (or
12   been omitted through markup minimization).

4.68 current element: The open element whose *start-tag*
2   [14] *314:1* most recently occurred (or was omitted through markup minimization).

4.4.1 Element Type Definition

A document type definition includes the definitions of the element types that can occur in the document. Element types are formally defined (in part) by "element type declarations" that associate a "generic identifier" (GI) with a definition of allowable content and markup minimization. Allowable attributes are defined in "attribute definition list declarations" that are associated with element types.

4   **4.115 element (type) definition:** Application-specific rules that apply SGML to the markup of elements of a particular type. An
6   element type definition includes a formal specification, expressed in element and attribute definition list declarations, of the content,
8   markup minimization, and attributes allowed for a specified element type.

10   NOTE — An element type definition is normally part of a document type definition.

12   **4.111 element declaration:** A markup declaration that contains the formal specification of the part of an element type definition that
14   deals with the content and markup minimization.

    4.116 element type parameter: A parameter of an element
16   declaration that identifies the type of element to which the definition applies.

18   NOTE — The specification can be direct, in the form of an individual *generic identifier* [30] *325:17* or member of a *name group* [69] *374:11* ,
20   or indirect, via a *ranked element* [118] *407:1* or member of a *ranked group* [119] *407:5* .

22   **4.145 generic identifier:** A name that identifies the element type of an element.

24   **4.146 GI:** Generic identifier.

    4.12 attribute (definition) list declaration: A markup declaration
26   that associates an attribute definition list with one or more element types.

4.14 attribute list declaration: Attribute definition list declaration.

2   **4.112 element set:** A set of element, attribute definition list, and notation declarations that are used together.

4   NOTE — An element set can be public text.

4.104 document type declaration subset: The element, entity,
6   and short reference sets occurring within the declaration subset of a document type declaration.

8   NOTE — The external entity referenced from the document type declaration is considered part of the declaration subset.

4.4.2 Content

In the element structure, the content of an element is data, other elements, or a mixture of both. In the text representation, it is the character string that occurs between the start-tag and end-tag.

10   **4.53 content:** Characters that occur between the start-tag and end-tag of an element in a document instance. They can be
12   interpreted as data, proper subelements, included subelements, other markup, or a mixture of them.

14   NOTE — If an element has an explicit content reference, or its declared content is "EMPTY", the content is empty. In such cases, the application
16   itself may generate data and process it as though it were content data.

An element type declaration can declare the element's content to be character data, replaceable character data, or empty (that is, without content). Alternatively, the declaration can contain a "content model" that states which subelement types and data can occur in the element.

4.309 subelement: An element that occurs in the content of
18   another element (the "containing element") in such a way that the subelement begins when the containing element is the current
20   element.

4.52 containing element: An element within which a subelement
22   occurs.

A content model has two parts:

a)   a *model group* ⸢ [127] *410:6* ⸥ , which uses a notation similar to regular expressions to specify the ordering of allowable subelements and data; and

b)   "exceptions" that modify the content model by excluding optional items allowed by the model and allowing optional items not mentioned in the model.

4.55 (content) model: Parameter of an element declaration that
2   specifies the *model group* ⸢ [127] *410:6* ⸥ and *exceptions* ⸢ [138] *418:1* ⸥ that define the allowed *content* ⸢ [24] *320:1* ⸥ of the element.

4   **4.193 model:** Content model.

4.4.2.1 Model Group

4.194 model group: A component of a content model that
6   specifies the order of occurrence of elements and character strings in an element's *content* ⸢ [24] *320:1* ⸥ , as modified by *exceptions*
8   ⸢ [138] *418:1* ⸥ specified in the *content model* ⸢ [126] *410:1* ⸥ of the element and in the content models of other open elements.

A model group consists of "content tokens" that represent elements and data that can occur in the document instance. A content token can be a generic identifier, a reserved name representing parsed character data, a nested model group, or a special form of nested model group called a "data tag group" (discussed later).

There is a concrete syntax limit on the depth of nesting of groups. Only normal model groups (not data tag groups) can contain nested groups; the other content tokens are therefore referred to as "primitive content tokens".

Groups are identified by paired opening and closing delimiters, mentioned in the definitions below: data tag groups by the *dtgo* and *dtgc* (square brackets), and other groups by the *grpo* and *grpc* (parentheses).

10   **4.66 corresponding content (of a content token):** The element(s) and/or data in a document instance that correspond to a
12   *content token* ⸢ [128] *410:17* ⸥ .

4.56 content model nesting level: The largest number of
2   successive ***grpo*** or ***dtgo*** delimiters that occur in a *content model*
    [126] *410:1* without a corresponding ***grpc*** or ***dtgc*** delimiter.

There are three kinds of model group, distinguished by the rules governing ordering and selection of the corresponding content:

seq	All must occur, in the order of the content tokens.
and	All must occur, in any order.
or	One and only one must occur.

The selected corresponding content must occur just once, unless the content token has one of the following "occurrence indicators":

opt	0 or 1 time (optional).
rep	0 or more times (optional and repeatable).
plus	1 or more times (required and repeatable).

A content model cannot be ambiguous.

4   **4.4 ambiguous content model:** A *content model* [126] *410:1* for
   which an element or character string occurring in the document
6   instance can satisfy more than one *primitive content token*
   [129] *410:20* without look-ahead.

8   NOTE — Ambiguous content models are prohibited in SGML.

4.4.2.2 Exceptions

4.130 exceptions: A parameter of an element declaration that
10   modifies the effect of the element's *content model* [126] *410:1* , and
   the content models of elements occurring within it, by permitting
12   inclusions and prohibiting exclusions.

4.157 inclusions: Elements that are allowed anywhere in the
14   content of an element or its subelements even though the
   applicable model does not permit them.

16   **4.131 exclusions:** Elements that are not allowed anywhere in the
   content of an element or its subelements even though the
18   applicable content model or inclusions would permit them
   optionally.

4.237 proper subelement: A subelement that is permitted by its
2 containing element's model.

NOTE — An included subelement is not a proper subelement.

4 **4.156 included subelement:** A subelement that is not permitted
by its containing element's model, but is permitted by an inclusion
6 exception.

Exceptions are intended for purposes that cannot easily be achieved
simply by modifying a DTD. Exclusions prevent unwanted recursions
and allow modification of "read-only" DTDs (see 11.2.5.2 ⟨419⟩), while
inclusions allow subelements to occur in the character string representation of an element's content that are not part of the element structure.

For example, a floating figure or sidebar is not part of an element's
content in the structural sense, but nevertheless could occur within it in
the source character string. SGML recognizes this distinction in its handling of record ends: an included subelement is not considered to be data
in its containing element, while a proper subelement is. A good application design will therefore treat a floating figure as a different element
type from a stationary ("inline") figure.

4.4.3 Attributes

An element type can have properties other than its content and generic identifier. These properties, called "attributes", are defined by an
attribute definition list declaration that associates an "attribute definition
list" with the element type. An element type can be associated with a
permanent attribute definition list in the DTD, and with process-specific
attributes in any LPD for which the DTD is the source.

As you might expect, an attribute definition list is made up of individual "attribute definitions". Each consists of an "attribute name", a
"declared value", and a "default value". The "declared value" defines the
representation of the attribute's allowable domain, and therefore appears
analogous to declaring a data type for a variable in a programming language. There is, however, a substantial difference, which is designed to
keep SGML from conflicting with the various text processing programs
with which it must work.

The difference is this: SGML can recognize only constructs that are
used in the SGML language itself, and so actual semantic domains cannot be declared. The declared value is only the *representation* of the
domain; in other words, a character string of one form or another. Moreover, the available forms of character string are only those that have been
defined for use in some part of the SGML language.

Of course, SGML as a language requires little of the function one normally associates with text processing, as it deals only with the representation of documents. In particular, SGML:

— Scans and tokenizes a character string in order to distinguish:

  — SGML markup,

  — data in a notation that must be interpreted specially, and

  — data that does not require special interpretation.

— Provides a method of identifying and referencing virtual storage objects, called "entities".

— Provides a method of identifying and referencing instances of structural elements by means of "ID" and "IDREF" attributes (discussed later).

These tasks effectively limit the possible declared values for attributes. Note that they do not require the language to define even such basic arithmetical constructs as "integer" and "increment". Although SGML has a construct called a "number", for example, it would more properly have been termed a "numeral". It is defined as a character string of a restricted length consisting solely of digit characters. As a result, the numbers "0" and "00" are not equivalent in SGML, even though the integers they could be taken to represent might be equivalent in some application.

The net result of this design is that an application is free to define its own semantics and the representation of its data types. The SGML parser can guarantee that the user's specified attribute values will meet the application's length and alphabet restrictions, so they will fit into the application's buffers and be valid input to the application's routines that convert them to internal representations. The application retains the responsibility of determining whether the converted values satisfy its semantic constraints.[4]

---

[4] There is no intention here to suggest that standardization of processing semantics and data type representations would not be a good thing — only that it should not be the province of SGML. Introducing semantic standards into SGML would only serve to limit the potential processing of a document, as a single semantic standard is no more likely to be optimal for all applications than is a single programming language.

4.4.3.1 Defining Attributes

4.10 attribute definition: A member of an attribute definition list; it
2   defines an attribute name, allowed values, and default value.

4.11 attribute definition list: A set of one or more attribute
4   definitions defined by the *attribute definition list* ⟨**[142]** *420:25*⟩
parameter of an attribute definition list declaration.

6   **4.8 associated element type:** An element type associated with
the subject of a markup declaration by its *associated element type*
8   ⟨**[72]** *377:1*⟩ parameter.

Attributes can also be associated with a data content notation, in
which case they are called "data attributes". The standard form of attribute list declaration is used, except that "associated notation names" are
specified, rather than element types.

4.8.1 associated notation (name): A notation name associated
10   with the subject of a markup declaration by its *associated notation
name* ⟨**[149.1]** *428:5*⟩ parameter.

Declared Value :

SGML recognizes the following declared values:

— A "CDATA" string consisting of any SGML characters.

— Four kinds of "name tokens", which are short strings containing
only characters that are permitted in an SGML name (chiefly letters
and digits).

— Lists of each of the four kinds of name token.

— A group of particular name tokens, with the value required to be a
member of the group.

— Certain SGML constructs: notation names, general entity names,
and unique identifiers of elements. (These are discussed later.)

It should be noted that the term "name token" cannot be abbreviated as "token". The latter term is applied to a member of a "group", which is a kind of markup declaration parameter (discussed later). However, it is possible for a name token to occur in a group, in which case it would (in that instance) also be a token.

4.202 name token: A character string, consisting solely of name characters, whose length is restricted by the NAMELEN quantity.

NOTE — A name token that occurs in a group is also a token; one that occurs as an attribute value is not.

4.198 name: A name token whose first character is a name start character.

4.215 number: A name token consisting solely of digits.

4.216 number token: A name token whose first character is a digit.

NOTE — A number token that occurs in a group is also a token; one that occurs as an attribute value is not.

4.199 name character: A character that can occur in a name: name start characters, digits, and others designated by the concrete syntax.

4.201 name start character: A character that can begin a name: letters, and others designated by the concrete syntax.

Default Value :

The minimal form of SGML, with no optional features, requires that an attribute specification include an explicit value unless the attribute was defined to be "impliable" by the application. Normally, though, optional features called "markup minimization" are used that allow attribute values to be defaulted. An attribute definition includes a default value parameter for this purpose.

4.84 default value: A portion of an attribute definition that specifies the attribute value to be used if there is no *attribute specification* [32] *327:19* for it.

A default value can be a specific value, specified in the way that attributes are normally specified (see below), or it can be a keyword that identifies the defaulting mechanism that is applicable to the attribute: impliable, required, or current.

2   **4.154 impliable attribute:** An attribute for which there need not be an *attribute specification* ⌐ **[32]** *327:19* ¬ , and whose value is defined by the application when it is not specified.

4   **4.268 required attribute:** An attribute for which there must always be an *attribute specification* ⌐ **[32]** *327:19* ¬ for the attribute value.

6   **4.67 current attribute:** An attribute whose current (that is, most recently specified) value becomes its default value.

8   NOTE — The start-tag cannot be omitted for the first occurrence of an element with a current attribute.

A keyword can be specified in conjunction with a specific value to establish a default that cannot be overridden.

10   **4.136 fixed attribute:** An attribute whose specified value (if any) must be identical to its default value.

4.4.3.2 Specifying Attribute Values

An attribute value is normally specified as a delimited string, called an "attribute value literal", which is interpreted to derive the actual attribute value. This technique can be used in both attribute definitions and attribute specifications.

When an attribute value contains only characters permitted in an SGML name, the value can be specified directly (that is, without an attribute value literal) within an attribute definition, and also within an attribute specification if the optional "SHORTTAG" feature is in use.

12   **4.17 attribute value literal:** A delimited character string that is interpreted as an *attribute value* ⌐ **[35]** *333:1* ¬ by replacing references
14   and ignoring or translating function characters.

Attribute values are specified in "attribute specification lists", which occur in start-tags, link rules, and entity declarations.

4.16 attribute (specification) list: Markup that is a set of one or
2   more attribute specifications.

NOTE — Attribute specification lists occur in start-tags, entity declarations,
4   and link sets.

4.13 attribute list: Attribute specification list.

6   **4.15 attribute specification:** A member of an attribute
specification list; it specifies the value of a single attribute.

The length of an attribute specification list is restricted by the concrete
syntax.

8   **4.210 normalized length (of an attribute specification list):** A
length calculated by ignoring the actual characters used for
10   delimiting and separating the components and counting an extra
fixed number per component instead.

4.4.3.3 Attributes Relating to SGML Constructs

Notation Attribute :

A "notation attribute" identifies the data content notation that applies
to an element's data. If no special interpretation of the data is required, or
if it is implicit in the processing of the element type, then a notation attribute would not normally be defined.

A "notation attribute" has a declared value that is a group of notation
names. The specified value must be a member of the group.

12   **4.211 notation attribute:** An attribute whose value is a *notation
name* [41] *333:33* that identifies the data content notation of the
14   element's *content* [24] *320:1* .

NOTE — A notation attribute does not apply when there is an explicit con-
16   tent reference, as the element's *content* [24] *320:1* will be empty.

ID Value and ID Reference :

Every element is inherently identifiable by means of its position in the document instance (for example, "the third paragraph of the second chapter"), in much the same way that program variables are identifiable by their memory addresses. In preference to these "absolute addresses" (as one might think of them), SGML identifies elements by SGML names, called "unique identifiers" (or "IDs").

An ID is assigned to an element by an "ID value" attribute. Other elements can refer to it by means of an "ID reference value" attribute. For example, a "figure reference" element could have a "referenced element" attribute whose value would be the ID of the figure referred to.

> **4.324 unique identifier:** A *name* [55] *346:17* that uniquely identi-
> 2   fies an element.

> **4.150 ID:** Unique identifier.

> 4   **4.153 ID value:** An attribute value that is a *name* [55] *346:17* that
> uniquely identifies the element; that is, it cannot be the same as
> 6   any other *id value* [36] *333:19* in the same document instance.

> **4.152 ID reference value:** An attribute value that is a *name*
> 8   [55] *346:17* specified as an *id value* [36] *333:19* of an element in
> the same document instance.

> 10   **4.151 ID reference list:** An attribute value that is a list of ID
> reference values.

General Entity Name :

It is possible to declare that an attribute value must be a general entity name, or a list of them. An SGML parser will check that the entity was declared properly, just as if it had occurred in a named entity reference, but it will not parse the entity.

General entity name attributes are often used to identify related sub-documents. For example, a link attribute called "font" could have as its value the name of an entity containing an ISO standard description of a font resource.

Content Reference Attribute :

A "content reference attribute" is not a kind of declared value. It is an attribute with the property that, if it is specified explicitly in a start-tag (rather than defaulted), then the content of that instance of the element is empty. Instead, the attribute value is used by the application (in some unspecified way) to produce content data.

A content reference attribute can have any declared value except ID value. Its special nature is indicated in the attribute definition by a keyword in the default value parameter.

A typical use of a content reference attribute is to allow the user to decide for any instance of an element, such as a figure, whether it will have normal SGML text content, or whether data in an external entity (such as a scanned image) will be used.

4.57 content reference (attribute): An impliable attribute whose
2   value is referenced by the application to generate content data.

NOTE — When an element has an explicit content reference, the element's
4   *content* [24] 320:1 in the document instance is empty.

4.132 explicit content reference: A content reference that was
6   specified in an *attribute specification* [32] 327:19 .

4.5 References

SGML offers three ways of referring to an entity:

a)   As a "named entity reference", which is an SGML name delimited to indicate that it is an entity reference.

     The reference is replaced by the entity text, which is parsed in the same syntactic and structural context in which the reference occurred.

b)   As a "short reference", which is a markup minimization technique by which a single character is treated as the equivalent of a named entity reference. (Short references are discussed later.)

c)   As the value of a general entity name attribute.

This method is not technically considered a reference, as it is not replaced by the entity's replacement text. Instead, a parser will normally pass a pointer to the entity text to the application, which can choose to treat the text as data. In the case of an SGML subdocument entity, the application might call the SGML parser recursively to parse the subdocument, but that would not be done in the context of parsing the original document.[5]

4.266 replacement text: The text of the entity that replaces an
2   entity reference.

To prevent the possibility of endless loops, replacement text cannot contain a reference to the same entity, or any other from which it was referenced (the "open" entities).

4.221 open entity: An entity that has been referenced but whose
4   entity end has not yet occurred.

SGML has rules designed to prevent entity references from obscuring the markup. In particular, if an entity reference occurs in delimited text (such as an attribute value literal), the closing delimiter will not be recognized within the entity's replacement text. Also, a delimiter string cannot cross an entity boundary.

4.5.1 Named Entity References

Two independent groups of entities can be declared and referenced: general and parameter. Parameter entities can be referenced only in markup declarations, so the end user need be aware only of those that the application allows one to override in, say, a document type declaration subset. General entities are those intended to be in the domain of the user doing the markup. The dual name space allows the end user to declare a general entity without fear that the new entity name will conflict with "internal" entity names used in the prolog.

---

[5] A subdocument looks to SGML like a single character; those seeking answers to the larger questions of existence may glean whatever insight they can from the fact that, in a well-designed document description language, a universe and an atom are treated identically. (The same may be true for page description languages, as a formatted page and a character glyph both look suspiciously like pictures.)

4.143 general entity: An entity that can be referenced from within
2   the content of an element or an attribute value literal.

4.144 general entity reference: A named entity reference to a
4   general entity.

4.225 parameter entity: An entity that can be referenced from a
6   markup declaration parameter.

4.226 parameter entity reference: A named entity reference to a
8   parameter entity.

A method (explained later) is provided for defaulting general entity
references, to facilitate the ad hoc creation of external entities during creation of the document.

4.205 named entity reference: An entity reference consisting of a
10   delimited name of a general entity or parameter entity (possibly
     qualified by a name group) that was declared by an entity
12   declaration.

NOTE — A general entity reference can have an undeclared name if a
14   default entity was declared.

4.83 default entity: The entity that is referenced by a general
16   entity reference with an undeclared name.

4.5.2 Character References

Characters and character sets will be discussed in some detail later. For now, things can be simplified by saying that a character is an idea represented by a number. Keyboards provide a direct means of entering the characters that are used most frequently, but there are always exceptions.

A general mechanism for dealing with unkeyable characters is to offer the end user a suitably mnemonic general entity reference to use. Such an entity is defined by using a "numeric character reference", which is replaced by the character represented by that number.

Some character numbers represent functions in the concrete syntax, such as tab or record end. If the function is wanted, a "named character reference" incorporating the function name is used; otherwise, a numeric character reference is used and the character is treated as data.

4.265 replacement character: The character that replaces a
2   *character reference* [62] *356:1* .

4.204 named character reference: A character reference
4   consisting of a delimited *function name* [63] *356:6* .

4.217 numeric character reference: A character reference
6   consisting of a delimited *character number* [64] *357:1* .

4.6 Markup Minimization

All markup minimization in SGML is optional. The SGML declaration
indicates which minimization features are usable in a document. Even
when minimization features can be used, it is always correct to enter the
full markup.

4.187 (markup) minimization feature: A feature of SGML that
8   allows markup to be minimized by shortening or omitting tags, or
shortening entity references.

10   NOTE — Markup minimization features do not affect the document type
definition, so a minimized document can be sent to a system that does not
12   support these features by first restoring the omitted markup. There are five
kinds: SHORTTAG, OMITTAG, SHORTREF, DATATAG, and RANK.

14   **4.192 minimization feature:** Markup minimization feature.

4.6.1 OMITTAG Feature

The standard identifies conditions under which tags can be omitted,
provided that the omission would not create an ambiguity. An application designer, however, could require that a technically valid omission be
reported as a markup error.

4.219 omitted tag minimization parameter: A parameter of an
16   element declaration that specifies whether a technically valid
omission of a start-tag or end-tag is considered a reportable
18   markup error.

4.6.1.1 End-tag Omission

The end-tag can be omitted for an element whose ending can be implied from the following circumstances:

— The end of the SGML document (or subdocument) entity.

— The end of the subject element's containing element (for example, a list item ends when its list ends).

— The occurrence of an element or SGML character that is not allowed in the subject element's content.

4.6.1.2 Start-tag Omission

A start-tag cannot be omitted if it is needed to specify a required attribute or to identify an element whose content requires special parsing (for example, an element with empty or declared content, such as character data or replaceable character data). Otherwise, the start-tag can be omitted for an element that is contextually required, as long as any other elements that could occur are contextually optional.

For example, if a content model called for an optional FRONTM followed by a required BODY, the start-tag of FRONTM could not be omitted because FRONTM is optional. The start-tag of BODY could be omitted, however, because BODY is required and the only other element that could occur (FRONTM) is optional.

When a start-tag is omitted, default values are used for its attributes.

Although the basic principles of start-tag omission are reasonably straightforward, the detailed requirements and definitions are highly technical. They hinge on the concepts "contextually optional element" and "contextually required element".

Contextually Optional Element :

4.59 contextually optional element: An element
2   a) that can occur only because it is an inclusion; or
     b) whose *content token* [128] *410:17* in the currently applicable
4   model group is a contextually optional token.

4.60 contextually optional token: A *content token* [128] *410:17*

2 that
a) is an inherently optional token; or
4 b) has a ***plus*** occurrence indicator and has been satisfied; or
c) is in a model group that is itself a contextually optional token,
6 no tokens of which have been satisfied.

4.159 inherently optional token: A *content token* [128] *410:17*

8 that:
a) has an ***opt*** or ***rep*** occurrence indicator; or
10 b) is an ***or*** group, one of whose tokens is inherently optional; or
c) is an ***and*** or ***seq*** group, all of whose tokens are inherently
12 optional.

Contextually Required Element :

4.61 contextually required element: An element that is not a

14 contextually optional element and
a) whose *generic identifier* [30] *325:17* is the *document type*
16 *name* [111] *404:4* ; or
b) whose currently applicable *content token* [128] *410:17* is a
18 contextually required token.

NOTE — An element could be neither contextually required nor

20 contextually optional; for example, an element whose currently applicable
content token [128] *410:17* is in an ***or*** group that has no inherently
22 optional tokens.

4.62 contextually required token: A *content token* [128] *410:17*

24 that
a) is the only one in its model group; or
26 b) is in a ***seq*** group
i)   that
28   — is itself a contextually required token; or
          — contains a token which has been satisfied;
30   and
ii) all preceding tokens of which
32   — have been satisfied; or
          — are contextually optional.

34 **4.274 satisfied token:** A *content token* [128] *410:17* whose corresponding content has occurred.

4.6.2 SHORTTAG Feature

This feature allows tags to be abbreviated in a variety of ways.

4.6.2.1 Empty Tags

SHORTTAG allows generic identifiers and attribute specifications to be omitted from start-tags. The GI is copied from the preceding element, and default values are used for the attributes.

The GI can also be omitted from an end-tag, in which case the GI of the current element is used.

4.6.2.2 Unclosed Tags

SHORTTAG allows closing delimiters of tags to be omitted when another tag follows.

4.6.2.3 Null End-tags

SHORTTAG permits a start-tag to enable a "null end-tag" — a single delimiter that will end the element.

4.6.3 Short references

A short reference is a delimiter, usually one or two characters long, that is replaced by an entity reference. The replacement text of the entity will typically be a start-tag so that, for example, a quotation mark character could represent the start of a quotation element, or an *RS,RE* sequence (empty record) could begin a paragraph.

The associations between short references and their entities are defined in short reference maps. Many maps can be defined, but at any given point in the element structure only one of them — the current map — applies.

4.291 short reference delimiter role: A delimiter role to which
2 zero or more strings can be assigned by the concrete syntax. When a short reference string is recognized, it is replaced by the general
4 entity to whose name it is mapped in the current map, or is treated as a separator or data if it is mapped to nothing.

4.295 short reference (string): A character string assigned to the
2   short reference delimiter role by the concrete syntax.

4.290 short reference (delimiter): Short reference string.

4   **4.292 (short reference) map:** A named set of associations,
declared by a *short reference mapping declaration* ⌈ **[150]** *429:8* ⌉ , in
6   which each short reference delimiter is mapped to a general entity
name or to nothing.

8   **4.177 map:** Short reference map.

It is possible for a "blank sequence" of spaces and separator characters
of unknown length to be recognized in a short reference. The blank
sequence is represented in the assigned delimiter string by a "B
sequence".

4.25 blank sequence: An uninterrupted sequence of *SPACE*
10   and/or *SEPCHAR* characters.

4.19 B sequence: An uninterrupted sequence of upper-case letter
12   "B" characters; in a string assigned as a short reference, it denotes
a blank sequence whose minimum length is the length of the B
14   sequence.

As with other markup minimization features, short references can be
removed from a document, in this case by replacing them with equivalent reference strings.

4.128 equivalent reference string: A character string, consisting
16   of an entity reference and possibly an *RE* and/or *RS*, that replaces
a short reference when a document is converted from a concrete
18   syntax that supports short references to one that does not.

4.6.3.1 Defining a Map

The set of short reference strings that can be mapped is fixed in the
concrete syntax. The set of character strings that potentially have special
meaning is therefore known for the entire document. A short reference
map indicates which of these strings will have meaning when the particular map is current, and which will have no special meaning because

they are not mapped ("mapped to nothing").

4.293 short reference mapping declaration: A markup
2 declaration that defines a short reference map.

4.118 empty map: A short reference map in which all delimiters
4 are mapped to nothing.

NOTE — The empty map need not (and cannot) be declared explicitly, but
6 can be referenced by its reserved name, which is "#EMPTY" in the
reference concrete syntax.

Short reference conventions for common element types can be defined and shared by means of short reference sets.

8 **4.294 short reference set:** A set of short reference mapping, short reference use, and entity declarations that are used together.

10 NOTE — A short reference set can be public text.

4.6.3.2 Associating a Map with an Element Type

Normally, a map is associated with an element type by a short reference use declaration in the DTD. Each time an element of that type occurs in the document instance, the associated map will be current. This approach allows a degree of context sensitivity, as an empty record, for example, could begin a row element within a table, but a paragraph elsewhere in the document.

Nonetheless, there is consistency for the person marking up the document, as the short references for a given element type are the same everywhere. However, if special markup techniques are needed in a specific place (for example, to enter character graphics in a particular figure), a short reference use declaration can be entered in the document instance.

4.70 current map: The short reference map associated with the
12 current element by a *short reference use declaration* [152] *430:10*
in the element content or document type definition. If the current
14 element has no associated map, the previous current map continues to be the current map.

16 **4.296 short reference use declaration:** A markup declaration that associates a short reference map with one or more element types,

or identifies a new current map for the current element.

Note that there is no inheritance of short reference associations from the maps of earlier open elements unless the entire map is inherited. For example, if lists have a short reference map, but list items do not, the list element map will be the current map for list items. However, if list items have their own map, none of the short references mapped in the list map will be recognized unless they are explicitly included in the list item map as well.

Obviously, the standard could have allowed short reference inheritance, as it did with link rules. The latter, however, are solely the province of the application designer, while short references are not. The standard therefore forces the application designer to consider and resolve all of the potential interactions between the maps of open elements, rather than leaving them for unwelcome discovery by the end user.

4.6.4 DATATAG Feature

A data tag, as its name implies, is a character string that that serves as both data and as the end-tag of the "target element" that preceded the data. Data tag minimization is defined in the context of the containing element, by including a data tag group in the containing element's content model. The group identifies the target element type that can be minimized, and specifies a pattern for the allowable data tag strings. [6]

2   **4.76 data tag:** A string that conforms to the data tag pattern of an open element. It serves both as the *end-tag* [[19] *317:4*] of the open
4   element and as *character data* [[47] *344:1*] in the element that contains it.

6   **4.77 data tag group:** A *content token* [[128] *410:17*] that associates a data tag pattern with a target element type.

8   NOTE — Within an instance of a target element, the data content and that of any subelements is scanned for a string that conforms to the pattern (a
10 "data tag").

---

[6] DATATAG is to some extent an accident of history. Most of what it was designed to accomplish can now be done more easily with short references, which I first proposed to the ANSI committee in 1984, years after DATATAG. The DATATAG feature was drastically curtailed during its later development (at one time it supported start-tags), but it is still quite complex for both user and implementer.

4.78 data tag pattern: A data tag group token that defines the
2 strings that, if they occurred in the proper context, would constitute
a data tag.

4 **4.315 target element:** An element whose *generic identifier*
[30] *325:17* is specified in a *data tag group* [133] *415:16* .

4.6.5 RANK Feature

RANK is a concession to application design practices in the early days
of generic coding, before GML introduced true nested element markup.
Designers then would represent nesting levels of an element by including
the level number as part of the GI; for example, P1, P2, and P3 for paragraphs that today might occur within three levels of nested list. Some
designs allowed different element types to share the same levels. For
example, P1, N2, and B3 might identify plain, numbered, and bulleted
items in those same three levels of nested list.

SGML supports ranked elements by allowing tags to contain only the
rank stem (P, N, or B in this case), omitting the rank suffix (the level
number), which is implied from the current rank. Ranked elements are
identified in element declarations by separating the rank stem from the
rank suffix. If a group of element types is to share the same current rank,
all of the group's rank stems are shown in the declaration.

6 **4.248 ranked element:** An element whose *generic identifier*
[30] *325:17* is composed of a *rank stem* [120] *407:17* and a *rank*
8 *suffix* [121] *407:19* . When a ranked element begins, its *rank suffix*
[121] *407:19* becomes the current rank for its *rank stem*
10 [120] *407:17* , and for the rank stems in the *ranked group*
[119] *407:5* (if any) of which the *rank stem* [120] *407:17* is a mem-
12 ber.

4.249 ranked group: A group of rank stems that share the same
14 current rank. When any ranked element whose stem is in the group
begins, its *rank suffix* [121] *407:19* becomes the current rank for all
16 rank stems in the group.

4.250 rank stem: A name from which a generic identifier can be
18 derived by appending a *rank suffix* [121] *407:19* .

4.251 rank suffix: A number that is appended to a rank stem to
20 form a *generic identifier* [30] *325:17* .

NOTE — The numbers are usually sequential, beginning with 1, so the resulting generic identifiers suggest the relative ranks of their elements (for example, H1, H2, and H3 for levels of heading elements, where "H" is the rank stem).

4.71 current rank: The *rank suffix* [121] *407:19* that, when appended to a rank stem in a tag, will derive the element's generic identifier. For a *start-tag* [14] *314:1* it is the *rank suffix* [121] *407:19* of the most recent element with the identical *rank stem* [120] *407:17*, or a *rank stem* [120] *407:17* in the same *ranked group* [119] *407:5*. For an *end-tag* [19] *317:4* it is the *rank suffix* [121] *407:19* of the most recent open element with the identical *rank stem* [120] *407:17*.

Chapter 5
Processing Model

The general model of processing in SGML is that there is a source document which is transformed by a link process into a result document. Normally, the source and result documents are of two different types, such as "magazine article" and "galley", "galley" and "formatted magazine", or "formatted book" and "index", to name a few.

The design of the application that the processing is in aid of must, in the general case, include document type definitions for the source and result, and a link process definition for the processing. Recall the meaning of "link process definition" (LPD):

> **4.167 link process definition:** Application-specific rules that apply
> 2 SGML to describe a link process. A link process definition includes
>   a formal specification, expressed in a *link type declaration*
> 4 [154] *434:1* , of the link between elements of the source and result,
>   including the definitions of source attributes applicable to the link
> 6 process ("link attributes").
>
> NOTES
>
> 8 1 A link process definition can also include comments that describe the
>   semantics of the process, including the meaning of the link attributes and
> 10 their effect on the process.
>
>   2 There are three kinds of link process definitions: simple, implicit, and
> 12 explicit.

It should be noted that the link attributes need not affect the process directly. They could simply identify external entities in which the actual processing specifications and/or the set of procedures that implement them can be found.

4.232 procedure: Processing defined by an application to operate
on elements of a particular type.

NOTES

1   A single procedure could be associated with more than one element
type, and/or more than one procedure could operate on the same element
type at different points in the document.

2   A procedure is usually part of a procedure set.

4.233 procedure set: The procedures that are used together for a
given application process.

NOTE — In SGML applications, a procedure set usually constitutes the
application processing for a link process definition.

It is also important to note that an LPD is merely a vehicle for specifying processing — as always, it is up to the application to determine what
the specifications mean. In particular, although the nominal result of processing is a document instance that conforms to the result DTD, this is
merely a conceptual device to permit specification of the processing in
terms of the result document instead of, or in addition to, the source document, if that should be desirable. The actual result could be anything at
all.

5.1 Link Type Declaration

The formal SGML inputs to a link process are:

a)   a source document type declaration;

b)   an instance of the source document type;

c)   a link type declaration; and

d)   a result document type declaration.

The link type declaration specifies the LPD by defining:

—   "Link attributes" that will apply to the source element types for the
purposes of this process alone.

— Entities, both parameter and general, that will exist only for this process. The LPD can also override the definitions of entities in the source DTD.

— "Link sets", containing the rules for linking the source and result elements. The link sets can be organized in a hierarchy so that different link rules can be applicable to the same element types at different points in the source document instance. (The means of associating link sets with portions of the source document are discussed later.)

2 **4.171 link type declaration subset:** The entity sets, link attribute sets, and link set declarations, that occur within the declaration subset of a link type declaration.

4 NOTE — The external entity referenced from the link type declaration is considered part of the declaration subset.

6 **4.165 link attribute:** An attribute of a source element type that is meaningful only in the context of a particular process that is 8 performed on the source document instance.

4.169 link set declaration: A markup declaration that defines a 10 link set.

4.168 link set: A named set of rules, declared in a *link set* 12 *declaration* [163] 441:6 , by which elements of the source document type are linked to elements of the result document type.

If no link rules are to apply to some portion of the source document, an empty link set can be used (that is, one with no link rules). When the empty link set is current, link attributes have their default values and the result element type is implied by the application.

14 **4.117 empty link set:** A link set that contains no link rules.

5.2 Link Rule

A link rule identifies a source element type, specifies the link attributes associated with it, and, for an explicit link, specifies the result element type and its attributes, if any.

2   **4.167.1 link rule:** A member of a link set; that is, for an implicit link, a *source element specification* [165] 443:1 , and for an explicit link, an *explicit link rule* [166.1] 445:1 .

4   **4.302 source element type (of a link):** An element type that is defined in the source document type declaration.

6   **4.272 result element type (of a link):** An element that is defined in the result document type declaration.

There can be more than one link rule for a given source element type, in which case the application decides among them in each instance by examining the link attributes.

The significance of designating a result element type depends upon the application. Typically, it would mean that an occurrence of the source element type would cause an instance of the result element type to be created.

The link attributes and result attributes in a link rule can specify processing in any of the following ways (or a mix of them):

— An attribute could have an application-defined meaning that affects processing directly (for example, FONT=Bodoni).

— An attribute could identify an entity (usually external), declared in the LPD, that contains a procedure that is to operate on the source element (for example, PROC=blockhi).

— An attribute could identify an entity (usually external), declared in the LPD, that contains a descriptive specification of the desired processing (for example, STYLE=slides). The specification could be a style sheet in the specialized notation of a word processor or desktop publishing program. Ideally, though, it would itself be an SGML document, and would include not only elements for expressing processing, but identification and comment elements that would describe what the specification is intended to accomplish. Such specifications could themselves be processed as documents to produce, for example, a user's guide to the application.

5.3 Link Set Context Sensitivity

In many applications, the desired processing for a given element type will depend on the context in which each instance of the element occurs. For example, a formatting style might call for ordered lists in the body of a book to be numbered, while those in the front matter were lettered. If the LPD defined a "counter" link attribute for ordered lists, its value would need to be "alpha" for lists in the front matter, and "numeric" for those in the body.

This requirement could be handled by defining separate link sets for the front matter and for the body. In each, the link rule for ordered list would have the appropriate value for the "counter" link attribute. SGML offers a number of techniques for associating link sets with portions of the source document instance:

— The link set that is current at the start of the document instance is identified as the "initial" link set in the LPD.

— The #USELINK link rule parameter associates a link set with the source element; its link rules apply to the content of the source element.

— The #POSTLINK link rule parameter associates a link set with the parent of the source element; its link rules apply to the younger siblings of the source element.

— A specially designated "ID link set" defines link rules that apply to a particular identified element, in preference to the link rules that would otherwise apply to an element of that type.

— As a last resort, a "link set use declaration" in the source document instance can override the normal link set.

If the current link set has no link rule for a source element, the link sets of open elements are searched, back to the initial link set.

4.69 current link set: The link set associated with the current
2 element by a *link set use declaration* [169] *448:1* in the element
   content or by a link process definition. If the current element has no
4 associated link set, the previous current link set continues to be the
   current link set.

6 **4.159.1 initial link set:** The link set that is current at the start of
   the document instance.

5.4 Explicitness of Link Process Design

The designer of a document type definition has to decide how much explicit structure to give to the document, and how much to leave to an application to decipher. Similar decisions must be made when designing a link process definition. A design could range, for example, from:

— Using simple link to associate a procedure set with a source document; to

— Using implicit link to associate context-sensitive style sheets with source elements; to

— Using a chain of explicit links to specify processing completely with link attributes and result attributes.

4.299 simple link (process definition): A link process definition in
2   which the result element types and their attributes are all implied by
the application, and link attribute values can be specified only for
4   the source document element.

4.155 implicit link (process definition): A link process definition
6   in which the result element types and their attributes are all implied
by the application, but link attribute values can be specified for
8   multiple source element types.

4.133 explicit link (process definition): A link process definition
10 in which the result element types and their attributes and link
attribute values can be specified for multiple source element types.

12 **4.30 chain of (link) processes:** Processes, performed
sequentially, that form a chain in which the source of the first
14 process is an instance of the base document type, and the result of
each process but the last is the source for the next. Any portion of
16 the chain can be iterated.

NOTE — For example, a complex page makeup application could include
18 three document types — logical, galley, and page — and two link
processes — justification and castoff. The justification process would
20 create an instance of a galley from an instance of a logical document, and
the castoff process would in turn create pages from the galleys. The two
22 processes could be iterated, as decisions made during castoff could require
rejustification of the galleys at different sizes.

In general, the benefits of exposing the structure of a processing specification in SGML are analogous to the benefits of exposing the document structure:

— The document originator can associate processing specifications with the source document in a standardized way, independent of the application or processing system.

— A recipient of the document can easily see the points where the processing specification changes, even if the semantics of the specification are not understood.

— The application implementer can rely on the SGML parser to manage context-dependent specification changes.

5.5 Concurrent Document Instances

Normally, the result of processing is a document that is completely independent of the source, and that is stored in a separate set of entities. When the result is an SGML document, however, and there is a substantial amount of text that is common to both the source and result, it may be desirable to retain the result as part of the source document.

This effect can be accomplished by means of the optional CONCUR feature of SGML, which allows instances of multiple document types to exist concurrently in the same document. (When the result is of the same document type as the source — for example, a new version — the CONCUR feature is not needed, as the same result can be achieved with marked section declarations, described later.)

The multiple document instances are distinguished from one another by means of a "document type specification" that occurs in the tags and entity references. The document can therefore be parsed with respect to any one instance exactly as if the others were not there. The relationship between the document instances is defined solely by the juxtaposition of markup and data in the document instance set, and not at all by the link process definitions that may have caused the instances to be generated in the first place.

Chapter 6
Storage Model

Within a document instance, SGML provides a uniform view of entity reference and replacement, in that the reference itself does not indicate the size or location of the replacement text. In this respect it differs from text processing systems that require a special form of reference when the replacement text is in a separate file from the reference (for example, a "file imbed" rather than a "symbol substitution").

The SGML approach is clearly superior, because it removes undesirable system dependencies from the document instance. However, one could question whether an interchange representation needs to deal with external references at all — could they not just be resolved so that the interchanged file need reflect only the element structure?

Reality, unfortunately, is not that simple. A table in a report, for example, could contain a dynamic reference ("hot link") to a cell range in a spreadsheet, the intention being that the report should always contain the latest version of the spreadsheet data. Resolving the reference to any particular version would defeat this intention.

Moreover, although applications may focus solely on the element structure of documents, users have to deal with documents on a physical level as well. They may choose to divide a document into parts that are convenient for manipulation and processing, and this division may have little or no connection with the element structure. For example, a number of short chapters might be grouped together for editing by a single person, while a larger chapter might be broken down into several parts. In a large work, the physical organization can be quite elaborate, and must be preserved during interchange.

SGML can deal with such requirements without introducing system dependencies because its storage model deals solely with virtual objects (entities), and not with actual storage objects, such as files. The mapping between virtual storage and actual is performed by an implementation's "entity manager", and is not standardized.

6.1 Virtual Storage

An SGML document consists of at least one entity. If other entities are declared within its prolog, their replacement text could either be contained directly within the entity declarations (internal entities) or not (external entities). For external entities, an external identifier, rather than the replacement text of the entity, is declared as the entity text parameter of the declaration. The external identifier can be system-specific, or, if the text belongs to a shared library of "public text" (discussed later), it can be universal.

4.160.1 internal entity: An entity whose replacement text is
2   incorporated in an entity declaration.

4.134 external entity: An entity whose text is not incorporated
4   directly in an entity declaration; its system identifier and/or public identifier is specified instead.

6.2 Mapping Virtual Storage to Actual

External identifiers are the vehicles for mapping between virtual and actual storage. In addition to their use in entity declarations, they can occur in notation declarations, where they identify the program that will interpret the data content or data entity that conforms to the notation. External identifiers can also be specified in document type and link type declarations, where they implicitly both declare and reference an external entity that contains all or part of the declaration subset.

6   **4.135 external identifier:** A parameter that identifies an external entity or data content notation.

8   NOTES

     1   There are two kinds: system identifier and public identifier.

10   2   A document type or link type declaration can include the identifier of an external entity containing all or part of the declaration subset; the external
12   identifier serves simultaneously as a declaration of that entity and as a reference to it.

As far as SGML is concerned, a system identifier need not be the actual identifier of the entity in the system storage. Like all system data, it is subject to interpretation by the implementation, and the system identifier could therefore contain more or less than the actual storage identifier.

In a subdocument entity declaration, for example, it could include parameters that identified the active document and link types, or, for hypertext applications, the location of specific text within the referenced document. Conversely, the system identifier could be empty or omitted, in which case the storage identifier would normally be generated from the entity name, using some system-specific convention.

4.313 system identifier: System data that specifies the file
2 identifier, storage location, program invocation, data stream position, or other system-specific information that locates an
4 external entity.

In contrast to a system identifier, a public identifier is not subject to interpretation. It is a unique non-system-specific identifier that can be converted to an actual storage identifier only by a table lookup. The universe in which a public identifier is unique depends upon whether it is a formal public identifier and upon its owner identifier (discussed later).

In order that a public identifier be usable in any SGML document, it is specified as a "minimum literal" — a delimited character string consisting solely of "minimum data" characters, which occur in all document character sets.

4.239 public identifier: A minimum literal that identifies public
6 text.

NOTES

8 1   The public identifiers in a document can optionally be interpretable as formal public identifiers.

10 2   The system is responsible for converting public identifiers to system identifiers.

An external identifier can include both a public identifier and a system identifier. In such cases, the way the system identifier would affect the normal table lookup of the public identifier is system-specific. Typically, it would be used in systems that have no public library as such, and would be used instead of a table lookup. (But there is a situation called "dual-role public text", discussed later, in which both identifiers are meaningful.)

6.3 Actual Storage

The system component that interprets external identifiers and makes the entity available to the SGML parser is known as the "entity manager".

The entity manager has complete freedom in mapping between virtual and actual storage. Several methods might be needed to meet different requirements; for example:

— Static local storage (file system)

Many external entities could be stored in a single file, or, conversely, a single entity could be spread over several files. In the former case, the entities could be intermixed; for example, by storing an external entity at its point of first reference. As long as the entity manager can present the virtual storage view to the SGML parser, no difficulties are presented.

— Dynamic local storage (memory management)

During the execution of a process, a document could be stored as a complex data structure in main memory, in order to facilitate direct access and modification.

— Communication between systems (interchange format)

For interchange between systems, it is frequently desirable to store all entities in a single object. However, the recipient must be able to segregate the entities and map them into its own real storage.

Moreover, systems whose communications conform to the Open Systems Interconnection (OSI) model may require the interchange object to meet their requirements for structure and identification.

An interchange format for SGML documents that satisfies all these needs has been standardized in ISO 9069. It is called the SGML Document Interchange Format (SDIF) and is discussed in detail later.

The SGML virtual storage model recognizes a record, if present, by its record start and record end characters. While some file systems do use two characters to separate records (typically, carrier return and line feed), others use only one. Still others use none, but have a data structure that shows the length of each record. It is the responsibility of the entity manager to present record start and record end characters to the SGML parser, regardless of the means by which records are distinguished in actual storage.

The entity manager is also responsible for identifying the end of an entity, which it can do in any manner convenient for the implementation. ISO 8879 does not dictate any representation of an entity end signal.

4.122 entity end (signal): A signal from the system that an
2   entity's replacement text has ended.

6.4 Public Text

The SGML term for shared text is "public text", although its owner may choose to restrict its availability to the public at large.

4.240 public text: Text that is known beyond the context of a
4   single document or system environment, and which can be accessed with a public identifier.

6   NOTES

1   Examples are standard or registered document type definitions, entity
8   sets, element sets, data content notations, and other markup constructs (see annex D (*498*)).

10   2   Public text is not equivalent to published text; there is no implication of unrestricted public access. In particular, the owner of public text may
12   choose to sell or license it to others, or to restrict its access to a single organization.

14   3   Public text simplifies access to shared constructs, reduces the amount of text that must be interchanged, and reduces the chance of copying
16   errors.

4.18 available public text: Public text that is available to the
18   general public, though its owner may require payment of a fee or performance of other conditions.

20   **4.323 unavailable public text:** Public text that is available only to a limited population, selected by its owner.

A formal public identifier indicates when the public text it identifies is unavailable.

6.4.1 Formal Public Identifier

An optional feature of SGML is the ability to impose a formal structure on the public identifiers used in a document. The structure allows the owner of the public text to be distinguished from the identification of the text itself.

4.137 formal public identifier: A public identifier that is
2   constructed according to rules defined in this International Standard so that its owner identifier and the components of its text identifier
4   can be distinguished.

6.4.1.1 Owner Identifier

An owner identifier is either registered or unregistered. If registered, it begins with a standardized registered owner prefix that identifies the owner uniquely. The rules for constructing a registered owner prefix are in a separate standard governing registration procedures for public text owner identifiers (ISO 9070).[1] An ISO owner identifier (mentioned in the definitions below but discussed later) is a special kind of registered owner identifier.

6   **4.223 owner identifier:** The portion of a public identifier that identifies the owner or originator of public text.

8   NOTE — There are three kinds: ISO, registered, and unregistered.

4.325 unregistered owner identifier: An owner identifier that can
10   be distinguished from registered owner identifiers and ISO owner identifiers. As it is not constructed according to a registration
12   standard, it could duplicate another unregistered owner identifier.

4.262 registered owner identifier: An owner identifier that was
14   constructed in accordance with ISO 9070. It is unique among

---

[1] The single definition from that standard appears in this section, its number suffixed with "R".

registered owner identifiers, and is distinguishable from ISO owner
2   identifiers and unregistered owner identifiers.

4.1R registered owner prefix: A sequence of characters
4   identifying a specific owner of public text and assigned in
accordance with the procedures defined in this International
6   Standard.

An owner identifier can optionally contain, in addition to the registered owner prefix, one or more owner-assigned names chosen by the
registered owner. These typically form a hierarchy that progressively
identifies the owner with greater precision. A corporation, for example,
could use owner-assigned names to identify the division, department
within division, and individual within department who owns the text.
Each department in such a scheme could assign names to individuals
without fear of conflicting with names assigned by other departments, as
the individuals would be distinguished by the department and division
names.

Similarly, a national organization that has a registered owner identifier
could designate regional organizations to assign owner-assigned names
to local organizations. As long as the regional names are unique within
the nation, and the local names within their respective regions, no problems are presented. For example:

```
USA/California/Saratoga
USA/New York/Saratoga
```

ISO 9070 establishes the American National Standards Institute
(ANSI) as a registration authority that will assign registered owner prefixes to those requesting them, upon payment of an administrative
charge. However, registration is not necessary if the owner already has
an acceptable prefix. These include:

a) Organization codes assigned in accordance with ISO 6523 (many
    banks have these, for example).

b) Official initialisms of recognized standards bodies (the ISO is a spe-
    cial case, discussed later).

A forthcoming amendment to ISO 9070 will allow registered owner
prefixes to be constructed from ISBN numbers and publisher identifiers
assigned in accordance with ISO 2108.

6.4.1.2 Text Identifier

4.317 text identifier: The portion of a public identifier that identifies a public text so that it can be distinguished from any other public text with the same owner identifier.

NOTE — It consists of a *public text class* [86] *386:5* , an optional *unavailable text indicator* [85] *385:17* , a *public text description* [87] *387:5* , a *public text language* [88] *388:1* , and an optional *public text display version* [90] *390:1* .

4.241 public text class: The portion of a text identifier that identifies the SGML markup construct to which the public text conforms.

4.242 public text description: The portion of a text identifier that describes the public text.

4.245 public text language: The portion of a text identifier that specifies the natural language in which the public text was written.

NOTE — It can be the language of the data, comments, and/or defined names.

The supported public text class constructs are:

— Document components
    SGML document
    SGML subdocument entity
    SGML text entity
    non-SGML data entity

Character data entity and specific character data entity are currently included in the "non-SGML data entity" category, but they will probably have their own in any future version of ISO 8879.

— DTD/LPD components
    entity set
    document type declaration subset
        element set
        short reference set
    link type declaration subset

— SGML declaration components
　　　capacity set
　　　concrete syntax

— Dual-role public text
　　　character set
　　　data content notation

When the public text is a character set, a public text designating sequence is included in the text identifier instead of a public text language. The designating sequence includes a formal identification of the character set as prescribed by the ISO 2022 standard for code extension (discussed later).

> **4.243 public text designating sequence:** The portion of a text
> identifier, used when public text is a character set, that contains an
> ISO 2022 escape sequence that designates the set.

2

6.4.2 Uniqueness of Public Identifiers

The form of owner identifier determines the universe in which a formal public identifier is unique. The following table summarizes the uniqueness of all forms of external identifier:

Form of Public ID	*Universe in Which Unique*
None (System ID)	System
Informal	Owner
Unregistered Formal	Owner + All Registered Formal
Registered Formal	All Formal

For obvious reasons, the use of the formal public identifier feature is highly recommended.[2]

6.4.3 Device-dependent Public Text

Public text other than SGML declaration components and dual-role public text may be device-dependent.

---

[2] Formal public identifiers would probably have been mandatory, except that they were introduced relatively late in the development cycle of ISO 8879.

4.93 device-dependent version (of public text): Public text
2   whose *formal public identifier* [79] 382:1 differs from that of
another public text only by the addition of a *public text display ver-*
4   *sion* [90] 390:1 , which identifies the display devices supported or
coding scheme used.

6   **4.244 public text display version:** An optional portion of a text
identifier that distinguishes among public text that has a common
8   *public text description* [87] 387:5 by describing the devices supported or coding scheme used. If omitted, the public text is not
10 device-dependent.

When the optional public text display version is omitted from a formal
public identifier, the entity manager will chose the best available device-
dependent version. This mechanism is particularly useful with character
entity sets.

4.35 character entity set: A public entity set consisting of general
12 entities that are graphic characters.

NOTES

14 1   Character entities are used for characters that have no coded
representation in the document character set, or that cannot be keyboarded
16 conveniently, or to achieve device independence for characters whose bit
combinations do not cause proper display on all output devices.

18 2   There are two kinds of character entity sets: definitional and display.

4.85 definitional (character) entity set: A character entity set
20 whose purpose is to define entity names for graphic characters, but
not actually to display them. Its *public identifier* [74] 379:8 does not
22 include a *public text display version* [90] 390:1 .

NOTE — During processing, the system replaces a definitional entity set
24 with a corresponding display character entity set for the appropriate output
device.

26 **4.95 display (character) entity set:** An entity set with the same
entity names as a corresponding definitional character entity set,
28 but which causes the characters to be displayed. It is a device-
dependent version of the corresponding definitional entity set.

6.4.4 Dual-role Public Text

Dual-role public text is so named because it is referenced both as a definition and as an implementation. Typically, an external identifier of dual-role public text will have both a public identifier and a system identifier. The public identifier refers to the definition, which is not usually system-specific, while the system identifier refers to the implementation (a program or internal data structure), which usually is.

The external identifier of a data content notation, for example, could include both a public identifier of a publication that describes the notation, and a system identifier of a program that will be called to interpret data that conforms to the notation.

Similarly, the public identifier of a character set would refer to its definition (usually in a national, international, or corporate standard, or in a registry of character sets maintained in accordance with such a standard), while the system identifier might refer to a translate table or similar system data structure.

6.4.5 ISO Documents

When public text is in an ISO publication, or is an ISO registered character set, special rules apply to the construction of the formal public identifier.

— The owner identifier is equivalent to a registered owner identifier, except that its form is defined in ISO 8879, rather than in ISO 9070.

— The form of the public text description is also defined in ISO 8879.[3]

2   **4.162 ISO owner identifier:** An *owner identifier* [80] 383:1 , consisting of an ISO publication number or character set registration
4   number, that is used when a *public identifier* [74] 379:8 identifies, or is assigned by, an ISO publication, or identifies an ISO regis-
6   tered character set.

     4.163 ISO text description: A *public text description* [87] 387:5 ,
8   consisting of the last element of an ISO publication title (without part designation, if any), that is used when a *public identifier*
10   [74] 379:8 identifies an ISO publication.

---

[3] I suppose this is just a special case of it being defined by the owner!

6.5 SGML Document Interchange Format (SDIF)

4.14S SGML Document Interchange Format: A data structure
that enables a main document and its related documents, each of
which might be stored in several entities, to be combined into a
single data stream for interchange in a manner that will permit the
recipient to reconstitute the separate entities.

4.8S SDIF: SGML Document Interchange Format

6.5.1 Contents of the Data Stream

In addition to the main document that is the subject of an interchange,
an SDIF data structure can include related documents. Each of the documents is subject to its own SGML declaration, whose concrete syntax definition, limits on subdocument nesting, and other restrictions apply.

4.5S main document: An SGML document that is the subject of
an interchange.

4.7S related document: An SGML document that is used in
conjunction with a main document, but is not referenced as part of
its content.

NOTE — Some examples are: a covering letter, transmittal form, catalog
card, formatting procedure, font resource, or document profile.

4.3S document profile: A transmittal form, defined by a document
architecture or application, that describes the characteristics of a
conforming document that are relevant to its management or
interchange.

6.5.2 Packing and Unpacking

The creation and decomposition of an SDIF structure are called "packing" and "unpacking", respectively. Packing requires the originator to
assign SDIF names (essentially entity names) to those entities for which
there are no entity declarations, and to the data stream itself.

4.12S SDIF packer: A program that creates an SDIF data stream.

NOTE — The parameters to an SDIF packer usually include the SDIF
2   name for the data stream, the SDIF names and system identifiers for the
main and related documents, and the order in which the documents should
4   be packed.

4.13S SDIF unpacker: A program that decomposes an SDIF data
6   stream into its constituent entities.

NOTE — If necessary, the SDIF unpacker will modify the system identifier
8   parameter of markup declarations to be consistent with storage addresses
in its environment.

10 **4.11S SDIF name:** An SGML name assigned in the SDIF data
stream to a document or to the data stream as a whole.

12 **4.1S data stream character set:** The character set used for all
document markup in an SDIF data stream, and for all SDIF names
14 and SDIF identifiers.

6.5.3 Data Stream Structure

ISO 9069 defines an SDIF data stream formally as an abstract definition, using the standard notation for OSI data structures, Abstract Syntax
Notation 1 (ASN.1), defined in ISO 8824. The components of the data
stream are document descriptors, in which entity descriptors can nest.
Each entity descriptor has an SDIF identifier that is unique in the data
stream, as the entity names may be duplicated in different documents or
subdocuments.

4.2S document descriptor: A component of an SDIF data stream
16 that contains an SGML document entity and entity descriptors for
all external entities that are directly or indirectly referenced from it.

18 **4.4S entity descriptor:** A component of an SDIF data stream that
represents an external entity.

20 **4.9S SDIF identifier:** A unique identifying sequence number
assigned to an entity descriptor in the SDIF data stream.

22 NOTE — It corresponds to the position of the entity's external identifier. For
example, the entity descriptor with the SDIF identifier "5" represents the
24 entity identified by the fifth markup declaration in the data stream that has
an external identifier.

4.10S SDIF identifier reference: An entity descriptor that contains
no text of its own, but instead refers to the SDIF identifier of
another entity descriptor. It represents a duplicate declaration of an
entity that either has already occurred in the data stream, or is
omitted public text.

4.6S omitted public text: An entity descriptor that has no text at
all; it represents public text that is part of the document, but is not
being interchanged because the recipient is expected to have a
copy.

6.5.4 Specific Encoding

A specific encoding for SDIF (as, indeed, for any structure defined in
ASN.1) can be derived automatically from the abstract syntax by applying the ASN.1 basic encoding rules, defined in ISO 8825. It is expected
that SDIF data streams in Open Systems Interconnection (OSI) environments will be encoded in this way. However, the standard allows any
encoding accepted by the medium of interchange.

6.5.5 Interchange in Open Systems

SGML documents in an SDIF data stream can be interchanged in
accordance with the OSI model in a variety of ways.

— SDIF is a standardized OSI Document Type (not the same as an
   SGML document type!) which can be used with the File Transfer,
   Access and Management(FTAM) protocol (ISO 8571) and the Job
   Transfer and Manipulation (JTM) protocol (ISO 8832).

— SDIF data streams can be transferred by the Message Handling Systems (MHS or X.400) protocol defined in CCITT Recommendation
   H.400.

— SDIF data streams can also be transferred using the Message Oriented Text Interchange System(MOTIS) functions defined in ISO
   8505 and ISO 8883, and in other similar message-handling standards and CCITT Recommendations.

SDIF data streams can also be interchanged on portable storage media,
such as magnetic disks and CD-ROM.

Chapter 7
Character Sets

7.1 General Concepts

The concepts related to character sets tend to be subtle, and the terminology is sometimes confusing, chiefly because important distinctions are often ignored in common parlance (and sometimes even in standards). ISO 8879, however, attempts to be meticulous in discussing character sets, as befits a standard whose own subject matter is full of subtle distinctions.[1]

Unfortunately, though, ISO 8879 does not exist in a vacuum. Ultimately, a document is a string of characters, and the meaning of those characters has to be defined somewhere. That somewhere is likely to be in national, international, or corporate standards, or in product documentation for the systems that process the document. Application designers and implementers will need to decipher those character set definitions and relate them to the character set specifications and concrete syntax definitions of SGML.

For this reason, the discussion here will range somewhat beyond the aspects of character sets that are addressed in ISO 8879. In particular, it will include some guidance on common uses (and misuses) of terminology that might be encountered in character set documentation.

---

[1] ISO 8879 uses terminology that was inspired by ISO character set standards (notably ISO 2022), but some definitions were revised for ISO 8879 in order to align them with SGML constructs. Others define terms that are used in ISO 2022, but not formally defined there.

192

7.1.1 Characters

A character is an atomic unit of information with no inherent meaning. It derives meaning only from its membership in a particular set of characters, called a "character repertoire", and/or from the context in which it occurs in a document.

4.31 character: An atom of information with an individual meaning,
2   defined by a character repertoire.

NOTES

4   1   There are two kinds: graphic character and control character.

2   A character can occur in a context in which it has a meaning, defined
6   by markup or a data content notation, that supersedes or supplements its
meaning in the character repertoire.

8   **4.38 character repertoire:** A set of characters that are used
together. Meanings are defined for each character, and can also be
10   defined for control sequences of multiple characters.

NOTE — When characters occur in a control sequence, the meaning of the
12   sequence supersedes the meanings of the individual characters.

Nor does a character have an inherent coded representation for machine processing — that is assigned only when the character becomes part of a character set.

4.39 character set: A mapping of a character repertoire onto a
14   code set such that each character in the repertoire is represented
by a bit combination in the code set.

A character set is sometimes called a "coded character set", or even a "code", although the latter term is more often (mis)used to mean "character", "bit combination", or "coded representation".[2] Some character set documentation uses the terms "character set", "character repertoire", and "code set" interchangeably, even when they have taken pains to distinguish the concepts.

---

2 I think "code" should be used only as an abbreviation for code set. ISO 8879 avoids it altogether (except for the adjective "multicode", which is applied to concrete syntaxes used with multiple coded character sets).

7.1.2 Code Set

In computers, all coded representations eventually reduce to sequences of binary digits (bits), officially termed "bit combinations" in ISO standards (but sometimes called "code points" by others).

> **4.23 bit:** Binary digit; that is, either zero or one.

2 **4.24 bit combination:** An ordered collection of bits, interpretable as a binary number.

4 NOTE — A bit combination should not be confused with a "byte", which is a name given to a particular size of bit string, typically seven or eight bits. A
6 single bit combination could contain several bytes.

The number of bits in a bit combination is called its "size". There are nicknames for some common sizes:

Size	Nickname
4	nibble
7	byte
8	byte
16	halfword
32	word
64	doubleword

Note that "byte" could refer to either seven or eight bits.

All of these nicknames for bit combination sizes are frequently used as nouns to refer to a bit string of the particular size. In that context, the nickname may or may not refer to a single complete bit combination. Character set documentation might say, for example, that the order of nibbles (or bytes) in a bit combination is device-dependent.

A code set is simply an ordered set of equal-size bit combinations. The maximum number of bit combinations in the set (the "code set size") is a function of the bit combination size (the "code set width"). At present, the most common code set width is 8-bit (6-bit and 7-bit once had their day). Where larger codes are needed, as in East Asia, their widths tend to be multiples of 8-bits (16-bit or 24-bit), rather than an arbitrary number of bits.

> **4.43 code set:** A set of bit combinations of equal size, ordered by
8 their numeric values, which must be consecutive.

NOTES

2 1   For example, a code set whose bit combinations have 8 bits (an "8-bit
      code") could consist of as many as 256 bit combinations, ranging in value
4   from 00000000 through 11111111 (0 through 255 in the decimal number
      base), or it could consist of any contiguous subset of those bit
6   combinations.

2   A compressed form of a bit combination, in which redundant bits are
8   omitted without ambiguity, is considered to be the same size as the
      uncompressed form. Such compression is possible when a character set
10 does not use all available bit combinations, as is common when the bit
      combinations contain several bytes.

12 **4.44 code set position:** The location of a bit combination in a
      code set; it corresponds to the numeric value of the bit
14 combination.

4.45 coded representation: The representation of a character as
16 a single bit combination in a code set.

NOTE — A coded representation is always a single bit combination, even
18 though the bit combination may be several 8-bit bytes in size.

When it is necessary to represent the coded representation of a character (as opposed to representing the character itself), as in a numeric character reference, SGML uses a decimal character number. Other standards
frequently use "nibble pairs", in which each four bit nibble of the coded
representation is represented by its own decimal number. In this scheme,
the bit combinations "00000000" in an 8-bit code and
"0000000000000000" in a 16-bit code are represented as "0/0" and "0/0
0/0", respectively. In SGML, in contrast, both bit combinations are represented as "0"; the representation does not depend on the code size.

4.36 character number: A *number* [56] *347:1* that represents the
20 base-10 integer equivalent of the coded representation of a charac-
      ter.

7.1.3 Character Repertoire

A single character repertoire could include both graphic and control
characters, but is frequently dedicated to one or the other.

4.147 graphic character: A character that is not a control character.

NOTE — For example, a letter, digit, or punctuation. It normally has a visual representation that is displayed when a document is presented.

4.63 control character: A character that controls the interpretation, presentation, or other processing of the characters that follow it; for example, a tab character.

4.64 control sequence: A sequence of characters, beginning with a control character, that controls the interpretation, presentation, or other processing of the characters that follow it; for example, an escape sequence.

4.129 escape sequence: A control sequence whose first character is escape (ESC).

An important use of escape sequences is to control code extension.

7.1.4 Code Extension

Code extension allows characters from multiple character sets to occur in the same document. For standardized character sets, the rules are defined in ISO 2022. For non-standardized character sets, some of the techniques may be similar, even though the details will differ.

4.42 code extension: Techniques for including in documents the coded representations of characters that are not in the document character set.

NOTE — When multiple national languages occur in a document, graphic repertoire code extension may be useful.

4.148 graphic repertoire code extension: Code extension in which multiple graphic character sets are mapped onto positions of the document code set by using shift functions to invoke virtual character sets.

4.289 shift function: In graphic repertoire code extension, a control sequence or control character that invokes a graphic character set.

NOTE — There are two kinds: single shift and locking shift.

2   **4.300 single shift:** A shift function that applies to the following character only.

4   **4.172 locking shift:** A shift function that applies until another locking shift function occurs.

ISO 2022 offers a large number of code extension techniques. Before you can begin to shift in and out of graphic character sets, it is usually necessary to "announce" which techniques will be used in the document, and to identify ("designate") the character sets. Announcing and designating are both done by escape sequences defined by ISO 2022. In SGML documents, these escape sequences must be entered in a manner that will prevent them accidentally being treated as markup, while still passing them on to the application. It may be possible to enter them in data, but it is probably safer to include them in processing instructions.

The announcement of code extension techniques includes identification of the "virtual character sets" used in the document.

6   **4.332 virtual character set:** In graphic repertoire code extension, one of the character sets, known as G0, G1, G2, or G3, that
8   represents the mapping of a real graphic character set, designated by an escape sequence, to a document code set position
10   previously announced by an escape sequence.

  4.141 G0 set: In graphic repertoire code extension, the virtual
12   character set that represents the document character set graphic characters whose character numbers are below 128, in their normal
14   code set positions.

Code extension must be managed very carefully to avoid markup recognition problems, and to preserve portability to systems that do not support ISO 2022, if that is desired. These points are discussed in E.3 〔537〕. Many of the considerations discussed there will be applicable to non-standardized character sets as well.

7.2 Character Sets in SGML

The syntax of SGML defines the rules for recognizing data and the various markup constructs so far discussed. The recognition occurs when delimiters and other characters occur in a specified order. Recall that, in order to maximize portability, the SGML syntax is defined in two levels:

a) Abstract Syntax

The abstract syntax defines markup constructs in terms of delimiter roles and character classes, but not (for the most part) specific characters.

b) Concrete Syntax

A user-defined concrete syntax assigns specific characters to the delimiter roles and character classes. The concrete syntax used in a document is identified in the SGML declaration, typically by referencing a public concrete syntax definition.

The concrete syntax is itself somewhat abstract, in that the characters are not mapped to coded representations. That task is performed by the document character set for every significant SGML character, whether it is assigned by the concrete syntax or is one of the few assigned by the abstract syntax.

4.298 significant   SGML   character: A *markup   character*
2   [51] *345:4* or *minimum data* [77] *381:8* character.

The document character set is described in the SGML declaration, typically by referencing a published character set description. It is normally the character set of the system in which the document resides.

4.98 document character set: The character set used for all
4   markup in an SGML document, and initially (at least) for data.

NOTE — When a document is interchanged between systems, its
6   character set is translated to the receiving system character set.

4.311 system character set: The character set used in an SGML
8   system.

Note that the document character set is not part of the abstract or concrete syntax. It serves to map the syntax characters to specific coded representations for a particular document. (It also maps some data characters to coded representations, but aside from minimum data characters, these are of no interest to the SGML parser. They are usually of substantial interest to the application, however!)

7.3 Character Classes

Every character in the document character set is a member of one of the eighteen character classes defined by the SGML syntax.

4.32 (character) class: A set of characters that have a common
2 purpose in the abstract syntax, such as non-SGML characters or separator characters.

4 NOTE — Specific characters are assigned to character classes in four different ways:
6 a) explicitly, by the abstract syntax (*Special*, *Digit*, *LC Letter*, and *UC Letter*);
8 b) explicitly, by the concrete syntax (*LCNMSTRT*, *FUNCHAR*, *SEPCHAR*, etc.);
10 c) implicitly, as a result of explicit assignments made to delimiter roles or other character classes (*DELMCHAR* and *DATACHAR*); or
12 d) explicitly, by the document character set (*NONSGML*).

4.41 class: Character class.

7.3.1 Non-SGML Characters

One character class is reserved for "non-SGML characters": those which do not occur in SGML entities and which therefore are not encountered by the SGML parser.

14 **4.207 non-SGML character:** A character in the document character set whose coded representation never occurs in an
16 SGML entity.

4.209 NONSGML: The class of non-SGML characters, defined by
18 the document character set.

7.3.2 Dedicated Data Characters

Characters that are not assigned explicitly to a delimiter role or character class are automatically classified as dedicated data characters.

> **4.82 dedicated data characters:** Character class consisting of
> 2 each *SGML character* [50] 345:1 that has no possible meaning as
> markup; a member is never treated as anything but a *data charac-*
> 4 *ter* [48] 344:3 .

7.3.3 Function Characters

Eight character classes are used for function characters. One of them is for characters whose SGML function is to do nothing. The others are used for "white space" and code extension functions.

> **4.139 function character:** A markup character, assigned by the
> 6 concrete syntax, that can perform some SGML function in addition
> to potentially being recognized as markup. If it is not recognized as
> 8 markup in a context in which data is allowed it is treated as data
> (unless the language dictates special treatment, as in the case of
> 10 the *RE* and *RS* function characters).

> **4.158 inert function characters:** Character class consisting of
> 12 function characters whose additional SGML "function" is to do
> nothing.

7.3.3.1 White Space Functions

White space functions are used in separator strings to make the document markup more readable. They are either discarded when the markup is parsed, or they are "normalized" into a single space so that markup strings can be compared without regard to record boundaries, spaces, etc.

The white space functions are the record start, record end, and space classes, each of which must have only a single character assigned to it, and the separator characters class.

> 14 **4.303 space:** A *function character* [54] 346:8 , assigned by the
> concrete syntax, that represents a space.

4.277 separator characters: A character class composed of
2   function characters other than ***RE***, ***RS***, and ***SPACE***, that are
allowed in separators and that will be replaced by ***SPACE*** in those
4   contexts in which ***RE*** is replaced by ***SPACE***.

7.3.3.2 Code Extension Functions

Three character classes are used to suppress markup recognition when
code extension is in use. Single shift characters are normally assigned as
markup-scan-suppress characters, locking shifts out of G0 are assigned
as markup-scan-out characters, and locking shifts back to G0 are
assigned as markup-scan-in characters. If a locking shift out of G0 is an
escape sequence, markup can be suppressed by assigning the escape
character to markup-scan-out characters; no special treatment is needed
for the rest of the sequence. (See figure 11 ⟨ *501* ⟩ for an example.)

4.190 markup-scan-suppress characters: A character class
6   consisting of function characters that suppress markup recognition
for the immediately following character in the same entity (if any).

8   **4.189 markup-scan-out characters:** Character class consisting of
function characters that suppress markup recognition until the
10   occurrence of a markup-scan-in character or entity end.

4.188 markup-scan-in characters: Character class consisting of
12   function characters that restore markup recognition if it was
suppressed by the occurrence of a markup-scan-out character.

7.3.4 Name Characters

Seven character classes are used for characters that can occur in name
tokens. The separate classes are needed to distinguish names from numbers, initial characters from others, and characters that occur in all concrete syntaxes from those that do not. The classes also serve to associate
lower-case characters with their corresponding upper-case forms so that
upper-case substitution can be performed on name tokens.

A name must begin with a character from one of the following classes
(a "name start character"):

14   **4.173 lower-case letters:** Character class composed of the 26
unaccented small letters from "a" through "z".

4.326 upper-case letters: Character class composed of the 26
2 capital letters from "A" through "Z".

4.175 lower-case name start characters: Character class
4 consisting of each lower-case *name start character* [53] 346:3
assigned by the concrete syntax.

6 **4.328 upper-case name start characters:** Character class
consisting of the upper-case forms of the corresponding lower-case
8 name start characters.

The remainder of the name can include name start characters and
characters from the following classes (collectively known as "name characters"):

4.94 digits: Character class composed of the 10 Arabic numerals
10 from "0" through "9".

4.174 lower-case name characters: Character class consisting of
12 each lower-case *name character* [52] 345:8 assigned by the concrete syntax.

14 **4.327 upper-case name characters:** Character class consisting of
the upper-case forms of the corresponding lower-case name
16 characters.

Some of the name character classes are defined by the abstract syntax
in order to guarantee that names can be constructed that will be usable
with all concrete syntaxes. They are shown in figure 1 [345]. (Note that
Ee really does not belong in this figure, as it is not a character class.)
The name character classes (and others) assigned by a concrete syntax
are shown in figure 2 [345]. The assignments illustrated are those made
by the two concrete syntaxes that are standardized in ISO 8879.
Normally, a character is assigned to a single character class. In the case
of name characters, though, there are two exceptions:

— An inert function or code extension function character can also be a
name character.

— An upper-case name or name start character can be the same as its
corresponding lower-case form.

7.3.5 Delimiter Characters

Each character that is assigned to a delimiter role is automatically assigned to the delimiter characters class (unless it is already a name character or function character). The general delimiter roles and the characters assigned to them by the "reference delimiter set" standardized in ISO 8879 are shown in figure 3 〔 *360* 〕. The characters assigned to the short reference delimiter role by the reference delimiter set are shown in figure 4 〔 *364* 〕.

4.86 delimiter characters: Character class that consists of each
2   *SGML character* 〔 **[50]** *345:1* 〕, other than a *name character*
〔 **[52]** *345:8* 〕 or *function character* 〔 **[54]** *346:8* 〕, that occurs in a string
4   assigned to a delimiter role by the concrete syntax.

4.142 general delimiter (role): A delimiter role other than short
6   reference.

4.89 delimiter set: A set of assignments of delimiter strings to the
8   abstract syntax delimiter roles.

4.259 reference delimiter set: The delimiter set, defined in this
10   International Standard, that is used in the reference concrete
syntax.

Chapter 8
Markup Declarations

8.1 Common Constructs

A markup declaration is composed of parameters, separated from one another by "ps separators" consisting of white space and/or comments.

> **4.224 parameter:** The portion of a markup declaration that is
> 2 bounded by ps separators (whether required or optional). A parameter can contain other parameters.

> 4 **4.238 ps (separator):** A parameter separator, occurring in markup declarations.

> 6 **4.46 comment:** A portion of a markup declaration that contains explanations or remarks intended to aid persons working with the
> 8 document.

A sequence of complete parameters can be in a parameter entity. The entity reference and corresponding entity end signal must both occur in ps separators in the same declaration.

A parameter can take the form of an undelimited name token, a delimited literal string, a group, a declaration subset, or a sequence of other parameters ("sub-parameters"). ISO 8879 indicates which forms are permissible for each parameter of each markup declaration.

8.1.1 Name Token Parameters

A name token parameter is undelimited. In some cases it is an application-defined name, in others it is a choice among reserved names ("keywords"), while in yet others both may be possible.

4.164 keyword: A parameter that is a reserved name.

2 NOTE — In parameters where either a keyword or a name defined by an
   application could be specified, the keyword is always preceded by the
4 reserved name indicator. An application is therefore able to define names
   without regard to whether those names are also used by the concrete
6 syntax.

4.269 reserved name: A name defined by the concrete syntax,
8 rather than by an application, such as a markup declaration name.

   NOTE — Such names appear in this International Standard as syntactic
10 literals (see 5.1 ⌐ 290 ⌐).

   There are also two cases of undelimited parameters that are not quite
name tokens:

— The allowable values for the omitted tag minimization parameters
   of the element declaration are either the keyword "O" or the *minus*
   delimiter.

— A default value parameter of an attribute definition list declaration
   can be an undelimited string of name characters. This is like a name
   token, but is subject to the length quantity of an attribute value,
   which is normally much longer than that of a name token.

8.1.2 Literals

   More or less arbitrary strings of SGML characters are specified as delimited parameter literals. A parameter literal is not really taken literally;
it can have references that are replaced when the declaration is parsed to
produce the actual parameter value.

4.227 parameter literal: A parameter or token consisting of
12 delimited replaceable parameter data.

4.161 interpreted parameter literal: The text of a *parameter*
14 *literal* ⌐ **[66]** *373:1* ⌐ , exclusive of the literal delimiters, in which character and parameter entity references have been replaced.

Some other kinds of literal can occur as parameters:

— Minimum literal.

It can contain only minimum data characters (members of the classes *LC Letter*, *UC Letter*, *Digit*, *Special*, *RS*, *RE*, and *SPACE*). Public identifiers are minimum literals.

— System identifier.

It contains system data, in which no markup is recognized except the closing delimiter.

— Attribute value literal.

Another literal that is not to be taken literally. It is first interpreted by resolving references, ignoring (that is, throwing out) entity ends and record starts, and replacing each record end and separator character with a space. The resulting attribute value is interpreted further if the declared value of the attribute is other than character data: it is "tokenized" by ignoring leading and trailing space sequences and replacing others with a single space.

An attribute value literal occurs as a default value parameter in attribute definition list declarations. As it can also occur in start-tags, general entity references — not parameter entity references — are used within it. Nonetheless, the references are resolved when the declaration is parsed, not when the default value is used in the document instance.

8.1.3 Groups

A parameter or sub-parameter could be a group. A group is a delimited sequence of tokens, which are usually name tokens but in some cases could also be nested groups. The tokens are separated by white space, but no comments are allowed. (In the case of a model group, a "connector" delimiter also occurs between tokens; it indicates whether the model group is an *and*, *or*, or *seq* group.)

4.149 group: The portion of a parameter that is bounded by a
2 balanced pair of **grpo** and **grpc** delimiters or **dtgo** and **dtgc** delimiters.

NOTE — There are five kinds: name group, name token group, model
2   group, data tag group, and data tag template group. A name, name token,
or data tag template group cannot contain a nested group, but a model
4   group can contain a nested model group or data tag group, and a data tag
group can contain a nested data tag template group.

6   **4.319 token:** The portion of a group, including a complete nested
group (but not a *connector* ⟨ **[131]** *413:4* ⟩), that is, or could be,
8   bounded by ts separators.

     4.321 ts (separator): A token separator, occurring in groups.

10   **4.200 name group:** A group whose tokens are required to be
names.

12   **4.203 name token group:** A group whose tokens are required to
be name tokens.

A sequence of complete tokens (including any intervening connectors)
can be in a parameter entity. The entity reference and corresponding
entity end signal must both occur in ts separators at the same level of the
same group.

8.1.4 Declaration Subsets

A declaration subset is a specially delimited portion of a document
type or link type declaration (one hesitates to call it a parameter) in
which other markup declarations can occur. The declarations are
separated by the usual white space, but processing instructions, marked
section declarations, and comment declarations are also allowed.

14   **4.107 ds (separator):** A declaration separator, occurring in
declaration subsets.

16   **4.47 comment declaration:** A markup declaration that contains
only comments.

A sequence of complete markup declarations and ds separators can be
in a parameter entity that is referenced from a declaration subset. The
entity reference and corresponding entity end signal must occur in ds
separators.

8.2 Marked Section

A marked section of a document is one that has been identified for a special purpose, such as ignoring it, treating some of the markup within it as data, or simply labeling it as temporary material that might need to be removed at a later time.

4.179 marked section: A section of the document that has been
2   identified for a special purpose, such as ignoring markup within it.

4.180 marked section declaration: A markup declaration that
4   identifies a marked section and specifies how it is to be treated.

The marked section is delimited by a marked section start and marked section end, and its special treatment is identified by status keywords. If the status keywords conflict, a priority scheme is used to determine the effective status.

4.182 marked section start: The opening delimiter sequence of a
6   marked section declaration.

4.181 marked section end: The closing delimiter sequence of a
8   marked section declaration.

4.222 open marked section declaration: A marked section
10   declaration whose *marked section start* [94] 392:3 has occurred
but whose *marked section end* [95] 392:6 has not yet occurred.

12   **4.307 status keyword:** A marked section declaration parameter
that specifies whether the marked section is to be ignored and, if
14   not, whether it is to be treated as character data, replaceable
character data, or normally.

16   **4.109 effective status (of a marked section):** The highest priority
status keyword specified on a marked section declaration.

8.3 SGML Declaration

The SGML declaration describes the properties of the SGML markup used in a given document, including the document character set, capacity set, concrete syntax, and optional features. Portability is enhanced by these properties being known at the start of the document, as it is easier to determine whether the document can be processed by a given system. The determination is assisted by an equivalent construct, called a "system declaration", that is part of the documentation of every conforming SGML system.

4.312 system declaration: A declaration, included in the
2   documentation for a conforming SGML system, that specifies the features, capacity set, concrete syntaxes, and character set that
4   the system supports, and any validation services that it can perform.

8.3.1 Concrete Syntax

The concrete syntax parameter of the SGML declaration identifies the concrete syntax used in the document. It does so either by describing ("declaring") the concrete syntax directly, or by referencing a description of a public concrete syntax.

6   **4.49 concrete syntax parameter:** A parameter of the SGML declaration that identifies the concrete syntax used in document
8   elements and (usually) prologs.

NOTE — The parameter consists of parameters that identify the syntax-
10 reference character set, function characters, shunned characters, naming rules, delimiter use, reserved name use, and quantitative characteristics.

12 **4.81 declared concrete syntax:** The concrete syntax described by the *concrete syntax* [182] *458:1* parameter of the *SGML decla-*
14 *ration* [171] *450:1* .

8.3.1.1 Character Set Considerations

The principal function of a concrete syntax description is to assign characters to various roles and classes defined by the abstract syntax. (Note that it is characters that are being assigned, and not their coded representations. The characters are mapped to coded representations on an individual document basis, by the document character set parameter of the SGML declaration.)

Of course, in order to refer to characters unambiguously, some coded representation is necessary. The "syntax-reference character set" is used for this purpose.

4.310 syntax-reference character set: A character set,
2   designated by a concrete syntax and known to all potential users of
the syntax, that contains every significant SGML character. It
4   enables a concrete syntax to be defined without regard to the
particular document or system character sets with which it might be
6   used.

A concrete syntax is designed with some set of potential users and their systems in mind. Some or all of these systems might act directly on certain bit combinations occurring in a data stream, without regard to their context (for example, the bit combination whose character number is 26 will end a file in some operating systems). The SGML declaration allows a designer to identify character numbers that should be shunned for such reasons when creating document character sets. A good document character set for a given concrete syntax will assign all shunned characters to the NONSGML character class.

4.297 shunned character (number): A character number,
8   identified by a concrete syntax, that should be avoided in
documents employing the syntax because some systems might
10   erroneously treat it as a control character.

8.3.1.2 Concrete Syntax Components

In addition to specifying a quantity set and identifying shunned characters, a concrete syntax description includes the following:

4.140 function character identification parameter: A parameter
12   of an SGML declaration that identifies the characters assigned to
the **RE**, **RS**, and **SPACE** functions, and allows additional functions
14   to be defined.

4.206 naming rules parameter: A parameter of an SGML
16   declaration that identifies additions to the standard name alphabet
character classes and specifies the case substitution.

18   **4.90 delimiter set parameter:** A parameter of an SGML
declaration that identifies the delimiter set used in the declared
20   concrete syntax.

2 **4.270 reserved name use parameter:** A parameter of the *SGML declaration* [171] 450:1 that specifies any replacement in the declared concrete syntax for a reference reserved name.

4 **4.261 reference reserved name:** A reserved name defined by this International Standard.

8.3.1.3 Public Concrete Syntaxes

ISO 8879 standardizes two public concrete syntaxes.

6 **4.258 reference concrete syntax:** A concrete syntax, defined in this International Standard, that is used in all SGML declarations.

8 **4.65 core concrete syntax:** A variant of the reference concrete syntax that has no short reference delimiters.

Users can define their own "variant" concrete syntaxes.

10 **4.330 variant concrete syntax:** A concrete syntax other than the reference concrete syntax or core concrete syntax.

ISO 8879 includes some examples of variant concrete syntaxes that can be used with code extension. As they are public text, they can be referenced in SGML declarations.

12 **4.196 multicode concrete syntax:** A concrete syntax that allows code extension control characters to be SGML characters.

14 **4.195 multicode basic concrete syntax:** A multicode variant of the basic concrete syntax in which markup is not recognized when
16 code extension is in use.

4.197 multicode core concrete syntax: A multicode variant of the
18 core concrete syntax in which markup is not recognized when code extension is in use.

8.3.1.4 Concrete Syntax Scope

An SGML declaration can declare a specified concrete syntax to be applicable to the entire document, or only to the document instances. In the latter case, the reference concrete syntax is used for the prologs, and the specified concrete syntax must meet certain criteria for compatibility with it.

8.3.2 Capacity

The SGML quantity set allows a concrete syntax to specify the size of buffers that contain such constructs as names, literals, and open element lists. However, in addition to knowing the size required for work areas to process individual constructs, a system must also know the total storage capacity that will be needed to accommodate all of the declared entities, elements, and other defined objects.

As the actual storage capacity required will depend upon programming techniques, SGML measures capacity in terms of a figure of merit called a "point". A system should be able to estimate real storage requirements for each type of object by multiplying the number of points by the number of bytes it uses per point, and adding its overhead value for that object type.

2 **4.26 capacity:** A named limit on some aspect of the size or complexity of a document, expressed as a number of points that can be accumulated for a kind of object or for all objects.

4 NOTE — The set of capacities is defined by the abstract syntax, but values are assigned to them by individual documents and SGML systems.

6 **4.231 point:** A unit of capacity measurement, roughly indicative of relative storage requirements.

8 **4.218 object capacity:** The capacity limit for a particular kind of object, such as entities defined or characters of entity text.

10 **4.320 total capacity:** A limit on the sum of all object capacities.

Capacity is independent of the concrete syntax. As a requirement, it is a property of an individual document, and is expressed in a capacity set in the SGML declaration. As a capability, it is a property of a system, and is expressed in a system declaration.

4.27 capacity set: A set of assignments of numeric values to
2 capacity names.

NOTE — In an SGML declaration, the capacity set identifies the maximum
4 capacity requirements of the document (its actual requirements may be
lower). A capacity set can also be defined by an application, to limit the
6 capacity requirements of documents that implementations of the application
must process, or by a system, to specify the capacity requirements that it is
8 capable of meeting.

ISO 8879 defines a reference capacity set that can be met by all conforming SGML systems (see figure 5 [*367*]).

4.257 reference capacity set: The capacity set defined in this
10 International Standard.

8.3.3 Application-specific Information

The division of labor among markup declarations is that the prolog
contains application-specific information for the SGML parser, while the
SGML declaration contains information for the parser that is not application-specific. Although the SGML declaration contains a parameter for
"application-specific information", it is of a different character from the
prolog. The parameter is intended for information that is passed to the
system or application directly, rather than affecting the behavior of the
SGML parser. Such information, for example, could be a keyword, specified by the application or by an architecture to which it conforms, that
signals the application to watch for violations of application markup
conventions.

4.7 application-specific information: A parameter of the *SGML*
12 *declaration* [**[171]** *450:1*] that specifies information required by an
application and/or its architecture.

14 NOTE — For example, the information could identify an architecture and/or
an application, or otherwise enable a system to determine whether it can
16 process the document.

Chapter 9
Conformance

Conformance to ISO 8879 is defined in the first instance in terms of conforming documents. Conformance of applications and systems is in turn based on their ability to process conforming documents, as well as other criteria.

9.1 Conforming Documents

4.51 conforming SGML document: An SGML document that
2 complies with all provisions of this International Standard.

NOTE — The provisions allow for choices in the use of optional features
4 and variant concrete syntaxes.

4.22 basic SGML document: A conforming SGML document that
6 uses the reference concrete syntax and capacity set and the
SHORTTAG and OMITTAG markup minimization features.

8 NOTE — It also uses the SHORTREF feature by virtue of using the
reference concrete syntax.

10 **4.191 minimal SGML document:** A conforming SGML document
that uses the core concrete syntax throughout, no features, and the
12 reference capacity set.

4.331 variant (conforming) SGML document: A conforming
14 SGML document that uses a variant concrete syntax.

9.2 Conforming Applications

4.50 conforming SGML application: An SGML application that requires documents to be conforming SGML documents, and whose documentation meets the requirements of this International Standard.

A conforming SGML application cannot prohibit markup that the standard would allow, nor adopt application conventions that affect areas not left open to specification by applications.

9.3 Conforming Systems

A conforming SGML system must be able to process any document that is not inconsistent with the system declaration. The reference concrete syntax must be supported at least to the same extent as any other concrete syntax. Parsing must be identical for all applications and processes that operate on a document.

Normally, there is no requirement that a system identify markup errors, only that it process conforming documents properly. This provision allows a back-end formatter to have a simpler parser than the front-end editor on which it relies to generate correct markup. A system that can report markup errors is said to have a "validating" SGML parser. Validating parsers can optionally report conditions that are not normally required to be reported.

4.329 validating SGML parser: A conforming SGML parser that can find and report a reportable markup error if (and only if) one exists.

4.267 reportable markup error: A failure of a document to conform to this International Standard when it is parsed with respect to the active document and link types, other than a semantic error (such as a generic identifier that does not accurately connote the element type) or:
    a) an ambiguous content model;
    b) an exclusion that could change a token's required or optional status in a model;
    c) exceeding a capacity limit;
    d) an error in the SGML declaration;

2   e) an otherwise allowable omission of a tag that creates an ambiguity;
     f) the occurrence of a non-SGML character; or
4   g) a formal public identifier error.

4.138 formal public identifier error: An error in the construction
6   or use of a *formal public identifier* ([79] *382:1*), other than an error
    that would prevent it being a valid *minimum literal* ([76] *381:1*) .

8   NOTE — A formal public identifier error can occur only if "FORMAL YES" is
    specified on the SGML declaration. A failure of a *public identifier*
10 ([74] *379:8*) to be a *minimum literal* ([76] *381:1*), however, is always an
    error.

9.4 Conformance Testing

ISO 8879 specifies the markup of a conforming SGML document, and
by implication, the set of information that an SGML parser gleans from
the document and passes to an application. For most of the requirements
of the standard, the correctness of an implementation can be validated by
a properly designed test suite and a suitable format for reporting the
information that the parser would pass to an application.

Not all aspects of conformance can be tested automatically, however.
Semantic errors, such as a generic identifier that does not accurately connote the element type, can only be detected by a human.

The standard also levies requirements on the documentation of conforming applications and systems, in order to promote user understanding of SGML that is transferrable among implementations. Conformance
to these requirements also requires human testing.

Part Three:

ISO 8879 Annotated

Part Three: ISO 8879 Annotated

Clause 0
Introduction

This clause explains the technical derivation of generalized markup languages and describes the user requirements that SGML was designed to meet. It also introduces the other clauses of the standard.

T–A.1 5

This International Standard specifies a language for document
2   representation referred to as the "Standard Generalized Markup Language" (SGML). SGML can be used for publishing in its
4   broadest definition, ranging from single medium conventional publishing to multi-media data base publishing. SGML can also be
6   used in office document processing when the benefits of human readability and interchange with publishing systems are required.

0.1 Background

8   A document can be viewed in the abstract as a structure of various types of element. An author organizes a book into chapters that
10 contain paragraphs, for example, and figures that contain figure captions. An editor organizes a magazine into articles that contain
12 paragraphs that contain words, and so on.

Processors treat these elements in different ways. A formatting
14 program might print headings in a prominent type face, leave space between paragraphs, and otherwise visually convey the structure
16 and other attributes to the reader. An information retrieval system would perhaps assign extra significance to words in a heading
18 when creating its dictionary.

Although this connection between a document's attributes and its
20 processing now seems obvious, it tended to be obscured by early

text processing methods. In the days before automated typesetting,
2 an editor would "mark up" a manuscript with the specific processing instructions that would create the desired format when executed by
4 a compositor. Any connection between the instructions and the document's structure was purely in the editor's head.

6 Early computerized systems continued this approach by adding the process-specific "markup" to the machine-readable document file.
8 The markup still consisted of specific processing instructions, but now they were in the language of a formatting program, rather than
10 a human compositor. The file could not easily be used for a different purpose, or on a different computer system, without
12 changing all the markup.

As users became more sophisticated, and as text processors
14 became more powerful, approaches were developed that alleviated this problem. "Macro calls" (or "format calls") were used to identify
16 points in the document where processing was to occur. The actual processing instructions were kept outside of the document, in
18 "procedures" (or "macro definitions" or "stored formats"), where they could more easily be changed.

20 While the macro calls could be placed anywhere in a document, users began to recognize that most were placed at the start or end
22 of document elements. It was natural, therefore, to choose names for such macros that were "generic identifiers" of the element types,
24 rather than names that suggested particular processing (for example, "heading" rather than "format-17"), and so the practice of
26 "generic coding" (or "generalized tagging") began.

Generic coding was a major step towards making automated text
28 processing systems reflect the natural relationship between document attributes and processing. The advent of "generalized
30 markup languages" in the early 1970's carried this trend further by providing a formal language base for generic coding. A generalized
32 markup language observes two main principles:

   a) Descriptive markup predominates and is distinguished from
34   processing instructions.

      Descriptive markup includes both generic identifiers and other
36   attributes of document elements that motivate processing instructions. The processing instructions, which can be in any
38   language, are normally collected outside of the document in procedures.

As the source file is scanned for markup and the various elements are recognized, the processing system executes the procedures associated with each element and attribute for that process. For other processes, different procedures can be associated with the same elements and attributes without changing the document markup.

When a processing instruction must be entered directly in a document, it is delimited differently from descriptive markup so that it can easily be located and changed for different processes.

b) Markup is formally defined for each type of document.

A generalized markup language formalizes document markup by incorporating "document type definitions". Type definitions include a specification (like a formal grammar) of which elements and attributes can occur in a document and in what order. With this information it is possible to determine whether the markup for an individual document is correct (that is, complies with the type definition) and also to supply markup that is missing, because it can be inferred unambiguously from other markup that is present.

NOTE — A more detailed introduction to the concepts of generic coding and the Standard Generalized Markup Language can be found in annex A
[5] .

0.2 Objectives

The Standard Generalized Markup Language standardizes the application of the generic coding and generalized markup concepts. It provides a coherent and unambiguous syntax for describing whatever a user chooses to identify within a document. The language includes:

— An "abstract syntax" for descriptive markup of document elements.
— A "reference concrete syntax" that binds the abstract syntax to particular delimiter characters and quantities. Users can define alternative concrete syntaxes to meet their requirements.

— Markup declarations that allow the user to define a specific vocabulary of generic identifiers and attributes for different document types.

— Provision for arbitrary data content. In generalized markup, "data" is anything that is not defined by the markup language. This can include specialized "data content notations" that require interpretation different from general text: formulas, images, non-Latin alphabets, previously formatted text, or graphics.

— Entity references: a non-system-specific technique for referring to content located outside the mainstream of the document, such as separately-written chapters, pi characters, photographs, etc.

— Special delimiters for processing instructions to distinguish them from descriptive markup. Processing instructions can be entered when needed for situations that cannot be handled by the procedures, but they can easily be found and modified later when a document is sent to a different processing system.

For a generalized markup language to be an acceptable standard, however, requires more than just providing the required functional capabilities. The language must have metalinguistic properties, in order to satisfy the constraints imposed by the need to use it in a multiplicity of environments. The major constraints, and the means by which the Standard Generalized Markup Language addresses them, can be summarized as follows:

a) Documents "marked up" with the language must be processable by a wide range of text processing and word processing systems.

The full form of the language, with all optional features, offers generality and flexibility that can be exploited by sophisticated systems; less powerful systems need not support the features. To facilitate interchange between dissimilar systems, an "SGML declaration" describes any markup features or concrete syntax variations used in a document.

b) The millions of existing text entry devices must be supported.

SGML documents, with the reference concrete syntax, can easily be keyboarded and understood by humans, without machine assistance. As a result:

— Use of SGML need not await the development and acceptance of a new generation of hardware — just software to process the documents on existing machines.

— Migration to such a new generation (when it comes) will be easier, as users will already be familiar with SGML.

c) There must be no character set dependency, as documents might be keyed on a variety of devices.

The language has no dependency on a particular character set. Any character set that has bit combinations for letters, numerals, space, and delimiters is acceptable.

d) There must be no processing, system, or device dependencies.

Generalized markup is predominantly descriptive and therefore inherently free of such dependencies. The occasional processing instruction is specially delimited so it can be found and converted for interchange, or when a different process renders the instruction irrelevant.

References to external parts of a document are indirect. The mappings to real system storage are made in "external entity declarations" that occur at the start of the document, where they can easily be modified for interchange.

The concrete syntax can be changed with the SGML declaration to accommodate any reserved system characters.

e) There must be no national language bias.

The characters used for names can be augmented by any special national characters. Generic identifiers, attribute names, and other names used in descriptive markup are defined by the user in element and entity declarations.

The declaration names and keywords used in markup declarations can also be changed.

Multiple character repertoires, as used in multi-lingual documents, are supported.

f) The language must accommodate familiar typewriter and word processor conventions.

The "short reference" and "data tag" capabilities support typewriter text entry conventions. Normal text containing paragraphs and quotations is interpretable as SGML although it is keyable with no visible markup.

g) The language must not depend on a particular data stream or physical file organization.

The markup language has a virtual storage model in which documents consist of one or more storage entities, each of which is a sequence of characters. All real file access is handled by the processing system, which can decide whether the character sequence should be viewed as continuous, or whether it should reflect physical record boundaries.

h) "Marked up" text must coexist with other data.

A processing system can allow text that conforms to this International Standard to occur in a data stream with other material, as long as the system can locate the start and end of the conforming text.

Similarly, a system can allow data content not defined by SGML to occur logically within a conforming document. The occurrence of such data is indicated by markup declarations to facilitate interchange.

i) The markup must be usable by both humans and programs.

The Standard Generalized Markup Language is intended as a suitable interface for keyboarding and interchange without preprocessors. It allows extensive tailoring to accommodate user preferences in text entry conventions and the requirements of a variety of keyboards and displays.

However, it is recognized that many implementers will want to take advantage of the language's information capture capabilities to provide intelligent editing or to create SGML documents from a word processing front-end environment. SGML accommodates such uses by providing the following capabilities:

2

— Element content can be stored separately from the markup.

— Control characters can be used as delimiters.

4

— Mixed modes of data representation are permitted in a document.

6

— Multiple concurrent logical and layout structures are supported.

0.3 Organization

8   The organization of this International Standard is as follows:

a) The physical organization of an SGML document as an entity
10   structure is specified in clause 6 ⎡ *293* ⎤ .

b) The logical organization of an SGML document as an element
12   structure, and its representation with descriptive markup, is
        specified in clause 7 ⎡ *302* ⎤ .

14 c) Processing instructions are discussed in clause 8 ⎡ *339* ⎤ .

d) Common markup constructs, such as characters, entity refer-
16   ences, and processing instructions, are covered in clause 9
        ⎡ *342* ⎤ .

18 e) Markup declarations with general applicability (comment,
        entity, and marked section) are specified in clause 10 ⎡ *370* ⎤ .

20 f) Markup declarations that are used primarily to specify docu-
        ment type definitions (document type, element, notation, short
22   reference mapping, and short reference use) are defined in
        clause 11 ⎡ *402* ⎤ .

24 g) Markup declarations that are used primarily to specify link pro-
        cess definitions (link type, link attribute, link set, and link set
26   use) are defined in clause 12 ⎡ *433* ⎤ .

h) The SGML declaration, which specifies the document charac-
28   ter set, capacity set, concrete syntax, and features, is defined
        in clause 13 ⎡ *450* ⎤ .

30 i) The reference concrete syntax is defined in clause 14 ⎡ *476* ⎤ .

j) Conformance of documents, applications, and systems is
32   defined in clause 15 ⎡ *478* ⎤ .

There are also a number of annexes containing additional
34 information; they are not integral parts of the body of this
International Standard.

36 NOTE — This International Standard is a formal specification of a computer
language, which may prove difficult reading for those whose expertise is in
38 the production of documents, rather than compilers. Annexes A, B, and C
discuss the main concepts in an informal tutorial style that should be more

accessible to most readers. However, the reader should be aware that
2   those annexes do not cover all SGML constructs, nor all details of those
covered, and subtle distinctions are frequently ignored in the interest of
4   presenting a clear overview.

Clause 1
Scope

The scope clause states clearly what is being standardized and what is not.

This International Standard:

2   a) Specifies an abstract syntax known as the Standard Generalized Markup Language (SGML). The language
4   expresses the description of a document's structure and other attributes, as well as other information that makes the markup
6   interpretable.
    b) Specifies a reference concrete syntax that binds the abstract
8   syntax to specific characters and numeric values, and criteria for defining variant concrete syntaxes.
10 c) Defines conforming documents in terms of their use of components of the language.
12 d) Defines conforming systems in terms of their ability to process conforming documents and to recognize markup errors in
14   them.
    e) Specifies how data not defined by this International Standard
16   (such as images, graphics, or formatted text) can be included in a conforming document.

18 NOTE — This International Standard does not:
    a) Identify or specify "standard" document types, document
20   architectures, or text structures.
    b) Specify the implementation, architecture, or markup error handling of
22   conforming systems.
    c) Specify how conforming documents are to be created.
24 d) Specify the data stream, message handling system, file structure, or other physical representation in which conforming documents are
26   stored or interchanged, or any character set or coding scheme into or from which conforming documents might be translated for such
28   purposes.

246

e) Specify the data content representation or notation for images, graphics, formatted text, etc., that are included in a conforming document.

Clause 2
Field of Application

This clause describes the expected areas of use of SGML.

O–4.318 *123:5*

2 The Standard Generalized Markup Language can be used for documents that are processed by any text processing or word processing system. It is particularly applicable to:

4 a) Documents that are interchanged among systems with differing text processing languages.

6 b) Documents that are processed in more than one way, even when the procedures use the same text processing language.

8 Documents that exist solely in final imaged form are not within the field of application of this International Standard.

Clause 3
References

This clause lists all of the ISO standards mentioned in ISO 8879. They can be purchased from the national standards bodies of most countries, and from other sources as well. (See Appendix D $\boxed{605}$ for bibliographic details on these and other sources of SGML information.)

ISO 639, *Codes for the representation of names of languages.*

2 ISO 646, *Information processing — ISO 7-bit coded character set for information interchange.*

4 ISO 9069, *Information processing — SGML support facilities — SGML Document Interchange Format (SDIF).*

6 ISO 9070, *Information processing — SGML support facilities — Registration procedures for public text.*

8 The following references are used in conjunction with illustrative material:

10 ISO 2022, *Information processing — ISO 7-bit and 8-bit coded character sets — Code extension techniques.*

12 ISO 3166, *Codes for the representation of names of countries.*

ISO 4873, *Information processing — ISO 8-bit code for information*
14 *interchange — Structure and rules for implementation.*

ISO 6937, *Information processing — Coded character sets for text*
16 *communication.*

2 ISO 8632/2, *Information processing systems — Computer graphics — Metafile for the storage and transfer of picture description information — Part 2: Character encoding.*

4 ISO 8632/4, *Information processing systems — Computer graphics — Metafile for the storage and transfer of picture description*
6 *information — Part 4: Clear text encoding.*

Clause 4
Definitions

ISO directives require that a standard include definitions for all terms that do not have their usual dictionary meaning. Here they all are, in alphabetic order for easy reference.

All of these terms are discussed in topical order in Part Two of this book.

NOTE — The typographic conventions described in 5.1 ⌊ *290* ⌋ are
2   employed in this clause.

For the purposes of this International Standard, the following
4   definitions apply:

4.1 abstract syntax (of SGML): Rules that define how markup is
6   added to the data of a document, without regard to the specific characters used to represent the markup.

8   **4.2 active document type (declaration):** A document type that the system has identified as being active.

10   NOTE — An SGML entity is parsed with respect to its active document types, if any, or if not, with respect to its base document type and any active
12   link types.

4.3 active link type (declaration): A link process that the system
14   has identified as being active.

4.4 ambiguous content model: A *content model* ⌊ **[126]** *410:1* ⌋ for
16   which an element or character string occurring in the document instance can satisfy more than one *primitive content token*
18   ⌊ **[129]** *410:20* ⌋ without look-ahead.

NOTE — Ambiguous content models are prohibited in SGML.

4.5 application: Text processing application.

4.6 application convention: Application-specific rule governing the text of a document in areas that SGML leaves to user choice.

NOTE — There are two kinds: content conventions and markup conventions.

4.7 application-specific information: A parameter of the *SGML declaration* [171] *450:1* that specifies information required by an application and/or its architecture.

NOTE — For example, the information could identify an architecture and/or an application, or otherwise enable a system to determine whether it can process the document.

4.8 associated element type: An element type associated with the subject of a markup declaration by its *associated element type* [72] *377:1* parameter.

4.8.1 associated notation (name): A notation name associated with the subject of a markup declaration by its *associated notation name* [149.1] *428:5* parameter.

4.9 attribute (of an element): A characteristic quality, other than type or content.

4.10 attribute definition: A member of an attribute definition list; it defines an attribute name, allowed values, and default value.

4.11 attribute definition list: A set of one or more attribute definitions defined by the *attribute definition list* [142] *420:25* parameter of an attribute definition list declaration.

4.12 attribute (definition) list declaration: A markup declaration that associates an attribute definition list with one or more element types.

4.13 attribute list: Attribute specification list.

4.14 attribute list declaration: Attribute definition list declaration.

4.15 attribute specification: A member of an attribute specification list; it specifies the value of a single attribute.

4.16 attribute (specification) list: Markup that is a set of one or
more attribute specifications.

NOTE — Attribute specification lists occur in start-tags, entity declarations,
and link sets.

4.17 attribute value literal: A delimited character string that is
interpreted as an _attribute value_ [35] _333:1_ by replacing references
and ignoring or translating function characters.

4.18 available public text: Public text that is available to the
general public, though its owner may require payment of a fee or
performance of other conditions.

4.19 B sequence: An uninterrupted sequence of upper-case letter
"B" characters; in a string assigned as a short reference, it denotes
a blank sequence whose minimum length is the length of the B
sequence.

4.20 base document element: A document element whose
document type is the base document type.

4.21 base document type: The document type specified by the
first document type declaration in a prolog.

4.22 basic SGML document: A conforming SGML document that
uses the reference concrete syntax and capacity set and the
SHORTTAG and OMITTAG markup minimization features.

NOTE — It also uses the SHORTREF feature by virtue of using the
reference concrete syntax.

4.23 bit: Binary digit; that is, either zero or one.

4.24 bit combination: An ordered collection of bits, interpretable
as a binary number.

NOTE — A bit combination should not be confused with a "byte", which is a
name given to a particular size of bit string, typically seven or eight bits. A
single bit combination could contain several bytes.

4.25 blank sequence: An uninterrupted sequence of _SPACE_
and/or _SEPCHAR_ characters.

4.26 capacity: A named limit on some aspect of the size or complexity of a document, expressed as a number of points that can be accumulated for a kind of object or for all objects.

NOTE — The set of capacities is defined by the abstract syntax, but values are assigned to them by individual documents and SGML systems.

4.27 capacity set: A set of assignments of numeric values to capacity names.

NOTE — In an SGML declaration, the capacity set identifies the maximum capacity requirements of the document (its actual requirements may be lower). A capacity set can also be defined by an application, to limit the capacity requirements of documents that implementations of the application must process, or by a system, to specify the capacity requirements that it is capable of meeting.

4.28 CDATA: Character data.

4.29 CDATA entity: Character data entity.

4.30 chain of (link) processes: Processes, performed sequentially, that form a chain in which the source of the first process is an instance of the base document type, and the result of each process but the last is the source for the next. Any portion of the chain can be iterated.

NOTE — For example, a complex page makeup application could include three document types — logical, galley, and page — and two link processes — justification and castoff. The justification process would create an instance of a galley from an instance of a logical document, and the castoff process would in turn create pages from the galleys. The two processes could be iterated, as decisions made during castoff could require re-justification of the galleys at different sizes.

4.31 character: An atom of information with an individual meaning, defined by a character repertoire.

NOTES

1   There are two kinds: graphic character and control character.

2   A character can occur in a context in which it has a meaning, defined by markup or a data content notation, that supercedes or supplements its meaning in the character repertoire.

4.32 (character) class: A set of characters that have a common purpose in the abstract syntax, such as non-SGML characters or separator characters.

NOTE — Specific characters are assigned to character classes in four different ways:

a) explicitly, by the abstract syntax (**Special**, **Digit**, **LC Letter**, and **UC Letter**);

b) explicitly, by the concrete syntax (**LCNMSTRT**, **FUNCHAR**, **SEPCHAR**, etc.);

c) implicitly, as a result of explicit assignments made to delimiter roles or other character classes (**DELMCHAR** and **DATACHAR**); or

d) explicitly, by the document character set (**NONSGML**).

4.33 character data: Zero or more characters that occur in a context in which no markup is recognized, other than the delimiters that end the *character data* [47] *344:1* . Such characters are classified as data characters because they were declared to be so.

4.34 character data entity: An entity whose text is treated as *character data* [47] *344:1* when referenced and is not dependent on a specific system, device, or application process.

4.35 character entity set: A public entity set consisting of general entities that are graphic characters.

NOTES

1   Character entities are used for characters that have no coded representation in the document character set, or that cannot be keyboarded conveniently, or to achieve device independence for characters whose bit combinations do not cause proper display on all output devices.

2   There are two kinds of character entity sets: definitional and display.

4.36 character number: A *number* [56] *347:1* that represents the base-10 integer equivalent of the coded representation of a character.

4.37 character reference: A reference that is replaced by a single character.

NOTE — There are two kinds: named character reference and numeric character reference.

4.38 character repertoire: A set of characters that are used together. Meanings are defined for each character, and can also be defined for control sequences of multiple characters.

NOTE — When characters occur in a control sequence, the meaning of the sequence supercedes the meanings of the individual characters.

4.39 character set: A mapping of a character repertoire onto a code set such that each character in the repertoire is represented by a bit combination in the code set.

4.40 (character) string: A sequence of characters.

4.41 class: Character class.

4.42 code extension: Techniques for including in documents the coded representations of characters that are not in the document character set.

NOTE — When multiple national languages occur in a document, graphic repertoire code extension may be useful.

4.43 code set: A set of bit combinations of equal size, ordered by their numeric values, which must be consecutive.

NOTES

1   For example, a code set whose bit combinations have 8 bits (an "8-bit code") could consist of as many as 256 bit combinations, ranging in value from 00000000 through 11111111 (0 through 255 in the decimal number base), or it could consist of any contiguous subset of those bit combinations.

2   A compressed form of a bit combination, in which redundant bits are omitted without ambiguity, is considered to be the same size as the uncompressed form. Such compression is possible when a character set does not use all available bit combinations, as is common when the bit combinations contain several bytes.

4.44 code set position: The location of a bit combination in a code set; it corresponds to the numeric value of the bit combination.

4.45 coded representation: The representation of a character as a single bit combination in a code set.

NOTE — A coded representation is always a single bit combination, even though the bit combination may be several 8-bit bytes in size.

4.46 comment: A portion of a markup declaration that contains explanations or remarks intended to aid persons working with the document.

4.47 comment declaration: A markup declaration that contains only comments.

4.48 concrete syntax (of SGML): A binding of the abstract syntax to particular delimiter characters, quantities, markup declaration names, etc.

4.49 concrete syntax parameter: A parameter of the SGML declaration that identifies the concrete syntax used in document elements and (usually) prologs.

NOTE — The parameter consists of parameters that identify the syntax-reference character set, function characters, shunned characters, naming rules, delimiter use, reserved name use, and quantitative characteristics.

4.50 conforming SGML application: An SGML application that requires documents to be conforming SGML documents, and whose documentation meets the requirements of this International Standard.

4.51 conforming SGML document: An SGML document that complies with all provisions of this International Standard.

NOTE — The provisions allow for choices in the use of optional features and variant concrete syntaxes.

4.52 containing element: An element within which a subelement occurs.

4.53 content: Characters that occur between the start-tag and end-tag of an element in a document instance. They can be interpreted as data, proper subelements, included subelements, other markup, or a mixture of them.

NOTE — If an element has an explicit content reference, or its declared content is "EMPTY", the content is empty. In such cases, the application itself may generate data and process it as though it were content data.

4.54 content convention: An application convention governing
2   data content, such as a restriction on length, allowable characters,
or use of upper-case and lower-case letters.

4   NOTE — A content convention is essentially an informal data content
notation, usually restricted to a single element type.

6   **4.55 (content) model:** Parameter of an element declaration that
specifies the *model group* [127] *410:6* and *exceptions* [138] *418:1*
8   that define the allowed *content* [24] *320:1* of the element.

4.56 content model nesting level: The largest number of
10   successive **grpo** or **dtgo** delimiters that occur in a *content model*
[126] *410:1* without a corresponding **grpc** or **dtgc** delimiter.

12   **4.57 content reference (attribute):** An impliable attribute whose
value is referenced by the application to generate content data.

14   NOTE — When an element has an explicit content reference, the element's
content [24] *320:1* in the document instance is empty.

16   **4.58 contextual sequence:** A sequence of one or more markup
characters that must follow a delimiter string within the same entity
18   in order for the string to be recognized as a delimiter.

4.59 contextually optional element: An element
20   a)   that can occur only because it is an inclusion; or
    b)   whose *content token* [128] *410:17* in the currently applicable
22   model group is a contextually optional token.

4.60 contextually optional token: A *content token* [128] *410:17*
24   that
    a)   is an inherently optional token; or
26   b)   has a **plus** occurrence indicator and has been satisfied; or
    c)   is in a model group that is itself a contextually optional token,
28   no tokens of which have been satisfied.

4.61 contextually required element: An element that is not a
30   contextually optional element and
    a)   whose *generic identifier* [30] *325:17* is the *document type*
32   *name* [111] *404:4* ; or
    b)   whose currently applicable *content token* [128] *410:17* is a
34   contextually required token.

NOTE — An element could be neither contextually required nor contextually optional; for example, an element whose currently applicable *content token* [128] *410:17* is in an *or* group that has no inherently optional tokens.

4.62 contextually required token: A *content token* [128] *410:17* that
a) is the only one in its model group; or
b) is in a *seq* group
   i) that

      — is itself a contextually required token; or
      — contains a token which has been satisfied;
   and
   ii) all preceding tokens of which

      — have been satisfied; or
      — are contextually optional.

4.63 control character: A character that controls the interpretation, presentation, or other processing of the characters that follow it; for example, a tab character.

4.64 control sequence: A sequence of characters, beginning with a control character, that controls the interpretation, presentation, or other processing of the characters that follow it; for example, an escape sequence.

4.65 core concrete syntax: A variant of the reference concrete syntax that has no short reference delimiters.

4.66 corresponding content (of a content token): The element(s) and/or data in a document instance that correspond to a *content token* [128] *410:17* .

4.67 current attribute: An attribute whose current (that is, most recently specified) value becomes its default value.

NOTE — The start-tag cannot be omitted for the first occurrence of an element with a current attribute.

4.68 current element: The open element whose *start-tag* [14] *314:1* most recently occurred (or was omitted through markup minimization).

4.69 current link set: The link set associated with the current

element by a *link set use declaration* [169] *448:1* in the element
2 content or by a link process definition. If the current element has no
associated link set, the previous current link set continues to be the
4 current link set.

4.70 current map: The short reference map associated with the
6 current element by a *short reference use declaration* [152] *430:10*
in the element content or document type definition. If the current
8 element has no associated map, the previous current map continues to be the current map.

10 **4.71 current rank:** The *rank suffix* [121] *407:19* that, when
appended to a rank stem in a tag, will derive the element's generic
12 identifier. For a *start-tag* [14] *314:1* it is the *rank suffix* [121] *407:19*
of the most recent element with the identical *rank stem*
14 [120] *407:17* , or a *rank stem* [120] *407:17* in the same *ranked*
group [119] *407:5* . For an *end-tag* [19] *317:4* it is the *rank suffix*
16 [121] *407:19* of the most recent open element with the identical
rank stem [120] *407:17* .

18 **4.72 data:** The characters of a document that represent the
inherent information content; characters that are not recognized as
20 markup.

4.72.1 data attribute: An attribute of the data conforming to a
22 particular data content notation.

NOTE — In most cases, the value of the data attributes must be known
24 before the data can be interpreted in accordance with the notation.

4.73 data character: An *SGML character* [50] *345:1* that is inter-
26 preted as data in the context in which it occurs, either because it
was declared to be data, or because it was not recognizable as
28 markup.

4.74 data content: The portion of an element's *content* [24] *320:1*
30 that is data rather than markup or a subelement.

4.75 data content notation: An application-specific interpretation
32 of an element's data content, or of a data entity, that usually
extends or differs from the normal meaning of the document
34 character set.

NOTE — It is specified for an element's *content* [24] *320:1* by a notation
36 attribute, and for a data entity by the *notation name* [41] *333:33* parameter

of the entity declaration.

4.75.1 data entity: An entity that was declared to be data and therefore is not parsed when referenced.

NOTES

1 There are three kinds: character data entity, specific character data entity, and non-SGML data entity.

2 The interpretation of a data entity may be governed by a data content notation, which may be defined by another International Standard.

4.76 data tag: A string that conforms to the data tag pattern of an open element. It serves both as the *end-tag* [19] *317:4* of the open element and as *character data* [47] *344:1* in the element that contains it.

4.77 data tag group: A *content token* [128] *410:17* that associates a data tag pattern with a target element type.

NOTE — Within an instance of a target element, the data content and that of any subelements is scanned for a string that conforms to the pattern (a "data tag").

4.78 data tag pattern: A data tag group token that defines the strings that, if they occurred in the proper context, would constitute a data tag.

4.79 declaration: Markup declaration.

4.80 declaration subset: A delimited portion of a markup declaration in which other declarations can occur.

NOTE — Declaration subsets occur only in document type, link type, and marked section declarations.

4.81 declared concrete syntax: The concrete syntax described by the *concrete syntax* [182] *458:1* parameter of the *SGML declaration* [171] *450:1*.

4.82 dedicated data characters: Character class consisting of each *SGML character* [50] *345:1* that has no possible meaning as markup; a member is never treated as anything but a *data character* [48] *344:3*.

4.83 default entity: The entity that is referenced by a general entity reference with an undeclared name.

4.84 default value: A portion of an attribute definition that specifies the attribute value to be used if there is no *attribute specification* [32] 327:19 for it.

4.85 definitional (character) entity set: A character entity set whose purpose is to define entity names for graphic characters, but not actually to display them. Its *public identifier* [74] 379:8 does not include a *public text display version* [90] 390:1 .

NOTE — During processing, the system replaces a definitional entity set with a corresponding display character entity set for the appropriate output device.

4.86 delimiter characters: Character class that consists of each *SGML character* [50] 345:1 , other than a *name character* [52] 345:8 or *function character* [54] 346:8 , that occurs in a string assigned to a delimiter role by the concrete syntax.

4.87 delimiter-in-context: A character string that consists of a delimiter string followed immediately in the same entity by a contextual sequence.

4.88 delimiter role: A role defined by the abstract syntax, and filled by a character string assigned by the concrete syntax, that involves identifying parts of the markup and/or distinguishing markup from data.

4.89 delimiter set: A set of assignments of delimiter strings to the abstract syntax delimiter roles.

4.90 delimiter set parameter: A parameter of an SGML declaration that identifies the delimiter set used in the declared concrete syntax.

4.91 delimiter (string): A character string assigned to a delimiter role by the concrete syntax.

4.92 descriptive markup: Markup that describes the structure and other attributes of a document in a non-system-specific manner, independently of any processing that may be performed on it. In particular, SGML descriptive markup uses tags to express the element structure.

4.93 device-dependent version (of public text): Public text whose *formal public identifier* [79] *382:1* differs from that of another public text only by the addition of a *public text display version* [90] *390:1* , which identifies the display devices supported or coding scheme used.

4.94 digits: Character class composed of the 10 Arabic numerals from "0" through "9".

4.95 display (character) entity set: An entity set with the same entity names as a corresponding definitional character entity set, but which causes the characters to be displayed. It is a device-dependent version of the corresponding definitional entity set.

4.96 document: A collection of information that is processed as a unit. A document is classified as being of a particular document type.

NOTE — In this International Standard, the term almost invariably means (without loss of accuracy) an SGML document.

4.97 document architecture: Rules for the formulation of text processing applications.

NOTE — For example, a document architecture can define:
a) attribute semantics for use in a variety of element definitions;
b) element classes, based on which attributes the elements have;
c) structural rules for defining document types in terms of element classes;
d) link processes, and how they are affected by the values of attributes; and/or
e) information to accompany a document during interchange (a "document profile").

4.98 document character set: The character set used for all markup in an SGML document, and initially (at least) for data.

NOTE — When a document is interchanged between systems, its character set is translated to the receiving system character set.

4.99 document element: The element that is the outermost element of an instance of a document type; that is, the element whose *generic identifier* [30] *325:17* is the *document type name* [111] *404:4* .

4.100 document instance: Instance of a document type.

2 **4.101 document instance set:** The portion of an *SGML document entity* [2] 295:13 or *SGML subdocument entity* [3] 296:1 in the 4 entity structure that contains one or more instances of document types. It is co-extensive with the base document element in the ele- 6 ment structure.

NOTE — When the concurrent instance feature is used, multiple instances 8 can exist in a document, and data and markup can be shared among them.

4.102 document type: A class of documents having similar 10 characteristics; for example, journal, article, technical manual, or memo.

12 **4.103 (document) type declaration:** A markup declaration that formally specifies a portion of a document type definition.

14 NOTE — A document type declaration does not specify all of a document type definition because part of the definition, such as the semantics of 16 elements and attributes, cannot be expressed in SGML. In addition, the application designer might choose not to use SGML in every possible 18 instance — for example, by using a data content notation to delineate the structure of an element in preference to defining subelements.

20 **4.104 document type declaration subset:** The element, entity, and short reference sets occurring within the declaration subset of 22 a document type declaration.

NOTE — The external entity referenced from the document type 24 declaration is considered part of the declaration subset.

4.105 document (type) definition: Rules, determined by an 26 application, that apply SGML to the markup of documents of a particular type.

28 NOTE — Part of a document type definition can be specified by an SGML document type declaration. Other parts, such as the semantics of elements 30 and attributes, or any application conventions, cannot be expressed formally in SGML. Comments can be used, however, to express them 32 informally.

4.106 document type specification: A portion of a tag that 34 identifies the document instances within which the tag will be processed.

NOTE — A *name group* [69] *374:11* performs the same function in an entity reference.

4.107 ds (separator): A declaration separator, occurring in declaration subsets.

4.108 DTD: Document type definition.

4.109 effective status (of a marked section): The highest priority status keyword specified on a marked section declaration.

4.110 element: A component of the hierarchical structure defined by a document type definition; it is identified in a document instance by descriptive markup, usually a start-tag and end-tag.

NOTE — An element is classified as being of a particular element type.

4.111 element declaration: A markup declaration that contains the formal specification of the part of an element type definition that deals with the content and markup minimization.

4.112 element set: A set of element, attribute definition list, and notation declarations that are used together.

NOTE — An element set can be public text.

4.113 element structure: The organization of a document into hierarchies of elements, with each hierarchy conforming to a different document type definition.

4.114 element type: A class of elements having similar characteristics; for example, paragraph, chapter, abstract, footnote, or bibliography.

4.115 element (type) definition: Application-specific rules that apply SGML to the markup of elements of a particular type. An element type definition includes a formal specification, expressed in element and attribute definition list declarations, of the content, markup minimization, and attributes allowed for a specified element type.

NOTE — An element type definition is normally part of a document type definition.

4.116 element type parameter: A parameter of an element declaration that identifies the type of element to which the definition applies.

NOTE — The specification can be direct, in the form of an individual *generic identifier* [30] *325:17* or member of a *name group* [69] *374:11* , or indirect, via a *ranked element* [118] *407:1* or member of a *ranked group* [119] *407:5* .

4.117 empty link set: A link set that contains no link rules.

4.118 empty map: A short reference map in which all delimiters are mapped to nothing.

NOTE — The empty map need not (and cannot) be declared explicitly, but can be referenced by its reserved name, which is "#EMPTY" in the reference concrete syntax.

4.119 end-tag: Descriptive markup that identifies the end of an element.

4.120 entity: A collection of characters that can be referenced as a unit.

NOTES

1   Objects such as book chapters written by different authors, pi characters, or photographs, are often best managed by maintaining them as individual entities.

2   The actual storage of entities is system-specific, and could take the form of files, members of a partitioned data set, components of a data structure, or entries in a symbol table.

4.121 entity declaration: A markup declaration that assigns an SGML name to an entity so that it can be referenced.

4.122 entity end (signal): A signal from the system that an entity's replacement text has ended.

4.123 entity manager: A program (or portion of a program or a combination of programs), such as a file system or symbol table, that can maintain and provide access to multiple entities.

4.124 entity reference: A reference that is replaced by an entity.

NOTE — There are two kinds: named entity reference and short reference.

4.125 entity set: A set of entity declarations that are used together.

NOTE — An entity set can be public text.

4.126 entity structure: The organization of a document into one or more separate entities.

NOTE — The first entity is an *SGML document entity* [2] *295:13* ; it contains entity references that indicate where the other entities belong with respect to it.

4.127 entity text: The entity declaration parameter that specifies the replacement text, either by including it in a parameter literal, or by pointing to it with an external identifier.

4.128 equivalent reference string: A character string, consisting of an entity reference and possibly an *RE* and/or *RS*, that replaces a short reference when a document is converted from a concrete syntax that supports short references to one that does not.

4.129 escape sequence: A control sequence whose first character is escape (ESC).

4.130 exceptions: A parameter of an element declaration that modifies the effect of the element's *content model* [126] *410:1* , and the content models of elements occurring within it, by permitting inclusions and prohibiting exclusions.

4.131 exclusions: Elements that are not allowed anywhere in the content of an element or its subelements even though the applicable content model or inclusions would permit them optionally.

4.132 explicit content reference: A content reference that was specified in an *attribute specification* [32] *327:19* .

4.133 explicit link (process definition): A link process definition in which the result element types and their attributes and link attribute values can be specified for multiple source element types.

4.134 external entity: An entity whose replacement text is not incorporated in an entity declaration; its system identifier and/or public identifier is specified instead.

4.135 external identifier: A parameter that identifies an external entity or data content notation.

NOTES

1   There are two kinds: system identifier and public identifier.

2   A document type or link type declaration can include the identifier of an external entity containing all or part of the declaration subset; the external identifier serves simultaneously as a declaration of that entity and as a reference to it.

4.136 fixed attribute: An attribute whose specified value (if any) must be identical to its default value.

4.137 formal public identifier: A public identifier that is constructed according to rules defined in this International Standard so that its owner identifier and the components of its text identifier can be distinguished.

4.138 formal public identifier error: An error in the construction or use of a *formal public identifier* [79] *382:1*, other than an error that would prevent it being a valid *minimum literal* [76] *381:1*.

NOTE — A formal public identifier error can occur only if "FORMAL YES" is specified on the SGML declaration. A failure of a *public identifier* [74] *379:8* to be a *minimum literal* [76] *381:1*, however, is always an error.

4.139 function character: A markup character, assigned by the concrete syntax, that can perform some SGML function in addition to potentially being recognized as markup. If it is not recognized as markup in a context in which data is allowed it is treated as data (unless the language dictates special treatment, as in the case of the *RE* and *RS* function characters).

4.140 function character identification parameter: A parameter of an SGML declaration that identifies the characters assigned to the *RE*, *RS*, and *SPACE* functions, and allows additional functions to be defined.

4.141 G0 set: In graphic repertoire code extension, the virtual character set that represents the document character set graphic characters whose character numbers are below 128, in their normal code set positions.

4.142 general delimiter (role): A delimiter role other than short reference.

4.143 general entity: An entity that can be referenced from within the content of an element or an attribute value literal.

4.144 general entity reference: A named entity reference to a general entity.

4.145 generic identifier: A name that identifies the element type of an element.

4.146 GI: Generic identifier.

4.147 graphic character: A character that is not a control character.

NOTE — For example, a letter, digit, or punctuation. It normally has a visual representation that is displayed when a document is presented.

4.148 graphic repertoire code extension: Code extension in which multiple graphic character sets are mapped onto positions of the document code set by using shift functions to invoke virtual character sets.

4.149 group: The portion of a parameter that is bounded by a balanced pair of *grpo* and *grpc* delimiters or *dtgo* and *dtgc* delimiters.

NOTE — There are five kinds: name group, name token group, model group, data tag group, and data tag template group. A name, name token, or data tag template group cannot contain a nested group, but a model group can contain a nested model group or data tag group, and a data tag group can contain a nested data tag template group.

4.150 ID: Unique identifier.

4.151 ID reference list: An attribute value that is a list of ID reference values.

4.152 ID reference value: An attribute value that is a *name* [55] *346:17* specified as an *id value* [36] *333:19* of an element in the same document instance.

4.153 ID value: An attribute value that is a *name* [55] *346:17* that
2 uniquely identifies the element; that is, it cannot be the same as
any other *id value* [36] *333:19* in the same document instance.

4 **4.154 impliable attribute:** An attribute for which there need not be
an *attribute specification* [32] *327:19* , and whose value is defined
6 by the application when it is not specified.

4.155 implicit link (process definition): A link process definition
8 in which the result element types and their attributes are all implied
by the application, but link attribute values can be specified for
10 multiple source element types.

4.156 included subelement: A subelement that is not permitted
12 by its containing element's model, but is permitted by an inclusion
exception.

14 **4.157 inclusions:** Elements that are allowed anywhere in the
content of an element or its subelements even though the
16 applicable model does not permit them.

4.158 inert function characters: Character class consisting of
18 function characters whose additional SGML "function" is to do
nothing.

20 **4.159 inherently optional token:** A model group token that:
    a)   has an *opt* or *rep* occurrence indicator; or
22   b)   is an *or* group, one of whose tokens is inherently optional; or
    c)   is an *and* or *seq* group, all of whose tokens are inherently
24   optional.

4.159.1 initial link set: The link set that is current at the start of
26 the document instance.

4.160 instance (of a document type): The data and markup for a
28 hierarchy of elements that conforms to a document type definition.

4.160.1 internal entity: An entity whose replacement text is
30 incorporated in an entity declaration.

4.161 interpreted parameter literal: The text of a *parameter*
32 *literal* [66] *373:1* , exclusive of the literal delimiters, in which character and parameter entity references have been replaced.

4.162 ISO owner identifier: An *owner identifier* [80] 383:1 , consisting of an ISO publication number or character set registration number, that is used when a *public identifier* [74] 379:8 identifies, or is assigned by, an ISO publication, or identifies an ISO registered character set.

4.163 ISO text description: A *public text description* [87] 387:5 , consisting of the last element of an ISO publication title (without part designation, if any), that is used when a *public identifier* [74] 379:8 identifies an ISO publication.

4.164 keyword: A parameter that is a reserved name.

NOTE — In parameters where either a keyword or a name defined by an application could be specified, the keyword is always preceded by the reserved name indicator. An application is therefore able to define names without regard to whether those names are also used by the concrete syntax.

4.165 link attribute: An attribute of a source element type that is meaningful only in the context of a particular process that is performed on the source document instance.

4.166 link process: A process that creates a new instance of some document type (the result) from an existing instance of the same or another document type (the source). Processes can be chained, so that the result of one is the source for the next.

NOTE — Examples of link processes include editing, in which the source and result document types are usually the same, and formatting, in which they are usually different.

4.167 link process definition: Application-specific rules that apply SGML to describe a link process. A link process definition includes a formal specification, expressed in a *link type declaration* [154] 434:1 , of the link between elements of the source and result, including the definitions of source attributes applicable to the link process ("link attributes").

NOTES

1   A link process definition can also include comments that describe the semantics of the process, including the meaning of the link attributes and their effect on the process.

2   There are three kinds of link process definitions: simple, implicit, and
2   explicit.

4.167.1 link rule: A member of a link set; that is, for an implicit
4   link, a *source element specification* [165] 443:1 , and for an explicit
link, an *explicit link rule* [166.1] 445:1 .

6   **4.168 link set:** A named set of rules, declared in a *link set
declaration* [163] 441:6 , by which elements of the source document
8   type are linked to elements of the result document type.

4.169 link set declaration: A markup declaration that defines a
10 link set.

4.170 link type declaration: A markup declaration that contains
12 the formal specification of a link process definition.

4.171 link type declaration subset: The entity sets, link attribute
14 sets, and link set declarations, that occur within the declaration
subset of a link type declaration.

16 NOTE — The external entity referenced from the link type declaration is
considered part of the declaration subset.

18 **4.172 locking shift:** A shift function that applies until another
locking shift function occurs.

20 **4.173 lower-case letters:** Character class composed of the 26
unaccented small letters from "a" through "z".

22 **4.174 lower-case name characters:** Character class consisting of
each lower-case *name character* [52] 345:8 assigned by the con-
24 crete syntax.

4.175 lower-case name start characters: Character class
26 consisting of each lower-case *name start character* [53] 346:3
assigned by the concrete syntax.

28 **4.176 LPD:** Link process definition.

4.177 map: Short reference map.

30 **4.178 mark up:** To add markup to a document.

4.179 marked section: A section of the document that has been
2 identified for a special purpose, such as ignoring markup within it.

4.180 marked section declaration: A markup declaration that
4 identifies a marked section and specifies how it is to be treated.

4.181 marked section end: The closing delimiter sequence of a
6 marked section declaration.

4.182 marked section start: The opening delimiter sequence of a
8 marked section declaration.

4.183 markup: Text that is added to the data of a document in
10 order to convey information about it.

NOTE — There are four kinds of markup: descriptive markup (tags),
12 references, markup declarations, and processing instructions.

4.184 markup character: An SGML character that, depending on
14 the context, could be interpreted either as markup or data.

4.185 markup convention: Application convention governing
16 markup, such as a rule for the formulation of an entity name, or a
preferred subset of allowed short reference delimiters.

18 **4.186 (markup) declaration:** Markup that controls how other
markup of a document is to be interpreted.

20 NOTE — There are 13 kinds: SGML, entity, element, attribute definition list,
notation, document type, link type, link set, link set use, marked section,
22 short reference mapping, short reference use, and comment.

4.187 (markup) minimization feature: A feature of SGML that
24 allows markup to be minimized by shortening or omitting tags, or
shortening entity references.

26 NOTE — Markup minimization features do not affect the document type
definition, so a minimized document can be sent to a system that does not
28 support these features by first restoring the omitted markup. There are five
kinds: SHORTTAG, OMITTAG, SHORTREF, DATATAG, and RANK.

30 **4.188 markup-scan-in characters:** Character class consisting of
function characters that restore markup recognition if it was
32 suppressed by the occurrence of a markup-scan-out character.

4.189 markup-scan-out characters: Character class consisting of function characters that suppress markup recognition until the occurrence of a markup-scan-in character or entity end.

4.190 markup-scan-suppress characters: A character class consisting of function characters that suppress markup recognition for the immediately following character in the same entity (if any).

4.191 minimal SGML document: A conforming SGML document that uses the core concrete syntax throughout, no features, and the reference capacity set.

4.192 minimization feature: Markup minimization feature.

4.193 model: Content model.

4.194 model group: A component of a content model that specifies the order of occurrence of elements and character strings in an element's *content* [24] *320:1* , as modified by *exceptions* [138] *418:1* specified in the *content model* [126] *410:1* of the element and in the content models of other open elements.

4.195 multicode basic concrete syntax: A multicode variant of the basic concrete syntax in which markup is not recognized when code extension is in use.

4.196 multicode concrete syntax: A concrete syntax that allows code extension control characters to be SGML characters.

4.197 multicode core concrete syntax: A multicode variant of the core concrete syntax in which markup is not recognized when code extension is in use.

4.198 name: A name token whose first character is a name start character.

4.199 name character: A character that can occur in a name: name start characters, digits, and others designated by the concrete syntax.

4.200 name group: A group whose tokens are required to be names.

4.201 name start character: A character that can begin a name: letters, and others designated by the concrete syntax.

4.202 name token: A character string, consisting solely of name characters, whose length is restricted by the NAMELEN quantity.

NOTE — A name token that occurs in a group is also a token; one that occurs as an attribute value is not.

4.203 name token group: A group whose tokens are required to be name tokens.

4.204 named character reference: A character reference consisting of a delimited *function name* [63] *356:6* .

4.205 named entity reference: An entity reference consisting of a delimited name of a general entity or parameter entity (possibly qualified by a name group) that was declared by an entity declaration.

NOTE — A general entity reference can have an undeclared name if a default entity was declared.

4.206 naming rules parameter: A parameter of an SGML declaration that identifies additions to the standard name alphabet character classes and specifies the case substitution.

4.207 non-SGML character: A character in the document character set whose coded representation never occurs in an SGML entity.

4.208 non-SGML data entity: A data entity in which a non-SGML character could occur.

4.209 NONSGML: The class of non-SGML characters, defined by the document character set.

4.210 normalized length (of an attribute specification list): A length calculated by ignoring the actual characters used for delimiting and separating the components and counting an extra fixed number per component instead.

4.211 notation attribute: An attribute whose value is a *notation name* [41] *333:33* that identifies the data content notation of the element's *content* [24] *320:1* .

NOTE — A notation attribute does not apply when there is an explicit content reference, as the element's *content* [24] *320:1* will be empty.

4.212 notation declaration: A markup declaration that associates
2 a name with a notation identifier.

4.213 notation identifier: An *external identifier* [73] 379:1 that
4 identifies a data content notation in a *notation declaration*
[148] 426:15 . It can be a *public identifier* [74] 379:8 if the notation
6 is public, and, if not, a description or other information sufficient to
invoke a program to interpret the notation.

8 **4.214 notation name:** The name assigned to a data content
notation by a notation declaration.

10 **4.215 number:** A name token consisting solely of digits.

4.216 number token: A name token whose first character is a
12 digit.

NOTE — A number token that occurs in a group is also a token; one that
14 occurs as an attribute value is not.

4.217 numeric character reference: A character reference
16 consisting of a delimited *character number* [64] 357:1 .

4.218 object capacity: The capacity limit for a particular kind of
18 object, such as entities defined or characters of entity text.

4.219 omitted tag minimization parameter: A parameter of an
20 element declaration that specifies whether a technically valid
omission of a start-tag or end-tag is considered a reportable
22 markup error.

4.220 open element: An *element* [13] 308:1 whose *start-tag*
24 [14] 314:1 has occurred (or been omitted through markup minimization), but whose *end-tag* [19] 317:4 has not yet occurred (or
26 been omitted through markup minimization).

4.221 open entity: An entity that has been referenced but whose
28 entity end has not yet occurred.

4.222 open marked section declaration: A marked section
30 declaration whose *marked section start* [94] 392:3 has occurred
but whose *marked section end* [95] 392:6 has not yet occurred.

32 **4.223 owner identifier:** The portion of a public identifier that
identifies the owner or originator of public text.

NOTE — There are three kinds: ISO, registered, and unregistered.

4.224 parameter: The portion of a markup declaration that is bounded by ps separators (whether required or optional). A parameter can contain other parameters.

4.225 parameter entity: An entity that can be referenced from a markup declaration parameter.

4.226 parameter entity reference: A named entity reference to a parameter entity.

4.227 parameter literal: A parameter or token consisting of delimited replaceable parameter data.

4.228 parsed character data: Zero or more characters that occur in a context in which text is parsed and markup is recognized. They are classified as data characters because they were not recognized as markup during parsing.

4.229 PCDATA: Parsed character data.

4.230 PI entity: Processing instruction entity.

4.231 point: A unit of capacity measurement, roughly indicative of relative storage requirements.

4.232 procedure: Processing defined by an application to operate on elements of a particular type.

NOTES

1   A single procedure could be associated with more than one element type, and/or more than one procedure could operate on the same element type at different points in the document.

2   A procedure is usually part of a procedure set.

4.233 procedure set: The procedures that are used together for a given application process.

NOTE — In SGML applications, a procedure set usually constitutes the application processing for a link process definition.

4.234 processing instruction: Markup consisting of system-specific data that controls how a document is to be processed.

4.235 processing instruction entity: An entity whose text is treated as the *system data* [45] 339:5 of a *processing instruction* [44] 339:1 when referenced.

4.236 prolog: The portion of an SGML document or SGML subdocument entity that contains document type and link type declarations.

4.237 proper subelement: A subelement that is permitted by its containing element's model.

NOTE — An included subelement is not a proper subelement.

4.238 ps (separator): A parameter separator, occurring in markup declarations.

4.239 public identifier: A minimum literal that identifies public text.

NOTES

1 The public identifiers in a document can optionally be interpretable as formal public identifiers.

2 The system is responsible for converting public identifiers to system identifiers.

4.240 public text: Text that is known beyond the context of a single document or system environment, and which can be accessed with a public identifier.

NOTES

1 Examples are standard or registered document type definitions, entity sets, element sets, data content notations, and other markup constructs (see annex D 498).

2 Public text is not equivalent to published text; there is no implication of unrestricted public access. In particular, the owner of public text may choose to sell or license it to others, or to restrict its access to a single organization.

3 Public text simplifies access to shared constructs, reduces the amount of text that must be interchanged, and reduces the chance of copying errors.

4.241 public text class: The portion of a text identifier that

identifies the SGML markup construct to which the public text
conforms.

4.242 public text description: The portion of a text identifier that
describes the public text.

4.243 public text designating sequence: The portion of a text
identifier, used when public text is a character set, that contains an
ISO 2022 escape sequence that designates the set.

4.244 public text display version: An optional portion of a text
identifier that distinguishes among public text that has a common
public text description [87] *387:5* by describing the devices supported or coding scheme used. If omitted, the public text is not
device-dependent.

4.245 public text language: The portion of a text identifier that
specifies the natural language in which the public text was written.

NOTE — It can be the language of the data, comments, and/or defined
names.

4.246 quantity: A numeric restriction on some aspect of markup,
such as the maximum length of a name or the maximum nesting
level of open elements.

NOTE — Quantities are defined by the abstract syntax, but specific values
are assigned to them by the concrete syntax.

4.247 quantity set: A set of assignments of numeric values to
quantity names.

4.248 ranked element: An element whose *generic identifier*
[30] *325:17* is composed of a *rank stem* [120] *407:17* and a *rank
suffix* [121] *407:19* . When a ranked element begins, its *rank suffix*
[121] *407:19* becomes the current rank for its *rank stem*
[120] *407:17* , and for the rank stems in the *ranked group*
[119] *407:5* (if any) of which the *rank stem* [120] *407:17* is a member.

4.249 ranked group: A group of rank stems that share the same
current rank. When any ranked element whose stem is in the group
begins, its *rank suffix* [121] *407:19* becomes the current rank for all
rank stems in the group.

4.250 rank stem: A name from which a generic identifier can be
2 derived by appending a *rank suffix* ⌐ **[121]** *407:19* ⌐ .

4.251 rank suffix: A number that is appended to a rank stem to
4 form a *generic identifier* ⌐ **[30]** *325:17* ⌐ .

NOTE — The numbers are usually sequential, beginning with 1, so the
6 resulting generic identifiers suggest the relative ranks of their elements (for
example, H1, H2, and H3 for levels of heading elements, where "H" is the
8 rank stem).

4.252 record: A division of an SGML entity, bounded by a record
10 start and a record end character, normally corresponding to an
input line on a text entry device.

12 NOTES

1   It is called a "record" rather than a "line" to distinguish it from the output
14 lines created by a text formatter.

2   An SGML entity could consist of many records, a single record, or text
16 with no record boundary characters at all (which can be thought of as being
part of a record or without records, depending on whether record boundary
18 characters occur elsewhere in the document).

4.253 record boundary (character): The record start (*RS*) or
20 record end (*RE*) character.

4.254 record end: A *function character* ⌐ **[54]** *346:8* ⌐ , assigned by
22 the concrete syntax, that represents the end of a record.

4.255 record start: A *function character* ⌐ **[54]** *346:8* ⌐ , assigned by
24 the concrete syntax, that represents the start of a record.

4.256 reference: Markup that is replaced by other text, either an
26 entity or a single character.

4.257 reference capacity set: The capacity set defined in this
28 International Standard.

4.258 reference concrete syntax: A concrete syntax, defined in
30 this International Standard, that is used in all SGML declarations.

4.259 reference delimiter set: The delimiter set, defined in this
32 International Standard, that is used in the reference concrete
syntax.

4.260 reference quantity set: The quantity set defined by this
International Standard.

4.261 reference reserved name: A reserved name defined by this
International Standard.

4.262 registered owner identifier: An owner identifier that was
constructed in accordance with ISO 9070. It is unique among
registered owner identifiers, and is distinguishable from ISO owner
identifiers and unregistered owner identifiers.

4.263 replaceable character data: Character data in which a
general entity reference [59] 350:17 or *character reference*
[62] 356:1 is recognized and replaced.

NOTE — Markup that would terminate *replaceable character data*
[46] 343:1 is not recognized in the replacement text of entities referenced
within it.

4.264 replaceable parameter data: Character data in which a
parameter entity reference [60] 350:22 or *character reference*
[62] 356:1 is recognized and replaced.

NOTE — Markup that would terminate *replaceable parameter data*
[67] 373:8 is not recognized in the replacement text of entities referenced
within it.

4.265 replacement character: The character that replaces a
character reference [62] 356:1 .

4.266 replacement text: The text of the entity that replaces an
entity reference.

4.267 reportable markup error: A failure of a document to
conform to this International Standard when it is parsed with
respect to the active document and link types, other than a
semantic error (such as a generic identifier that does not accurately
connote the element type) or:
a) an ambiguous content model;
b) an exclusion that could change a token's required or optional
status in a model;
c) exceeding a capacity limit;
d) an error in the SGML declaration;

e) an otherwise allowable omission of a tag that creates an ambiguity;

f) the occurrence of a non-SGML character; or

g) a formal public identifier error.

4.268 required attribute: An attribute for which there must always be an *attribute specification* [32] *327:19* for the attribute value.

4.269 reserved name: A name defined by the concrete syntax, rather than by an application, such as a markup declaration name.

NOTE — Such names appear in this International Standard as syntactic literals (see 5.1 *290*).

4.270 reserved name use parameter: A parameter of the *SGML declaration* [171] *450:1* that specifies any replacement in the declared concrete syntax for a reference reserved name.

4.271 result document type (of a link): A document type, a new instance of which is created as the result of a link process.

4.272 result element type (of a link): An element that is defined in the result document type declaration.

4.273 s (separator): A separator, consisting of separator characters and other non-printing function characters, that occurs in markup and in *element content* [26] *320:10* .

4.274 satisfied token: A *content token* [128] *410:17* whose corresponding content has occurred.

4.275 SDATA entity: Specific character data entity.

4.276 separator: A character string that separates markup components from one another.

NOTES

1 There are four kinds *s* [5] *297:23* , *ds* [71] *376:1* , *ps* [65] *372:1* , and *ts* [70] *375:3* .

2 A separator cannot occur in data.

4.277 separator characters: A character class composed of function characters other than *RE*, *RS*, and *SPACE*, that are allowed in separators and that will be replaced by *SPACE* in those contexts in which *RE* is replaced by *SPACE*.

4.278 SGML: Standard Generalized Markup Language

4.279 SGML application: Rules that apply SGML to a text processing application. An SGML application includes a formal specification of the markup constructs used in the application, expressed in SGML. It can also include a non-SGML definition of semantics, application conventions, and/or processing.

NOTES

1   The formal specification of an SGML application normally includes document type definitions, data content notations, and entity sets, and possibly a concrete syntax or capacity set. If processing is defined by the application, the formal specification could also include link process definitions.

2   The formal specification of an SGML application constitutes the common portions of the documents processed by the application. These common portions are frequently made available as public text.

3   The formal specification is usually accompanied by comments and/or documentation that explains the semantics, application conventions, and processing specifications of the application.

4   An SGML application exists independently of any implementation. However, if processing is defined by the application, the non-SGML definition could include application procedures, implemented in a programming or text processing language.

4.280 SGML character: A character that is permitted in an SGML entity.

4.281 SGML declaration: A markup declaration that specifies the character set, concrete syntax, optional features, and capacity requirements of a document's markup. It applies to all of the SGML entities of a document.

4.282 SGML document: A document that is represented as a sequence of characters, organized physically into an entity structure and logically into an element structure, essentially as described in this International Standard. An SGML document consists of data characters, which represent its information content, and markup characters, which represent the structure of the data and other information useful for processing it. In particular, the markup describes at least one document type definition, and an instance of a structure conforming to the definition.

4.283 SGML document entity: The SGML entity that begins an SGML document. It contains, at a minimum, an SGML declaration, a base document type declaration, and the start and end (if not all) of a base document element.

4.284 SGML entity: An entity whose characters are interpreted as markup or data in accordance with this International Standard.

NOTE — There are three types of SGML entity: *SGML document entity* [2] *295:13* , *SGML subdocument entity* [3] *296:1* , and *SGML text entity* [4] *296:5* .

4.285 SGML parser: A program (or portion of a program or a combination of programs) that recognizes markup in SGML documents.

NOTE — If an analogy were to be drawn to programming language processors, an SGML parser would be said to perform the functions of both a lexical analyzer and a parser with respect to SGML documents.

4.286 SGML subdocument entity: An SGML entity that conforms to the SGML declaration of the SGML document entity, while conforming to its own document type and link type declarations. It contains, at a minimum, a base document type declaration and the start and end of a base document element.

4.287 SGML system: A system that includes an SGML parser, an entity manager, and both or either of:
  a) an implementation of one or more SGML applications; and/or
  b) facilities for a user to implement SGML applications, with access to the SGML parser and entity manager.

4.288 SGML text entity: An SGML entity that conforms to the SGML declaration of the SGML document entity, and to the document type and link type declarations to which the entity from which it is referenced conforms.

4.289 shift function: In graphic repertoire code extension, a control sequence or control character that invokes a graphic character set.

NOTE — There are two kinds: single shift and locking shift.

4.290 short reference (delimiter): Short reference string.

4.291 short reference delimiter role: A delimiter role to which zero or more strings can be assigned by the concrete syntax. When a short reference string is recognized, it is replaced by the general entity to whose name it is mapped in the current map, or is treated as a separator or data if it is mapped to nothing.

4.292 (short reference) map: A named set of associations, declared by a _short reference mapping declaration_ ⌈[150] _429:8_⌉ , in which each short reference delimiter is mapped to a general entity name or to nothing.

4.293 short reference mapping declaration: A markup declaration that defines a short reference map.

4.294 short reference set: A set of short reference mapping, short reference use, and entity declarations that are used together.

NOTE — A short reference set can be public text.

4.295 short reference (string): A character string assigned to the short reference delimiter role by the concrete syntax.

4.296 short reference use declaration: A markup declaration that associates a short reference map with one or more element types, or identifies a new current map for the current element.

4.297 shunned character (number): A character number, identified by a concrete syntax, that should be avoided in documents employing the syntax because some systems might erroneously treat it as a control character.

4.298 significant SGML character: A _markup character_ ⌈[51] _345:4_⌉ or _minimum data_ ⌈[77] _381:8_⌉ character.

4.299 simple link (process definition): A link process definition in which the result element types and their attributes are all implied by the application, and link attribute values can be specified only for the source document element.

4.300 single shift: A shift function that applies to the following character only.

4.301 source document type (of a link): A document type, an existing instance of which is the source of a link process.

4.302 source element type (of a link): An element type that is
2 defined in the source document type declaration.

4.303 space: A *function character* [54] 346:8 , assigned by the
4 concrete syntax, that represents a space.

4.304 specific character data entity: An entity whose text is
6 treated as *system data* [45] 339:5 when referenced. The text is
dependent on a specific system, device, or application process.

8 NOTE — A specific character data entity would normally be redefined for
different applications, systems, or output devices.

10 **4.305 Standard Generalized Markup Language:** A language for
document representation that formalizes markup and frees it of
12 system and processing dependencies.

4.306 start-tag: Descriptive markup that identifies the start of an
14 element and specifies its generic identifier and attributes.

4.307 status keyword: A marked section declaration parameter
16 that specifies whether the marked section is to be ignored and, if
not, whether it is to be treated as character data, replaceable
18 character data, or normally.

4.308 string: Character string.

20 **4.309 subelement:** An element that occurs in the content of
another element (the "containing element") in such a way that the
22 subelement begins when the containing element is the current
element.

24 **4.310 syntax-reference character set:** A character set,
designated by a concrete syntax and known to all potential users of
26 the syntax, that contains every significant SGML character. It
enables a concrete syntax to be defined without regard to the
28 particular document or system character sets with which it might be
used.

30 **4.311 system character set:** The character set used in an SGML
system.

32 **4.312 system declaration:** A declaration, included in the
documentation for a conforming SGML system, that specifies the
34 features, capacity set, concrete syntaxes, and character set that

the system supports, and any validation services that it can perform.

4.313 system identifier: System data that specifies the file identifier, storage location, program invocation, data stream position, or other system-specific information that locates an external entity.

4.314 tag: Descriptive markup.

NOTE — There are two kinds: start-tag and end-tag.

4.315 target element: An element whose *generic identifier* [30] *325:17* is specified in a *data tag group* [133] *415:16* .

4.316 text: Characters.

NOTE — The characters could have their normal character set meaning, or they could be interpreted in accordance with a data content notation as the representation of graphics, images, etc.

4.317 text identifier: The portion of a public identifier that identifies a public text so that it can be distinguished from any other public text with the same owner identifier.

NOTE — It consists of a *public text class* [86] *386:5* , an optional *unavailable text indicator* [85] *385:17* , a *public text description* [87] *387:5* , a *public text language* [88] *388:1* , and an optional *public text display version* [90] *390:1* .

4.318 text processing application: A related set of processes performed on documents of related types.

NOTE — Some examples are:
a) Publication of technical manuals for a software developer: document types include installation, operation, and maintenance manuals; processes include creation, revision, formatting, and page layout for a variety of output devices.
b) Preparation of manuscripts by independent authors for members of an association of publishers: document types include book, journal, and article; creation is the only defined process, as each publisher has its own methods of formatting and printing.
c) Office correspondence: document types include memos, mail logs, and reports; processes include creation, revision, simple formatting, storage and retrieval, memo log update, and report generation.

4.319 token: The portion of a group, including a complete nested group (but not a *connector* ⸢ [131] *413:4* ⸣), that is, or could be, bounded by ts separators.

4.320 total capacity: A limit on the sum of all object capacities.

4.321 ts (separator): A token separator, occurring in groups.

4.322 type definition: Document type definition.

4.323 unavailable public text: Public text that is available only to a limited population, selected by its owner.

4.324 unique identifier: A *name* ⸢ [55] *346:17* ⸣ that uniquely identifies an element.

4.325 unregistered owner identifier: An owner identifier that can be distinguished from registered owner identifiers and ISO owner identifiers. As it is not constructed according to a registration standard, it could duplicate another unregistered owner identifier.

4.326 upper-case letters: Character class composed of the 26 capital letters from "A" through "Z".

4.327 upper-case name characters: Character class consisting of the upper-case forms of the corresponding lower-case name characters.

4.328 upper-case name start characters: Character class consisting of the upper-case forms of the corresponding lower-case name start characters.

4.329 validating SGML parser: A conforming SGML parser that can find and report a reportable markup error if (and only if) one exists.

4.330 variant concrete syntax: A concrete syntax other than the reference concrete syntax or core concrete syntax.

4.331 variant (conforming) SGML document: A conforming SGML document that uses a variant concrete syntax.

4.332 virtual character set: In graphic repertoire code extension, one of the character sets, known as G0, G1, G2, or G3, that represents the mapping of a real graphic character set, designated

by an escape sequence, to a document code set position
2   previously announced by an escape sequence.

Clause 5
Notation

This clause describes the typographic conventions employed in ISO 8879, and the notation that is used to define the SGML language formally.

NOTE — This clause describes the notation used in this International Standard to define the Standard Generalized Markup Language. This notation is not part of SGML itself (although there are some similarities between them), and therefore this clause should be considered as affecting only the presentation of this International Standard, not the substance.

The SGML abstract syntax is specified by formal syntax productions, each of which defines a "syntactic variable". A production consists of a reference number (in square brackets), the name of the syntactic variable being defined, an equals sign, and an expression that constitutes the definition.

[number] syntactic variable = expression

The expression is composed of one or more "syntactic tokens", parenthesized expressions, and symbols that define the ordering and selection among them.

5.1 Syntactic Tokens

The following list shows the syntactic token types using the typographic conventions employed for them in this International Standard, together with the source of their definitions:

syntactic variable. A syntactic token that is defined by a syntax production.

"SYNTACTIC LITERAL". A syntactic token consisting of a reserved name that is to be entered in markup exactly as it is shown in the syntax production, except that corresponding lower-case letters can be used if upper-case translation of general names is specified by the concrete syntax. Syntactic literals are defined whenever they occur in a syntax production, and the definition is applicable only in the context of that production.

delimiter role. A syntactic token that represents a delimiter string. Delimiter roles are defined in figure 3 [360] , which also lists the strings assigned to general delimiter roles by the reference concrete syntax. Strings assigned to the **shortref** delimiter role are shown in figure 4 [364] .

TERMINAL VARIABLE. A syntactic token that represents a character class whose members are not necessarily the same in all SGML documents. Terminal variables whose members are assigned by the concrete syntax are defined in figure 2 [345] . (The **NONSGML** variable, whose members are assigned by the document character set, is defined in 13.1.2 [455] .)

Terminal Constant. A syntactic token that represents either an entity end signal, or a character class whose members are the same in all SGML documents. Terminal constants are defined in figure 1 [345] .

5.2 Ordering and Selection Symbols

If there is more than one syntactic token in an expression, the ordering and selection among them is determined by symbols that connect them, as follows:

,   All must occur, in the order shown.
&   All must occur, in any order.
| One and only one must occur.

Each selected syntactic token must occur once and only once unless the contrary is indicated by a suffix consisting of one of the following symbols:

?   Optional (0 or 1 time).
+   Required and repeatable (1 or more times).
*   Optional and repeatable (0 or more times).

2 Successive instances of a syntactic token are deemed to be repetitions of a repeatable token, where permissible, rather than instances of multiple tokens.

4 The occurrence suffixes are applied first, then the ordering connectors. Parentheses can be used as in mathematics to change

6 these priorities.

Clause 6
Entity Structure

People who work with long documents invariably want to break them into smaller pieces. There may be a number of people working on different parts; or, for practical reasons, there may be a need to distinguish portions that came from a scanner or are graphical from parts that are character text.

> **T–B.2** *21*
> **O–4.282** *132:3*

6.1 SGML Document

SGML has no restrictions on whether the character text, graphics, or other notations comprising a document are in separate units of storage on a physical system or in a single file. (Some word processing systems, for example, are capable of mixing different notations within a single file.) On the other hand, in a system where it is necessary to keep arbitrary binary data, such as raster or geometric graphics, in separate files from one another and from your character text, each entity can be a separate file in a file system. The techniques for this storage are considered an implementation decision.

Whether or not they are stored in one physical object, then, component entities — text or graphics or whatever — are considered to be a single SGML document. At the same time, they are considered to be in separate entities because the entity boundaries are used to distinguish between different notations. The SGML parser must be able to tell whether to parse an entity, or to pass it directly to an application for processing.

> **O–4.134** *179:3*

Three operational levels may be distinguished:
— At the document level, everything is part of a single logical structure. During a production process, for example, all entities will be handled appropriately and, on the printed page, all traces of the separateness of entities will have disappeared.

— At the entity level, what will be handled separately and how is controlled by the application and user decisions during the writing and editing process.

— At the implementation level, the system designer decides whether all the entities are in one file or are in separate files.

One method for combining the entities into a single storage object while still maintaining the entity structure is defined in a separate international standard, ISO 9069, the SGML Document Interchange Format (SDIF). In SDIF, the entities are essentially concatenated together. Some systems might prefer to store an entity at the first point where it is referenced, and that is possible also. All of this is done below the level of the SGML parser, in what is called the entity manager. $\boxed{\text{O–4.123 } 129{:}9}$
$\boxed{\text{A–15.6.3 } 492{:}33}$

An SGML document does not have to be the only thing in a data stream. The Standard does not constrain what may precede or follow an SGML document and therefore you can take an entire SGML document and have it be a portion of some other document that is encoded in some other way entirely.

The major division of entities is into SGML entities and data entities.

An *SGML document* $\boxed{\text{[1] } 294{:}5}$ is physically organized in an entity
2   structure. The first entity is an *SGML document entity* $\boxed{\text{[2] } 295{:}13}$; it
    contains entity references that indicate where the other entities
4   belong with respect to it.
$\boxed{\text{O–4.283 } 142{:}1}$

    [1] SGML document =
6   *SGML document entity,* $\boxed{\text{[2] } 295{:}13}$
            (*SGML subdocument entity* | $\boxed{\text{[3] } 296{:}1}$
8   *SGML text entity* | $\boxed{\text{[4] } 296{:}5}$
            character data entity | $\boxed{\text{[5.1] } 300{:}1}$
10   *specific character data entity* | $\boxed{\text{[5.2] } 300{:}4}$
            non-SGML data entity   )* $\boxed{\text{[6] } 300{:}7}$

NOTES

2   1   This International Standard does not constrain the physical organization of the document within the data stream, message handling protocol, file
4   system, etc., that contains it. In particular, separate entities could occur in
the same physical object, a single entity could be divided between multiple
6   objects, and the objects could occur in any order.

  2   This International Standard does not constrain the characters that can
8   occur in a data stream outside of the SGML entities. Such characters would
be interpreted according to applicable standards and conventions.

10   3   The SGML Document Interchange Format (SDIF) standardized in ISO
9069 allows an SGML document to be managed conveniently as a single
12   object, while still preserving the entity structure.

6.2 SGML Entities

An SGML entity is one that is parsed in accordance with the SGML
standard. In the course of doing so, the parser is distinguishing the
markup — the special characters that contain information intended for
the parser to understand — from those characters which are the actual
data to be processed by the application.

The SGML standard does not dictate which characters will indicate
the markup in an SGML entity. The SGML declaration defines them as
part of the concrete syntax.

> **O–4.48** *136:1*
> **A–13.4** *457:24*

As this sub-clause indicates, there are three kinds of SGML entity:
SGML document entity, SGML subdocument entity, and SGML text
entity.

    [2] SGML document entity =
14   *s**,   **[5]** *297:23*
        SGML declaration,   **[171]** *450:1*
16   *prolog*,   **[7]** *303:1*
        document instance set,   **[10]** *306:10*
18   ***Ee***

All of the rules that the SGML parser follows are laid out at the beginning of an SGML document entity.

> **O–4.283** *142:1*

An SGML document entity contains an SGML declaration, a prolog, and a document instance set. The SGML declaration defines the concrete syntax. The prolog contains the application-specific rules for the parser: the document type definitions and link process definitions. The prolog is followed by the document instance set, which contains an instance of one or more of the defined document types.

> **T–B.14.1** *63*
> **O–4.236** *143:1*
> **A–7.1** *302:1*

```
     [3] SGML subdocument entity =
2          prolog,                                    [7] 303:1
           document instance set,                     [10] 306:10
4          Ee
```

An SGML subdocument entity differs from the SGML document entity only in that it must use the same concrete syntax as the entity from which it is referenced. It can have its own application-specific definitions, but assumes the current SGML declaration. At the same time, the SGML subdocument entity, because it has its own prolog, sets up its own name space completely. It cannot refer to the element types and attributes and IDs and entities that are defined in the SGML entity from which it was referenced, nor can that entity refer to any names that are defined within the subdocument.

The subdocument can be thought of as analogous to a function defined in a programming language that has only local variables and no ability to refer to any global variables defined by the calling function. There are techniques that an application can use to reference names internal to a subdocument from elsewhere in the document, but those are outside the scope of the SGML parser itself.

```
     [4] SGML text entity =
6          SGML character*,                           [50] 345:1
           Ee
```

An SGML text entity, unlike an SGML subdocument entity, is governed by the same application-specific rules and the same syntax rules as the entity from which it is referenced. Therefore, all of the components that have been defined in the referencing entity — such as element types, entity names, and unique identifiers — will apply to the referenced SGML text entities.

This sub-clause also spells out the order of the testing of a character to see whether it is markup or data. In so doing it defines a ubiquitous class of characters called "s separators".

The characters of an SGML entity are parsed in accordance with
2 this International Standard to recognize the *SGML declaration*
[171] *450:1* , *prolog* [7] *303:1* , and *document instance set*
4 [10] *306:10* , and their constituent parts.

Each *SGML character* [50] *345:1* is parsed in the order it occurs, in
6 the following manner:
  a) The character is tested to see if it is part of a delimiter string
8   (see 9.6 357). If a general delimiter string is recognized, the
      ensuing markup is parsed (see item d 297:17 , below). If a
10   short reference is recognized, it is treated as specified in 9.4.6
      353 .
12 b) If the character is not part of a delimiter string, or it is part of
      an unmapped short reference, it is tested to see if it is a sepa-
14   rator; if so, it is ignored.
  c) If the character is not part of a delimiter or a separator, it is
16   treated as data.
  d) Within markup, a character is tested to see if it is part of a del-
18   imiter string, a separator, delimited literal data, or a token (see
      9.6.6 364).

20 If an *SGML character* [50] *345:1* is a *function character*
   [54] *346:8* , its function is performed in addition to any other treat-
22 ment it may receive.

6.2.1 S Separator

An *s* [5] *297:23* separator is blank space that is inserted by the user to "format" an SGML document — that is, to make it more readable and convenient for editing and revision. An *s* [5] *297:23* separator could be significant to the SGML parser as a means of separating markup constructs, such as declaration parameters, from one another, or it could be redundant. In either case, it is never treated as data for the application to process.

O–4.273 *139:7*
A–10.1 *370:5*

[5] s =
24   **SPACE** |
          RE |

RS |

2   ***SEPCHAR***

An *SGML character* ⎡ **[50]** *345:1* ⎤ is not considered part of an *s*
4   ⎡ **[5]** *297:23* ⎤ if it can be interpreted as some other markup. If it is
considered part of an *s* ⎡ **[5]** *297:23* ⎤ it is ignored.

6.2.2 Entity End

A system must be able to indicate to an SGML parser that an entity is
ended. The entity end is the signal to the parser to resume parsing from
the end of the original entity reference. Just as the storage represention of
entities is not defined by the standard, however, representation of the
entity end will depend on the characteristics of the system:

⎡ **O–4.122** *182:1* ⎤

— A character may be used, but only if it is guaranteed not to show up
   in the SGML entities. Accordingly, during the creation of the SGML
   declaration, attention must be paid to the declaration of the non-
   SGML characters; it is only one of those whose bit combination can
   be used for representing an entity end.

— In the case where no such bit combinations are available, a system
   can represent the entity end by counting the length of the entity and
   simply indicating through a return code or some other means that
   the entity has ended. In other words, in that situation, no bit combination (that is, no special character) would have to be dedicated to
   fulfilling the role of the entity end.

The choice between these techniques is a matter left to the implementer. All that the SGML parser cares about is that, upon recognizing
an entity reference, it can have the entity manager begin processing in
that entity, and that finally it can be told that the entity has ended.

⎡ **O–4.123** *129:9* ⎤

6   An ***Ee*** is an entity end signal.

     NOTE — An ***Ee*** is not a character and is never treated as data. It can occur
8   only where expressly permitted.

A system can represent an *Ee* in any manner that will allow it to be
2 distinguished from SGML characters.

NOTE — For example, an *Ee* could be represented by the bit combination
4 of a non-SGML character, if any have been assigned.

6.2.3 Implied SGML Declaration

Although the definition of an SGML document entity says that it must
include an SGML declaration, in a given system environment, the SGML
declaration is likely to be omitted. The real purpose of the SGML declaration is to state what capabilities are required of the SGML parser, in the
sense of saying "Here are the concrete syntax and the quantity restrictions and so on to which this document conforms."

In practice, one can assume that in any given system, one concrete
syntax would be used for all documents. A document would be
translated if it were brought into that environment from a system built
on a different concrete syntax.

It remains to be seen whether this assumption will remain valid for
non-Latin character sets, and for mixing non-Latin documents with
Latin-alphabet documents. Should it prove necessary for the average
implementation of SGML to be able to deal with multiple concrete syntaxes simultaneously, then it may be appropriate in the future to parti-
tion the SGML declaration so that particular aspects of a concrete syntax
can easily be modified. The topic, clearly, needs future study based on
the experience of users over the next few years.

While a document is processed exclusively by a single system, the
6 system can imply the *SGML declaration* [171] *450:1* . The declaration must be present explicitly, however, if the document is subse-
8 quently sent to another system.

6.3 Data Entities

Data entities are not parsed by an SGML parser. They are passed
directly to an application, which uses a notation parameter to determine
the nature of the processing that must take place.

The standard distinguishes among three kinds of data entity: character
data entity, specific character data entity, and non-SGML data entity.

```
    [5.1] character data entity =
2          SGML character*,                          [50] 345:1
           Ee
```

A character data entity is in a notation that is not system-specific and therefore can be transported to other environments without change.

> T–B.13.1 *58*
> O–4.34 *145:17*

```
4   [5.2] specific character data entity =
           SGML character*,                          [50] 345:1
6          Ee
```

A specific character data entity is like a processing instruction: it contains material in a notation that is understood by the particular processing system in which the document exists. The assumption is that a specific character data entity would not be transferred to another environment. If it were transferred, it would have to be modified, perhaps by humans who would create their own specific character data entity containing the commands native to their own processing system.

> O–4.304 *146:2*

```
    [6] non-SGML data entity =
8          character*,                               [49] 344:5
           Ee
```

A non-SGML data entity could contain anything. By differentiating non-SGML data from SGML data, one is effectively saying: "It is not safe to have this entity examined in any way by an SGML parser; the entity may contain bit combinations which have been declared to be non-SGML characters and which therefore may be reserved by the system to indicate, for example, an end-of-file or some other condition, which, if it were misinterpreted, might be dangerous."

> T–B.13.1.2 *59*
> O–4.208 *146:8*

The distinction between the non-SGML data entity, the character data entity, and the specific character data entity is there in case you want to use SGML-based utilities to deal with these entities in some fashion other than the normal processing of them as part of an SGML document. For example, a utility that counted words might be able to process a character data entity without being able to interpret its notation, but probably could not process a non-SGML data entity.

The interpretation of any of these data entities is governed by a declared data content notation. As far as SGML is concerned, anything can go on in a data entity, including references to other entities, but the notation in which all of these things is expressed is a notation other than the SGML markup defined in ISO 8879.

T–B.13.2 *60*

O–4.75 *139:15*

NOTE — A data entity is declared with a notation parameter that identifies
2   how the data is to be interpreted.

The purpose of declaring a data content notation is to associate it with a program. During the processing of the document, when an implementation recognizes a reference to a data entity, it can look up the notation declaration and find, in the external identifier, the name of a program that interprets that data. It can then invoke that program to process the data and pass the appropriate information on to the application.

Clause 7
Element Structure

Entities, as discussed in clause 6 (293), are essentially objects of convenience. There may be little or no relationship between what a reader or a writer might intuitively think of as a document's organizational structure and the same document's entity structure — the set of files, images, textual substitutions, and so on, that reflect the bits and pieces that went into its creation.

It is coincidence if the entity structure matches the organizational, or "element", structure; more likely, they are superimposed in a haphazard manner — two different ways of viewing the same document.

The element structure consists of objects organized into one or more hierarchies; each hierarchy conforms to a document type definition. This "document type definition" is an abstraction, the description of a class of documents that an application designer is using SGML to represent. The document type declaration, which is part of the prolog, is the set of statements that rigorously describes that definition. The document type definition, usually abbreviated "DTD", is what makes the term "conform" meaningful in SGML.

T–B.4 *26*

O–4.113 *133:5*

7.1 Prolog

Parsing cannot occur in a vacuum. In order to make sense out of a document, it must be parsed with respect to some model that defines what is allowed in the document. In SGML, that information is contained in the prolog.

Although the prolog may contain other constructs, at a minimum there will be one document type declaration, called the "base" document type declaration. In a typical application without optional features, that will be the only document type declaration in the prolog. Parsing is done with respect to that base document type declaration.

> T–B.12 *56*
>
> O–4.236 *143:1*
>
> A–11.1 *402:1*

```
     [7] prolog =
2              other prolog*,
               base document type declaration,
4              ( document type declaration |
                 other prolog  )*,
6              ( link type declaration |
                 other prolog  )*

8  [8] other prolog =
               comment declaration |
10             processing instruction |
               s

12 [9] base document type declaration =
               document type declaration
```

> [8] *303:8*
>
> [9] *303:12*
>
> [110] *403:1*
>
> [8] *303:8*
>
> [154] *434:1*
>
> [8] *303:8*

> [91] *391:1*
>
> [44] *339:1*
>
> [5] *297:23*

> [110] *403:1*

The rest of 7.1 is significant only when using an optional feature of SGML that allows more than one document type declaration or that allows one or more link type declarations. Either "CONCUR" (the concurrent document instance feature) or "EXPLICIT" (which stands for the explicit link feature) must be indicated as being supported in the SGML declaration.

> T–B.14.1 *63*
>
> O–4.281 *135:16*
>
> A–13 *450:1*

There are three SGML link features: simple, implicit and explicit, and each of these features has different implications for what can occur in the prolog. If any of these features are used, the prolog can have any number of link type declarations in it. When it is time to process the document the user has to communicate to the system in some fashion which of the link type declarations are to be active with respect to this particular processing of the document.

> T–C.2 *87*
>
> O–4.171 *173:1*
>
> A–12.1 *433:1*

In the case of the concurrent document instance feature, there are not only multiple document type declarations in the prolog, but also instances of those document types in the SGML document entity — that is, there are multiple document elements (entire element structures) in the entity at one time. As a result it is necessary for the user to indicate to the system which of those document types are going to be active for any given processing of the document. That way the system knows how to match the document with the document type declarations for parsing.

In summary, there are three ways to parse a document:

a) With respect to the base document type alone (the common, simple case); or

b) With respect to the base document type and one or more active link types; or

c) With respect to two or more active document types. In that case, for the base document type to be one of them, it must be named as an active document type.

Note the distinction between base document type and active document type. The term "active document type" is only significant if the concurrent instance feature is being used to parse two or more document types at the same time. In all other cases — whether or not the link feature is being used — only the base document type matters.

T–C.3.1 *88*

O–4.101 *144:5*

A–13.5.3 *473:28*

The original idea behind the CONCUR feature was to allow the results of one or more formatting processes to coexist with the unformatted source document. Savings in storage could be obtained if there was minimal difference in the text between source and result; that is, little boilerplate generated and an essentially one-to-one mapping between source character codes and font glyph identifiers. These conditions frequently obtain in simple word processing applications (so-called "formatted processable" documents).

In light of this expected use of CONCUR, it was reasonable to assume that there would no longer be direct human manipulation of the document once one or more concurrent instances were generated, since changing the source would require the document to be reprocessed in order for the (presumably formatted) concurrent instances to be accurate. As a result, certain awkward implications of CONCUR were deemed acceptable. For example, strings that are recognized as short references in the base document instance will be treated as data in the others unless protected by a suitable marked section. It was expected that the formatter would generate such marked sections during processing.

I therefore recommend that CONCUR not be used to create multiple logical views of a document, such as verse-oriented and speech-oriented views of poetry. Hypertext links are more appropriate for such applications, and can be created easily by taking advantage of unique identifiers and external references.[1]

2   An SGML document or subdocument entity conforms to the document type and link process definitions that are specified by the document type and link type declarations, respectively, in its *prolog*

4   [7] 303:1 . An SGML text entity conforms to the *prolog* [7] 303:1 to which the entity from which it is referenced conforms. An SGML

6   entity is parsed with respect to its base document type and any active link types unless one or more active document types are

8   identified, in which case it is parsed only with respect to them.

   NOTE — The system normally identifies the active document and link types

10   to the SGML parser during initialization (see F.2 548).

   Document type declarations in addition to the base are permitted

12   only if "CONCUR YES" or "EXPLICIT YES" is specified on the *SGML declaration* [171] 450:1 . There can be an active document

14   type only if "CONCUR YES" is specified on the *SGML declaration* [171] 450:1 . The base document type can be active only if at least

16   one other document type is active.

   NOTE — Parsing with respect to the base document type alone is accom-

18   plished by not identifying an active document type.

There are rules concerning the number of link type declarations that can be active at one time. For simple links, that limit is expressed on the SGML declaration. For implicit links, only one can be active, while for explicit links several can be active if they form a chain of processes.

The intention is that simple links be used to set up background parameters for the processing. For example, one simple link declaration could specify properties of the output printer, while another establishes general page layout parameters.

Simple links could suffice for an application. However, for processing specifications to be context-sensitive — that is, to vary at different places in the element structure — implicit or explicit links must be used. These declarations can be used alone, or in conjunction with simple links.

   There can be an active link type for an entity if it has at least one

20   link process definition. The possibility of simultaneous active link types depends on the class of link type, as follows:

---

[1] The "Hypermedia/Time-based Document Representation Language (HyTime)" is an American National Standard, in development as of this writing, that includes a core of SGML element definitions for hypertext links.

simple		More than one simple link type can be active, in
2		addition to any implicit and explicit links.
implicit		Only one can be active.
4	**explicit**	More than one can be active only if they form a
		chain of processes in which the source document
6		type of the first is the base document type, the
		source document type of the second is the result
8		document type of the first, etc. The last link type
		in the chain can be an implicit link.

7.2 Document Element

The discussion of SGML documents in Clause 6 sets the stage for this clause. For all practical purposes, an SGML document consists of an optional SGML declaration, a prolog (which contains DTDs) and instances of the document types defined in the prolog. In the common straightforward case, there is only a single DTD (the "base") and an instance of it. The instance of the first (or only) DTD is what you might consider (informally!) to be the "real document".

> O–4.101 *144:5*

The document element is the highest level element in a document. The document element for this book, for example, is "handbook", which in turn contains the elements front matter, body, appendices and rear matter.

```
10   [10] document instance set =
              base document element,              [11] 306:13
12            other prolog*                        [8] 303:8

     [11] base document element =
14            document element                    [12] 306:15

     [12] document element =
16            element                             [13] 308:1
```

Some of the terminology here may be somewhat misleading. Although the syntactic variables have names such as "document element" and "base element" in fact what they are describing is the entire one-dimensional character string that represents an element structure. For this reason, productions 10 and 11 may seem strange; the document instance set appears to have only a single document element in it. This is correct: in cases in which there are concurrent instances, the character strings which are the tags that identify the other document elements are all contained within the base document element.

7.2.1 Limits

The limits clause is poorly worded. The word "instances" in the phrase "instances of document type declarations" means document instances — entire document elements that occur in the document instance set. It doesn't mean occurrences of document type declarations.

> 2   Instances of document type declarations other than the base are permitted only to the limit specified on the "CONCUR" parameter of the *SGML declaration* [171] 450:1 .

There really is no limitation on the number of document types that can be declared in the prolog. What is limited is the number of full-blown instances of those document types that can occur in the document instance set. The number of document type declarations in the prolog is in fact unlimited as long as multiple document type declarations are permitted at all.

7.3 Element

An element has a start-tag, content, and an end-tag, but there are situations in which any one of those might not be there.

The syntax production shows content as required because technically the content always exists, even if it is empty and looks as if it isn't there.

O-4.53 *149:10*

There are several reasons to have such an "empty" element as a placeholder for content that will be generated. A table of contents or an index in a publishing application, for example, might be created from other text. Alternatively, the element might be a marker for a figure that will be brought in by the system during composition or pasted in by a human. A third type of empty element can act as a "point", signifying the location of a footnote reference, for example, or of endpoints in a hypertext link.

T–B.4.2 *27*

For reasons of common sense — and, as the note points out, this has nothing to do with markup minimization— when an element is declared to be empty then the end-tag must be omitted. This is the one case in

SGML when it is not right to include full markup.

```
      [13] element =
2                 start-tag?,                                    [14] 314:1
                  content,                                       [24] 320:1
4                 end-tag?                                       [19] 317:4
```

If an element has a *declared content* [125] 409:3 of "EMPTY", or
6   an explicit content reference, the *end-tag* [19] 317:4 must be omitted.

8   NOTE — This requirement has nothing to do with markup minimization.

T–B.10 53

7.3.1 Omitted Tag Minimization

The rather legalistic wording of this clause states that omitted tag minimization is possible only when the OMITTAG feature is specified on the
SGML declaration, and only if an ambiguity is not created when the tag
is omitted. However, the rules in the clause pretty much make it impossible for an omitted tag to create an ambiguity. The wording here was just
a safety net.

O–4.187 162:7
A–13.5.1 471:12

A tag can be omitted only as provided in this sub-sub-clause, and
10   only if the omission would not create an ambiguity, and if
"OMITTAG YES" is specified on the *SGML declaration* [171] 450:1 .

12   NOTE — A document type definition may consider a technically valid omission to be a markup error (see 11.2.2 408).

As the note points out, the document type designer might still prohibit
users from minimization even when the standard permits it and no
ambiguity would be created. However, an SGML parser applies the rules
for omission in 7.3.1 without consideration of what the document type
definition says about tag omission for any elements.

7.3.1.1 Start-tag Omission

The rules about start-tag omission can be summarized informally: A start-tag can be omitted only for an element that must occur when any other elements that could occur at the same time are optional. In other words, it is not unreasonable to assume that the element that must come along at some point is the one we do not have the start-tag to identify.

> **T–C.1.2.5** *74*
>
> **O–4.59** *163:1*

During the development of the standard there was a lot of controversy over whether start-tag omission should be allowed for the element y in the following example:

```
<!ELEMENT x    - O (y*) >
<!ELEMENT y    O O (#PCDATA) >
```

The idea was rejected because even though nothing could occur within element x except y's, no y had to occur. Therefore, a conflict would be created in the following case:

```
<!ELEMENT document  - - (x, z) >
<!ELEMENT x              - O (y*) >
<!ELEMENT (y|z)       O O (#PCDATA) >
```

if the text were:

```
<x><y>some data</y>additional data
```

By the rule in the standard, the additional data would imply a z element, not a y element, because z is contextually required at that point. The z would itself imply the end of the x.

There are some cases where you cannot omit a start-tag even where it would otherwise be allowed:

a) If there is a required attribute because, obviously, there would be no way to specify the attribute.

> **O–4.268** *156:4*

b) If the element is subject to specialized parsing. For example, if the element contains declared content such as character data or replaceable character data, there is no way to know that the parser must respond differently unless the start-tag is there. As another instance of this general principle, you cannot omit a start-tag if the content

begins with a short reference string and the mapping of that string
is changed by the element's short reference map.

O–4.33 *140:9*

c) If that particular instance of the element has empty content. In that
case, there would either be no visible evidence that the element has
occurred at all, or else you would have the strange situation of having an end-tag without a start-tag.

The *start-tag* [14] *314:1* can be omitted if the element is a contex-
2   tually required element and any other elements that could occur are
contextually optional elements, except if:
4   a)   the element type has a required attribute or *declared content*
[125] *409:3* ; or
6   b)   the *content* [24] *320:1* of the instance of the element is
empty.

8   It is ambiguous to omit the start-tag of an element whose content
begins with a short reference string whose mapping is changed by
10 the element's associated short reference map.

An omitted *start-tag* [14] *314:1* is treated as having an empty *attri-*
12 *bute specification list* [31] *327:17* .

7.3.1.2 End-tag Omission

Basically an end-tag can be omitted either:

a)   when a document has come to an end; or

b)   when an element that contains this one has ended; or

c)   when something (for example, data or an element) shows up that is
not allowed inside the current element.

T–C.1.2.3 *73*

The *end-tag* [19] *317:4* can be omitted for an element that is fol-
14 lowed either

2
   a) by the end of an *SGML document entity* ⌈ [2] *295:13* ⌉ or *SGML subdocument entity* ⌈ [3] *296:1* ⌉;

4
   b) by the *end-tag* ⌈ [19] *317:4* ⌉ of another open *element* ⌈ [13] *308:1* ⌉ ; or

6
   c) by an *element* ⌈ [13] *308:1* ⌉ or *SGML character* ⌈ [50] *345:1* ⌉ that is not allowed in its *content* ⌈ [24] *320:1* ⌉.

8
    NOTE — An element that is not allowed because it is an exclusion has the same effect as one that is not allowed because no token appears for it in the model group.

7.3.2 Data Tag Minimization

Data tag minimization is an optional feature of SGML. I do not usually recommend it because, frankly, it was invented rather early during the development of the language and most of its benefits can now be accomplished more simply and flexibly using the short reference feature.

The fundamental idea behind data tag minimization is that some data can represent the end-tag of an element. As a simple example: You might declare an element type of "word" with a data tag of a space. An element called sentence would be defined to contain zero or more words. Each time a space came up in the sentence it would act as the end-tag for word; you could think of the space either as being the end-tag, or as implying that a word end-tag occurred just before it, because the space itself does not go away. It is treated as data in the sentence element that contains the words.

⌈ **T–C.1.4** *82* ⌉
⌈ **O–4.76** *168:3* ⌉

Data tags are very localized. That is, in this example of a word element, it is only within a sentence that the data tag is possible. If a word occurs somewhere else in the document structure, that same data tag will not necessarily apply there unless it is declared in that context as well.

The character string that serves as a data tag has to conform to a pattern that is defined in the document type definition. Unlike a short reference character, that pattern can be a little richer than just a single character string. The pattern can give you a choice of strings; in addition, it can have what is called a "data tag padding template". So, for example, taking advantage of this additional capability, the data tag for word could be defined so that a word was terminated either by the data tag "one or more spaces" or the data tag "comma followed by one or more spaces".

⌈ **A–11.2.4.4** *415:16* ⌉

If "DATATAG YES" is specified on the *SGML declaration*
2 ⎡ [171] *450:1* ⎤ , data can serve as the *end-tag* ⎡ [19] *317:4* ⎤ of an element that is the corresponding content of a data tag group.

4 The data content of the (target) element and its subelements is
scanned for a string that conforms to one of the data tag templates
6 in the element's *data tag pattern* ⎡ [134] *416:9* ⎤ . That string, plus any
succeeding characters that conform to the *data tag padding tem-*
8 *plate* ⎡ [137] *416:28* ⎤ , are considered the element's data tag. The data
tag is treated both as the *end-tag* ⎡ [19] *317:4* ⎤ of the target element
10 and as *character data* ⎡ [47] *344:1* ⎤ in its containing element.

NOTE — A *generic identifier* ⎡ [30] *325:17* ⎤ that occurs as a target element
12 in a *data tag group* ⎡ [133] *415:16* ⎤ could also occur in other contexts as an
element token ⎡ [130] *410:25* ⎤ . In those contexts, it would not be scanned for
14 a data tag. It could also occur in other data tag groups, possibly with different data tag patterns.

16 The data content of the target element is scanned a character at a
time. At each character, the longest possible *data tag template*
18 ⎡ [136] *416:26* ⎤ in the *data tag pattern* ⎡ [134] *416:9* ⎤ is matched. If more
than one target element is an open element, then at each character
20 the templates of the most recently opened target element are
tested first. If there is no match, the templates of the next most
22 recently opened target element are tested, and so on.

NOTE — A data tag will therefore terminate the most recently opened tar-
24 get element whose data tag pattern it satisfies.

The matching of a *data tag pattern* ⎡ [134] *416:9* ⎤ to the content
26 occurs after recognition of markup and replacement of references
in the content, but before any *RE* or *RS* characters are ignored.

28 NOTE — The *data tag pattern* ⎡ [134] *416:9* ⎤ can therefore contain named
character references to *RE* and *RS*.

30 A data tag cannot be recognized in any context in which end-tags
are not recognized; for example, within a CDATA marked section.

32 In matching the *data tag padding template* ⎡ [137] *416:28* ⎤ , the template characters can be omitted, used once, or repeated indefi-
34 nitely. The last (or only) use can stop short of the full template.

An element that has a data tag is not treated as having an omitted
36 *end-tag* ⎡ [19] *317:4* ⎤ .

7.3.3 Quantities

SGML provides, through the mechanism of the concrete syntax, values for delimiter characters, quantities, and other reassignable parts of SGML syntax. Within the concrete syntax, the quantity set assigns maximum lengths (in characters) to element, attribute and entity names, to attribute values, to complete attribute specification lists, and to a variety of other aspects of markup.

This clause reminds application and system designers that values assignable in the quantity set have an impact on element nesting levels and on how data tags are used.

O-4.247 *136:16*

A-13.4.8 *469:26*

2   The number of open elements cannot exceed the "TAGLVL" quantity.

The length of a data tag cannot exceed the "DTAGLEN" quantity.

7.4 Start-tag

Start-tags basically come in two flavors:

T–A.2 *8*

a)   A complete start-tag consists of a generic identifier and possibly attributes, and the tag is delimited by a start-tag open and a tag close delimiter. The syntax production also calls for a document type specification to indicate the DTD to which the element belongs. The document type specification is only required if the document uses the concurrent document feature. Otherwise the document type specification is considered to be there but will always be empty.

O-4.306 *138:2*

b)   All other start-tags are "minimized". The start-tag is not left out; rather, it is included in an abbreviated form. Minimized tags can be used only if the SGML declaration indicates that the document uses the short tag feature.

O-4.187 *162:7*

[14] start-tag =

2   (**stago**,   [**<**]
                 document type specification,   [28] *325:1*
4   generic identifier specification,   [29] *325:14*
                 attribute specification list,   [31] *327:17*
6   s*,   [5] *297:23*
                 tagc) | [**>**]
8   minimized start-tag   [15] *314:9*

                                                           T–B.3.1 *22*

7.4.1 Minimization

Start-tag minimization is optional and based on the short tag feature. There are three types: empty, unclosed, and net-enabling.

[15] minimized start-tag =

10   empty start-tag | [16] *315:1*
               unclosed start-tag | [17] *316:1*
12   net-enabling start-tag   [18] *316:11*

A *start-tag* [14] *314:1* can be a *minimized start-tag* [15] *314:9* only
14 if "SHORTTAG YES" is specified on the *SGML declaration*
    [171] *450:1* .

7.4.1.1 Empty Start-tag

An empty start-tag is just what it says: <>
Since there is no way for an empty start-tag to indicate which of a number of concurrent instances it belongs to, the rule is that an empty start-tag can only be in the base document instance.

It has been suggested that an empty start-tag should be called a "repeat-tag" because of the way it works — its purpose is to repeat the previous element. For example, in marking up a row of a table you could tag the first cell in the table and then just have empty start-tags to begin the following cells. You could even go a step further and define a short reference, let us say, of a tab character, that would stand for an empty start-tag. Then your table markup would look very WYSIWYGish indeed.

                                                           T–C.1.1.2 *68*

(Of course, the tab character could be mapped directly to an entity whose text was a table cell start-tag, but then new maps would be needed for other contexts in which this technique could be used, such as list items within a list.)

Because of the working of the OMITTAG feature, the precise definition of what an empty start-tag repeats is technical, but the net effect is the same. That is to say, it repeats the previous element. If OMITTAG is not in use, an empty start-tag repeats the element that just ended. Otherwise, it repeats the element that just started. Because in the latter case the empty start-tag will, in fact, be implying and enforcing the ending of the previous element, the net result is the same.

T–C.1.2.6 *75*

[16] empty start-tag =
2   **stago**,   `<`
    tagc   `>`

4 A *start-tag* [14] *314:1* can be an *empty start-tag* [16] *315:1* only if the *element* [13] *308:1* is in the base document instance, in which
6 case the tag's *generic identifier specification* [29] *325:14* is assumed to be:
8   a) if "OMITTAG YES" is specified on the *SGML declaration*
       [171] *450:1*, the *generic identifier* [30] *325:17* of the most
10   recently started open element in the base document type; or
    b) if "OMITTAG NO" is specified on the *SGML declaration*
12   [171] *450:1*, the *generic identifier* [30] *325:17* of the most
       recently ended element in the base document type; or
14   c) if there was no such previous applicable element, the *generic identifier* [30] *325:17* of the *document element* [12] *306:15* .

16 NOTE — A *generic identifier specification* [29] *325:14* is implied for an *empty start-tag* [16] *315:1* prior to determining whether any tags were
18 omitted before it.

    An *empty start-tag* [16] *315:1* is treated as having an empty *attri-*
20 *bute specification list* [31] *327:17* .

7.4.1.2 Unclosed Start-tag

The unclosed start-tag allows the closing delimiter of a tag to be omitted when it is followed immediately by another tag. For example, a chapter opening with a paragraph could be minimized as: `<CHP<P>`

T–C.1.1.1 *68*

[17] unclosed start-tag =

2   ***stago***,   `< `

     document type specification,   **[28]** *325:1*

4   *generic identifier specification,*   **[29]** *325:14*

     attribute specification list,   **[31]** *327:17*

6   *s**   **[5]** *297:23*

A *start-tag* **[14]** *314:1* can be an *unclosed start-tag* **[17]** *316:1* only
8   if it is followed immediately by the character string assigned to the
stago or ***etago*** delimiter role, regardless of whether the string
10   begins a valid delimiter-in-context sequence.

7.4.1.3 NET-enabling Start-tag

This subject will be discussed in conjunction with the null end-tag in
7.5.1.3 *319* .

T–C.1.1.2 *68*

A–7.5.1.3 *319:2*

[18] net-enabling start-tag =

12   ***stago***,   `< `

     generic identifier specification,   **[29]** *325:14*

14   *attribute specification list,*   **[31]** *327:17*

     s*,   **[5]** *297:23*

16   ***net***   `/ `

A *start-tag* **[14]** *314:1* can be a *net-enabling start-tag* **[18]** *316:11*
18   only if its *element* **[13]** *308:1* is in the base document instance.

7.4.2 Quantities

Application and system designers are reminded that the length of a
start-tag — including all its attribute specifications — is governed by the
value assigned in the quantity set.

TAGLEN is not to be confused with the length assigned to just the
generic identifier within the start-tag. That value cannot exceed
NAMELEN.

O–4.247 *136:16*

A–13.4.8 *469:26*

The length of a *start-tag* **[14]** *314:1* , before interpretation of attri-

2   bute value literals in the *attribute specification list* [31] *327:17* and
exclusive of the ***stago*** and ***tagc*** or ***net*** delimiters, cannot exceed
the "TAGLEN" quantity.

7.5 End-tag

End tags, like start-tags, come in two varieties: complete or minimized. In a complete end-tag, when using the CONCUR feature, there
may be a document type specification. Empty or not, it will always be
followed by a generic identifier specification. The technical wording just
explains that the end-tag and start-tag have to match one another with
respect to the document type specification and the generic identifier
specification.

     T–B.3.1 *22*
     O–4.119 *138:4*

4   [19] end-tag =
6   (***etago***,   ⟨ </ ⟩
              document type specification,   [28] *325:1*
              generic identifier specification,   [29] *325:14*
8   *s**,   [5] *297:23*
              tagc   ) | ⟨ > ⟩
10   *minimized end-tag*   [20] *317:15*

An *end-tag* [19] *317:4* ends the most recently started open *element*
12   [13] *308:1* , within the instance of the document type specified by
the *document type specification* [28] *325:1* , whose generic identif-
14   ier is specified by the *generic identifier specification* [29] *325:14* .

7.5.1 Minimization

End-tag minimization is optional and based on the same SHORTTAG
feature that makes possible start-tag minimization. The three types of
minimization correspond to those used for start-tags.

     T–C.1.1 *67*

     [20] minimized end-tag =
16   *empty end-tag* | [21] *318:5*
          unclosed end-tag | [22] *318:12*

null end-tag   [23] *319:2*

2   An *end-tag* [19] *317:4* can be a *minimized end-tag* [20] *317:15*
only if "SHORTTAG YES" is specified on the *SGML declaration*
4   [171] *450:1* .

7.5.1.1 Empty End-tag

An empty end-tag </> terminates the most recently started open element. As with an empty start-tag, it has to be in the base document
instance because there is no way to specify any other document instance.

T–C.1.1.2 *68*

[21] empty end-tag =
6   ***etago*,**   </
           tagc   >

8   If an *end-tag* [19] *317:4* is an *empty end-tag* [21] *318:5* , its *generic
identifier* [30] *325:17* is that of the most recently started open ele-
10   ment in the base document instance. If there was no such element,
the *end-tag* [19] *317:4* is an error.

7.5.1.2 Unclosed End-tag

The unclosed end-tag is the same concession to sloppy typists as the
unclosed start-tag — the closing delimiter can be left out if it is followed
by another tag.

T–C.1.1.1 *68*

12   [22] unclosed end-tag =
           ***etago*,**   </
14   *document type specification*,   [28] *325:1*
           generic identifier specification,   [29] *325:14*
16   *s**   [5] *297:23*

An *end-tag* [19] *317:4* can be an *unclosed end-tag* [22] *318:12*
18   only if it is followed immediately by the character string assigned to
the ***stago*** or ***etago*** delimiter role, regardless of whether the string

begins a valid delimiter-in-context sequence.

You might want to notice the small print there — in determining whether or not another tag is coming along, a parser does not look beyond the delimiter string to see whether it is really valid in context. So technically there does not really have to be another tag — just the delimiter of a tag. In a situation where a paragraph is ending — for example, </para<qwerty — the start-tag open delimiter ensures the integrity of the para end-tag even though qwerty may not be a valid generic identifier, or even part of a properly-formed tag.

7.5.1.3 Null End-tag

The null end-tag is an interesting idea for short elements. It lets you terminate those elements with a single character null end-tag delimiter, but only if the start-tag of the element enabled the use of the null end-tag by ending with the same delimiter. This form of start-tag is the NET-enabling start-tag mentioned in 7.4.1.3 ⌐316⌐. In the reference concrete syntax that delimiter is a virgule (or slash or solidus) and so, for something short like a quotation you might use:

```
He said <q/hello/ to me.
```

⌐ **T–C.1.1.2** *68* ⌐
⌐ **A–7.4.1.3** *316:11* ⌐

2 [23] null end-tag =
          net   ⌐ *l* ⌐

4 The ***net*** is recognized as a *null end-tag* ⌐ **[23]** *319:2* ⌐ only if the *start-tag* ⌐ **[14]** *314:1* ⌐ of an open element in the base document type was
6 a *net-enabling start-tag* ⌐ **[18]** *316:11* ⌐. It is assumed to be the *end-tag* ⌐ **[19]** *317:4* ⌐ of the most recently started such element.

7.6 Content

The text of an SGML document is classified in either of two ways: as markup characters or as data characters that are passed to an application for processing. The job of the SGML parser is to figure out which is which.

As part of the instructions to the parser, the declaration for an element either *declares* the content to be data only, or includes a *content model* that allows the content to contain either subordinate elements only ("element content") or an unpredictable mixture of subordinate elements and/or data ("mixed content").

If the content is declared to be data, it will be one of two specialized types: character data (indicated by the keyword CDATA in the declaration), or replaceable character data (indicated by RCDATA). In CDATA and RCDATA, most normal markup characters are not recognized. Only markup that would appear to end the element is actually detected as markup. (CDATA and RCDATA are discussed in clause 9 (342).)

In mixed content, the possibility of data occurring is indicated by the keywords #PCDATA ("parsed character data") or ANY. As subordinate elements and other content markup constructs could also occur, it is up to the SGML parser to determine which content characters, if any, are data.

In element content, data cannot occur, but other markup constructs can.

		T–B.13.1 *58*
		O–4.34 *145:17*
		A–9.1 *342:1*

```
    [24] content =
2       mixed content |                              [25] 320:6
        element content |                            [26] 320:10
4       replaceable character data |                 [46] 343:1
        character data                               [47] 344:1

6   [25] mixed content =
        (  data character |                          [48] 344:3
8          element |                                 [13] 308:1
           other content   )*                        [27] 320:14

10  [26] element content =
        (  element |                                 [13] 308:1
12         other content |                           [27] 320:14
           s  )*                                      [5] 297:23

14  [27] other content =
        comment declaration |                        [91] 391:1
16      short reference use declaration |            [152] 430:10
        link set use declaration |                   [169] 448:1
18      processing instruction |                     [44] 339:1
        shortref |                                    364
20      character reference |                        [62] 356:1
        general entity reference |                   [59] 350:17
22      marked section declaration |                 [93] 391:13
        Ee
```

An element's *declared content* [125] *409:3* or *content model*

2   [126] *410:1* determines which of the four types of *content* [24] *320:1* it has, or whether it is empty, except that the *content*

4   [24] *320:1* must be empty if the element has an explicit content reference.

6   The *content* [24] *320:1* of an element declared to be *character data* [47] *344:1* or *replaceable character data* [46] *343:1* is ter-

8   minated only by an **etago** delimiter-in-context (which need not open a valid *end-tag* [19] *317:4*) or a valid **net**. Such termination is an

10   error if it would have been an error had the *content* [24] *320:1* been *mixed content* [25] *320:6*.

12   NOTE — Content characters could be classed as data content for either of two reasons:

14   a)   Declared character data.

      The element's entire content was declared to be *character data*

16   [47] *344:1* or *replaceable character data* [46] *343:1* by the *declared content* [125] *409:3* parameter of the *element declaration*

18   [116] *405:6*.

   b)   Parsed character data.

20   The element was declared to have *mixed content* [25] *320:6*, and an *SGML character* [50] *345:1* within it was parsed as data

22   because it was not recognized as markup.

7.6.1 Record Boundaries

T–B.3.3 *24*

O–4.252 *145:1*

Some text editors and word processors require that each line of input end with a carriage return or line feed character or both. Others "wrap" the text by themselves within margins, often inserting returns secretly. Clearly, identical data, even though created in such different ways, needs to be processed as though the input text (data plus carriage returns and line feeds) were identical. [2]

SGML achieves the needed consistency by representing each source input line as a "record", bounded by a record start (RS) and record end character (RE), regardless of the codes used by the editor to display the

---

[2] The problem is compounded by the inexorable operation of Goldfarb's first law of text processing, which states that if a text processor has bugs, at least one of them will have to do with the handling of input line endings.

input. In the reference concrete syntax, the record start character is the ASCII character 10, or line feed, and the record end character is the ASCII character 13, the carriage return. Within content, unless those characters have meaning as markup, a record start will simply be ignored and a record end treated in one of several ways.

If the record end is there solely because of something in the markup, it is ignored; if not, it is passed along as data to an application. An application such as a formatting system would typically treat a record end as though it were an inter-word space — but SGML makes no assumptions about that. [3]

2   If an **RS** in *content* [24] *320:1* is not interpreted as markup, it is ignored.

4   Within *content* [24] *320:1* , an **RE** remaining after replacement of all references and recognition of markup is treated as data unless its presence can be attributed solely to markup. That is:

6   a) The first **RE** in an element is ignored if no **RS**, data, or proper subelement preceded it.

8   b) The last **RE** in an element is ignored if no data or proper subelement follows it.

10   c) An **RE** that does not immediately follow an **RS** or **RE** is ignored if no data or proper subelement intervened.

An area that can cause difficulties for users if designers are not careful is improperly formed mixed content. The only reliable way to define mixed content is as a repeatable "OR" group; in other words, the data can occur anywhere within the content, intermixed with whatever subelements are also permitted.

In adherence to the principle that a record end that is caused by markup is ignored, the first record end in the content, if it comes right after a start-tag, will be ignored. Similarly, a record end that is followed by the end-tag is ignored.

12   NOTE — The determination that an **RE** is data is made during recognition of markup. Markup recognition, which includes recognition of omitted tags,

14   occurs before the determination of whether an **RE** can be ignored according to the above rules. This sequence produces intuitive results in

16   the normal case, where data can occur anywhere in the *content*

---

[3] SGML has these rules about record boundaries so that if implementations have bugs, they will result from poor coding rather than from poor understanding of what to do. Since the first rule is that an SGML document does not have to be divided into records, if your text editor will let you avoid this whole mess, more power to it.

     [24] *320:1*   of an element, as in:

2   (quote | #PCDATA) *

In content models where the occurrence of data is restricted, however, as in

4   (x, #PCDATA)

the situations described in items a) and b) would be treated as errors during
6   markup recognition. The use of such content models is normally
unnecessary and therefore not normally recommended (see 11.2.4 *409*).

In determining whether a record end occurred because of markup or
because of data, a subelement is treated as an atom, as though it were a
single character. Whether that atom is a character of data or a character
of markup depends on whether it was a proper subelement (one that was
declared in the content model of the containing element) or whether it
was an included subelement. Included subelements — known as inclusions — are treated as if they did not belong. So, if one causes a record
end to occur, that record end is treated as one that was created by
markup, just as if the included element had been a processing instruction.   **T–B.11.1** *55*

                                      O–4.157 *151:13*

                                      A–11.2.5 *417:16*

This implication of designating an element to either be an inclusion or
a proper subelement should be kept in mind when designing document
types. It can have a significant impact on the likelihood that users will
create record boundary errors.

8   In applying these rules to an element, subelement content is
ignored; that is, a proper or included subelement is treated as an
10   atom that ends in the same record in which it begins.

12   NOTE — For example, in the following three records:

```
   record 1 data<outer><sub>
14 record 2 data</sub>
   record 3 data</outer>
```

16   the first ***RE*** in the outer element is at the end of record 2. It is treated as
data if "sub" is a proper subelement of "outer", but is ignored if "sub" is an
18   included element, because no data or proper subelement would have
preceded it in the outer element.

20   In either case, the first ***RE*** in the subelement is at the end of record 1; it is
ignored because no data or proper subelement preceded it in the

subelement.

In order to avoid long parser look-aheads when the last record end is followed by markup declarations or processing instructions, the standard provides that the record end is deemed to occur immediately prior to the next following data or proper subelement. Because of that rule, a parser can simply hold on to a record end and wait to see whether data shows up before the end-tag of the element. That way if data does arrive, the parser will pass the record end on to the application, but if the end-tag of the element arrives, then the parser will simply ignore the record end.

2 An **RE** is deemed to occur immediately prior to the first data or proper subelement that follows it (that is, after any intervening
4 markup declaration, processing instruction, or included subelement).

6 NOTES

1 A specific character data entity, non-SGML data entity, or SGML
8 subdocument entity, is treated as data, while a processing instruction entity is not.

10 2 Although the handling of record boundaries is defined by SGML, there is no requirement that SGML documents must be organized in records.

12 3 No entity, including the *SGML document entity* [2] *295:13* and external entities, is deemed to start with an **RS** or end with an **RE** unless it really
14 does.

7.7 Document Type Specification

A document type specification is something that shows up in start-tags and end-tags when the concurrent document instance feature is in use. It indicates which document type definition or definitions the partic-ular tag conforms to, and therefore to which document instance or instances the tag belongs. If no document type named in the specification is active then the tag is ignored. If a name is active, or if there are no names at all — in other words if the document type specification is empty — then the tag is processed. This rule means that a tag without a document type specification will be processed as part of every document type.

T–C.3.1 *88*
O–4.106 *138:6*

[28] document type specification =

2   *name group*?   [69] *374:11*

Markup containing a *document type specification* [28] *325:1* is pro-
4   cessed only if:
     a) a *name* [55] *346:17* in the *name group* [69] *374:11* is that of
6   an active document type; or
     b) there is no *name group* [69] *374:11* (that is, the *document*
8   *type specification* [28] *325:1* is empty).

     NOTE — An effect of this requirement is that markup with an empty
10   document type specification (that is, no *name group* [69] *374:11*) will
     apply to all document instances (or the only one).

12   A *name group* [69] *374:11* can be specified only if "CONCUR YES"
     is specified on the *SGML declaration* [171] *450:1* .

7.8 Generic Identifier (GI) Specification

   This clause is the technical wording that gives meaning to the concept
of a content model. It establishes the fact that a particular generic identifier specification is only valid when an element of that type is allowed in
the current content model or an applicable inclusion, or is the document
element.   T–B.4.2.1 *27*

                                                             O–4.145 *148:22*

                                                             A–9.6.2 *361:12*

14   [29] generic identifier specification =
               generic identifier | [30] *325:17*
16   *rank stem*   [120] *407:17*

     [30] generic identifier =
18   *name*   [55] *346:17*

     A *generic identifier* [30] *325:17* is valid in a *generic identifier speci-*
20   *fication* [29] *325:14* only if it was specified as an *element type*
     [117] *406:1* in the document type definition and:
22   a) it was named in the *content model* [126] *410:1* of the *element*
         declaration [116] *405:6* for the element in which it occurred; or
24   b) it was named in an applicable *inclusions* [139] *418:11* excep-
         tion; or

c) it is the *document type name* [111] *404:4* and it occurred in
2   the *start-tag* [14] *314:1* or *end-tag* [19] *317:4* of the document element.

7.8.1 Rank Feature

RANK is an optional markup minimization feature that can be applied
to the generic identifier specification. Like data tag, it showed up early in
the development and stayed in the final standard. I think, however, there
is even less justification for using RANK.

In the early days of generic markup, some applications labeled different kinds of paragraphs with numbers that indicated their hierarchical
relationship. For example, P1, P2 and P3 might indicate three levels of
paragraphs based on their importance: Each level would get a different
type face or some other distinction when the document was formatted.
Levels B1, B2 and B3 could identify bulleted paragraphs that were
designed to be nested. A characteristic of these approaches was that a
paragraph that did not have a level number on it would be given the
level of the last paragraph that did have a number. This technique gave
you some ability to edit the document and move paragraphs around
without having to renumber all of them if their position in the hierarchy
was changed.

In the SGML rank feature, a ranked element is declared by separating
the generic identifier into two parts in the element declaration. The two
parts are called the rank stem and the rank suffix, and the rank suffix
must be a number.

In a start-tag, when the generic identifier specification for an element
that is a ranked element contains the entire generic identifier, then that
ranked suffix becomes the current rank for the element. Subsequent tags
that have only the rank stem for that element will be treated as if the current suffix were attached to it.

Ranked elements can be combined, when they are defined, into a
ranked group, which means that all of their stems will share the same
rank suffix. In our previous example, if we combined paragraph and bulleted paragraph into the same ranked group, then if an element of P1
occurred and then an element B, the B would be treated as a B1.

It should be noted that SGML does not know anything about arithme-
tic and that a number to a parser is just a character string composed of
digits. Therefore, there is no requirement that ranked suffixes actually
form some numerical hierarchy. It is possible to define ranked elements
B1 and B27, for example, and SGML will not care because the parser is
not called upon to calculate a ranked suffix. The parser always takes the
most recently used rank suffix without regard to what suffixes were used
before that.

T–C.1.5 *85*
O–4.248 *169:6*
A–11.2.1 *405:24*

If "RANK YES" is specified on the *SGML declaration* [171] *450:1* ,
2 the provisions of this sub-sub-clause apply.

7.8.1.1 Full Generic Identifier

If the full *generic identifier* [30] *325:17* is specified for the start-tag
4 of a ranked element, its *rank suffix* [121] *407:19* becomes the current rank for its *rank stem* [120] *407:17* , and for the rank stems in
6 any *ranked group* [119] *407:5* of which the *rank stem* [120] *407:17*
is a member.

7.8.1.2 Rank Stem

8 A *generic identifier specification* [29] *325:14* can be a *rank stem*
[120] *407:17* if it was declared via a *ranked element* [118] *407:1* or
10 member of a *ranked group* [119] *407:5* in an applicable *element
declaration* [116] *405:6* .

12 Specifying a *rank stem* [120] *407:17* is equivalent to specifying the
generic identifier [30] *325:17* that is derived by appending the cur-
14 rent rank to it. It is an error to specify a *rank stem* [120] *407:17* if no
element previously occurred to establish the current rank for that
16 stem.

7.9 Attribute Specification List

Attribute specification lists occur in start-tags, link rules, and entity
declarations. Technically, the attribute specification list is always present,
but it must be empty if no attributes have been defined in a corresponding attribute definition list declaration.

[31] attribute specification list =
18   *attribute specification**   [32] *327:19*

[32] attribute specification =
20   *s**,   [5] *297:23*
            (*name*,   [55] *346:17*

2

s*,	[5] *297:23*
vi,	=
s*)?,	[5] *297:23*
attribute value specification	[33] *331:1*

4

The validity of the attribute specification list is determined by the
6   *attribute definition list* [142] *420:25* associated with the element. If
there is no associated *attribute definition list* [142] *420:25* , the *attri-*
8   *bute specification list* [31] *327:17* must be empty.

An attribute can be defined either:

a)   as a normal or "fixed" attribute with a default value;

O–4.84 *155:17*

b)   as a required attribute (meaning that it can never be left with a
default value);

O–4.268 *156:4*

c)   as a normal or "content reference" form of "impliable" attribute
(meaning that if it is not specified then the application will imply a
value); or

O–4.154 *156:1*

d)   as a "current" attribute (meaning that it is initially required, but
that any value specified for it becomes the default value for subsequent occasions when the attribute is not specified).

O–4.67 *156:6*

A value must be specified in the attribute specification list for every
defined attribute, except for those which are impliable. However, there
are markup minimization techniques that can be used to reduce the set of
attributes that have to be specified.   T–C.1.1.3 *69*

Every attribute for which there is an *attribute definition* [143] *421:1* ,
10   other than an impliable attribute, must be specified (unless markup
minimization is used, as described in 7.9.1.1 329).

12   There can be only one *attribute specification* [32] *327:19* for each
attribute definition [143] *421:1* .

14   The leading s [5] *297:23* can only be omitted from an *attribute*
specification [32] *327:19* that follows a delimiter.

7.9.1 Minimization

The cases of start-tag minimization described above, where a start-tag was omitted or was empty, are also examples of minimization of attribute specifications, as the entire attribute specification lists were omitted and the default values of the attributes were used. There are also methods of omitting all or part of individual attribute specifications while specifying others in full.

> A–7.3.1.1 *309:1*

7.9.1.1 Omitted Attribute Specification

If you are using either the short tag or the omit tag feature then you have to specify an attribute only if it is required. In other cases, you can omit the attribute specification and the default value will be used.

With a current attribute, its first occurrence is required and afterwards it is treated as though the most recent specified value is the default value.

If "SHORTTAG YES" or "OMITTAG YES" is specified on the *SGML*
2   *declaration* [171] *450:1* :
     a)   There need be an *attribute specification* [32] *327:19* only for a
4   required attribute, and for a current attribute on the first occurrence of any element in whose *attribute definition list*
6   [142] *420:25* it appears. Other attributes will be treated as though specified with an *attribute value* [35] *333:1* equal to
8   the declared *default value* [147] *425:1* .
     b)   If there is an *attribute value specification* [33] *331:1* for a current attribute, the specified *attribute value* [35] *333:1* will
10   become the default value. The new default affects all elements associated with the *attribute definition list* [142] *420:25*
12   in which the attribute was defined.

7.9.1.2 Omitted Attribute Name

Another form of minimization is possible with the short tag feature. SGML allows the value declared for an attribute to be a set of name tokens, chosen to be self-describing — in other words, to imply the attribute name as well as the value. For example, with an attribute named "color" whose possible values are red, white and blue, it is sufficient to say "red" or "blue" and know that it is a color. For this reason, only the value is required when specifying the attribute.

> T–C.1.1.3 *69*

It is a requirement of SGML (even without SHORTTAG) that if you have more than one such attribute in a single definition list, name tokens must not be duplicated within the list. Otherwise you would not know which attribute the value applied to if the name were omitted.

[**A–11.3.2** *421:14*]

2   If "SHORTTAG YES" is specified on the *SGML declaration* [**[171]** *450:1*] , the *name* [**[55]** *346:17*] and *vi* can be omitted if the *attribute value specification* [**[33]** *331:1*] is an undelimited *name*
4   *token* [**[57]** *347:3*] that is a member of a group specified in the *declared value* [**[145]** *422:6*] for that attribute.

6   NOTE — A *name token* [**[57]** *347:3*] can occur in only one group in an *attribute definition list* [**[142]** *420:25*] (see 11.3.3 [*422*]).

7.9.2 Quantities

Because an attribute specification list can have an arbitrary amount of space between the names and the values, the quantity requirement here has rules for normalizing the lengths so that these extraneous separator characters can be ignored. The purpose of quantity restrictions is to give a parser developer some notion of the buffer sizes needed for different purposes, and since these separator characters do not have to be preserved in storage, they are not counted in calculating the quantity.

[**A–13.4.8** *469:26*]

8   The normalized length of the *attribute specification list* [**[31]** *327:17*] is the sum of the normalized lengths of each attribute name and
10   attribute value specified, which cannot exceed the "ATTSPLEN" quantity.

12   The normalized length of an attribute name is the "NORMSEP" quantity plus the number of characters in the name.

7.9.3 Attribute Value Specification

The attribute value specification is either an attribute value or an attribute value literal. This is a very important and sometimes misunderstood distinction.

[**T–B.5.2** *35*]
[**O–4.16** *157:1*]

The *attribute value literal* [34] 331:4 is what you type in between quotation marks. The *attribute value* [35] 333:1 is something that the parser derives from the attribute value literal. The interpretation is accomplished by replacing any entity references or character references within the literal and then normalizing the resulting attribute value by throwing out any entity ends and record starts and replacing any record end or separator characters with a space. This work is all done before the parser considers what the declared value of the attribute is.

At this point, if the declared value of the attribute is character data (CDATA), derivation of the attribute value is complete. If the declared value is anything else, such as an ID or a name or a general entity name list, for example, then there is a further process in which any sequence of space characters is replaced by a single space. Also, if there are any space characters at the beginning or end of the attribute value, those are deleted.

T–B.9 52
O–4.150 158:3

The result of this process is, at the end of the first step, a normalized character string, and at the end of the second step, a tokenized version of that character string. Obviously, the order of the tokens is significant and must be preserved during interpretation.

```
      [33] attribute value specification =
2            attribute value |
             attribute value literal
```
[35] 333:1
[34] 331:4

```
4     [34] attribute value literal =
         ( lit,
6            replaceable character data*,
             lit   ) |
8         ( lita,
             replaceable character data*,
10           lita   )
```
"
[46] 343:1
"
'
[46] 343:1
'

An *attribute value literal* [34] 331:4 is interpreted as an *attribute*
12 *value* [35] 333:1 by replacing references within it, ignoring **Ee** and **RS**, and replacing an **RE** or **SEPCHAR** with a **SPACE**.

14 NOTE — Interpretation of an *attribute value literal* [34] 331:4 occurs as though the attribute were *character data* [47] 344:1 , regardless of its
16 actual declared value.

An attribute value other than *character data* [47] 344:1 is tokenized

2 by replacing a sequence of **SPACE** characters with a single **SPACE** character and ignoring leading or trailing **SPACE** characters.

4 NOTE — Tokenization is performed without regard to the original literal; for example, whether CDATA or SDATA entities were used is irrelevant.

7.9.3.1 Minimization

There is one case in which an attribute value can be entered directly, rather than entering an attribute value literal: when the attribute value has nothing in it except name characters and either you are using the short tag feature or the value is being entered as the default value in an attribute definition list. Although the value can have nothing but name characters, it is not restricted to the normal length of a name.

> **T–C.1.1.3** *69*

6 An *attribute value specification* ⌐ **[33]** *331:1* ⌐ can be an *attribute value* ⌐ **[35]** *333:1* ⌐ (that is, not an *attribute value literal* ⌐ **[34]** *331:4* ⌐) only if it
8 contains nothing but name characters and either:
  a) it occurs in an *attribute definition list* ⌐ **[142]** *420:25* ⌐ ; or
10 b) "SHORTTAG YES" is specified on the *SGML declaration* ⌐ **[171]** *450:1* ⌐ .

7.9.4 Attribute Value

There are fifteen types of attribute value. Which one applies to a given attribute is specified in the attribute definition as the declared value parameter of that definition.

> **O–4.10** *154:1*

The fifteen values actually syntactically break down into a smaller group because some of them — such as ID value, ID reference list and ID reference value — are really names or name lists. It should be re-emphasized that in the attribute value literal there can be any number of spaces or record ends between the names in a name list. But after the parser's interpretation of the attribute value literal and after tokenization, there will only be a single space between each of them. That is why, for example, production 39 shows a single space between the names and the name list; this space is the result of interpreting the attribute value literal to produce the attribute value.

[35] attribute value =
2   *character data* | [47] *344:1*
                general entity name | [103] *395:4*
4   *general entity name list* | [35.1] *333:17*
                id value | [36] *333:19*
6   *id reference value* | [38] *333:23*
                id reference list | [37] *333:21*
8   *name* | [55] *346:17*
                name list | [39] *333:25*
10   *name token* | [57] *347:3*
                name token list | [40] *333:29*
12   *notation name* | [41] *333:33*
                number | [56] *347:1*
14   *number list* | [42] *333:35*
                number token | [58] *347:5*
16   *number token list*   [43] *334:2*

        [35.1] general entity name list =
18   *name list*   [39] *333:25*

        [36] id value =
20   *name*   [55] *346:17*

        [37] id reference list =
22   *name list*   [39] *333:25*

        [38] id reference value =
24   *name*   [55] *346:17*

        [39] name list =
26   *name,*   [55] *346:17*
                (**SPACE**,
28   *name*   )*   [55] *346:17*

        [40] name token list =
30   *name token,*   [57] *347:3*
                (**SPACE**,
32   *name token*   )*   [57] *347:3*

        [41] notation name =
34   *name*   [55] *346:17*

        [42] number list =
36   *number,*   [56] *347:1*
                (**SPACE**,

          number)*   [56] *347:1*

2   [43] number token list =
          number token,   [58] *347:5*
4   (**SPACE**,
              number token)*   [58] *347:5*

6   The *declared value* [145] *422:6* parameter of an *attribute definition*
    [143] *421:1* determines which of the fifteen types of *attribute value*
8   [35] *333:1* must be specified.

7.9.4.1 Syntactic Requirements

This clause is straightforward. However, it is worth noting that an
empty string is a valid value for character data attributes but not for
attribute values of the various tokenized types. There is no such thing as
an empty token.

      An *attribute value* [35] *333:1* must conform to the *declared value*
10   [145] *422:6* .

      If the *declared value* [145] *422:6* includes a group, the *attribute*
12   *value* [35] *333:1* must be a token in that group.

      An empty *attribute value literal* [34] *331:4* can be specified only for
14   an *attribute value* [35] *333:1* whose type is *character data*
      [47] *344:1* .

7.9.4.2 Fixed Attribute

Fixed attributes are those whose default value is declared to be the
only allowable value for the attribute. In other words, every occurrence
of the attribute will have that value.

16   The specified *attribute value* [35] *333:1* for a fixed attribute must
      be its *default value* [147] *425:1* .

One might well ask, if there is just the one value permitted for the
attribute, why bother to declare the attribute at all? The answer is that
fixed attributes are normally used when the application is conforming to
an architecture that requires certain attributes to be present for every element.

For example, in the Office Document Architecture (ISO 8613) an attribute called "object type" must be specified for every element. So, in using SGML to represent a formatted page that conforms to the ODA architecture, the allowed value for object type might be "page", or "frame" (an area of the page), or "block" (an area with data in it). The application might distinguish between recto and verso pages by defining them as two different element types. Each of those elements would have the attribute "object type" defined for it; in both cases that attribute would have a fixed value of "page". In that way, a processor that implemented ODA semantics would know that the element types "recto" and "verso" should be treated semantically like objects of type "page" in the ODA architecture.

O–4.136 *156:10*

A–11.3.4 *424:16*

7.9.4.3 General Entity Name

An entity whose name occurs as the value of an attribute is not treated as part of the content of the element, and therefore it is not parsed in the context of the document. An application processor may reinvoke the parser as part of the application to parse that entity, but that is done independently of the parsing of the main document and any markup errors that are in the entity will not show up as markup errors in the main document.

If these entities are to be parsed, they must be SGML subdocument entities; that is, they must have their own document type definitions. Alternatively, the attribute value may be a data entity which is not parsed by SGML at all; so it too satisfies the requirement that it not be parsed in the context of the current document.

T–B.13.1.2 *59*

The value of a *general entity name* [103] *395:4* attribute, and of
2 each *name* [55] *346:17* in a *general entity name list* [35.1] *333:17* ,
must be the *name* [55] *346:17* of a data entity or an SGML subdo-
4 cument entity. Such a name must be declared as though it
occurred in a *general entity reference* [59] *350:17* with no *name*
6 *group* [69] *374:11* specified (see 9.4.4.1 *351*).

In my opinion, the last sentence of this clause is erroneous because it conflicts with 9.4.4.1 *351* . For example, when a general entity name attribute occurs in a start-tag that is being parsed with respect to two or more active document types, the entity could have a different declaration in each of the applicable DTDs. In such a case, the applicable declaration would be that of the DTD with respect to which the tag is parsed. So for document type "A", the entity would have the declaration that occurred in DTD "A" and be resolved accordingly; for document type "B", the entity would have the declaration that occurred in DTD "B".

7.9.4.4 Notation

When an attribute value is declared to be a notation name, the SGML parser will check to make sure that the notation was declared in the same document type declaration. The first paragraph of this clause provides the basis for that checking.

O–4.211 *157:12*

A–11.4 *426:15*

2   The *attribute value* [35] *333:1* of a notation attribute must be a *notation name* [41] *333:33* that was declared in the same document type declaration as the element.

Notation attributes are frequently used in conjunction with content reference attributes. A content reference attribute is an impliable attribute with the property that, if a value is specified for it, the content of that instance of the element must be empty. A value cannot be specified for a notation attribute if one is specified for a content reference attribute, as the following examples will illustrate.

T–B.13.2.3 *62*

Consider this DTD fragment:

```
<!NOTATION cgmbin   SYSTEM    "Program to interpret CGM binary    ▼
                                  notation">
<!NOTATION cgmclear SYSTEM    "Program to interpret CGM clear     ▼
                                  text">
<!NOTATION iges     SYSTEM    "Program to interpret IGES clear    ▼
                                  text">
<!ENTITY   fig42    SYSTEM    "fig42.cgm" NDATA cgmbin>
<!ELEMENT  figure   - O       CDATA>
<!ATTLIST  figure   notation NOTATION(cgmbin|cgmclear|iges)       ▼
                                  #REQUIRED
                    location ENTITY #CONREF>
```

Three data content notations are defined, and an NDATA entity that uses one of them. There is an element, "figure", for which a notation attribute and a content reference attribute ("location") are defined. The intention of these declarations is to allow the user to enter the data of a figure either between the start-tag and end-tag in the usual manner, or as a separate external entity.

Here is how the data could be entered as content:

```
<figure notation=iges>
...Some IGES statements...
</figure>
```

Here is how the data might be entered as a separate entity:

```
<figure location=fig42>
```

Because this start-tag includes a specification of a content reference attribute (an "explicit content reference"), the notation attribute was not specified, even though it is normally required. As the content has no data, it is meaningless to specify a data notation for the content. The external entity, of course, does have data, but its notation is specified on the entity declaration.   A–11.3.4 *424:16*

2   It is an error to specify a value for a notation attribute if there is an explicit content reference.

4   NOTE — As the element's *content* [24] *320:1* will be empty, it is pointless to specify a notation for it. Even if the content reference were to a non-SGML data entity, the applicable notation would be specified by the *nota-*
6   *tion name* [41] *333:33* parameter of the entity declaration.

7.9.4.5 Quantities

An attribute value literal could have separator characters in it that are ignored after the literal is interpreted and the attribute value is tokenized. In order for the quantities to reflect this, rules are given for a normalized length calculation for attribute values.

A–13.4.8 *469:26*

8   The normalized length of an *attribute value* [35] *333:1* , whether specified directly or interpreted from an *attribute value literal* [34] *331:4* , is the "NORMSEP" quantity plus:
10   a)   for a *general entity name list* [35.1] *333:17* , *id reference list* [37] *333:21* , *name list* [39] *333:25* , *name token list*
12   [40] *333:29* , *number list* [42] *333:35* , or *number token list* [43] *334:2* (even if there is only one token in the list), the sum
14   of the number of characters in each token in the list, plus the "NORMSEP" quantity for each token in the list; or

2   b)   for all others, the number of characters in the value, plus the "NORMSEP" quantity for each reference to a "CDATA" or "SDATA" entity.

4   The normalized length of an *attribute value* [35] *333:1* cannot exceed the "LITLEN" quantity.

6   In a single *start-tag* [14] *314:1* , the total number of names in *id reference value* [38] *333:23* and *id reference list* [37] *333:21* attribute
8   values, whether defaulted or specified, cannot exceed the "GRPCNT" quantity.

10   In a single *attribute specification list* [31] *327:17* , the total number of names in *general entity name* [103] *395:4* and *general entity*
12   *name list* [35.1] *333:17* attribute values, whether defaulted or specified, cannot exceed the "GRPCNT" quantity.

Clause 8
Processing Instruction

The uses for SGML span a continuum: at one end is a future oriented to information culled from databases, gathered in response to a particular need, and processed for any purpose by any available system in accordance with rules that react to the structure inherent in the stored information. At the other is the past, built on non-rule-based one-time formatting of text and images onto pages.

In one sense, the SGML processing instruction construct can be viewed as a throwback to that past, as it gives a user the opportunity to send system-specific markup to an application in its own language. In practice, though, processing instructions serve as a useful escape valve for failures of rule-based application design or implementation. In a perfect world, they would not be needed, but, as you may have noticed, the world is not perfect.

> T–B.2 *21*
> O–4.234 *139:10*

```
     [44] processing instruction =
2          pio,
           system data,
4          pic

     [45] system data =
6          character data
```

> `<?`
> [45] *339:5*
> `>`

> [47] *344:1*

However, there are good and bad ways of communicating system-specific data to the system. The simplest — but worst — is the processing instruction that can occur anywhere in the document. This was a very early invention in the development of SGML and was a response to people who wanted, for example, to force page breaks in the right place when an application's normal processing did them incorrectly.

Later on, two improvements were designed: the processing instruction PI entity and the SDATA entity. Because they are entities, they must be declared in the prolog. Accordingly, it is a straightforward task to locate these system-specific strings. A recipient of the document can modify them far more easily than direct processing instructions that are scattered throughout a document instance.

> Processing instructions are deprecated, as they reduce portability
> of the document. If a processing instruction must be used, it should
> be defined as an entity, so that the *system data* [[45] *339:5*] will be
> confined to the *prolog* [[7] *303:1*] , where a recipient of the document
> can more easily locate and modify it.

By definition, the data of a processing instruction must be acted upon by a processing system. SGML allows the user to indicate when such action will generate data that the application will treat as though it had occurred in the document content. Data-generating instructions must be entered in SDATA entities, while instructions that change the processing environment must be entered in PI entities or direct processing instructions. (For example, instructions with functions like "begin new page" or "use a special font for the next character".)

> [**T–B.6.2.1** *41*]
> [**O–4.235** *147:5*]
> [**A–10.5.3** *397:9*]

The distinction between processing instructions that return data to the application and those that do not is very important because of the method by which an SGML parser handles record ends. It was stated in 7.6.1 [*321*] that a record end that follows data is treated as data and passed on to an application, while a record end that is caused solely by markup — such as a processing instruction — is not. Therefore, if a processing instruction generates data it must be defined as an SDATA entity; that way, if a record end follows it, the SGML parser will treat that as a significant record end and pass it to the application just as if a word had preceded it in the text.

> [**T–B.3.3.1** *25*]
> [**O–4.275** *146:7*]

On the other hand, if the processing instruction does not return data — if it merely sets a switch in the environment or performs some similar action — then it should be put into a processing instruction entity instead. The SGML parser will ignore a record end that is preceded in a record only by a processing instruction entity.

The term "returns data" can be confusing because the generated data is returned to the application program, not to the SGML parser. It does not affect the replacement text of the SDATA entity in any way.

2   A *processing instruction* [44] *339:1* that returns data must be defined as an "SDATA" entity and entered with an entity reference. One that does not return data should be defined as a "PI" entity.

System data is another of those special cases like character data and replaceable character data. That is, the normal parsing rules are changed and most delimiters will not be recognized. In this case, only the processing instruction close delimiter that terminates the system data is recognized. If the processing system wants to allow the processing instruction close delimiter character to occur within a processing instruction, then the processing system has to provide some other way of entering it so that the SGML parser will not confuse it with a real processing instruction close. (In the reference concrete syntax, this means that a processing instruction cannot contain a ">".)   **A–10.5.3** *397:9*

4   No markup is recognized in system data other than the delimiter that would terminate it.

6   NOTE — The characters allowed in *system data* [45] *339:5* and their interpretation are defined by the system. If it is desired to allow non-SGML

8   characters or the *pic* delimiter character in *system data* [45] *339:5*, an alternative way of entering them should be provided so that the actual char-

10 acters do not occur in the document.

8.1 Quantities

The length of a *processing instruction* [44] *339:1*, exclusive of its

12 delimiters, cannot exceed the "PILEN" quantity.

                                                        A–13.4.8 *469:26*

Clause 9
Common Constructs

This chapter covers some constructs that are common to many aspects of SGML. They include:

— Delimiter and name recognition, and some of the conditions under which normal delimiter recognition rules do not apply.

A–11.2.3 *409:3*

— References to entities and characters.

— Capacity.

9.1 Replaceable Character Data

The sub-clauses 9.4 ⟨*347*⟩ and 9.5 ⟨*356*⟩ define a pair of valuable markup constructs — entity and character references. There are circumstances in which it is important to recognize these constructs, and no others, as markup. That function can be accomplished by identifying certain text as "replaceable character data".

O–4.263 *140:14*

In replaceable character data, all characters are treated as data characters except for those necessary to recognize a character or a general entity reference, as well as the characters that would terminate the replaceable character data. This means that the parser must recognize the delimiter characters, which might be literal delimiters or some other kind of delimiters, depending on where the replaceable character data occurs.

T–B.8.3 *50*

A–7.9.3 *330:14*

[46] replaceable character data =

2   (*data character* | [48] *344:3*

           character reference | [62] *356:1*

4   *general entity reference* | [59] *350:17*

        Ee)*

The most significant rule about entity references in replaceable character data is that markup that would terminate the replaceable character data is not recognized in one of those entities. In other words, an entity cannot begin inside of a replaceable character data string and have the character string end inside that entity. Entities cannot overlap with replaceable character data: they must nest cleanly within the replaceable character data and the replaceable character data must begin and end in the same entity.

6   Markup that would terminate *replaceable character data* [46] *343:1* is not recognized in an entity that was referenced from within the

8   same *replaceable character data* [46] *343:1* .

An *Ee* can occur in *replaceable character data* [46] *343:1* only if

10   the reference to the entity it terminates occurred in the same *replaceable character data* [46] *343:1* .

The replacement text of an entity reference has to be valid in the replaceable character data. Therefore the entity could be a CDATA or an SDATA entity because those simply resolve to data, but it cannot be a non-SGML data entity or a processing instruction entity or a subdocument entity because those constructs would not be allowed in replaceable character data.   T–B.13.1 *58*

12   A reference to a non-SGML data entity, PI entity, or, SGML subdocument entity, is prohibited in *replaceable character data*

14   [46] *343:1* . A reference to a CDATA entity or SDATA entity is permitted.

16   NOTE — An effect of this sub-clause is to require that an element or marked section that is declared to be *replaceable character data*

18   [46] *343:1* must start and end in the same entity.

9.2 Character Data

Character data is a lot simpler than replaceable character data. Nothing is allowed in character data except data characters.

Even though SGML characters normally have the potential of being either markup characters or data characters, we know that in text that is declared as character data that they are data characters — or to put it another way, no markup will be recognized in character data other than the delimiters that would terminate the character data.

> T–B.8.3 *50*
> O–4.33 *140:9*

| | [47] character data = | |
| 2 | *data character** | [48] *344:3* |

| | [48] data character = | |
| 4 | *SGML character* | [50] *345:1* |

Certain characters may be declared to be non-SGML characters in the document character set. These can never appear in an SGML entity. All others are considered to be SGML characters.

> T–B.13.1.2 *59*
> O–4.208 *146:8*

	[49] character =	
6	*SGML character* |	[50] *345:1*
	NONSGML	

8 NOTE — A non-SGML character can be entered as a data character within an SGML entity by using a *character reference* [62] *356:1* .

9.2.1 SGML Character

Every character in the document character set is a member of one of the eighteen character classes defined by the SGML syntax and listed in figures 1 and 2.

> O–4.32 *199:1*

The classes listed in figure 1 [*345*] are those assigned by SGML itself as part of the abstract syntax. In most cases, that simply means acknowledging that SGML follows accepted conventions: Digits are the characters zero to nine. Lower-case letters are the characters a through z, and upper-case are A though Z.

In figure 2 [*345*] are listed the fourteen classes that are assigned by the

Variable	Characters	Numbers	Description
Digit	0 – 9	48 – 57	Digits
Ee	(system signal; not a character)		Entity end signal
LC Letter	a – z	97 – 122	Lower-case letters
Special	' ( ) + , - . / : = ?	39 – 41 43 – 47 58 61 63	Special minimum data characters
UC Letter	A – Z	65 – 90	Upper-case letters

Figure 1 — Character Classes: Abstract Syntax

Variable	Characters	Numbers	Description
DATACHAR	(implicit)	(implicit)	Dedicated data characters
DELMCHAR	(implicit)	(implicit)	Delimiter characters
FUNCHAR	(none)	(none)	Inert function characters
LCNMCHAR	- .	45 46	Lower-case name characters
LCNMSTRT	(none)	(none)	Lower-case name start characters
MSICHAR	(none)	(none)	Markup-scan-in characters
MSOCHAR	(none)	(none)	Markup-scan-out characters
MSSCHAR	(none)	(none)	Markup-scan-suppress characters
RE		13	Record end character
RS		10	Record start character
SEPCHAR		9	Separator characters
SPACE		32	Space character
UCNMCHAR	- .	45 46	Upper-case name characters
UCNMSTRT	(none)	(none)	Upper-case name start characters

Figure 2 — Character Classes: Concrete Syntax

concrete syntax and therefore are reassignable, if necessary, by an SGML application.

The purpose of this clause is simply to group some of the character classes in the abstract and concrete syntaxes into useful categories that can be referenced elsewhere.   O–4.280 *134:18*

2   [50] SGML character =
         markup character | [51] *345:4*
         DATACHAR

4   [51] markup character =
         name character | [52] *345:8*
6   function character | [54] *346:8*
         DELMCHAR

8   [52] name character =
         name start character | [53] *346:3*
10   **Digit** |

2
        LCNMCHAR |
        UCNMCHAR

[53] name start character =
4
        LC Letter |
        UC Letter |
6
        LCNMSTRT |
        UCNMSTRT

9.2.2 Function Character

This clause identifies the classes from figure 2 ⟨ *345* ⟩ that are function characters; that is, characters that can serve as markup or perform some useful SGML function — indicating record starts and record ends, for instance.
        ⟨ **O–4.139** *200:5* ⟩

8   [54] function character =
        RE |
10
        RS |
        SPACE |
12
        SEPCHAR |
        MSOCHAR |
14
        MSICHAR |
        MSSCHAR |
16
        FUNCHAR

9.3 Name

This clause probably should have been entitled "Name Token" since each item in it — name, number, name token and number token — is in fact a name token. A name token is one or more name characters, and a name is a special case of a name token in which the first character is a name start character. Similarly, a number token is a special case of a name token in which the first character is a digit, and a number is simply a number token or a name token in which all the characters are digits.

[55] name =
18
        name start character,   ⟨ **[53]** *346:3* ⟩
        name character*   ⟨ **[52]** *345:8* ⟩

[56] number =
2   **Digit**+

[57] name token =
4   *name character*+   [**52**] *345:8*

[58] number token =
6   **Digit**,
       *name character******   [**52**] *345:8*

Depending on whether an application's declared concrete syntax respects the case of names or not, the upper-case form of each character in a name token or its derivatives would be substituted for the lower case equivalent if that was entered.   **T–B.5.1.1** *33*

               O–4.198 *155:5*

8   The upper-case form of each character in a *name* [**55**] *346:17*,
name token [**57**] *347:3*, *number* [**56**] *347:1*, or *number token*
10   [**58**] *347:5*, as specified by the "NAMECASE" parameter of the
SGML declaration [**171**] *450:1*, is substituted for the character actu-
12   ally entered.

NOTE — A *number* [**56**] *347:1* or *number token* [**58**] *347:5* is not a
14   quantity but a character string, like a *name* [**55**] *346:17* or *name token*
[**57**] *347:3*; therefore, "01" and "1", for example, are not equivalent.

9.3.1 Quantities

16   The length of a *name* [**55**] *346:17*, *name token* [**57**] *347:3*, *number*
[**56**] *347:1*, or *number token* [**58**] *347:5*, cannot exceed the
18   "NAMELEN" quantity.

               A–13.4.8 *469:26*

9.4 Entity References

The fundamental idea behind entity references is that they are transparent. What the SGML parser sees should be, with few exceptions, the
same as if the entity's replacement text had been entered directly. The
fact that the text was accessed by an entity reference should not be significant. One exception, stated in 9.1 *342*, is that when an entity reference
occurs in replaceable character data, any markup that might have ter-

minated the replaceable character data is not recognized in the replacement text.

Note that, in the second sentence, the word "non-SGML" is an error and should have been deleted by the amendment, as was done in similar cases. O–4.124 *138:13*

2 The replacement text of an entity reference must comply with the syntactic and semantic requirements that govern the context of the reference. For purposes of this rule, a reference to an *SGML*
4 *subdocument entity* [3] *296:1* or a *non-SGML data entity* [6] *300:7* is treated like a reference to a *data character* [48] *344:3* .

6 NOTE — Such entities can also be accessed by a *general entity name* [103] *395:4* attribute.

8 A reference to an undeclared entity is an error unless there is an applicable default entity (see 9.4.4 350).

10 A reference to an entity that has already been referenced and has not yet ended is invalid (i.e., entities cannot be referenced recur-
12 sively).

9.4.1 Quantities

14 The number of open entities (except for the unreferenced *SGML document entity* [2] *295:13* in which the document begins) cannot exceed the "ENTLVL" quantity.

Note that this limitation does not apply to an entity named in an attribute value. Such an entity does not meet the definition of an "open entity" as it is not referenced.

O–4.221 *160:3*
A–13.4.8 *469:26*

9.4.2 Limits

16 The number of open SGML subdocument entities cannot exceed the quantity specified on the "SUBDOC" parameter of the *SGML*
18 *declaration* [171] *450:1* .

This limitation is particularly significant because each open subdocument entity is essentially a recursive call to the SGML parser. Such calls could have a substantial impact on the overhead of a system. This limit is interesting also because it is very unusual: an SGML parser is never aware that a subdocument was called from anywhere else. The very essence of a subdocument entity is that it is not parsed in the context of a document from which it is referenced, but with respect to its own document type definition.

Therefore something outside the SGML parser — the entity manager, in fact — has to keep track of the open subdocument entities because the parser will never be aware of more than one. Once it opens a subdocument entity everything else that goes on is done without reference to the environment of the original document.

T–B.6.2.3 *42*

O–4.123 *129:9*

Note that the limitation on open subdocument entities, like the limitation on open entities in general, does not apply to an entity named in an attribute value.

9.4.3 Obfuscatory Entity References

Obfuscatory is one of those wonderful words that describes itself. For many readers, it will not be at all clear what the word means, and the objective of this clause is to prevent any use of entity references that makes it not clear what the markup means.

The basic principle of eschewing obfuscation is to keep things balanced between the element structure and the entity structure. In other words, start elements in the same entities as they end, and end marked sections in the same entities as they begin. Apply those same principles to balance structures that occur within markup declarations; for example, make sure that groups start and end in the same entity.

In most of these cases, there is no choice; the requirements of the standard enforce these principles. There are cases however where it was felt necessary to give the user flexibility or it was just too burdensome to have a parser check for compliance. There the user must simply exercise good judgment.

Any use of entity references that obscures the markup is deprecated.

NOTE — Most such abuses are prohibited by the syntax of SGML. The following principles should be observed (those that say "must" are restatements of syntax rules, stated formally elsewhere, that enforce the principles):

a)   The opening delimiter of a tag, *processing instruction* [44] *339:1* , declaration, literal, or other delimited text, must be in the same entity as the closing delimiter. An entity must not end in delimited text unless it began there, and an entity that begins there must end there.

2   b)   The content of an element or marked section that was declared to be *character data* [47] 344:1 or *replaceable character data*

4   [46] 343:1 , or of a marked section that is ignored, must (and the content of other elements and marked sections should) start and end

6   in the same entity.

    c)   For other elements and marked sections, the *start-tag* [14] 314:1

8   and *end-tag* [19] 317:4 (or *marked section start* [94] 392:3 and *marked section end* [95] 392:6) should be in the same entity, or

10   they should be the replacement text of entities whose references are in the same entity.

12   d)   In a markup declaration, a reference must be replaced either by zero or more consecutive complete parameters (with any intervening *ps*

14   [65] 372:1 separators), or, within a group, by one or more consecutive complete tokens (with any intervening *ts* [70] 375:3 separators

16   and/or connectors).

9.4.4 Named Entity Reference

There are two kinds of named entity reference: general entity references, which occur in document instances and in attribute values (e.g.: • and &file1;) and parameter entity references, which occur in prologs and in markup declarations that occur in the document instance (e.g.: %lists; and %emph;).

T–B.6 38

[59] general entity reference =

18   ***ero***,   &
        name group?,   [69] 374:11
20   *name*,   [55] 346:17
        reference end   [61] 352:29

22   [60] parameter entity reference =
        pero,   %
24   *name group?*,   [69] 374:11
        name,   [55] 346:17
26   *reference end*   [61] 352:29

The name group in a named entity reference serves the same purpose as a document type specification in a start-tag. That is, if there are active document types named in the group then the entity reference is recognized as such; otherwise it is ignored. Unlike the start-tag, though, the named entity reference group will be processed if the name group contains either the name of an active link type or that of an active document type.   ⌐O–4.205 *161:9* ¬

A *name group* ⌐ **[69]** *374:11* ¬ can be specified only if "CONCUR
2   YES", "SIMPLE YES", "IMPLICIT YES", or "EXPLICIT YES" is
     specified on the *SGML declaration* ⌐ **[171]** *450:1* ¬ , and the reference
4   does not occur within a *start-tag* ⌐ **[14]** *314:1* ¬ or *prolog* ⌐ **[7]** *303:1* ¬ .

     NOTE — This requirement does not prohibit specifying a *name group*
6   ⌐ **[69]** *374:11* ¬ for a *parameter entity reference* ⌐ **[60]** *350:22* ¬ within a *marked*
     section start ⌐ **[94]** *392:3* ¬ in a document instance.

8   If a *name group* ⌐ **[69]** *374:11* ¬ is specified, the entity reference is
     ignored unless a *name* ⌐ **[55]** *346:17* ¬ in the *name group* ⌐ **[69]** *374:11* ¬
10 is that of an active document type or link type.

9.4.4.1 Applicable Entity Declaration

This clause consists of complex technical rules designed to sort out which entity declaration is applicable to a given entity reference when there could be more than one. The rules also apply to entities named in the value of general entity name and general entity name list attributes, although such attribute values are not considered references.

In the usual case, when there is only a single document type declaration in the prolog, the rules are simple: there must be one or more declarations in the prolog and the first of these will apply. For a general entity, there is the additional provision that, if there was no declaration for that entity by name, then a default entity declaration will be used if there was one of those.

     NOTE — The following requirements apply to entity names used in the
12 value of general entity name and general entity name list attributes, as well
     as to named entity references.

14 Before an *entity name* ⌐ **[102]** *395:1* ¬ can be used, it must be
     declared by an *entity declaration* ⌐ **[101]** *394:18* ¬ in all applicable
16 DTDs, except that a *general entity name* ⌐ **[103]** *395:4* ¬ that is unde-
     clared in a particular DTD is treated as though it had been declared
18 for the default entity if that DTD has one.

Where there are multiple document type declarations and the CONCUR feature is being used, rules a), b), and c) apply.

Where there are active link types, rules b) and e) will always apply, and for explicit link types rule d) applies as well.

The applicable DTDs depend on the context in which the *entity
name* [102] 395:1 occurs, as follows:

a) Within a start-tag, all DTDs applicable to the tag.

NOTE — That is, either the base DTD or those of active document
types named in the tag's *document type specification* [28] 325:1 .

b) Elsewhere in a document instance, the DTDs of active
document types or the source DTDs of active link types
specified in a named entity reference's *name group*
[69] 374:11 , or, for any name that is undeclared in such a
DTD, or if no *name group* [69] 374:11 is specified, the base
DTD.

NOTE — An effect of this requirement is that an entity declared in the
base document type can be referenced in an instance of any document type in which no entity with the same name was defined, and in
which, for a general entity, no default entity was defined.

c) Within a DTD, the same DTD.

d) Within a *result attribute specification* [168] 446:8 , the result
DTD.

e) Elsewhere in an LPD, the source DTD.

NOTE — An LPD is parsed as though entity declarations within it had
occurred in its source DTD.

NOTES

1   An effect of these requirements is that a default entity declared in the
base document type will be referenced by an undeclared general entity
name in an instance of any document type that does not itself have a
default entity.

2   If an entity declaration specifies a data content notation, the notation
must be declared in the same DTD as the entity.

9.4.5 Reference End

[61] reference end =
   (**refc** |
   RE)?   ;

NOTE — Ending a reference with an **RE** has the effect of suppressing the
2   record end.

The **refc** or **RE** can be omitted only if the reference is not followed
4   by a character that could occur in the reference, or by a character
that could be interpreted as the omitted *reference end* [**[61]** *352:29*] .

This funny definition of reference end was designed to solve a problem that occurs in record-oriented systems. When there is data in a
source record, the record end will be passed on by the SGML parser to
the application as significant data. Sometimes it is desirable to prevent
that — in other words, to treat two different records as though they were
a single record.

This effect can be achieved by ending the first record with an entity
reference that is terminated by the record end, rather than by an explicit
reference close delimiter. In this way, the record end is treated as part of
the markup of the entity reference and is not available to be treated as a
data character. As it is unlikely an entity reference will show up just
when you need it, the recommended practice is to define an entity whose
replacement text is an empty string, just for the purpose of using it to
suppress record ends.

[**T–B.6.2** *40*]

9.4.6 Short Reference

Short references are a markup minimization capability in which a
short reference delimiter, usually one or two characters, is replaced by a
general entity reference. The general entity reference that replaces the
short reference can vary in different parts of the document, but the set of
characters that are usable as short references stays the same because it is
defined in the concrete syntax.

This approach gives the user the benefit of knowing that only a fixed
set of characters can potentially have special meaning as short references,
while still giving the application designer the flexibility to reinterpret
what those characters mean at different places. For example, a short reference of a blank line in the body of a document might mean a new paragraph, while the same blank line occurring in a table could mean a new
row.

[**T–C.1.3** *76*]
[**O–4.290** *166:3*]
[**A–13.4.6.2** *466:20*]

The indirect mapping of short references through entity names, rather
than directly to the entity text, offers a number of benefits:

— Entities and short reference maps can be redefined independently of one another.

— Short references can be converted to entity references if a document is sent to a system that does not support short references. Without the indirection, the receiving system could only redefine the entity text by changing every occurrence of the text in the document instance, and there would be no way to distinguish the occurrences that were due to the short references from any other occurrences.

— The language is simpler because there is no need to fit the rather complex definition of entity text into the structure of a short reference map.

If a short reference is mapped to a general entity name in the
2 current map, it is treated as markup and replaced by the named entity. If the short reference is mapped to nothing, each character
4 in the delimiter string is treated as an *s* 〔 [5] *297:23* 〕 separator if it can be recognized as such, and if not it is treated as data.

9.4.6.1 Equivalent Reference String

As with other markup minimization capabilities in SGML, it must be possible to create a document that does not use minimization but will be parsed to produce the same results as a document that does.

6 A short reference can be removed from a document by replacing it with an equivalent reference string that contains a named entity
8 reference. The *entity name* 〔 [102] *395:1* 〕 must be that to which the short reference is mapped in the current map.

In the case of short references, a potential problem arises in record-oriented systems that have an inherent system limitation on the length of a record. A short reference that has record boundaries in it, when replaced by a general entity reference, will have the effect of concatenating records together and possibly exceeding the maximum length. This clause provides rules that will prevent that from happening.

The general technique is to replace the short reference with an "equivalent reference string" that includes the record boundaries as well as the general entity reference.

〔 **O–4.128** *166:15* 〕

For example, consider a "row" element of a "table", within which the short reference delimiter "leading blanks" (record start followed by one or more blanks) is mapped to the general entity "row". An example with short references in use might appear as follows:

```
<table>
     First row of table.
     Second row of table.
</table>
```

Without short references, it would appear as:

```
<table>
&row;First row of table.
&row;Second row of table.
</table>
```

rather than:

```
<table>&row;First row of table.&row;Second row of table.
</table>
```

If the short reference contains any quantity of **RS** or **RE** characters, the equivalent reference string will include a single **RS** or **RE**, or both, as shown in the following list:

Short Reference	**Equivalent Reference String**
No *RS* or *RE*	*ero*, *name* [55] *346:17* , *refc*
RS*; no *RE	***RS**, ero*, *name* [55] *346:17* , *refc*
RE*; no *RS	*ero*, *name* [55] *346:17* , **RE**
Both *RS* and *RE*	***RS**, ero*, *name* [55] *346:17* , **RE**

NOTES

1   Equivalent reference strings are used when a document is converted from a concrete syntax that supports short references to one that does not.

2   A single **RS** and/or **RE** is preserved in the equivalent reference string to prevent records from becoming joined, and possibly exceeding a system's maximum length restriction. They are not recognized as data: the **RS** because it never is, and the **RE** because it serves as the *reference end* [61] *352:29* .

9.5 Character Reference

"Character reference" sounds like something that you would look for when hiring a butler, but in SGML it simply means a reference that is replaced by a single character rather than an entity.

> **T–B.7.2** *45*
> **O–4.37** *138:15*

There are two kinds of character reference — a numeric character reference, which consists of a delimited character number, and a named character reference, which consists of a delimited function name. Both are intended to be used when you could not otherwise enter a character conveniently in the text (perhaps because there is no key for it on your keyboard).

A numeric character reference has the special property that it is always treated as a data character at the point where it is entered. Therefore, if you put a numeric character reference into an entity text string in an entity declaration, at that point it would be treated as data. Subsequently, when you reference that entity and it is replaced by the entity text, there is no longer a record of the fact that the character was originally entered with a numeric character reference. Therefore, whether it is treated as data or not will depend on what that character is and the context that is established when the entity reference is resolved.

> **O–4.217** *162:5*

Some characters are functions in the concrete syntax, such as tab or record end. If the function is wanted, a named character reference incorporating the function name is used; otherwise, a numeric character reference is used and the function is not performed.

> **O–4.204** *162:3*

```
   [62] character reference =
2       cro,                                    &#
           ( function name |                    [63] 356:6
4              character number   ),            [64] 357:1
           reference end                        [61] 352:29

6  [63] function name =
           "RE" |
8          "RS" |
           "SPACE" |
10         name                                 [55] 346:17
```

[64] character number =

2   *number*   [**56**] *347:1*

4   A *name* [**55**] *346:17* specified as a *function name* [**63**] *356:6* must have been specified as an *added function* [**187**] *462:10* in the concrete syntax.

6   A *character reference* [**62**] *356:1* should be used when a character could not otherwise be entered conveniently in the text.

8   A replacement character is considered to be in the same entity as its reference.

10   A replacement character is treated as though it were entered directly except that the replacement for a numeric *character refer-*

12   *ence* [**62**] *356:1* is always treated as data in the context in which the replacement occurs.

14   NOTES

1   A system can determine its own internal representation for a replace-

16   ment character. Care should be taken to distinguish a normal *function char-acter* [**54**] *346:8* (entered directly or as a replacement for a named char-

18   acter reference) from one that replaces a numeric character reference.

2   When a document is translated to a different document character set,

20   the *character number* [**64**] *357:1* of each numeric character reference must be changed to the corresponding *character number* [**64**] *357:1* of

22   the new set.

9.6 Delimiter Recognition

One of the design criteria for SGML was to strike a balance between the requirements of computer programs that process documents and those of users who are keyboarding documents without the assistance of intelligent SGML-sensitive editing programs; that is, using conventional text editors or word processing programs. This conflict of interest becomes very evident in the area of delimiter recognition.

The processing programs would like a simple set of delimiters, explicit and unambiguous, making very clear what is markup and what is data. On the other hand, the human being entering documents is aware of context and knows, for example, when he is entering data and therefore becomes annoyed if a computer program tries to treat that data as though it were markup. To minimize that sort of annoyance, the SGML delimiter recognition design takes into account that there are different modes of recognition, and that certain delimiter roles are only recognized within certain modes. (See also F.1.2 [545] .)

Another protection for the user is that, even within the correct mode, certain delimiters are not recognized unless they satisfy what is called a "contextual constraint". Usually that constraint means that certain other characters have to follow the delimiter in order for the delimiter to be recognized as valid. For example, a start-tag open delimiter is not recognized unless it is followed by a character that is allowed to occur as the first character of a start-tag, such as a name start character for a generic identifier.

[**T–B.7.3** *46*]
[**O–4.58** *136:13*]

To explain these techniques, let us look at how one uses the table in figure 3 [360]. The first column of the table, labeled "Name", gives the names of all of the delimiter roles that are defined in the abstract syntax of SGML. For example, the third one on the list — CRO — is the delimiter that begins a character reference. As we can see from the right-most column of the table, its purpose is to be a character reference open delimiter.

The second column of the table, headed "String", shows the character string assigned to this role by the reference concrete syntax — in this case an & followed by a #. The next column, "Number", shows the character numbers for these characters in the syntax-reference character set of the reference concrete syntax.

The fourth column, headed "Mode", indicates in which modes a CRO is recognized. Those modes are CON and LIT. Now look up those names in the listing in 9.6.1 [359]. We can see that CON means that a delimiter string is recognized in content and in the marked section of marked section declarations that occur in content, while LIT means that it is recognized in a literal. A CRO, therefore, would not be recognized in other places, such as in a declaration subset, a markup declaration, or a processing instruction.

The next column, headed "Constraint", indicates whether there are any contextual constraints. These are listed in 9.6.2 [361]. In the case of the CRO delimiter, there is the constraint CREF, which means that in order for a CRO to be recognized, it must be followed by either a name start character or a digit. This constraint, of course, is consistent with what we know about character references, which is that they contain either a function character name or a character number.

Because of the operation of this contextual constraint, if the content of an element included the string &#* (ampersand, number sign, asterisk), the parser would treat it as data. The string would not be treated as an erroneously constructed character reference because the contextual constraint was not satisfied.

$\boxed{\textbf{T–B.7.2}\ 45}$

$\boxed{\textbf{A–9.6.2}\ 361{:}12}$

Except as otherwise provided in this International Standard, a
delimiter string is recognized as satisfying a delimiter role only
within the particular recognition mode (or modes) in which the role
is meaningful and, in some cases, only if a contextual constraint is
satisfied. The roles, their recognition modes, and any contextual
constraints on their recognition, are listed in figure 3 $\boxed{360}$. Also
shown are the strings assigned to general delimiters in the reference delimiter set, and the character numbers of those strings in
the *syntax-reference character set* $\boxed{\textbf{[185]}\ 461{:}1}$ of the reference
concrete syntax. The strings assigned as short reference delimiters
in the reference delimiter set are shown in figure 4 $\boxed{364}$.

NOTE — A named character reference can be used to enter the first character of a delimiter string or delimiter-in-context, but only the first character.

All characters of a delimiter string or delimiter-in-context (see 9.6.2
$\boxed{361}$) must occur in the same entity.

9.6.1 Recognition Modes

The recognition modes are:

Mode	Meaning
CON	Recognized in *content* $\boxed{\textbf{[24]}\ 320{:}1}$ and in the *marked section* $\boxed{\textbf{[96]}\ 392{:}9}$ of marked section declarations that occur in *content* $\boxed{\textbf{[24]}\ 320{:}1}$.
	NOTE — Most delimiters will not be recognized when the *content* $\boxed{\textbf{[24]}\ 320{:}1}$ is *character data* $\boxed{\textbf{[47]}\ 344{:}1}$ or *replaceable character data* $\boxed{\textbf{[46]}\ 343{:}1}$.
CXT	Recognized as part of the contextual sequence of a "CON" or "DSM" mode delimiter-in-context. (See below.)
DS	Recognized in a declaration subset.
DSM	Recognized in a declaration subset or in the *marked section* $\boxed{\textbf{[96]}\ 392{:}9}$ of marked section declarations that occur in a declaration subset.
GRP	Recognized in a group.
LIT	Recognized in a literal.
MD	Recognized in a markup declaration.

Name	String	Number	Mode	Constraint	Description of Role
AND	&	38	GRP		And connector
COM	--	45 45	CXT MD		Comment start or end
CRO	&#	38 35	CON LIT	CREF	Character reference open
DSC	]	93	DS MD	ENT	Declaration subset close
DSO	[	91	CXT MD		Declaration subset open
DTGC	]	93	GRP		Data tag group close
DTGO	[	91	GRP		Data tag group open
ERO	&	38	CON LIT		Entity reference open
ETAGO	</	60 47	CON TAG	NMS	End-tag open
GRPC	)	41	GRP	GI	Group close
GRPO	(	40	CXT GRP MD		Group open
LIT	"	34	GRP LIT MD TAG		Literal start or end
LITA	'	39	GRP LIT MD TAG		Literal start or end (alternative)
MDC	>	62	CXT MD		Markup declaration close
MDO	<!	60 33	CON DSM	DCL	Markup declaration open
MINUS	-	45	MD	EX	Exclusion
MSC	]]	93 93	CON DSM	MSE	Marked section close
NET	/	47	CON TAG	ELEM	Null end-tag
OPT	?	63	GRP		Optional occurrence indicator
OR	|	124	GRP		Or connector
PERO	%	37	DSM GRP LIT MD	NMS	Parameter entity reference open
PIC	>	62	PI		Processing instruction close
PIO	<?	60 63	CON DSM		Processing instruction open
PLUS	+	43	GRP MD	EX	Required and repeatable; inclusion
REFC	;	59	REF		Reference close
REP	*	42	GRP		Optional and repeatable
RNI	#	35	GRP MD		Reserved name indicator
SEQ	,	44	GRP		Sequence connector
SHORTREF			CON		Short reference (see Figure 4)
STAGO	<	60	CON TAG	GI	Start-tag open
TAGC	>	62	CXT TAG		Tag close
VI	=	61	TAG		Value indicator

Figure 3 — Reference Delimiter Set: General

	PI	Recognized in a *processing instruction* [44] *339:1* .
2	**REF**	Recognized in a *general entity reference* [59] *350:17* , *parameter entity reference* [60] *350:22* , or *character ref-*
4		*erence* [62] *356:1* .
	TAG	recognized in a *start-tag* [14] *314:1* or *end-tag*
6		[19] *317:4* .

8 NOTE — Recognition modes can nest. For example, when a markup decla- ration begins, the recognition mode becomes "MD". If a **GRPO** occurs in the declaration, the mode will become "GRP", and an **MDC** (for example)
10 will not be recognizable. When a **GRPC** occurs, the "GRP" mode ends and the recognition mode again becomes "MD".

9.6.2 Contextual Constraints

12 The most common constraint is that the delimiter string must start a delimiter-in-context in which it is followed by one of the listed
14 contextual sequences:

	CREF	*name start character* [53] *346:3* or **Digit**
16	**DCL**	*name start character* [53] *346:3* , **com**, **dso**, or **mdc**
	GI	*name start character* [53] *346:3* , or, if "SHORTTAG
18		YES" is specified on the *SGML declaration* [171] *450:1* , **tagc**, or, if "CONCUR YES" is specified on the *SGML*
20		*declaration* [171] *450:1* , **grpo**
	MSE	**mdc**
22	**NMS**	*name start character* [53] *346:3* , or, if "CONCUR YES", "SIMPLE YES", "IMPLICIT YES", or "EXPLICIT YES", is
24		specified on the *SGML declaration* [171] *450:1* , **grpo**

Other contextual constraints are:

26	**ELEM**	In "CON" mode, recognized only within an element whose *start-tag* [14] *314:1* was a *net-enabling start-tag*
28		[18] *316:11* ; in "TAG" mode, no constraints.
	EX	In "MD" mode, recognized only at the start of a delim-
30		iter-in-context in which it is followed by **grpo**; in "GRP" mode, no constraints.
32	**ENT**	Recognized only in the same entity as the corresponding **dso**.

9.6.3 Order of Recognition

This clause tries to resolve in a practical, implementable way some odd problems that can occur in theory but are less likely to occur in practice. The basic principle is to let the recognition of delimiters be resolved independently of whether or not the delimiters are actually useful. For example, as long as it is legal for a short reference to be recognized in a certain context, it will be recognized even though it may not be mapped to anything (and therefore is useless), even though the recognition of the short reference might prevent recognition of some other delimiter that could be useful.

O–4.58 *136:13*

2 Delimiter strings (including any required contextual sequences) are recognized in the order they occur, with no overlap.

4 NOTE — For example, if "abc" and "bcd" are delimiter strings, and the document contains "abcde", then "abc" will be recognized and parsing will continue at "d", so "bcd" will not be recognized.

6 This rule holds true even if the recognized delimiter is semantically incorrect, or is a short reference that is mapped to nothing.

8 NOTE — For example, in the reference delimiter set, the solidus (/) will be recognized as part of an ***etago*** delimiter-in-context rather than as the ***net***,
10 even if the *end-tag* [19] *317:4* GI was not declared, or is not the GI of an open element.

9.6.4 Delimiters Starting with the Same Character

This sub-clause, like the previous one, is one in which unusual situations are being resolved. Once again the principle is followed that delimiter recognition conflicts are resolved independently of whether the delimiters are semantically useful at that time.

12 If multiple delimiter strings start with the same character, only the longest delimiter string or delimiter-in-context among them will be
14 recognized at a given point in the document.

16 NOTE — For example, if "ab" and "abc" are delimiters and the document contains "abcd", then "abc" will be recognized and parsing will continue at "d", so "ab" will not be recognized.

18 This rule holds true even if the longer delimiter is semantically incorrect, or is a short reference that is mapped to nothing.

NOTE — If, in the previous example, "ab" and "abc" were short reference delimiters, short reference "abc" alone would be recognized and short reference "ab" would not be, even if short reference "abc" were mapped to nothing in the current map and short reference "ab" were mapped to an entity.

9.6.5 Short References with Blank Sequences

In figure 4 (364) is the list of short reference delimiter strings that are defined for the reference concrete syntax. The first column lists all the strings, the second column shows the character numbers for those strings in the syntax-reference character set of the reference concrete syntax, and the last column is a textual name for the string.

The fifth and sixth strings warrant discussion. The fifth is an empty record — a record start followed by a record end; the sixth is a blank record — a record start followed by a "B" and then followed by a record end.

"B" in a short reference string has a special meaning. It says that a blank sequence will be recognized in the content wherever a sequence of B's appears in the short reference delimiter. A blank sequence is an uninterrupted sequence of space characters, possibly intermixed with function characters acting as separator characters (that is, of the type SEPCHAR). In the reference concrete syntax, a tab character is a SEPCHAR.

The distinction, then, between an empty record as a short reference and a blank record as a short reference is that the empty record can have no characters in between the record start and record end while the blank record can have spaces and separator characters.

T–C.1.3.2 77

If there is a B sequence in the definition of a short reference delimiter, it will cause recognition of a blank sequence in the content ([24] 320:1). The minimum length of the blank sequence is the length of the B sequence.

NOTE — That is, one B means one or more blanks, two B's means two or more blanks, etc.

A string that could be recognized as more than one delimiter will be considered the string of the most specific delimiter that it satisfies.

NOTE — For example, a tab character would be recognized as "&#TAB;" in preference to "B", and three spaces would be recognized as "BBB" in preference to "BB".

String	Number	Description
&#TAB;	9	Horizontal tab
&#RE;	13	Record end
&#RS;	10	Record start
&#RS;B	10 66	Leading blanks
&#RS;&#RE;	10 13	Empty record
&#RS;B&#RE;	10 66 13	Blank record
B&#RE;	66 13	Trailing blanks
&#SPACE;	32	Space
BB	66 66	Two or more blanks
"	34	Quotation mark
#	35	Number sign
%	37	Percent sign
'	39	Apostrophe
(	40	Left parenthesis
)	41	Right parenthesis
*	42	Asterisk
+	43	Plus sign
,	44	Comma
-	45	Hyphen
--	45 45	Two hyphens
:	58	Colon
;	59	Semicolon
=	61	Equals sign
@	64	Commercial at
[	91	Left square bracket
]	93	Right square bracket
^	94	Circumflex accent
_	95	Low line
{	123	Left curly bracket
|	124	Vertical line
}	125	Right curly bracket
~	126	Tilde

Figure 4 — Reference Delimiter Set: Short References

9.6.5.1 Quantities

2 The length of a blank sequence recognized as a short reference cannot exceed the "BSEQLEN" quantity. If an actual blank sequence is longer, only the first "BSEQLEN" characters will be
4 included in the short reference string, and parsing will resume with the following character.

> A–13.4.8 *469:26*

9.6.6 Name Characters

Although it is technically possible to assign a name character to a delimiter role, it is not a good idea to do so. This clause states how the ambiguity will be resolved in cases where it is. Normally, the name character will be recognized as a delimiter in preference to recognition as a name character, but if a name token has already begun then it will be treated as a name character. The normal rules about case sensitivity for name characters also apply when a name character is being used as a delimiter.

T–B.7.1 *43*

O–4.119 *138:4*

2   If a *name character* [52] *345:8* is assigned to a delimiter role, it will be recognized as a delimiter (in preference to recognition as a *name character* [52] *345:8*) if a *name token* [57] *347:3* has not
4   already begun; if found within a *name token* [57] *347:3* , it will be treated as a *name character* [52] *345:8* .

6   If general upper-case substitution is specified by the "NAMECASE" parameter of the *SGML declaration* [171] *450:1* , then for purposes
8   of delimiter recognition, a *name character* [52] *345:8* assigned to a delimiter role is treated as though it were its upper-case form.

9.7 Markup Suppression

Certain function characters can suppress recognition of markup or reinstate it. There are no characters of this nature defined as part of the reference concrete syntax, but some are defined in the multicode basic concrete syntax which is a registered concrete syntax that is published as part of the SGML standard. It is shown in figure 11 *501* .

T–B.7.1 *43*

These markup suppression function character types are used when graphic repertoire code extension is in use. Graphic repertoire code extension temporarily redefines the meaning of a particular character number. As a result, a character number that normally is associated with a character that is assigned to a delimiter role might temporarily be assigned to a character that is not a delimiter. In order to prevent that character from being treated as a delimiter while code extension is in effect, the markup suppression function characters are used to suppress markup recognition. As figure 11 *501* illustrates, the markup suppression functions are assigned to those characters that are used to invoke and cancel the graphic repertoire code extension. (See also E.3 *537* .)

O–4.148 *196:19*

10   An **MSOCHAR** suppresses recognition of markup until an **MSICHAR** or entity end occurs. An **MSSCHAR** does so for the
12   next character in the same entity (if any).

NOTE — An **MSOCHAR** occurring in *character data* ⟨ **[47]** *344:1* ⟩ or other
2   delimited text will therefore suppress recognition of the closing delimiter. An
MSSCHAR could do so if it preceded the delimiter.

4   If markup recognition has not been suppressed by an **MSOCHAR**,
an **MSICHAR** has no effect on markup recognition, but is not an
6   error.

If markup recognition has been suppressed by an **MSOCHAR**, a
8   subsequent **MSOCHAR** or **MSSCHAR** has no effect on markup
recognition, but is not an error.

10   An **MSOCHAR** that follows an **MSSCHAR** has no effect on markup
recognition.

9.8 Capacity

One of the most frustrating experiences that a user can have with a
supposedly portable and standardized object, like a document in SGML
or a program written in a portable language like C, is to find that the document or program that he receives from someone else is syntactically
correct and parsable by his system, but so large or complex that his system environment can not handle it. For example, the C program might
have too many variables defined for the receiving system's symbol table
to handle. Or, in the case of SGML, there may be so many entities and
elements defined in some document that originated on a mainframe, that
the system on a personal computer will not have enough storage to store
all those definitions.

It was to address such concerns that the concept of "capacity" was
introduced in SGML. Capacity points are assigned to certain objects that
occur in an SGML document, with a point being roughly indicative of a
storage location. There will not be an exact match because different
implementations handle storage differently, but the capacity points give
some idea of the relative amount of storage that each class of object
requires. Accordingly, it should be possible to predict fairly accurately
how much actual storage a particular system requires to handle an
SGML document of a given capacity.

⟨ **O–4.26** *212:1* ⟩
⟨ **A–13.2** *456:2* ⟩

Capacity values are expressed in a "capacity set", which is a table of
pairs of capacity categories and points allocated to them. The method by
which the points are calculated is illustrated in the table in figure 5 ⟨ *367* ⟩,

Name	Value	Points	Object for which capacity points are counted
TOTALCAP	35000	(total)	Grand total of individual capacity points.
ENTCAP	35000	NAMELEN	Entity defined.
ENTCHCAP	35000	1	Character of entity text.
ELEMCAP	35000	NAMELEN	Element defined.
GRPCAP	35000	NAMELEN	Content token at any level of a content model (a data tag group is three tokens).
EXGRPCAP	35000	NAMELEN	Exclusion or inclusion exceptions group.
EXNMCAP	35000	NAMELEN	Name in an exclusion or inclusion exceptions group.
ATTCAP	35000	NAMELEN	Attribute defined, plus NAMELEN for each occurrence (whether or not the attribute is specified) in a link set declaration of an element type associated with the definition, or, in an entity declaration, of a notation name associated with the definition.
ATTCHCAP	35000	1	Character of normalized length of an attribute value defined as a default value, or explicitly specified (not defaulted) in a link set declaration or data attribute specification.
AVGRPCAP	35000	NAMELEN	Token defined in an attribute value name group or name token group.
NOTCAP	35000	NAMELEN	Data content notation defined.
NOTCHCAP	35000	1	Character in a notation identifier.
IDCAP	35000	NAMELEN	ID attribute specified.
IDREFCAP	35000	NAMELEN	IDREF attribute specified (explicitly or by default).
MAPCAP	35000	NAMELEN	Short reference map declared, plus, for each map declared, NAMELEN for each short reference delimiter in the concrete syntax (whether or not the delimiter is specified in the map).
LKSETCAP	35000	NAMELEN	Link types or link sets defined.
LKNMCAP	35000	NAMELEN	Document type or element in a link type or link set declaration.

Figure 5 — Reference Capacity Set

which incorporates the reference capacity set in its first and second columns. The first column of the table has the name of a capacity category — the first one is TOTALCAP which, as the last column of the table says, is the grand total of individual capacity points. Below that line in the table are the individual capacities. Each individual capacity listed in the "Name" column is allocated the number of points indicated in the second column, "Value". The number in the third column, "Points", is multiplied by the number of occurrences of the object described in column four. The total is considered the value for that type of capacity and can not exceed the limit given in the second column.

For example, the second item in the table, ENTCAP, counts, for each entity defined, the number of points represented by the keyword NAMELEN, which is the name of a quantity in the SGML quantity set. The reference quantity set in the reference concrete syntax assigns NAMELEN a value of 8. The second column of the table states that the total points for all the defined entities can not exceed 35,000.

The next row of the table, the capacity called ENTCHCAP, indicates that 1 point will be counted for each character of entity text — again with a maximum of 35,000 points for all entity text in the document.

As figure 5 [367] indicates, in the reference capacity set every individual type of capacity could potentially use up the value for total capacity. This is another way of saying that the reference capacity set does not care how the capacity requirements are distributed over the different kinds of object that use capacity points. To put it another way, the storage could be distributed arbitrarily among entity definitions and element definitions and so on. Systems that lack such flexibility can assign different limits to the various individual capacities, and the sum of those limits to the total capacity.

Capacity sets are used in two different ways. There is one in the SGML declaration of every document stating how much capacity is required for that particular document. That is, it states that the capacity requirements of the document are no greater than the values in the capacity set. As every conforming SGML system must handle the reference capacity set, as long as your document does not exceed those limits, there is no need to state exactly what its requirements are.

The other use for a capacity set is when describing a particular system. There the capacity set states the maximum amount that the system can handle. By comparing its system capacity set with the capacity set of an incoming document, a receiving system can get a fairly good idea whether that document can be handled or whether some human intervention will be required (to break the document up into smaller processable pieces, for instance).

Note the difference between capacities and quantities. Quantities affect the size of buffers that are used by an implementation to store individual markup constructs. The NAMELEN quantity, for example, indicates how large a buffer is needed to store a name. Capacities, on the other hand, have to do with the overall memory that may be required in a system to deal with all the components and constructs of an SGML document.

2   The size and complexity of a document must not exceed the number of capacity points allowed by the document capacity set for the objects occurring in the document.

4   The names of the total and individual capacities, together with the values assigned to them in the reference capacity set, are shown in
6   figure 5 [367] . The set's public identifier is:

```
ISO 8879:1986//CAPACITY Reference//EN
```

2 The points accumulated for each type of object cannot exceed the value of that object's individual capacity, and the total points for all objects cannot exceed the "TOTALCAP" value.

4 The capacity values must be sufficient for the greatest capacity requirement among the possible sets of concurrent instances or
6 chains of link processes that could be processed at once.

Points are counted for the SGML document entity and SGML text
8 entities referenced from it, plus the set of possible open subdocument entities and SGML text entities referenced from them
10 that would require the largest capacity.

NOTE — As an example of capacity calculation, when a concrete syntax
12 with 32 short references and a "NAMELEN" of 8 is used, a capacity of 30818 or more would be required to accommodate a document with 100
14 entities averaging 70 characters (800+7000), 200 element types (1600) with 2000 tokens in content models (16000) and 25 exceptions groups with
16 a total of 50 names (200+400), 50 attributes with default values averaging 20 characters (400+1000) and 100 attribute name tokens (800), 5 data
18 content notations with identifiers averaging 50 characters (40+250), 50 ID and 50 IDREF attributes (400+400), 5 short reference maps
20 (5x(8+(8x32))=1320), and a single implicit link type declaration with 4 link sets, each containing 5 source element names (40+168).

Clause 10
Markup Declarations: General

Most markup declarations in SGML are related either to document structure or to link processes. This chapter discusses those declarations which are related to neither: comment declarations, marked section declarations, and entity declarations. Also discussed are constructs that are common to many types of declarations, such as parameters, groups, separators, literals, and external identifiers.

The note that begins the clause serves to remind application and system designers that even some names that appear in syntax productions (and therefore give the impression of being immutable) may be reassigned by variant concrete syntaxes. Such a reminder might have been equally appropriate at the head of other clauses as well.

> T–B.14.1 *63*
>
> O–4.330 *211:10*
>
> A–15.5.4 *487:20*

NOTE — The declaration names and keywords in the syntax productions
2   are reference reserved names that can be redefined for a variant concrete syntax with the *reserved name use* [193] *468:9* parameter of the *SGML*
4   *declaration* [171] *450:1* .

10.1 Parts of Declarations

The term "parameter", as used in ISO 8879, is somewhat problematical because of its hierarchical nature. An entity declaration, for example, has two parameters: an entity name and the entity text. The entity text parameter, however, could comprise two subordinate parameters: a keyword and a parameter literal.

Examination of an individual markup declaration may give no hint of this hierarchy. For example, in

```
<!ENTITY cat CDATA "puss">
```

there is no sign that "CDATA 'puss'" is a single parameter as well as being two individual parameters. One has to look to the actual syntax productions in ISO 8879 to identify the hierarchy of parameters.

10.1.1 Parameter Separator

A parameter separator, logically enough, is a character string that separates the parameters of a markup declaration. The rules for parameter separators are designed to avoid obfuscatory markup by prohibiting a parameter from occurring partly in one entity and partly in another. The objective is to make it very clear what is going on when a human examines the markup declaration.

| **O–4.224** *204:1* |

To illustrate, the element declaration in the following example is prohibited because the entity reference obscures the markup; that is, the reference causes the declaration to appear to a human reader to have a markup error — unbalanced group delimiters (parentheses).

```
<!ENTITY % test "(abc">
...
...
<!ELEMENT test %abc)>
```

In contrast, consider the following example:

```
<!ENTITY % lpart "(abc">
<!ENTITY % rpart ")">
<!ENTITY % abc "%lpart;%rpart">
...
...
<!ELEMENT test %abc>
```

Although the entity structure of this example is pointlessly complex, the markup is perfectly clear. In no case does a valid declaration appear to a human reader to have a markup error.

| **O–4.226** *161:7* |

[65] ps =

2   s | [5] *297:23*

     Ee |

4   *parameter entity reference* | [60] *350:22*

     comment   [92] *391:7*

6   A *parameter entity reference* [60] *350:22* can be used wherever a parameter could occur. The entity must consist of zero or more of
8   the consecutive complete parameters that follow the *ps* [65] *372:1* in which the reference occurs, together with any surrounding or
10   intervening *ps* [65] *372:1* separators. The entity must end within the same declaration.

12   An *Ee* can occur in a *ps* [65] *372:1* only if the reference to the entity it terminates occurs in a *ps* [65] *372:1* in the same declara-
14   tion.

   A required *ps* [65] *372:1* that is adjacent to a delimiter or another
16   *ps* [65] *372:1* can be omitted if no ambiguity would be created thereby.

18   A *ps* [65] *372:1* must begin with an *s* [5] *297:23* if omitting it would create an ambiguity.

10.1.2 Parameter Literal

A parameter literal consists of replaceable parameter data delimited by the literal or alternative literal delimiter characters. (In the reference concrete syntax, these are the conventional typewriter double and single quotation marks, the ASCII characters numbered 34 and 39). "Replaceable parameter data" simply means that whatever is between the quotes acts just as replaceable character data does, except that the entity references that are recognized within it are parameter entity references rather than general entity references. As in replaceable character data, no markup is recognized in replaceable parameter data other than references and the delimiters that would terminate the literal, and the latter are not recognized in the replacement text of an entity reference.

T–B.6.2 *40*

O–4.227 *205:11*

It is important to remember that parameter literals are interpreted at the time the markup declaration that they occur in is parsed. For most markup declarations, that is the only time they could be interpreted.

Parameter literals are used, however, for specifying the replacement text of an entity, and there the question could arise of whether the references are interpreted when the entity declaration is parsed, or later on when a reference is made to that entity. This clause makes it quite clear that the interpretation occurs at entity declaration time, not at entity reference time.   O-4.227 *205:11*

[66] parameter literal =

2   (*lit*,   "
              replaceable parameter data,   [67] *373:8*
4   *lit*) | "
         (*lita*,   '
6   *replaceable parameter data*,   [67] *373:8*
              lita)   '

8 [67] replaceable parameter data =
         (*data character* | [48] *344:3*
10   *character reference* | [62] *356:1*
              parameter entity reference | [60] *350:22*
12   *Ee*)*

A *parameter literal* [66] *373:1* is interpreted as a parameter (or
14 token) by replacing references while the declaration is being processed.

16 Except for parameter entity and character references, no markup is
recognized in a *parameter literal* [66] *373:1* other than the terminal
18 *lit* or *lita*, and those are not recognized within the replacement text
of a reference.

20 NOTE — If the literal is in the *entity text* [105] *396:18* parameter of an
entity declaration [101] *394:18*, markup characters in its text could be
22 recognized when the entity is referenced.

An *Ee* can occur in *replaceable parameter data* [67] *373:8* only if
24 the reference to the entity it terminates occurred in the same
replaceable parameter data [67] *373:8* .

10.1.2.1 Quantities

26 The length of an interpreted *parameter literal* [66] *373:1* cannot
exceed the "LITLEN" quantity (unless some other restriction is
28 applied in the context in which it is used).

10.1.3 Group

A group is a list of names or name tokens that in the reference concrete syntax is delimited by parentheses.

T–B.4.2 *27*
O–4.149 *206:1*

The name tokens or names in the list are separated by connector delimiters. There are three kinds: AND, OR, and SEQ. Normally only one of the three is used in a given group. The convention is to use the OR connector unless there is a reason to use one of the others. The exceptions to these conventions occur when a group is the replacement text of a parameter entity, and the entity is referenced as both a name group and a model group.

The connectors and the name tokens in a group can optionally be separated by token separator (ts) strings. A token separator is just like a parameter separator except that comments are not permitted in it. When a parameter entity reference is used in a token separator it must follow rules, similar to those for a parameter separator, that will guarantee the clearest possible expression for the human reader of the markup. The rules require that the entity contain one or more complete tokens with their intervening or surrounding separators and any intervening connectors. In other words, you cannot have a token that will be in more than one entity, nor can a group be partly in one entity and partly in another.

O–4.149 *206:1*

```
[68] name token group =
2          grpo,                                              (
           ts*,                                        [70] 375:3
4          name token,                                 [57] 347:3
           ( ts*,                                      [70] 375:3
6            connector,                                [131] 413:4
             ts*,                                      [70] 375:3
8            name token )*,                            [57] 347:3
           ts*,                                        [70] 375:3
10         grpc                                              )

[69] name group =
12         grpo,                                            (
           ts*,                                        [70] 375:3
14         name,                                       [55] 346:17
           ( ts*,                                      [70] 375:3
16           connector,                                [131] 413:4
             ts*,                                      [70] 375:3
18           name )*,                                  [55] 346:17
```

```
              ts*,                                    [70] 375:3
2             grpc                                        )
```

```
      [70] ts =
4             s |                                     [5] 297:23
              Ee |
6             parameter entity reference             [60] 350:22
```

Only one type of *connector* [131] 413:4 should be used in a single
8 *name group* [69] 374:11 or *name token group* [68] 374:1 .

NOTE — No specific type of *connector* [131] 413:4 is mandated, so that a
10 group defined in an entity can be referenced as both a *model group*
[127] 410:6 (where the specific connector is meaningful) and a *name
12 group* [69] 374:11 (where it is not).

A token can occur only once in a single *name group* [69] 374:11 or
14 *name token group* [68] 374:1 .

A *parameter entity reference* [60] 350:22 can be used anywhere in
16 a group that a token could occur. The entity must consist of one or
more of the consecutive complete tokens that follow the *ts*
18 [70] 375:3 in which the reference occurs in the same group (i.e., at
the same nesting level), together with any surrounding or interven-
20 ing *ts* [70] 375:3 separators and any intervening connectors. The
entity must end within the same group.

22 An **Ee** can occur in a *ts* [70] 375:3 only if:

— the *ts* [70] 375:3 follows a token (as opposed to a *connector*
24   [131] 413:4 , **grpo**, or **dtgo**); and
— the reference to the entity the **Ee** terminates occurs in the
26   same group (i.e., at the same nesting level).

10.1.3.1 Quantities

The number of tokens in a group cannot exceed the "GRPCNT"
28 quantity.

A–13.4.8 469:26

10.1.4 Declaration Separator

Declaration separators, as the name implies, are used to separate markup declarations within the declaration subset of a document type declaration or a link type declaration. While declaration separators are invariably optional, the normal practice is to begin each declaration on a new source record.

> **O–4.107** *207:14*

Like the parameter separator and token separator, a declaration separator permits parameter entity references and entity ends. Here, too, the rule about maintaining balance and clarity applies: The parameter entity reference must refer to an entity that has complete markup declarations in it, or anything else that is normally allowed in a declaration separator. A markup declaration cannot occur partly in one parameter entity and partly in another.

Since a declaration separator occurs between markup declarations rather than within, it allows different things to occur. For example, instead of a comment, a full comment declaration is allowed in a declaration separator. Also, processing instructions and marked section declarations are allowed.

	[71] ds =	
2	*s* |	**[5]** *297:23*
	Ee |	
4	*parameter entity reference* |	**[60]** *350:22*
	comment declaration |	**[91]** *391:1*
6	*processing instruction* |	**[44]** *339:1*
	marked section declaration	**[93]** *391:13*

8   A *parameter entity reference* ⌈ **[60]** *350:22* ⌉ in a *ds* ⌈ **[71]** *376:1* ⌉ must refer to an entity that consists of zero or more complete markup
10   declarations and/or *ds* ⌈ **[71]** *376:1* ⌉ separators.

An ***Ee*** can occur in a *ds* ⌈ **[71]** *376:1* ⌉ only if the reference to the
12   entity it terminates occurs in a *ds* ⌈ **[71]** *376:1* ⌉ in the same parameter.

10.1.5 Associated Element Type

An associated element type is, simply, the name or names of the element types to which a markup declaration applies. It can occur in an attribute definition declaration, a short reference use declaration, or in a link rule. It is either a single generic identifier or a group of them.

2   [72] associated element type =
        generic identifier | `[30]` *325:17*
        name group   `[69]` *374:11*

4   Each *name* `[55]` *346:17* in the *name group* `[69]` *374:11* must be a
generic identifier `[30]` *325:17* .

The interesting point to note here is that the generic identifier does not have to be that of a defined element type. In other words, you can associate short reference maps or attributes with elements that do not exist. This provision is to enable the effective use of public shared document type definitions that are modified for local use.

For example, a public document type definition could exist for a core multimedia structure that could be used in a variety of applications. The multimedia core might allow a large set of multimedia element types, such as audio, video, lighting controls, slide projector controls, and so on, and it might define a common set of attributes that would be associated with all of the element types. Let us say further that this core document type definition does not include the element declarations for each of these multimedia element types because the declarations could vary substantially from one application to another. In your application, you might choose to support only two of these multimedia types and you would create element declarations for them. The attribute definition list, however, which you were using by reference to the public document type, would still be associated with a much larger set of element types — most of which would not exist.

                                      `O–4.8` *154:6*

6   A *generic identifier* `[30]` *325:17* can be a valid *associated element type* `[72]` *377:1* whether or not it is specified as an *element type*
8   `[117]` *406:1* in the document type definition.

NOTE — This provision makes it easier to use public definitions that name
10   a large set of generic identifiers in conjunction with a more restrictive document type that does not permit all of them.

10.1.6 External Identifier

Entities can be categorized as either internal or external. An internal entity is one whose replacement text occurs within the declaration of the entity. An external entity is one where the replacement text itself does not appear in the entity declaration. Instead, there is an external identifier that locates the replacement text in some entity other than the one in which the entity declaration appears. The external identifier can contain either a system identifier or a public identifier or both.

> **T–B.12** *56*
>
> **O–4.135** *179:6*

A *system identifier* is system-specific information that enables the entity manager component of an SGML system to locate the file or the memory location or the pointer within a file where the entity can be found. (It is important to recall that entities enable the user to think of the document as being physically segmented for convenience, although there is no requirement that a system really physically segment the document; all the entities could, in fact, be in a single file.) It should also be noted that a system identifier could be an invocation of a program that controls access to an entity that is being identified. This possibility is particularly important when the entity uses a data content notation.

A *public identifier* is a name that is intended to be meaningful across systems and different user environments. Typically it will be a name that has a registered owner associated with it, so that public identifiers will be guaranteed unique and no two entities will have the same public identifier. This uniqueness can only be achieved when the public identifiers are "formal public identifiers", which is an optional feature that can be specified on the SGML declaration.

It is the responsibility of the entity manager to use the information in the system identifier, and elsewhere in the entity declaration or other declaration in which the external identifier appears, to determine the actual storage identifier in the system. The storage identifier could be a file name, or a record key in a data base, or an offset into storage, or something similar. The system identifier itself need not be the full storage identifier; it is just a method of expressing information that the entity manager can use to determine the storage identifier.

In that regard, it would be very sensible for an implementation to devise a defaulting scheme in which the storage identifier could be determined from the entity name alone. SGML encourages this by providing syntactically that the keyword SYSTEM can be specified for an external identifier without actually specifying a system identifier parameter at all. This form of an external identifier is particularly useful in a default general entity declaration. What it means is that references can be made throughout the document to undeclared general entities, and the system will be able to determine their storage identifiers just by the entity name that appears in the reference.

The system identifier parameter can also be used to pass parameters to the entity manager that deal with matters other than determining the storage identifier. Some systems, for example, support more than one text editor, and these editors may have different approaches to dealing with record starts and record ends at the start and end of an entity. The popular MS-DOS operating system for personal computers, for example, has some editors that leave a record end and record start at the end of a file. That way if two files are concatenated, the second file will begin on a new record. Other MS-DOS editors, however, do not follow this convention, so two files that are concatenated will merge the last record of the first file with the first record of the second file.

Recall from the discussion in 7.6.1 ⌐321⌐ that an SGML parser does not imply record starts or record ends at the start or ends of entities. Therefore, in order to obtain consistent parsing regardless of which text editor may have created a given entity, it may be desirable to establish, as part of the system identifier, a code that indicates whether the entity manager should ensure that an entity begins with a record start and ends with a record end.

```
    [73] external identifier =
2           ( "SYSTEM" |
              ( "PUBLIC",
4               ps+,                                    [65] 372:1
                public identifier   ) ),               [74] 379:8
6               ( ps+,                                  [65] 372:1
                system identifier )?                    [75] 379:10


8   [74] public identifier =
              minimum literal                           [76] 381:1


10  [75] system identifier =
              ( lit,
12              system data,                            [45] 339:5
              lit   ) |
14            ( lita,                                    '
                system data,                           [45] 339:5
16            lita   )                                   '
```

The *system identifier* ⌐[75] 379:10⌐ can be omitted if the system can generate it from the *public identifier* ⌐[74] 379:8⌐ and/or other information available to it. The generated *system identifier* ⌐[75] 379:10⌐ must be the same for all uses of the *external identifier* ⌐[73] 379:1⌐, except in the case of a default entity, where it must be the same for all references with a given undeclared entity name.

The previous paragraph of the standard is confusing. As discussed above, the system does not generate an omitted *system identifier* ⌐[75] 379:10⌐; it uses the other information available to it to determine the actual storage location identifier, which must be the same for all uses of the *external identifier* [73] *379:1* .

2   If "FORMAL YES" is specified on the *SGML declaration* [171] *450:1* , a *public identifier* [74] *379:8* is interpreted as a *formal public identifier* [79] *382:1* (see 10.2 *381*) and a formal public
4   identifier error can occur.

     NOTE — It is still a *minimum literal* [76] *381:1* , and all requirements per-
6   taining to minimum literals apply.

10.1.6.1 Quantities

     The length of a *system identifier* [75] *379:10* , exclusive of delim-
8   iters, cannot exceed the "LITLEN" quantity.

                                                              A–13.4.8 *469:26*

10.1.6.2 Capacities

     The number of characters of *entity text* [105] *396:18* counted
10   towards the ENTCHCAP capacity for an *external identifier*
     [73] *379:1* is that of its *system identifier* [75] *379:10* component,
12   added to that of its *public identifier* [74] *379:8* component (and
     exclusive of delimiters).

                                                              A–13.2 *456:2*

10.1.7 Minimum Literal

A minimum literal is data that is delimited by the literal or alternative literal delimiters. It contains only "minimum data"; that is, digits, the upper- and lower-case letters, and special characters listed in figure 1 *345* in Chapter 9, as well as the space and the record start and end characters.

Minimum literals are used for information that is expected to be meaningful for all concrete syntaxes, character sets, and system environments. The SGML declaration, for example, makes extensive use of minimum literals, and a public identifier is also a minimum literal.

                                                              O–4.239 *180:5*

As a minimum literal is sometimes used by applications for comparisons, particularly when it occurs in a public identifier, the literal is normalized by ignoring record starts, condensing record end and space sequences to a single space, and stripping spaces that occurred at the start or end of the minimum literal.

[76] minimum literal =
2   (*lit,*   "

        minimum data,   [77] *381:8*

4   *lit*   ) | "

        (*lita,*   '

6   *minimum data,*   [77] *381:8*

        lita   )   '

8   [77] minimum data =
        *minimum data character**   [78] *381:10*

10   [78] minimum data character =
        RS |
12   *RE* |
        SPACE |
14   *LC Letter* |
        UC Letter |
16   *Digit* |
        Special

18   A *minimum literal* [76] *381:1* is interpreted by ignoring **RS** and replacing a sequence of one or more **RE** and/or **SPACE** characters
20   with a single **SPACE**, except that such a sequence is ignored if it occurs at the start or end of the *minimum literal* [76] *381:1* .

10.1.7.1 Quantities

22   The length of an interpreted *minimum literal* [76] *381:1* , exclusive of delimiters, cannot exceed the "LITLEN" quantity of the reference
24   quantity set, regardless of the concrete syntax used. A–13.4.8 *469:26*

10.2 Formal Public Identifier

A formal public identifier is constructed so that a reader can distinguish between the owner of the public text, and the identification of the public text itself. The idea behind this is to permit owners to be given unique identifiers that will distinguish all owners from one another. The owner can then determine how the individual public text objects that it

owns can be distinguished from one another within the same owner
identifier.

T–C.3.3 *90*
O–4.137 *183:1*

To accomplish this objective, the formal public identifier is, first of all,
a minimum literal. That means that it will be interpreted and normalized
by reducing spaces to a single space character, stripping the leading and
trailing blanks, and so on. Secondly, the interpreted and normalized literal is broken up into fields by means of a double solidus (two slashes).
(Accordingly, the standard prohibits any other use of that character
string in a formal public identifier.)

The double solidus and other delimiter strings that occur in formal
public identifiers, unlike normal SGML delimiter strings, are defined by
ISO 8879 and cannot be changed in an SGML declaration. The reason for
this rule is that public identifiers (formal and informal) must not change
from one system or application to another (except for character set translation, which is unambiguous for the minimum data characters of which
a public identifier is composed).

Incidentally, the syntactic variable "formal public identifier" does not
appear in the definition of *public identifier* (**[74]** *379:8*), as you might
expect. The reason is that "public identifier" is defined to be a "minimum
literal". As a formal public identifier is indeed a minimum literal, that
definition is technically satisfied. The formal public identifier structure
defined in this sub-clause is simply an optional method of interpreting
the minimum literal, and therefore does not appear in the definition of
any syntactic variable.

```
     [79] formal public identifier =
2            owner identifier,                              [80] 383:1
             "//",
4            text identifier                               [84] 385:7
```

A *formal public identifier* (**[79]** *382:1*) cannot contain consecutive
6   solidi ("//") except where expressly permitted by this sub-clause.

NOTE — As a *public identifier* (**[74]** *379:8*) is a *minimum literal*
8   (**[76]** *381:1*), **RS** characters are removed, and sequences of one or more
RE and/or **SPACE** characters replaced by a single **SPACE**, prior to inter-
10   pretation as a *formal public identifier* (**[79]** *382:1*). The *minimum literal*
(**[76]** *381:1*) length limitation applies to the interpreted text (see 10.1.7.1
12   (*381*)).

10.2.1 Owner Identifier

Owner identifiers come in three varieties: ISO owner identifiers, registered owner identifiers, and unregistered owner identifiers. The significance of these categories is that registered owner identifiers are guaranteed to be different from one another, and therefore unique, while unregistered owner identifiers are only guaranteed to be different from all registered identifiers and not necessarily from one another.

The ISO owner identifier is a special case of registered owner identifier that was defined in this standard to make sure that there would be some way of providing registered ownership, and therefore unique identification, for the document type definitions, concrete syntaxes, and other objects that are defined in ISO 8879.

> **T–C.3.3** *90*
> **O–4.223** *183:6*

```
[80] owner identifier =
2        ISO owner identifier |                    [81] 383:7
         registered owner identifier |             [82] 384:8
4        unregistered owner identifier             [83] 385:1
```

NOTE — In formulating an *owner identifier* [80] *383:1* , standards such as
6   ISO 3166 can be helpful.

10.2.1.1 ISO Owner Identifier

An ISO owner identifier is the ISO publication number without the language suffix. The style of ISO publication numbers has changed since the standard was published, and for this standard it would now be "ISO 8879:1986" (which is the way it is shown in the ISO text in this book).

```
[81] ISO owner identifier =
8        minimum data                             [77] 381:8
```

The usual form of *ISO owner identifier* [81] *383:7* can be used only
10   when the *public identifier* [74] *379:8* identifies an ISO publication or
     is assigned within one. It consists of the ISO publication number,
12   without the language suffix.

NOTE — For example, the *ISO owner identifier* [81] *383:7* for public text
14   defined in this document is "ISO 8879:1986" in all translations. If the public

2 text is translated, that fact is indicated by specifying the appropriate *public text language* [88] *388:1* in the *text identifier* [84] *385:7* .

4 A special form of *ISO owner identifier* [81] *383:7* can be used only when the public text is an ISO registered character set and the *public text class* [86] *386:5* is "CHARSET". It consists of the string
6 "ISO Registration Number" , followed by the registration number of the character set.

10.2.1.2 Registered Owner Identifier

ISO 9070, the standard for the registration of SGML public text owner identifiers, provides a number of techniques for assigning unique identifiers. These include standards body identifiers for national or industry standards organizations (similar to the ISO owner identifier), and unique codes that may have been assigned to organizations by other standards.

An amendment to ISO 9070 is being developed that would allow the use of the international standard book numbering (ISBN) prefixes as a basis for registered owner identifiers.

O–4.262 *183:13*

8 [82] registered owner identifier =
           "+//",
10   minimum data

[77] *381:8*

12 NOTE — A registered owner identifier could be a citation of a national or industry standard, or some other unique identifier assigned in accordance with ISO 9070.

10.2.1.3 Unregistered Owner Identifier

An unregistered owner identifier can be any minimum data string. It is distinguished from the registered owner identifier because it begins with a minus sign rather than a plus sign. The ISO owner identifier is distinguished from both of them because it begins with the letters "ISO".

T–C.3.3 *90*

O–4.325 *183:9*

```
     [83] unregistered owner identifier =
2            "-//",
             minimum data                                    [77] 381:8
```

4   NOTE — An unregistered owner identifier could be a (presumably unique)
    designation created by a trade organization or other user community, or by
6   an individual.

10.2.2 Text Identifier

The text identifier component of a formal public identifier describes
the text and adds some useful information about it. One of the latter
items is an indicator that states whether the public text is available to the
general public, or only within the owner's organization. There are actually two forms of text identifiers, one for public character sets and the
other for public text in general, but the difference between them is slight.

O–4.317 *185:1*

```
     [84] text identifier =
8            public text class,                              [86] 386:5
             SPACE,
10           unavailable text indicator?,                    [85] 385:17
             public text description,                        [87] 387:5
12           "//",
             ( public text language |                        [88] 388:1
14             public text designating sequence   ),         [89] 388:14
             ( "//",
16             public text display version )?                [90] 390:1

     [85] unavailable text indicator =
18           "-//"
```

If the *unavailable text indicator* [85] *385:17* is present, the text is
20 unavailable public text; otherwise, it is available public text.

If the *public text class* [86] *386:5* is "CHARSET", the *text identifier*
22 [84] *385:7* includes a *public text designating sequence*
    [89] *388:14* ; otherwise, it includes a *public text language*
24 [88] *388:1* .

A *text identifier* [84] *385:7* cannot be the same as another *text*

identifier [84] *385:7* in a *formal public identifier* [79] *382:1* that has
2 the same *owner identifier* [80] *383:1* .

NOTE — If two public texts with the same owner have the same public text
4 description, they must be of different classes, versions, etc.

10.2.2.1 Public Text Class

The public text class identifies which one, out of those SGML constructs that might usefully be made "public", a particular piece of public
text is. The class could range from an entire document to a set of entity
declarations, or it might be a specialized resource such as the description
of a character set, or the specification of a data content notation. Different
public text classes may require slightly differing forms of public identifier. (For examples, see 10.2.2 385 and 10.2.2.4 388 .)

> **T–C.3.3** *90*
> **O–4.241** *185:8*

[86] public text class =
6   *name*   [55] *346:17*

The *name* [55] *346:17* must be one that identifies an SGML con-
8 struct in the following list:

Name	SGML Construct
10 **CAPACITY**	*capacity set* [180] *456:2*
CHARSET	*character data* [47] *344:1*
12 **DOCUMENT**	*SGML document* [1] *294:5*
DTD	*document type declaration subset*
14	[112] *404:6*
ELEMENTS	*element set* [114] *404:13*
16 **ENTITIES**	*entity set* [113] *404:10*
LPD	*link type declaration subset* [161] *437:1*
18 **NONSGML**	*non-SGML data entity* [6] *300:7*
NOTATION	*character data* [47] *344:1*
20 **SHORTREF**	*short reference set* [115] *404:18*
SUBDOC	*SGML subdocument entity* [3] *296:1*
22 **SYNTAX**	*concrete syntax* [182] *458:1*
TEXT	*SGML text entity* [4] *296:5*

24 The *name* [55] *346:17* must be entered with upper-case letters.

NOTE — When appropriate, a system can use the *public text class*
2   [86] *386:5* to determine strategies for converting the public text from its
interchange form into a referenceable entity that uses the system character
4   set and concrete syntax.

10.2.2.2 Public Text Description

A public text description can be any string of minimum data except
when the public text is an ISO publication. In that case, there is a rule for
extracting a portion of the title of the ISO publication and using it as the
public text description. Other owners of public text might want to adopt
similar rules for their own organizations' publications.

[87] public text description =
6   *ISO text description* | [87.1] *387:8*
           minimum data   [77] *381:8*

8   [87.1] ISO text description =
           minimum data   [77] *381:8*

10   An *ISO text description* [87.1] *387:8* can be used only when the
public identifier [74] *379:8* identifies an ISO publication. It consists
12   of the last element of the publication title, without the part number
designation (if any).

14   NOTE — For example, the *ISO text description* [87.1] *387:8* for ISO
8632/4 is "Clear text encoding".

10.2.2.3 Public Text Language

The public text language is simply an indicator of which natural language was used in the public text. It is normally a two-character ISO
standardized code for the language. You will note that in this clause, and
most of the others within 10.2, the word "should" is used rather than
"must", as was used elsewhere in the standard. Most of the requirements
in this clause are beyond the capabilities of an SGML parser to test effi-
ciently. The word "should" here is an ISO convention that means
"strongly recommended". By stopping short of "required", the standard
frees validating parsers from the burden of checking conformance. This
approach also permits user extensibility in an area where it cannot compromise the integrity of SGML.

                                               O–4.245 *185:13*

[88] public text language =
2   *name*   [55] *346:17*

The *public text language* [88] *388:1* must be a *name* [55] *346:17*,
4 entered with upper-case letters. The *name* [55] *346:17* should be
the two-character language code from ISO 639 that identifies the
6 principal natural language used in the public text.

NOTES

8 1   The natural language will affect the usability of some public text classes
more than others.

10 2   The portions of text most likely to be influenced by a natural language
include the data, defined names, and comments.

12 3   A system can use the *public text language* [88] *388:1* to facilitate
automatic language translation.

10.2.2.4 Public Text Designating Sequence

A public text designating sequence is always specified in lieu of a public text language when the public text is a character set definition. A
designating sequence is a character string that is defined by ISO 2022 as a
means of identifying a character set.

                                    O–4.243 *186:1*

14   [89] public text designating sequence =
              minimum data   [77] *381:8*

16   The *minimum data* [77] *381:8* should be the external form of a
designating escape sequence prescribed by ISO 2022 for the char-
18   acter set referenced by the *public identifier* [74] *379:8*. If the public
text is an ISO registered character set, the designating escape
20   sequence should be a registered escape sequence for that set.

NOTES

22   1   For example, the external form of the registered G0 designating
sequence for the graphic characters of ISO 646 IRV (registered character
24   set 002) is:

     ESC 2/8 4/0

The full set of 128 characters, which is not registered, should be
2   designated by:

```
ESC 2/5 4/0
```

4   2   For registered character sets, the *public text designating*
     sequence [89] *388:14* uniquely identifies the public text. For other
6   character sets, it should uniquely identify the public text with
     respect to a particular *owner identifier* [80] *383:1* .

10.2.2.5 Public Text Display Version

The public text display version provides a method of distinguishing
versions of public text that would be identical except for coding that is
system or device dependent. The mechanism was designed for character
entity sets, which are public entity sets consisting of general entities that
are graphic characters.

O–4.244 *187:6*

Character entities are used for characters that have no coded representation in the document character set, or that cannot be keyboarded conveniently, or to achieve device independence for characters whose bit
combinations do not cause proper display on all output devices.

There are two kinds of character entity set: definitional and display. In
the definitional character entity set the replacement text of an entity declaration is a description of the graphic character rather than a bit combination that would cause a glyph that depicts the graphic character to be
displayed. In a display entity set, of course, the reverse is true.

In the public identifier of a display character entity set, the public text
display version is specified, which serves to distinguish the different display versions of the character entity set from one another. In the definitional character entity set, no public text display version is specified. The
author of a document will typically reference the definitional version of
the entity set; that is, no public text display version would be specified in
the public identifier. As part of the processing of that entity reference, the
entity manager would substitute the display version of the entity set that
is most appropriate for the processing that is being performed and the
output device that is being used.

A large group of definitional character entity sets can be found in
annex D 498 . These entity sets have formal public identifiers that are
unique; they can therefore be referenced unambiguously from other documents.

An important use of character entity sets is to preserve system independence for documents that are shared among system environments
whose system character sets differ from one another. As the document

character set is normally the same as a system character set, the document character set will have to be translated when the document is shipped from one of these systems to another.

SGML requires that a document character set have a character number for every markup character and minimum data character, the so-called "significant SGML characters". SGML does not require that the document character set have a character number for every data character — that would be impossible because there are tens of thousands of them. For data characters that have no direct representation in the document character set, a system must adopt some other method of representation, such as a standardized means of code extension or proprietary or device-dependent techniques. In order to maintain portability of the document, and to keep such proprietary techniques out of it, an entity reference should be used to enter data characters that are not significant SGML characters. Each system sharing the document would then have its own display version of the character entity set in which these character entities were declared.

```
       [90] public text display version =
2                minimum data                              [77] 381:8
```

The *public text display version* [90] 390:1 must be omitted if the
4   *public text class* [86] 386:5 is "CAPACITY", "CHARSET", "NOTA-
    TION", or "SYNTAX". For other classes, if the public text is device-
6   dependent, the text identifier must include a *public text display ver-
    sion* [90] 390:1 that describes the devices supported or coding
8   scheme used.

When a system accesses public text for which a *public text display*
10 *version* [90] 390:1 could have been specified but was not, it must
    substitute the best available device-dependent version for the dis-
12 play device in use. If there is none, no substitution occurs.

NOTE — This mechanism is particularly useful with character entity sets.

10.3 Comment Declaration

A comment is a string of SGML characters that is used in the parameter separators of markup declarations to explain what the declaration is doing.

```
                                                    O–4.47 207:16
                                                    A–10.1.4 376:1
```

It is also possible to have a declaration that contains nothing but comments; this is called a comment declaration. Comment declarations are frequently used in markup declaration subsets to separate the declarations from one another and to explain what each group of declarations is for. They can also be used by authors in the document instance to provide instructions to other people working with the document, or reminders for themselves.

> T–B.5.2 *35*

```
[91] comment declaration =
2        mdo,
         ( comment,
4          ( s |
             comment  )*  )?,
6          mdc
```

> `<!`
> [92] *391:7*
> [5] *297:23*
> [92] *391:7*
> `>`

```
[92] comment =
8        com,
         SGML character*,
10       com
```

> `--`
> [50] *345:1*
> `--`

No markup is recognized in a *comment* [92] *391:7* , other than the
12 **com** delimiter that terminates it.

10.4 Marked Section Declaration

A marked section of a document is a portion of the document that is set off distinctively by surrounding it with the start and end of a marked section declaration. In between the start of the declaration and the marked section itself there can be one or more status keywords that indicate why the section is being marked. Even though a section is marked, it still must conform to the requirements for the context in which it occurs, just as if the marked section declaration were not there.

> T–B.8 *47*
> O–4.180 *208:3*

```
[93] marked section declaration =
14       marked section start,
         status keyword specification,
16       dso,
```

> [94] *392:3*
> [97] *393:1*
> `[`

	marked section,	[96] *392:9*
2	*marked section end*	[95] *392:6*

[94] marked section start =

4	**mdo**,	<!
	dso	[

6 [95] marked section end =

8	**msc**,	]]
	mdc	>

[96] marked section =

10	*SGML character**	[50] *345:1*

The *marked section* ⟨ [96] *392:9* ⟩ must comply with the syntactic and
12 semantic requirements that govern the context in which the *marked
section declaration* ⟨ [93] *391:13* ⟩ occurs.

14 A *marked section end* ⟨ [95] *392:6* ⟩ that occurs outside of a *marked
section declaration* ⟨ [93] *391:13* ⟩ is an error.

10.4.1 Quantities

16 The number of open marked section declarations cannot exceed
the "TAGLVL" quantity.

⟨ A–13.4.8 *469:26* ⟩

10.4.2 Status Keyword Specification

The status keywords indicate why the section is being marked:

a) because it is to be ignored completely; or

b) because it is to be parsed in a special way, such as treating it as
character data or replaceable character data; or

c) to indicate that the section is a temporary part of the document that
might need to be removed at a later time.

The IGNORE and INCLUDE keywords are typically entered as the
replacement text of entity references. The entities would be defined to
have the value of either IGNORE or INCLUDE in, let us say, link type

declarations. That way, depending on which link process is active, parts of the document will be included or ignored. This technique can be used to support multiple versions of a document; for example, a product manual in which there are slight variations depending on which model of the product is being described.

$\boxed{\text{O–4.307 } 208{:}12}$

[97] status keyword specification =
2   (ps+, $\boxed{\textbf{[65]} 372{:}1}$
              (*status keyword* | $\boxed{\textbf{[100]} 393{:}6}$
4   "TEMP"   ))*,
              ps* $\boxed{\textbf{[65]} 372{:}1}$

6 [100] status keyword =
              "CDATA" |
8   "IGNORE" |
              "INCLUDE" |
10   "RCDATA"

        where

12 **IGNORE**   specifies that the section is treated as though
                        there were no characters in the *marked section*
14                      $\boxed{\textbf{[96]} 392{:}9}$, except that a nested *marked section*
                        start $\boxed{\textbf{[94]} 392{:}3}$ or *marked section end*
16                      $\boxed{\textbf{[95]} 392{:}6}$ is recognized so that the correct end-
                        ing can be found.
18 **INCLUDE**   specifies that the *marked section* $\boxed{\textbf{[96]} 392{:}9}$ is
                        not to be ignored.
20 **CDATA**   specifies that the *marked section* $\boxed{\textbf{[96]} 392{:}9}$ is
                        treated as *character data* $\boxed{\textbf{[47]} 344{:}1}$.
22 **RCDATA**   specifies that the *marked section* $\boxed{\textbf{[96]} 392{:}9}$ is
                        treated as *replaceable character data* $\boxed{\textbf{[46]} 343{:}1}$.
24 **TEMP**   identifies the section as a temporary part of the
                        document that might need to be removed at a
26   later time.

        In the event of a conflicting specification, the status keywords have
28 the following priority (highest shown first):
              "IGNORE"
30   "CDATA"
              "RCDATA"

"INCLUDE"

2   If none is specified, "INCLUDE" is assumed.

    If the effective status is "CDATA" or "RCDATA", a *marked section*
4   *declaration* [93] *391:13* is terminated by the first *marked section*
    end [95] *392:6* .

6   NOTE — A nested *marked section declaration* [93] *391:13* within the
    CDATA or RCDATA marked section in the same entity could not occur, as
8   the markup would not be recognized.

    If the effective status is "IGNORE", an *Ee* is not allowed in the
10 *marked section* [96] *392:9* .

    NOTE — The scan of an "IGNORE", "CDATA", or "RCDATA" marked sec-
12 tion ignores virtually all markup but marked section ends. As a result, pro-
    cessing instructions, attribute values, literals, character data elements, and
14 comments are not recognized to be such, so their characters are also
    scanned. This could cause erroneous results if the characters look like
16 marked sections. In most cases, problems can be avoided by entering such
    characters with references, instead of directly.

10.5 Entity Declaration

An entity declaration defines an entity by associating an entity name
with its replacement text.

T–B.6.2 *40*
O–4.121 *141:11*
A–9.4.4 *350:17*

18 [101] entity declaration =
        mdo,   <!
20   "ENTITY",
        ps+,   [65] *372:1*
22   *entity name*,   [102] *395:1*
        ps+,   [65] *372:1*
24   *entity text*,   [105] *396:18*
        ps*,   [65] *372:1*
26   ***mdc***   >

10.5.1 Entity Name

The general rule is that for every entity reference in a document there must be a declaration. If there is more than one declaration for the same entity name, the first one governs. This rule is different from the usual programming language rule that says the latest definition of a variable governs. However, entities are not considered to be variables, they are considered to be constants. A principal benefit for the user is that he can be sure of the first definition of an entity that he encounters. There is no fear that it can be overridden later in the DTD, although it can of course be redefined by a link process definition.

There is one situation in which it is not necessary to declare an entity before referencing it: A default general entity may be declared. Its declaration looks normal except that the entity name is the keyword "#DEFAULT". If a default entity has been declared, then any reference to an undeclared general entity will be treated as though the default declaration had been made for that entity.

Although a default entity declaration can be used when a document stays within its system of origin, it cannot be used if the document is to be transferred to another system by means of the SGML Document Interchange Format described in ISO 9069. The "SDIF packer" software that creates the transferable file structure will only know which entities to include in the data stream by virtue of finding external identifiers for them in declarations. Therefore there must be an entity declaration for each entity that is to be included in an SDIF data stream.

```
[102] entity name =
2          general entity name |                          [103] 395:4
           parameter entity name                          [104] 395:8


4   [103] general entity name =
           name |                                         [55] 346:17
6          ( rni,                                              #
             "DEFAULT"   )


8   [104] parameter entity name =
           pero,                                               %
10         ps+,                                           [65] 372:1
           name                                           [55] 346:17



12  where
```

DEFAULT   means the entity is the default entity.

2 The **pero** in production 104 is recognized as a delimiter in this context without a contextual constraint.

4 An attempt to redefine an entity is ignored, but is not an error.

NOTE — This requirement allows an entity declaration in a document type
6 declaration subset to take priority over a later declaration of the same entity in a public document type definition.

8 The *ps* [65] 372:1 in a *parameter entity name* [104] 395:8 is required, even though it follows a delimiter.

10.5.1.1 Quantities

10 A *name* [55] 346:17 in a *parameter entity name* [104] 395:8 must be at least the number of characters in a **pero** delimiter string
12 shorter than the "NAMELEN" quantity.   A–13.4.8 469:26

10.5.1.2 Capacities

Points are counted towards the "ENTCAP" capacity for the default
14 entity, and for each unique entity name that is defaulted in one or more references.

16 Points are counted towards the "ENTCHCAP" capacity for the default entity.   A–13.2 456:2

10.5.2 Entity Text

There are four ways to specify the entity text, one for external entities and three for internal. The external entity specification is discussed in 10.5.5 [399]. The entity text for an internal entity is either a parameter literal that is interpreted when the declaration is parsed, data text, or bracketed text.   0–4.127 141:13

18 [105] entity text =
              parameter literal | [66] 373:1
20   *data text* | [106] 397:14
              bracketed text | [107] 399:1
22   *external entity specification*   [108] 400:1

2 If a *parameter literal* [66] *373:1* alone is specified as the *entity text*
[105] *396:18*, the interpreted *parameter literal* [66] *373:1* is the
replacement text of the entity.

4 An **Ee** is deemed to be present at the end of the replacement text;
it is not entered explicitly.

6 NOTE — An entity whose text includes a *parameter literal* [66] *373:1* is
considered a single entity even if the literal contained entity references that
8 were resolved when the literal was interpreted.

10.5.3 Data Text

A data text entity, as the name implies, will always be treated as character data when it is referenced. It is possible, through the use of keywords, to distinguish between normal character data and character data
that is system-dependent.

T–B.7.1 *43*

A–8 *339:1*

There are two system-dependent types: SDATA, or "specific character
data", and PI, or "processing instruction". The distinction between these
two is significant only in the way that SGML handles record boundaries.
A processing instruction entity reference will be treated as if no data had
occurred; therefore a record end that follows it would be suppressed and
not passed to the application. An SDATA entity, on the other hand, is
treated as though it contained data; therefore, a record end that follows it
is considered significant and is passed to the application as data.

Data text is treated as *character data* [47] *344:1* when referenced,
10 regardless of the context in which the entity reference occurs. It is
specified as a *parameter literal* [66] *373:1*, whose characters, after
12 resolution of references in the usual manner, will comprise the
entity text [105] *396:18* .

14 [106] data text =
     ("CDATA" |
16   "SDATA" |
          "PI"   ),
18   ps+,   [65] *372:1*
          parameter literal   [66] *373:1*

20 where

	CDATA	means the interpreted *parameter literal*
2		[66] 373:1 is the replacement text of a character data entity.
4	**SDATA**	means the interpreted *parameter literal*
		[66] 373:1 is the replacement text of a specific character data entity.
6		
	PI	means the interpreted *parameter literal*
8		[66] 373:1 is the replacement text of a processing instruction entity.

10 "CDATA" or "SDATA" can be specified only if the *entity name* [102] 395:1 is a *general entity name* [103] 395:4 .

12 A *processing instruction* [44] 339:1 that returns data must be defined as an "SDATA" entity.

14 NOTES

1 A "CDATA" or "SDATA" entity must be referenced in a context in which
16 a data character can occur, and a "PI" entity in a context in which a *processing instruction* [44] 339:1 could occur.

18 2 "SDATA" is normally specified if the entity would be redefined for different applications, systems, or output devices; for example, if the data con-
20 tained processing instructions, or characters not present in the *syntax-reference character set* [185] 461:1 .

22 3 No data content notation applies to an internal data entity that is the subject of an explicit content reference. To specify a notation, the entity
24 must be declared as an external data entity.

10.5.4 Bracketed Text

Bracketed text offers a minor convenience when declaring entities whose entity text is markup. It lets the SGML parser supply certain delimiters that would otherwise have to be entered by the user in the parameter literal. More important, though, by declaring the purpose of the entity it improves communication with a human reader of the entity declaration, and allows a system to optimize the storage of the entity.

Note that it is not an error to declare the entity text to be, for example, a start-tag, and then create a parameter literal that is not a valid start-tag. Therefore, if a system is optimizing the storage based on the type of bracketed text, it must check internally and make sure that the entity text truly is a start-tag before storing it in whatever specialized form it might use for start-tags.

T–B.8.6 *51*

```
     [107] bracketed text =
2            (  "STARTTAG" |
                "ENDTAG" |
4               "MS" |
                "MD"   ),
6            ps+,                                         [65] 372:1
             parameter literal                           [66] 373:1
```

8   where the keywords mean that the entity consists of the interpreted *parameter literal* [66] 373:1 bracketed with delimiters, as follows:

10   **STARTTAG**   means preceded by ***stago*** and followed by ***tagc***.

12   **ENDTAG**   means preceded by ***etago*** and followed by ***tagc***.

14   **MS**   means preceded by a *marked section start* [94] 392:3 and followed by a *marked section*

16   *end* [95] 392:6 .

    MD   means preceded by ***mdo*** and followed by

18   ***mdc***.

NOTE — Bracketed text is simply text with delimiter characters; there is no
20   requirement that the entities form valid start-tags or other constructs. As usual, the validity of the entity is determined in context whenever the entity
22   is referenced.

10.5.4.1 Quantities

The length of an interpreted *parameter literal* [66] 373:1 in
24   *bracketed text* [107] 399:1 cannot exceed the "LITLEN" quantity, less the length of the bracketing delimiters.

A–13.4.8 469:26

10.5.5 External Entity Specification

When an external entity is declared, the declaration can also state whether the entity is an SGML subdocument entity, a data entity, or by default, an SGML text entity.

O–4.288 142:10

If it is a data entity, a data content notation can be declared for it and data attributes can be specified. These attributes are typically parameters to the program that will access this specialized data. For example, in the case of an image notation, they might tell the accessing program whether the data represents a horizontally ordered image or a vertically ordered one, and the number of pixels in each dimension.

O–4.75.1 *134:11*

It is worth noting again that an external entity does not necessarily mean an external file. The mapping of entities to storage is performed by the entity manager component of an SGML system. All entities could be in a single file or, conversely, an entity might comprise a number of concatenated files. The purpose of the entity structure is to allow the user or application designer to conceive of the document as being distributed in a number of segments independently of the element structure. The extent to which that virtual segmentation reflects the physical reality of the storage system is entirely system-dependent.

T–B.6.2 *40*

[108] external entity specification =

2 *external identifier,*   [73] *379:1*

(*ps+,*   [65] *372:1*

4 *entity type*)?   [109] *400:5*

[109] entity type =

6 "SUBDOC" |

(("CDATA" |

8 "NDATA" |

"SDATA"),

10 *ps+,*   [65] *372:1*

notation name,   [41] *333:33*

12 *data attribute specification?*)   [149.2] *428:20*

where

14 **SUBDOC**   means the entity is an *SGML subdocument entity* [3] *296:1* .

16 **NDATA**   means the entity is a *non-SGML data entity* [6] *300:7* .

18 **CDATA**   means the entity is a *character data entity* [5.1] *300:1* .

20 **SDATA**   means the entity is a *specific character data entity* [5.2] *300:4* .

The *entity type* [109] *400:5* can be specified only if the *entity name*
2   [102] *395:1* is a *general entity name* [103] *395:4* .

If the *entity type* [109] *400:5* is omitted, the entity is an *SGML text*
4   *entity* [4] *296:5* .

The *notation name* [41] *333:33* must be declared in the same docu-
6   ment type definition as the entity. It need not have been defined
prior to this declaration, but must be defined prior to a reference to
8   the entity.

A data entity can reference (in its own notation) other data entities
10   and SGML subdocument entities. The referenced entities, and any
data entities referenced within a nested structure of data entities,
12   should be declared in the same document type definitions as the
original data entity.

14   "SUBDOC" can be specified only if "SUBDOC YES" is specified on
the *SGML declaration* [171] *450:1* .

A–13.5.3 *473:28*

Clause 11
Markup Declarations: Document Type Definition

11.1 Document Type Declaration

Most markup declarations associate one parameter (an element type name, for example) with related parameters (a content model, for example, or an attribute definition list). The document type declaration is no different, as it associates a document type name with a document type definition, or "DTD". The document type definition is expressed as element, attribute definition list, notation, entity, short reference, and comment declarations of various kinds, all of which are contained within a portion of the document type declaration called the "document type declaration subset".

> **T–B.4.1** *26*
> **O–4.103** *143:4*
> **A–7.1** *302:1*

The declaration subset could occur entirely within the same entity as the document type declaration. In the reference concrete syntax, that would mean between the square brackets of the declaration. More often, though, all or part of the subset is in an external entity. This raises an interesting problem: in order to reference an entity, there has to be an entity declaration and the entity declaration has to occur within the document type declaration subset. The problem could be handled simply by including an entity declaration and a reference to that entity within the square brackets. However, in order to simplify the case where a document simply references a public document type definition and has no internal declaration subset, provision is made for including an external identifier as part of the document type declaration. That external identifier can be thought of as an entity declaration for an unnamed entity that contains the document type definition. You can think of the end of the document type declaration as being the reference to that entity.

This relationship between the document type declaration and an external document type definition is important to understand. The document type declaration occurs in the document and it identifies the DTD that applies. The external document type definition must not itself contain a document type declaration as that would not only be syntactically incorrect but also illogical and redundant. It is the document type declaration that incorporates the document type definition, not the reverse.

When an external document type definition is used, the internal declaration subset can be used for two purposes:

a)   One use of the internal subset is to include modifications or additions to the external DTD that will apply to this particular document. That is typically done by declaring parameter entities in the internal subset that are the same as parameter entities in the external definition. The declarations in the internal subset will take precedence because the internal subset is processed before the external. (Remember, the external subset acts as if it is referenced at the end of the document type declaration.)

b)   The other use of the internal subset is to declare entities that are used only in this document. It stretches the terminology a bit to think of such entities as part of the document type definition, but from a purely mechanical standpoint there is no real distinction between declarations that tailor an external definition and those that introduce new material for a specific document. A user can make this distinction, if it is important to him, by introducing the local entity declarations with a suitable comment declaration.

	[110] document type declaration =	
2	**mdo**,	`<!`
	"DOCTYPE",	
4	ps+,	[65] 372:1
	document type name,	[111] 404:4
6	(ps+,	[65] 372:1
	external identifier)?,	[73] 379:1
8	(ps+,	[65] 372:1
	dso,	`[`
10	document type declaration subset,	[112] 404:6

2
　　　　　　　　dsc　)?,　　　　　　　　　　　　　　　　　]
　　　　　　　　ps*,　　　　　　　　　　　　　　　　　 [65] *372:1*
　　　　　　　　mdc　　　　　　　　　　　　　　　　　　 >

4　[111] document type name =
　　　　　　generic identifier　　　　　　　　　　　　 [30] *325:17*

6　[112] document type declaration subset =
　　　　　　(*entity set* |　　　　　　　　　　　　 [113] *404:10*
8　　　　　　　*element set* |　　　　　　　　　　　 [114] *404:13*
　　　　　　　short reference set　)*　　　　　 [115] *404:18*

10　[113] entity set =
　　　　　　(*entity declaration* |　　　　　　　 [101] *394:18*
12　　　　　*ds*　)*　　　　　　　　　　　　　　　 [71] *376:1*

　　[114] element set =
14　　　　　(*element declaration* |　　　　　　 [116] *405:6*
　　　　　　attribute definition list declaration |　 [141] *420:15*
16　　　　　*notation declaration* |　　　　　　　 [148] *426:15*
　　　　　　ds　)*　　　　　　　　　　　　　　　 [71] *376:1*

18　[115] short reference set =
　　　　　　(*entity declaration* |　　　　　　　 [101] *394:18*
20　　　　　*short reference mapping declaration* |　 [150] *429:8*
　　　　　　short reference use declaration |　 [152] *430:10*
22　　　　　*ds*　)*　　　　　　　　　　　　　　　 [71] *376:1*

The *document type name* [111] *404:4* must be a *generic identifier*
24　[30] *325:17* that does not occur as a *document type name*
　　[111] *404:4* or *link type name* [155] *434:18* in the same *prolog*
26　[7] *303:1* .

The *external identifier* [73] *379:1* points to an entity that is refer-
28　enced at the end of the declaration subset and is considered to be
　　part (or all) of it. The effective document type definition is the com-
30　bination of the declarations entered in the subset and the external
　　ones.

32　NOTE — A parameter entity declaration in the subset will have priority over
　　another declaration for that entity in the external entity, as the external entity
34　is parsed later.

A *document type declaration* [110] *403:1* must contain an *element*
36　*declaration* [116] *405:6* for the *document type name* [111] *404:4* .

A *short reference set* [115] *404:18* is permitted only in the base
2   document type declaration.

An **Ee** or *parameter entity reference* [60] *350:22* cannot occur in a
4   *document type declaration* [110] *403:1* , except within the *document
type declaration subset* [112] *404:6* .

11.2 Element Declaration

An element declaration associates an element type with its element
definition.   T–B.4.2 *27*

O–4.111 *148:12*

6   [116] element declaration =
        mdo,   <!
8   "ELEMENT",
        ps+,   [65] *372:1*
10   element type,   [117] *406:1*
        (ps+,   [65] *372:1*
12   omitted tag minimization   )?,   [122] *408:1*
        ps+,   [65] *372:1*
14   (declared content | [125] *409:3*
            content model   ),   [126] *410:1*
16   ps*,   [65] *372:1*
        mdc   >

18 The order in which elements and characters occur within an ele-
    ment in the document instance must comply with the element type
20 definition specified in the element declaration.

    The *omitted tag minimization* [122] *408:1* parameter and its preced-
22 ing *ps* [65] *372:1* can be omitted only if "OMITTAG NO" is specified
    on the *SGML declaration* [171] *450:1* .

11.2.1 Element Type

An element type is normally a generic identifier or, when the same element definition is to apply to all of them, it could be a name group containing many generic identifiers. This latter approach is most often used
when a document type definition provides for user extensibility. The

method used is to define a parameter entity that is a list of elements — for example, one might define "titlepg" to be a list of elements that could appear on the title page of a book, such as author, document number, date, and so on.

T–B.4.2 *27*

O–4.114 *127:18*

The end-user of this document type definition would, in the internal document type declaration subset, also define that entity, but this time to include only those element types that his publisher accepted on a title page. As the designer of the document type definition cannot know what those specific element types are, he would create an element declaration in which the element type parameter was "%titlepg;", a reference to the parameter entity containing the group of title page elements. As the internal declaration has precedence over the external one, the more specific element list would be in effect.

```
[117] element type =
2          generic identifier |
           name group |
4          ranked element |
           ranked group
```

[30] *325:17*
[69] *374:11*
[118] *407:1*
[119] *407:5*

6 Within a document type definition, a *generic identifier* **[30]** *325:17* can be specified only once in an *element type* **[117]** *406:1* parame-
8 ter, and it cannot be the same as a *rank stem* **[120]** *407:17* , or as the *generic identifier* **[30]** *325:17* that is derived by appending the
10 *rank suffix* **[121]** *407:19* of a *ranked element* **[118]** *407:1* to its *rank stem* **[120]** *407:17* .

12 If the *element type* **[117]** *406:1* is a group, the group members are defined in the order their names occur, and the definition applies to
14 each of them.

If the *element type* **[117]** *406:1* is a *name group* **[69]** *374:11* , each
16 *name* **[55]** *346:17* is a *generic identifier* **[30]** *325:17* .

11.2.1.1 Ranked Element

An element type can be specified as a separate ranked stem and ranked suffix in order to support the use of the rank feature. Note that it is possible to enter ranked elements in the document type definition even when the document is not using RANK. In this way, the designer of a public document type definition can support the use of RANK by those who want it, while others can ignore the feature. When the rank feature is not used — or even when it is used but is not being applied in a particular tag — a ranked element can be treated as a normal generic identifier simply by concatenating the rank stem with the rank suffix.

> T–C.1.5 *85*
> O–4.250 *169:17*
> A–7.8.1 *326:4*

```
      [118] ranked element =
2              rank stem,                                          [120] 407:17
               ps+,                                                 [65] 372:1
4              rank suffix                                         [121] 407:19

      [119] ranked group =
6              grpo,                                                      (
               ts*,                                                 [70] 375:3
8              rank stem,                                          [120] 407:17
               ( ts*,                                              [70] 375:3
10                 connector,                                     [131] 413:4
                   ts*,                                            [70] 375:3
12                 rank stem   )*,                                [120] 407:17
               ts*,                                                [70] 375:3
14             grpc,                                                      )
               ps+,                                                 [65] 372:1
16             rank suffix                                         [121] 407:19

      [120] rank stem =
18             name                                                [55] 346:17

      [121] rank suffix =
20             number                                              [56] 347:1
```

The *generic identifier* [30] *325:17* specified by a *ranked element* [118] *407:1* or member of a *ranked group* [119] *407:5* is the *rank stem* [120] *407:17* with the *rank suffix* [121] *407:19* appended.

11.2.1.2 Quantities

The length of a *generic identifier* [30] *325:17* cannot exceed the "NAMELEN" quantity.

A–13.4.8 *469:26*

11.2.2 Omitted Tag Minimization

The omitted tag minimization parameter indicates whether omission of a tag is to be treated as a markup error. This parameter is not considered by the SGML parser in determining whether a tag was omitted properly. Its sole purpose is to indicate whether an error message should be issued by a validating parser.

T–C.1.2 *71*
O–4.210 *157:8*
A–7.3.1 *308:9*

```
    [122] omitted tag minimization =
2          start-tag minimization,                         [123] 408:5
           ps+,                                             [65] 372:1
4          end-tag minimization                            [124] 408:8

    [123] start-tag minimization =
6          "O" |
           minus                                              -

8   [124] end-tag minimization =
           "O" |
10         minus                                              -
```

where

12 **O**   means that omission of the tag under the conditions
                 specified in 7.3.1 [308] is not a markup error.
14 **minus**   means that omission of the tag under the conditions
                 specified in 7.3.1 [308] is a markup error.
16   The **minus** in productions 123 and 124 is recognized as
                 a delimiter in this context without a contextual constraint.

18 **minus** should be specified for start-tag minimization if omission is
    prohibited by 7.3.1 [308] .

20 "O" should be specified for end-tag minimization if the element has
    a content reference attribute or a declared value of "EMPTY".

NOTE — Specifying "O" serves as a reminder that empty elements do not
2   have end-tags (although this has nothing to do with markup minimization).

11.2.3 Declared Content

Declared content is used in an element definition when the content of
the element is to be parsed in a special way, either because it is character
data or replaceable character data, or because the content is empty.

> **T–B.4.2.6** *31*
>
> **A–9.1** *342:1*

[125] declared content =
4   "CDATA" |
           "RCDATA" |
6   "EMPTY"

where

8   **RCDATA**   means that the *content* [24] *320:1* is *replaceable*
                   character data [46] *343:1* .
10 **CDATA**   means that the *content* [24] *320:1* is *character*
                   data [47] *344:1* .
12 **EMPTY**   means the *content* [24] *320:1* is empty.

11.2.4 Content Model

The content model defines where subelements and data can occur in
the content of an element, and which subelement types are permitted.
There are two parts to a content model: a model group, and optional
exceptions to the model group.

a)   A model group consists of tokens that represent elements and that
     are separated by connectors that indicate the relationship among
     the tokens. For example, an OR connector would mean that either
     of two elements could occur, while an AND connector would mean
     that both of them had to occur. Model groups can be nested within
     one another so that complex relationships can be described.

> **T–B.4.2.1** *27*
>
> **O–4.194** *150:5*

Alternatively, the keyword ANY can be used to represent a model group that allows data or any element type to occur.

b)   The exceptions modify the content model by excluding optional elements allowed by the model group and allowing optional elements not mentioned in the model group. The exceptions also apply to the content models of subordinate elements.

> **O–4.130** *151:9*
>
> **A–11.2.5** *417:16*

[126] content model =		
2	(*model group* |	**[127]** *410:6*
	"ANY"),	
4	(*ps+*,	**[65]** *372:1*
	exceptions)?	**[138]** *418:1*
6	[127] model group =	
	grpo,	(
8	*ts**,	**[70]** *375:3*
	content token,	**[128]** *410:17*
10	(*ts**,	**[70]** *375:3*
	connector,	**[131]** *413:4*
12	*ts**,	**[70]** *375:3*
	content token)*,	**[128]** *410:17*
14	*ts**,	**[70]** *375:3*
	grpc,	)
16	*occurrence indicator*?	**[132]** *413:20*
	[128] content token =	
18	*primitive content token* |	**[129]** *410:20*
	model group	**[127]** *410:6*
20	[129] primitive content token =	
	(*rni*,	#
22	"PCDATA") |	
	element token |	**[130]** *410:25*
24	*data tag group*	**[133]** *415:16*
	[130] element token =	
26	*generic identifier*,	**[30]** *325:17*
	occurrence indicator?	**[132]** *413:20*

where

2 **ANY** means the *content model* [126] *410:1* is an optional and repeatable *or* group whose members are
4 "#PCDATA" and all of the GIs specified as element types in the same document type definition.
6 **PCDATA** means parsed character data is allowed.

8 NOTE — The *rni* distinguishes this keyword from an *element token* [130] *410:25* of "PCDATA".

The rules for parsing the content of an element are defined in 7.6 319, which distinguishes between "element content" and "mixed content". The content model indicates whether the content of an element is element content or mixed content by use of the reserved content token #PCDATA (which stands for "parsed character data"). If that token is present, the content is mixed content; otherwise, it is element content.

The token #PCDATA indicates that data characters are expected but the text must first be parsed to see if other markup is present — such as entity references or short references. #PCDATA therefore differs from declared content of CDATA or RCDATA, where only limited parsing occurs.

If "#PCDATA" or a *data tag group* [133] *415:16* is present in a
10 *model group* [127] *410:6* , the element's *content* [24] *320:1* is *mixed content* [25] *320:6* ; if not, it is *element content* [26] *320:10* .

As was pointed out in 7.6.1 321 , #PCDATA should be used in a content model only when the intention of the content model is to allow intermixed data with whatever elements are permitted — in other words, where the content model is a repeatable OR group. Incidentally, the explanation for this rule in the note is somewhat unclear. The unwritten assumption is that the content model of the element x is simply "(#PCDATA)".

A–7.6.1 *321:23*

12 NOTE — It is recommended that "#PCDATA" be used only when data characters are to be permitted anywhere in the *content* [24] *320:1* of the
14 element; that is, in a *content model* [126] *410:1* where it is the sole token, or where *or* is the only connector used in any *model group* [127] *410:6* .

16 This recommendation is made because separator characters, which are recognized as separators in *element content* [26] *320:10* , are treated as

data in *mixed content* [25] *320:6* . In content models where this recom-
2 mendation is not followed, such as

```
(x, #PCDATA)
```

4 an **RE** occurring before the start-tag of "x" would (because it is data) imply
the start of an "x" element (because an "x" is contextually required). The
6 actual start-tag for "x" would then be treated as an error (because a second
"x" is not permitted).

8 An equivalent for a non-recommended content model can normally be
obtained by replacing "#PCDATA" with the GI of an element whose content
10 is "#PCDATA" and both of whose tags can be omitted.

This recommendation should not be construed as deprecating the use of
12 the data tag feature (see the note in 11.2.4.4 415), but care should be
taken with separator characters.

14 The elements and data characters of the *content* [24] *320:1* must
conform to the *content model* [126] *410:1* by satisfying *model*
16 *group* [127] *410:6* tokens and *exceptions* [138] *418:1* in the following order of priority:
18 a) a repetition of the most recent satisfied token, if it has a **rep**
or **plus** occurrence indicator; or
20 b) some other token in a *model group* [127] *410:6* , possibly as
modified by exclusion *exceptions* [138] *418:1* (see 11.2.5
22 417); or
c) a token in an inclusion *exceptions* [138] *418:1* group (see
24 11.2.5.1 418).

NOTE — For example, in an instance of the following element

26 `<!element e (a+ | b)+>`

successive "a" elements will satisfy repetitions of the element token, rather
28 than repetitions of the model group.

All data characters occurring between successive tags are
30 considered to satisfy a single "#PCDATA" token, even if some were
declared to be character data by a marked section declaration.

32 A *generic identifier* [30] *325:17* can be a valid *element token*
[130] *410:25* whether or not it is specified as an *element type*
34 [117] *406:1* in the document type definition.

2 NOTE — This provision makes it easier to use public definitions that name a large set of generic identifiers in conjunction with a more restrictive document type that does not permit all of them.

11.2.4.1 Connector

4 [131] connector =
      and |

6   *or* |
      seq

| & |
| | |
| , |

T–B.4.2.2 *28*

8 If there is more than one *content token* [128] *410:17* in a *model group* [127] *410:6*, the ordering and selection among their corre-
10 sponding content is determined by the *connector* [131] *413:4*, as follows:

12 **seq**   All must occur, in the order entered.
    and   All must occur, in any order.
14 **or**   One and only one must occur.

Only one kind of *connector* [131] *413:4* can occur in a single *model*
16 *group* [127] *410:6* (but a *model group* [127] *410:6* nested within it could have a different *connector* [131] *413:4*).

The following rule is necessary in order to apply the definitions of optional and required elements and tokens that are used to determine whether start-tag omission is possible. The definitions vary depending upon the type of group that a token is, or is a member of.

T–C.1.2 *71*

O–4.159 *164:7*

18 A *model group* [127] *410:6* with a single *content token* [128] *410:17* is regarded as a **seq** group.

11.2.4.2 Occurrence Indicator

20 [132] occurrence indicator =
      opt |

22   *plus* |
      rep

| ? |
| + |
| * |

T–B.4.2.2 *28*

2   The corresponding content of each selected *content token* [128] *410:17* must occur once and only once unless the contrary is indicated by the token's *occurrence indicator* [132] *413:20* , as fol-
4   lows:

opt   Optional (0 or 1 time).
6   **plus**   Required and repeatable (1 or more times).
rep   Optional and repeatable (0 or more times).

The following paragraphs are used in applying the priority rules in 11.2.4 *409* , and also the definitions of required and optional elements and tokens that are used for application of the start-tag omission rules.

O–4.274 *164:34*

8   The "#PCDATA" content token is regarded as having an *occurrence indicator* [132] *413:20* of **rep**.

10 An inherently optional token is treated as having an **opt** occurrence indicator if none is specified, or as having a **rep** occurrence indica-
12 tor if **plus** is specified.

11.2.4.3 Ambiguous Content Model

This area of the standard is one of those where the power of the computer to deal with abstractions was compromised in favor of the tendency of human beings to become confused by them.

O–4.4 *151:4*

The purpose of the content model is, in effect, to state an agreement between human beings and computer programs as to what will occur in a given element. Although a computer could make sense of a content model that SGML prohibits, a human is likely to encounter difficulties with it.

For example, the first content model in the note is likely to be less intuitive to a human than the pair of content models shown later. That is because the additional generic identifier "f" will provide semantic cues for the human reader that will make the content model more intuitive. In the first example, there is only the parenthesized sequence group and it may be difficult to see at a glance what role it plays in the document.

A *content model* [126] *410:1* cannot be ambiguous; that is, an ele-

2   ment or character string that occurs in the document instance must be able to satisfy only one *primitive content token* [**[129]** *410:20*] without looking ahead in the document instance. The priority rules

4   stated earlier in 11.2.4 [*409*] are not considered in determining whether a content model is ambigous.

6   NOTE — For example, the content model in

```
<!element e ((a, b?), b) >
```

8   is ambiguous because after an "a" element occurs, a "b" element could satisfy either of the remaining tokens. The ambiguity can be avoided by

10 using intermediate elements, as in:

```
<!element e (f, b) >
<!element f (a, b?) >
```

12

Here the token satisfied by "b" is determined unambiguously by whether the

14 "f" element ends before the "b" occurs. (The theoretical basis of content models is discussed in annex H [*556*] .)

11.2.4.4 Data Tag Group

A data tag group is a special form of token that is allowed in model groups in order to support the data tag minimization feature (see 7.3.2 [*311*]). It is a *seq* group consisting of a generic identifier and a data tag pattern that defines the set of character strings that will be treated as the data tag.

The data tag pattern itself has two parts. The first part is a character string or an *or* group of character strings, one of which has to occur completely in order for the data tag to be recognized. The second part of the data tag pattern is an optional padding template — a character string that does not have to occur at all, or that could occur any number of times, including fractional times in which only the initial characters of it occur. For example, if you wanted the data tag that terminated the element to be, let us say, a comma followed by one or more spaces, the data tag template would consist of a comma and a space and the data tag padding template would consist of a single space.

[**T–C.1.4** *82*]
[**O–4.76** *168:3*]

16 [133] data tag group =
            ***dtgo*,**   [[ ]

18   *ts**,   [**[70]** *375:3*]

	generic identifier,	[30] *325:17*
2	*ts*,*	[70] *375:3*
	seq,	,
4	*ts*,*	[70] *375:3*
	data tag pattern,	[134] *416:9*
6	*ts*,*	[70] *375:3*
	dtgc,	]
8	*occurrence indicator?*	[132] *413:20*

	[134] data tag pattern =	
10	(*data tag template group* |	[135] *416:16*
	data tag template),	[136] *416:26*
12	(*ts*,*	[70] *375:3*
	seq,	,
14	*ts*,*	[70] *375:3*
	data tag padding template)?	[137] *416:28*

16	[135] data tag template group =	
	grpo,	(
18	*ts*,*	[70] *375:3*
	data tag template,	[136] *416:26*
20	(*ts*,*	[70] *375:3*
	or,	|
22	*ts*,*	[70] *375:3*
	data tag template)*,	[136] *416:26*
24	*ts*,*	[70] *375:3*
	grpc	)

26	[136] data tag template =	
	parameter literal	[66] *373:1*

28	[137] data tag padding template =	
	parameter literal	[66] *373:1*

A data tag group is treated effectively as a special form of model group. If the data tag feature is not supported then the data tag pattern is simply treated as though #PCDATA had been specified.

30   A *data tag group* [133] *415:16* is interpreted as a **seq** group with two tokens: an element GI followed by "#PCDATA".

32   NOTE — For example, with the reference delimiter set, the *model group* [127] *410:6*

```
([hours, (" :" | ":"), " "], minutes)
```

2   is treated as though it were

```
((hours, #PCDATA), minutes)
```

4   A *data tag group* [133] *415:16* can only be present in the base *doc-
     ument type declaration* [110] *403:1* .

6   A *parameter literal* [66] *373:1* in a *data tag pattern* [134] *416:9* is
     interpreted in the normal manner, except that a numeric character
8   reference to a non-SGML character or *function character*
     [54] *346:8* is prohibited.

11.2.4.5 Quantities

10   The content model nesting level cannot exceed the "GRPLVL"
     quantity.

12   The grand total of the content tokens at all levels of a content
     model cannot exceed the "GRPGTCNT" quantity.

14   The length of an interpreted *parameter literal* [66] *373:1* in a *data
     tag pattern* [134] *416:9* cannot exceed the "DTEMPLEN" quantity.

A–13.4.8 *469:26*

11.2.5 Exceptions

   Exceptions are a shorthand method of defining a content model that
can avoid the need for complex model groups throughout an element's
subelements. Like many good power tools, however, if used improperly
they can cause significant damage. They should always be specified as
low in the element structure as possible, in order to make their effect
clear to a reader of the DTD, and the specific considerations described
below for exclusions and inclusions should be observed.

T–B.11 *54*

O–4.130 *151:9*

[138] exceptions =

2   (*exclusions,*   `[140] 419:8`

            (*ps+,*   `[65] 372:1`

4   *inclusions*)?) | `[139] 418:11`

           inclusions   `[139] 418:11`

6   The *exceptions* `[138] 418:1` apply anywhere in an instance of the element, including subelements whose *content* `[24] 320:1` is *mixed*

8   *content* `[25] 320:6` or *element content* `[26] 320:10` .

At any point in a document instance, if an element is both an appli-

10   cable inclusion and an exclusion, it is treated as an exclusion.

11.2.5.1 Inclusions

Elements named in an inclusion can occur anywhere within the content of the element being defined, including anywhere in the content of its subelements.

                                   `T–B.11.1 55`

                              `O–4.157 151:13`

[139] inclusions =

12   **plus**,   `+`

           name group   `[69] 374:11`

14   Inclusions modify the effect of model groups to which they apply in the manner shown in the following example: given that "Q" is a gen-

16   eric identifier or group in the model group, "x" is its occurrence indi-cator (or empty if there is no occurrence indicator), and "R1"

18   through "Rn" are applicable inclusions, then a token

    Qx

20   is treated as though it were

    `(R1|R2|...|Rn)*, (Q, (R1|R2|...|Rn)*)x`

22   An element that can satisfy an element token in the content model is considered to do so, even if the element is also an inclusion.

An inclusion differs from an optional token in a model group in the way that record ends following an inclusion are handled. They are normally ignored, which is to say the inclusion is not treated as though it were data. A record end that follows a proper subelement, however, is treated as data. Inclusions should therefore be used only for "floating" elements, such as sidebars, that are not part of the element structure at the point where they occur in the content. Conversely, such elements should never be specified in a model group.

An implication of this rule is that the distinction between a floating figure and a stationary ("inline") one should be made by defining two element types, not by defining a "float/nofloat" attribute.

NOTES

2   1   Inclusions should not be used for contextual subelements. They should
        be used only for elements that are not logically part of the content at the
4   point where they occur in the document, such as index entries or floating
        figures.

6   2   An **RE** that follows an inclusion will normally be ignored, while one that
        follows a proper subelement will be treated as data (see 7.6.1 [*321*]).

11.2.5.2 Exclusions

Exclusions have the effect of removing optional tokens from the model groups to which the exclusions apply. They are intended for "document management" purposes; for example, to prohibit selected elements defined in a referenced public DTD without physically modifying the DTD. The DTD would make this possible by defining a parameter entity for the exclusions.

[**T–B.11.2** *55*]
[**O–4.131** *151:16*]

Exclusions can also be used to avoid unwanted recursion. Consider a "duration" element whose content is "seconds" or "expression" or "range". If a "range" consists of "duration" followed by "duration", it is necessary to specify that a "duration" nested in a "range" cannot itself contain a "range". Excluding "range" in the content model for "range" expresses this restriction clearly and simply.

8   [140] exclusions =
            minus,   [-]
10   *name group*   [**[69]** *374:11*]

Exclusions modify the effect of model groups to which they apply
2   by precluding options that would otherwise have been available
(just as though the user had chosen to leave optional elements out
4   of the document).

An exclusion cannot affect a specification in a model group that indicates that an element is required.

It is an error if an exclusion attempts to modify the effect of a model
6   group in any other way. In particular, it is an error if:
   a)   an exclusion applies to tokens other than those in *inclusions*
8   ⌈ **[139]** *418:11* ⌉, those having an ***opt*** or ***rep*** occurrence indica-
       tor, or those that are members of ***or*** groups; or
10   b)   an exclusion attempts to change a token's required or optional
       status.

12   NOTE — For example, it is prohibited to exclude all members of a
       required *model group* ⌈ **[127]** *410:6* ⌉, as the group would then no
14   longer be required.

11.3 Attribute Definition List Declaration

An attribute definition list declaration defines an attribute definition
list for one or more elements or data content notations.

⌈ **T–B.5.2** *35* ⌉
⌈ **O–4.12** *148:25* ⌉

[141] attribute definition list declaration =
16   ***mdo*,**   ⌈ **<!** ⌉
       "ATTLIST",
18   *ps+,*   ⌈ **[65]** *372:1* ⌉
       (*associated element type* | ⌈ **[72]** *377:1* ⌉
20   *associated notation name*),   ⌈ **[149.1]** *428:5* ⌉
       ps+,   ⌈ **[65]** *372:1* ⌉
22   *attribute definition list,*   ⌈ **[142]** *420:25* ⌉
       ps,*   ⌈ **[65]** *372:1* ⌉
24   ***mdc***   ⌈ **>** ⌉

[142] attribute definition list =
26   *attribute definition,*   ⌈ **[143]** *421:1* ⌉
       (*ps+,*   ⌈ **[65]** *372:1* ⌉
28   *attribute definition*)*   ⌈ **[143]** *421:1* ⌉

An attribute definition consists of an attribute name, a declared value that states the type of attribute that it is, and a default value.

[143] attribute definition =

2   *attribute name,*   [144] *421:14*

           ps+,   [65] *372:1*

4   *declared value,*   [145] *422:6*

           ps+,   [65] *372:1*

6   *default value*   [147] *425:1*

An individual associated element type cannot be associated with
8   another attribute definition list in the same declaration subset in which this list occurs.

11.3.1 Quantities

10   The total number of attribute names and name tokens in the *attribute definition list* [142] *420:25* cannot exceed the "ATTCNT"
12   quantity.

NOTE — Default values should not be considered in applying this rule.

A–13.4.8 *469:26*

11.3.2 Attribute Name

An attribute name can occur only once in an attribute definition list and it cannot be specified more than once. To define an attribute that can have more than one value for an element, the declared value that you choose for it should be one that permits a number of values to be specified — for example, a list or a character data string.

T–B.5.1 *33*

14   [144] attribute name =

           name   [55] *346:17*

16   An *attribute name* [144] *421:14* can be specified only once in the same *attribute definition list* [142] *420:25* .

By convention, the name "ID" is used for attributes whose declared value is a unique identifier (that is, "ID").

T–B.9 *52*

2   Within a document type definition, the same *attribute name* [144] *421:14* should be used for all attributes having a *declared value* [145] *422:6* of "ID".

4   NOTE — Use of a common name for all ID attributes emphasizes the requirement that an ID value must be unique within a document instance.

11.3.3 Declared Value

The declared value parameter of an attribute definition determines which of the fifteen types of attribute value must occur when the attribute is specified. (See 7.9.4 *332*.) The declared values can be classified in two categories:

A–7.9.4 *332:12*

a)   Declared values whose semantics are meaningful to the SGML parser — ENTITY, ENTITIES, ID, IDREF, IDREFS and NOTATION. For these six, the SGML parser performs all of the necessary semantic checking.

b)   Declared values for which checking is the responsibility of the application.

For the latter group, if there were no other declared value type but CDATA, that would really be sufficient. However, because an SGML parser must already have code for recognizing names, name tokens, numbers, and number tokens, the eight tokenized forms of attribute value were supplied.

It must be emphasized that the checking done for these eight declared values is purely lexical and not semantic. Number, for example, means a character string consisting of digits — not a numeric quantity. Therefore, "1" and "01" are two different values.

T–B.5.2.2 *36*

```
6   [145] declared value =
            "CDATA" |
8           "ENTITY" |
            "ENTITIES" |
10          "ID" |
```

```
 2        "IDREF" |
          "IDREFS" |
          "NAME" |
 4        "NAMES" |
          "NMTOKEN" |
 6        "NMTOKENS" |
          "NUMBER" |
 8        "NUMBERS" |
          "NUTOKEN" |
10        "NUTOKENS" |
          notation |                              [146] 423:13
12        name token group                        [68] 374:1


    [146] notation =
14        "NOTATION",
          ps+,                                     [65] 372:1
16        name group                               [69] 374:11
```

where

18 **CDATA**	means the *attribute value* [35] 333:1 is *character data* [47] 344:1 .
20 **ENTITY**	means the *attribute value* [35] 333:1 is a *general entity name* [103] 395:4 .
22 **ENTITIES**	means the *attribute value* [35] 333:1 is a *general entity name list* [35.1] 333:17 .
24 **ID**	means the *attribute value* [35] 333:1 is an *id value* [36] 333:19 .
26 **IDREF**	means the *attribute value* [35] 333:1 is an *id reference value* [38] 333:23 .
28 **IDREFS**	means the *attribute value* [35] 333:1 is an *id reference list* [37] 333:21 .
30 **NAME**	means the *attribute value* [35] 333:1 is a *name* [55] 346:17 .
32 **NAMES**	means the *attribute value* [35] 333:1 is a *name list* [39] 333:25 .
34 **NMTOKEN**	means the *attribute value* [35] 333:1 is a *name token* [57] 347:3 .
36 **NMTOKENS**	means the *attribute value* [35] 333:1 is a *name token list* [40] 333:29 .
38 **NOTATION**	means the *attribute value* [35] 333:1 is a *notation name* [41] 333:33 that identifies the data content notation of the element's *content* [24] 320:1 . The *name group* [69] 374:11

specifies the permissible notation names.

2　**NUMBER**　　　means the *attribute value* ⌈ **[35]** *333:1* ⌉ is a *number* ⌈ **[56]** *347:1* ⌉ .

4　**NUMBERS**　　means the *attribute value* ⌈ **[35]** *333:1* ⌉ is a *number list* ⌈ **[42]** *333:35* ⌉ .

6　**NUTOKEN**　　means the *attribute value* ⌈ **[35]** *333:1* ⌉ is a *number token* ⌈ **[58]** *347:5* ⌉ .

8　**NUTOKENS**　means the *attribute value* ⌈ **[35]** *333:1* ⌉ is a *number token list* ⌈ **[43]** *334:2* ⌉ .

10　"ID" and "NOTATION" can each be declared only once in the *attribute definition list* ⌈ **[142]** *420:25* ⌉ .

The requirement in the following paragraph supports the omitted name markup minimization described in 7.9.1.2 ⌈ *329* ⌉ . It also represents another compromise between humans and computers. While some unambiguous rule could no doubt be created that would allow unminimized specification of an attribute where the tokens are duplicated between attributes, such a rule would not be in the best interests of the user. The intention is that these name tokens be self-describing attribute values. They should imply the attribute name as well as the value. When properly designed, they should be meaningless as values of a different attribute. (I might add, in general, that markup minimization is an appropriate area for making such compromises in favor of people, since markup minimization is there principally to support direct human markup. A computer program would be happier with a fully marked up document and no need to check for minimization.)

⌈ **A–7.9.1.2** *329:14* ⌉

12　A token cannot occur more than once in an *attribute definition list* ⌈ **[142]** *420:25* ⌉ , even in different groups.

14　"NOTATION" cannot be declared for an element whose *declared content* ⌈ **[125]** *409:3* ⌉ is "EMPTY".

11.3.4 Default Value

The default value parameter of a attribute definition indicates when an attribute value must be specified and when it can be omitted. It also indicates what value will be used if the attribute is not specified. When no markup minimization features are used, an attribute must always be specified unless its default value is either of the keywords IMPLIED or CONREF. When the SHORTTAG or OMITTAG features are used, it is possible to omit some or all of an attribute specification list, except for those attributes whose default value is specified as REQUIRED. A default value specified as CURRENT is the equivalent of REQUIRED for the first occurrence of the defined attribute list, but for subsequent occurrences the most recent specification is used as a default value.

T–B.5.2.4 *38*

O–4.84 *155:17*

When an attribute value specification is the default value, the attribute value literal is interpreted and references are resolved at the time of the attribute definition list declaration. However, testing for general entity names and notations is deferred until the default value is used in an attribute specification because those objects may not have been declared until after the attribute definition list.

If an attribute value specification is prefixed by the keyword FIXED, then any specification of the attribute must have the identical value. (The purpose of fixed attributes is explained in 7.9.4.2 334 .)

O–4.136 *156:10*

A–7.9.4.2 *334:16*

```
[147] default value =
  2          ( (  rni,                                          #
                 "FIXED",
  4             ps+   )?,                                    [65] 372:1
             attribute value specification   )|             [33] 331:1
  6          ( rni,                                             #
               ( "REQUIRED" |
  8             "CURRENT" |
                "CONREF" |
 10             "IMPLIED"   )  )
```

where

12	**FIXED**	means the attribute is a fixed attribute.
	REQUIRED	means the attribute is a required attribute.
14	**CURRENT**	means the attribute is a current attribute.
	CONREF	means the attribute is a content reference
16		attribute.
	IMPLIED	means the attribute is an impliable attribute.

18   NOTE — Specifying an empty literal is not equivalent to specifying "IMPLIED".

2   If an attribute value is specified in this parameter, it must conform to the syntactic requirements specified in 7.9.4.1 ⌐334⌐.

4   NOTE — Further testing of general entity name, general entity name list, and notation values is performed when the default value is used in an attribute specification.

6   If the *declared value* ⌐**[145]** *422:6*⌐ is "ID", the *default value* ⌐**[147]** *425:1*⌐ must be "IMPLIED" or "REQUIRED".

8   "CONREF" cannot be declared for an element whose *declared content* ⌐**[125]** *409:3*⌐ is "EMPTY".

11.3.4.1 Quantities

10   "CONREF", "REQUIRED", and "IMPLIED" have normalized lengths of zero.

⌐**A–13.4.8** *469:26*⌐

11.3.4.2 Capacities

12   In calculating "ATTCHCAP" requirements, the default value of a current attribute is given the length of the longest value specified
14   for the attribute in the document.

⌐**A–13.2** *456:2*⌐

11.4 Notation Declaration

A notation declaration assigns a unique notation name to a notation identifier.

[148] notation declaration =
16	**mdo**,	⌐ <! ⌐
	"NOTATION",	
18	ps+,	⌐**[65]** *372:1*⌐
	notation name,	⌐**[41]** *333:33*⌐
20	ps+,	⌐**[65]** *372:1*⌐
	notation identifier,	⌐**[149]** *427:1*⌐
22	ps*,	⌐**[65]** *372:1*⌐
	mdc	⌐ > ⌐

A notation identifier is an external identifier and can therefore contain a public identifier, a system identifier, or both. It is best to specify both a public identifier and a system identifier. The public identifier should identify the document that specifies the notation; in other words, that explains how the notation is to be interpreted. The system identifier should identify the program that will access the data in order to process it. In hypertext and hypermedia applications, for example, the notation might be an interpretive command language that is used in hypertext scripts. In this case, the system identifier would identify the program that interprets the scripts.   <kbd>**T–B.13.2.3** *62*</kbd>

<kbd>**O–4.213** *146:14*</kbd>

```
[149] notation identifier =
         external identifier
```
2   <kbd>**[73]** *379:1*</kbd>

The *notation name* <kbd>**[41]** *333:33*</kbd> cannot be specified on another
4 *notation declaration* <kbd>**[148]** *426:15*</kbd> in the same document type definition.

6 If a *notation identifier* <kbd>**[149]** *427:1*</kbd> includes a *public identifier*
<kbd>**[74]** *379:8*</kbd> and "FORMAL YES" is specified on the *SGML declara-*
8 *tion* <kbd>**[171]** *450:1*</kbd>, the *public text class* <kbd>**[86]** *386:5*</kbd> must be "NOTA-
TION".

11.4.1 Data Attributes

The purpose of data attributes is to pass parameters to the program that controls access to data in a particular notation. Typically, such parameters govern the interpretation of the notation, not the processing of the data. For example, in a raster notation, the data attributes might indicate the order of the pixels — whether horizontal or vertical — as well as the number of pixels in each dimension. However, data attributes would not indicate whether the image is to be scaled or rotated. That information does not affect how to interpret the notation, and therefore would be specified in attributes on the start-tag of the element in which the data occurred. Or, if the scaling and rotation were to vary for different processes, they would be specified as link attributes.   <kbd>**T–B.13.2.3** *62*</kbd>

<kbd>**O–4.8.1** *154:9*</kbd>

10 NOTE — Data attributes are defined for a data content notation. Values can
be specified for them on the entity declarations for data entities conforming

to the notation.

2 The *declared value* [145] *422:6* of a data attribute cannot be "ENTITY", "ENTITIES", "ID", "IDREF", "IDREFS", or "NOTATION".

4 "CURRENT" or "CONREF" cannot be specified for a data attribute.

11.4.1.1 Associated Notation Name

An associated notation name is used in an attribute definition list declaration when the defined attributes are data attributes.

[149.1] associated notation name =
6   ***rni*,**   #
         "NOTATION",
8   *ps+,*   [65] *372:1*
         (*notation name* | [41] *333:33*
10   *name group*   )   [69] *374:11*

where

12 **NOTATION**   means the attributes being defined are data attributes.

14 Each *name* [55] *346:17* in the *name group* [69] *374:11* must be a *notation name* [41] *333:33* defined in the same document type defi-
16 nition in which this attribute definition list occurs, and not specified for any other attribute definition list. It need not have been defined
18 prior to this declaration, but must be defined prior to a reference to an entity for which it was declared to be the notation.

11.4.1.2 Data Attribute Specification

A data attribute specification is simply an attribute specification list that occurs in an entity declaration when the entity is subject to a data content notation.

20 [149.2] data attribute specification =
         ps+,   [65] *372:1*
22   ***dso*,**   [
         attribute specification list,   [31] *327:17*
24   *s*,*   [5] *297:23*

dsc   ⌐] ⌐

2   The validity of a data *attribute specification list* ⌐ **[31]** *327:17* ⌐ is deter-
    mined by the attribute definition list associated with the data con-
4   tent notation. The attribute definition list must have been declared
    prior to this declaration.

6   The *data attribute specification* ⌐ **[149.2]** *428:20* ⌐ must be omitted if its
    attribute specification list ⌐ **[31]** *327:17* ⌐ is empty.

11.5 Short Reference Mapping Declaration

A short reference mapping declaration defines a named mapping of
short reference delimiter strings to corresponding general entity names.
When a short reference is recognized, it is treated as a reference to the
general entity that corresponds to it in the current map. (See 9.4.6 ⌐ *353* ⌐)

⌐ **T–C.1.3** *76* ⌐
⌐ **O–4.293** *167:1* ⌐
⌐ **A–9.4.6** *353:6* ⌐

8   [150] short reference mapping declaration =
        mdo,   ⌐ <! ⌐
10   "SHORTREF",
         ps+,   ⌐ **[65]** *372:1* ⌐
12   *map name*,   ⌐ **[151]** *429:19* ⌐
         (*ps+*,   ⌐ **[65]** *372:1* ⌐
14   *parameter literal*,   ⌐ **[66]** *373:1* ⌐
            ps+,   ⌐ **[65]** *372:1* ⌐
16   *name*   )+,   ⌐ **[55]** *346:17* ⌐
         ps*,   ⌐ **[65]** *372:1* ⌐
18   **mdc**   ⌐ > ⌐

    [151] map name =
20   *name*   ⌐ **[55]** *346:17* ⌐

The *map name* ⌐ **[151]** *429:19* ⌐ cannot be specified on another *short
22 reference mapping declaration* ⌐ **[150]** *429:8* ⌐ in the same document
    type definition.

24 The interpreted *parameter literal* ⌐ **[66]** *373:1* ⌐ is a short reference
    delimiter that is mapped to the *name* ⌐ **[55]** *346:17* ⌐ of a general entity

that is defined in the same document type definition.

2   NOTE — A general entity is required because the short reference will be
    replaced by a named entity reference if the document is sent to a system
4   that does not support short references, and parameter entity references are
    not permitted in *content* [24] *320:1* .

6   A short reference delimiter can be mapped only once in a *short
    reference mapping declaration* [150] *429:8* .

8   If a short reference delimiter is not specified it is considered to be
    mapped to nothing.

11.6 Short Reference Use Declaration

A short reference use declaration indicates when a given short reference map becomes current. If the keyword EMPTY is used instead of a
map name, it means that no short reference mappings will be recognized
while that empty map is current.

A short reference use declaration can occur in either a document type
declaration or a document instance. These two possibilities are discussed
in detail below.

T–C.1.3.3 *78*

O–4.296 *167:16*

A–9.4.6 *353:6*

10   [152] short reference use declaration =
           mdo,   <!
12   "USEMAP",
             ps+,   [65] *372:1*
14   map specification,   [153] *430:19*
             (ps+,   [65] *372:1*
16   associated element type   )?,   [72] *377:1*
             ps*,   [65] *372:1*
18   **mdc**   >

     [153] map specification =
20   map name | [151] *429:19*
           (**rni**,   #
22   "EMPTY"   )

where

2   **EMPTY**   means the map is the empty map.

11.6.1 Use in Document Type Declaration

When short reference use declarations occur in a document type declaration, they have the effect of creating context sensitive short reference
mappings. That is, each short reference map is associated with one or
more element types. When an element of one of those types begins, the
map becomes current and stays current until the end of the element —
unless it is temporarily superseded by the map of some subelement.

> T–C.1.3.2 *77*
> O–4.70 *167:11*

Each map is complete in itself and does not inherit any mappings from
its parent or any other open elements. This characteristic of short reference maps was a deliberate design decision, another in the series of
compromises in the area of markup minimization between what human
beings are comfortable with and what computers are capable of doing.
Obviously, nested or hierarchical symbol tables that inherit definitions
from their ancestors are a well-understood feature of programming languages, and could easily have been used for short reference maps.

However, it was felt that the application designer could best work out
the potential interactions between short references in the context of various paths of open elements that could occur, and then design the maps
for each of those elements to provide the most consistency and simplicity
of use for the end-user. The alternative would have been to require the
end-user to be aware of all current maps of open elements, rather than
just being able to deal with one map at a time.

4   If the declaration occurs in a *document type declaration*
    [110] *403:1* , the *associated element type* [72] *377:1* must be
6   specified. The named map will become the current map whenever
    an element of an associated type becomes the current element.

8   The *map name* [151] *429:19* must be defined on a *short reference
    mapping declaration* [150] *429:8* in the same *document type decla-
    ration* [110] *403:1* .

10 NOTE — It need not have been defined prior to this declaration, but must
    be defined prior to becoming the current map.

12 Specifying an associated element type that is already associated

with a map is not an error, but is ignored.

11.6.2 Use in Document Instance

A short reference use declaration in the document instance can handle special situations that require a temporary remapping of the keyboard. For example, if a section of a document contains many special characters that would normally be entered with entity references, a short reference map can temporarily assign short reference characters as equivalents of the longer general entity references.

T–C.1.3.2 *77*

2   If the declaration occurs in a document instance, an *associated element type* [72] *377:1* cannot be specified. The map becomes
4   the current map for this instance of the current element.

The *map name* [151] *429:19* must have been defined on a *short ref-*
6   *erence mapping declaration* [150] *429:8* in the document type definition to which the instance conforms.

11.6.3 Current Map

8   A map is the current map as long as its associated element is the current element. It can become superceded for an instance of the
10 element: either temporarily by a subelement becoming the current element, or permanently by a *short reference use declaration*
12 [152] *430:10* occurring in an instance of the element.

If an element type has no associated short reference map, the cur-
14 rent map for an instance of the element is the map that is current when the instance begins. If the element is a document element,
16 the current map will be the empty map.

A short reference use declaration that occurs in an element perma-
nently changes the element's current short reference map. That is, the map that was current when the element began is replaced by the new map. The new map, like any other, can be replaced temporarily as the current map by that of a subelement. The new map is considered "per-manent", though, because at the end of the subelement the new map — and not the original map — will again become the current map.

T–C.1.3.3 *78*

O–4.70 *167:11*

Clause 12
Markup Declarations: Link Process Definition

SGML's optional LINK feature allows specific processing (types of formatting, for instance) to be associated with start-tags without having to put instructions in either the DTD or the document instance. Instead, an application designer has the opportunity to place a link process definition (or "LPD") in the prolog, which adds processing-oriented attributes to the set of attributes already defined in the DTD.

> **O–4.166** *124:22*

I recommend that you read Tutorial D ⎡ *92* ⎤ as an introduction to this chapter.

> **T–D** *92*

> **O–4.170** *143:12*

12.1 Link Type Declaration

As with most other markup declarations, the link type declaration's job is to associate one parameter — in this case, the link type name — with related parameters — here, a link process definition.

> **O–4.167** *171:1*

The link process definition is represented by markup declarations that occur in a declaration subset. Although the declaration types differ, the relationship between a link type declaration and the declaration subset that contains the LPD is exactly the same as the relationship between a document type declaration and its subset. (See 11.1 ⎡ *402* ⎤.) In particular, the two declarations operate the same way as far as distributing the definition across multiple entities, modifying the definition in the current document, and preempting entity declarations in the external definition by defining them in the internal subset.

A link type declaration also includes a specification indicating which of the three SGML link features is being used. These are: simple, implicit, or explicit link. The link specification parameter also identifies the source and result document types that are applicable to the link process.

T–C.2 *87*

```
    [154] link type declaration =
2        mdo,                                              <!
         "LINKTYPE",
4        ps+,                                            [65] 372:1
         link type name,                                 [155] 434:18
6        ps+,                                            [65] 372:1
         ( simple link specification |                   [156] 435:1
8          implicit link specification |                 [157] 435:18
           explicit link specification  ),               [158] 436:8
10       ( ps+,                                          [65] 372:1
           external identifier  )?,                      [73] 379:1
12       ( ps+,                                          [65] 372:1
           dso,                                            [
14         link type declaration subset,                 [161] 437:1
           dsc  )?,                                        ]
16       ps*,                                            [65] 372:1
         mdc                                               >

18  [155] link type name =
         name                                           [55] 346:17
```

20 The *link type name* [155] *434:18* must be different from any other *link type name* [155] *434:18* or *document type name* [111] *404:4* in
22 the same *prolog* [7] *303:1* .

The *external identifier* [73] *379:1* points to an entity that is refer-
24 enced at the end of the declaration subset and is considered to be part (or all) of it. The effective link process definition is the combina-
26 tion of the declarations entered in the subset and the external ones.

NOTE — A parameter entity declaration in the subset will have priority over
28 another declaration for that entity in the external entity, as the external entity is parsed later.

30 An *Ee* or *parameter entity reference* [60] *350:22* cannot occur in a *link type declaration* [154] *434:1* , except within the *link type decla-*
32 *ration subset* [161] *437:1* .

12.1.1 Simple Link Specification

[156] simple link specification =

2   *rni*,   `#`
           "SIMPLE",
4   *ps*+,   `[65]` *372:1*
           rni,   `#`
6   "IMPLIED"

`T–D.8` *105*

`O–4.299` *176:1*

where

8   **SIMPLE**   means the link is a simple link.
     IMPLIED   means the *result document type name*
10   `[160]` *436:14* is implied by the application.

If a simple link is specified, "SIMPLE YES" must be specified on the
12   SGML declaration link type features parameter.

The source document type is the base document type.

12.1.1.1 Limits

14   The number of simple link processes that can be active
     simultaneously cannot exceed the quantity specified for "SIMPLE"
16   on the *link type features* `[197]` *472:29* parameter of the *SGML dec-*
     laration `[171]` *450:1* .

12.1.2 Implicit Link Specification

18   [157] implicit link specification =
           source document type name,   `[159]` *436:12*
20   *ps*+,   `[65]` *372:1*
           rni,   `#`
22   "IMPLIED"

`O–4.155` *176:5*

where

IMPLIED   means the *result document type name*
2   [160] *436:14* is implied by the application.

If an implicit link is specified, "IMPLICIT YES" must be specified on
4   the SGML declaration link type features parameter.

The *source document type name* [159] *436:12* must be the base
6   document type, or another document type that is the last result
document type in a chain of processes

12.1.3 Explicit Link Specification

8   [158] explicit link specification =
     source document type name,   [159] *436:12*
10   ps+,   [65] *372:1*
     result document type name   [160] *436:14*

12   [159] source document type name =
     document type name   [111] *404:4*

14   [160] result document type name =
     document type name   [111] *404:4*

                                                   T–D.7 *104*
                                                   O–4.133 *176:9*

16   If an explicit link is specified, "EXPLICIT YES" must be specified on
the SGML declaration *link type features* [197] *472:29* parameter.

18   The *source document type name* [159] *436:12* must be the base
document type, or another document type that is a result document
20   type in a chain of processes.

Each *document type name* [111] *404:4* must previously have been
22   specified on a *document type declaration* [110] *403:1* in the same
prolog [7] *303:1* .

12.1.3.1 Limits

24   The number of link processes in the longest chain cannot exceed
the quantity specified for "EXPLICIT" on the *link type features*
26   [197] *472:29* parameter of the *SGML declaration* [171] *450:1* .

12.1.4 Link Type Declaration Subset

The declaration subset of a link type declaration includes intermixed sets of link attribute definitions and link set declarations, and optionally a single specialized link set declaration called an "ID link set declaration".

O–4.171 *173:1*

[161] link type declaration subset =
2   (*link attribute set* |
            link set declaration)*,

[162] *437:7*
[163] *441:6*

4   *ID link set declaration*?,

[168.1] *447:1*

          (*link attribute set* |
6   *link set declaration*)*

[162] *437:7*
[163] *441:6*

[162] link attribute set =
8   (*attribute definition list declaration* |
            entity set)*)

[141] *420:15*
[113] *404:10*

12.1.4.1 Entities

Entity declarations in a link type declaration subset are treated as though they occurred in the source document type declaration subset, but are given priority over any declarations that did. This principle is important in determining the applicable entity declaration for a reference (see 9.4.4.1 351).

T–D.9.1 *107*

For example, an application could change the default value of an attribute when a particular link process was active, in the following manner: The default value would be specified using an entity reference and the entity would be defined in the source document type definition. The same entity would then be defined in each LPD that will be used with that source DTD. As the entity declarations in the LPDs will have priority, they will have the effect of changing the default value of the attribute.

It is expected that a good application design will make sure that the same entity is not defined in more than one link type declaration subset that can be active at one time. For example, if an application has defined some simple link processes that have to do with different output devices, and another set of simple link processes that have to do with page layouts, each of the page layout processes could define the same entities because only one of those would be active for a given processing run. Similarly, each of the output device link processes could define the same entities, but those entities should be different from the entities defined for the page layout definitions, as both the page layout link process and an output device link process will be active at the same time.

In the event that an application designer does not follow this sensible approach, the standard provides a tie-breaking rule for conflicting entity declarations. The rule is that in determining which entity declaration is applicable, priority is based on the order in which they occur in the document prolog.

For example, assume a prolog that contains a document type declaration followed by link type declarations "A" and "B", in that order, and that both link types are active. If all three declarations contain internal and external subsets, there are six places in which entity declarations can occur. For the purpose of determining the applicable declaration for an entity, the priority of those six places is as follows:

a)   internal subset of link type A;

b)   external subset of link type A;

c)   internal subset of link type B;

d)   external subset of link type B;

e)   internal subset of the document type declaration;

f)   external subset of the document type declaration.

> When this link type is active, the entity declarations are treated as if
> 2   they occurred at the start of the source document type declaration
> subset, but after the entity declarations of any preceding active link
> 4   type declarations.

> A link type declaration can contain parameter entity references to
> 6   entities defined in the source document type declaration, as well as
> in its own declaration subset.

On the surface, the preceding two paragraphs of the standard appear to contradict one another. On the one hand, entity declarations in an LPD are treated as if they preceded the entity declarations in the source DTD. On the other, declarations in the LPD (presumably including entity declarations) can reference entities declared in the DTD.

The confusion arises because the first paragraph applies only to the order for determining the applicability of the declarations, not the order in which the declarations are interpreted. The DTD declarations are interpreted ahead of the LPDs, except that applicable declarations from LPDs replace the DTD declarations that they supersede.

For example, consider a DTD that begins with entity declarations for X, Y, and Z, in that order, and an active LPD that begins with an entity declaration for Y. The order of priority for applicability places the LPD ahead of the DTD, so the declaration of Y in the LPD preempts that of the DTD. The order of *applicability* of the declarations will therefore be:

a)   declaration of Y in LPD;

b)   remaining declarations of LPD;

c)   declaration of X in DTD;

d)   declaration of Y in DTD (preempted);

e)   declaration of Z in DTD;

f)   remaining declarations of DTD;

However, as the DTD is interpreted ahead of the LPD, the order of *interpretation* of the declarations will be:

a)   declaration of X in DTD;

b)   declaration of Y in LPD;

c)   declaration of Z in DTD;

d)   remaining declarations of DTD;

e)   remaining declarations of LPD;

In practice, a parser would implement these requirements by scanning the active LPDs for entity declarations prior to interpreting the prolog. During interpretation of the source DTD, entities that were declared in both the DTD and an LPD would be given the LPD definition. The LPDs would be interpreted in the usual manner, ignoring declarations for entities that had previously been declared.

12.1.4.2 Link Attributes

Link attributes, conceptually, are attributes that would have been on a start-tag except that they are specific to a particular process that is performed on the document, rather than being applicable to the document itself. The specification of the attribute occurs as part of a link rule within which the attribute specification list is associated with the source element type. Link rules are collected into link sets, and the particular link rule that is used for any instance of a source element type depends on which link set is current at that time.

T–D.1 *93*

O–4.165 *173:6*

There are a number of ways in which a link attribute specification can specify processing:

a)   with an attribute for each processing parameter, such as, in the case of formatting: indention, type font, leading, and so on;

b)   with a single attribute to identify the name of an executable procedure that will perform the processing;

c)   with a single attribute that identifies a description of the processing that is required, such as a style sheet. The style sheet could either be in a natural language (instructions to a compositor, for instance) or it could be in the form of a formal specification that could be interpreted by a computer program to create procedures for a processing program.

T–D.4 *99*

An associated element type of an attribute definition list must be a
2   source element type.

The *declared value* [145] *422:6* of a link attribute cannot be "ID",
4   "IDREF", "IDREFS", or "NOTATION".

"CURRENT" or "CONREF" cannot be specified for a link attribute.

12.1.4.3 Simple Link

For simple link types there is only one attribute definition list declaration. It has fixed attributes, which means that the default values are the only values and the list applies to the document as a whole. The mechanism is designed simply to pass a global set of parameters to an application.

T–D.8 *105*

If the declaration defines a simple link, the declaration subset must
2 consist solely of a *link attribute set* [162] 437:7 that contains no
more than one *attribute definition list declaration* [141] 420:15 . The
4 list must be associated with the base document element type, and
can define only fixed attributes.

12.2 Link Set Declaration

A link set declaration gives a name to a set of link rules. One link set
declaration is always named by the keyword #INITIAL. This is the link
set that is current when processing of the document instance begins. Subsequently, other link sets may become current as a result of parameters
that occur in the link rules.

T–C.2.1 *87*

O–4.69 *175:1*

6 [163] link set declaration =
mdo, ⏍ <!
8 "LINK",
ps+, [65] *372:1*
10 link set name, [164] *441:18*
(ps+, [65] *372:1*
12 link rule)+, [163.1] *441:15*
ps*, [65] *372:1*
14 **mdc** ⏍ >

[163.1] link rule =
16 source element specification | [165] *443:1*
explicit link rule [166.1] *445:1*

18 [164] link set name =
name | [55] *346:17*
20 (**rni**, ⏍ #
"INITIAL")

22 where

INITIAL identifies the link set that is current when the
24 document instance begins.

The *link set name* [164] *441:18* cannot be specified on another *link set declaration* [163] *441:6* in the same link type declaration.

2 "#INITIAL" must be specified for exactly one *link set declaration* [163] *441:6* in a *link type declaration subset* [161] *437:1* .

Within an explicit LPD, all link rules are "explicit link rules", which can include both a "source element specification" and a "result element specification". SGML has no construct called an "implicit link rule". Therefore, within an implicit LPD, all link rules are simply source element specifications. O–4.167.1 *174:1*

4 If an implicit link is specified, a *link rule* [163.1] *441:15* must be a *source element specification* [165] *443:1* ; if an explicit link is speci-
6 fied, it must be an *explicit link rule* [166.1] *445:1* .

12.2.1 Source Element Specification

A source element specification names one or more element types found in the source document and associates them with an attribute specification list. In an implicit link process definition, the source element specification is the complete link rule. In an explicit link process definition, however, the source element specification is only the first part of an explicit link rule that also contains a result element specification.

A source element specification can include a #USELINK parameter, which establishes a link set for its subelements, and a #POSTLINK parameter, which does the same for its younger siblings.

T–D.3 *96*

The link set identified by a #USELINK or #POSTLINK parameter could be the empty link set — a link set with no link rules. When the empty link set is current, it has the effect of supplying default link rules, constructed from the default values of the link attributes, if any. The result element type is always #IMPLIED. The use of the default link rule applies regardless of whether markup minimization is used for the document.

O–4.117 *173:14*

When a source element occurs, the SGML parser determines if a link rule exists for that element type. It first examines the link rules in the current link set and, if unsuccessful, it then examines all of the current link sets of open elements starting with the parent of the current open element and going on backwards to the initial link set. If no link rule is found in any of the open link sets, a default link rule is constructed as described above. Except for the #USELINK and #POSTLINK parameters, which are only of interest to the SGML parser, the link rule or link rules are passed to the application.

O–4.302 *174:4*

[165] source element specification =
2   *associated element type*,　　　　　　　　　　[72] *377:1*
　　　　　(ps+,　　　　　　　　　　　　　　　　　　[65] *372:1*
4   **rni**,　　　　　　　　　　　　　　　　　　　#
　　　　　　"USELINK",
6   ps+,　　　　　　　　　　　　　　　　　　　[65] *372:1*
　　　　　　(*link set name* |　　　　　　　　　　　　[164] *441:18*
8   (**rni**,　　　　　　　　　　　　　　　　#
　　　　　　　"EMPTY")))?,
10   (ps+,　　　　　　　　　　　　　　　　　[65] *372:1*
　　　　　　　rni,　　　　　　　　　　　　　　　　#
12   "POSTLINK",
　　　　　　ps+,　　　　　　　　　　　　　　　　　[65] *372:1*
14   *link set specification*)?,　　　　　[170] *448:10*
　　　　　link attribute specification?　　　　　　　[166] *443:16*

16 [166] link attribute specification =
　　　　　ps+,　　　　　　　　　　　　　　　　　　[65] *372:1*
18   **dso**,　　　　　　　　　　　　　　　　　　[
　　　　　attribute specification list,　　　　　　　[31] *327:17*
20   s*,　　　　　　　　　　　　　　　　　　　[5] *297:23*
　　　　　dsc　　　　　　　　　　　　　　　　　　]

22 where

USELINK　　　　means that the specified link set will become the
24   current link set when an element of an associated type becomes the current element.

26   NOTE — The "#USELINK" parameter acts like a link
set use declaration that occurs immediately after the
28   start-tag; that is, it affects the subelements of an element. It has no effect if an element is empty.

30 **POSTLINK**　　means that the specified link set will become the
current link set when an element of an
32   associated type ceases to be the current
element.

34   NOTE — The "#POSTLINK" parameter acts like a link
set use declaration that occurs immediately after the

2 end-tag (or after the start-tag if the element is empty and has no end-tag); that is, it affects succeeding elements within the same containing element.

4 The specified link set must be defined by a *link set declaration* [163] *441:6* in the same *link type declaration* [154] *434:1* .

It is possible for a link set to have conflicting link rules; that is, two or more link rules that name the same source element type. In such cases, the link rules must contain an attribute specification and the application must determine from the attributes which link rule applies. The application must advise the SGML parser which of the conflicting rules was chosen, so that the parser can act on the #USELINK and #POSTLINK parameters. (The method of advising the parser is specific to the implementation.)

6 An element type can be an *associated element type* [72] *377:1* in only one link rule in a link set, unless in each such link rule there is
8 a *link attribute specification* [166] *443:16* .

NOTE — An application must be able to determine from the link attributes
10 which rule applies to a given instance of the element type. For example, the application could define a "usage" attribute whose value is an expression
12 that tests source attribute values and the state of processing; the rule would apply if the expression were true.

14 The validity of a link *attribute specification list* [31] *327:17* is determined by the attribute definition list associated with the source ele-
16 ment type in the link type declaration subset. The attribute definition list must have been declared prior to this declaration. All element
18 types associated with an attribute specification must be associated with the same definition.

20 The *link attribute specification* [166] *443:16* must be omitted if its *attribute specification list* [31] *327:17* is empty.

12.2.2 Explicit Link Rule

An explicit link rule can occur only in link sets that are part of an explicit link process definition. The explicit link process need not actually produce an instance of the result document type, but for purposes of specifying the processing, it is useful to think about the process as if it did.

O–4.272 *174:6*

An explicit link rule consists of a source element specification and also a result element specification. The latter consists of a generic identifier and an attribute specification list, just as they might appear on a start-tag for that element in an instance of the result document type. In those cases where the result element type is not known because the application has to determine it based on the state of processing, the keyword #IMPLIED is used as the result element specification.

There are also situations in which it may be desirable to specify the attributes for a particular result element type without knowing the conditions under which those result elements will occur. For example, in a multi-column page layout application there might be a result element type called a "column" for which certain attribute values must be specified, but for which the source element types or processing conditions that cause a column to begin are not known. For those situations, the source element specification can be specified as the keyword #IMPLIED and a result element specification can be associated with it.

The implication of specifying a result generic identifier in an explicit link rule is that when the associated source element type occurs, the processor will begin an instance of the specified result element type. The generic identifier of the result element type, and the attribute specification list for the result (if there is one), are passed to the application along with the rest of the link rule and the information about the source element start-tag.

Link rules whose source element type is implied must be handled differently. They are all passed to the application when the link set becomes current. Whenever the application creates a result element, other than by operation of a link rule, it checks the result element type against the list of those for which link rules with implied source elements exist. If the element cannot be found among the implied source link rules for the current link set, then the link sets of open elements are examined, starting with the parent and going back up to the initial link set. If the result element type cannot be found in any of those link sets then the instance of the result element is created using the default attribute values from the result DTD.

[166.1] explicit link rule =
      2   (*source element specification,*   [165] *443:1*
                     ps+,   [65] *372:1*
      4   *result element specification*) | [167] *446:5*
                     (*source element specification,*   [165] *443:1*
      6   *ps+,*   [65] *372:1*
                     rni,   #
      8   "IMPLIED") |

```
          (  rni,                                                      #
2            "IMPLIED",
             ps+,                                                 [65] 372:1
4            result element specification   )                    [167] 446:5


       [167] result element specification =
6            generic identifier,                                  [30] 325:17
             result attribute specification?                     [168] 446:8

8      [168] result attribute specification =
             ps+,                                                 [65] 372:1
10           dso,                                                        [
             attribute specification list,                       [31] 327:17
12           s*,                                                   [5] 297:23
             dsc                                                         ]


14     where
```

IMPLIED   means the source or result element is implied by
16   the application.

"#IMPLIED" can be linked to a given result element type only once
18 in a link set.

The validity of the result *attribute specification list* [31] 327:17 is
20 determined by the *attribute definition list* [142] 420:25 associated
with the result element in the result element document type decla-
22 ration.

The *result attribute specification* [168] 446:8 must be omitted if its
24 *attribute specification list* [31] 327:17 is empty.

12.2.3 ID Link Set Declaration

   One of the benefits of SGML is its ability to provide uniform processing for elements of the same type. This type of processing is called "rule-
based" because it follows well-defined rules that are specified for elements of various types. Sometimes, however, it is necessary to single out
an individual element and specify unique processing for it. The ID link
set declaration meets this need by allowing a link set to be associated
with a particular instance of an element type without regard to what the
current link set would otherwise have been.
   An ID link set declaration consists of one or more link rules, each of

which is associated with the unique identifier of a source element in the source document instance. The link rule will apply to the processing of the identified element. It can also control the processing of subordinate elements by including a #USELINK parameter.

A typical application of ID link rules in formatting would be the placement of individual figures. Frequently, it is only with knowledge of the contents and size of a particular figure and the contents of the surrounding text that a user can determine where the figure should be placed — at the top of the page, for example, or at the bottom of the next page. An ID link rule provides a convenient method of specifying this processing.

It is preferable that an LPD not refer to specific element IDs, as that limits its general usefulness. Instead, an ID link set should be created in the link type declaration internal subset in the source document instance. In the previous example of figures, there could be a separate ID link set for each LPD so that the specified placements could vary depending upon the layout produced by each of the LPDs.   T–D.6 *102*

```
     [168.1] ID link set declaration =
2          mdo,                                                    <!
           "IDLINK",
4          ( ps+,                                          [65] 372:1
             name,                                         [55] 346:17
6            ps+,                                          [65] 372:1
             link rule  )+,                                [163.1] 441:15
8          ps*,                                            [65] 372:1
           mdc                                                   >
```

10   The *name* [55] *346:17* should be the unique identifier of a source element. The corresponding *link rule* [163.1] *441:15* will apply to that
12   element regardless of the current link set. The *associated element type* [72] *377:1* of the *link rule* [163.1] *441:15* must be that of the
14   identified source element.

     A *name* [55] *346:17* can be associated with only one *link rule*
16   [163.1] *441:15* in an ID link set, unless in each such *link rule*
     [163.1] *441:15* there is a *link attribute specification* [166] *443:16* .

12.3 Link Set Use Declaration

The link set use declaration offers another means of departing from rule-based processing specifications. It is intended for use only where a link rule in an ID link set is not practical.

[169] link set use declaration =

2   **mdo**,   `<!`
        "USELINK",

4   *ps+*,   [65] *372:1*
        link set specification,   [170] *448:10*

6   *ps+*,   [65] *372:1*
        link type name,   [155] *434:18*

8   *ps**,   [65] *372:1*
        mdc   `>`

10   [170] link set specification =
        link set name | [164] *441:18*

12   (**rni**,   `#`
          "EMPTY"   ) |

14   (**rni**,   `#`
          "RESTORE"   )

16   where

        EMPTY   means the link set is the empty link set.
18   **RESTORE**   means the link set is that associated with the current
                         element or, if there is none, the link set that was cur-
20   rent when the current element began.

        The link set becomes the current link set for this instance of the
22   current element.

        NOTE — As an aid to revision of the document, a declaration such as

24   `<!USELINK #RESTORE linktype>`

        should be specified at the point where the link set activated by a *link set*
26   *use declaration* [169] *448:1* is no longer required.

        The *link type name* [155] *434:18* must be that of the *link type decla-*
28   *ration* [154] *434:1* in which the link set was defined. If the *link type*
        name [155] *434:18* is not an active link type, the declaration is
30   ignored.

12.4 Current Link Set

The principles for determining the current link set are similar to those for determining the current short reference map (see 11.6.3 (432)). Unlike short reference maps, however, where the current map is the only one that is considered at any point in time, the current link set is only the first to be searched for an applicable link rule. If not found, the link set of the parent element is searched and so on backward to the initial link set.

(**O–4.69** *175:1*)

As determination of the applicable link rule is not an activity performed by the end-user of the document, there is no problem here in resolving the trade-off between computer power and simplicity for humans in favor of the computer. The designer of the application is presumed to be capable of understanding the effect of a hierarchy of open link sets. The user's involvement is typically restricted to the creation of ID link rules in order to deal with problems that arise in the handling of individual elements. Since an ID link rule supersedes the hierarchy of open link sets, the user can be certain that whatever he puts into an ID link rule will apply to that particular element regardless of what other link sets and link rules may have been created by the application designer. The ID link mechanism is therefore a simple construct with which an end-user can deal comfortably, as it avoids the complexity of determining the current link set.

(**T–D.6** *102*)

A link set is the current link set as long as its element is the current
2   element. It can become superceded for an instance of the element: either temporarily by a subelement becoming the current element,
4   or permanently by a *link set use declaration* (**[169]** *448:1*) occurring in an instance of the element.

6   If an element type has no associated link set, the current link set for an instance of the element is the link set that is current when the
8   instance begins. If the element is a document element, the current link set is the initial link set.

Clause 13
SGML Declaration

The SGML declaration contains instructions to the SGML parser that are independent of the document types and the link processes. (See the typical SGML declaration in figure 8 [479].)

The minimum literal parameter identifies the version of the standard to which the document conforms. At this writing there is only one version of the standard, but ISO directives require a review at least every five years to determine whether a standard is still applicable. Such reviews frequently result in the publication of a revised standard, so this parameter anticipates that possibility.

T–B.14.1 *63*

O–4.281 *135:16*

```
      [171] SGML declaration =
 2          mdo,
            "SGML",
 4          ps+,
            minimum literal,
 6          ps+,
            document character set,
 8          ps+,
            capacity set,
10          ps+,
            concrete syntax scope,
12          ps+,
            concrete syntax,
14          ps+,
            feature use,
16          ps+,
            application-specific information,
18          ps*,
            mdc
```

<!

[65] *372:1*
[76] *381:1*
[65] *372:1*
[172] *452:1*
[65] *372:1*
[180] *456:2*
[65] *372:1*
[181] *457:4*
[65] *372:1*
[182] *458:1*
[65] *372:1*
[195] *471:4*
[65] *372:1*
[199] *474:27*
[65] *372:1*
>

The *minimum data* [77] *381:8* of the *minimum literal* [76] *381:1*
2   must be "ISO 8879:1986".

The reference concrete syntax must be used in the *SGML declara-*
4   *tion* [171] *450:1* , regardless of the concrete syntax used in the
remainder of the document.

6   Only markup characters (in the reference concrete syntax) and
minimum data [77] *381:8* characters can be used in the parame-
8   ters and comments, although the replacement text of a character
reference could be an SGML character other than a markup or min-
10 imum data character.

NOTES

12 1   The *SGML declaration* [171] *450:1* is intended for human consump-
tion (in printed form!) as well as for machine processing, as it enables the
14 recipient of a document to determine whether a system can process it "as
is", whether character translation or other algorithmic conversion is needed
16 (for example, if markup minimization features or a different delimiter set
were used), or whether conversion that could require manual intervention is
18 needed (for example, if the document quantity set required larger values
than were available in the system quantity set).

20 2   A character reference such as "Þ" is valid because the reference
consists solely of markup and minimum data characters, even though the
22 replacement text does not.

3   No entity references can occur in an SGML declaration (because no
24 entities could have been declared).

13.1 Document Character Set

A character set is a mapping between a set of constructs, such as
letters of the alphabet, and a scheme for representing them. The set of
constructs is called a "character repertoire" and the scheme for representing them is called a "code set" or simply a "code". The coded representation of a character is an integer number known as a "character number".
A machine-readable document is simply a sequence of character numbers. The purpose of the document character set parameter of the SGML
declaration is to state what each of those character numbers normally
represents (that is, when they are not subject to a data content notation).
Such a statement is called a "character set description".
A full explanation of character set concepts is given in the overview.

O–4.39 *193:13*

[172] document character set =
2   "CHARSET",
          ps+,   [65] *372:1*
4   *character set description*   [173] *453:1*

The document character set must include one and only one coded
6   representation, that is, a single bit combination, for each significant
SGML character.

8   NOTE — If the document uses two concrete syntaxes, the markup characters of both are significant SGML characters.

10   As part of the translation of a document to a new character set, the
character numbers in this parameter and any numeric character
12   references in the document must be changed.

For this reason, a numeric character reference should not be used in
the document instance if an entity reference can be substituted. The
entity would have a name suggestive of the character, and the entity text
would consist of the numeric character reference.   **O–4.217** *162:5*
                                                                 A–9.5 *356:1*

NOTE — It is recognized that the recipient of a document must be able to
14   translate it to his system character set before the document can be
processed by machine. There are two basic approaches to communicating
16   this information:
          a)   If the character set is standard, registered, or otherwise capable of
18   being referenced by an identifying name or number, that identifier can
                be communicated to the recipient of the document. The
20   communication must necessarily occur outside of the document; for
                example, in a field of the document interchange data stream, or via
22   other (probably non-electronic) media.
          b)   For other character sets, a human-readable copy of the SGML
24   declaration will provide sufficient information.

As the last note implies, the document character set parameter is
ignored by the SGML parser because the document is already in the document character set. The parameter is intended for a human to read in
printed form, in order to determine how to translate an incoming document to the local system character set.   **O–4.311** *198:7*

13.1.1 Character Set Description

A character set description is a list of all of the character numbers that occur in the document and a description of the character represented by each. (See figure 8 [479] for examples of usage.) There are three ways that a character can be described:

[O–4.98 *198:3*]

— With a descriptive string. For example, if a character number represented the SGML Users' Group logo, the string could simply say "SGML Users' Group logo".

— By reference to a character number in some known character set. That character set is called a "base" character set. It is typically a standardized or registered character set.

— With the keyword "UNUSED", which means that no meaning is assigned to that character.

[173] character set description =
2   *base character set,*   [174] *453:12*
           ps+,   [65] *372:1*
4   *described character set portion,*   [175] *454:7*
           (*ps+,*   [65] *372:1*
6   *base character set,*   [174] *453:12*
               ps+,   [65] *372:1*
8   *described character set portion*)*   [175] *454:7*

The described character set portions must collectively describe
10   each character number in the described character set once and
only once.

13.1.1.1 Base Character Set

12   [174] base character set =
           "BASESET",
14   *ps+,*   [65] *372:1*
           public identifier   [74] *379:8*

16   The *public identifier* [74] *379:8* is a human-readable identifier of the

base character set ⌐**[174]** *453:12* ⌐ .

2   NOTE — For example, a standard or registered name or number, or other
designation that will be understood by the expected recipients of the docu-
4   ment.

The *public identifier* ⌐ **[74]** *379:8* ⌐ should be a *formal public identifier*
6   ⌐ **[79]** *382:1* ⌐ with a *public text class* ⌐ **[86]** *386:5* ⌐ of "CHARSET".

13.1.1.2 Described Character Set Portion

[175] described character set portion =
8   "DESCSET",
              (*ps+*,   ⌐ **[65]** *372:1* ⌐
10   *character description*)+   ⌐ **[176]** *454:11* ⌐

[176] character description =
12   *described set character number*,   ⌐ **[177]** *454:19* ⌐
               ps+,   ⌐ **[65]** *372:1* ⌐
14   *number of characters*,   ⌐ **[179]** *454:23* ⌐
               ps+,   ⌐ **[65]** *372:1* ⌐
16   (*base set character number* | ⌐ **[178]** *454:21* ⌐
                 minimum literal | ⌐ **[76]** *381:1* ⌐
18   "UNUSED")

[177] described set character number =
20   *character number*   ⌐ **[64]** *357:1* ⌐

[178] base set character number =
22   *character number*   ⌐ **[64]** *357:1* ⌐

[179] number of characters =
24   *number*   ⌐ **[56]** *347:1* ⌐

where

26   **UNUSED**   means that no meaning is assigned to the specified
                     character numbers in the described set.

28   The specified *number of characters* ⌐ **[179]** *454:23* ⌐ in the described
     character set, beginning with the specified *described set character*
30   *number* ⌐ **[177]** *454:19* ⌐ , are assigned meanings as follows:

a) If a *base set character number* [178] 454:21 is specified, the
meanings are those of the corresponding characters in the
base character set [174] 453:12 , beginning with the specified
base set character number [178] 454:21 .

NOTE — If a base set character number is unused, no meaning is
assigned to the corresponding described set character number.

b) If a *minimum literal* [76] 381:1 is specified, the meaning or
meanings are as described in the literal.

NOTE — A *minimum literal* [76] 381:1 should be specified only if no
character in the *base character set* [174] 453:12 has the desired
meaning.

c) If "UNUSED" is specified, no meanings are assigned.

13.1.2 Non-SGML Character Identification

In a document character set, every character number that is unused is
considered a non-SGML character. Any character number that is
shunned by the concrete syntax (see 13.4.2 459) must be defined as
UNUSED, and therefore as a non-SGML character, unless it is a markup
character or a minimum data character. In other words, a shunned character can never occur in a document character set simply as an ordinary
data character. It must either be a non-SGML character or a significant
SGML character.   T–B.7.1 43

O–4.207 199:14

Each *character number* [64] 357:1 to which no meaning is
assigned by the *character set description* [173] 453:1 is assigned
to **NONSGML**, thereby identifying it as a non-SGML character.

NOTE — After receipt and translation of a document, the non-SGML characters may be different because the new document character set may map
control characters to different coded representations.

A shunned character must be identified as a non-SGML character,
unless it is a significant SGML character.

NOTES

1   For example, in figure 8 479 , characters numbered 9, 10, and 13,
which are shunned characters, are nevertheless not assigned as non-
SGML characters because they are function characters.

2   If the document uses two concrete syntaxes, the shunned characters of

both are subject to this requirement.

13.2 Capacity Set

This topic was discussed in detail in 9.8 ⌜ 366 ⌝ . See figure 5 ⌜ 367 ⌝ .

⌜ **O–4.27** *213:1* ⌝

2   [180] capacity set =
           "CAPACITY",
4   *ps+*,   ⌜ **[65]** *372:1* ⌝
           (("PUBLIC",
6   *ps+*,   ⌜ **[65]** *372:1* ⌝
               public identifier   ) | ⌜ **[74]** *379:8* ⌝
8   ("SGMLREF",
              (*ps+*,   ⌜ **[65]** *372:1* ⌝
10   *name*,   ⌜ **[55]** *346:17* ⌝
              ps+,   ⌜ **[65]** *372:1* ⌝
12   *number*)+))   ⌜ **[56]** *347:1* ⌝

The specified *name* ⌜ **[55]** *346:17* ⌝ is a name given to a capacity in
14 figure 5 ⌜ 367 ⌝ . The capacity is assigned the value indicated by the
specified *number* ⌜ **[56]** *347:1* ⌝ .

16 The reference capacity set value is used for any capacity for which
no replacement is assigned by this parameter.

18 NOTE — The "SGMLREF" keyword, which is required (and therefore
redundant) when a public identifier is not used, is a reminder of this rule for
20 human readers of the SGML declaration.

The capacity values must express limits that are not exceeded by
22 the document. They must be sufficient for the greatest capacity
requirement among the possible sets of concurrent instances or
24 chains of link processes that could be processed at once.

The value assigned to "TOTALCAP" must equal or exceed the
26 largest individual capacity.

The *public identifier* ⌜ **[74]** *379:8* ⌝ should be a *formal public identifier*
28 ⌜ **[79]** *382:1* ⌝ with a *public text class* ⌜ **[86]** *386:5* ⌝ of "CAPACITY".

13.3 Concrete Syntax Scope

Normally the same concrete syntax is used for both the prolog of a document and the document instance set. This parameter supports situations where the prolog — perhaps because it contains a public document type definition — must be in the reference concrete syntax, while at the same time a variant concrete syntax is used for the document instance set.

> **O–4.258** *211:6*
>
> **A–15.6** *487:22*

2   This parameter specifies whether a declared concrete syntax must be used for the entire document, or whether the reference concrete syntax can be used in the prologs.

4   [181] concrete syntax scope =
     "SCOPE",

6   *ps*+,   **[65]** *372:1*
        ("DOCUMENT" |
8   "INSTANCE"   )

    where

10 **DOCUMENT**   means the declared concrete syntax is used
                           throughout the document.
12 **INSTANCE**   means the reference concrete syntax is used
                           in prologs and the declared concrete syntax is
14   used in document instance sets.

    If "INSTANCE" is specified, the declared concrete syntax must
16 meet the following requirements:
    a) the syntax-reference character set must be the same as that
18   of the reference concrete syntax;
    b) the significant SGML characters must be such that the start of
20   a document instance set is always distinguishable from the
        end of its prolog; and
22 c) the quantity set values must equal or exceed those of the ref-
        erence quantity set.

13.4 Concrete Syntax

A concrete syntax is defined either by referencing a public concrete syntax, or by declaring a concrete syntax in detail in the SGML declaration. Systems and applications designers must make a trade-off between, on the one hand, creating a variant concrete syntax to meet the specific needs of users or system environments or national languages; or, on the other hand, adhering to the reference concrete syntax in order to promote the widest possible interchange of the documents. As every conforming SGML system must support the reference concrete syntax or core concrete syntax, it is best, when declaring a variant concrete syntax, to design it for ease of conversion to and from the reference or core concrete syntax. (See also D.3 ⌐ *500* ⌐).

	T–B.14.1.2 *64*
	O–4.49 *209:6*

```
      [182] concrete syntax =
2              "SYNTAX",
               ps+,                                              [65] 372:1
4              ( public concrete syntax |                        [183] 458:22
                  ( shunned character number identification,     [184] 459:22
6                  ps+,                                          [65] 372:1
                   syntax-reference character set,               [185] 461:1
8                  ps+,                                          [65] 372:1
                   function character identification,            [186] 461:6
10                 ps+,                                          [65] 372:1
                   naming rules,                                 [189] 463:3
12                 ps+,                                          [65] 372:1
                   delimiter set,                                [190] 465:8
14                 ps+,                                          [65] 372:1
                   reserved name use,                            [193] 468:9
16                 ps+,                                          [65] 372:1
                   quantity set   )   )                          [194] 470:1
```

18   The reference concrete syntax or core concrete syntax should be
      used unless a variant concrete syntax is necessitated by such
20   requirements as the keyboard, display capabilities, or characteristics of the national language.

13.4.1 Public Concrete Syntax

A public concrete syntax can be referenced either as is, or with substitutions of some of the character numbers.

```
22    [183] public concrete syntax =
              "PUBLIC",
24            ps+,                                               [65] 372:1
```

```
      public identifier,                        [74] 379:8
2     (  ps+,                                   [65] 372:1
         "SWITCHES",
4        (  ps+,                                [65] 372:1
            character number,                   [64] 357:1
6        ps+,                                    [65] 372:1
            character number   )+   )?          [64] 357:1
```

8   where

SWITCHES   means that markup characters in the speci-
10   fied concrete syntax have been switched.

The pairs of character numbers are in the *syntax-reference charac-*
12 *ter set* [185] 461:1 of the *public concrete syntax* [183] 458:22. The
first of each pair is a markup character other than a **Digit**, **LC**
14 **Letter**, or **UC Letter** in the identified concrete syntax and the second is a character other than a **Digit**, **LC Letter**, or **UC Letter** that
16 substitutes for it in every instance in which the first character was
used.

18 NOTE — The concrete syntax that results from the switches must meet all
the usual requirements, just as if it had been declared explicitly.

20 The *public identifier* [74] 379:8 should be a *formal public identifier*
[79] 382:1 with a *public text class* [86] 386:5 of "SYNTAX".

13.4.2 Shunned Character Number Identification

The designer of a concrete syntax can identify character numbers that
should be shunned in the character set of any document that uses the
syntax. These are the numbers that the designer expects could cause difficulties in some system environments in which the document will be processed. Shunned character numbers should never be used to represent
ordinary data characters. They should be either unused (i.e., as non-
SGML characters) or, if unavoidable, used to represent markup or minimum data characters. (For usage example, see figure 7 [477] and discussion in D.3 [500].)   O-4.297 210:7

```
22  [184] shunned character number identification =
         "SHUNCHAR",
24       ps+,                                         [65] 372:1
         (  "NONE" |
```

```
        (  (  "CONTROLS" |
2              character number   ),          [64] 357:1
            (  ps+,                           [65] 372:1
4              character number   )*  )  )    [64] 357:1
```

where

6 **NONE**   means there are no shunned character num-
                       bers.
8 **CONTROLS**   means that any character number that the
                       system character set considers to be the
10   coded representation of a control character,
                       and not a graphic character, is a shunned
12   character.

Note that shunned character numbers represent bit combinations, not characters, and therefore this parameter is not changed even if the SGML declaration is translated from one character set to another.

Each specified *character number* [64] 357:1 is identified as a
14 shunned character number.

NOTE — Character numbers in this parameter need not (and should not)
16 be changed when a document is translated to another character set.

13.4.3 Syntax-reference Character Set

If you are designing character set descriptions or concrete syntaxes, the material in Chapter 7 192 should prove helpful. In particular, 7.1 is good prerequisite reading for this annotation, as is 13.1.1 453 .

O–4.310 *210:1*
A–13.1.1 *453:1*

A concrete syntax assigns specific characters to the various delimiter roles and character classes defined by the abstract syntax. However, it does not assign coded representations of the characters. In other words, a concrete syntax definition is independent of the character sets that are used in the documents that conform to the syntax.

How is this independence accomplished, given that a character can only be referenced unambiguously by a coded representation in some known character set? The answer is the syntax-reference character set, which is defined using a character set description in the same way that a document character set is defined (see 13.1.1 453). Both a syntax-reference character set and a document character set must have coded representations (character numbers) for all markup characters, thereby permitting unambiguous translation between the two.

When declaring a concrete syntax, all parameters that require character numbers are specified using character numbers from the syntax-reference character set. Within a document conforming to the syntax, of course, those same characters are represented by the document character set character numbers.

Some concrete syntax parameters require a parameter literal rather than a character number. The interpreted literal is treated as though its character set were the syntax-reference character set. That is, the character numbers that represent the interpreted literal are treated as specified character numbers in the syntax-reference character set. This treatment produces the expected results when numeric character references are used in the literal. However, a character cannot be entered directly in the literal unless its character number is the same in both the syntax-reference character set and the document character set of the document that contains the concrete syntax definition.

```
      [185] syntax-reference character set =
2            character set description                    [173] 453:1
```

```
      The document character set must include one and only one coded
4     representation, that is, a single bit combination, for each significant
      SGML character.
```

13.4.4 Function Character Identification

This parameter identifies the characters that represent the record end, record start, and space functions, plus any other functions that are defined for the concrete syntax. (See example of usage in figure 7 `477` .)

```
6     [186] function character identification =
            "FUNCTION",
8           ps+,                                          [65] 372:1
            "RE",
10          ps+,                                          [65] 372:1
            character number,                             [64] 357:1
12          ps+,                                          [65] 372:1
            "RS",
14          ps+,                                          [65] 372:1
            character number,                             [64] 357:1
16          ps+,                                          [65] 372:1
```

"SPACE",

2   *ps+,*   [65] *372:1*
         character number,   [64] *357:1*
4   (*ps+,*   [65] *372:1*
            added function,   [187] *462:10*
6   *ps+,*   [65] *372:1*
         function class,   [188] *462:12*
8   *ps+,*   [65] *372:1*
         character number   )*   [64] *357:1*

10   [187] added function =
          name   [55] *346:17*

12   [188] function class =
          "FUNCHAR" |
14   "MSICHAR" |
          "MSOCHAR" |
16   "MSSCHAR" |
          "SEPCHAR"

18   where the keywords identify the *added function* [187] *462:10* , as
     follows:

20   **FUNCHAR**   means an inert function character.
     SEPCHAR   means a separator character.
22   **MSOCHAR**   means a markup-scan-out character.
     MSICHAR   means a markup-scan-in character.
24   **MSSCHAR**   means a markup-scan-suppress character.

     The character with the specified *character number* [64] *357:1* in
26   the *syntax-reference character set* [185] *461:1* is assigned to the
     function.

28   A character can be assigned to only one function.

     An *added function* [187] *462:10* cannot be "RE", "RS", "SPACE", or
30   another *added function* [187] *462:10* .

     "MSICHAR" must be specified for at least one *added function*
32   [187] *462:10* if "MSOCHAR" is specified for an *added function*
      [187] *462:10* .

34   NOTE — When code extension is used, shift characters could be assigned
     to markup suppression functions to avoid false delimiter recognition, but

only by sacrificing the ability to use entity references to obtain device inde-
2   pendence (see clause E.3 ⌈ *537* ⌉).

13.4.5 Naming Rules

The naming rules parameter identifies name characters and name start characters in addition to those specified in 9.2.1 ⌈ *344* ⌉. A given character may be assigned once and only once as a lower-case name or name-start character (that is, specified once only in either the "LCNMCHAR" or "LCNMSTRT" parameters, but not both). (See example of usage in figure 7 ⌈ *477* ⌉.)

The parameter also specifies the upper-case substitution for the added name characters by providing corresponding upper-case and lower-case forms of the name start and name character parameters. A character can be assigned more than once as an upper-case name or name-start character, so that different lower-case characters can be associated with the same upper-case form. In particular, a **UC Letter** can be specified in the "UCNMCHAR" and "UCNMSTRT" parameters.

If the upper and lower-case forms of a character are the same (as for special characters, or languages that have no concept of capitalization), then the same character number should be entered into the corresponding positions of the upper and lower-case parameters. ⌈ **T–B.7.1** *43* ⌉

⌈ **A–9.6.6** *364:6* ⌉


```
     [189] naming rules =
4              "NAMING",
               ps+,                                        [65] 372:1
6              "LCNMSTRT",
               (  ps+,                                     [65] 372:1
8                 parameter literal  )+,                   [66] 373:1
               ps+,                                        [65] 372:1
10             "UCNMSTRT",
               (  ps+,                                     [65] 372:1
12                parameter literal  )+,                   [66] 373:1
               ps+,                                        [65] 372:1
14             "LCNMCHAR",
               (  ps+,                                     [65] 372:1
16                parameter literal  )+,                   [66] 373:1
               ps+,                                        [65] 372:1
18             "UCNMCHAR",
               (  ps+,                                     [65] 372:1
20                parameter literal  )+,                   [66] 373:1
               ps+,                                        [65] 372:1
22             "NAMECASE",
```

```
 2      ps+,                          [65] 372:1
        "GENERAL",
                                      [65] 372:1
 4      ps+,
        (  "NO" |
           "YES"  ),
 6      ps+,                          [65] 372:1
        "ENTITY",
                                      [65] 372:1
 8      ps+,
        (  "NO" |
10         "YES"  )
```

where

12 **LCNMSTRT** means each *character* [49] 344:5 in the literals (if any) is assigned to **LCNMSTRT**.

14 **UCNMSTRT** Each *character* [49] 344:5 in the literals (if any) is assigned to **UCNMSTRT** as the associated upper-case form of the character in the corresponding position of **LCNMSTRT**.

18 **LCNMCHAR** means each *character* [49] 344:5 in the literals (if any) is assigned to **LCNMCHAR**.

20 **UCNMCHAR** Each *character* [49] 344:5 in the literals (if any) is assigned to **UCNMCHAR** as the associated upper-case form of the character in the corresponding position of **LCNMCHAR**.

24 **NAMECASE** specifies whether upper-case substitution is to be performed for entity references and entity names ("ENTITY") and/or for all other names, name tokens, number tokens, and delimiter strings ("GENERAL").

    YES means an *LC Letter* will be replaced by the corresponding **UC Letter**, and a *character* [49] 344:5 in **LCNMSTRT** or **LCNMCHAR** will be replaced by its associated upper-case form.

    NO means no upper-case substitution will take place.

The upper-case form of a name character can be the same as the lower-case.

A *character* [49] 344:5 assigned to **LCNMCHAR**, **UCNMCHAR**,

2　*LCNMSTRT*, or *UCNMSTRT* cannot be an *LC Letter*, *UC Letter*, *Digit*, *RE*, *RS*, *SPACE*, or *SEPCHAR*.

4　A *character* [49] *344:5* assigned to *LCNMCHAR* or *UCNMCHAR* cannot be assigned to *LCNMSTRT* or *UCNMSTRT*.

6　*UCNMCHAR* must have the same number of characters as *LCNMCHAR*; *UCNMSTRT* must have the same number of characters as *LCNMSTRT*.

13.4.6 Delimiter Set

The delimiter set parameter assigns delimiter strings to the general delimiter roles and zero or more strings to the role of short reference delimiter. (See example of usage in figure 7 [477].)

8　[190] delimiter set =
　　　　"DELIM",
10　　　　ps+,　　　　　　　　　　　　　　　　　　[65] *372:1*
　　　　general delimiters,　　　　　　　　　　　[191] *466:1*
12　　　　ps+,　　　　　　　　　　　　　　　　　　[65] *372:1*
　　　　short reference delimiters　　　　　　　[192] *467:1*

14　A delimiter or delimiter-in-context must differ from every other delimiter and delimiter-in-context that can be recognized in the same
16　mode.

NOTE — Different delimiter roles with the same character string can occur
18　in CXT mode, as long as the resulting delimiters in context are unique.

The next paragraph deprecates delimiters such as "<e" for an end-tag open delimiter, since that would effectively prevent the letter "e" from being the first character of any generic identifier.

The use of a *name start character* [53] *346:3* or *Digit* in a delimiter
20　string is deprecated.

The length of a delimiter string in the delimiter set cannot exceed
22　the "NAMELEN" quantity of the quantity set.

13.4.6.1 General Delimiters

This parameter specifies general delimiter assignments that are different from those in the reference delimiter set defined in figure 3 [*360*] .

```
     [191] general delimiters =
2              "GENERAL",
               ps+,                                            [65] 372:1
4              "SGMLREF",
               (  ps+,                                         [65] 372:1
6                 name,                                        [55] 346:17
                  ps+,                                         [65] 372:1
8                 parameter literal   )*                       [66] 373:1
```

The specified *name* [55] *346:17* is a name given to a general del-
10 imiter role in figure 3 [*360*] . The interpreted parameter literal is
assigned to the role.

12 General delimiter roles not assigned by this parameter are
assigned as in the reference delimiter set.

14 NOTE — The "SGMLREF" keyword, which is required (and therefore
redundant), is a reminder of this rule for human readers of the SGML decla-
16 ration.

Using a function character, such as a record start or tab, as a general
delimiter is prohibited, although such characters can be used in short reference delimiter strings. Combinations of function characters with others
are not flatly prohibited, but are deprecated as throw-backs to primitive
implementations of early text processing systems. The classic example is
"record start followed by a period" as the delimiter for a processing
instruction, the so-called "dot control word".

A general delimiter string cannot consist solely of function
18 characters. A general delimiter string that contains such characters
in combination with others is permitted, but is deprecated.

13.4.6.2 Short Reference Delimiters

This parameter allows additional short reference delimiter strings to
be added to those in the reference delimiter set, or a totally new set of
strings to be defined.

[192] short reference delimiters =
2   "SHORTREF",
             ps+,   [65] *372:1*
4   ("SGMLREF" |
             "NONE"   ),
6   (*ps+*,   [65] *372:1*
             parameter literal   )*   [66] *373:1*

8   where

     SGMLREF   means that the short references assigned by the
10   reference delimiter set are included in this delim-
                             iter set.
12   **NONE**   means that no short reference delimiters are
                             assigned except for those assigned by this
14   parameter.

     The interpreted parameter literal is assigned as a short reference
16   delimiter string.

     The restriction in the next paragraph that prohibits characters that can
     occur in a blank sequence from being adjacent to a B sequence relieves
     the user from distinguishing between characters that all look like white
     space — in other words, it prohibits strings such as "tab followed by one
     or more blanks" because to the user the tab will be indistinguishable
     from a sequence of blanks.

     A *parameter literal* [66] *373:1* can have a single B sequence, which
18   cannot immediately be preceded or followed by a blank sequence
     or by a reference to a character that can occur in a blank
20   sequence.

     The following paragraph is simply an attempt to keep short references
     short. There are some multi-character sequences that are common key-
     boarding conventions, such as the use of two hyphens to stand for an
     em-dash, and these are not deprecated.

     A short reference string longer than a single character is
22   deprecated unless the string is a common keyboarding convention
     or coding sequence.

     The last paragraph deprecates short references that look like general
     delimiters — for example, "record start followed by a less than". That
     string would keep a start-tag from occurring at the beginning of a record.

Moreover, when this short reference is not mapped, it gives the impression that start-tags at the beginning of records are ignored.

A short reference string is deprecated if:
2 a) it contains all, or the start, of a delimiter or delimiter-in-context that is recognized in CON mode; and
4 b) it is likely to create the impression that the delimiter was erroneously ignored.

6 NOTE — In applying this requirement, remember that a short reference is recognized as a delimiter even when it is not mapped to an entity.
8 Therefore, a general delimiter within it will never be recognized as such.

13.4.7 Reserved Name Use

The reserved name use parameter allows the concrete syntax to substitute its own reserved names for those used in the reference concrete syntax. The replacement name is actually entered as a parameter literal, which is then interpreted to produce the replacement name. Otherwise there would be no way to enter character numbers that were valid name characters in the declared concrete syntax, but not in the reference concrete syntax. The parameter literal allows character references to be used for such characters. (See example of usage in figure 7 [477].)

[193] reserved name use =
10   "NAMES",
         ps+,   [65] 372:1
12   "SGMLREF",
         (ps+,   [65] 372:1
14   name,   [55] 346:17
           ps+,   [65] 372:1
16   parameter literal)*   [66] 373:1

The *name* [55] 346:17 is a reference reserved name that is
18 replaced in the declared concrete syntax by the interpreted *parameter literal* [66] 373:1, which must be a valid *name* [55] 346:17 in
20 the declared concrete syntax.

NOTES

22 1   The list of reference reserved names that can be replaced in a declared concrete syntax is:

	ANY	IDLINK	NMTOKEN	REQUIRED
2	ATTLIST	IDREF	NMTOKENS	RESTORE
	CDATA	IDREFS	NOTATION	RS
4	CONREF	IGNORE	NUMBER	SDATA
	CURRENT	IMPLIED	NUMBERS	SHORTREF
6	DEFAULT	INCLUDE	NUTOKEN	SIMPLE
	DOCTYPE	INITIAL	NUTOKENS	SPACE
8	ELEMENT	LINK	O	STARTTAG
	EMPTY	LINKTYPE	PCDATA	SUBDOC
10	ENDTAG	MD	PI	SYSTEM
	ENTITIES	MS	POSTLINK	TEMP
12	ENTITY	NAME	PUBLIC	USELINK
	FIXED	NAMES	RCDATA	USEMAP
14	ID	NDATA	RE	

16 2   Reserved names that occur only in the *SGML declaration* [171] 450:1 ,
including delimiter role, quantity, and capacity names, cannot be replaced,
as the *SGML declaration* [171] 450:1 is always in the reference concrete
18 syntax.

The reference reserved name is used for any reserved name for
20 which no replacement is assigned by this parameter.

NOTE — The "SGMLREF" keyword, which is required (and therefore
22 redundant), is a reminder of this rule for human readers of the SGML
declaration.

24 The replacement for a reference reserved name cannot be another
reference reserved name, or a replacement for one.

13.4.8 Quantity Set

A quantity set is a list of pairs of quantity names and their associated
values. The quantity set parameter allows a declared concrete syntax to
alter some or all of the quantities in the reference quantity set. The table
in figure 6 470 incorporates the reference quantity set in its first two columns. The first column is the name of a quantity, the second column is
its value, and the third column describes it. For example, the quantity
ATTCNT states that 40 attribute names and name tokens is the maximum permitted in an attribute definition list. Similarly, the quantity
ATTSPLEN restricts the normalized length of an attribute specification
list to 960 characters. (See example of usage in figure 7 477 .)

O–4.247 136:16

Name	Value	Description of Quantity
ATTCNT	40	Number of attribute names and name tokens in an *attribute definition list*.
ATTSPLEN	960	Normalized length of a start-tag's *attribute specifications list*.
BSEQLEN	960	Length of a blank sequence in a short reference string.
DTAGLEN	16	Length of a data tag.
DTEMPLEN	16	Length of a data tag template or pattern template (undelimited).
ENTLVL	16	Nesting level of entities (other than primary).
GRPCNT	32	Number of tokens in a group.
GRPGTCNT	96	Grand total of content tokens at all levels of a content model (a data tag group is three tokens).
GRPLVL	16	Nesting level of model groups (including first level).
LITLEN	240	Length of a *parameter literal* or *attribute value literal* (interpreted and undelimited).
NAMELEN	8	Length of a *name, name token, number*, etc.
NORMSEP	2	Used in lieu of counting separators in calculating normalized lengths.
PILEN	240	Length of a *processing instruction* (undelimited).
TAGLEN	960	Length of a *start-tag* (undelimited).
TAGLVL	24	Nesting level of open elements.

Figure 6 — Reference Quantity Set

[194] quantity set =
2   "QUANTITY",
          ps+,   [65] *372:1*
4   "SGMLREF",
          (*ps*+,   [65] *372:1*
6   *name*,   [55] *346:17*
          ps+,   [65] *372:1*
8   *number*)*   [56] *347:1*

The specified *name* [55] *346:17* is a name given to a quantity in fig-
10   ure 6 [470], which also shows the value assignments that consti-
     tute the reference quantity set. The designated quantity is assigned
12   the value indicated by the specified *number* [56] *347:1*, which must
     exceed the reference value. The resulting quantity set must be
14   rational.

     NOTE — For example, "TAGLEN" must be greater than "LITLEN" because
16   literals occur in start-tags. Similarly, "LITLEN" must exceed "NAMELEN"
     because names occur in literals.

18   The reference quantity set value is used for any quantity for which
     no replacement is assigned by this parameter.

2   NOTE — The "SGMLREF" keyword, which is required (and therefore redundant), is a reminder of this rule for human readers of the SGML declaration.

13.5 Feature Use

4   [195] feature use =
           "FEATURES",
6   ps+,   `[65]` *372:1*
           markup minimization features,   `[196]` *471:12*
8   ps+,   `[65]` *372:1*
           link type features,   `[197]` *472:29*
10   ps+,   `[65]` *372:1*
           other features   `[198]` *473:28*

13.5.1 Markup Minimization Features

This parameter indicates which markup minimization features are used in the document instance set. Markup minimization features have two properties that distinguish them from other features:

a)   A document type definition can always be written as if the feature is permitted in the document instance, whether or not it actually is.

b)   A document instance that employs markup minimization can be converted to one that does not without changing the element structure information that is passed to an application (see attachment 1 of Appendix B `571`).

These properties of markup minimization features allow DTDs and entire documents to be shared among users who employ differing markup minimization techniques. (See the typical SGML declaration in figure 8 `479`.)

12   [196] markup minimization features =
           "MINIMIZE",
14   ps+,   `[65]` *372:1*
           "DATATAG",
16   ps+,   `[65]` *372:1*
           ("NO" |
18   "YES"),

2	*ps*+, "OMITTAG",	[65] *372:1*
4	*ps*+, ("NO" | "YES"),	[65] *372:1*
6	*ps*+, "RANK",	[65] *372:1*
8 10	*ps*+, ("NO" | "YES"),	[65] *372:1*
12	*ps*+, "SHORTTAG",	[65] *372:1*
14	*ps*+, ("NO" | "YES")	[65] *372:1*

16   where

18	**NO** **YES**	means the feature is not used. means the feature is used.
20	**DATATAG**	means data characters may serve simulta- neously as tags.
22	**OMITTAG** **RANK**	means some tags may be omitted altogether. means element ranks may be omitted from tags.
24 26	**SHORTTAG**	means short tags with omitted delimiters, attribute specifications, or generic identifiers may be used.

28   NOTE — The use of short references is not specified in this parameter because it is specified by the "SHORTREF" parameter.

13.5.2 Link Type Features

This parameter indicates which link type features are used in the document and establishes limits on the use of explicit and simple links. (See the typical SGML declaration in figure 8 [479].)

30	[197] link type features = "LINK",	
32	*ps*+, "SIMPLE",	[65] *372:1*
	ps+,	[65] *372:1*

```
          (  "NO" |
2           (  "YES",
                ps+,                                    [65] 372:1
4               number  )  ),                           [56] 347:1
            ps+,                                        [65] 372:1
6         "IMPLICIT",
            ps+,                                        [65] 372:1
8         (  "NO" |
            "YES"  ),
10          ps+,                                        [65] 372:1
          "EXPLICIT",
12          ps+,                                        [65] 372:1
          (  "NO" |
14          (  "YES",
                ps+,                                    [65] 372:1
16              number  )  )                            [56] 347:1
```

where

18	**NO**	means the feature is not used.
	YES	means the feature is used.
20	**EXPLICIT**	means explicit link process definitions may be used and the longest chain of link processes has
22		the specified number of links (1 or more).
	IMPLICIT	means implicit link process definitions may be
24		used.
	SIMPLE	means simple link process definitions may be
26		used and the specified number can be active simultaneously (1 or more).

13.5.3 Other Features

This parameter identifies whether the CONCUR, SUBDOC, and/or FORMAL features are used, and specifies a limit on the concurrent document instance feature. (See the typical SGML declaration in figure 8 479 .)

```
28   [198] other features =
            "OTHER",
30          ps+,                                        [65] 372:1
          "CONCUR",
32          ps+,                                        [65] 372:1
          (  "NO" |
```

```
                ( "YES",
2                   ps+,                                          [65] 372:1
                    number ) ),                                   [56] 347:1
4               ps+,                                              [65] 372:1
                "SUBDOC",
6               ps+,                                              [65] 372:1
                ( "NO" |
8                 ( "YES",
                    ps+,                                          [65] 372:1
10                  number ) ),                                   [56] 347:1
                  ps+,                                            [65] 372:1
12              "FORMAL",
                ps+,                                              [65] 372:1
14              ( "NO" |
                "YES"  )
```

16   where

NO	means the feature is not used.
YES	means the feature is used.
CONCUR	means instances of the specified number of document types (1 or more) may occur concurrently with an instance of the base document type.
SUBDOC	means the specified number of SGML subdocument entities (1 or more) may be open at one time.
FORMAL	means that public identifiers are interpreted as formal public identifiers.

13.6 Application-specific Information

This parameter specifies application-specific information that is independent of the document type and link process definitions. For example, it could specify the architecture to which the document conforms. (See the typical SGML declaration in figure 8 [479].)   [O-4.7 213:11]

```
      [199] application-specific information =
28              "APPINFO",
                ps+,                                              [65] 372:1
30              ( "NONE" |
                  minimum literal   )                            [76] 381:1
```

where

2 **NONE**   means that no application-specific information
                         has been specified.

4 The *minimum literal* [76] *381:1* specifies application-specific information that is applicable to the document.

Clause 14

Reference and Core Concrete Syntaxes

This clause defines the reference and core concrete syntaxes, one of which must be supported by every conforming SGML system. The two are identical, except that the core concrete syntax does not support short references. (See 13.4.2 ⌈ *459* ⌋ through 13.4.8 ⌈ *469* ⌋ for discussion of the parts of figure 7 ⌈ *477* ⌋ .)

⌈ O–4.49 209:6 ⌋

2 The reference concrete syntax is defined by the SGML declaration *concrete syntax* ⌈ **[182]** *458:1* ⌋ parameter shown in figure 7 ⌈ *477* ⌋ . Its *public identifier* ⌈ **[74]** *379:8* ⌋ is:

4   `"ISO 8879:1986//SYNTAX Reference//EN"`

6 The core concrete syntax is the same as the reference concrete syntax, except that "NONE" is specified for the "SHORTREF" parameter. Its *public identifier* ⌈ **[74]** *379:8* ⌋ is:

8   `"ISO 8879:1986//SYNTAX Core//EN"`

10 NOTE — The *syntax-reference character set* ⌈ **[185]** *461:1* ⌋ of the reference concrete syntax is ISO 646 IRV. That set consists of characters numbered 0 through 127, which correspond to the like-numbered characters in ISO

12 4873 and ISO 6937. The set was chosen because it is the simplest standard character set that contains all of the significant SGML characters used

14 in the reference concrete syntax. This choice does not restrict the document character sets that can be used, nor their size.

```
           SYNTAX

SHUNCHAR CONTROLS 0 1 2 3 4 5 6 7 8 9 10 11 12 13 14 15 16 17
          18 19 20 21 22 23 24 25 26 27 28 29 30 31 127 255
BASESET  "ISO 646-1983//CHARSET
          International Reference Version (IRV)//ESC 2/5 4/0"
DESCSET  0 128 0
FUNCTION RE               13
         RS               10
         SPACE            32
         TAB     SEPCHAR   9
NAMING   LCNMSTRT ""
         UCNMSTRT ""
         LCNMCHAR "-."     -- Lower-case hyphen, period are --
         UCNMCHAR "-."     -- same as upper-case (45 46).    --
         NAMECASE GENERAL  YES
                  ENTITY   NO
DELIM    GENERAL  SGMLREF
         SHORTREF SGMLREF
NAMES    SGMLREF
QUANTITY SGMLREF
```

Figure 7 — Reference Concrete Syntax

Clause 15
Conformance

This clause defines conformance to ISO 8879 for SGML documents, SGML applications, and SGML systems. As the purpose of SGML is to describe documents, it is logical that conformance of applications and systems is defined primarily in terms of their ability to handle conforming SGML documents.

15.1 Conforming SGML Document

If an SGML document complies with all the provisions of the standard, it is a conforming SGML document. If it comes close, it is still an SGML document but not a conforming one. There are different categories of conforming SGML document depending upon what concrete syntax is supported and which optional features. ⌊ **O–4.51** *214:1* ⌋

2   If an SGML document complies with all provisions of this International Standard it is a conforming SGML document.

15.1.1 Basic SGML Document

4   If a conforming SGML document uses the reference concrete syntax throughout, the reference capacity set, and only the SHORTTAG and OMITTAG features, it is a basic SGML document.

6   NOTE — A typical SGML declaration for a basic SGML document is shown in figure 8 ⌊ *479* ⌋ . Only the *document character set* ⌊ **[172]** *452:1* ⌋ parameter
8   can differ from one basic SGML document to another.

478

```
                    <!SGML "ISO 8879-1986"
          -- This document is a basic SGML document. --

                            CHARSET
          -- 8-bit document character set whose first 128 characters
             are the same as the syntax-reference character set. --
BASESET   "ISO 646-1983//CHARSET
           International Reference Version (IRV)//ESC 2/5 4/0"
DESCSET    0    9   UNUSED
           9    2   9
           11   2   UNUSED
           13   1   13
           14   18  UNUSED
           32   95  32
           127  1   UNUSED
BASESET   "ISO Registration Number 109//CHARSET
           ECMA-94 Right Part of Latin Alphabet Nr. 3//ESC 2/9 4/3"
DESCSET    128  32  UNUSED
           160  5   32
           165  1   "SGML User's Group logo"
           166  88  38         -- Includes 5 unused for NONSGML --
           254  1   127        -- Move 127 to unused position as --
           255  1   UNUSED     -- 255 is shunned character number --

CAPACITY  PUBLIC "ISO 8879-1986//CAPACITY Reference//EN"
SCOPE     DOCUMENT
SYNTAX    PUBLIC "ISO 8879-1986//SYNTAX Reference//EN"

                            FEATURES
MINIMIZE DATATAG NO  OMITTAG  YES  RANK     NO   SHORTTAG YES
LINK     SIMPLE  NO  IMPLICIT NO   EXPLICIT NO
OTHER    CONCUR  NO  SUBDOC   NO   FORMAL   NO

                    APPINFO NONE>
```

Figure 8 — Typical SGML Declaration for Basic SGML Document

15.1.2 Minimal SGML Document

2 If a conforming SGML document uses the core concrete syntax, the reference capacity set, and no features, it is a minimal SGML document.

15.1.3 Variant Conforming SGML Document

4 If a conforming SGML document uses a variant concrete syntax, it is a variant conforming SGML document.

15.2 Conforming SGML Application

A conforming SGML application cannot change the standard; however, it can require that options that are open to the user be done in a certain way. A conforming application must also meet the requirements for conforming documentation — that is, documentation describing the application itself, not the documents processed by the application.

O–4.50 *215:1*

If an SGML application meets the requirements of this sub-clause it
2   is a conforming SGML application.

15.2.1 Application Conventions

A conforming SGML application's conventions can affect only areas
4   that are left open to specification by applications.

NOTE — Some examples are: naming conventions for elements and
6   entities, or a content convention that data characters not in the syntax-reference character set always be entered by references rather than
8   directly.

15.2.2 Conformance of Documents

A conforming SGML application shall require its documents to be
10   conforming SGML documents, and shall not prohibit any markup that this International Standard would allow in such documents.

12   NOTE — For example, an application markup convention could recommend that only certain minimization functions be used, but could not
14   prohibit the use of other functions if they are allowed by the formal specification.

15.2.3 Conformance of Documentation

16   A conforming SGML application's documentation shall meet the requirements of this International Standard (see 15.5 485).

O–4.51 *214:1*

15.3 Conforming SGML System

A conforming SGML system must also have conforming documentation. In addition, it must be able to conform to its own system declaration. In other words, it has to be able to handle everything it promises to handle. In order to promote the maximum capability for document interchange among systems, every conforming system must be able to support the reference or core concrete syntax and the reference capacity set.

O-4.312 *209:1*

If an SGML system meets the requirements of this sub-clause it is a conforming SGML system.

NOTE — An effect of this sub-clause is to require that a conforming SGML system be able to process a minimal SGML document.

15.3.1 Conformance of Documentation

A conforming SGML system's documentation shall meet the requirements of this International Standard (see 15.5 *485*).

15.3.2 Conformance to System Declaration

A conforming SGML system shall be capable of processing any conforming SGML document that is not inconsistent with the system's *system declaration* [200] *488:1* (see 15.6 *487*).

NOTE — As this International Standard does not define data content notations or system data, a system's inability to process such text does not affect whether it is a conforming SGML system.

15.3.3 Support for Reference Concrete Syntax

A conforming SGML system shall be able to parse documents in the reference concrete syntax in addition to any variant concrete syntax that it may support.

NOTE — This requirement can be satisfied by converting from the reference to the system concrete syntax when a document is received.

A conforming SGML system that can create or revise SGML

documents shall be able to do so for SGML documents that use the
2   reference concrete syntax.

NOTE — This requirement can be satisfied by converting from the system
4   to the reference concrete syntax when a document is to be exported.

If a conforming SGML system allows a user to edit SGML markup
6   directly, it must also allow the reference concrete syntax to be
edited directly.

8   If an SGML system does not support short references in any
syntax, the core concrete syntax can be used instead of the
10 reference concrete syntax.

NOTES

12 1   A system can meet the requirement to support the reference concrete
syntax by using separate programs or modules.

14 2   This requirement should not be interpreted to require that interchange
be restricted to the reference concrete syntax; documents can be
16 interchanged in variant concrete syntaxes as well.

15.3.4 Support for Reference Capacity Set

A conforming SGML system shall be able to parse documents
18 whose capacities are no greater than those of the reference
capacity set. If SGML documents can be created with the system,
20 the system shall be able to create documents whose capacities are
no greater than those of the reference capacity set.

15.3.5 Consistency of Parsing

A major objective of SGML is that markup, once known to be correct,
should not have to be changed in order to use different applications that
support that document type definition. There are bad practices that a system designer could engage in that would make it possible for applications to produce inconsistent results even when the markup is correct.
The purpose of this clause is to prevent those possibilities.

Consider as an example an application that collects bibliographic citations occurring throughout a technical report and then prints them as a
bibliography at the back of the report. There are a number of ways the
application could handle that. One way might be for the user who
wanted such a collected bibliography to put a "bibliography list" tag at

the end of the document. The application, as it collected the items for the bibliography, would generate a file with bibliography items in it, suitably tagged in SGML. At the end of the processing run, it would simply embed that file as though an entity reference had been made to it, and treat it as part of the original source document.

If the above application did its job properly, the user would never know what had gone on and it would not necessarily have caused any problems. On the other hand, if the application developer made a mistake, the user might find error messages saying "bibliography item tag found outside of a bibliography list", when in fact no such tag had ever been entered. Worse, the user might try to fix the problem by inserting a bibliography list tag elsewhere in the document. Another application, operating on the same document, might then report an error for having a bibliography list tag out of place.

The problem could have been avoided if the original application had generated the bibliography strictly as output, and not by feeding information back into the parser's input stream. In a conforming system, generating text which must then be parsed is prohibited.

A conforming SGML system shall parse the same document
2   identically for all applications and processes that operate on it.

NOTES

4   1   An application program, using normal interfaces to the SGML parser, should not be able to affect the state of the parse, such as by generating
6   text and causing it to be parsed as though it were part of the document. Documentation for application developers should make them aware of this
8   requirement.

2   This requirement enables a system to be tested for conformance
10   without having to test every application.

15.3.6 Application Conventions

This clause is motivated by the same considerations as the requirement for conforming documentation — to encourage an informed user community with a body of knowledge about SGML. To accomplish this goal, the user must know when something is a requirement of SGML and when it is a requirement of a particular application. Otherwise he could not port his knowledge of SGML from one application to another. Therefore, when a system advises the user of an error in some application convention, it must be made quite clear that the error is not an SGML error.

A   conforming   SGML   system   shall   not   enforce   application

conventions as though they were requirements of this International
2 Standard.

NOTE — Warnings of the violation of application conventions can be given,
4 but they must be distinguished from reports of markup errors.

15.4 Validating SGML Parser

A system can be a conforming SGML system even if it is unable to
detect errors. In other words, there are two tiers of system conformance:
one is the ability to process an error-free (i.e., conforming) SGML document correctly; the other is the ability to recognize errors in a non-conforming SGML document. ⌐ **O–4.329** *215:5* ⌐

If an SGML parser in a conforming SGML system meets the
6 requirements of this sub-clause, it is a validating SGML parser.

NOTE — A conforming SGML system need not have a validating SGML
8 parser. Implementors can therefore decide whether to incur the overhead of
validation in a given system. A user whose text editing system allowed the
10 validation and correction of SGML documents, for example, would not
require the validation process to be repeated when the documents are
12 processed by a formatting system.

15.4.1 Error Recognition

A validating SGML parser shall find and report a reportable markup
14 error if one exists, and shall not report an error when none exists.

A validating SGML parser can optionally report other errors (see
16 4.267).

NOTE — This International Standard does not specify how a markup error
18 should be handled, beyond the requirement for reporting it. In particular, it
does not state whether the erroneous text should be treated as data, and/or
20 whether an attempt should be made to continue processing after an error is
found.

22 A validating SGML parser may warn of conditions that are
potentially, but not necessarily, errors.

NOTE — For example, a generic identifier that is an optional token in a
2   *model group* ⟨ **[127]** *410:6* ⟩ but is not declared, could be an error if its element occurred in the document instance.

15.4.2 Identification of SGML Messages

As with 15.3.6 ⟨ *483* ⟩, the purpose of this clause is to maintain the
integrity of SGML across multiple systems and applications, and to further the users' awareness of it.

4   Reports of SGML markup errors, including optional reports, shall be
identified as SGML messages in such a manner as to distinguish
6   them clearly from all other messages, including warnings of
potential SGML errors.

15.4.3 Content of SGML Messages

8   A report of an SGML markup error, including an optional report,
shall state the nature and location of the error in sufficient detail to
10   permit its correction.

NOTE — This requirement is worded to allow implementors maximum
12   flexibility to meet their user and system requirements. More precise
suggestions are made in clause F.4 ⟨ *549* ⟩ .

15.5 Documentation Requirements

It has been said that "Eternal vigilance is the price of liberty". In the
same way, the best enforcement of a standard is an informed user community that can tell when the standard is being applied properly. The
purpose of the documentation requirements clause is to further the
growth of a pool of educated users who are aware of when they are
using SGML, and to enable them to distinguish SGML constructs from
the constructs of a particular implementation or application. The user
community benefits by avoiding expensive re-education efforts when
going from one system or application to another. The SGML vendor
community benefits for the same reason.

14   The objectives of this International Standard will be met most
effectively if users, at all levels, are aware that SGML documents
16   conform to an International Standard that is independent of any

2 application or parser. The documentation of a conforming SGML system or application shall further such awareness.

4 NOTE — These requirements are intended to help users apply knowledge gained from one SGML system to the use of other systems, not to inhibit a casual and friendly writing style.

15.5.1 Standard Identification

6 Standard identification shall be in the national language of the documentation.

8 Standard identification text shall be displayed prominently
   a) in a prominent location in the front matter of all publications
10 (normally the title page and cover page);
   b) on all identifying display screens of programs; and
12 c) in all promotional and training material.

For applications, the identification text is:

```
14 An SGML Application Conforming to
   International Standard ISO 8879 —
16 Standard Generalized Markup Language
```

For systems, the identification text is:

```
18 An SGML System Conforming to
   International Standard ISO 8879 —
20 Standard Generalized Markup Language
```

The documentation for a conforming SGML system shall include a
22 system declaration (see 15.6 [487]).

15.5.2 Identification of SGML Constructs

The documentation shall distinguish SGML constructs from
24 application conventions and system functions, and shall identify the SGML constructs as being part of the Standard Generalized
26 Markup Language.

NOTE — The objective of this requirement is for the user to be aware of
2   which constructs are common to all SGML systems, and which are unique
to this one. This will reduce the experienced user's learning time for a new
4   system or application.

This International Standard shall be cited as a reference for
6   supported SGML constructs that are not specifically documented
for the system or application. For example, if, for simplicity's sake,
8   only a subset of some function is presented (such as by omitting
some of the options of the entity declaration), it shall be stated
10   clearly that other options exist and can be found in this International
Standard.

15.5.3 Terminology

12   All SGML constructs shall be introduced using the terminology of
this International Standard, translated to the national language
14   used by the publication or program.

Such standard terminology should be used throughout the
16   documentation. If, notwithstanding, a non-standard equivalent is
used for a standard term, it must be introduced in context and it
18   shall not conflict with any standard SGML terms, including terms for
unsupported or undocumented constructs.

15.5.4 Variant Concrete Syntax

20   If a variant concrete syntax is used, that fact shall be made clear to
the user. The rules of that syntax shall not be attributed to SGML.

15.6 System Declaration

A system declaration is the complement of an SGML declaration.
While an SGML declaration identifies the features that a parser requires
in order to deal with a particular document, the system declaration identifies the set of SGML declarations that a system can deal with.

O–4.312 *209:1*

A–13 *450:1*

[200] system declaration =

2	**mdo**,	`<!`
	"SYSTEM",	
4	ps+,	[65] *372:1*
	minimum literal,	[76] *381:1*
6	ps+,	[65] *372:1*
	document character set,	[172] *452:1*
8	ps+,	[65] *372:1*
	capacity set,	[180] *456:2*
10	ps+,	[65] *372:1*
	feature use,	[195] *471:4*
12	ps+,	[65] *372:1*
	concrete syntax scope,	[181] *457:4*
14	ps+,	[65] *372:1*
	concrete syntaxes supported,	[201] *489:12*
16	ps+,	[65] *372:1*
	validation services,	[203] *491:8*
18	ps+,	[65] *372:1*
	SDIF support,	[204] *493:4*
20	ps*,	[65] *372:1*
	mdc	`>`

22   A *system declaration* [200] *488:1* must meet the same syntax requirements as an *SGML declaration* [171] *450:1* with respect to
24   the concrete syntax used, data characters allowed, etc.

The *minimum data* [77] *381:8* of the *minimum literal* [76] *381:1*
26   must be "ISO 8879:1986"

The *document character set* [172] *452:1* parameter is specified as
28   on the *SGML declaration* [171] *450:1*, except that the system character set is being described, rather than that of a document. The
30   system character set must include one and only one coded representation, that is, a single bit combination, for each significant
32   SGML character in every concrete syntax described by the *concrete syntaxes supported* [201] *489:12* parameter.

34   The *capacity set* [180] *456:2* parameter is specified as on the *SGML declaration* [171] *450:1*, except that the capacity of the sys-
36   tem is being described, rather than the capacity requirements of a document.

38   The *feature use* [195] *471:4* parameter is specified as on the *SGML declaration* [171] *450:1*, except that the ability of the system

to support a feature is being described, rather than the characteris-
2   tics of a document that uses the feature.

The *concrete syntax scope* [181] *457:4* parameter is specified as
4   on the *SGML declaration* [171] *450:1* , except that the ability of the
system to support two syntaxes at once is being described, rather
6   than whether a document uses two syntaxes.

NOTE — The *system declaration* [200] *488:1* should include comments
8   to indicate which data content notations and types of *system data*
[45] *339:5* the system can support.

15.6.1 Concrete Syntaxes Supported

A conforming system must support either the core concrete syntax or,
if any concrete syntax that it supports includes short references, the reference concrete syntax.   O–4.49 *209:6*

10   This parameter specifies the concrete syntaxes that the system
SGML parser can parse and any allowed variations.

12   [201] concrete syntaxes supported =
               (*ps+*,   [65] *372:1*
14   *concrete syntax*,   [182] *458:1*
               (*ps+*,   [65] *372:1*
16   *concrete syntax changes*)?)+   [202] *490:5*

A *concrete syntax* [182] *458:1* parameter is specified, as on the
18   *SGML declaration* [171] *450:1* , for each concrete syntax that the
system can parse. One of the specified concrete syntaxes must be
20   either the reference concrete syntax, if short references are supported for any concrete syntax, or the core concrete syntax if they
22   are not.

15.6.1.1 Concrete Syntax Changes

This parameter describes concrete syntaxes that can be supported that
are minor modifications of other concrete syntaxes. In effect, the parameter is a shorthand technique for describing a large set of concrete syntaxes.
The options offered in this parameter also serve to recommend a reasonable range of variation from the reference concrete syntax. Remem-

ber, the greater the set of concrete syntaxes in the world and the more they vary from the reference concrete syntax, the more difficult it will be to achieve universal document interchange.

2   This parameter describes concrete syntaxes that the system can parse, that are minor modifications of the specified *concrete syntax* [182] *458:1*. The keywords define the nature and extent of the per-
4   mitted changes.

```
     [202] concrete syntax changes =
6            "CHANGES",
             ps+,                                        [65] 372:1
8            ( "SWITCHES" |
               ( "DELIMLEN",
10               ps+,                                    [65] 372:1
                 number,                                 [56] 347:1
12               ps+,                                    [65] 372:1
                 "SEQUENCE",
14               ps+,                                    [65] 372:1
               ( "YES" |
16                "NO"  ),
                 ps+,                                    [65] 372:1
18               "SRCNT",
                 ps+,                                    [65] 372:1
20               number,                                 [56] 347:1
                 ps+,                                    [65] 372:1
22               "SRLEN",
                 ps+,                                    [65] 372:1
24               number )  )                             [56] 347:1
```

where

26 **SWITCHES**   means that changes specified by use of the "SWITCHES" parameter of the *SGML decla-*
28   *ration* [171] *450:1* are permitted.
   DELIMLEN   means new strings that do not exceed the
30   specified number of characters (1 or more) can be assigned to the general delimiter
32   roles.
   SEQUENCE   indicates whether a blank sequence can be
34   used in short reference delimiters. If so, it is considered to have a length of 1 character.
36 **SRCNT**   means that a different set of short reference strings can be assigned, as long as it does

		not exceed the specified number (0 or more).
2	**SRLEN**	means that any new short reference strings
		must not exceed the specified number of
4		characters (1 or more).

15.6.2 Validation Services

This parameter specifies the validation capabilities of a conforming SGML system.

O–4.329 *215:5*

Note that a system need not report the optional errors in models until parsing of the document instance is complete. It might be easier for a system, for example, to recognize an invalid exclusion when it becomes applicable during parsing of the document instance, than to try to detect the possibility of it by analyzing the document type definition.

The *validation services* [203] *491:8* parameter specifies whether a
6 system has a validating SGML parser, and which, if any, optional validation services it provides.

8   [203] validation services =
         "VALIDATE",
10   ps+,   [65] *372:1*
         "GENERAL",
12   ps+,   [65] *372:1*
         ("NO" |
14   "YES"),
         ps+,   [65] *372:1*
16   "MODEL",
         ps+,   [65] *372:1*
18   ("NO" |
            "YES"),
20   ps+,   [65] *372:1*
         "EXCLUDE",
22   ps+,   [65] *372:1*
         ("NO" |
24   "YES"),
         ps+,   [65] *372:1*
26   "CAPACITY",
         ps+,   [65] *372:1*
28   ("NO" |·
            "YES"),
30   ps+,   [65] *372:1*
         "NONSGML",

2	*ps*+, ("NO" | "YES"),	[65] *372:1*
4	*ps*+, "SGML",	[65] *372:1*
6 8	*ps*+, ("NO" | "YES"),	[65] *372:1*
10	*ps*+, "FORMAL",	[65] *372:1*
12	*ps*+, ("NO" | "YES")	[65] *372:1*

14   where:

16	**NO**	means the service is not provided.
	YES	means the service is provided.
18	**GENERAL**	means a reportable markup error will be found and reported.
20	**MODEL**	means an ambiguous content model will be reported.
22	**EXCLUDE**	means an exclusion that could change a token's required or optional status in a model will be reported.
24	**CAPACITY**	means that exceeding a capacity limit will be reported.
26 28	**NONSGML**	means the occurrence of at least one non-SGML character, but not necessarily all, will be reported.
30	**SGML**	means an error in the SGML declaration will be reported.
32	**FORMAL**	means a formal public identifier error will be reported.

15.6.3 SDIF Support

This parameter specifies whether a system can use the SGML Document Interchange Format either to transmit documents or to receive them.

O–4.14S *189:1*

SDIF is defined using the Abstract Syntax Notation 1 (ISO 8824). There exists a set of basic encoding rules for ASN.1 (ISO 8825) that can be applied to an abstract definition such as SDIF to produce a specific encoding automatically. This parameter indicates whether that specific encoding is supported by an SGML system. The SDIF standard (ISO 9069) recommends the use of the ASN.1 basic encoding rules but does not require them. Other encodings can be supported in place of, or in addition to, the ASN.1 basic encoding.

2 The *SDIF support* [204] *493:4* parameter specifies whether the system can interchange documents by means of the SGML Document Interchange Format (SDIF) defined in ISO 9069.

4 [204] SDIF support =
      "SDIF",
6   *ps*+,   **[65]** *372:1*
      "PACK",
8   *ps*+,   **[65]** *372:1*
    ("NO" |
10   ("YES",
        (*ps*+,   **[65]** *372:1*
12   "ASN1")?)),
      ps+,   **[65]** *372:1*
14   "UNPACK",
      ps+,   **[65]** *372:1*
16   ("NO" |
      ("YES",
18   (*ps*+,   **[65]** *372:1*
          "ASN1")?))

20 where

PACK	is the function of creating an SDIF data stream from one or more entities.
UNPACK	is the function of decomposing an SDIF data stream into its constituent entities.
NO	means that the specified SDIF function is not supported.
YES	means the specified SDIF function is supported.
ASN1	means the specified SDIF function is supported for SDIF data streams encoded according to the ASN.1 basic encoding rules specified in ISO 8825.

Part Four:

ISO 8879 Annexes

Part Four: ISO 8879 Annexes

Annex D
Public Text

This annex covers three main subjects:

a) Possible uses for public text;

b) Variant concrete syntaxes, including the definitions of two public variant syntaxes for use with code extension;

c) Character entity sets, including definitions of 19 public entity sets for Latin, Greek, and Cyrillic alphabetic characters, special characters for publishing and technical use, and mathematical symbols.

(This annex does not form an integral part of this International Standard.)

2   SGML specifies how markup such as generic identifiers, attributes, and entity references is recognized, but no *specific* GIs or other
4   names are part of the language. The vocabulary is made up by users to meet their needs, and is defined in the document type and
6   link process definitions.

Substantial benefit can be derived from individual use of SGML (as
8   was the case with earlier generic coding and generalized markup language designs). However, trade organizations, technical
10   societies, and similar groups desiring to interchange documents could benefit further by sharing document type definitions and other
12   markup constructs.

To this end, SGML includes a syntax for referencing text with public
14   identifiers. This annex describes some applications for public text, and defines some public entity sets for immediate use.

D.1 Element Sets

2 Sets of element declarations can be created for elements that normally do not exist as independent documents, but which can occur in a variety of document types.

D.1.1 Common Element Types

4 There are certain elements that have well-recognized common forms that can occur in a variety of documents. Some involve
6 specialized data content notations as well (see below).

8 Some examples from the United States, with sources of existing specifications, are:
   a) Legal citations (Harvard Law Review)
10 b) Mathematical formulas (Association of American Publishers)
   c) Chemical formulas (American Chemical Society)
12 d) Bibliography entries (Library of Congress)
   e) Name and address (direct mail organizations, directory
14   publishers, telephone companies)

D.1.2 Pro Forma Element Types

There are a number of element configurations that occur in a
16 variety of documents and elements, but usually with differences in the GIs, or other variations. Public *pro forma* descriptions of such
18 configurations would serve as guides for constructing specific descriptions that a user might require.

20 Examples of such elements are:
   a) Paragraph (for typical formatting applications)
22 b) Paragraph (for detailed syntactic or other analysis)
   c) Tables
24 d) Nested ranked paragraph structures
   e) Lists

D.2 Data Content Notations

26 There are commonly used data content notations that could be adapted for use with SGML and given public identifiers.

For example, the EQN mathematical notation could be adapted as
follows:

a) The commands that indicate the start and end of an EQN
statement are not needed, as the tags for a formula element
would serve that function.

b) The remainder of EQN could be used unmodified as the data
content notation (possibly supplemented by descriptive
markup for some of the mathematical elements).

```
<p>The formula,
<q><formula notation=EQN>E equals m
times c squared</formula></q>
should provide speedy enlightenment.</p>
```

D.3 Variant Concrete Syntaxes

The *shunned character identification* and *function character
identification* parameters of the reference concrete syntax were
chosen to maximize the chance of successful interchange with the
widest possible set of SGML systems. Unlike dedicated word
processors, text processing applications frequently reside in
operating system environments over which they have no control,
and which do not necessarily conform to ISO standards governing
system architecture and communications. In such cases, a bit
combination that SGML would treat as data might be interpreted as
a control character by the operating system, resulting in abnormal
behavior. To prevent such errors, the reference concrete syntax
prohibits direct occurrence in the document of any bit combinations
that might be construed as controls, except for four universally
recognized function characters.

For some national languages, however, additional function
characters are needed so that code extension techniques can be
used to allow keyboards and displays to respond to changes in the
character repertoire as text is entered or revised. This sub-clause
defines two public variant concrete syntaxes that allow function
characters for code extension to occur in SGML entities in a
manner that prevents them, or the additional graphic characters,
from mistakenly being interpreted as markup.

```
          SYNTAX

SHUNCHAR CONTROLS 0 1 2 3 4 5 6 7 8 9 10 11 12 13 14 15 16 17
          18 19 20 21 22 23 24 25 26 27 28 29 30 31 127 255
BASESET  "ISO 646-1983//CHARSET
          International Reference Version (IRV)//ESC 2/5 4/0"
DESCSET   0  14  0
          14   1 "LS0 in ISO 2022"
          15   1 "LS1 in ISO 2022"
          16 112 16
          128 14 UNUSED
          142  1 "SS2 in ISO 2022"
          143  1 "SS3 in ISO 2022"
          144 112 UNUSED
FUNCTION RE                13
         RS                10
         SPACE             32
         TAB       SEPCHAR  9
         -- Functions for graphic repertoire code extension --
         -- Markup is recognized only in the G0 set. --
         ESC       MSOCHAR  27 -- Escape --
         LS0       MSICHAR  15 -- Locking-shift zero (G0 set) --
         LS1       MSOCHAR  14 -- Locking-shift one (G1 set) --
                            -- LS1R, LS2, LS2R, LS3, and
                               LS3R are ESC sequences --
         SS2       MSSCHAR 142 -- Single-shift two (G2 set) --
         SS3       MSSCHAR 143 -- Single-shift three (G3 set) --
NAMING   LCNMSTRT ""
         UCNMSTRT ""
         LCNMCHAR "-."        -- Lower-case hyphen, period are --
         UCNMCHAR "-."        -- same as upper-case (45 46).   --
         NAMECASE GENERAL YES
                  ENTITY  NO
DELIM    GENERAL  SGMLREF
         SHORTREF SGMLREF
NAMES    SGMLREF
QUANTITY SGMLREF
```

Figure 11 — Multicode Basic Concrete Syntax

D.3.1 Multicode Concrete Syntaxes

The multicode basic concrete syntax is described by the SGML
declaration *concrete syntax* parameter shown in figure 11 ⟨*501*⟩. Its
public identifier is:

`"ISO 8879:1986//SYNTAX Multicode Basic//EN"`

The multicode core concrete syntax is the same as the multicode
basic concrete syntax, except that "NONE" is specified for the
"SHORTREF" parameter. Its *public identifier* is:

```
"ISO 8879:1986//SYNTAX Multicode Core//EN"
```

2 These syntaxes allow markup to be recognized only in the G0 set because a shift to G1, G2, or G3 begins with a function character 4 that suppresses markup recognition.

The LS0 function restores markup recognition while shifting back to 6 G0. It must be entered after an escape sequence occurs to allow further markup recognition.

8 NOTE — Techniques for device-independent code extension that allow mixed use of ISO 2022 and non-ISO 2022 devices are discussed in clause 10 E.3 ⌷537⌷ .

D.4 Entity Sets

Tens of thousands of graphic characters are used in the publishing 12 of text, of which relatively few have been incorporated into standard coded character sets. Even where standard coded representations 14 exist, however, there may be situations in which they cannot be keyboarded conveniently, or in which it is not possible to display the 16 desired visual depiction of the characters.

To help overcome these barriers to successful interchange of 18 SGML documents, this sub-clause defines character entity sets for some of the widely-used special graphic characters. The entity 20 repertoires are based on applicable published and proposed International Standards for coded character sets, and current 22 industry and professional society practice.

NOTE — Entity repertoires are necessarily larger and more repetitious than 24 character sets, as they deal in general with higher-level constructs. For example, unique entities have been defined for each accented Latin 26 alphabetic character, while a character set might represent such characters as combinations of letters and diacritical mark characters. These public 28 entity sets should therefore not be construed as requirements for new standard coded character sets.

D.4.1 General Considerations

30 This sub-sub-clause discusses design criteria applicable to the public entity sets included in this annex.

D.4.1.1 Format of Declarations

The entity sets published here are definitional; the entity text simply
2   consists of the entity name in square brackets, and there is a
comment describing the symbol, rather than a (possibly) device-
4   dependent coded representation of it:

```
<!ENTITY frac78 SDATA "[frac78]"--=fraction seven-
                                      eighths-->
```

6   ▼

If, as in the above example, the comment contains an equals sign,
8   the description is essentially that given the character in ISO 6937,
which also contains a visual depiction of the character.

10   If, as in the following example, the comment includes a name (of
any length) preceded by a solidus, the name is an identifier of a
12   visual depiction of the character in *MathSci, an expansion of
mathfile*, 26-Apr-85, published by the American Mathematical
14   Society, 201 Charles St., Providence, RI 02940, U.S.A. [1]

```
<!ENTITY frown  SDATA "[frown ]"--/frown R: down
                                      curve-->
```

16   ▼

A comment can include an ISO 6937 description, one or more
18   MathSci identifiers, or none or all of them.

NOTE — In the MathSci document, an identifier is preceded by a reverse
20   solidus, rather than a solidus.

A comment can include a single upper-case letter, followed by a
22   colon, as in the previous example. The letter indicates that in
conventional mathematical typesetting, the character is treated
24   differently from an ordinary character, as follows:

Letter	***Treated as:***
26 **A**	Relation (arrow)
B	Binary operator
28 **C**	Closing delimiter
L	Large operator
30 **N**	Relation (negated)

---

[1] A better source is Joan Smith and Robert Stutely's *SGML: The User's Guide to ISO 8879* (see Appendix D ⌐605⌐). It illustrates every one of the entities — not just the math symbols — and indexes them in a number of useful ways.

	O	Opening delimiter
2	**P**	Punctuation
	R	Relation

D.4.1.2 Corresponding Display Entity Sets

4   A system will need to provide corresponding display entity sets for the output devices it supports, in which the entity text is replaced by
6   processing instructions or character sequences that will produce the desired visual depiction. The entity name and descriptive
8   comment would, of course, remain the same. For example, the declaration

10 ```
    <!ENTITY frac78 SDATA "7/8"--=fraction seven-eighths-->
    ```

    might be used in a display character entity set for output devices
12  that did not support ISO 6937/2, while

    ```
    <!ENTITY frac78 SDATA "ß"--=fraction seven-
    ```
14  ```
                                          eighths-->
    ```

    might be used in an entity set for 8-bit coded devices that did. For a
16 text formatter driving a photocomposer, a declaration like the following might be used:

18 ```
    <!ENTITY frac78 SDATA "?bf pi;&#14;?pf"--=fraction
    ```
    ```
                                          7/8-->
    ```

20  NOTE — All of the entity declarations use the "SDATA" keyword as a reminder that the entity text could be system-specific character data that
22  might require modification for different output devices and applications.

### D.4.1.3 Entity Names

    The entity names are derived from the English language. They
24  were chosen for maximum mnemonic value, consistent with the logical and systematic use of abbreviations.

26  NOTE — Translations may be desired for other languages.

    The entity names are case-sensitive, so the case of letters within
28  the name can identify the case of the character, indicate the
    ```

doubling of a line, or be used for some other convention.

2 The entity names are limited to six characters in length, and employ only letters and numerals, so they can be used with a variety of
4 concrete syntaxes.

NOTE — If shorter names are desired for frequently used entities, they can
6 be defined in the documents where the frequent use occurs.

Some characters have different semantic connotations in different
8 application contexts. Multiple entities were defined for some of them.

10 NOTE — If a different name would be more expressive in the context of a particular document, the entity can be redefined within the document.

D.4.1.4 Organization of Entity Sets

12 The entity sets were organized principally to reflect the structure of the ISO 6937 character sets, or to group large numbers of similar
14 characters together. This organization is not likely to be optimal for most applications, which will normally require a mix of entities from
16 a number of sets. Permission is granted to copy all or part of the public entity sets in this sub-clause in any form for use with
18 conforming SGML systems and applications, provided the ISO copyright notice (including the permission-to-copy text) is included
20 in all copies. In particular, entities can be copied from a number of public sets to form a new set, provided the ISO copyright notice is
22 included in the new set.

NOTE — If the same entity name occurs in more than one public set, and
24 both are needed in a document, an entity with a different name should be declared for one of them within the document.

D.4.2 Alphabetic Characters

26 This group of character entity sets uses a consistent naming scheme in which the character, or a transliteration of it, is followed
28 by an abbreviation for the accent, and/or a designator of a non-Latin alphabet. The character is capitalized in the entity name when
30 the entity represents its capital form.

D.4.2.1 Latin

2   This entity set consists of Latin alphabetic characters used in Western European languages, other than those in *UC Letter* and *LC Letter*.

```
<!-- (C) International Organization for Standardization 1986
     Permission to copy in any form is granted for use with
     conforming SGML systems and applications as defined in
     ISO 8879, provided this notice is included in all copies.
-->
<!-- Character entity set. Typical invocation:
     <!ENTITY % ISOlat1 PUBLIC
       "ISO 8879-1986//ENTITIES Added Latin 1//EN">
     %ISOlat1;
-->
<!ENTITY aacute SDATA "[aacute]"--=small a, acute accent-->
<!ENTITY Aacute SDATA "[Aacute]"--=capital A, acute accent-->
<!ENTITY acirc  SDATA "[acirc ]"--=small a, circumflex accent-->
<!ENTITY Acirc  SDATA "[Acirc ]"--=capital A, circumflex accent-->
<!ENTITY agrave SDATA "[agrave]"--=small a, grave accent-->
<!ENTITY Agrave SDATA "[Agrave]"--=capital A, grave accent-->
<!ENTITY aring  SDATA "[aring ]"--=small a, ring-->
<!ENTITY Aring  SDATA "[Aring ]"--=capital A, ring-->
<!ENTITY atilde SDATA "[atilde]"--=small a, tilde-->
<!ENTITY Atilde SDATA "[Atilde]"--=capital A, tilde-->
<!ENTITY auml   SDATA "[auml  ]"--=small a, dieresis or umlaut mark-->
<!ENTITY Auml   SDATA "[Auml  ]"--=capital A, dieresis or umlaut mark-->
<!ENTITY aelig  SDATA "[aelig ]"--=small ae diphthong (ligature)-->
<!ENTITY AElig  SDATA "[AElig ]"--=capital AE diphthong (ligature)-->
<!ENTITY ccedil SDATA "[ccedil]"--=small c, cedilla-->
<!ENTITY Ccedil SDATA "[Ccedil]"--=capital C, cedilla-->
<!ENTITY eth    SDATA "[eth   ]"--=small eth, Icelandic-->
<!ENTITY ETH    SDATA "[ETH   ]"--=capital Eth, Icelandic-->
<!ENTITY eacute SDATA "[eacute]"--=small e, acute accent-->
<!ENTITY Eacute SDATA "[Eacute]"--=capital E, acute accent-->
<!ENTITY ecirc  SDATA "[ecirc ]"--=small e, circumflex accent-->
<!ENTITY Ecirc  SDATA "[Ecirc ]"--=capital E, circumflex accent-->
<!ENTITY egrave SDATA "[egrave]"--=small e, grave accent-->
<!ENTITY Egrave SDATA "[Egrave]"--=capital E, grave accent-->
<!ENTITY euml   SDATA "[euml  ]"--=small e, dieresis or umlaut mark-->
<!ENTITY Euml   SDATA "[Euml  ]"--=capital E, dieresis or umlaut mark-->
<!ENTITY iacute SDATA "[iacute]"--=small i, acute accent-->
<!ENTITY Iacute SDATA "[Iacute]"--=capital I, acute accent-->
<!ENTITY icirc  SDATA "[icirc ]"--=small i, circumflex accent-->
<!ENTITY Icirc  SDATA "[Icirc ]"--=capital I, circumflex accent-->
<!ENTITY igrave SDATA "[igrave]"--=small i, grave accent-->
<!ENTITY Igrave SDATA "[Igrave]"--=capital I, grave accent-->
<!ENTITY iuml   SDATA "[iuml  ]"--=small i, dieresis or umlaut mark-->
<!ENTITY Iuml   SDATA "[Iuml  ]"--=capital I, dieresis or umlaut mark-->
<!ENTITY ntilde SDATA "[ntilde]"--=small n, tilde-->
<!ENTITY Ntilde SDATA "[Ntilde]"--=capital N, tilde-->
<!ENTITY oacute SDATA "[oacute]"--=small o, acute accent-->
<!ENTITY Oacute SDATA "[Oacute]"--=capital O, acute accent-->
<!ENTITY ocirc  SDATA "[ocirc ]"--=small o, circumflex accent-->
<!ENTITY Ocirc  SDATA "[Ocirc ]"--=capital O, circumflex accent-->
<!ENTITY ograve SDATA "[ograve]"--=small o, grave accent-->
<!ENTITY Ograve SDATA "[Ograve]"--=capital O, grave accent-->
```

```
<!ENTITY oslash SDATA "[oslash]"--=small o, slash-->
<!ENTITY Oslash SDATA "[Oslash]"--=capital O, slash-->
<!ENTITY otilde SDATA "[otilde]"--=small o, tilde-->
<!ENTITY Otilde SDATA "[Otilde]"--=capital O, tilde-->
<!ENTITY ouml   SDATA "[ouml ]"--=small o, dieresis or umlaut mark-->
<!ENTITY Ouml   SDATA "[Ouml ]"--=capital O, dieresis or umlaut mark-->
<!ENTITY szlig  SDATA "[szlig ]"--=small sharp s, German (sz ligature)-->
<!ENTITY thorn  SDATA "[thorn ]"--=small thorn, Icelandic-->
<!ENTITY THORN  SDATA "[THORN ]"--=capital THORN, Icelandic-->
<!ENTITY uacute SDATA "[uacute]"--=small u, acute accent-->
<!ENTITY Uacute SDATA "[Uacute]"--=capital U, acute accent-->
<!ENTITY ucirc  SDATA "[ucirc ]"--=small u, circumflex accent-->
<!ENTITY Ucirc  SDATA "[Ucirc ]"--=capital U, circumflex accent-->
<!ENTITY ugrave SDATA "[ugrave]"--=small u, grave accent-->
<!ENTITY Ugrave SDATA "[Ugrave]"--=capital U, grave accent-->
<!ENTITY uuml   SDATA "[uuml ]"--=small u, dieresis or umlaut mark-->
<!ENTITY Uuml   SDATA "[Uuml ]"--=capital U, dieresis or umlaut mark-->
<!ENTITY yacute SDATA "[yacute]"--=small y, acute accent-->
<!ENTITY Yacute SDATA "[Yacute]"--=capital Y, acute accent-->
<!ENTITY yuml   SDATA "[yuml ]"--=small y, dieresis or umlaut mark-->
```

This entity set contains additional Latin alphabetic characters.

```
<!-- (C) International Organization for Standardization 1986
     Permission to copy in any form is granted for use with
     conforming SGML systems and applications as defined in
     ISO 8879, provided this notice is included in all copies.
-->
<!-- Character entity set. Typical invocation:
     <!ENTITY % ISOlat2 PUBLIC
       "ISO 8879-1986//ENTITIES Added Latin 2//EN">
     %ISOlat2;
-->
<!ENTITY abreve SDATA "[abreve]"--=small a, breve-->
<!ENTITY Abreve SDATA "[Abreve]"--=capital A, breve-->
<!ENTITY amacr  SDATA "[amacr ]"--=small a, macron-->
<!ENTITY Amacr  SDATA "[Amacr ]"--=capital A, macron-->
<!ENTITY aogon  SDATA "[aogon ]"--=small a, ogonek-->
<!ENTITY Aogon  SDATA "[Aogon ]"--=capital A, ogonek-->
<!ENTITY cacute SDATA "[cacute]"--=small c, acute accent-->
<!ENTITY Cacute SDATA "[Cacute]"--=capital C, acute accent-->
<!ENTITY ccaron SDATA "[ccaron]"--=small c, caron-->
<!ENTITY Ccaron SDATA "[Ccaron]"--=capital C, caron-->
<!ENTITY ccirc  SDATA "[ccirc ]"--=small c, circumflex accent-->
<!ENTITY Ccirc  SDATA "[Ccirc ]"--=capital C, circumflex accent-->
<!ENTITY cdot   SDATA "[cdot  ]"--=small c, dot above-->
<!ENTITY Cdot   SDATA "[Cdot  ]"--=capital C, dot above-->
<!ENTITY dcaron SDATA "[dcaron]"--=small d, caron-->
<!ENTITY Dcaron SDATA "[Dcaron]"--=capital D, caron-->
<!ENTITY dstrok SDATA "[dstrok]"--=small d, stroke-->
<!ENTITY Dstrok SDATA "[Dstrok]"--=capital D, stroke-->
<!ENTITY ecaron SDATA "[ecaron]"--=small e, caron-->
<!ENTITY Ecaron SDATA "[Ecaron]"--=capital E, caron-->
<!ENTITY edot   SDATA "[edot  ]"--=small e, dot above-->
<!ENTITY Edot   SDATA "[Edot  ]"--=capital E, dot above-->
<!ENTITY emacr  SDATA "[emacr ]"--=small e, macron-->
<!ENTITY Emacr  SDATA "[Emacr ]"--=capital E, macron-->
<!ENTITY eogon  SDATA "[eogon ]"--=small e, ogonek-->
<!ENTITY Eogon  SDATA "[Eogon ]"--=capital E, ogonek-->
<!ENTITY gacute SDATA "[gacute]"--=small g, acute accent-->
```

```
<!ENTITY gbreve SDATA "[gbreve]"--=small g, breve-->
<!ENTITY Gbreve SDATA "[Gbreve]"--=capital G, breve-->
<!ENTITY Gcedil SDATA "[Gcedil]"--=capital G, cedilla-->
<!ENTITY gcirc  SDATA "[gcirc ]"--=small g, circumflex accent-->
<!ENTITY Gcirc  SDATA "[Gcirc ]"--=capital G, circumflex accent-->
<!ENTITY gdot   SDATA "[gdot  ]"--=small g, dot above-->
<!ENTITY Gdot   SDATA "[Gdot  ]"--=capital G, dot above-->
<!ENTITY hcirc  SDATA "[hcirc ]"--=small h, circumflex accent-->
<!ENTITY Hcirc  SDATA "[Hcirc ]"--=capital H, circumflex accent-->
<!ENTITY hstrok SDATA "[hstrok]"--=small h, stroke-->
<!ENTITY Hstrok SDATA "[Hstrok]"--=capital H, stroke-->
<!ENTITY Idot   SDATA "[Idot  ]"--=capital I, dot above-->
<!ENTITY Imacr  SDATA "[Imacr ]"--=capital I, macron-->
<!ENTITY imacr  SDATA "[imacr ]"--=small i, macron-->
<!ENTITY ijlig  SDATA "[ijlig ]"--=small ij ligature-->
<!ENTITY IJlig  SDATA "[IJlig ]"--=capital IJ ligature-->
<!ENTITY inodot SDATA "[inodot]"--=small i without dot-->
<!ENTITY iogon  SDATA "[iogon ]"--=small i, ogonek-->
<!ENTITY Iogon  SDATA "[Iogon ]"--=capital I, ogonek-->
<!ENTITY itilde SDATA "[itilde]"--=small i, tilde-->
<!ENTITY Itilde SDATA "[Itilde]"--=capital I, tilde-->
<!ENTITY jcirc  SDATA "[jcirc ]"--=small j, circumflex accent-->
<!ENTITY Jcirc  SDATA "[Jcirc ]"--=capital J, circumflex accent-->
<!ENTITY kcedil SDATA "[kcedil]"--=small k, cedilla-->
<!ENTITY Kcedil SDATA "[Kcedil]"--=capital K, cedilla-->
<!ENTITY kgreen SDATA "[kgreen]"--=small k, Greenlandic-->
<!ENTITY lacute SDATA "[lacute]"--=small l, acute accent-->
<!ENTITY Lacute SDATA "[Lacute]"--=capital L, acute accent-->
<!ENTITY lcaron SDATA "[lcaron]"--=small l, caron-->
<!ENTITY Lcaron SDATA "[Lcaron]"--=capital L, caron-->
<!ENTITY lcedil SDATA "[lcedil]"--=small l, cedilla-->
<!ENTITY Lcedil SDATA "[Lcedil]"--=capital L, cedilla-->
<!ENTITY lmidot SDATA "[lmidot]"--=small l, middle dot-->
<!ENTITY Lmidot SDATA "[Lmidot]"--=capital L, middle dot-->
<!ENTITY lstrok SDATA "[lstrok]"--=small l, stroke-->
<!ENTITY Lstrok SDATA "[Lstrok]"--=capital L, stroke-->
<!ENTITY nacute SDATA "[nacute]"--=small n, acute accent-->
<!ENTITY Nacute SDATA "[Nacute]"--=capital N, acute accent-->
<!ENTITY eng    SDATA "[eng   ]"--=small eng, Lapp-->
<!ENTITY ENG    SDATA "[ENG   ]"--=capital ENG, Lapp-->
<!ENTITY napos  SDATA "[napos ]"--=small n, apostrophe-->
<!ENTITY ncaron SDATA "[ncaron]"--=small n, caron-->
<!ENTITY Ncaron SDATA "[Ncaron]"--=capital N, caron-->
<!ENTITY ncedil SDATA "[ncedil]"--=small n, cedilla-->
<!ENTITY Ncedil SDATA "[Ncedil]"--=capital N, cedilla-->
<!ENTITY odblac SDATA "[odblac]"--=small o, double acute accent-->
<!ENTITY Odblac SDATA "[Odblac]"--=capital O, double acute accent-->
<!ENTITY Omacr  SDATA "[Omacr ]"--=capital O, macron-->
<!ENTITY omacr  SDATA "[omacr ]"--=small o, macron-->
<!ENTITY oelig  SDATA "[oelig ]"--=small oe ligature-->
<!ENTITY OElig  SDATA "[OElig ]"--=capital OE ligature-->
<!ENTITY racute SDATA "[racute]"--=small r, acute accent-->
<!ENTITY Racute SDATA "[Racute]"--=capital R, acute accent-->
<!ENTITY rcaron SDATA "[rcaron]"--=small r, caron-->
<!ENTITY Rcaron SDATA "[Rcaron]"--=capital R, caron-->
<!ENTITY rcedil SDATA "[rcedil]"--=small r, cedilla-->
<!ENTITY Rcedil SDATA "[Rcedil]"--=capital R, cedilla-->
<!ENTITY sacute SDATA "[sacute]"--=small s, acute accent-->
<!ENTITY Sacute SDATA "[Sacute]"--=capital S, acute accent-->
<!ENTITY scaron SDATA "[scaron]"--=small s, caron-->
<!ENTITY Scaron SDATA "[Scaron]"--=capital S, caron-->
```

```
<!ENTITY scedil SDATA "[scedil]"--=small s, cedilla-->
<!ENTITY Scedil SDATA "[Scedil]"--=capital S, cedilla-->
<!ENTITY scirc  SDATA "[scirc ]"--=small s, circumflex accent-->
<!ENTITY Scirc  SDATA "[Scirc ]"--=capital S, circumflex accent-->
<!ENTITY tcaron SDATA "[tcaron]"--=small t, caron-->
<!ENTITY Tcaron SDATA "[Tcaron]"--=capital T, caron-->
<!ENTITY tcedil SDATA "[tcedil]"--=small t, cedilla-->
<!ENTITY Tcedil SDATA "[Tcedil]"--=capital T, cedilla-->
<!ENTITY tstrok SDATA "[tstrok]"--=small t, stroke-->
<!ENTITY Tstrok SDATA "[Tstrok]"--=capital T, stroke-->
<!ENTITY ubreve SDATA "[ubreve]"--=small u, breve-->
<!ENTITY Ubreve SDATA "[Ubreve]"--=capital U, breve-->
<!ENTITY udblac SDATA "[udblac]"--=small u, double acute accent-->
<!ENTITY Udblac SDATA "[Udblac]"--=capital U, double acute accent-->
<!ENTITY umacr  SDATA "[umacr ]"--=small u, macron-->
<!ENTITY Umacr  SDATA "[Umacr ]"--=capital U, macron-->
<!ENTITY uogon  SDATA "[uogon ]"--=small u, ogonek-->
<!ENTITY Uogon  SDATA "[Uogon ]"--=capital U, ogonek-->
<!ENTITY uring  SDATA "[uring ]"--=small u, ring-->
<!ENTITY Uring  SDATA "[Uring ]"--=capital U, ring-->
<!ENTITY utilde SDATA "[utilde]"--=small u, tilde-->
<!ENTITY Utilde SDATA "[Utilde]"--=capital U, tilde-->
<!ENTITY wcirc  SDATA "[wcirc ]"--=small w, circumflex accent-->
<!ENTITY Wcirc  SDATA "[Wcirc ]"--=capital W, circumflex accent-->
<!ENTITY ycirc  SDATA "[ycirc ]"--=small y, circumflex accent-->
<!ENTITY Ycirc  SDATA "[Ycirc ]"--=capital Y, circumflex accent-->
<!ENTITY Yuml   SDATA "[Yuml  ]"--=capital Y, dieresis or umlaut mark-->
<!ENTITY zacute SDATA "[zacute]"--=small z, acute accent-->
<!ENTITY Zacute SDATA "[Zacute]"--=capital Z, acute accent-->
<!ENTITY zcaron SDATA "[zcaron]"--=small z, caron-->
<!ENTITY Zcaron SDATA "[Zcaron]"--=capital Z, caron-->
<!ENTITY zdot   SDATA "[zdot  ]"--=small z, dot above-->
<!ENTITY Zdot   SDATA "[Zdot  ]"--=capital Z, dot above-->
```

D.4.2.2 Greek Alphabetic Characters

2   This entity set consists of the letters of the Greek alphabet. The entity names reflect their intended use as language characters, rather than as symbols in formulas. (Greek character entities for
4   technical use are defined below.)

```
<!-- (C) International Organization for Standardization 1986
     Permission to copy in any form is granted for use with
     conforming SGML systems and applications as defined in
     ISO 8879, provided this notice is included in all copies.
-->
<!-- Character entity set. Typical invocation:
     <!ENTITY % ISOgrk1 PUBLIC
       "ISO 8879-1986//ENTITIES Greek Letters//EN">
     %ISOgrk1;
-->
<!ENTITY agr    SDATA "[agr   ]"--=small alpha, Greek-->
<!ENTITY Agr    SDATA "[Agr   ]"--=capital Alpha, Greek-->
<!ENTITY bgr    SDATA "[bgr   ]"--=small beta, Greek-->
<!ENTITY Bgr    SDATA "[Bgr   ]"--=capital Beta, Greek-->
```

```
<!ENTITY ggr     SDATA "[ggr   ]"--=small gamma, Greek-->
<!ENTITY Ggr     SDATA "[Ggr   ]"--=capital Gamma, Greek-->
<!ENTITY dgr     SDATA "[dgr   ]"--=small delta, Greek-->
<!ENTITY Dgr     SDATA "[Dgr   ]"--=capital Delta, Greek-->
<!ENTITY egr     SDATA "[egr   ]"--=small epsilon, Greek-->
<!ENTITY Egr     SDATA "[Egr   ]"--=capital Epsilon, Greek-->
<!ENTITY zgr     SDATA "[zgr   ]"--=small zeta, Greek-->
<!ENTITY Zgr     SDATA "[Zgr   ]"--=capital Zeta, Greek-->
<!ENTITY eegr    SDATA "[eegr  ]"--=small eta, Greek-->
<!ENTITY EEgr    SDATA "[EEgr  ]"--=capital Eta, Greek-->
<!ENTITY thgr    SDATA "[thgr  ]"--=small theta, Greek-->
<!ENTITY THgr    SDATA "[THgr  ]"--=capital Theta, Greek-->
<!ENTITY igr     SDATA "[igr   ]"--=small iota, Greek-->
<!ENTITY Igr     SDATA "[Igr   ]"--=capital Iota, Greek-->
<!ENTITY kgr     SDATA "[kgr   ]"--=small kappa, Greek-->
<!ENTITY Kgr     SDATA "[Kgr   ]"--=capital Kappa, Greek-->
<!ENTITY lgr     SDATA "[lgr   ]"--=small lambda, Greek-->
<!ENTITY Lgr     SDATA "[Lgr   ]"--=capital Lambda, Greek-->
<!ENTITY mgr     SDATA "[mgr   ]"--=small mu, Greek-->
<!ENTITY Mgr     SDATA "[Mgr   ]"--=capital Mu, Greek-->
<!ENTITY ngr     SDATA "[ngr   ]"--=small nu, Greek-->
<!ENTITY Ngr     SDATA "[Ngr   ]"--=capital Nu, Greek-->
<!ENTITY xgr     SDATA "[xgr   ]"--=small xi, Greek-->
<!ENTITY Xgr     SDATA "[Xgr   ]"--=capital Xi, Greek-->
<!ENTITY ogr     SDATA "[ogr   ]"--=small omicron, Greek-->
<!ENTITY Ogr     SDATA "[Ogr   ]"--=capital Omicron, Greek-->
<!ENTITY pgr     SDATA "[pgr   ]"--=small pi, Greek-->
<!ENTITY Pgr     SDATA "[Pgr   ]"--=capital Pi, Greek-->
<!ENTITY rgr     SDATA "[rgr   ]"--=small rho, Greek-->
<!ENTITY Rgr     SDATA "[Rgr   ]"--=capital Rho, Greek-->
<!ENTITY sgr     SDATA "[sgr   ]"--=small sigma, Greek-->
<!ENTITY Sgr     SDATA "[Sgr   ]"--=capital Sigma, Greek-->
<!ENTITY sfgr    SDATA "[sfgr  ]"--=final small sigma, Greek-->
<!ENTITY tgr     SDATA "[tgr   ]"--=small tau, Greek-->
<!ENTITY Tgr     SDATA "[Tgr   ]"--=capital Tau, Greek-->
<!ENTITY ugr     SDATA "[ugr   ]"--=small upsilon, Greek-->
<!ENTITY Ugr     SDATA "[Ugr   ]"--=capital Upsilon, Greek-->
<!ENTITY phgr    SDATA "[phgr  ]"--=small phi, Greek-->
<!ENTITY PHgr    SDATA "[PHgr  ]"--=capital Phi, Greek-->
<!ENTITY khgr    SDATA "[khgr  ]"--=small chi, Greek-->
<!ENTITY KHgr    SDATA "[KHgr  ]"--=capital Chi, Greek-->
<!ENTITY psgr    SDATA "[psgr  ]"--=small psi, Greek-->
<!ENTITY PSgr    SDATA "[PSgr  ]"--=capital Psi, Greek-->
<!ENTITY ohgr    SDATA "[ohgr  ]"--=small omega, Greek-->
<!ENTITY OHgr    SDATA "[OHgr  ]"--=capital Omega, Greek-->
```

This entity set contains additional characters needed for Monotoniko Greek.

```
<!-- (C) International Organization for Standardization 1986
     Permission to copy in any form is granted for use with
     conforming SGML systems and applications as defined in
     ISO 8879, provided this notice is included in all copies.
-->
<!-- Character entity set. Typical invocation:
     <!ENTITY % ISOgrk2 PUBLIC
       "ISO 8879-1986//ENTITIES Monotoniko Greek//EN">
     %ISOgrk2;
-->
```

```
<!ENTITY aacgr  SDATA "[aacgr ]"--=small alpha, accent, Greek-->
<!ENTITY Aacgr  SDATA "[Aacgr ]"--=capital Alpha, accent, Greek-->
<!ENTITY eacgr  SDATA "[eacgr ]"--=small epsilon, accent, Greek-->
<!ENTITY Eacgr  SDATA "[Eacgr ]"--=capital Epsilon, accent, Greek-->
<!ENTITY eeacgr SDATA "[eeacgr]"--=small eta, accent, Greek-->
<!ENTITY EEacgr SDATA "[EEacgr]"--=capital Eta, accent, Greek-->
<!ENTITY idigr  SDATA "[idigr ]"--=small iota, dieresis, Greek-->
<!ENTITY Idigr  SDATA "[Idigr ]"--=capital Iota, dieresis, Greek-->
<!ENTITY iacgr  SDATA "[iacgr ]"--=small iota, accent, Greek-->
<!ENTITY Iacgr  SDATA "[Iacgr ]"--=capital Iota, accent, Greek-->
<!ENTITY idiagr SDATA "[idiagr]"--=small iota, dieresis, accent, Greek-->
<!ENTITY oacgr  SDATA "[oacgr ]"--=small omicron, accent, Greek-->
<!ENTITY Oacgr  SDATA "[Oacgr ]"--=capital Omicron, accent, Greek-->
<!ENTITY udigr  SDATA "[udigr ]"--=small upsilon, dieresis, Greek-->
<!ENTITY Udigr  SDATA "[Udigr ]"--=capital Upsilon, dieresis, Greek-->
<!ENTITY uacgr  SDATA "[uacgr ]"--=small upsilon, accent, Greek-->
<!ENTITY Uacgr  SDATA "[Uacgr ]"--=capital Upsilon, accent, Greek-->
<!ENTITY udiagr SDATA "[udiagr]"--=small upsilon, dieresis, accent, Greek-->
<!ENTITY ohacgr SDATA "[ohacgr]"--=small omega, accent, Greek-->
<!ENTITY OHacgr SDATA "[OHacgr]"--=capital Omega, accent, Greek-->
```

D.4.2.3 Cyrillic Alphabetic Characters

This entity set consists of Cyrillic characters used in the Russian
language.

```
<!-- (C) International Organization for Standardization 1986
     Permission to copy in any form is granted for use with
     conforming SGML systems and applications as defined in
     ISO 8879, provided this notice is included in all copies.
-->
<!-- Character entity set. Typical invocation:
     <!ENTITY % ISOcyr1 PUBLIC
       "ISO 8879-1986//ENTITIES Russian Cyrillic//EN">
     %ISOcyr1;
-->
<!ENTITY acy   SDATA "[acy  ]"--=small a, Cyrillic-->
<!ENTITY Acy   SDATA "[Acy  ]"--=capital A, Cyrillic-->
<!ENTITY bcy   SDATA "[bcy  ]"--=small be, Cyrillic-->
<!ENTITY Bcy   SDATA "[Bcy  ]"--=capital BE, Cyrillic-->
<!ENTITY vcy   SDATA "[vcy  ]"--=small ve, Cyrillic-->
<!ENTITY Vcy   SDATA "[Vcy  ]"--=capital VE, Cyrillic-->
<!ENTITY gcy   SDATA "[gcy  ]"--=small ghe, Cyrillic-->
<!ENTITY Gcy   SDATA "[Gcy  ]"--=capital GHE, Cyrillic-->
<!ENTITY dcy   SDATA "[dcy  ]"--=small de, Cyrillic-->
<!ENTITY Dcy   SDATA "[Dcy  ]"--=capital DE, Cyrillic-->
<!ENTITY iecy  SDATA "[iecy ]"--=small ie, Cyrillic-->
<!ENTITY IEcy  SDATA "[IEcy ]"--=capital IE, Cyrillic-->
<!ENTITY iocy  SDATA "[iocy ]"--=small io, Russian-->
<!ENTITY IOcy  SDATA "[IOcy ]"--=capital IO, Russian-->
<!ENTITY zhcy  SDATA "[zhcy ]"--=small zhe, Cyrillic-->
<!ENTITY ZHcy  SDATA "[ZHcy ]"--=capital ZHE, Cyrillic-->
<!ENTITY zcy   SDATA "[zcy  ]"--=small ze, Cyrillic-->
<!ENTITY Zcy   SDATA "[Zcy  ]"--=capital ZE, Cyrillic-->
<!ENTITY icy   SDATA "[icy  ]"--=small i, Cyrillic-->
<!ENTITY Icy   SDATA "[Icy  ]"--=capital I, Cyrillic-->
```

```
<!ENTITY jcy     SDATA "[jcy   ]"--=small short i, Cyrillic-->
<!ENTITY Jcy     SDATA "[Jcy   ]"--=capital short I, Cyrillic-->
<!ENTITY kcy     SDATA "[kcy   ]"--=small ka, Cyrillic-->
<!ENTITY Kcy     SDATA "[Kcy   ]"--=capital KA, Cyrillic-->
<!ENTITY lcy     SDATA "[lcy   ]"--=small el, Cyrillic-->
<!ENTITY Lcy     SDATA "[Lcy   ]"--=capital EL, Cyrillic-->
<!ENTITY mcy     SDATA "[mcy   ]"--=small em, Cyrillic-->
<!ENTITY Mcy     SDATA "[Mcy   ]"--=capital EM, Cyrillic-->
<!ENTITY ncy     SDATA "[ncy   ]"--=small en, Cyrillic-->
<!ENTITY Ncy     SDATA "[Ncy   ]"--=capital EN, Cyrillic-->
<!ENTITY ocy     SDATA "[ocy   ]"--=small o, Cyrillic-->
<!ENTITY Ocy     SDATA "[Ocy   ]"--=capital O, Cyrillic-->
<!ENTITY pcy     SDATA "[pcy   ]"--=small pe, Cyrillic-->
<!ENTITY Pcy     SDATA "[Pcy   ]"--=capital PE, Cyrillic-->
<!ENTITY rcy     SDATA "[rcy   ]"--=small er, Cyrillic-->
<!ENTITY Rcy     SDATA "[Rcy   ]"--=capital ER, Cyrillic-->
<!ENTITY scy     SDATA "[scy   ]"--=small es, Cyrillic-->
<!ENTITY Scy     SDATA "[Scy   ]"--=capital ES, Cyrillic-->
<!ENTITY tcy     SDATA "[tcy   ]"--=small te, Cyrillic-->
<!ENTITY Tcy     SDATA "[Tcy   ]"--=capital TE, Cyrillic-->
<!ENTITY ucy     SDATA "[ucy   ]"--=small u, Cyrillic-->
<!ENTITY Ucy     SDATA "[Ucy   ]"--=capital U, Cyrillic-->
<!ENTITY fcy     SDATA "[fcy   ]"--=small ef, Cyrillic-->
<!ENTITY Fcy     SDATA "[Fcy   ]"--=capital EF, Cyrillic-->
<!ENTITY khcy    SDATA "[khcy  ]"--=small ha, Cyrillic-->
<!ENTITY KHcy    SDATA "[KHcy  ]"--=capital HA, Cyrillic-->
<!ENTITY tscy    SDATA "[tscy  ]"--=small tse, Cyrillic-->
<!ENTITY TScy    SDATA "[TScy  ]"--=capital TSE, Cyrillic-->
<!ENTITY chcy    SDATA "[chcy  ]"--=small che, Cyrillic-->
<!ENTITY CHcy    SDATA "[CHcy  ]"--=capital CHE, Cyrillic-->
<!ENTITY shcy    SDATA "[shcy  ]"--=small sha, Cyrillic-->
<!ENTITY SHcy    SDATA "[SHcy  ]"--=capital SHA, Cyrillic-->
<!ENTITY shchcy  SDATA "[shchcy]"--=small shcha, Cyrillic-->
<!ENTITY SHCHcy  SDATA "[SHCHcy]"--=capital SHCHA, Cyrillic-->
<!ENTITY hardcy  SDATA "[hardcy]"--=small hard sign, Cyrillic-->
<!ENTITY HARDcy  SDATA "[HARDcy]"--=capital HARD sign, Cyrillic-->
<!ENTITY ycy     SDATA "[ycy   ]"--=small yeru, Cyrillic-->
<!ENTITY Ycy     SDATA "[Ycy   ]"--=capital YERU, Cyrillic-->
<!ENTITY softcy  SDATA "[softcy]"--=small soft sign, Cyrillic-->
<!ENTITY SOFTcy  SDATA "[SOFTcy]"--=capital SOFT sign, Cyrillic-->
<!ENTITY ecy     SDATA "[ecy   ]"--=small e, Cyrillic-->
<!ENTITY Ecy     SDATA "[Ecy   ]"--=capital E, Cyrillic-->
<!ENTITY yucy    SDATA "[yucy  ]"--=small yu, Cyrillic-->
<!ENTITY YUcy    SDATA "[YUcy  ]"--=capital YU, Cyrillic-->
<!ENTITY yacy    SDATA "[yacy  ]"--=small ya, Cyrillic-->
<!ENTITY YAcy    SDATA "[YAcy  ]"--=capital YA, Cyrillic-->
<!ENTITY numero  SDATA "[numero]"--=numero sign-->
```

This entity set consists of Cyrillic characters that are not used in the Russian language.

```
<!-- (C) International Organization for Standardization 1986
     Permission to copy in any form is granted for use with
     conforming SGML systems and applications as defined in
     ISO 8879, provided this notice is included in all copies.
-->
<!-- Character entity set. Typical invocation:
     <!ENTITY % ISOcyr2 PUBLIC
       "ISO 8879-1986//ENTITIES Non-Russian Cyrillic//EN">
```

```
      %ISOcyr2;
-->
<!ENTITY djcy   SDATA "[djcy  ]"--=small dje, Serbian-->
<!ENTITY DJcy   SDATA "[DJcy  ]"--=capital DJE, Serbian-->
<!ENTITY gjcy   SDATA "[gjcy  ]"--=small gje, Macedonian-->
<!ENTITY GJcy   SDATA "[GJcy  ]"--=capital GJE Macedonian-->
<!ENTITY jukcy  SDATA "[jukcy ]"--=small je, Ukrainian-->
<!ENTITY Jukcy  SDATA "[Jukcy ]"--=capital JE, Ukrainian-->
<!ENTITY dscy   SDATA "[dscy  ]"--=small dse, Macedonian-->
<!ENTITY DScy   SDATA "[DScy  ]"--=capital DSE, Macedonian-->
<!ENTITY iukcy  SDATA "[iukcy ]"--=small i, Ukrainian-->
<!ENTITY Iukcy  SDATA "[Iukcy ]"--=capital I, Ukrainian-->
<!ENTITY yicy   SDATA "[yicy  ]"--=small yi, Ukrainian-->
<!ENTITY YIcy   SDATA "[YIcy  ]"--=capital YI, Ukrainian-->
<!ENTITY jsercy SDATA "[jsercy]"--=small je, Serbian-->
<!ENTITY Jsercy SDATA "[Jsercy]"--=capital JE, Serbian-->
<!ENTITY ljcy   SDATA "[ljcy  ]"--=small lje, Serbian-->
<!ENTITY LJcy   SDATA "[LJcy  ]"--=capital LJE, Serbian-->
<!ENTITY njcy   SDATA "[njcy  ]"--=small nje, Serbian-->
<!ENTITY NJcy   SDATA "[NJcy  ]"--=capital NJE, Serbian-->
<!ENTITY tshcy  SDATA "[tshcy ]"--=small tshe, Serbian-->
<!ENTITY TSHcy  SDATA "[TSHcy ]"--=capital TSHE, Serbian-->
<!ENTITY kjcy   SDATA "[kjcy  ]"--=small kje Macedonian-->
<!ENTITY KJcy   SDATA "[KJcy  ]"--=capital KJE, Macedonian-->
<!ENTITY ubrcy  SDATA "[ubrcy ]"--=small u, Byelorussian-->
<!ENTITY Ubrcy  SDATA "[Ubrcy ]"--=capital U, Byelorussian-->
<!ENTITY dzcy   SDATA "[dzcy  ]"--=small dze, Serbian-->
<!ENTITY DZcy   SDATA "[DZcy  ]"--=capital dze, Serbian-->
```

D.4.3 General Use

D.4.3.1 Numeric and Special Graphic Characters

2 This set includes, among others, minimum data characters and reference concrete syntax markup characters. Such characters are normally directly keyable, but when they are assigned to delimiter 4 roles, an entity reference may be needed to enter them as data.

```
<!-- (C) International Organization for Standardization 1986
     Permission to copy in any form is granted for use with
     conforming SGML systems and applications as defined in
     ISO 8879, provided this notice is included in all copies.
-->
<!-- Character entity set. Typical invocation:
     <!ENTITY % ISOnum PUBLIC
       "ISO 8879-1986//ENTITIES Numeric and Special Graphic//EN">
     %ISOnum;
-->
<!ENTITY half   SDATA "[half  ]"--=fraction one-half-->
<!ENTITY frac12 SDATA "[frac12]"--=fraction one-half-->
<!ENTITY frac14 SDATA "[frac14]"--=fraction one-quarter-->
<!ENTITY frac34 SDATA "[frac34]"--=fraction three-quarters-->
<!ENTITY frac18 SDATA "[frac18]"--=fraction one-eighth-->
```

```
<!ENTITY frac38 SDATA "[frac38]"--=fraction three-eighths-->
<!ENTITY frac58 SDATA "[frac58]"--=fraction five-eighths-->
<!ENTITY frac78 SDATA "[frac78]"--=fraction seven-eighths-->

<!ENTITY sup1   SDATA "[sup1  ]"--=superscript one-->
<!ENTITY sup2   SDATA "[sup2  ]"--=superscript two-->
<!ENTITY sup3   SDATA "[sup3  ]"--=superscript three-->

<!ENTITY plus   SDATA "[plus  ]"--=plus sign B:-- >
<!ENTITY plusmn SDATA "[plusmn]"--/pm B: =plus-or-minus sign-->
<!ENTITY lt     SDATA "[lt    ]"--=less-than sign R:-->
<!ENTITY equals SDATA "[equals]"--=equals sign R:-->
<!ENTITY gt     SDATA "[gt    ]"--=greater-than sign R:-->
<!ENTITY divide SDATA "[divide]"--/div B: =divide sign-->
<!ENTITY times  SDATA "[times ]"--/times B: =multiply sign-->

<!ENTITY curren SDATA "[curren]"--=general currency sign-->
<!ENTITY pound  SDATA "[pound ]"--=pound sign-->
<!ENTITY dollar SDATA "[dollar]"--=dollar sign-->
<!ENTITY cent   SDATA "[cent  ]"--=cent sign-->
<!ENTITY yen    SDATA "[yen   ]"--/yen =yen sign-->

<!ENTITY num    SDATA "[num   ]"--=number sign-->
<!ENTITY percnt SDATA "[percnt]"--=percent sign-->
<!ENTITY amp    SDATA "[amp   ]"--=ampersand-->
<!ENTITY ast    SDATA "[ast   ]"--/ast B: =asterisk-->
<!ENTITY commat SDATA "[commat]"--=commercial at-->
<!ENTITY lsqb   SDATA "[lsqb  ]"--/lbrack O: =left square bracket-->
<!ENTITY bsol   SDATA "[bsol  ]"--/backslash =reverse solidus-->
<!ENTITY rsqb   SDATA "[rsqb  ]"--/rbrack C: =right square bracket-->
<!ENTITY lcub   SDATA "[lcub  ]"--/lbrace O: =left curly bracket-->
<!ENTITY horbar SDATA "[horbar]"--=horizontal bar-->
<!ENTITY verbar SDATA "[verbar]"--/vert =vertical bar-->
<!ENTITY rcub   SDATA "[rcub  ]"--/rbrace C: =right curly bracket-->
<!ENTITY micro  SDATA "[micro ]"--=micro sign-->
<!ENTITY ohm    SDATA "[ohm   ]"--=ohm sign-->
<!ENTITY deg    SDATA "[deg   ]"--=degree sign-->
<!ENTITY ordm   SDATA "[ordm  ]"--=ordinal indicator, masculine-->
<!ENTITY ordf   SDATA "[ordf  ]"--=ordinal indicator, feminine-->
<!ENTITY sect   SDATA "[sect  ]"--=section sign-->
<!ENTITY para   SDATA "[para  ]"--=pilcrow (paragraph sign)-->
<!ENTITY middot SDATA "[middot]"--/centerdot B: =middle dot-->
<!ENTITY larr   SDATA "[larr  ]"--/leftarrow /gets A: =leftward arrow-->
<!ENTITY rarr   SDATA "[rarr  ]"--/rightarrow /to A: =rightward arrow-->
<!ENTITY uarr   SDATA "[uarr  ]"--/uparrow A: =upward arrow-->
<!ENTITY darr   SDATA "[darr  ]"--/downarrow A: =downward arrow-->
<!ENTITY copy   SDATA "[copy  ]"--=copyright sign-->
<!ENTITY reg    SDATA "[reg   ]"--/circledR =registered sign-->
<!ENTITY trade  SDATA "[trade ]"--=trade mark sign-->
<!ENTITY brvbar SDATA "[brvbar]"--=broken (vertical) bar-->
<!ENTITY not    SDATA "[not   ]"--/neg /lnot =not sign-->
<!ENTITY sung   SDATA "[sung  ]"--=music note (sung text sign)-->

<!ENTITY excl   SDATA "[excl  ]"--=exclamation mark-->
<!ENTITY iexcl  SDATA "[iexcl ]"--=inverted exclamation mark-->
<!ENTITY quot   SDATA "[quot  ]"--=quotation mark-->
<!ENTITY apos   SDATA "[apos  ]"--=apostrophe-->
<!ENTITY lpar   SDATA "[lpar  ]"--O: =left parenthesis-->
<!ENTITY rpar   SDATA "[rpar  ]"--C: =right parenthesis-->
<!ENTITY comma  SDATA "[comma ]"--P: =comma-->
<!ENTITY lowbar SDATA "[lowbar]"--=low line-->
```

```
<!ENTITY hyphen SDATA "[hyphen]"--=hyphen-->
<!ENTITY period SDATA "[period]"--=full stop, period-->
<!ENTITY sol    SDATA "[sol   ]"--=solidus-->
<!ENTITY colon  SDATA "[colon ]"--/colon P:-->
<!ENTITY semi   SDATA "[semi  ]"--=semicolon P:-->
<!ENTITY quest  SDATA "[quest ]"--=question mark-->
<!ENTITY iquest SDATA "[iquest]"--=inverted question mark-->
<!ENTITY laquo  SDATA "[laquo ]"--=angle quotation mark, left-->
<!ENTITY raquo  SDATA "[raquo ]"--=angle quotation mark, right-->
<!ENTITY lsquo  SDATA "[lsquo ]"--=single quotation mark, left-->
<!ENTITY rsquo  SDATA "[rsquo ]"--=single quotation mark, right-->
<!ENTITY ldquo  SDATA "[ldquo ]"--=double quotation mark, left-->
<!ENTITY rdquo  SDATA "[rdquo ]"--=double quotation mark, right-->
<!ENTITY nbsp   SDATA "[nbsp  ]"--=no break (required) space-->
<!ENTITY shy    SDATA "[shy   ]"--=soft hyphen-->
```

D.4.3.2 Diacritical Mark Characters

These entities are considered to represent independent characters.

```
<!-- (C) International Organization for Standardization 1986
     Permission to copy in any form is granted for use with
     conforming SGML systems and applications as defined in
     ISO 8879, provided this notice is included in all copies.
-->
<!-- Character entity set. Typical invocation:
     <!ENTITY % ISOdia PUBLIC
       "ISO 8879-1986//ENTITIES Diacritical Marks//EN">
     %ISOdia;
-->
<!ENTITY acute  SDATA "[acute ]"--=acute accent-->
<!ENTITY breve  SDATA "[breve ]"--=breve-->
<!ENTITY caron  SDATA "[caron ]"--=caron-->
<!ENTITY cedil  SDATA "[cedil ]"--=cedilla-->
<!ENTITY circ   SDATA "[circ  ]"--=circumflex accent-->
<!ENTITY dblac  SDATA "[dblac ]"--=double acute accent-->
<!ENTITY die    SDATA "[die   ]"--=dieresis-->
<!ENTITY dot    SDATA "[dot   ]"--=dot above-->
<!ENTITY grave  SDATA "[grave ]"--=grave accent-->
<!ENTITY macr   SDATA "[macr  ]"--=macron-->
<!ENTITY ogon   SDATA "[ogon  ]"--=ogonek-->
<!ENTITY ring   SDATA "[ring  ]"--=ring-->
<!ENTITY tilde  SDATA "[tilde ]"--=tilde-->
<!ENTITY uml    SDATA "[uml   ]"--=umlaut mark-->
```

D.4.3.3 Publishing Characters

```
<!-- (C) International Organization for Standardization 1986
     Permission to copy in any form is granted for use with
     conforming SGML systems and applications as defined in
     ISO 8879, provided this notice is included in all copies.
-->
```

```
<!-- Character entity set. Typical invocation:
     <!ENTITY % ISOpub PUBLIC
       "ISO 8879-1986//ENTITIES Publishing//EN">
     %ISOpub;
-->
<!ENTITY emsp   SDATA "[emsp ]"--=em space-->
<!ENTITY ensp   SDATA "[ensp ]"--=en space (1/2-em)-->
<!ENTITY emsp13 SDATA "[emsp3]"--=1/3-em space-->
<!ENTITY emsp14 SDATA "[emsp4]"--=1/4-em space-->
<!ENTITY numsp  SDATA "[numsp]"--=digit space (width of a number)-->
<!ENTITY puncsp SDATA "[puncsp]"--=punctuation space (width of comma)-->
<!ENTITY thinsp SDATA "[thinsp]"--=thin space (1/6-em)-->
<!ENTITY hairsp SDATA "[hairsp]"--=hair space-->
<!ENTITY mdash  SDATA "[mdash ]"--=em dash-->
<!ENTITY ndash  SDATA "[ndash ]"--=en dash-->
<!ENTITY dash   SDATA "[dash ]"--=hyphen (true graphic)-->
<!ENTITY blank  SDATA "[blank ]"--=significant blank symbol-->
<!ENTITY hellip SDATA "[hellip]"--=ellipsis (horizontal)-->
<!ENTITY nldr   SDATA "[nldr ]"--=double baseline dot (en leader)-->
<!ENTITY frac13 SDATA "[frac13]"--=fraction one-third-->
<!ENTITY frac23 SDATA "[frac23]"--=fraction two-thirds-->
<!ENTITY frac15 SDATA "[frac15]"--=fraction one-fifth-->
<!ENTITY frac25 SDATA "[frac25]"--=fraction two-fifths-->
<!ENTITY frac35 SDATA "[frac35]"--=fraction three-fifths-->
<!ENTITY frac45 SDATA "[frac45]"--=fraction four-fifths-->
<!ENTITY frac16 SDATA "[frac16]"--=fraction one-sixth-->
<!ENTITY frac56 SDATA "[frac56]"--=fraction five-sixths-->
<!ENTITY incare SDATA "[incare]"--=in-care-of symbol-->
<!ENTITY block  SDATA "[block ]"--=full block-->
<!ENTITY uhblk  SDATA "[uhblk ]"--=upper half block-->
<!ENTITY lhblk  SDATA "[lhblk ]"--=lower half block-->
<!ENTITY blk14  SDATA "[blk14 ]"--=25% shaded block-->
<!ENTITY blk12  SDATA "[blk12 ]"--=50% shaded block-->
<!ENTITY blk34  SDATA "[blk34 ]"--=75% shaded block-->
<!ENTITY marker SDATA "[marker]"--=histogram marker-->
<!ENTITY cir    SDATA "[cir ]"--/circ B: =circle, open-->
<!ENTITY squ    SDATA "[squ ]"--=square, open-->
<!ENTITY rect   SDATA "[rect ]"--=rectangle, open-->
<!ENTITY utri   SDATA "[utri ]"--/triangle =up triangle, open-->
<!ENTITY dtri   SDATA "[dtri ]"--/triangledown =down triangle, open-->
<!ENTITY star   SDATA "[star ]"--=star, open-->
<!ENTITY bull   SDATA "[bull ]"--/bullet B: =round bullet, filled-->
<!ENTITY squf   SDATA "[squf ]"--/blacksquare =sq bullet, filled-->
<!ENTITY utrif  SDATA "[utrif ]"--/blacktriangle =up tri, filled-->
<!ENTITY dtrif  SDATA "[dtrif ]"--/blacktriangledown =dn tri, filled-->
<!ENTITY ltrif  SDATA "[ltrif ]"--/blacktriangleleft R: =l tri, filled-->
<!ENTITY rtrif  SDATA "[rtrif ]"--/blacktriangleright R: =r tri, filled-->
<!ENTITY clubs  SDATA "[clubs ]"--/clubsuit =club suit symbol-->
<!ENTITY diams  SDATA "[diams ]"--/diamondsuit =diamond suit symbol-->
<!ENTITY hearts SDATA "[hearts]"--/heartsuit =heart suit symbol-->
<!ENTITY spades SDATA "[spades]"--/spadesuit =spades suit symbol-->
<!ENTITY malt   SDATA "[malt ]"--/maltese =maltese cross-->
<!ENTITY dagger SDATA "[dagger]"--/dagger B: =dagger-->
<!ENTITY Dagger SDATA "[Dagger]"--/ddagger B: =double dagger-->
<!ENTITY check  SDATA "[check ]"--/checkmark =tick, check mark-->
<!ENTITY cross  SDATA "[ballot]"--=ballot cross-->
<!ENTITY sharp  SDATA "[sharp ]"--/sharp =musical sharp-->
<!ENTITY flat   SDATA "[flat ]"--/flat =musical flat-->
<!ENTITY male   SDATA "[male ]"--=male symbol-->
<!ENTITY female SDATA "[female]"--=female symbol-->
<!ENTITY phone  SDATA "[phone ]"--=telephone symbol-->
```

```
<!ENTITY telrec SDATA "[telrec]"-=telephone recorder symbol-->
<!ENTITY copysr SDATA "[copysr]"-=sound recording copyright sign-->
<!ENTITY caret  SDATA "[caret ]"-=caret (insertion mark)-->
<!ENTITY lsquor SDATA "[lsquor]"-=rising single quote, left (low)-->
<!ENTITY ldquor SDATA "[ldquor]"-=rising dbl quote, left (low)-->

<!ENTITY fflig  SDATA "[fflig ]"--small ff ligature-->
<!ENTITY filig  SDATA "[filig ]"--small fi ligature-->
<!ENTITY fjlig  SDATA "[fjlig ]"--small fj ligature-->
<!ENTITY ffilig SDATA "[ffilig]"--small ffi ligature-->
<!ENTITY ffllig SDATA "[ffllig]"--small ffl ligature-->
<!ENTITY fllig  SDATA "[fllig ]"--small fl ligature-->

<!ENTITY mldr   SDATA "[mldr  ]"--em leader-->
<!ENTITY rdquor SDATA "[rdquor]"--rising dbl quote, right (high)-->
<!ENTITY rsquor SDATA "[rsquor]"--rising single quote, right (high)-->
<!ENTITY vellip SDATA "[vellip]"--vertical ellipsis-->

<!ENTITY hybull SDATA "[hybull]"--rectangle, filled (hyphen bullet)-->
<!ENTITY loz    SDATA "[loz   ]"--/lozenge - lozenge or total mark-->
<!ENTITY lozf   SDATA "[lozf  ]"--/blacklozenge - lozenge, filled-->
<!ENTITY ltri   SDATA "[ltri  ]"--/triangleleft B: l triangle, open-->
<!ENTITY rtri   SDATA "[rtri  ]"--/triangleright B: r triangle, open-->
<!ENTITY starf  SDATA "[starf ]"--/bigstar - star, filled-->

<!ENTITY natur  SDATA "[natur ]"--/natural - music natural-->
<!ENTITY rx     SDATA "[rx    ]"--pharmaceutical prescription (Rx)-->
<!ENTITY sext   SDATA "[sext  ]"--sextile (6-pointed star)-->

<!ENTITY target SDATA "[target]"--register mark or target-->
<!ENTITY dlcrop SDATA "[dlcrop]"--downward left crop mark -->
<!ENTITY drcrop SDATA "[drcrop]"--downward right crop mark -->
<!ENTITY ulcrop SDATA "[ulcrop]"--upward left crop mark -->
<!ENTITY urcrop SDATA "[urcrop]"--upward right crop mark -->
```

D.4.3.4 Box and Line Drawing Characters

```
<!-- (C) International Organization for Standardization 1986
     Permission to copy in any form is granted for use with
     conforming SGML systems and applications as defined in
     ISO 8879, provided this notice is included in all copies.
-->
<!-- Character entity set. Typical invocation:
     <!ENTITY % ISObox PUBLIC
       "ISO 8879-1986//ENTITIES Box and Line Drawing//EN">
     %ISObox;
-->
<!-- All names are in the form: box1234, where:
     box = constants that identify a box drawing entity.
     1&2 = v, V, u, U, d, D, Ud, or uD, as follows:
       v = vertical line for full height.
       u = upper half of vertical line.
       d = downward (lower) half of vertical line.
     3&4 = h, H, l, L, r, R, Lr, or lR, as follows:
       h = horizontal line for full width.
       l = left half of horizontal line.
       r = right half of horizontal line.
```

```
         In all cases, an upper-case letter means a double or heavy line.
-->
<!ENTITY boxh    SDATA "[boxh  ]"--horizontal line -->
<!ENTITY boxv    SDATA "[boxv  ]"--vertical line-->
<!ENTITY boxur   SDATA "[boxur ]"--upper right quadrant-->
<!ENTITY boxul   SDATA "[boxul ]"--upper left quadrant-->
<!ENTITY boxdl   SDATA "[boxdl ]"--lower left quadrant-->
<!ENTITY boxdr   SDATA "[boxdr ]"--lower right quadrant-->
<!ENTITY boxvr   SDATA "[boxvr ]"--upper and lower right quadrants-->
<!ENTITY boxhu   SDATA "[boxhu ]"--upper left and right quadrants-->
<!ENTITY boxvl   SDATA "[boxvl ]"--upper and lower left quadrants-->
<!ENTITY boxhd   SDATA "[boxhd ]"--lower left and right quadrants-->
<!ENTITY boxvh   SDATA "[boxvh ]"--all four quadrants-->
<!ENTITY boxvR   SDATA "[boxvR ]"--upper and lower right quadrants-->
<!ENTITY boxhU   SDATA "[boxhU ]"--upper left and right quadrants-->
<!ENTITY boxvL   SDATA "[boxvL ]"--upper and lower left quadrants-->
<!ENTITY boxhD   SDATA "[boxhD ]"--lower left and right quadrants-->
<!ENTITY boxvH   SDATA "[boxvH ]"--all four quadrants-->
<!ENTITY boxH    SDATA "[boxH  ]"--horizontal line-->
<!ENTITY boxV    SDATA "[boxV  ]"--vertical line-->
<!ENTITY boxUR   SDATA "[boxUR ]"--upper right quadrant-->
<!ENTITY boxUL   SDATA "[boxUL ]"--upper left quadrant-->
<!ENTITY boxDL   SDATA "[boxDL ]"--lower left quadrant-->
<!ENTITY boxDR   SDATA "[boxDR ]"--lower right quadrant-->
<!ENTITY boxVR   SDATA "[boxVR ]"--upper and lower right quadrants-->
<!ENTITY boxHU   SDATA "[boxHU ]"--upper left and right quadrants-->
<!ENTITY boxVL   SDATA "[boxVL ]"--upper and lower left quadrants-->
<!ENTITY boxHD   SDATA "[boxHD ]"--lower left and right quadrants-->
<!ENTITY boxVH   SDATA "[boxVH ]"--all four quadrants-->
<!ENTITY boxVr   SDATA "[boxVr ]"--upper and lower right quadrants-->
<!ENTITY boxHu   SDATA "[boxHu ]"--upper left and right quadrants-->
<!ENTITY boxVl   SDATA "[boxVl ]"--upper and lower left quadrants-->
<!ENTITY boxHd   SDATA "[boxHd ]"--lower left and right quadrants-->
<!ENTITY boxVh   SDATA "[boxVh ]"--all four quadrants-->
<!ENTITY boxuR   SDATA "[boxuR ]"--upper right quadrant-->
<!ENTITY boxUl   SDATA "[boxUl ]"--upper left quadrant-->
<!ENTITY boxdL   SDATA "[boxdL ]"--lower left quadrant-->
<!ENTITY boxDr   SDATA "[boxDr ]"--lower right quadrant-->
<!ENTITY boxUr   SDATA "[boxUr ]"--upper right quadrant-->
<!ENTITY boxuL   SDATA "[boxuL ]"--upper left quadrant-->
<!ENTITY boxDl   SDATA "[boxDl ]"--lower left quadrant-->
<!ENTITY boxdR   SDATA "[boxdR ]"--lower right quadrant-->
```

D.4.4 Technical Use

As many technical symbols can be used in more than one context,
the entity names in this category normally describe the graphic
visually, rather than attempting to convey the semantic concept that
is usually associated with it.

The following abbreviations are used with substantial consistency:
Prefixes:
l=left; r=right; u=up; d=down; h=horizontal; v=vertical

```
        b=back, reversed
2       cu=curly
        g=greater than; l=less than;
4       n=negated;
        o=in circle
6       s=small, short;
        sq=square shaped
8       thk=thick;
        x=extended, long, big;
10    Bodies:
        ap=approx;
12      arr=arrow; har=harpoon
        pr=precedes; sc=succeeds
14      sub=subset; sup=superset
      Suffixes:
16      b=boxed;
        f=filled, black, solid
18      e=single equals; E=double equals;
        hk=hook
20      s=slant
        t=tail
22      w=wavy, squiggly;
        2=two of
24    Upper-case letter means "doubled" (or sometimes "two of")
```

NOTE — Visual depictions of most of the technical use entities are
26 identified by their entity names in *Association of American Publishers
    Electronic Manuscript Series: Markup of Mathematical Formulas*, published
28 by the Association of American Publishers, Inc., 2005 Massachusetts
    Avenue, N.W., Washington, DC 20036, U.S.A.

D.4.4.1 General

```
<!-- (C) International Organization for Standardization 1986
     Permission to copy in any form is granted for use with
     conforming SGML systems and applications as defined in
     ISO 8879, provided this notice is included in all copies.
-->
<!-- Character entity set. Typical invocation:
     <!ENTITY % ISOtech PUBLIC
       "ISO 8879-1986//ENTITIES General Technical//EN">
     %ISOtech;
-->
<!ENTITY aleph  SDATA "[aleph ]"--/aleph =aleph, Hebrew-->
<!ENTITY and    SDATA "[and   ]"--/wedge /land B: =logical and-->
<!ENTITY ang90  SDATA "[ang90 ]"--=right (90 degree) angle-->
<!ENTITY angsph SDATA "[angsph]"--/sphericalangle =angle-spherical-->
<!ENTITY ap     SDATA "[ap    ]"--/approx R: =approximate-->
```

```
<!ENTITY becaus SDATA "[becaus]"--/because R: =because-->
<!ENTITY bottom SDATA "[bottom]"--/bot B: =perpendicular-->
<!ENTITY cap    SDATA "[cap   ]"--/cap B: =intersection-->
<!ENTITY cong   SDATA "[cong  ]"--/cong R: =congruent with-->
<!ENTITY conint SDATA "[conint]"--/oint L: =contour integral operator-->
<!ENTITY cup    SDATA "[cup   ]"--/cup B: =union or logical sum-->
<!ENTITY equiv  SDATA "[equiv ]"--/equiv R: =identical with-->
<!ENTITY exist  SDATA "[exist ]"--/exists =at least one exists-->
<!ENTITY forall SDATA "[forall]"--/forall =for all-->
<!ENTITY fnof   SDATA "[fnof  ]"--=function of (italic small f)-->
<!ENTITY ge     SDATA "[ge    ]"--/geq /ge R: =greater-than-or-equal-->
<!ENTITY iff    SDATA "[iff   ]"--/iff =if and only if-->
<!ENTITY infin  SDATA "[infin ]"--/infty =infinity-->
<!ENTITY int    SDATA "[int   ]"--/int L: =integral operator-->
<!ENTITY isin   SDATA "[isin  ]"--/in R: =set membership-->
<!ENTITY lang   SDATA "[lang  ]"--/langle O: =left angle bracket-->
<!ENTITY lArr   SDATA "[lArr  ]"--/Leftarrow A: =is implied by-->
<!ENTITY le     SDATA "[le    ]"--/leq /le R: =less-than-or-equal-->
<!ENTITY minus  SDATA "[minus ]"--B: =minus sign-->
<!ENTITY mnplus SDATA "[mnplus]"--/mp B: =minus-or-plus sign-->
<!ENTITY nabla  SDATA "[nabla ]"--/nabla =del, Hamilton operator-->
<!ENTITY ne     SDATA "[ne    ]"--/ne /neq R: =not equal-->
<!ENTITY ni     SDATA "[ni    ]"--/ni /owns R: =contains-->
<!ENTITY or     SDATA "[or    ]"--/vee /lor B: =logical or-->
<!ENTITY par    SDATA "[par   ]"--/parallel R: =parallel-->
<!ENTITY part   SDATA "[part  ]"--/partial =partial differential-->
<!ENTITY permil SDATA "[permil]"--=per thousand-->
<!ENTITY perp   SDATA "[perp  ]"--/perp R: =perpendicular-->
<!ENTITY prime  SDATA "[prime ]"--/prime =prime or minute-->
<!ENTITY Prime  SDATA "[Prime ]"--=double prime or second-->
<!ENTITY prop   SDATA "[prop  ]"--/propto R: =is proportional to-->
<!ENTITY radic  SDATA "[radic ]"--/surd =radical-->
<!ENTITY rang   SDATA "[rang  ]"--/rangle C: =right angle bracket-->
<!ENTITY rArr   SDATA "[rArr  ]"--/Rightarrow A: =implies-->
<!ENTITY sim    SDATA "[sim   ]"--/sim R: =similar-->
<!ENTITY sime   SDATA "[sime  ]"--/simeq R: =similar, equals-->
<!ENTITY square SDATA "[square]"--/square B: =square-->
<!ENTITY sub    SDATA "[sub   ]"--/subset R: =subset or is implied by-->
<!ENTITY sube   SDATA "[sube  ]"--/subseteq R: =subset, equals-->
<!ENTITY sup    SDATA "[sup   ]"--/supset R: =superset or implies-->
<!ENTITY supe   SDATA "[supe  ]"--/supseteq R: =superset, equals-->
<!ENTITY there4 SDATA "[there4]"--/therefore R: =therefore-->
<!ENTITY Verbar SDATA "[Verbar]"--/Vert =dbl vertical bar-->


<!ENTITY angst  SDATA "[angst ]"--Angstrom =capital A, ring-->
<!ENTITY bernou SDATA "[bernou]"--Bernoulli function (script capital B)-->
<!ENTITY compfn SDATA "[compfn]"--B: composite function (small circle)-->
<!ENTITY Dot    SDATA "[Dot   ]"--=dieresis or umlaut mark-->
<!ENTITY DotDot SDATA "[DotDot]"--four dots above-->
<!ENTITY hamilt SDATA "[hamilt]"--Hamiltonian (script capital H)-->
<!ENTITY lagran SDATA "[lagran]"--Lagrangian (script capital L)-->
<!ENTITY lowast SDATA "[lowast]"--low asterisk-->
<!ENTITY notin  SDATA "[notin ]"--N: negated set membership-->
<!ENTITY order  SDATA "[order ]"--order of (script small o)-->
<!ENTITY phmmat SDATA "[phmmat]"--physics M-matrix (script capital M)-->
<!ENTITY tdot   SDATA "[tdot  ]"--three dots above-->
<!ENTITY tprime SDATA "[tprime]"--triple prime-->
<!ENTITY wedgeq SDATA "[wedgeq]"--R: corresponds to (wedge, equals)-->
```

D.4.4.2 Greek Symbols

2 This entity set defines the Greek character names for use as variable names in technical applications.

```
<!-- (C) International Organization for Standardization 1986
     Permission to copy in any form is granted for use with
     conforming SGML systems and applications as defined in
     ISO 8879, provided this notice is included in all copies.
-->
<!-- Character entity set. Typical invocation:
     <!ENTITY % ISOgrk3 PUBLIC
       "ISO 8879-1986//ENTITIES Greek Symbols//EN">
     %ISOgrk3;
-->
<!ENTITY alpha     SDATA "[alpha ]"-==small alpha, Greek-->
<!ENTITY beta      SDATA "[beta  ]"-==small beta, Greek-->
<!ENTITY gamma     SDATA "[gamma ]"-==small gamma, Greek-->
<!ENTITY Gamma     SDATA "[Gamma ]"-==capital Gamma, Greek-->
<!ENTITY gammad    SDATA "[gammad]"--/digamma-->
<!ENTITY delta     SDATA "[delta ]"-==small delta, Greek-->
<!ENTITY Delta     SDATA "[Delta ]"-==capital Delta, Greek-->
<!ENTITY epsi      SDATA "[epsi  ]"-==small epsilon, Greek-->
<!ENTITY epsiv     SDATA "[epsiv ]"--/varepsilon-->
<!ENTITY epsis     SDATA "[epsis ]"--/straightepsilon-->
<!ENTITY zeta      SDATA "[zeta  ]"-==small zeta, Greek-->
<!ENTITY eta       SDATA "[eta   ]"-==small eta, Greek-->
<!ENTITY thetas    SDATA "[thetas]"--straight theta-->
<!ENTITY Theta     SDATA "[Theta ]"-==capital Theta, Greek-->
<!ENTITY thetav    SDATA "[thetav]"--/vartheta - curly or open theta-->
<!ENTITY iota      SDATA "[iota  ]"-==small iota, Greek-->
<!ENTITY kappa     SDATA "[kappa ]"-==small kappa, Greek-->
<!ENTITY kappav    SDATA "[kappav]"--/varkappa-->
<!ENTITY lambda    SDATA "[lambda]"-==small lambda, Greek-->
<!ENTITY Lambda    SDATA "[Lambda]"-==capital Lambda, Greek-->
<!ENTITY mu        SDATA "[mu    ]"-==small mu, Greek-->
<!ENTITY nu        SDATA "[nu    ]"-==small nu, Greek-->
<!ENTITY xi        SDATA "[xi    ]"-==small xi, Greek-->
<!ENTITY Xi        SDATA "[Xi    ]"-==capital Xi, Greek-->
<!ENTITY pi        SDATA "[pi    ]"-==small pi, Greek-->
<!ENTITY piv       SDATA "[piv   ]"--/varpi-->
<!ENTITY Pi        SDATA "[Pi    ]"-==capital Pi, Greek-->
<!ENTITY rho       SDATA "[rho   ]"-==small rho, Greek-->
<!ENTITY rhov      SDATA "[rhov  ]"--/varrho-->
<!ENTITY sigma     SDATA "[sigma ]"-==small sigma, Greek-->
<!ENTITY Sigma     SDATA "[Sigma ]"-==capital Sigma, Greek-->
<!ENTITY sigmav    SDATA "[sigmav]"--/varsigma-->
<!ENTITY tau       SDATA "[tau   ]"-==small tau, Greek-->
<!ENTITY upsi      SDATA "[upsi  ]"-==small upsilon, Greek-->
<!ENTITY Upsi      SDATA "[Upsi  ]"-==capital Upsilon, Greek-->
<!ENTITY phis      SDATA "[phis  ]"--/straightphi - straight phi-->
<!ENTITY Phi       SDATA "[Phi   ]"-==capital Phi, Greek-->
<!ENTITY phiv      SDATA "[phiv  ]"--/varphi - curly or open phi-->
<!ENTITY chi       SDATA "[chi   ]"-==small chi, Greek-->
<!ENTITY psi       SDATA "[psi   ]"-==small psi, Greek-->
<!ENTITY Psi       SDATA "[Psi   ]"-==capital Psi, Greek-->
<!ENTITY omega     SDATA "[omega ]"-==small omega, Greek-->
<!ENTITY Omega     SDATA "[Omega ]"-==capital Omega, Greek-->
```

D.4.4.3 Alternative Greek Symbols

2

4

The characters in this entity set can be used in conjunction with the preceding one when a separate class of variables is required. By convention, they are displayed in a different font or style (usually emboldened).

```
<!-- (C) International Organization for Standardization 1986
     Permission to copy in any form is granted for use with
     conforming SGML systems and applications as defined in
     ISO 8879, provided this notice is included in all copies.
-->
<!-- Character entity set. Typical invocation:
     <!ENTITY % ISOgrk4 PUBLIC
       "ISO 8879-1986//ENTITIES Alternative Greek Symbols//EN">
     %ISOgrk4;
-->
<!ENTITY b.alpha  SDATA "[b.alpha ]"--=small alpha, Greek-->
<!ENTITY b.beta   SDATA "[b.beta  ]"--=small beta, Greek-->
<!ENTITY b.gamma  SDATA "[b.gamma ]"--=small gamma, Greek-->
<!ENTITY b.Gamma  SDATA "[b.Gamma ]"--=capital Gamma, Greek-->
<!ENTITY b.gammad SDATA "[b.gammad]"--/digamma-->
<!ENTITY b.delta  SDATA "[b.delta ]"--=small delta, Greek-->
<!ENTITY b.Delta  SDATA "[b.Delta ]"--=capital Delta, Greek-->
<!ENTITY b.epsi   SDATA "[b.epsi  ]"--=small epsilon, Greek-->
<!ENTITY b.epsiv  SDATA "[b.epsiv ]"--/varepsilon-->
<!ENTITY b.epsis  SDATA "[b.epsis ]"--/straightepsilon-->
<!ENTITY b.zeta   SDATA "[b.zeta  ]"--=small zeta, Greek-->
<!ENTITY b.eta    SDATA "[b.eta   ]"--=small eta, Greek-->
<!ENTITY b.thetas SDATA "[b.thetas]"--straight theta-->
<!ENTITY b.Theta  SDATA "[b.Theta ]"--=capital Theta, Greek-->
<!ENTITY b.thetav SDATA "[b.thetav]"--/vartheta - curly or open theta-->
<!ENTITY b.iota   SDATA "[b.iota  ]"--=small iota, Greek-->
<!ENTITY b.kappa  SDATA "[b.kappa ]"--=small kappa, Greek-->
<!ENTITY b.kappav SDATA "[b.kappav]"--/varkappa-->
<!ENTITY b.lambda SDATA "[b.lambda]"--=small lambda, Greek-->
<!ENTITY b.Lambda SDATA "[b.Lambda]"--=capital Lambda, Greek-->
<!ENTITY b.mu     SDATA "[b.mu    ]"--=small mu, Greek-->
<!ENTITY b.nu     SDATA "[b.nu    ]"--=small nu, Greek-->
<!ENTITY b.xi     SDATA "[b.xi    ]"--=small xi, Greek-->
<!ENTITY b.Xi     SDATA "[b.Xi    ]"--=capital Xi, Greek-->
<!ENTITY b.pi     SDATA "[b.pi    ]"--=small pi, Greek-->
<!ENTITY b.Pi     SDATA "[b.Pi    ]"--=capital Pi, Greek-->
<!ENTITY b.piv    SDATA "[b.piv   ]"--/varpi-->
<!ENTITY b.rho    SDATA "[b.rho   ]"--=small rho, Greek-->
<!ENTITY b.rhov   SDATA "[b.rhov  ]"--/varrho-->
<!ENTITY b.sigma  SDATA "[b.sigma ]"--=small sigma, Greek-->
<!ENTITY b.Sigma  SDATA "[b.Sigma ]"--=capital Sigma, Greek-->
<!ENTITY b.sigmav SDATA "[b.sigmav]"--/varsigma-->
<!ENTITY b.tau    SDATA "[b.tau   ]"--=small tau, Greek-->
<!ENTITY b.upsi   SDATA "[b.upsi  ]"--=small upsilon, Greek-->
<!ENTITY b.Upsi   SDATA "[b.Upsi  ]"--=capital Upsilon, Greek-->
<!ENTITY b.phis   SDATA "[b.phis  ]"--/straightphi - straight phi-->
<!ENTITY b.Phi    SDATA "[b.Phi   ]"--=capital Phi, Greek-->
<!ENTITY b.phiv   SDATA "[b.phiv  ]"--/varphi - curly or open phi-->
<!ENTITY b.chi    SDATA "[b.chi   ]"--=small chi, Greek-->
<!ENTITY b.psi    SDATA "[b.psi   ]"--=small psi, Greek-->
<!ENTITY b.Psi    SDATA "[b.Psi   ]"--=capital Psi, Greek-->
```

```
<!ENTITY b.omega   SDATA "[b.omega ]"--=small omega, Greek-->
<!ENTITY b.Omega   SDATA "[b.Omega ]"--=capital Omega, Greek-->
```

D.4.5 Additional Mathematical Symbols

D.4.5.1 Ordinary Symbols

```
<!-- (C) International Organization for Standardization 1986
     Permission to copy in any form is granted for use with
     conforming SGML systems and applications as defined in
     ISO 8879, provided this notice is included in all copies.
-->
<!-- Character entity set. Typical invocation:
     <!ENTITY % ISOamso PUBLIC
       "ISO 8879-1986//ENTITIES Added Math Symbols: Ordinary//EN">
     %ISOamso;
-->
<!ENTITY ang    SDATA "[ang   ]"--/angle - angle-->
<!ENTITY angmsd SDATA "[angmsd]"--/measuredangle - angle-measured-->
<!ENTITY beth   SDATA "[beth  ]"--/beth - beth, Hebrew-->
<!ENTITY bprime SDATA "[bprime]"--/backprime - reverse prime-->
<!ENTITY comp   SDATA "[comp  ]"--/complement - complement sign-->
<!ENTITY daleth SDATA "[daleth]"--/daleth - daleth, Hebrew-->
<!ENTITY ell    SDATA "[ell   ]"--/ell - cursive small l-->
<!ENTITY empty  SDATA "[empty ]"--/emptyset /varnothing =small o, slash-->
<!ENTITY gimel  SDATA "[gimel ]"--/gimel - gimel, Hebrew-->
<!ENTITY image  SDATA "[image ]"--/Im - imaginary-->
<!ENTITY inodot SDATA "[inodot]"--/imath =small i, no dot-->
<!ENTITY jnodot SDATA "[jnodot]"--/jmath - small j, no dot-->
<!ENTITY nexist SDATA "[nexist]"--/nexists - negated exists-->
<!ENTITY oS     SDATA "[oS    ]"--/circledS - capital S in circle-->
<!ENTITY planck SDATA "[planck]"--/hbar /hslash - Planck's over 2pi-->
<!ENTITY real   SDATA "[real  ]"--/Re - real-->
<!ENTITY sbsol  SDATA "[sbsol ]"--/sbs - short reverse solidus-->
<!ENTITY vprime SDATA "[vprime]"--/varprime - prime, variant-->
<!ENTITY weierp SDATA "[weierp]"--/wp - Weierstrass p-->
```

D.4.5.2 Binary and Large Operators

```
<!-- (C) International Organization for Standardization 1986
     Permission to copy in any form is granted for use with
     conforming SGML systems and applications as defined in
     ISO 8879, provided this notice is included in all copies.
-->
<!-- Character entity set. Typical invocation:
     <!ENTITY % ISOamsb PUBLIC
       "ISO 8879-1986//ENTITIES Added Math Symbols: Binary Operators//EN">
     %ISOamsb;
-->
<!ENTITY amalg  SDATA "[amalg ]"--/amalg B: amalgamation or coproduct-->
<!ENTITY Barwed SDATA "[Barwed]"--/doublebarwedge B: log and, dbl bar-->
```

```
<!ENTITY barwed SDATA "[barwed]"--/barwedge B: logical and, bar above-->
<!ENTITY Cap    SDATA "[Cap  ]"--/Cap /doublecap B: dbl intersection-->
<!ENTITY Cup    SDATA "[Cup  ]"--/Cup /doublecup B: dbl union-->
<!ENTITY cuvee  SDATA "[cuvee ]"--/curlyvee B: curly logical or-->
<!ENTITY cuwed  SDATA "[cuwed ]"--/curlywedge B: curly logical and-->
<!ENTITY diam   SDATA "[diam  ]"--/diamond B: open diamond-->
<!ENTITY divonx SDATA "[divonx]"--/divideontimes B: division on times-->
<!ENTITY intcal SDATA "[intcal]"--/intercal B: intercal-->
<!ENTITY lthree SDATA "[lthree]"--/leftthreetimes B:-->
<!ENTITY ltimes SDATA "[ltimes]"--/ltimes B: times sign, left closed-->
<!ENTITY minusb SDATA "[minusb]"--/boxminus B: minus sign in box-->
<!ENTITY oast   SDATA "[oast  ]"--/circledast B: asterisk in circle-->
<!ENTITY ocir   SDATA "[ocir  ]"--/circledcirc B: open dot in circle-->
<!ENTITY odash  SDATA "[odash ]"--/circleddash B: hyphen in circle-->
<!ENTITY odot   SDATA "[odot  ]"--/odot B: middle dot in circle-->
<!ENTITY ominus SDATA "[ominus]"--/ominus B: minus sign in circle-->
<!ENTITY oplus  SDATA "[oplus ]"--/oplus B: plus sign in circle-->
<!ENTITY osol   SDATA "[osol  ]"--/oslash B: solidus in circle-->
<!ENTITY otimes SDATA "[otimes]"--/otimes B: multiply sign in circle-->
<!ENTITY plusb  SDATA "[plusb ]"--/boxplus B: plus sign in box-->
<!ENTITY plusdo SDATA "[plusdo]"--/dotplus B: plus sign, dot above-->
<!ENTITY rthree SDATA "[rthree]"--/rightthreetimes B:-->
<!ENTITY rtimes SDATA "[rtimes]"--/rtimes B: times sign, right closed-->
<!ENTITY sdot   SDATA "[sdot  ]"--/cdot B: small middle dot-->
<!ENTITY sdotb  SDATA "[sdotb ]"--/dotsquare /boxdot B: small dot in box-->
<!ENTITY setmn  SDATA "[setmn ]"--/setminus B: reverse solidus-->
<!ENTITY sqcap  SDATA "[sqcap ]"--/sqcap B: square intersection-->
<!ENTITY sqcup  SDATA "[sqcup ]"--/sqcup B: square union-->
<!ENTITY ssetmn SDATA "[ssetmn]"--/smallsetminus B: sm reverse solidus-->
<!ENTITY sstarf SDATA "[sstarf]"--/star B: small star, filled-->
<!ENTITY timesb SDATA "[timesb]"--/boxtimes B: multiply sign in box-->
<!ENTITY top    SDATA "[top  ]"--/top B: inverted perpendicular-->
<!ENTITY uplus  SDATA "[uplus ]"--/uplus B: plus sign in union-->
<!ENTITY wreath SDATA "[wreath]"--/wr B: wreath product-->
<!ENTITY xcirc  SDATA "[xcirc ]"--/bigcirc B: large circle-->
<!ENTITY xdtri  SDATA "[xdtri ]"--/bigtriangledown B: big dn tri, open-->
<!ENTITY xutri  SDATA "[xutri ]"--/bigtriangleup B: big up tri, open-->
<!ENTITY coprod SDATA "[coprod]"--/coprod L: coproduct operator-->
<!ENTITY prod   SDATA "[prod  ]"--/prod L: product operator-->
<!ENTITY sum    SDATA "[sum  ]"--/sum L: summation operator-->
```

D.4.5.3 Relations

```
<!-- (C) International Organization for Standardization 1986
     Permission to copy in any form is granted for use with
     conforming SGML systems and applications as defined in
     ISO 8879, provided this notice is included in all copies.
-->
<!-- Character entity set. Typical invocation:
     <!ENTITY % ISOamsr PUBLIC
       "ISO 8879-1986//ENTITIES Added Math Symbols: Relations//EN">
     %ISOamsr;
-->
<!ENTITY ape    SDATA "[ape  ]"--/approxeq R: approximate, equals-->
<!ENTITY asymp  SDATA "[asymp ]"--/asymp R: asymptotically equal to-->
<!ENTITY bcong  SDATA "[bcong ]"--/backcong R: reverse congruent-->
<!ENTITY bepsi  SDATA "[bepsi ]"--/backepsilon R: such that-->
```

```
<!ENTITY bowtie SDATA "[bowtie]"--/bowtie R:-->
<!ENTITY bsim   SDATA "[bsim  ]"--/backsim R: reverse similar-->
<!ENTITY bsime  SDATA "[bsime ]"--/backsimeq R: reverse similar, eq-->
<!ENTITY bump   SDATA "[bump  ]"--/Bumpeq R: bumpy equals-->
<!ENTITY bumpe  SDATA "[bumpe ]"--/bumpeq R: bumpy equals, equals-->
<!ENTITY cire   SDATA "[cire  ]"--/circeq R: circle, equals-->
<!ENTITY colone SDATA "[colone]"--/coloneq R: colon, equals-->
<!ENTITY cuepr  SDATA "[cuepr ]"--/curlyeqprec R: curly eq, precedes-->
<!ENTITY cuesc  SDATA "[cuesc ]"--/curlyeqsucc R: curly eq, succeeds-->
<!ENTITY cupre  SDATA "[cupre ]"--/curlypreceq R: curly precedes, eq-->
<!ENTITY dashv  SDATA "[dashv ]"--/dashv R: dash, vertical-->
<!ENTITY ecir   SDATA "[ecir  ]"--/eqcirc R: circle on equals sign-->
<!ENTITY ecolon SDATA "[ecolon]"--/eqcolon R: equals, colon-->
<!ENTITY eDot   SDATA "[eDot  ]"--/doteqdot /Doteq R: eq, even dots-->
<!ENTITY esdot  SDATA "[esdot ]"--/doteq R: equals, single dot above-->
<!ENTITY efDot  SDATA "[efDot ]"--/fallingdotseq R: eq, falling dots-->
<!ENTITY egs    SDATA "[egs   ]"--/eqslantgtr R: equal-or-gtr, slanted-->
<!ENTITY els    SDATA "[els   ]"--/eqslantless R: eq-or-less, slanted-->
<!ENTITY erDot  SDATA "[erDot ]"--/risingdotseq R: eq, rising dots-->
<!ENTITY fork   SDATA "[fork  ]"--/pitchfork R: pitchfork-->
<!ENTITY frown  SDATA "[frown ]"--/frown R: down curve-->
<!ENTITY gap    SDATA "[gap   ]"--/gtrapprox R: greater, approximate-->
<!ENTITY gsdot  SDATA "[gsdot ]"--/gtrdot R: greater than, single dot-->
<!ENTITY gE     SDATA "[gE    ]"--/geqq R: greater, double equals-->
<!ENTITY gel    SDATA "[gel   ]"--/gtreqless R: greater, equals, less-->
<!ENTITY gEl    SDATA "[gEl   ]"--/gtreqqless R: gt, dbl equals, less-->
<!ENTITY ges    SDATA "[ges   ]"--/geqslant R: gt-or-equal, slanted-->
<!ENTITY Gg     SDATA "[Gg    ]"--/ggg /Gg /gggtr R: triple gtr-than-->
<!ENTITY gl     SDATA "[gl    ]"--/gtrless R: greater, less-->
<!ENTITY gsim   SDATA "[gsim  ]"--/gtrsim R: greater, similar-->
<!ENTITY Gt     SDATA "[Gt    ]"--/gg R: dbl greater-than sign-->
<!ENTITY lap    SDATA "[lap   ]"--/lessapprox R: less, approximate-->
<!ENTITY ldot   SDATA "[ldot  ]"--/lessdot R: less than, with dot-->
<!ENTITY lE     SDATA "[lE    ]"--/leqq R: less, double equals-->
<!ENTITY lEg    SDATA "[lEg   ]"--/lesseqqgtr R: less, dbl eq, greater-->
<!ENTITY leg    SDATA "[leg   ]"--/lesseqgtr R: less, eq, greater-->
<!ENTITY les    SDATA "[les   ]"--/leqslant R: less-than-or-eq, slant-->
<!ENTITY lg     SDATA "[lg    ]"--/lessgtr R: less, greater-->
<!ENTITY Ll     SDATA "[Ll    ]"--/Ll /lll /llless R: triple less-than-->
<!ENTITY lsim   SDATA "[lsim  ]"--/lesssim R: less, similar-->
<!ENTITY Lt     SDATA "[Lt    ]"--/ll R: double less-than sign-->
<!ENTITY ltrie  SDATA "[ltrie ]"--/trianglelefteq R: left triangle, eq-->
<!ENTITY mid    SDATA "[mid   ]"--/mid R:-->
<!ENTITY models SDATA "[models]"--/models R:-->
<!ENTITY pr     SDATA "[pr    ]"--/prec R: precedes-->
<!ENTITY prap   SDATA "[prap  ]"--/precapprox R: precedes, approximate-->
<!ENTITY pre    SDATA "[pre   ]"--/preceq R: precedes, equals-->
<!ENTITY prsim  SDATA "[prsim ]"--/precsim R: precedes, similar-->
<!ENTITY rtrie  SDATA "[rtrie ]"--/trianglerighteq R: right tri, eq-->
<!ENTITY samalg SDATA "[samalg]"--/smallamalg R: small amalg-->
<!ENTITY sc     SDATA "[sc    ]"--/succ R: succeeds-->
<!ENTITY scap   SDATA "[scap  ]"--/succapprox R: succeeds, approximate-->
<!ENTITY sccue  SDATA "[sccue ]"--/succcurlyeq R: succeeds, curly eq-->
<!ENTITY sce    SDATA "[sce   ]"--/succeq R: succeeds, equals-->
<!ENTITY scsim  SDATA "[scsim ]"--/succsim R: succeeds, similar-->
<!ENTITY sfrown SDATA "[sfrown]"--/smallfrown R: small down curve-->
<!ENTITY smid   SDATA "[smid  ]"--/shortmid R:-->
<!ENTITY smile  SDATA "[smile ]"--/smile R: up curve-->
<!ENTITY spar   SDATA "[spar  ]"--/shortparallel R: short parallel-->
<!ENTITY sqsub  SDATA "[sqsub ]"--/sqsubset R: square subset-->
<!ENTITY sqsube SDATA "[sqsube]"--/sqsubseteq R: square subset, equals-->
```

```
<!ENTITY sqsup  SDATA "[sqsup ]"--/sqsupset R: square superset-->
<!ENTITY sqsupe SDATA "[sqsupe]"--/sqsupseteq R: square superset, eq-->
<!ENTITY ssmile SDATA "[ssmile]"--/smallsmile R: small up curve-->
<!ENTITY Sub    SDATA "[Sub   ]"--/Subset R: double subset-->
<!ENTITY subE   SDATA "[subE  ]"--/subseteqq R: subset, dbl equals-->
<!ENTITY Sup    SDATA "[Sup   ]"--/Supset R: dbl superset-->
<!ENTITY supE   SDATA "[supE  ]"--/supseteqq R: superset, dbl equals-->
<!ENTITY thkap  SDATA "[thkap ]"--/thickapprox R: thick approximate-->
<!ENTITY thksim SDATA "[thksim]"--/thicksim R: thick similar-->
<!ENTITY trie   SDATA "[trie  ]"--/triangleq R: triangle, equals-->
<!ENTITY twixt  SDATA "[twixt ]"--/between R: between-->
<!ENTITY vdash  SDATA "[vdash ]"--/vdash R: vertical, dash-->
<!ENTITY Vdash  SDATA "[Vdash ]"--/Vdash R: dbl vertical, dash-->
<!ENTITY vDash  SDATA "[vDash ]"--/vDash R: vertical, dbl dash-->
<!ENTITY veebar SDATA "[veebar]"--/veebar R: logical or, bar below-->
<!ENTITY vltri  SDATA "[vltri ]"--/vartriangleleft R: l tri, open, var-->
<!ENTITY vprop  SDATA "[vprop ]"--/varpropto R: proportional, variant-->
<!ENTITY vrtri  SDATA "[vrtri ]"--/vartriangleright R: r tri, open, var-->
<!ENTITY Vvdash SDATA "[Vvdash]"--/Vvdash R: triple vertical, dash-->
```

D.4.5.4 Negated Relations

```
<!-- (C) International Organization for Standardization 1986
     Permission to copy in any form is granted for use with
     conforming SGML systems and applications as defined in
     ISO 8879, provided this notice is included in all copies.
-->
<!-- Character entity set. Typical invocation:
     <!ENTITY % ISOamsn PUBLIC
       "ISO 8879-1986//ENTITIES
        Added Math Symbols: Negated Relations//EN">
     %ISOamsn;
-->
<!ENTITY gnap   SDATA "[gnap  ]"--/gnapprox N: greater, not approximate-->
<!ENTITY gne    SDATA "[gne   ]"--/gneq N: greater, not equals-->
<!ENTITY gnE    SDATA "[gnE   ]"--/gneqq N: greater, not dbl equals-->
<!ENTITY gnsim  SDATA "[gnsim ]"--/gnsim N: greater, not similar-->
<!ENTITY gvnE   SDATA "[gvnE  ]"--/gvertneqq N: gt, vert, not dbl eq-->
<!ENTITY lnap   SDATA "[lnap  ]"--/lnapprox N: less, not approximate-->
<!ENTITY lnE    SDATA "[lnE   ]"--/lneqq N: less, not double equals-->
<!ENTITY lne    SDATA "[lne   ]"--/lneq N: less, not equals-->
<!ENTITY lnsim  SDATA "[lnsim ]"--/lnsim N: less, not similar-->
<!ENTITY lvnE   SDATA "[lvnE  ]"--/lvertneqq N: less, vert, not dbl eq-->
<!ENTITY nap    SDATA "[nap   ]"--/napprox N: not approximate-->
<!ENTITY ncong  SDATA "[ncong ]"--/ncong N: not congruent with-->
<!ENTITY nequiv SDATA "[nequiv]"--/nequiv N: not identical with-->
<!ENTITY ngE    SDATA "[ngE   ]"--/ngeqq N: not greater, dbl equals-->
<!ENTITY nge    SDATA "[nge   ]"--/ngeq N: not greater-than-or-equal-->
<!ENTITY nges   SDATA "[nges  ]"--/ngeqslant N: not gt-or-eq, slanted-->
<!ENTITY ngt    SDATA "[ngt   ]"--/ngtr N: not greater-than-->
<!ENTITY nle    SDATA "[nle   ]"--/nleq N: not less-than-or-equal-->
<!ENTITY nlE    SDATA "[nlE   ]"--/nleqq N: not less, dbl equals-->
<!ENTITY nles   SDATA "[nles  ]"--/nleqslant N: not less-or-eq, slant-->
<!ENTITY nlt    SDATA "[nlt   ]"--/nless N: not less-than-->
<!ENTITY nltri  SDATA "[nltri ]"--/ntriangleleft N: not left triangle-->
<!ENTITY nltrie SDATA "[nltrie]"--/ntrianglelefteq N: not l tri, eq-->
<!ENTITY nmid   SDATA "[nmid  ]"--/nmid-->
```

```
<!ENTITY npar    SDATA "[npar  ]"--/nparallel N: not parallel-->
<!ENTITY npr     SDATA "[npr   ]"--/nprec N: not precedes-->
<!ENTITY npre    SDATA "[npre  ]"--/npreceq N: not precedes, equals-->
<!ENTITY nrtri   SDATA "[nrtri ]"--/ntriangleright N: not rt triangle-->
<!ENTITY nrtrie  SDATA "[nrtrie]"--/ntrianglerighteq N: not r tri, eq-->
<!ENTITY nsc     SDATA "[nsc   ]"--/nsucc N: not succeeds-->
<!ENTITY nsce    SDATA "[nsce  ]"--/nsucceq N: not succeeds, equals-->
<!ENTITY nsim    SDATA "[nsim  ]"--/nsim N: not similar-->
<!ENTITY nsime   SDATA "[nsime ]"--/nsimeq N: not similar, equals-->
<!ENTITY nsmid   SDATA "[nsmid ]"--/nshortmid-->
<!ENTITY nspar   SDATA "[nspar ]"--/nshortparallel N: not short par-->
<!ENTITY nsub    SDATA "[nsub  ]"--/nsubset N: not subset-->
<!ENTITY nsube   SDATA "[nsube ]"--/nsubseteq N: not subset, equals-->
<!ENTITY nsubE   SDATA "[nsubE ]"--/nsubseteqq N: not subset, dbl eq-->
<!ENTITY nsup    SDATA "[nsup  ]"--/nsupset N: not superset-->
<!ENTITY nsupE   SDATA "[nsupE ]"--/nsupseteqq N: not superset, dbl eq-->
<!ENTITY nsupe   SDATA "[nsupe ]"--/nsupseteq N: not superset, equals-->
<!ENTITY nvdash  SDATA "[nvdash]"--/nvdash N: not vertical, dash-->
<!ENTITY nvDash  SDATA "[nvDash]"--/nvDash N: not vertical, dbl dash-->
<!ENTITY nVDash  SDATA "[nVDash]"--/nVDash N: not dbl vert, dbl dash-->
<!ENTITY nVdash  SDATA "[nVdash]"--/nVdash N: not dbl vertical, dash-->
<!ENTITY prnap   SDATA "[prnap ]"--/precnapprox N: precedes, not approx-->
<!ENTITY prnE    SDATA "[prnE  ]"--/precneqq N: precedes, not dbl eq-->
<!ENTITY prnsim  SDATA "[prnsim]"--/precnsim N: precedes, not similar-->
<!ENTITY scnap   SDATA "[scnap ]"--/succnapprox N: succeeds, not approx-->
<!ENTITY scnE    SDATA "[scnE  ]"--/succneqq N: succeeds, not dbl eq-->
<!ENTITY scnsim  SDATA "[scnsim]"--/succnsim N: succeeds, not similar-->
<!ENTITY subne   SDATA "[subne ]"--/subsetneq N: subset, not equals-->
<!ENTITY subnE   SDATA "[subnE ]"--/subsetneqq N: subset, not dbl eq-->
<!ENTITY supne   SDATA "[supne ]"--/supsetneq N: superset, not equals-->
<!ENTITY supnE   SDATA "[supnE ]"--/supsetneqq N: superset, not dbl eq-->
<!ENTITY vsubnE  SDATA "[vsubnE]"--/subsetneqq N: subset not dbl eq, var-->
<!ENTITY vsubne  SDATA "[vsubne]"--/subsetneq N: subset, not eq, var-->
<!ENTITY vsupne  SDATA "[vsupne]"--/supsetneq N: superset, not eq, var-->
<!ENTITY vsupnE  SDATA "[vsupnE]"--/supsetneqq N: super not dbl eq, var-->
```

D.4.5.5 Arrow Relations

```
<!-- (C) International Organization for Standardization 1986
     Permission to copy in any form is granted for use with
     conforming SGML systems and applications as defined in
     ISO 8879, provided this notice is included in all copies.
-->
<!-- Character entity set. Typical invocation:
     <!ENTITY % ISOamsa PUBLIC
       "ISO 8879-1986//ENTITIES Added Math Symbols: Arrow Relations//EN">
     %ISOamsa;
-->
<!ENTITY cularr  SDATA "[cularr]"--/curvearrowleft A: left curved arrow -->
<!ENTITY curarr  SDATA "[curarr]"--/curvearrowright A: rt curved arrow -->
<!ENTITY dArr    SDATA "[dArr  ]"--/Downarrow A: down dbl arrow -->
<!ENTITY darr2   SDATA "[darr2 ]"--/downdownarrows A: two down arrows -->
<!ENTITY dharl   SDATA "[dharl ]"--/downleftharpoon A: dn harpoon-left -->
<!ENTITY dharr   SDATA "[dharr ]"--/downrightharpoon A: down harpoon-rt -->
<!ENTITY lAarr   SDATA "[lAarr ]"--/Lleftarrow A: left triple arrow -->
<!ENTITY Larr    SDATA "[Larr  ]"--/twoheadleftarrow A:-->
<!ENTITY larr2   SDATA "[larr2 ]"--/leftleftarrows A: two left arrows -->
```

```
<!ENTITY larrhk SDATA "[larrhk]"--/hookleftarrow A: left arrow-hooked -->
<!ENTITY larrlp SDATA "[larrlp]"--/looparrowleft A: left arrow-looped -->
<!ENTITY larrtl SDATA "[larrtl]"--/leftarrowtail A: left arrow-tailed -->
<!ENTITY lhard  SDATA "[lhard ]"--/leftharpoondown A: l harpoon-down -->
<!ENTITY lharu  SDATA "[lharu ]"--/leftharpoonup A: left harpoon-up -->
<!ENTITY hArr   SDATA "[hArr  ]"--/Leftrightarrow A: l&r dbl arrow -->
<!ENTITY harr   SDATA "[harr  ]"--/leftrightarrow A: l&r arrow -->
<!ENTITY lrarr2 SDATA "[lrarr2]"--/leftrightarrows A: l arr over r arr -->
<!ENTITY rlarr2 SDATA "[rlarr2]"--/rightleftarrows A: r arr over l arr -->
<!ENTITY harrw  SDATA "[harrw ]"--/leftrightsquigarrow A: l&r arr-wavy -->
<!ENTITY rlhar2 SDATA "[rlhar2]"--/rightleftharpoons A: r harp over l -->
<!ENTITY lrhar2 SDATA "[lrhar2]"--/leftrightharpoons A: l harp over r -->
<!ENTITY lsh    SDATA "[lsh   ]"--/Lsh A:-->
<!ENTITY map    SDATA "[map   ]"--/mapsto A:-->
<!ENTITY mumap  SDATA "[mumap ]"--/multimap A:-->
<!ENTITY nearr  SDATA "[nearr ]"--/nearrow A: NE pointing arrow -->
<!ENTITY nlArr  SDATA "[nlArr ]"--/nLeftarrow A: not implied by -->
<!ENTITY nlarr  SDATA "[nlarr ]"--/nleftarrow A: not left arrow -->
<!ENTITY nhArr  SDATA "[nhArr ]"--/nLeftrightarrow A: not l&r dbl arr -->
<!ENTITY nharr  SDATA "[nharr ]"--/nleftrightarrow A: not l&r arrow -->
<!ENTITY nrarr  SDATA "[nrarr ]"--/nrightarrow A: not right arrow -->
<!ENTITY nrArr  SDATA "[nrArr ]"--/nRightarrow A: not implies -->
<!ENTITY nwarr  SDATA "[nwarr ]"--/nwarrow A: NW pointing arrow -->
<!ENTITY olarr  SDATA "[olarr ]"--/circlearrowleft A: l arr in circle -->
<!ENTITY orarr  SDATA "[orarr ]"--/circlearrowright A: r arr in circle -->
<!ENTITY rAarr  SDATA "[rAarr ]"--/Rrightarrow A: right triple arrow -->
<!ENTITY Rarr   SDATA "[Rarr  ]"--/twoheadrightarrow A:-->
<!ENTITY rarr2  SDATA "[rarr2 ]"--/rightrightarrows A: two rt arrows -->
<!ENTITY rarrhk SDATA "[rarrhk]"--/hookrightarrow A: rt arrow-hooked -->
<!ENTITY rarrlp SDATA "[rarrlp]"--/looparrowright A: rt arrow-looped -->
<!ENTITY rarrtl SDATA "[rarrtl]"--/rightarrowtail A: rt arrow-tailed -->
<!ENTITY rarrw  SDATA "[rarrw ]"--/squigarrowright A: rt arrow-wavy -->
<!ENTITY rhard  SDATA "[rhard ]"--/rightharpoondown A: rt harpoon-down -->
<!ENTITY rharu  SDATA "[rharu ]"--/rightharpoonup A: rt harpoon-up -->
<!ENTITY rsh    SDATA "[rsh   ]"--/Rsh A:-->
<!ENTITY drarr  SDATA "[drarr ]"--/searrow A: downward rt arrow -->
<!ENTITY dlarr  SDATA "[dlarr ]"--/swarrow A: downward l arrow -->
<!ENTITY uArr   SDATA "[uArr  ]"--/Uparrow A: up dbl arrow -->
<!ENTITY uarr2  SDATA "[uarr2 ]"--/upuparrows A: two up arrows -->
<!ENTITY vArr   SDATA "[vArr  ]"--/Updownarrow A: up&down dbl arrow -->
<!ENTITY varr   SDATA "[varr  ]"--/updownarrow A: up&down arrow -->
<!ENTITY uharl  SDATA "[uharl ]"--/upleftharpoon A: up harpoon-left -->
<!ENTITY uharr  SDATA "[uharr ]"--/uprightharpoon A: up harp-r-->
<!ENTITY xlArr  SDATA "[xlArr ]"--/Longleftarrow A: long l dbl arrow -->
<!ENTITY xhArr  SDATA "[xhArr ]"--/Longleftrightarrow A: long l&r dbl arr-->
<!ENTITY xharr  SDATA "[xharr ]"--/longleftrightarrow A: long l&r arr -->
<!ENTITY xrArr  SDATA "[xrArr ]"--/Longrightarrow A: long rt dbl arr -->
```

D.4.5.6 Opening and Closing Delimiters

```
<!-- (C) International Organization for Standardization 1986
     Permission to copy in any form is granted for use with
     conforming SGML systems and applications as defined in
     ISO 8879, provided this notice is included in all copies.
-->
<!-- Character entity set. Typical invocation:
     <!ENTITY % ISOamsc PUBLIC
```

```
        "ISO 8879-1986//ENTITIES Added Math Symbols: Delimiters//EN">
     %ISOamsc;
-->
<!ENTITY rceil  SDATA "[rceil ]"--/rceil C: right ceiling-->
<!ENTITY rfloor SDATA "[rfloor]"--/rfloor C: right floor-->
<!ENTITY rpargt SDATA "[rpargt]"--/rightparengtr C: right paren, gt-->
<!ENTITY urcorn SDATA "[urcorn]"--/urcorner C: upper right corner-->
<!ENTITY drcorn SDATA "[drcorn]"--/lrcorner C: downward right corner-->
<!ENTITY lceil  SDATA "[lceil ]"--/lceil O: left ceiling-->
<!ENTITY lfloor SDATA "[lfloor]"--/lfloor O: left floor-->
<!ENTITY lpargt SDATA "[lpargt]"--/leftparengtr O: left parenthesis, gt-->
<!ENTITY ulcorn SDATA "[ulcorn]"--/ulcorner O: upper left corner-->
<!ENTITY dlcorn SDATA "[dlcorn]"--/llcorner O: downward left corner-->
```

Annex E
Application Examples

This annex covers three main subjects:

a) A practical document type definition, which can be referenced as public text. This DTD is explained in detail in a separate publication, ISO TR 9573, *Techniques for Using SGML*.

b) Using SGML with graphics represented in the Computer Graphics Metafile data content notation. This subject is explored in far greater depth in a paper that I wrote with Donald D. Chamberlin, of the IBM Almaden Research Center, entitled "Graphic Applications of the Standard Generalized Markup Language (SGML)". The paper appeared in *Computers & Graphics* vol. 11, No. 4, pp.343-358, 1987.

c) How to preserve device independence when using ISO 2022 techniques for code extension.

(This annex does not form an integral part of this International Standard.)

E.1 Document Type Definition

2   The following example is supplied as an illustration of a practical document type definition. It is primarily intended to illustrate the
4   correct use of markup declarations, but it follows good design practices as well.

```
<!-- (C) International Organization for Standardization 1986
   Permission to copy in any form is granted for use with
```

```
      conforming SGML systems and applications as defined in
      ISO 8879, provided this notice is included in all copies.
-->
<!-- Public document type definition. Typical invocation:
<!DOCTYPE general PUBLIC "ISO 8879-1986//DTD General Document//EN" [
  <!ENTITY % ISOnum PUBLIC
    "ISO 8879-1986//ENTITIES Numeric and Special Graphic//EN">
  <!ENTITY % ISOpub PUBLIC
    "ISO 8879-1986//ENTITIES Publishing//EN">
  %ISOnum; %ISOpub;
      (Parameter entities and additional elements can be defined here.)
]>
-->
<!ENTITY % doctype "general" -- Document type generic identifier -->
<!--This is a document type definition for a "general" document.
It contains the necessary elements for use in many applications, and is
organized so that other elements can be added in the document type
declaration subset. -->

                    <!-- Entity Naming Conventions -->
<!--
                Prefix = where used:
      p.  = in paragraphs (also in phrases if .ph suffix)
      s.  = in sections (i.e., among paragraphs)
      ps. = in paragraphs and sections
      i.  = where allowed by inclusion exceptions
      m.  = content model or declared content
      a.  = attribute definition
      NONE= specific use defined in models
                Suffix = allowed content:
      .ph = elements whose content is %m.ph
      .d  = elements whose content has same definition
      NONE= elements with unique definitions
-->
                    <!-- Element Tokens -->
<!ENTITY % p.em.ph "hp1|hp2|hp3|hp0|cit" -- Emphasized phrases -->
<!ENTITY % p.rf.ph "hdref|figref" -- Reference phrases -->
<!ENTITY % p.rf.d  "fnref|liref" -- References (empty) -->
<!ENTITY % p.zz.ph "q|(%p.em.ph;)|(%p.rf.ph;)|(%p.rf.d;)" -- All phrases -->
<!ENTITY % ps.ul.d "ol|sl|ul|nl" -- Unit-item lists -->
<!ENTITY % ps.list "%ps.ul.d;|dl|gl" -- All lists -->
<!ENTITY % ps.elem "xmp|lq|lines|tbl|address|artwork" -- Other elements -->
<!ENTITY % ps.zz   "(%ps.elem;)|(%ps.list;)" -- Para/sect subelements -->
<!ENTITY % s.p.d   "p|note" -- Simple paragraphs -->
<!ENTITY % s.top   "top1|top2|top3|top4" -- Topics -->
```

```
<!ENTITY % s.zz     "(%s.p.d;)|(%ps.zz;)|(%s.top;)" -- Section subelements -->
<!ENTITY % i.float  "fig|fn" -- Floating elements -->
<!ENTITY % fm.d     "abstract|preface" --Front matter-->
<!ENTITY % bm.d     "glossary|bibliog" -- Back matter -->


                    <!-- Model Groups -->
<!ENTITY % m.ph     "(#PCDATA|(%p.zz.ph;))*" -- Phrase model -->
<!ENTITY % m.p      "(#PCDATA|(%p.zz.ph;)|(%ps.zz;))*" -- Paragraph model -->
<!ENTITY % m.pseq   "(p, ((%s.p.d;)|(%ps.zz;))*)" -- Paragraph sequence -->
<!ENTITY % m.top    "(th?, p, (%s.zz;)*)" -- Topic model -->


                    <!-- Document Structure -->
<!--        ELEMENTS   MIN  CONTENT (EXCEPTIONS) -->
<!ELEMENT %doctype;    - -  (frontm?, body, appendix?, backm?)
                            +(ix|%i.float;)>
<!ELEMENT frontm       - O  (titlep, (%fm.d;|h1)*, toc?, figlist?)>
<!ELEMENT body         - O  (h0+|h1+)>
<!ELEMENT appendix     - O  (h1+)>
<!ELEMENT backm        - O  ((%bm.d;|h1)*, index?)>
<!ELEMENT (toc|figlist|index)    -- Table of contents, figure list, --
                       - O  EMPTY -- and index have generated content -->


                    <!-- Title Page Elements -->
<!--        ELEMENTS   MIN  CONTENT (EXCEPTIONS) -->
<!ELEMENT titlep       - O  (title & docnum? & date? & abstract? &
                            (author|address|%s.zz;)*)>
<!ELEMENT (docnum|date|author)
                       - O  (#PCDATA) -- Document number, etc. -->
<!ELEMENT title        - O  (tline+) -- Document title -->
<!ELEMENT tline        O O  %m.ph; -- Title line -->


                    <!-- Headed Sections -->
<!--        ELEMENTS   MIN  CONTENT (EXCEPTIONS) -->
<!ELEMENT h0           - O  (h0t, (%s.zz;)*, h1+) -- Part -->
<!ELEMENT (h1|%bm.d;|%fm.d;)
                       - O  (h1t, (%s.zz;)*, h2*) -- Chapter -->
<!ELEMENT h2           - O  (h2t, (%s.zz;)*, h3*) -- Section -->
<!ELEMENT h3           - O  (h3t, (%s.zz;)*, h4*) -- Subsection -->
<!ELEMENT h4           - O  (h4t, (%s.zz;)*) -- Sub-subsection -->
<!ELEMENT (h0t|h1t|h2t|h3t|h4t)
                       O O  %m.ph;    -- Headed section titles -->


                <!-- Topics (Captioned Subsections) -->
<!--        ELEMENTS   MIN  CONTENT (EXCEPTIONS) -->
<!ELEMENT top1         - O  %m.top; -(top1) -- Topic 1 -->
```

```
<!ELEMENT top2          - O  %m.top; -(top2) -- Topic 2 -->
<!ELEMENT top3          - O  %m.top; -(top3) -- Topic 3 -->
<!ELEMENT top4          - O  %m.top; -(top4) -- Topic 4 -->
<!ELEMENT th            - O  %m.ph; -- Topic heading -->


                 <!-- Elements in Sections or Paragraphs -->
<!--      ELEMENTS   MIN  CONTENT (EXCEPTIONS) -->
<!ELEMENT address       - -  (aline+)>
<!ELEMENT aline         O O  %m.ph; -- Address line -->
<!ELEMENT artwork       - O  EMPTY>
<!ELEMENT dl            - -  ((dthd+, ddhd)?, (dt+, dd)*)>
<!ELEMENT dt            - O  %m.ph; -- Definition term -->
<!ELEMENT (dthd|ddhd)- O  (#PCDATA) -- Headings for dt and dd -->
<!ELEMENT dd            - O  %m.pseq; -- Definition description -->
<!ELEMENT gl            - -  (gt, (gd|gdg))* -- Glossary list -->
<!ELEMENT gt            - O  (#PCDATA) -- Glossary term -->
<!ELEMENT gdg           - O  (gd+) -- Glossary definition group -->
<!ELEMENT gd            - O  %m.pseq; -- Glossary definition -->
<!ELEMENT (%ps.ul.d;) - -  (li*) -- Unit item lists -->
<!ELEMENT li            - O  %m.pseq; -- List item -->
<!ELEMENT lines         O O  %m.pseq; -- Line elements -->
<!ELEMENT (lq|xmp)      - -  %m.pseq; -(%i.float;) -- Long quote -->
<!ELEMENT (%s.p.d;)     O O  %m.p; -- Paragraphs -->


                      <!-- Table -->
<!--      ELEMENTS   MIN  CONTENT (EXCEPTIONS) -->
<!ELEMENT tbl           - -  (hr*, fr*, r+)>
<!ELEMENT hr            - O  (h+) -- Heading row -->
<!ELEMENT fr            - O  (f+) -- Footing row -->
<!ELEMENT r             O O  (c+) -- Row (body of table) -->
<!ELEMENT c             O O  %m.pseq; -- Cell in body row -->
<!ELEMENT (f|h)         O O  (#PCDATA) -- Cell in fr or hr -->


                      <!-- Phrases -->
<!--      ELEMENTS   MIN  CONTENT (EXCEPTIONS) -->
<!ELEMENT (%p.em.ph;) - -  %m.ph;  -- Emphasized phrases -->
<!ELEMENT q             - -  %m.ph;  -- Quotation -->
<!ELEMENT (%p.rf.ph;) - -  %m.ph;  -- Reference phrases -->
<!ELEMENT (%p.rf.d;)    - O  EMPTY    -- Generated references -->


                 <!-- Includable Subelements -->
<!--      ELEMENTS   MIN  CONTENT (EXCEPTIONS) -->
<!ELEMENT fig           - -  (figbody, (figcap, figdesc?)?) -(%i.float;)>
<!ELEMENT figbody       O O  %m.pseq; -- Figure body -->
<!ELEMENT figcap        - O  %m.ph; -- Figure caption -->
```

```
<!ELEMENT  figdesc    - O  %m.pseq; -- Figure description -->
<!ELEMENT fn          - -  %m.pseq; -(%i.float;) -- Footnote -->
<!ELEMENT ix          - O  (#PCDATA) -- Index entry -->


              <!-- Attribute Definition Lists -->
<!-- As this document type definition is intended for basic SGML
     documents, in which the LINK features are not supported, it was
     necessary to include link attributes in the definitions.
-->
<!--      ELEMENTS    NAME     VALUE     DEFAULT -->
<!ATTLIST %doctype;   security CDATA     #IMPLIED
                      status   CDATA     ""
                      version  CDATA     #IMPLIED>
<!ATTLIST title       stitle   CDATA     #IMPLIED>
<!ATTLIST (h0|h1|h2|%bm.d;|%fm.d;)
                      id       ID        #IMPLIED
                      stitle   CDATA     #IMPLIED>
<!ATTLIST (h3|h4)     id       ID        #IMPLIED>
<!ATTLIST artwork     sizex    NMTOKEN   textsize
          -- Default is current text width in column. --
                      sizey    NUTOKEN   #REQUIRED
          -- (Sizes are specified in the units supported by the
             application in which this declaration appears;
             for sizex, the keyword "textsize" can be used
             to mean "the width at which previous text was set").
          -->
<!ATTLIST gl          compact  (compact) #IMPLIED
                      termhi   NUMBER    2>
<!ATTLIST dl          compact  (compact) #IMPLIED
                      headhi   NUMBER    2
                      termhi   NUMBER    2
                      tsize    NUMBERS   9
          -- The number of dt elements per dd must equal the
             number of numbers specified for tsize (here 1).
             The number of dthd elements must be the same.
          -->
<!ATTLIST gd          source   CDATA     #IMPLIED>
<!ATTLIST (%ps.ul.d;) compact  (compact) #IMPLIED>
<!ATTLIST li          id       ID        #IMPLIED>
<!ATTLIST xmp         depth    NUTOKEN   #IMPLIED
                      keep     NMTOKEN   all
                      lines    (flow|lines) lines>
<!ATTLIST tbl         cols     NUMBERS   #REQUIRED
             -- The number of c elements per r must equal
                the number of numbers specified for cols
```

```
              (similarly, the number of h per hr and f per fr).
        -->
<!ATTLIST c          heading  (h)       #IMPLIED
        -- If h is specified, cell is row heading.
        -->
<!ATTLIST (%p.rf.ph;) refid   IDREF     #CONREF
                     page    (yes|no)  yes>
<!ATTLIST fnref      refid    IDREF     #REQUIRED>
<!ATTLIST liref      refid    IDREF     #REQUIRED
                     page    (yes|no)  yes>
<!ATTLIST fig        id       ID        #IMPLIED
                     frame   (box|rule|none)     none
                     place   (top|fixed|bottom)  top
                     width   (column|page)       page
                     align   (left|center|right) center
                     lines   (flow|lines)        lines>
<!ATTLIST ix         id       ID        #IMPLIED
                     print    CDATA     #IMPLIED
                     see      CDATA     #IMPLIED
                     seeid    IDREF     #IMPLIED>
<!ATTLIST fn         id       ID        #IMPLIED>


           <!-- Entities for Short References -->
<!ENTITY    ptag   STARTTAG "p"     -- Paragraph start-tag -->
<!ENTITY    qtag   STARTTAG "q"     -- Quoted phrase start-tag -->
<!ENTITY    qetag  ENDTAG   "q"     -- Quoted phrase end-tag -->
<!ENTITY    endtag ENDTAG   ""      -- Empty end-tag for any element -->


<!SHORTREF docmap                   -- Map for general use --
              "&#RS;&#RE;" ptag     -- Blank line is <p> --
              '"'          qtag     -- " is <q> -->
<!USEMAP    docmap %doctype;>
<!SHORTREF qmap                     -- Map for quoted phrases' --
              '"'          qetag    -- " is </q> -->
<!USEMAP    qmap q>
<!SHORTREF ixmap                    -- Map for index entries --
              "&#RE;"      endtag   -- Record end is </> -->
<!USEMAP    ixmap ix>
```

The capacity calculation for this document type definition is as
follows:

```
         23 entities declared with 732 characters of
                                   text.
```

▼

```
        78 element types declared with 696 model
2                                         tokens and
        8 exception groups with 13 names.
4       39 attributes declared with 23 group members
                                             and
6          80 characters of default value text.
        0 IDs and 0 ID references specified.
8          0 data content notations with 0 text
                                       characters.
10         3 short reference maps declared.
     8644 capacity points required (24% of 35000
12                                   permitted).
```

E.2 Computer Graphics Metafile

14 Pictures generated by a computer graphics program can be included in an SGML document by the techniques illustrated in figure 12 ⌈ 537 ⌉ and figure 13 ⌈ 539 ⌉.

16 The illustrated notations are encodings of the Computer Graphics Metafile (CGM). As SGML delimiters could occur in such a file, it 18 should be incorporated with a content reference so that it will not be scanned by the SGML parser. It can safely be merged into an 20 SGML entity only if it was examined and found not to contain delimiters that would be recognized in replaceable character data, or if it 22 was pre-processed to convert such delimiters to entity references.

Note that the "graphic" element contains no attributes for position-24 ing or referencing it. The element is analagous to formatted text or to white space left for paste-in art (like the "artwork" element in the 26 document type definition in E.1 ⌈ 530 ⌉), in that it normally is formatted at the same point in the logical document as it is entered. To 28 move it elsewhere, or to frame it, or to give it an ID by which it can be referenced, it is necessary to include it in the body of a figure 30 element.

If the element declaration for "graphic" were stored in the file 32 "graphic.etd", the following declaration would allow graphic metafiles to occur in figures within a "general" document:

34 <!DOCTYPE general PUBLIC "ISO 8879-1986//DTD General

```
<!NOTATION cgmchar    PUBLIC
               "ISO 8632/2//NOTATION Character encoding//EN" >
<!NOTATION cgmclear    PUBLIC
               "ISO 8632/4//NOTATION Clear text encoding//EN" >
<!ELEMENT graphic     - O  RCDATA>
<!ATTLIST graphic
    --         NAME        VALUE                        DEFAULT --
               file        ENTITY                       #CONREF
               -- The external entity containing the metafile.
                  If not specified, the metafile is the syntactic
                  content of the element.
               --
               coding      NOTATION (cgmclear|cgmchar) cgmclear
               -- Data content notation when the metafile is not
                  external.  Ignored if it is external because
                  notation is specified on the entity declaration.
               --
               picnum      NUMBER                       1
               -- Sequence number of picture if the metafile
                  contains more than one.
               --
               x0          CDATA --lower left corner-- #IMPLIED
               x1          CDATA                        #IMPLIED
               y0          CDATA --upper right corner--#IMPLIED
               y1          CDATA                        #IMPLIED
               -- Coordinates of view port into picture, in
                  virtual device coordinates (a real number in
                  the format -n.nEn).  Defaults are the numbers
                  that refer to the VDC extent.
               --
```

Figure 12 — Graphics Metafile Attributes (1 of 2): Encoding and View

```
                                          Document//EN"
2   [<!ENTITY % ps.elem "graphic|xmp|lq|lines|tbl|address
                                       |artwork">
4   <!ENTITY % graphic SYSTEM "graphic.etd">
    %graphic;
6   ]>
```

E.3 Device-Independent Code Extension

NOTE — This clause is intended only to exemplify approaches to using
ISO 2022 graphic repertoire code extension techniques with SGML; not all
combinations of the techniques are discussed, nor is a complete design
offered for any one of them. The reader is assumed to have a knowledge of
ISO 2022, ISO 4873, and ISO 6937.

SGML documents can contain multiple graphic character
2 repertoires by employing the code extension techniques of ISO
2022. Moreover, these techniques can be supplemented with
4 SGML entity references and short references to achieve a degree
of freedom from device and code dependencies that is not possible
6 with code extension alone.

The basic principle behind code extension is that a bit combination
8 can represent more than one character: which character depends
on the control characters and escape sequences that have
10 preceded it. When using code extension with SGML, then, it is
necessary to allow code extension control characters in SGML
12 entities in a manner that precludes confusing delimiters with them,
or with the extended characters.

E.3.1 Code Extension Facilities

14 Those facilities that require the least user effort and parsing
overhead to avoid confusion with delimiters when markup
16 suppression is not used, are those in which all graphic markup
characters are in the G0 set, which occupies the left (or only) side
18 of the code table, and the code is:
 a) 8-bit, with a G1 set always occupying the right. The G1
20 character repertoire can be changed as needed with the
appropriate designating escape sequence. No locking shifts
22 are used.
 b) 8-bit, with G1, G2, and G3 sets invoked by locking shifts into
24 the right side of the code table. If more than three
supplementary sets are needed, the G1, G2, and G3
26 character repertoires can be changed with the appropriate
designating escape sequences.
28 c) 7-bit or 8-bit, with characters from the G2 and G3 sets
invoked by single shifts into the left (or only) side of the code
30 table. As above, the G2 and G3 character repertoires can be
changed as needed. In 8-bit codes, this facility can be
32 combined with either of the other two.

Illustrated in figure 14 ⌐539⌐ is the *function character identification*
34 parameter that should replace that of the multicode basic concrete
syntax when using the above code extension facilities.

```
            sizex      NMTOKEN                          #IMPLIED
            sizey      NUTOKEN                          #IMPLIED
            -- Either sizex or sizey can be specified, or both
               (in the units supported by the DTD in
               which this declaration appears; for sizex, the
               keyword "textsize" can be used to mean "the
               width at which previous text was set").
               If either is specified alone, the scaling,
               alignx, and aligny attributes are ignored,
               as scaling will necessarily be uniform.
            --
            scaling    (uniform|nonunif)              uniform
            alignx     (left|center|right)            center
            aligny     (top|middle|bottom)            middle
            -- If both sizex and sizey are specified, then
               if scaling is nonuniform, alignx and aligny
               are ignored as the actual x and y will equal
               the specified sizex and sizey.  Else, the
               actual x and y will be such that one will
               equal its specified size and the other will
               be less than its specified size.  The alignx
               or aligny attribute will apply to the one
               that is less than its specified size.
            --
            --*-*-*-*-*-*-*-*-*-*-*-*-*-*-*-*-*-*-*-*--
            -- The following table summarizes the
               relationship between the size, scaling,
               and alignment attributes:

            SizeX  SizeY  Scaling  AlignX      AlignY
            (yes)  (no)
            (no)   (yes)
            (yes)  (yes)  nonunif
            (yes)  (yes)  uniform  if x<SizeX  if y<SizeY --
            --*-*-*-*-*-*-*-*-*-*-*-*-*-*-*-*-*-*-*-*--
            orient     (0|90|180|270)                   0
            -- Angle of rotation in degrees. --
    >
```

Figure 13 — Graphics Metafile Attributes (2 of 2): Size and Rotation

```
    FUNCTION RE                 13
             RS                 10
             SPACE              32
             TAB      SEPCHAR    9
             -- Functions for graphic repertoire code extension --
             -- Markup is recognized while they are in use. --
             ESC      FUNCHAR  27 -- Escape --
             LS0      FUNCHAR  15 -- Locking-shift zero (G0 set) --
                                  -- LS1R, LS2R, and LS3R
                                     are ESC sequences --
             SS2      FUNCHAR 142 -- Single-shift two (G2 set) --
             SS3      FUNCHAR 143 -- Single-shift three (G3 set) --
```

Figure 14 — Function Characters for Device-Independent Multicode Concrete Syntaxes

E.3.1.1 Avoiding False Delimiter Recognition

When code extension is done with a single G1 set in conformance
with ISO 4873 there is little or no possibility of false delimiter
recognition. Other code extension techniques introduce a greater
possibility, which can be avoided if the implementor and/ôr user
observe the following practices:

a) All markup, including short references and entity references,
    must be done in the G0 set.

b) If an entity shifts to a supplementary set, it must return to the
    G0 set (unless the purpose of the entity was to effect the
    shift).

c) Escape sequences other than shift functions (for example,
    designator and announcer sequences) should be entered in
    comment declarations.

A ***com*** delimiter string should be assigned that does not
appear in any of the non-shifting escape sequences. With the
reference delimiter set, for example, all public escape
sequences up to five characters long, and private ones of up
to three characters, can be entered in comment declarations
with no possibility of false delimiter recognition.

Non-shifting escape sequences can also be entered in *mixed
content*, but only if they contain no delimiter strings that could
be recognized, or if short references are defined to prevent
false recognition, as explained below.

d) Strings that occur in shift functions should not be assigned to
    delimiter roles recognized in the CON recognition mode
    unless short references are defined to prevent false
    recognition.

For example, in the reference delimiter set, the right curly
bracket, the tilde, and the vertical bar are short reference
delimiters, but they are also found in the LS1R, LS2R, and
LS3R shift sequences required when G2 and G3 sets are
used. As they are short reference delimiters, they could easily
be disabled by simply never mapping them to entities. But if
they are needed, they can be kept available by defining the
LS2R and LS3R sequences to be short references that are
never mapped to entities.

The following parameters would be added to the *short
reference delimiters* parameter of the *SGML declaration*:

```
       SHORTREF SGMLREF
2                  -- Added SHORTREFs to prevent false recognition      ▼
                                                      of --
4                  -- single-character SHORTREFs when preceded by        ▼
                                                     ESC --
6          "&#ESC;|" -- LS3R contains SHORTREF "|" --
           "&#ESC;}" -- LS2R contains SHORTREF "}" --
8          "&#ESC;~" -- LS2R contains SHORTREF "~" --
```

As a longer delimiter string is always recognized in preference
10   to a shorter one contained in it (even if the longer is a short
reference that is mapped to nothing), the vertical bar and right
12   curly bracket will not erroneously be recognized as delimiters
when they occur within shift sequences.

14   e) If single shifts are used, each sequence comprised of SS2 or
SS3 followed by the bit combination of the first character of a
16   delimiter string recognized in CON mode must be defined as a
short reference to prevent false recognition of the delimiter, in
18   the manner previously described.

In the reference delimiter set, the affected characters are the
20   ampersand (&), less-than sign (<), right square
bracket (]), and solidus (/), plus the first character
22   of the short reference delimiters that begin with a graphic
character.

E.3.1.2 Eliminating Device and Code Dependencies

24   An SGML document that uses ISO 2022 code extension facilities
can be submitted to other systems or devices that use the same
26   facilities. In such cases, the concrete syntaxes described in D.3.1
⸢501⸣ can be used, and the techniques described in this sub-clause
28   are not needed. However, not all systems or devices to which an
SGML document might be directed will support all of the ISO 2022
30   code extension techniques. Many formatters and photocomposers,
for example, will require specialized font change and positioning
32   commands to accomplish what code extension achieves with
escape sequences and shifts.

34   The usual SGML technique for achieving output independence is to
use an entity reference for any character that is not in both the G0
36   set and the *syntax-reference character set*. While the entity name
remains constant, the definition varies depending on the output
38   system, in the manner explained in D.4 ⸢502⸣. The public entity

sets defined in that clause can be used for this purpose; they con-

2   tain entity names for the present and proposed character repertoires defined by ISO 6937, among others.

4   When code extension is used for document creation, the burden of
entering entity references can greatly be reduced, as each supple-

6   mentary set character can be defined as a short reference and
mapped to the appropriate entity. This is not possible, however,

8   when the characters occur in a context in which short references
are not recognized, such as a *character data* element or marked

10   section, or where markup recognition has been suppressed by
function characters.

Annex F
Implementation
Considerations

This annex describes one possible model of an SGML implementation, as a means of emphasizing and clarifiying some of the subtleties of SGML parsing. A complementary discussion, "The ISO 8879 Element Structure Information Set (ESIS)", appears in attachment 1 of Appendix B 588 .

(This annex does not form an integral part of this International Standard.)

2 An SGML system presents two faces — one to the marked up document and one to the application programs that process the
4 marked up document.

The requirements and permitted variations for the document
6 interface are specified in the body of this International Standard. The interface to the application programs is not standardized, but
8 this annex identifies some useful markup support functions for SGML systems that allow user-developed programs access to the
10 SGML parser and entity manager.

The discussion is in general terms and does not cover all aspects
12 of implementation. It is intended solely to provide the flavor of some implementation issues, and in no sense should it be considered a
14 specification.

F.1 A Model of SGML Parsing

As a background for the discussion of functions, it is necessary to
2 have in mind a model of the SGML parsing process.

NOTE — This section should not be construed as a requirement for a
4 particular SGML parser architecture or implementation techniques. Any
terms that might suggest the contrary (such as, for example, procedure,
6 stack, service routine) are used only as a means of expressing functional
capabilities.

8 Moreover, the model described here is merely one the developers of SGML
have found useful during design discussions: it is not the only model
10 possible, may not be the best, is certainly incomplete, and may even be
internally inconsistent. It is helpful, though, for understanding how an SGML
12 parser can relate to other components of a system, and is offered for that
purpose only.

F.1.1 Physical Input

14 The SGML parser does not read a physical input stream. All input
management is handled by the entity manager. The parser is
16 invoked by the system and given characters to parse.

F.1.1.1 Entities

When the parser recognizes an entity reference it tells the entity
18 manager, which treats the new entity as the physical input source
until the entity ends, at which point the entity manager advises the
20 parser (i.e., it generates an *Ee*). The entity manager will then obtain
succeeding input from the original entity.

22 The parser considers entity boundaries to be significant when
recognizing multi-character delimiters and delimiters-in-context, and
24 when ensuring that entity references in delimited text do not violate
the prescriptions of the language. Otherwise, it sees only a
26 continuous string of characters, without regard to the entities in
which they occur.

F.1.1.2 Record Boundaries

If the document contains record boundaries, they are processed as
2 defined in this International Standard. The recognition of delimiter
strings that contain record boundaries is done during the initial
4 parse of the input. The determination that a data **RE** should be
ignored (as required by 7.6.1 ⟮ 321 ⟯), however, cannot be done until
6 all references have been resolved and minimized markup has been
normalized.

F.1.2 Recognition Modes

8 A significant property of SGML is the distinction among delimiter
recognition modes, as described in 9.6.1 ⟮ 359 ⟯. After the prolog,
10 the document is initially scanned in CON mode, with text characters
processed as defined in 7.6 ⟮ 319 ⟯, until one of the following occur-
12 rences causes a change of mode:

— Descriptive markup (start-tag or end-tag):

14   Parsing continues in TAG mode.

     The GI is identified and the attributes and their values are vali-
16   dated and saved, with defaults supplied for the unspecified
     attributes. The procedure associated with the GI is then given
18   control, along with a pointer to the attribute names and val-
     ues.

20   Depending upon the application, the procedure might need to
     save all of the element's content before processing it, or it
22   could simply modify the application state and then return con-
     trol. When an element's procedure saves the content, the pro-
24   cedures for elements nested within it must also process their
     content and return it to the saved text.

26   NOTE — It is a violation of this International Standard for a system to
     save unparsed text and later parse it as though it had occurred at a
28   different place in the document. Instead, the text must be parsed as it
     is found, and the internal form of the parsed text (including informa-
30   tion about GIs, attributes, etc.) is what should be saved for later use.

     After the system returns control, parsing resumes in CON
32   mode after the **tagc** (or equivalent).

— Processing instruction:

The instruction is parsed as CDATA (in PI mode) and the resulting character string, after removal of the delimiters, is passed to the application program. The program executes the instruction and returns control. Parsing resumes in CON mode after the ***pic***.

— Markup declaration:

The start and name are identified; parsing proceeds in MD mode to identify the individual parameters and the end of the declaration. The individual declaration's semantic routine is then called to execute the declaration, and control is returned.

— References:

The reference is parsed in REF mode to determine the name (or character number) and find the reference close.

If it is a character reference, the parser replaces it with the correct character within the current entity. If the reference is to a non-SGML character or to a function character as data, the character is flagged to keep it from being confused with a normal character.

If it is an entity reference, the entity name is passed to the entity manager, which updates the pointer to the input buffers and returns control. For short references not mapped to an entity, the reference is treated as described in 9.4.6 $\boxed{353}$.

— Data: Data characters can be passed to the procedure as they are found, or they can be buffered until some markup occurs. In the latter case, the location and length of the data are passed to the procedure, and parsing continues at the markup.

The passed data string may contain flagged characters from character references, which the system must be able to handle.

F.1.3 Markup Minimization

Markup minimization allows a user to omit all or part of an

element's start-tag or end-tag.

2 For SHORTTAG minimization, a system must keep track of the
current location in the element structure, typically by maintaining a
4 record of GIs of open elements. It is also necessary to interpret
attribute definitions, but it is not necessary to understand the
6 content models unless validation services are provided.

For the OMITTAG and DATATAG features, however, knowledge of
8 the content models is essential.

NOTE — It is a violation of this International Standard to allow markup
10 minimization support to be handled by user-written application programs, as
that introduces the possibility that a document will be parsed differently by
12 different applications.

F.1.4 Translation

SGML assumes that the document character set is the same as the
14 system character set; that is, that the SGML parser need not be
cognizant of any translation. Any required translation is done by the
16 system prior to processing, or during processing in a manner that is
transparent to the SGML parser.

F.1.5 Command Language Analogy

18 SGML descriptive tags are the antithesis of procedural language
commands, and document type designers, in particular, should be
20 discouraged from thinking of them as similar. Nonetheless, there
are analogies that can be drawn between an element's attributes
22 and a command's parameters that might aid an implementor's
understanding.

SGML Term	Programming Term
attribute definition list	formal parameter list
attribute definition	formal parameter
attribute specification list	actual parameter list
attribute specification	actual parameter

24 (SGML Term) / *Programming Term*
26
28

Note that, unlike many formal parameter lists, the order of the
30 individual attribute definitions does not prescribe an order in which
the attribute specifications must occur.

F.2 Initialization

The user must be able to specify certain information to the system
2 at the start of a run, some of which, like the active document types
and link types, must be made available to the SGML parser. The
4 manner of passing the information is system-specific.

F.2.1 Initial Procedure Mapping

The user must specify the mappings between element types, on
6 the one hand, and the procedures to be executed for them, on the
other.

8 This could be in the form of the name of a single procedure (for
example, the procedure for the document element) which would set
10 up the mappings for the other elements. The parser itself does not
need this information, but if it were available the parser could return
12 the appropriate procedure name whenever it returned descriptive
tag information.

F.2.2 Link Process Specification

14 In formatting, the document type of the unformatted document is
often called the "logical structure", and the document type of the
16 formatted document is called the "layout structure". An SGML
document that is to be formatted will always contain a logical
18 structure (normally the base document type). If an explicit link
process is to be used, it will also contain the document type
20 definition for a layout structure ("generic layout structure"), and
possibly a fully formatted instance of one.

22 For a formatting application, the user must specify, when invoking
processing, the link type that will generate an instance of the
24 desired layout structure from the logical structure, together with any
parameters needed by the application. This information is not
26 maintained as part of the document markup because it varies from
one application run to another. However, the markup does contain
28 the link type declarations that specify which elements of the layout
structure are produced from the elements of the logical structure.

F.2.3 Concurrent Document Instances

A fully formatted instance is not normally used for a formatting
2 application, as it is the result of such an application. It is more likely
to be used in an indexing or cataloging process, where line and
4 page numbers from the layout structure are used in conjunction
with information from the logical structure. Here, the linkage
6 between the two structures at the top level and between
subelements is a permanent characteristic of the document, and is
8 expressed by the juxtaposition of tags from the two document
types. At initialization time, the user must specify the two document
10 types whose instances are to be processed.

F.3 Dynamic Procedure Mapping

A system should support procedure mapping as a dynamic process
12 available to procedures, since, in some applications, the procedure
for an element type might specify the processing of its
14 subelements. For example, in a formatting application, the
procedure for an element of the type "body" might specify that
16 elements of the type "heading" are to be set in a Roman font, while
the procedure for the generic identifier "appendix" might specify
18 that "heading" elements occurring within it should be set in italics.

In other words, the heading element can be thought of as being
20 qualified by the type of elements within whose bounds it occurs.
The model of a surname and personal name suggests itself: the
22 heading shares something in common with all other headings
(same personal name), but that is modified by the fact that it is part
24 of a body or an appendix (two different surnames).

F.4 Error Handling

This International Standard requires that a report of a markup error
26 include its nature and location. Implementors are free to decide on
the best means of satisfying that requirement, given their unique
28 system environments and user interfaces.

Some general considerations to keep in mind are:
30   a) The location in the entity structure can be expressed as an
         entity name, and a record number and character position

within it. The location could also include:

    i)   a list of open entities;

    ii) the location in the entity structure where each open entity was referenced;

    iii) for each open entity accessed by a short reference, the map name and short reference string.

b) The location in the element structure may be just as useful as that in the entity structure. It can be expressed as a list of currently open elements.

c) When reporting the nature of an error, consideration should be given to markup minimization or other features that may be in use that could affect the user's perception of the error.

Annex G
Conformance Classification and Certification

This annex discusses some of the considerations involved in certifying SGML systems, and describes a classification scheme for the options and variations under test.

(This annex does not form an integral part of this International Standard.)

2　This International Standard offers a variety of conformance options to SGML systems. It is expected that agencies that certify
4　conformance will want to define a meaningful subset of these options for testing. They will also need a simple way to classify
6　certified systems that will precisely identify the features and syntax variations that the systems support.

8　This annex describes a classification scheme that satisfies both these objectives, and discusses some of the implications for
10　certification agencies.

G.1 Classification Code

　The classification scheme is summarized in figure 15 ⎡ 552 ⎤ . The
12　scheme assigns SGML systems a conformance classification code that consists of three subordinate codes: feature, syntax, and vali-
14　dation. For this reason, the conformance classification code can be called an "FSV".

Conformance Class Name	Feature Code: F	Syntax Code: S	Validation Code: V	Validation Suffix
Minimal	0000	CS	000	non-validating
Minimal with options	0001-0767	CS	000	
Basic	0768	RS	000	
Basic with options	0769-1022	RS	000	
Full	1023	RS	000	
Multicode minimal	0000	MC	000	
Multicode minimal with options	0001-0767	MC	000	
Multicode basic	0768	MB	000	
Multicode basic with options	0769-1022	MB	000	
Multicode full	1023	MB	000	
Minimal	0000	CS	064	validating
Minimal with options	0001-0767	CS	064	
Basic	0768	RS	064	
Basic with options	0769-1022	RS	064	
Full	1023	RS	064	
Multicode minimal	0000	MC	064	
Multicode minimal with options	0001-0767	MC	064	
Multicode basic	0768	MB	064	
Multicode basic with options	0769-1022	MB	064	
Multicode full	1023	MB	064	
Minimal	0000	CS	065-127	validating with options
Minimal with options	0001-0767	CS	065-127	
Basic	0768	RS	065-127	
Basic with options	0769-1022	RS	065-127	
Full	1023	RS	065-127	
Multicode minimal	0000	MC	065-127	
Multicode minimal with options	0001-0767	MC	065-127	
Multicode basic	0768	MB	065-127	
Multicode basic with options	0769-1022	MB	065-127	
Multicode full	1023	MB	065-127	

Figure 15 — FSV Conformance Classification

For example, the FSV "0768RS064" is composed of feature code "0768", syntax code "RS", and validation code "064". It is the classification code for a system that can validate basic SGML documents with no features or validation options.

According to the figure, the classification name is "basic, validating". If the validation code were "000", the validation suffix would change, and the classification name would be "basic, non-validating".

As the features, concrete syntax, and validation options of a conforming system can vary independently of one another, it is not possible to define a single conformance classification hierarchy. Instead, there are two hierarchies, one based on the feature code and one on the validation code, as shown in the figure.

G.1.1 Feature Code

The feature code is determined by summing the factors assigned in the following list to each supported feature:

Feature	Weight
FORMAL	1
CONCUR	2
EXPLICIT	4
IMPLICIT	8
SIMPLE	16
SUBDOC	32
RANK	64
DATATAG	128
OMITTAG	256
SHORTTAG	512

If necessary, the code is padded with high-order zeros to make it the same length as the largest possible code.

The feature numbers are weighted (they are powers of two) so that the feature code will uniquely identify the features that are supported. For example, a feature code of 0384 means that the DATATAG and OMITTAG features are supported, and no others.

NOTE — The method described works when all features are specified independently and each is either supported or unsupported; that is, there are two possible values for each feature, 0 (unsupported) and 1 (supported). In the general case, there are N possible values, V, ranging from V=0 through V=N-1. For each feature, there is a factor, F, which is the product of N times the previous feature's factor, G (G is 1 for the first feature). The weight for a given value, W(V), is the product of V times G. (To summarize: $F=N*G$ and $W(V)=V*G$, where the asterisk means multiplication.)

G.1.2 Validation Code

The validation code is determined by summing the factors assigned in the following list to each supported validation feature:

Feature	Weight
CAPACITY	1
EXCLUDE	2
SGML	4

	MODEL	8
2	**FORMAL**	16
	NONSGML	32
4	**GENERAL**	64

If necessary, the code is padded with high-order zeros to make it
6   the same length as the largest possible code.

A system that did only general validation would have a validation
8   code of 064. As this International Standard requires general
validation as a prerequisite to any of the validation options, the only
10   possible validation codes would be 000, and 064 through 127.

NOTE — If modifying this scheme, GENERAL must have the highest
12   weight, and no validation code can be lower than the weight for GENERAL,
unless it is 0.

G.1.3 Syntax Code

14   The code for the concrete syntax is one of those in the following
list:

16   **Code**   *Concrete Syntax*

	CS	Core concrete syntax
18	**RS**	Reference concrete syntax
	MC	Multicode core concrete syntax
20	**MB**	Multicode basic concrete syntax

The listed syntaxes are those defined in this document.

22   The classification scheme assumes that conformance will be tested
for a single concrete syntax used in both the prolog and the
24   document element.

G.2 Certification Considerations

It is important to note that a conformance classification scheme is
26   not a constraint on either certification agencies or implementors.
Conformance is defined in clause 15 $\boxed{478}$ of this International
28   Standard, and is expressed formally in a system declaration, for
which a conformance classification code is only an informal partial
30   summary.

An implementor can choose to offer as many features and concrete
2   syntax variations as it thinks its users will require. A certification
agency can offer testing for as narrow or wide a group of these as it
4   wishes. As a result, a given certification may not include all of the
function that the tested system claims to offer, but that does not
6   mean the system failed to conform to this International Standard. It
simply means that, with respect to certain functions of the system,
8   the certification agency offers no opinion on whether it conforms.

Certification agencies should feel free to modify the suggested
10   classification scheme to meet their requirements, or to ignore it
altogether. An agency, however, regardless of the classification
12   scheme it adopts, must recognize that it cannot declare a system to
be conforming or nonconforming by any criteria other than those
14   specified in this International Standard. In particular, it cannot consider a system to be non-conforming solely because its mix of func-
16   tions does not fit the agency's classification scheme. The agency
must certify (or not, as the testing indicates) as to those functions
18   that it is willing to test, and declare that it has no opinion as to the
others.

Annex H
Theoretical Basis for the SGML Content Model

One role of SGML is to serve as the common language between an application designer and an application programmer. For this reason, the SGML model group notation, which was designed to be as intuitive for document type designers as a non-graphic formal language could be, was also designed to mimic the regular expression notation of automata theory. The predictable (in retrospect, at least) result was a chorus of complaints from implementors regarding the "mistakes" in SGML's use of regular expressions.

The purpose of this annex is to describe, in terms of automata theory, how SGML model group notation differs from regular expressions. During the ISO committee discussions on the annex, Robert Tischer of the Danish standards committee, who was not a party to the SGML design, contributed an eloquent explanation of SGML's design rationale. Here it is (slightly edited for clarity):

> SGML is a closed set of analytical constructs, coherent in themselves, defining an analytical formal world, useful to some population of information processing people. As is the case in all constructed languages, from mathematics to programming languages, the generated semantics and syntax of the constituent elements of SGML cross-reference one another and build upon one another in an ordered manner.
>
> There is, however, no constructed language that does not in some manner tie into the real world of natural language, with all of its historically derived, often contradictory, semantics and syntax.
>
> SGML solves this problem in the following manner: Correspondence to the real world takes place by allowing the intuitive understanding apparatus of the native speaker to

infiltrate strategically SGML's formal analytical world of coherent constructs. In the case where SGML's formal world is at conflict with the intuitive semantics of natural language, both are respected without sacrificing the internal coherency of SGML.

This subtle connection to the real world of understanding deserves clarification. Take, for instance, the task of constructing an SGML element declaration. The function of the omitted-tag-minimization of element types was intentionally made to be descriptive, instead of prescriptive, with respect to the SGML user. Instead, the user is allowed to express himself in the body of the document.

To further illustrate, a document type designer might wish to have a document with optional front matter, followed by a body of text, and ended by optional back matter. First, appropriate generic identifiers are constructed, retaining their mnemonic connection to the semantics in a natural language. Next, these terms are imbedded in SGML occurrence syntax, which, too, has its concommitants to natural language. The result might be

```
<!ELEMENT ...  (frontm?, body, backm?) ... >
```

which to the SGML user is both intuitively understandable, as well as being SGML-formally correct.

Another example is found in the attention given to "short references". The degrees of freedom these constructs give the user permit the formalities of SGML to all but disappear, allowing the real world of the user to dominate at the appropriate times.

Thus, it can be seen how the theoretical world of SGML is bound, in an integrated manner, to the world of everyday language, usage, and understanding.

Because of this necessary binding, SGML syntax cannot be treated formally as corresponding to regular mathematical expressions, whose validity, by definition, has no correspondence to the real world. Therefore, SGML cannot be manipulated, as such, to advance any sort of mathematical proof by, for example, transforming a model group from one form to another.

(This annex does not form an integral part of this International Standard.)

2   The SGML *model group* notation was deliberately designed to resemble the regular expression notation of automata theory,

because automata theory provides a theoretical foundation for
2   some aspects of the notion of conformance to a *content model*.
This annex defines the relationship between *model group* notation
4   and regular expressions, and discusses some ways in which model
groups behave like automata and some ways in which they do not.

H.1 Model Group Notation

6   The SGML *model group* notation corresponds to the regular
expression notation of automata theory, or reduces to it in the
8   following manner:

   a) **and** groups reduce to an **or** group of **seq** group permutations;
10   for example:

      (a & b)

12   is equivalent to the regular expression (or SGML *model group*):

14   ((a, b) | (b, a))

   b) a token with an **opt** occurrence indicator reduces to the same
16   token in an **or** group with the null token; for example:

      (a?)

18   is equivalent to the regular expression:

      (a |)

20   (which, incidentally, is not a valid SGML *model group*).

H.2 Application of Automata Theory

Checking for conformance to a *content model* is essentially
22   equivalent to the problem of recognizing (accepting or rejecting)
regular expressions, and regular expressions therefore provide a
24   useful theoretical basis for some aspects of context checking in
SGML.

26   It can be shown (by Kleene's theorem) that a regular expression is

equivalent to a deterministic finite automaton (DFA). A parser could in theory, therefore, handle any *model group* by reducing it to a regular expression and constructing a DFA with state transition paths corresponding to the tokens of the *model group*. Practice, however, presents some difficulties.

One problem arises in the reduction of **and** groups. Since the number of required **seq** group permutations is a factorial function, even small **and** groups can lead to an intractably large number of corresponding **seq** groups. An **and** group with six members, for example, would require 6!, or 720, **seq** groups.

Another problem lies with the construction of the DFA. One method is first to construct a nondeterministic finite automaton (NFA) directly from the regular expression, then to derive a deterministic equivalent. Although this and other algorithms for DFA construction are non-polynomial and hardly intractable for the human-readable models envisaged by SGML, they may be too resource-intensive for some implementations.

This International Standard avoids these problems by eliminating the need to construct a DFA. This it does by prohibiting models that are ambiguous or require "look-ahead"; that is, a *model group* is restricted so that, in any given context, an element (or character string) in the document can correspond to one and only one primitive content token (see 11.2.4.3 414). In effect, the allowable set of regular expressions is reduced to those whose corresponding NFA can be traversed deterministically, because either:

a) from a given node there can leave only one arc sequence that contains but a single labeled arc whose label is that of the corresponding content; or

b) if more than one such arc sequence can leave the node, only one of them can enter it, and this sequence is given priority by the rules of SGML.

As a result, context checking can be done by simplified algorithms that use only NFAs.

The restriction is justifiable in principle because human beings must also perform context checking when creating the document, and they are more likely to do this successfully if the regular expressions are kept simple. The restriction is also justifiable in practice because a desired document structure can always be obtained, despite the restriction, by introducing intermediate elements.

H.3 Divergence from Automata Theory

No assumptions should be made about the general applicability of
2 automata theory to content models. For example, it should be
noted that content models that reduce to equivalent regular
4 expressions are not necessarily equivalent for other purposes. In
particular, the determination of whether a start-tag is technically
6 omissible depends on the exact form of expression of the content
model. Minimization would be permitted for "b" in

8 ` (a?, b)`

while it would not be permitted in

10 ` ((a,b)|b)`

even though both models reduce to equivalent regular expressions.

Annex I
Nonconforming Variations

During the early development of SGML, there was some fear of "quick and dirty" implementations giving SGML a bad name before conforming systems could be produced. This annex was developed to warn of possible corner-cutting and to explain why the real thing was superior. Today, the annex is useful chiefly as an explanation of some of the design rationale.

(This annex does not form an integral part of this International Standard.)

2 Historically, many of the benefits of generalized markup have been obtained by using a procedural text processing language as though
4 it were a descriptive language. That approach is necessarily less effective than using the Standard Generalized Markup Language,
6 which was designed specifically for the purpose of describing documents.

8 This annex discusses some common departures from this International Standard that occur when procedural languages are
10 used for descriptive markup.

I.1 Fixed-length Generic Identifiers

In a fixed-length GI language, no attributes are supported, and
12 there is no *tagc*. The *content* begins with the first character after the start-tag GI.

The following example uses 2-character GIs:

```
2   <paThis is a paragraph with
    a <sqshort quotation</sqin it.</pa
```

4   Some drawbacks to fixed-length GIs are:

— The source document can be difficult for a human to read
6   (although machines have no trouble).
— Some "natural" tag mnemonics will be unusable in
8   combination because of their length (e.g., "p" for paragraph
        and "h1" for head-level-1 cannot be used together).
10 — Document types that have attributes cannot be processed.

A document created with fixed-length GIs can be converted to an
12 SGML document (provided no other differences exist) by inserting
the *tagc* delimiter.

I.2 Single Delimiter

14 In a single delimiter language, the same character is used for the
stago, *etago*, *ero*, *mdo*, and *pio* delimiter roles.

16 This approach introduces a number of restrictions:

— GIs, entity names, declaration names, processing instruction
18   names, and processing macro names must all be different
        from one another, as there is no other way to distinguish
20   them.
— End-tags can be entered only when the context offers no
22   possibility of confusing them with start-tags, as they look the
        same.

24 Some drawbacks to the use of a single delimiter are:

— The structure of the document is no longer apparent to a
26   human reader because descriptive tags cannot easily be
        distinguished from processing instructions, markup
28   declarations, or entity references.
— Processing instructions, which apply only to a single
30   application and system, cannot easily be located for
        modification if the document is used in a different application
32   or system.

— A document type designer must be aware of every processing
instruction and macro name and cannot use the same names
for GIs. Similarly, a text programmer cannot create a new
macro without making sure that no GI exists with the same
name.

— Document interchange is severely limited because of the
difficulty in preventing a document's GIs from conflicting with
a receiving system's macro names.

An obvious solution to these problems is to use naming
conventions to distinguish the types of name. For example,
declaration names could begin with an exclamation mark,
processing instruction names with a question mark, and so on.

```
<!ENTITY abc SYSTEM>
<?NEWPAGE>
```

The SGML reference concrete syntax uses multiple-character
strings as delimiters, thereby creating the visual effect of a single
delimiter with naming conventions, but with none of the drawbacks.

Appendices

Appendices

Appendix A
A Brief History of the Development of SGML

SGML, in its present form, is the result of the efforts of many people, channelled into four major activities that occurred over the past twenty years: generic coding, the GML and SGML languages, the SGML standard, and major SGML applications.

The Generic Coding Concept

Historically, electronic manuscripts contained control codes or macros that caused the document to be formatted in a particular way ("specific coding"). In contrast, generic coding, which began in the late 1960s, uses descriptive tags (for example, "heading", rather than "format-17"). Many credit the start of the generic coding movement to a presentation made by William Tunnicliffe, chairman of the Graphic Communications Association (GCA) Composition Committee, during a meeting at the Canadian Government Printing Office in September 1967: his topic — the separation of the information content of documents from their format.

Also in the late 1960s, a New York book designer named Stanley Rice proposed the idea of a universal catalog of parameterized "editorial structure" tags. Norman Scharpf, director of the GCA, recognized the significance of these trends, and established a generic coding project in the Composition Committee.

The committee developed the "GenCode® concept", recognizing that different generic codes were needed for different kinds of documents, and that smaller documents could be incorporated as elements of larger ones. The project evolved into the GenCode Committee, which later played an instrumental role in the development of the SGML standard.

GML and SGML: Languages for Generic Coding

In 1969, Charles Goldfarb was leading an IBM research project on integrated law office information systems. Together with Edward Mosher and Raymond Lorie he invented the Generalized Markup Language (GML) as a means of allowing the text editing, formatting, and information retrieval subsystems to share documents.

GML (which, not coincidentally, comprises the initials of its three inventors) was based on the generic coding ideas of Rice and Tunnicliffe. Instead of a simple tagging scheme, however, GML introduced the concept of a formally-defined document type with an explicit nested element structure.

Major portions of GML were implemented in mainframe "industrial strength" publishing systems by IBM and others and achieved substantial industry acceptance. IBM itself, reckoned to be the world's second largest publisher, adopted GML and now produces over 90% of its documents with it.

After the completion of GML, Goldfarb continued his research on document structures, creating additional concepts, such as short references, link processes, and concurrent document types, that were not part of GML but were later to be developed as part of SGML.

Development of SGML as an International Standard

In 1978, the American National Standards Institute (ANSI) committee on Information Processing established the Computer Languages for the Processing of Text committee, chaired by Charles Card, then of Univac, with Norman Scharpf as a member. Goldfarb was asked to join the committee and eventually to lead a project for a text description language standard based on GML. The GCA GenCode committee supported the effort and provided a nucleus of dedicated people for the task of developing Goldfarb's basic language design for SGML into a standard.

The first working draft of the SGML standard was published in 1980.

By 1983, the GCA was able to recommend the sixth working draft as an industry standard (GCA 101-1983). Major adopters included the US Internal Revenue Service (IRS) and the US Department of Defense.

In 1984, with feedback from the GCA standard in hand, three more working drafts were produced. The project, which had been authorized by the International Organization for Standardization (ISO) as well as ANSI, reorganized. It began regular international meetings as what is now called ISO/IEC JTC1/SC18/WG8, chaired by James Mason of the US Oak Ridge National Laboratory. Work also continued in the ANSI committee, now called X3V1.8, chaired by William Davis of SGML Associates, and supported by the GCA GenCode committee, chaired by Sharon Adler of IBM. Alignment between ISO and ANSI was maintained by Goldfarb continuing as technical leader, serving as project editor for both groups.

In 1985, a draft proposal for an international standard was published and the international SGML Users' Group was founded in the the UK by Joan Smith, who became its first president. Together with the GCA in North America, it played a vital role in educating the public about SGML and communicating user reactions and comments back to the development project.

A draft international standard was published in October 1985, and was adopted by the Office of Official Publications of the European Community. Another year of review and comment resulted in the final text, which — using an SGML system developed by Anders Berglund, then of the European Particle Physics Laboratory (CERN) — was published in record time after approval (ISO 8879:1986).

Important Early Applications of SGML

SGML applications are frequently developed for use by a single organization or a small community of users. Two early applications were developed with much broader participation: the Electronic Manuscript Project of the Association of American Publishers (AAP), and the documentation component of the Computer-aided Acquisition and Logistic Support (CALS) initiative of the US Department of Defense.

Electronic Manuscript Project

From 1983 to 1987, an AAP committee, chaired by Nicholas Alter of University Microfilms, developed an initial SGML application for book, journal, and article creation. The application is intended for manuscript interchange between authors and their publishers, among other uses, and includes optional element definitions for complex tables and scientific formulas.

The technical work was led by Joan Knoerdel of Aspen Systems, with participation by over thirty information processing organizations, including the IEEE, Council on Library Resources, American Society of Indexers, US Library of Congress, American Chemical Society, American Institute of Physics, Council of Biology Editors, and American Mathematical Society.

The AAP industry application standard has achieved significant acceptance, and has particularly been embraced by the emerging CD-ROM publishing industry. It has been adopted as a formal ANSI application standard (Z39.59) and a corresponding ISO standard is under development.

Computer-aided Acquisition and Logistic Support (CALS)

The SGML portion of CALS was initiated in February 1987 when Bruce Lepisto of the Department of Defense organized a committee to address the subject. The committee consisted of John Bean of Northrup, Pam Gennusa of Datalogics, Ed Herl of the US Army, and Mary McCarthy and Dave Plimier of the US Navy. They were subsequently joined by hundreds of representatives of military contractors and military commands, who participated in additional development and review. Their efforts led to the publication of a military standard (MIL-M-28001) in February 1988.

Similar SGML projects are under way in the defense departments of Canada, Sweden, and Australia, and are under consideration by other countries.

Appendix B
ISO/IEC JTC1/SC18/WG8/N1035: Recommendations for a Possible Revision of ISO 8879

Introduction

ISO/IEC standards are reviewed at least once every five years to determine whether they are still applicable or whether they should be withdrawn. Such reviews frequently result in the publication of a revised edition of the standard.

ISO 8879 was published October 15, 1986. It is the expectation of its developers (ISO/IEC JTC1/SC18/WG8) that a review will result in republication with editorial changes and possibly some new technical enhancements. The purpose of this document is to record in one place all such changes that have been agreed to by the developers. Accordingly, this document incorporates and replaces WG8 N931 and WG8 N1013.

NOTE — This document should be read carefully and taken at face value. In particular, it cannot be stated with certainty that a revision of ISO 8879 will ever be published, or that, if one is published, that any of these "accepted" items will find their way unmodified into the final draft.

Items are listed in order by clause number. General comments precede those relating to specific clauses. Each item is preceded by a two-letter code indicating the status of the item and the type of change involved. If the source of the item is a WG8 document, the document number and item number within that document, if any, are given in parentheses. (The attachments to WG8 N680 are N680A, N680B, and N680C.)

The status codes are:

A   Accepted as editing instructions for first draft of revision.
F   Accepted for further study in preparation of revision.

The types of change code are:

E   Editorial: correction of typographical errors, restatement of
         unclear text, and changes made for consistency or to facilitate
         maintenance of the document.
R   Resolution of ambiguity (conflict within text of ISO 8879)
T   Technical: innovation, or change to existing function

Items coded "E" and "R" reflect the developers' understanding of SGML as defined by the existing text of ISO 8879. Items coded "T" represent modifications to the SGML language that will not come into effect unless and until a revision of ISO 8879 is published.

General Editorial

AE   Delete some annexes and move them to technical
                 report on Techniques for using SGML (ISO/IEC TR
                 9573) under indicated topics:
                 Annex B: Tutorial on basic SGML concepts
                 Annex C: Tutorial on additional SGML concepts
                 Annex D.3: Variant concrete syntaxes, including mul-
                 ticode concrete syntaxes
                 Annex D (except D.3): Public entity sets
                 Annex E.1: Example of document type definition
                 Annex E.2: Computer graphics metafile
                 Annex E.3: Device-independent techniques for code
                 extension

AE (N680B 81)	Change public identifiers on any revised public text.
AE	All references to ISO standards should change "-" before year to ":". For example, "ISO 8879-1986" should be "ISO 8879:1986".
AE	Avoid "instance of an element". It should be "element", or "instance of an element type" when emphasis on the type is desired.
AE (N680B 38a)	13.4.1 onward, keywords in "where" lists are in medium font while in earlier lists they are in bold.
AE (N924)	Examples of multiple-byte codes in ISO 8879 (none at present) or in technical reports should be modified to follow the recommendation in WG8 N924.
AE	Clauses should be further subdivided and renumbered to isolate individual requirements as much as possible, in order to facilitate correlation of test cases with the standard.
AE (N680B 3)	Clarify that SHORTREF is semantically a named feature, but syntactically is not.
AE (N680B 2)	Rationalize use of italicized phrases in body of standard and annexes.

General Technical

AT	Create an ASN.1 description of SGML for binary encoding (SGML-B) as a normative annex. SGML-B should not require delimiter recognition and should not employ markup minimization. However, it should be capable of preserving information about markup minimization, comments, etc., so that transformations in either direction between SGML and SGML-B can be made without loss of information.

Clause 3 (AE)

The footnotes identifying certain references as being "at present at the stage of draft" should be deleted, as those standards are now available in final form.

Clause 4: Definitions

The full text of the revised definitions is given, rather than change instructions. Although this approach adds to the size of this report, it makes it easier to see the effect of the changes. All definitions are coded "AE". (N680B 20 23-24 26-28, N680C 1 7 11)

4.16 attribute (specification) list: Markup that is a set of one or more attribute specifications.

NOTE — Attribute specification lists occur in start-tags, entity declarations, and link sets.

4.24 bit combination: An ordered collection of bits, interpretable as a binary number.

NOTE — A bit combination should not be confused with a "byte", which is a name given to a particular size of bit string, typically seven or eight bits. A single bit combination could contain several bytes.

4.36 character number: A *number* that represents the base-10 integer equivalent of the coded representation of a character.

4.38 character repertoire: A set of characters that are used together. Meanings are defined for each character, and can also be defined for control sequences of multiple characters.

NOTE — When characters occur in a control sequence, the meaning of the sequence supercedes the meanings of the individual characters.

4.39 character set: A mapping of a character repertoire onto a code set such that each character in the repertoire is represented by a bit combination in the code set.

4.42 code extension: Techniques for including in documents the coded representations of characters that are not in the document character set.

NOTE — When multiple national languages occur in a document, graphic repertoire code extension may be useful.

4.43 code set: A set of bit combinations of equal size, ordered by their numeric values, which must be consecutive.

NOTES

1   For example, a code set whose bit combinations have 8 bits (an "8-bit code") could consist of as many as 256 bit combinations, ranging in value from 00000000 through 11111111 (0 through 255 in the decimal number base), or it could consist of any contiguous subset of those bit combinations.

2   A compressed form of a bit combination, in which redundant bits are omitted without ambiguity, is considered to be the same size as the uncompressed form. Such compression is possible when a character set does not use all available bit combinations, as is common when the bit combinations contain several bytes.

4.44 code set position: The location of a bit combination in a code set; it corresponds to the numeric value of the bit combination.

4.45 coded representation: The representation of a character as a single bit combination in a code set.

NOTE — A coded representation is always a single bit combination, even though the bit combination may be several 8-bit bytes in size.

4.51 conforming SGML document: An SGML document that complies with all provisions of this International Standard.

NOTE — The provisions allow for choices in the use of optional features and variant concrete syntaxes.

4.61 contextually required element: An element that is not a contextually optional element and

a)   whose *generic identifier* is the *document type name*; or

b)   whose currently applicable *content token* is a contextually required token.

NOTE — An element could be neither contextually required nor contextually optional; for example, an element whose currently applicable *content token* is in an *or* group that has no inherently optional tokens.

4.71 current rank: The *rank suffix* that, when appended to a rank stem in a tag, will derive the element's generic identifier. For a *start-tag* it is the *rank suffix* of the most recent element with the identical *rank stem*, or a *rank stem* in the same *ranked group*. For an *end-tag* it is the *rank suffix* of the most recent open element with the identical *rank stem*.

4.75.1 data entity: An entity that was declared to be data and therefore is not parsed when referenced.

NOTES

1   There are three kinds: character data entity, specific character data entity, and non-SGML data entity.

2   The interpretation of a data entity may be governed by a data content notation, which may be defined by another International Standard.

4.77 data tag group: A *content token* that associates a data tag pattern with a target element type.

NOTE — Within an instance of a target element, the data content and that of any subelements is scanned for a string that conforms to the pattern (a "data tag").

4.92 descriptive markup: Markup that describes the structure and other attributes of a document in a non-system-specific manner, independently of any processing that may be performed on it. In particular, SGML descriptive markup uses tags to express the element structure.

4.103 (document) type declaration: A markup declaration that formally specifies a portion of a document type definition.

NOTE — A document type declaration does not specify all of a document type definition because part of the definition, such as the semantics of elements and attributes, cannot be expressed in SGML. In addition, the application designer might choose not to use SGML in every possible instance — for example, by using a data content notation to delineate the structure of an element in preference to defining subelements.

4.105 document (type) definition: Rules, determined by an application, that apply SGML to the markup of documents of a particular type.

NOTE — Part of a document type definition can be specified by an SGML document type declaration. Other parts, such as the semantics of elements and attributes, or any application conventions, cannot be expressed formally in SGML. Comments can be used, however, to express them informally.

4.106 document type specification: A portion of a tag that identifies the document instances within which the tag will be processed.

NOTE — A *name group* performs the same function in an entity reference.

4.112 element set: A set of element, attribute definition list, and notation declarations that are used together.

NOTE — An element set can be public text.

4.117 empty link set: A link set that contains no link rules.

4.120 entity: A collection of characters that can be referenced as a unit.

NOTES

1 Objects such as book chapters written by different authors, pi characters, or photographs, are often best managed by maintaining them as individual entities.

2 The actual storage of entities is system-specific, and could take the form of files, members of a partitioned data set, components of a data structure, or entries in a symbol table.

4.133 explicit link (process definition): A link process definition in which the result element types and their attributes and link attribute values can be specified for multiple source element types.

4.134 external entity: An entity whose replacement text is not incorporated in an entity declaration; its system identifier and/or public identifier is specified instead.

4.135 external identifier: A parameter that identifies an external entity or data content notation.

NOTES

1   There are two kinds: system identifier and public identifier.

2   A document type or link type declaration can include the identifier of an external entity containing all or part of the declaration subset; the external identifier serves simultaneously as a declaration of that entity and as a reference to it.

4.138 formal public identifier error: An error in the construction or use of a *formal public identifier*, other than an error that would prevent it being a valid *minimum literal*.

NOTE — A formal public identifier error can occur only if "FORMAL YES" is specified on the SGML declaration. A failure of a *public identifier* to be a *minimum literal*, however, is always an error.

4.142 general delimiter (role): A delimiter role other than short reference.

4.147 graphic character: A character that is not a control character.

NOTE — For example, a letter, digit, or punctuation. It normally has a visual representation that is displayed when a document is presented.

4.149 group: The portion of a parameter that is bounded by a balanced pair of *grpo* and *grpc* delimiters or *dtgo* and *dtgc* delimiters.

NOTE — There are five kinds: name group, name token group, model group, data tag group, and data tag template group. A name, name token, or data tag template group cannot contain a nested group, but a model group can contain a nested model group or data tag group, and a data tag group can contain a nested data tag template group.

4.155 implicit link (process definition): A link process definition in which the result element types and their attributes are all implied by the application, but link attribute values can be specified for multiple source element types.

4.160.1 internal entity: An entity whose replacement text is incorporated in an entity declaration.

4.164 keyword: A parameter that is a reserved name.

NOTE — In parameters where either a keyword or a name defined by an application could be specified, the keyword is always preceded by the reserved name indicator. An application is therefore able to define names without regard to whether those names are also used by the concrete syntax.

4.167.1 link rule: A member of a link set; that is, for an implicit link, a *source element specification*, and for an explicit link, an *explicit link rule*.

4.168 link set: A named set of rules, declared in a *link set declaration*, by which elements of the source document type are linked to elements of the result document type.

4.171 link type declaration subset: The entity sets, link attribute sets, and link set declarations, that occur within the declaration subset of a link type declaration.

NOTE — The external entity referenced from the link type declaration is considered part of the declaration subset.

4.174 lower-case name characters: Character class consisting of each lower-case *name character* assigned by the concrete syntax.

4.175 lower-case name start characters: Character class consisting of each lower-case *name start character* assigned by the concrete syntax.

4.186 (markup) declaration: Markup that controls how other markup of a document is to be interpreted.

NOTE — There are 13 kinds: SGML, entity, element, attribute definition list, notation, document type, link type, link set, link set use, marked section, short reference mapping, short reference use, and comment.

4.205 named entity reference: An entity reference consisting of a delimited name of a general entity or parameter entity (possibly qualified by a name group) that was declared by an entity declaration.

NOTE — A general entity reference can have an undeclared name if a default entity was declared.

4.208 non-SGML data entity: A data entity in which a non-SGML character could occur.

4.224 parameter: The portion of a markup declaration that is bounded by ps separators (whether required or optional). A parameter can contain other parameters.

4.237 proper subelement: A subelement that is permitted by its containing element's model.

NOTE — An included subelement is not a proper subelement.

4.250 rank stem: A name from which a generic identifier can be derived by appending a *rank suffix*.

4.267 reportable markup error: A failure of a document to conform to this International Standard when it is parsed with respect to the active document and link types, other than a semantic error (such as a generic identifier that does not accurately connote the element type) or:

a) an ambiguous content model;

b) an exclusion that could change a token's required or optional status in a model;

c) exceeding a capacity limit;

d) an error in the SGML declaration;

e) an otherwise allowable omission of a tag that creates an ambiguity;

f)   the occurrence of a non-SGML character; or

g)   a formal public identifier error.

4.276 separator: A character string that separates markup components from one another.

NOTES

1   There are four kinds *s*, *ds*, *ps*, and *ts*.

2   A separator cannot occur in data.

4.277 separator characters: A character class composed of function characters other than *RE*, *RS*, and *SPACE*, that are allowed in separators and that will be replaced by *SPACE* in those contexts in which *RE* is replaced by *SPACE*.

4.285 SGML parser: A program (or portion of a program or a combination of programs) that recognizes markup in SGML documents.

NOTE — If an analogy were to be drawn to programming language processors, an SGML parser would be said to perform the functions of both a lexical analyzer and a parser with respect to SGML documents.

4.290 short reference (delimiter): Short reference string.

4.299 simple link (process definition): A link process definition in which the result element types and their attributes are all implied by the application, and link attribute values can be specified only for the source document element.

4.304 specific character data entity: An entity whose text is treated as *system data* when referenced. The text is dependent on a specific system, device, or application process.

NOTE — A specific character data entity would normally be redefined for different applications, systems, or output devices.

4.312 system declaration: A declaration, included in the documentation for a conforming SGML system, that specifies the features, capacity set, concrete syntaxes, and character set that the system supports, and any validation services that it can perform.

4.315 target element: An element whose *generic identifier* is specified in a *data tag group*.

4.319 token: The portion of a group, including a complete nested group (but not a *connector*), that is, or could be, bounded by ts separators.

Clause 7

AE 7.1 (N680A 5, N701 2)
Clarify governing principle that the parsing of a document instance shall not be affected by the concurrent parsing of other document instances. For example, the replacement text of an entity reference could differ from one active concurrent instance to another. Also, a record end could be ignored in one instance and not in another.

AE 7.1
Caution the user that short references in the base document instance are treated as data in other concurrent instances.

AE 7.6.1, first note
Replace:
For example, in

```
record 1<outer><sub>
record 2</sub>
</outer>record 3
```

with:
For example, in the following three records:

```
record 1 data<outer><sub>
record 2 data</sub>
record 3 data</outer>
```

AE 7.9.3
Clarify that the order of the tokens is significant and cannot be changed by a parser.

Clause 9

AE 9.2.1 Add note clarifying that character classes in productions 52 and 53 are defined in Figures 1 and 2.

Clause 10

AR 10.1.6 Clarify that system must determine storage location of entity or notation from the name and external identifier; it does not "generate" a modified system identifier.

AE 10.1.7 Add note clarifying that character classes in production 78 are defined in Figure 1.

Clause 13

AE 13 In Note 1, change "document markup features" to: markup minimization features

AE 13 In Note 1, change last parenthesized phrase to: (for example, if the document quantity set required larger values than were available in the system quantity set)

FE 13 (N759 12, N790 2)
Clarify relationship between document character set and syntax-reference character set. In particular, that concrete syntax is defined in terms of characters, not bit combinations. (Contributions invited: a short explanation for this clause; examples and discussion for a technical report.)

AE 13.1 In first sentence, change "a coded" to: one and only one coded

AE 13.1 In first sentence, change "as" to: that is,

AE 13.1.1.1 Replace last paragraph with:
The *public identifier* should be a *formal public identifier* with a *public text class* of "CHARSET".

AE 13.1.2 In first paragraph, change "added" to: assigned

AR 13.2 Replace last paragraph with:
The *public identifier* should be a *formal public identifier* with a *public text class* of "CAPACITY".

AE 13.4.1   Replace last paragraph with:
The *public identifier* should be a *formal public identifier* with a *public text class* of "SYNTAX".

AE 13.4.3   Change "a coded" to: one and only one coded

AE 13.4.3   Change "as" to: that is

AE 13.4.3   Change "of" to: for

AR 13.4.3   Clarify that a parameter literal in the SGML declaration is interpreted as though its character set were the syntax-reference character set. Therefore, a character can be entered directly in a parameter literal only if it has the same character number in the document character set as in the syntax-reference character set. If not, it must be entered as a character reference.

AR 13.4.5 (N927 1)

Resolve conflict between intent of text and syntax production rule, which restricts the declared concrete syntax, by treating production 189 as though each occurrence of "*ps+, parameter literal*" were replaced by "(*ps+, parameter literal*)+", and by replacing each occurrence of the word "literal" in the text with "literals".

AE 13.4.5   Change all occurrences of "added" to: assigned

AE 13.4.5   Clarify that a character can be assigned only once as a lower-case name or name-start character (that is, assigned once only to either LCNMCHAR or LCNMSTRT, but not both).

AR 13.4.5 (N759 7, N790 5)

Clarify that different lower-case characters can be associated with the same upper-case form, which can be a UC Letter. The associated upper-case forms can be the same as the lower-case, for languages (or special characters) where the concept of capitalization does not apply.

FT 13.4.5 (N759 10, N790 1 4)

Allow the set of Digit characters to be extended by a concrete syntax (NUCHAR for "numeral characters"?). A character could not be assigned to more than one of NUCHAR, LCNMSTRT, and LCNMCHAR.

FT 13.4.5 (N927 1)

Devise a less burdensome method of declaring long sequences of character numbers.

AR 13.4.6 (N759 2)

Add new paragraph:
The length of a delimiter string in the delimiter set cannot exceed the NAMELEN quantity of the quantity set.

AR 13.4.7 (N759 1)

In production 193, replace second *name* with *parameter literal* and replace first paragraph with:
The *name* is a reference reserved name that is replaced in the declared concrete syntax by the interpreted *parameter literal*, which must be a valid *name* in the declared concrete syntax.

AE 13.4.7

Add new note before the existing first note:

NOTE — The list of reference reserved names that can be replaced in a declared concrete syntax is:

ANY	IDLINK	NMTOKEN	REQUIRED
ATTLIST	IDREF	NMTOKENS	RESTORE
CDATA	IDREFS	NOTATION	RS
CONREF	IGNORE	NUMBER	SDATA
CURRENT	IMPLIED	NUMBERS	SHORTREF
DEFAULT	INCLUDE	NUTOKEN	SIMPLE
DOCTYPE	INITIAL	NUTOKENS	SPACE
ELEMENT	LINK	O	STARTTAG
EMPTY	LINKTYPE	PCDATA	SUBDOC
ENDTAG	MD	PI	SYSTEM
ENTITIES	MS	POSTLINK	TEMP
ENTITY	NAME	PUBLIC	USELINK
FIXED	NAMES	RCDATA	USEMAP
ID	NDATA	RE	

AR 13.4.8 (N759 3)

In last sentence of first paragraph, change the period to: , which must exceed the reference value. The resulting quantity set must be rational.

NOTE — For example, "TAGLEN" must be greater than "LITLEN" because literals occur in start-tags. Similarly, "LITLEN" must exceed "NAMELEN" because names occur in literals.

Clause 15

FE 15 (N680B 38b-41)
> Make editorial changes.

AE 15.6, third paragraph
> In second sentence, change "a coded" to: one and only one coded

AR 15.6, third paragraph
> In the second sentence, change "as" to: that is,

AE 15.6.1.1, production 202
> Before "SRLEN", insert: *ps+,*

Figures in Body

AE Fig. 6   For ATTSPLEN, replace description with: Normalized length of an *attribute specification list*.

Annex A

FE A (N680B 42) Make editorial change.
FE A   Add some key examples from current annexes B and C.

Annex C (for TR 9573)

AE C.1.1.2   Replace

```
<!ELEMENT -- CONTENT       EXCEPTIONS? --
1  list      (item+)
2  item      (p | list)*
```

with

```
<!--         ELEMENTS         CONTENT          -->
<!ELEMENT list               (item+) >
<!ELEMENT item               (p | list)*
```

AE C.1.4, first example
In line 1, "jobitem" should be delimited by LIT.

AE C.1.4, first example
Replace last two lines:

```
Kit von Suck,          Member
</joblist>
```

with

```
Kit von Suck,          Member</joblist>
```

AE C.1.4, p.105
Delete last example and its discussion, which begins at the last paragraph of p.105 and continues through "I wonder whether Mrs. G will read this" on p.106.

AE C.3.1
Replace example with:

```
<(source)item>
<(layout)block indent=5>Text of list item.
</(source)item>
</(layout)block>
```

Annex F

AR F
Add explicit statement of information exchanged between SGML parser and application, based on Attachment 1 (Element Structure Information Set).

FE F.1 (N680B 74-75)
Make editorial changes.

Annex G

AE G   Delete and move to new standard on "Conformance
                 Testing" if project for it is approved.
FE G (N680B 76-79)
                 Make editorial changes.

Attachment 1: The ISO 8879 Element Structure Information Set (ESIS)

There are two kinds of SGML application (and therefore two kinds of conforming SGML application):

a) A structure-controlled SGML application operates only on the element structure that is described by SGML markup, never on the markup itself.

b) A markup-sensitive SGML application can act on the actual SGML markup and can act on element structure information as well. Examples include SGML-sensitive editors and markup validators.

The set of information that is acted upon by implementations of structure-controlled applications is called the "element structure information set" (ESIS). ESIS is implicit in ISO 8879, but is not defined there explicitly. The purpose of this paper is to provide that explicit definition.

ESIS is particularly significant for SGML conformance testing because two SGML documents are equivalent documents if, when they are parsed with respect to identical DTDs and LPDs, their ESIS is identical. All structure-controlled applications must therefore produce identical results for all equivalent SGML documents. In contrast, not all markup-sensitive applications will produce identical results from equivalent documents. (For example, a program that prints comment declarations, or that counts the number of omitted end-tags.)

ESIS information is exchanged between an SGML parser and the rest of an SGML system that implements a structure-controlled application. Although an implementation may choose to "wire in" some of ESIS, such as the names of attributes, a structure-controlled application need have no other knowledge of the prolog than what ESIS provides.

A system implementing a structure-controlled application is required to act only on ESIS information and on the APPINFO parameter of the

SGML declaration.

NOTES

1 This requirement does not prohibit a parser from providing the same interface to both structure-controlled and markup-sensitive applications, which could include non-ESIS information (e.g., the date), and/or information that could be derived from ESIS information (e.g., the list of open elements).

2 The documentation of a conforming SGML system that supports user-developed structure-controlled applications should make application developers aware of this requirement. Such a system should facilitate conformance to this requirement by distinguishing ESIS information from non-ESIS in its interface to applications. Note 1 in 15.3.5 ⌐482⌐ of ISO 8879 applies only to structure-controlled applications.

In the following description of ESIS, information is identified as being available at a particular point in the parsed document. This identification should not be interpreted as a requirement that the information actually be exchanged at that point — all or part of it could have been exchanged at some other point. Similarly, there is no constraint on the manner (e.g., number of function calls) or format in which the exchanges take place.

The ESIS description includes the information associated with all of the SGML optional features. When a given feature is not in use, corresponding information is not present in the document. ESIS information is transmitted from the parser to the application unless otherwise indicated.

ESIS information applies to a single parsed document instance. Therefore, if concurrent instances are being parsed, the applicable document type name must be identified. This requirement also applies when parsing intermediate instances in a chain of active links.

ESIS information consists of the identification of the following occurrences, and the passing of the indicated information for each:

a) Initialization

The application must inform the SGML parser of the active document types, the active link types, or that parsing is to occur only with respect to the base document type.

b) Start of document instance set

For each active LPD, the link type name and link set information (see l ⌐593⌐ below) for the initial link set.

c)   Start of document element only

For each active simple link, the link type name and attribute information (see i ⌐591⌐ below) for the link attributes.

d)   Start of any element
— Generic identifier

— Attribute information for the start-tag.

— For each link rule for which this element is an associated element type, attribute information for the link attributes.

— The application must inform the SGML parser which applicable link rule it chose.

— For the chosen link rule, the result GI and attribute information for the result element.

— If the element has an associated link set, the link set information.

e)   End of any element, including elements declared to be empty

Generic identifier

NOTE — If the element was empty, ESIS does not indicate why it was empty; that is, whether it was declared to be empty, or whether an explicit content reference occurred, or whether it just happened to contain no data characters.

f)   End of document instance set

NOTE — Processing instructions could occur between the end of the document element and the end of the document instance set.

g)   Processing instruction

System data

h) Data

Includes no ignored characters (e.g., record starts).

Includes only significant record ends, with no indication of how significance was determined. Characters entered via character references are not distinguished in any way. Implementation-specific means can be used to represent bit combinations that the application cannot accept directly.

NOTES

1 Such bit combinations may be those of non-SGML characters entered via character references, but no significance is attached to this coincidence.

2 Bit combinations of non-SGML characters that occurred directly in the source text would have been flagged as errors, and would therefore never be treated as data.

i) Attribute information

All attribute values must be reported and associated with their attribute names.

NOTES

1 For example, a parser could supply the attribute names with each value, or supply the values in an order that corresponds to a previously-supplied list of names.

2 The order of the tokens in a tokenized attribute value shall be preserved as originally specified.

Each unspecified impliable attribute must be identified.

NOTE — For example, a parser could identify such attributes explicitly, or it could allow the application to determine them by comparing the identified specified attribute values to a previously-supplied list of attribute names.

There shall be no indication of whether an attribute value was the default value.

The order in which attributes are specified in the attribute specification list is not part of the ESIS.

General entity name attribute values include the entity name and entity text. The entities themselves are not treated as having been referenced.

NOTE — An application can use system services to parse the entities, but such parsing is outside the context of the current document.

For notation attributes, the attribute value includes the notation name and notation identifier.

For CDATA attributes, references to SDATA entities in attribute value literals are resolved. The replacement text is distinguished from the surrounding text and identified as an individual SDATA entity.

For CDATA attributes, references to CDATA entities in attribute value literals are resolved. The replacement text is not distinguished from the surrounding text.

j)   References to internal entities

The information passed to the application depends on the entity type:

SDATA   replacement text, identified as an individual
                   SDATA entity.
PI   replacement text, identified as a processing
                   instruction but not as an entity.

For other references, nothing is passed to the application.

NOTE — The replacement text is parsed in the context in which the reference occurred, which can result in other ESIS information being passed.

k)   References to external entities

The information passed to the application depends on the entity type:

— For data entities, the entity name and entity text are passed. If a notation is named, the notation name, notation identifier, and attribute information for the data attributes are also passed.

— For SGML text entities, nothing is passed to the application.

NOTE — The replacement text is parsed in the context in which the reference occurred, which can result in other ESIS information being passed.

— For SUBDOC entities, the entity name and entity text are passed. The application can require that the subdocument entity be parsed at the point at which the reference occurred.

NOTE — Parsing of the subdocument entity can result in other ESIS information being passed. The occurrence of the end of the document instance set of the subdocument entity will indicate that subsequent ESIS information applies to the element from which the subdocument entity was referenced.

l) Link set information

All link rules whose source element specification is implied.

Appendix C
About the ISO 8879 Text

ISO 8879 was published on October 15, 1986. After some 18 months of public use, an amendment, whose purpose was "to improve the expression of the design of SGML, not to change that design", was published July 1, 1988. The amendment corrected typographic errors and omissions, provided clarifying notes for unclear areas, and resolved some ambiguities.

Further public use of the amended standard unearthed additional areas where editorial clarification would be helpful. The ISO SGML committee documented these on January 19, 1990 in WG8 N1035, and they are reprinted in their entirety in Appendix B (571). [1] These changes are intended to clarify the standard and not to modify the SGML language. It is expected that they will be incorporated in the next revision of ISO 8879.

The text of ISO 8879 that appears in this book is the official text of October 15, 1986, as amended by the amendment of July 1, 1988. In addition, the recommendations of WG8 N1035 were followed in the following manner:

a) Where clarification of the text was recommended, the annotations provide the needed clarification.

---

[1] The remainder of this appendix will not aid your quest for knowledge of SGML. It is included because I promised you the complete official text of the standard, some of which was replaced in the body of this book by ISO SGML committee recommendations. On the other hand, if you are seeking evidence of the human frailty of standards committees and the endlessness of the task of editing a standard, read on.

b) Where additional or revised definitions were recommended, the recommendations were followed exactly and identified as such by change bars in the right margin. The original definitions are provided in this appendix for completeness.

c) Where precise recommendations were made for changes in the wording of requirements or production rules, the recommendations were followed exactly and identified as such by change bars in the right margin. The original text of large changes and deletions is provided in this appendix for completeness.

Clause 4

The replacement definitions recommended by N1035 were incorporated in clause 4 and in the structured overview. For the record, the original text of the modified definitions is reproduced here:

4.16 attribute (specification) list: Markup that is a set of one or more attribute specifications.

NOTE — Attribute specification lists occur in start-tags and link sets.

4.24 bit combination: An ordered collection of bits, interpretable as a binary number.

4.36 character number: A *number* that represents the base-10 integer equivalent of the coded representation of a character, obtained by treating the sequence of bit combinations as a single base-2 integer.

4.38 character repertoire: A set of characters that are used together. Meanings are defined for each character, and can also be defined for control sequences of multiple characters.

NOTE — When characters occur in a control sequence, the meaning of the sequence supercedes the meanings of the individual characters.

4.39 character set: A mapping of a character repertoire onto a code set such that each character is associated with its coded representation.

4.42 code extension: The use of a single coded representation for more than one character, without changing the document character set.

NOTE — When multiple national languages occur in a document, graphic repertoire code extension may be useful.

4.43 code set: A set of bit combinations of equal size, ordered by their numeric values, which must be consecutive.

NOTE — For example, a code set whose bit combinations have 8 bits (an "8-bit code") could consist of as many as 256 bit combinations, ranging in value from 00000000 through 11111111 (0 through 255 in the decimal number base), or it could consist of any contiguous subset of those bit combinations.

4.44 code set position: The numeric value of a bit combination in a code set.

4.45 coded representation: The representation of a character as a sequence of one or more bit combinations of equal size.

4.51 conforming SGML document: An SGML document that complies with all provisions of this International Standard.

4.61 contextually required element: An element that is not a contextually optional element and

a) whose *generic identifier* is the *document type name*; or

b) whose currently applicable model token is a contextually required token.

NOTE — An element could be neither contextually required nor contextually optional; for example, an element whose currently applicable model token is in an *or* group that has no inherently optional tokens.

4.71 current rank: A number that is appended to a rank stem in a tag to derive the generic identifier. For a *start-tag* it is the *rank suffix* of the most recent element with the identical *rank stem*, or a *rank stem* in the same *ranked group*. For an *end-tag* it is the *rank suffix* of the most recent open element with the identical *rank stem*.

4.75.1 data entity: An entity that was declared to be data and therefore is not parsed when referenced.

NOTE — There are three kinds: character data entity, specific character data entity, and non-SGML data entity.

4.77 data tag group: A model group token that associates a data tag pattern with a target element type.

NOTE — Within an instance of a target element, the data content and that of any subelements is scanned for a string that conforms to the pattern (a "data tag").

4.92 descriptive markup: Markup that describes the structure and other attributes of a document in a non-system-specific manner, independently of any processing that may be performed on it. In particular, it uses tags to express the element structure.

4.103 (document) type declaration: A markup declaration that contains the formal specification of a document type definition.

4.105 document (type) definition: Rules, determined by an application, that apply SGML to the markup of documents of a particular type. A document type definition includes a formal specification, expressed in a document type declaration, of the element types, element relationships and attributes, and references that can be represented by markup. It thereby defines the vocabulary of the markup for which SGML defines the syntax.

NOTE — A document type definition can also include comments that describe the semantics of elements and attributes, and any application conventions.

4.106 document type specification: A portion of a tag that identifies the document instances within which the tag or entity reference will be processed.

4.112 element set: A set of element declarations that are used together.

NOTE — An element set can be public text.

4.117 empty link set: A link set in which all result element types are implied and no attributes are specified.

4.120 entity: A collection of characters that can be referenced as a unit.

NOTES

1   Objects such as book chapters written by different authors, pi characters, or photographs, are often best managed by maintaining them as individual entities.

2   The physical organization of entities is system-specific, and could take the form of files, members of a partitioned data set, components of a data structure, or entries in a symbol table.

4.133 explicit link (process definition): A link process definition in which the result element types and their attributes and multiple sets of link attribute values can be specified.

4.134 external entity: An entity whose text is not incorporated directly in an entity declaration; its system identifier and/or public identifier is specified instead.

NOTE — A document type or link type declaration can include the identifier of an external entity containing all or part of the declaration subset; the external identifier serves simultaneously as both the entity declaration and the entity reference.

4.135 external identifier: A parameter that identifies an external entity or data content notation.

NOTE — There are two kinds: system identifier and public identifer.

4.138 formal public identifier error: An error in the construction or use of a *formal public identifer*, other than an error that would prevent it being a valid *minimum literal*.

NOTE — A formal public identifier error can occur only if "FORMAL YES" is specified on the SGML declaration. A failure of a *public identifier* to be a *minimum literal*, however, is always an error.

4.142 general delimiter (role): A delimiter role other than a short reference.

4.147 graphic character: A character, such as a letter, digit, or punctuation, that normally occupies a single position when text is displayed.

4.149 group: The portion of a parameter that is bounded by a balanced pair of *grpo* and *grpc* delimiters or *dtgo* and *dtgc* delimiters.

NOTE — There are five kinds: name group, name token group, model group, data tag group, and data tag template group. A name, name token, or data tag template group cannot contain a group, but a model group can contain a model group and a data tag group can contain a data tag template group.

4.155 implicit link (process definition): A link process definition in which the result element types and their attributes are all implied by the application, but multiple sets of link attribute values can be specified.

4.164 keyword: A parameter that is a reserved name defined by the concrete syntax, as opposed to arbitrary text.

NOTE — In parameters where either a keyword or a name defined by an application could be specified, the keyword is always preceded by the reserved name indicator. An application is therefore able to define names without regard to whether those names are also used by the concrete syntax.

4.168 link set: A named set of associations, declared by a *link set declaration*, in which elements of the source document type are linked to elements of the result document type. For each element link, source link attributes and result element attributes can be specified.

4.171 link type declaration subset: The entity sets, link attribute sets, and link set and link set use declarations, that occur within the declaration subset of a link type declaration.

NOTE — The external entity referenced from the link type declaration is considered part of the declaration subset.

4.174 lower-case name characters: Character class consisting of each additional lower-case *name character* assigned by the concrete syntax.

4.175 lower-case name start characters: Character class consisting of each additional lower-case *name start character* assigned by the concrete syntax.

4.186 (markup) declaration: Markup that controls how other markup of a document is to be interpreted.

NOTE — There are 13 kinds: SGML, entity, element, attribute definition list, notation, document type, link type, link set, link use, marked section, short reference mapping, short reference use, and comment.

4.205 named entity reference: An entity reference consisting of a delimited name of a general entity or parameter entity (possibly qualified by a document type specification) that was declared by an entity declaration.

NOTE — A general entity reference can have an undeclared name if a default entity was declared.

4.208 non-SGML data entity: An entity whose characters are not interpreted in accordance with this International Standard, and in which, therefore, no SGML markup can be recognized.

NOTE — The interpretation of a non-SGML data entity is governed by a data content notation, which may be defined by another International Standard.

4.224 parameter: The portion of a markup declaration that is bounded by parameter separators (whether required or optional). A parameter can contain other parameters.

4.237 proper subelement: A subelement that is permitted by its containing element's model.

4.250 rank stem: A name from which a generic identifier can be derived by appending the current rank.

4.267 reportable markup error: A failure of a document to conform to this International Standard when it is parsed with respect to the active document and link types, other than a semantic error (such as a generic identifier that does not identify an element type) or:

a)   an ambiguous content model;

b)   an exclusion that could change a token's required or optional status in a model;

c)   exceeding a capacity limit;

d)   an error in the SGML declaration;

e)   an otherwise allowable omission of a tag that creates an ambiguity;

f)   the occurrence of a non-SGML character; or

g)   a formal public identifier error.

4.276 separator: An s, ds, ps, or ts.

4.277 separator characters: A character class that consists of function characters that are allowed in separators and that will be replaced by *Space* in those contexts in which *RE* is replaced by *Space*.

4.285 SGML parser: A program (or portion of a program or a combination of programs) that recognizes markup in conforming SGML documents.

NOTE — If an analogy were to be drawn to programming language processors, an SGML parser would be said to perform the functions of both a lexical analyzer and a parser with respect to SGML documents.

4.290 short reference: Short reference string.

4.299 simple link (process definition): A link process definition in which the result element types and their attributes are all implied by the application, and only one set of link attribute values can be specified. The source document type must be the base.

4.304 specific character data entity: An entity whose text is treated as *character data* when referenced. The text is dependent on a specific system, device, or application process.

NOTE — A specific character data entity would normally be redefined for different applications, systems, or output devices.

4.312 system declaration: A declaration, included in the documentation for a conforming SGML system, that specifies the features, capacity set, concrete syntaxes, and character set that the system supports, the data content notations that it can interpret, and any validation services that it can perform.

4.315 target element: An element whose *generic identifier* is specified in a *data tag group*

4.319 token: The portion of a group, including a complete nested group (but not a *connector*), that is bounded by token separators (whether required or optional).

Clause 13

As recommended in N1035, all terms in "where" lists are presented in the same type font.

For the record, the text that N1035 replaced in 13.4.5 is reproduced here:

[189] naming rules =
        "NAMING",
        ps+,
        "LCNMSTRT",
        ps+,
        parameter literal,
        ps+,
        "UCNMSTRT",
        ps+,
        parameter literal,
        ps+,
        "LCNMCHAR",
        ps+,
        parameter literal,
        ps+,
        "UCNMCHAR",
        ps+,
        parameter literal,

> *ps+*,
> "NAMECASE",
> *ps+*,
> "GENERAL",
> *ps+*,
> ("NO" |
>   "YES"),
> *ps+*,
> "ENTITY",
> *ps+*,
> ("NO" |
>   "YES")

where

LCNMSTRT	means each *character* in the literal (if any) is added to *LCNMSTRT*.
UCNMSTRT	Each *character* in the literal (if any) is added to *UCNMSTRT* as the associated upper-case form of the character in the corresponding position of *LCNMSTRT*.
LCNMCHAR	means each *character* in the literal (if any) is added to *LCNMCHAR*.
UCNMCHAR	Each *character* in the literal (if any) is added to *UCNMCHAR* as the associated upper-case form of the character in the corresponding position of *LCNMCHAR*.

Here is the text that N1035 replaced in 13.4.7:

[193] reserved name use =
       "NAMES",
       ps+,
       "SGMLREF",
       (*ps+*,
         name,
         ps+,
         name)*

The first of each pair of names is a reference reserved name, and the second is a name that is to replace it in the declared concrete syntax.

Annex C

Here is the text that N1035 deleted from C.1.4:

Data tag minimization is useful for applications that analyze text. The following example uses data tags to identify sentences and words within a paragraph:

```
<!ENTITY % stop '( ".&#RE;" | ".   " | ".)&#RE;" | ".)   " |
                  "?&#RE;" | "?   " | "?)&#RE;" | "?)   " |
                  "!&#RE;" | "!   " | "!)&#RE;" | "!)   " )' >
<!ENTITY % pause '( "  "  | "&#RE;"   | ", "  | ",&#RE;"  |
                   "; "  | ";&#RE;"  | ": "  | ":&#RE;"  |
                   ") "  | ")&#RE;"  | ",) " | ",)&#RE;" |
                   ";) " | ";)&#RE;" | ":) " | ":)&#RE;" |
                   "), " | "),&#RE;" | "); " | ");&#RE;" |
                   "): " | "):&#RE;" )' >
<!ELEMENT p        - O    ([sentence, %stop;]+)>
<!ELEMENT sentence O O    ([word, %pause;, "  "]+)>
<!ELEMENT word     O O    (#PCDATA)>
<p>The first sentence ends here.
The second sentence ends
here.
This is the third sentence.  The
fourth sentence ends, not here!, but here!
</p>
```

In the example, a word end-tag is a "pause" character string followed by zero or more spaces. All words but the last in each sentence have a data tag that conforms to this pattern.

The sentence end-tag is a "stop" character string that ends with either a record end or two spaces. When the tag is recognized, an omitted end-tag for the last word is implied by the usual "end of containing element" rule.

Care must be taken with text entry when using data tag minimization. In the following example, an abbreviation will erroneously be treated as a sentence end-tag:

```
I wonder whether Mrs. G.
will read this.
```

Appendix D
Sources of SGML Information

International SGML Users' Group

The SGML Users' Group is the principal organization dedicated to the furtherance of SGML. It has national chapters in a number of countries, and special interest groups on such topics as SGML data bases and the U.S. Department of Defense CALS application. The group has an active program of conferences and publications. For information, contact the Secretary:

Stephen G. Downie
c/o SoftQuad Inc.
720 Spadina Avenue
Toronto Ontario M5S 2T9
Canada

Graphic Communications Association (GCA)

The Graphic Communications Association, an affiliate of the Printing Industries of America, supports its members with conferences and publications on all aspects of commercial and in-house publishing. The GCA has been a major contributor to the development of SGML (see Appendix A (567)), and conducts an active program of SGML seminars, tutorials, and publication sales, the latter including most SGML-related standards. Together with the SGML Users' Group, the GCA sponsors the preeminent international SGML conference — the annual Markup series.

Graphic Communications Association
1730 North Lynn Street,
Suite 604,
Arlington, VA 22209-2085
United States

International Organization for Standardization (ISO)

The ISO standards mentioned in this book can be purchased from the national standards body in most countries, and from other sources as well. Information regarding the purchase of ISO standards can be obtained from:

ISO Central Secretariat
1, rue de Varembe
CH-1211 Geneva 20
Switzerland

Periodicals

a) "TAG: The Technical Journal of the SGML Community" is a monthly publication covering activities of interest to SGML users and product developers. It has a strong technical orientation and frequently features detailed reports by SGML users and product developers. TAG is edited by Dale Waldt and Bill Davis. Subscription arrangements are handled by the GCA (see above).

b) "The EPSIG Newsletter" is the quarterly publication of the Electronic Publishing Special Interest Group of the Association of American Publishers (AAP) in collaboration with OCLC Online Computer Library Center, Inc. Its primary interest is the Electronic Manuscript Project standard, an SGML application that was developed by the AAP and approved in 1988 as an American National Standard. However, general SGML and electronic publishing matters are covered as well. The editor is Betsy Kiser. For subscription information, contact:

EPSIG News (MC 278)
c/o OCLC
6565 Frantz Road

Dublin Ohio 43017-0702
United States

Video

Rubinsky, Yuri and Giacomelli, Marc. *SGML: The Movie*, videotape
17mins., SGML Users' Group and Graphic Communications Association
(1990).

Yuri Rubinsky and Marc Giacomelli have, as they say in Hollywood,
conceived, written, produced, and directed an exciting fun-filled introduction to SGML, with dazzling special effects and a host of fascinating
characters. (It is no substitute for *Hitchhiker's Guide to the Galaxy*,
although it does have aliens!) The video can be purchased from the GCA
in North America or from the SGML Users' Group in the rest of the
world.

Books

a) Berglund, Anders (Editor). *Information processing — SGML support
    facilities — Techniques for using SGML*, 124pp., ISO/IEC/TR 9573
    (1988).

    Anders Berglund has edited a technical report, with contributions
    from himself and other users and developers of SGML applications.
    The report includes techniques and examples for both publishing
    and office documents, mathematical formulas, complex tables,
    graphics, and spreadsheets. There is a special emphasis on the
    problems of multilingual documents and linguistic scholarship,
    with examples ranging from intermixed Kanji and English to Scan-
    dinavian Runes.

b) Bryan, Martin. *SGML: An author's guide to the Standard Generalized
    Markup Language*, 364pp., Addison-Wesley (1988). ISBN
    0-201-17535-5

    Martin Bryan has written an in-depth tutorial on SGML for authors
    and document type designers. He includes a complete explanation
    of the DTD that he used to produce the book.

c)   Smith, Joan M. and Stutely, Robert. *SGML: The User's Guide to ISO 8879*, 176pp., Ellis Horwood (1988). ISBN 0-7458-0221-4

Joan Smith and Robert Stutely have prepared a comprehensive index and other access tools for readers of ISO 8879. The book includes illustrative glyphs for all of the public character entity sets defined in annex D of the standard.

d)   Van Herwijnen, Eric. *Practical SGML*, 307pp., Kluwer Academic Publishers (1990). ISBN 0-7923-0635-X

This book, by Eric Van Herwijnen of the European Particle Physics Laboratory (CERN), supplements a basic SGML tutorial with discussion of such applications as graphics, CALS, and EDI. He includes bibliographies for each chapter.

Index

The typographic conventions of ISO 8879 are not followed in the index, in order to avoid dividing a single subject into multiple index entries. All entries are in lower-case, except for keywords and other terms that normally include upper-case letters, which appear as distinct entries.

In lieu of the typographic conventions, specialized uses of an index term are distinguished by sub-entries, as follows:

— defined in glossary

> The index term is a glossary term. The first page reference refers to the contextual discussion in the overview; the second to the alphabetic listing in clause 4 of the standard.

— defined in [XX]

> The index term is a syntactic variable defined in the indicated production at the given location (page and line number).

— used in definition

> The index term is a syntactic variable. The locations of all productions in which it is part of the definition are listed.

— clause XX

> The index term is the subject of the indicated normative clause of ISO 8879, beginning at the listed page number.

— tutorial XX *or* annex XX

> The index term is the subject of the indicated informative clause of ISO 8879, beginning at the listed page number.

— overview XX *or* appendix XX

> The index term is the subject of the indicated chapter or appendix of this book, beginning at the listed page number.

Other sub-entries should be self-explanatory.

Special character sequences appear ahead of the alphabetic entries. Each has an alphabetic description (in curly brackets) by which the entries are sorted. There are two exceptions:

— Named character references, although they begin with the {ampersand, number sign} sequence, are listed in the alphabetic index as sub-entries to their function names. For example, &#RS; appears under the entry for RS.

— Keywords that are specified with a reserved name indicator are listed in the main index without it. For example, #PCDATA appears in the alphabetic index as PCDATA.

Symbols

A

D

document capacity set, *See* capacity set

document character set
See also character set
—344, 389, 455, 460, 478:7, 488:27
clause 13.1, 451
defined in [172], 452:1
defined in glossary, 198:3, 263:28
parameter of the SGML declaration, 209
used in production, 450:7, 488:7

document definition, *See* document type definition

document descriptor, defined in glossary, 190:15

document element
—18:13, 315:15
clause 7.2, 306
defined in [12], 306:15
defined in glossary, 144:12, 263:32
used in production, 306:14

document instance
—350, 391
and document type specification, 324
and local entity declarations, 403
defined in glossary, 137:12, 264:1

document instance set
—297:3, 457, 471
defined in [10], 306:10
defined in glossary, 144:5, 264:2
overview 4.3.2.2, 144
used in production, 295:17, 296:3

document profile
—130:11
defined in glossary, 189:14

document structure
overview 3.2.1, 127
tutorial annex B.4, 26

Document Style Semantics and Specification Language, *See* DSSSL

document type
See also DTD
—406
defined in glossary, 124:19, 264:9
not specified by SGML, 246:19

document type declaration
—27:1, 143, 179, 207, 376, 404:35, 405:4, 417:5, 431:3, 431:9, 436:22, 438
and subdocument feature, 90:8
clause 11.1, 402
defined in [110], 403:1
defined in glossary, 143:4, 264:12
tutorial annex B.12, 56
used in production, 303:4, 303:13

document type declaration subset
—386:13, 402, 405:5
and public text, 386
and public text class, 185
defined in [112], 404:6
defined in glossary, 149:5, 264:20
used in production, 403:10

document type definition
See also DTD
—13:4, 19:27, 26:16, 240:13, 335, 402, 405
and elements that do not exist, 377
and the rank feature, 406
annex E.1, 530
defined in glossary, 126:22, 264:25
tutorial annex B.1.2, 19
tutorial annex B.4.1, 26

document type name
—144:14, 164:16, 258:32, 263:34, 326:1, 404:23, 404:24, 404:36, 434:21, 436:21
defined in [111], 404:4
used in production, 403:5, 436:13, 436:15

F

feature code, annex G.1.1, 553
feature use
   —488:38
   clause 13.5, 471
   defined in [195], 471:4
   used in production, 450:15, 488:11
FEATURES, keyword, 471:5
figure
   element type, 152
   tutorial example of, 12:6
figure reference, 158
file imbedding, 21:20
file structure, not specified by
   SGML, 246:24
File Transfer, Access and Management, *See* FTAM
FIXED
   keyword, 425:3, 425:12
   reserved name, 469:13
fixed attribute
   —328
   clause 7.9.4.2, 334
   defined in glossary, 156:10, 268:9
fixed-length generic identifiers,
   nonconforming variation,
   annex I.1, 561
floating element, 419
FORMAL
   conformance classification, 553:4,
   554:2
   feature, 64:1, 88:21
   keyword, 216:8, 268:18, 380:1,
   427:7, 454:5, 456:27, 459:20,
   474:12, 474:25, 492:10, 492:31
formal public identifier
   —187:2, 216:6, 263:2, 268:16, 378,
   380:3, 382:5, 382:10, 386:1,
   454:5, 456:27, 459:20
   clause 10.2, 381
   defined in [79], 382:1
   defined in glossary, 183:1, 268:11
   overview 6.4.1, 183
   tutorial annex C.3.3, 90

formal public identifier error,
   defined in glossary, 216:5,
   268:15
formal specification, 244:36
format of declarations, in public
   entity sets in annex D.4.1.1, 503
formatted text, 61
formatting, 20:8
FSV conformance classification,
   figure 15 on 552
FTAM, 191
full conformance class, figure 15
   on 552
full generic identifier, clause
   7.8.1.1, 327
FUNCHAR
   concrete syntax character class,
   199:8, 255:8, 346:16, figure 2 on
   345
   keyword, 462:13, 462:20
FUNCTION
   in reference concrete syntax, 476
   keyword, 461:7
   variant concrete syntax example,
   figure 11 on 501
function character
   —43:29, 145:13, 145:15, 200:14,
   203:3, 209:10, 262:15, 280:21,
   280:23, 286:3, 297:20, 357:17,
   363, 417:8
   and markup suppression, 365
   clause 9.2.2, 346
   defined in [54], 346:8
   defined in glossary, 200:5, 268:22
   device-independent multicode
   concrete syntaxes, figure 14 on
   539
   overview 7.3.3, 200
   used in production, 345:6
**function character as a general
   delimiter**, 466

function character identification
clause 13.4.4, 461
defined in [186], 461:6
used in production, 458:9
function character identification parameter, defined in glossary, 210:11, 268:28
function class
defined in [188], 462:12
used in production, 462:7
function name
—162:4, 275:8, 357:3
defined in [63], 356:6
used in production, 356:3

G

G0 set
—201
defined in glossary, 197:11, 268:32
GCA, appendix D, 605
GENERAL
conformance classification, 554:4
in reference concrete syntax, 476
keyword, 464:2, 464:28, 466:2, 491:11, 492:17
general concepts, overview 7.1, 192
general considerations, public entity sets in annex D.4.1, 502
general delimiter role, defined in glossary, 203:5, 269:1
general delimiters
See also general delimiter role
clause 13.4.6.1, 466
defined in [191], 466:1
used in production, 465:11

general entity
—429
defined in glossary, 161:1, 269:3
graphic characters, 389
general entity name
—158, 335:1, 338:11, 348:6, 351, 351:16, 398:11, 401:2, 423:21
clause 7.9.4.3, 335
declared attribute value, 331
defined in [103], 395:4
used in production, 333:3, 395:2
general entity name attribute, 159
general entity name list
—335:2, 337:10, 338:12, 351, 423:23
defined in [35.1], 333:17
used in production, 333:4
general entity reference
—140:15, 206, 281:10, 335:5, 353, 361:2
defined in [59], 350:17
defined in glossary, 161:3, 269:5
used in production, 320:21, 343:4
general use, public entity sets in annex D.4.3, 513
generalized markup, tutorial introduction to, 5
Generalized Markup Language, *See* GML
generalized markup languages, 238
generated data, 149:16
generated text, 483
generic coding
—10:36, 239:26, 326
appendix A, 567

H

hierarchical structure, 12:2
history of the development of SGML, appendix A, 567
horizontal tab, short reference, figure 4 on 364
hypermedia application, 427
hypertext, 133, 180, 427
hypertext link, 307
hyphen, short reference, figure 4 on 364

I

ID
  —422
  and subdocument feature, 90:8
  declared attribute value, 331
  defined in glossary, 158:3, 269:26
  keyword, 422:3, 422:10, 423:24, 424:10, 426:6, 428:3, 440:3
  reserved name, 469:14
ID attribute, 14:31
ID link rule, 449
ID link set, 175
id link set declaration
  clause 12.2.3, 446
  defined in [168.1], 447:1
  used in production, 437:4
ID reference list, defined in glossary, 158:10, 269:27
id reference list
  —337:10, 338:7, 423:29
  defined in [37], 333:21
  used in production, 333:7
ID reference value, defined in glossary, 158:7, 269:29
id reference value
  —338:7, 423:27
  used in production, 333:6
  defined in [38], 333:23

ID value
  and ID reference, 158
  defined in glossary, 158:4, 270:1
id value
  —158:6, 158:8, 269:30, 270:3, 423:25
  defined in [36], 333:19
  used in production, 333:5
IDCAP, capacity, figure 5 on 367
identification of SGML constructs, clause 15.5.2, 486
identification of SGML messages, clause 15.4.2, 485
IDLINK
  keyword, 447:3
  reserved name, 469:1
  tutorial D.6, 102
IDREF
  —422
  keyword, 423:1, 423:26, 428:3, 440:3
  reserved name, 469:2
IDREFCAP, capacity, figure 5 on 367
IDREFS
  —422
  keyword, 423:2, 423:28, 428:3, 440:4
  reserved name, 469:3
IGES, notation example, 337
IGNORE
  —392
  keyword, 49:6, 89:15, 393:8, 393:12, 393:29, 394:9, 394:11
  reserved name, 469:4
ignored record end, 322
ignoring a marked section, tutorial annex B.8.1, 48
image notation, not specified by SGML, 247:2
impact of customization, tutorial annex B.14.2, 64

interchange in open systems,
  overview 6.5.5, 191
internal declaration subset, 143,
  403
internal entity
  —377
  defined in glossary, 179:1, 270:29
International Organization for
  Standardization (ISO),
  appendix D, 606
International SGML Users'
  Group, appendix D, 605
interpretation, 439
interpreted parameter literal,
  defined in glossary, 205:13,
  270:31
introduction
  clause 0, 238
  overview 1, 121
introduction to generalized
  markup, tutorial annex A, 5
ISBN, 384
ISO, keyword, 451:2
ISO 639, 249:1
ISO 646, 249:2
ISO 2022, 186, 192:1, 196, 249:10,
  388
ISO 2108, 184
ISO 3166, 249:12
ISO 4873, 249:13
ISO 6523, 184
ISO 6937, 249:15
ISO 8505, 191
ISO 8571, 191
ISO 8613, 131, 335
ISO 8632-2, 250:1
ISO 8632-4, 250:4
ISO 8824, 190, 492
ISO 8825, 191, 493
ISO 8832, 191
ISO 8879
  —122
  scope of, clause 1, 246
  sources of text in this book, appen-
    dix C, 594

ISO 8879:1986, keyword, 488:26
ISO 8883, 191
ISO 9069, 122, 181, 189:4, 249:4,
  294, 395, 493
ISO 9070, 183, 188, 249:6, 384
ISO 10179, 131
ISO 10180, 131
ISO copyright, 122
ISO documents, overview 6.4.5,
  188
ISO owner identifier
  —183, 383, 383:9, 383:13, 384:3
  clause 10.2.1.1, 383
  defined in [81], 383:7
  defined in glossary, 188:2, 271:1
  used in production, 383:2
ISO Registration Number, keyword, 384:6
ISO standards, 249
ISO text description
  —387:10, 387:14
  defined in [87.1], 387:8
  defined in glossary, 188:7, 271:6
  used in production, 387:6

J

Job Transfer and Manipulation
  (JTM), 191

K

keyboard remapping, 432
keyword
  —31:18, 208, 213, 242:30, 370
  and marked sections, 391
  attribute default value, 156
  defined in glossary, 205:1, 271:10
keyword specification, tutorial
  annex B.8.5, 51

L

Latin, public entity sets in annex
    D.4.2.1, 506
LC Letter, abstract syntax character class, 199:6, 206, 255:6,
    346:4, 381:14, 459:13, 459:15,
    464:29, 465:1, figure 1 on 345
LCNMCHAR
    concrete syntax character class,
    346:1, 464:19, 464:23, 464:32,
    464:39, 465:3, 465:5, figure 2 on
    345
    in reference concrete syntax, 476
    keyword, 463, 463:14, 464:18
LCNMSTRT
    concrete syntax character class,
    199:8, 255:8, 346:6, 464:13,
    464:17, 464:32, 464:39, 465:4,
    465:7, figure 2 on 345
    in reference concrete syntax, 476
    keyword, 463, 463:6, 464:12
leading blanks, short reference,
    figure 4 on 364
leading space, 206
limits
    clause 12.1.1.1, 435
    clause 12.1.3.1, 436
    clause 7.2.1, 307
    clause 9.4.2, 348
line, input, 145:3
line feed character, 321
LINK
    keyword, 441:8, 472:30
    reserved name, 469:8
link attribute
    —93, 171:6, 174, 427
    and POSTLINK, 98
    and USELINK, 97
    clause 12.1.4.2, 439
    defined in glossary, 173:6, 271:16
link attribute set
    —441:2
    defined in [162], 437:7
    used in production, 437:2, 437:5

link attribute specification
    —444:8, 444:20, 447:17
    defined in [166], 443:16
    used in production, 443:15
link feature
    —171, 433
    tutorial D, 92
    tutorial annex C.2, 87
link process
    —130:8, 171
    defined in glossary, 124:22, 271:19
link process definition
    —152, 171, 433, 87:17, 93
    defined in glossary, 128:1, 171:1,
    271:26
    tutorial annex C.2.1, 87
link process specification, annex
    F.2.2, 548
link rule
    —377, 442:4, 447:11, 447:13,
    447:15, 447:16
    and attribute specification list,
    327
    defined in [163.1], 441:15
    defined in glossary, 174:1, 272:3
    overview 5.2, 174
    tutorial example of, 94
    used in production, 441:12, 447:7
link set
    and attribute specification list,
    157:3
    and context sensitivity, 449
    and context sensitivity, overview
    5.3, 175
    defined in glossary, 173:11, 272:6
    initial, 175
    tutorial D.1, 93
link set activation
    mixing manual and automatic
    methods, tutorial D.5, 101
    tutorial example of, 97
link set declaration
    —173:12, 272:7, 442:1, 442:2,
    444:4
    clause 12.2, 441

lower-case, in attribute names, 33:25

lower-case letters
abstract syntax character class, figure 1 on 345
defined in glossary, 201:14, 272:20
notation in ISO 8879, 291

lower-case name, 463

lower-case name characters, defined in glossary, 202:11, 272:22

lower-case name start charac-ters, defined in glossary, 202:3, 272:25

LPD
See also link process definition
and public text, 386
and public text class, 185
defined in glossary, 128:13, 272:28
public text class, 386:17

M

main document, defined in glossary, 189:7

map
See also short reference map
defined in glossary, 166:8, 272:29

map name
—429:21, 431:7, 432:5
defined in [151], 429:19
used in production, 429:12, 430:20

map specification
defined in [153], 430:19
used in production, 430:14

MAPCAP, capacity, figure 5 on 367

mapping, *See* short reference map-ping declaration

mark up
See also markup
—239:2
defined in glossary, 125:5, 272:30

marked section
—47:28, 359:19, 359:28, 392:11, 393:13, 393:18, 393:20, 393:22, 394:10
defined in [96], 392:9
defined in glossary, 208:1, 273:1
overview 8.2, 208
tutorial annex B.8, 47
used in production, 392:1

marked section close, delimiter role, figure 3 on 360

marked section declaration
—47:29, 207, 370, 392:13, 392:15, 394:4, 394:6
clause 10.4, 391
defined in [93], 391:13
defined in glossary, 208:3, 273:3
used in production, 320:22, 376:7

marked section end
—48:20, 208:11, 276:31, 350:9, 392:14, 393:15, 394:5, 399:16
defined in [95], 392:6
defined in glossary, 208:7, 273:5
used in production, 392:2

marked section entity, 398

marked section start
—48:9, 208:10, 276:30, 350:8, 351:7, 393:15, 399:14
defined in [94], 392:3
defined in glossary, 208:5, 273:7
used in production, 391:14

markup
See also mark up
—21:1, 322
defined in glossary, 125:1, 273:9
tutorial annex B.2, 21

markup character
—198:1, 285:24, 390, 455
and shunned character numbers, 459
defined in [51], 345:4
defined in glossary, 135:1, 273:13
used in production, 345:2

markup convention, defined in glossary, 127:11, 273:15

O

Q

quantities

—240:32

clause 7.3.3, 313

clause 7.4.2, 316

clause 7.9.2, 330

clause 7.9.4.5, 337

clause 8.1, 341

clause 9.3.1, 347

clause 9.4.1, 348

clause 9.6.5.1, 364

clause 10.1.2.1, 373

clause 10.1.3.1, 375

clause 10.1.6.1, 380

clause 10.1.7.1, 381

clause 10.4.1, 392

clause 10.5.1.1, 396

clause 10.5.4.1, 399

clause 11.2.1.2, 407

clause 11.2.4.5, 417

clause 11.3.1, 421

clause 11.3.4.1, 426

QUANTITY

in reference concrete syntax, 476

keyword, 470:2

variant concrete syntax example, figure 11 on 501

quantity

—299

and capacity, 368

defined in glossary, 136:18, 279:17

in concrete syntax parameter, 209:11

quantity set

See also reference quantity set

—33:30, 210, 212

clause 13.4.8, 469

defined in [194], 470:1

defined in glossary, 136:16, 279:22

used in production, 458:17

R

RANK

conformance classification, 553:10

keyword, 327:1, 472:7, 472:22

rank feature

—63:26, 67:27

and subdocument feature, 90:8

clause 7.8.1, 326

overview 4.6.5, 169

tutorial annex C.1.5, 85

tutorial example of, 85:15

rank stem

—86:2, 169:7, 169:9, 169:11, 170:8, 170:9, 170:12, 260:13, 260:14, 260:17, 279:25, 279:27, 279:29, 326, 327:5, 327:6, 327:8, 327:12, 327:14, 406:8, 406:11, 407:23

clause 7.8.1.2, 327

defined in [120], 407:17

defined in glossary, 169:17, 280:1

used in production, 325:16, 407:2, 407:8, 407:12

rank suffix

—86:3, 169:8, 169:15, 169:18, 170:5, 170:7, 170:10, 260:10, 260:12, 260:15, 279:26, 279:33, 280:2, 326, 327:4, 406:10, 407:23

defined in [121], 407:19

defined in glossary, 169:19, 280:3

used in production, 407:4, 407:16

ranked element

—86:2, 148:20, 266:6, 326, 327:9, 406:10, 407:21

clause 11.2.1.1, 406

defined in [118], 407:1

defined in glossary, 169:6, 279:24

used in production, 406:4

ranked group

—86:19, 148:20, 169:10, 170:10, 260:15, 266:6, 279:28, 326, 327:6, 327:10, 407:22

defined in [119], 407:5

S

s

—139:4, 282:27, 297, 298:3, 298:5, 328:14, 354:4, 372:18

clause 6.2.1, 297

defined in [5], 297:23

defined in glossary, 139:7, 282:18

used in production, 295:14, 303:11, 314:6, 316:6, 316:15, 317:8, 318:16, 320:13, 327:20, 328:1, 328:3, 372:2, 375:4, 376:2, 391:4, 428:24, 443:20, 446:12

s separator, *See* s

satisfied token, defined in glossary, 164:34, 282:21

scientific notations, 61

SCOPE, keyword, 457:5

Scribe text processing system, 10:34

SDATA

keyword, 338:2, 341:2, 397:16, 398:4, 398:10, 398:13, 398:15, 398:18, 400:9, 400:20

reserved name, 469:4

SDATA entity

—147, 340, 343

defined in glossary, 146:7, 282:23

SDIF

—181, 189:5, 249:5, 294, 493

defined in glossary, 189:6

keyword, 493:5

SDIF data stream character set, defined in glossary, 190:12

SDIF data stream contents, overview 6.5.1, 189

SDIF data stream packing and unpacking, overview 6.5.2, 189

SDIF data stream structure, overview 6.5.3, 190

SDIF data structure, 189

SDIF identifier, defined in glossary, 190:20

SDIF identifier reference, defined in glossary, 191:1

SDIF name, defined in glossary, 190:10

SDIF packer, defined in glossary, 189:18

SDIF support

—493:1

clause 15.6.3, 492

defined in [204], 493:4

used in production, 488:19

SDIF unpacker, defined in glossary, 190:5

semantic error, 216

separator

—297:13

defined in glossary, 139:1, 282:24

overview 4.2.3.2, 139

separator characters

—206, 331, 363, 461

defined in glossary, 201:1, 282:30

in attribute value literal, 337

SEPCHAR

—363

concrete syntax character class, figure 2 on 345

function, 166:10, 199:8, 253:31, 255:8, 298:2, 331:13, 346:12, 465:2

in reference concrete syntax, 476

keyword, 462:17, 462:21

seq

defined in overview 4.4.2.1, 151

delimiter role, 28:2, 29:12, 32:22, 84:16, 164:11, 164:26, 206, 259:8, 270:23, 374, 413:7, 413:12, 413:19, 415, 416:3, 416:13, 416:30, figure 3 on 360

U

UC Letter, abstract syntax character class, 199:6, 206, 255:6, 346:5, 381:15, 459:14, 459:15, 463, 464:30, 465:1, figure 1 on 345

UCNMCHAR
concrete syntax character class, 346:2, 464:21, 464:39, 465:3, 465:5, figure 2 on 345
in reference concrete syntax, 476
keyword, 463, 463:18, 464:20

UCNMSTRT
concrete syntax character class, 346:7, 464:15, 465:1, 465:4, 465:6, figure 2 on 345
in reference concrete syntax, 476
keyword, 463, 463:10, 464:14

unavailable public text, defined in glossary, 182:20, 288:7

unavailable text indicator
—185:5, 287:19, 385:19
defined in [85], 385:17
used in production, 385:10

unclosed end-tag
—318:17
clause 7.5.1.2, 318
defined in [22], 318:12
used in production, 317:17

unclosed short tag, tutorial annex C.1.1.1, 68

unclosed start-tag
—316:7
clause 7.4.1.2, 315
defined in [17], 316:1
used in production, 314:11

unclosed tag, overview 4.6.2.2, 165

undefined character, 62

undelimited name token, 204

unique identifier
—422
defined in glossary, 158:1, 288:9

unique identifier attribute, tutorial annex B.9, 52

uniqueness of public identifier, overview 6.4.2, 186

unkeyable character, 161

UNPACK, keyword, 493:14, 493:23

unpacking of SDIF data stream, 189

unparsable section, tutorial annex B.8.3, 50

unregistered owner identifier
—383
clause 10.2.1.3, 384
defined in [83], 385:1
defined in glossary, 183:9, 288:11
used in production, 383:4

UNUSED, keyword, 453, 454:18, 454:26, 455:12

upper-case, in attribute name, 33:25

upper-case letters
abstract syntax character class, figure 1 on 345
defined in glossary, 202:1, 288:15

upper-case name characters, defined in glossary, 202:14, 288:17

upper-case name start characters, defined in glossary, 202:6, 288:20

upper-case substitution, 463

USELINK
keyword, 443:5, 443:23, 443:26, 448:3
parameter, 175, 442, 447
parameter, tutorial D.3.1, 97
reserved name, 469:12

USEMAP
keyword, 81:28, 430:12
reserved name, 469:13

user requirements of SGML, 240:25

user-defined concrete syntax, *See* variant concrete syntax

V

W

X

Y

Colophon

The SGML Handbook was created from two sets of files: parts (including the original text of ISO 8879) keyed in using IBM GML and converted to SGML using the *GML2SGML* converter developed by Wayne Wohler of IBM; and new material, dictated by the author, transcribed and keyboarded using *SoftQuad Author/Editor*, an SGML-sensitive text editor.

The merged files were parsed to ensure their conformance using the validating SGML parser originally programmed by Charles Goldfarb to test ISO 8879 during its development, and by the parser used in *Author/Editor*.

Interim proofs of portions of the book were produced by IBM's Document Composition Facility. Conversion for final formatting was performed by SoftQuad's *SQML* program; the book was typeset using *SoftQuad Publishing Software v.2.9*. Mechanicals of the composed pages were imaged by Philippe Robitaille at Agfa Canada Inc. using the *Agfa 9600PS Imagesetter* and the *Agfa CAPS* corporate publishing system.

The excerpts from ISO 8879 are set in Helvetica, the preferred typeface for ISO documents. The remainder of the text, including the annotations, is set in Adobe's Palatino font (based on Hermann Zapf's original typeface).